THE ECONOMICS
OF LABOR
AND COLLECTIVE
BARGAINING

THE ECONOMICS OF LABOR AND COLLECTIVE BARGAINING

SECOND EDITION

William H. Miernyk
West Virginia University

D. C. HEATH AND COMPANY
Lexington, Massachusetts   Toronto   London

FOR
JAN, JUDY
JEANNE
AND
JAMES

PREFACE

Labor economics has undergone significant change since the first edition of this book appeared in 1965. Reviewing the literature of the past decade, one is struck by the methodological changes that have occurred. In the early 1960s, papers in the IRRA *Proceedings* and the leading labor journals rarely contained mathematical notation; even descriptive statistical tables were few and far between. In the 1970s, however, an appreciable proportion of articles bristle with equations and mathematical symbols, and one is able to speak of a "new" labor economics, which makes extensive use of statistical and econometric methods.

Quantitative techniques have been used to analyze such diverse issues as the participation rates of various subgroups in the labor force, the relative impacts of unions on wage levels, and the causes of trade-union growth, to name but a few. The increased use of sophisticated quantitative methods has not been viewed by all labor economists as an unmixed blessing.[1] But today's student of labor economics should be familiar with the results of quantitative studies relevant to modern labor problems and issues. The results of a number of econometric studies are summarized in the present text although they are not always accepted uncritically.

Another kind of change in the study of labor economics is perhaps less obvious than the one just mentioned. This is the tendency toward more rigorous theoretical analysis. The recent books by Fleisher and Richard Perlman which focus on labor theory exemplify this trend. This is a change of degree rather than of kind. Labor economics has always included a certain amount of theory, but the institutional bias in the field has been strong. This is no longer true. Today's student would miss an important part of the discipline of labor economics by reading only the institutional material available. The revised edition of this text includes a good bit more theory than the original, although an effort has been made to maintain a balance among the historical, institutional, and theoretical approaches.

Another change in labor economics in recent years has been substantive rather than methodological. Manpower economics has become a specialized part of labor economics due, in part, to increasing government involvement in training, retraining, and job placement. This is another area in which labor economists have always had an interest, but labor market problems have received more emphasis during the past few years than formerly. Indeed, three chapters of the present version of this text are devoted to manpower problems and policies, whereas this topic claimed no extraordinary amount of attention in the first edition.

Finally, labor economics today must be more concerned with unionized

---

1. See, for example, the acerbic comments by Sar A. Levitan in the *Proceedings,* Twenty-Third Annual Meeting, Industrial Relations Research Association (1970), p. 319.

public employees than it was a decade ago. Federal, state, and local government workers have belonged to unions for some time. But the most rapid growth of American union membership in the 1960s was in the public sector. At the last count, government employees made up 10 per cent of total union membership, and that proportion will no doubt increase. The rise of unionism in the public sector has raised a host of new problems in the collective bargaining arena. These problems are discussed in several places in the present text.

The author of a textbook has many debts. First, I would like to thank Macmillan & Company, Ltd., the RAND Corporation, McGraw-Hill Book Co., Inc., and the National Bureau of Economic Research, Inc. for permission to use copyrighted materials. The many scholars upon whose work I have drawn are acknowledged throughout the text. In addition, I would like to thank those of my colleagues who used the first edition in class and took the trouble to send me helpful comments and suggestions. Authors who published reviews of the earlier edition also helped shape this revision. The anonymous reviewers arranged for by the publisher substantially improved the material they commented upon as well. Professor Neil Palomba was kind enough to give me the benefit of his comments on portions of this text. Professor Raymond McKay brought to my attention several studies I otherwise might have missed, and his detailed criticism of the new material in this revision led to many improvements. Miss Seetha N. Hampapur not only provided invaluable research assistance, but also helped with the secretarial chores. Mr. Robert Benton assisted with sundry research tasks and with proofreading. Mrs. Ada Marlier handled most of the secretarial details. My sincere thanks go to everyone who helped with this book. I am responsible, of course, for any errors that remain, and for the interpretations and conclusions set forth in this volume.

Writing is a lonely occupation, but the author of a text has the benefit of association with the work and ideas of scholars. His family is usually unable to share in this fringe benefit. I am grateful to my children, to whom this book is dedicated, for their willingness to accept a set of priorities that at times interfered with their plans. My wife as always was a constant source of encouragement and support.

William H. Miernyk

CONTENTS

V
Collective Bargaining

THE ECONOMICS
OF LABOR
AND COLLECTIVE
BARGAINING

Introduction

A century ago the United States was predominantly an urban-agrarian economy. The total population in 1870 was less than 40 million, and more than half the nation's residents were concentrated in three regions: New England, the Middle Atlantic states, and the Great Lakes region. The rest of the nation was sparsely populated. The labor force at that time included about 12.5 million persons. Of these, more than half (53 percent) were engaged in farming, fishing, forestry, and mining; about one fourth were employed in providing services; and 21 per cent were in manufacturing.[1]

Labor in a Dynamic Economy

By 1972, the population of the United States had passed the 207 million mark. There were more than 84 million workers in the civilian labor force, but fewer than 3.4 million, or 3.9 per cent of the total, were in agriculture. America had become a heavily urban (and suburban) society. The nature of work was also vastly different from the way it had been in the nineteenth century. In 1972, only 35 per cent of all wage and salary workers outside of agriculture were engaged in the production of goods; the rest were employed in a wide range of professional and service occupations.

The American economy has grown rapidly during the past century, occasioning significant changes in economic organization. When society was predominantly rural and the economy heavily dependent upon agriculture, few large enterprises were in existence. And there were no strong or well-entrenched unions in this country a century ago.

America in the 1870s was not a highly structured society. There were few laws dealing with the activities of businessmen, and none dealing with organized labor. Indeed, government activity of all kinds was minimal. The pre-

---

1. Harvey S. Perloff et al., *Regions, Resources, and Economic Growth* (Baltimore: The Johns Hopkins Press, 1960), pp. 12–13; 131.

vailing philosophy was that "the government which governed least governed best." The economy was also relatively simple. Transportation was slow, and communication was limited. Under these circumstances many markets were local in character; there was much less specialization and exchange than there is today.

It is easy to exaggerate the joys of life in nineteenth-century America. Many of the problems which leaders of government, business, and labor wrestle with today were unheard of at that time, but so were many of the material advantages that we take for granted in the more highly specialized and institutionalized society of today. Hours of work were long, and work itself was usually arduous; only the well-to-do had the time and means to take advantage of the available cultural and recreational facilities.

The Emergence of Large-Scale Organizations

One important institutional change in the economy was well under way before the end of the nineteenth century. This was the rise of the corporation, and an increase in the size of many enterprises. This change in the form of business organization eventually led to a separation of ownership and control. As corporations grew in size and complexity, a class of professional managers emerged to guide their destinies, and this in turn led to a change in the relationship between employers and employees.

In an earlier day, there had been personal contact between the owner-manager of a firm and his workers. The owner did the hiring; he also supervised training and maintained discipline on the job; and it was up to him to make job assignments and promotions. He dealt directly with disgruntled workers either by settling their grievances or by dismissing them. From the point of view of the worker, this was not necessarily the best of all possible worlds, but he always knew where he stood. Moreover, if the employer was interested in making a profit—and in economics this is the standard assumption we make about employers—he paid close attention to the actions and attitudes of his employees. He served his own best interests by trying to keep his workers satisfied.

As some firms grew in size and adopted the corporate structure, the personal relationship between employer and employee disappeared. The growth of the corporation was one factor contributing to the development of stable trade unionism in the United States. Workers recognized that as individuals they had to accept wages, hours, and working conditions on a take-it-or-leave-it basis, and they sought to match the strength of large employers by dealing with them collectively through representatives of their choosing.

The Great Depression of the 1930s brought another change in economic organization. For the first time in American history, excluding wartime periods, government began to play an increasingly important role in economic life. Among other things, the government laid down the rules governing labor-management relations; and this, as we will see, had an important impact on the growth of trade unions. The change from an economy made up of many small farms, small businesses, and a small government to one in which business, government, and labor have all become big was gradual. But viewed over a fairly long period of time—a century or even a half century—the contrasts are dramatic indeed.

The principal focus of this book is one of the major institutions in modern industrial society—namely, trade unions. This is not because most workers belong to unions. As a matter of fact, union members in the United States are a minority of the work force. In 1968, union members in this country accounted for only 23 per cent of the labor force, and 28 per cent of workers employed in nonagricultural establishments. But the influence of unions is greater than their minority status might suggest. They have an effect upon wage structure and wage levels of the entire economy. Also, in a society in which many decisions are the product of organized group activity, the political and social influence of unions cannot be ignored.

Regardless of how individuals or specific groups might feel, the institution of trade unionism is accepted by government. Political leaders make appropriate obeisances to organized labor, particularly during election years, although it is far from clear that union leaders can actually "deliver the vote." More important, labor representatives serve on various governmental advisory committees. When President Nixon instituted Phase II of his program to combat inflation in 1971, for example, he saw to it that organized labor played an active part. One third of the members of the Pay Board, set up to establish and administer wage guidelines, were union leaders. The tenure of four of the five original labor members of the Pay Board was brief, but they left voluntarily after a disagreement over basic policy. Finally, labor leaders regularly appear before legislative committees to present the views of organized labor on impending legislation.

A Profile of American Trade Unionism

There were about 18.9 million union members in the United States in 1968. Most of them were members of the 189 national or international unions with headquarters in the United States, and 15.6 million belonged to the 126 unions affiliated with the AFL–CIO.[2]

Three unions in the United States have more than 1 million members each; these are the Teamsters, Automobile Workers, and Steelworkers. But most American unions are relatively small. In 1968, 117 of the nation's unions, or about 62 per cent of the total, claimed fewer than 50,000 members each. Collectively, they accounted for less than 8 per cent of total union member-

2. U.S. Department of Labor, Bureau of Labor Statistics, *Directory of National and International Labor Unions In the United States, 1969,* Bulletin No. 1665 (1970), pp. 64–67.

ship. Another 47 unions reported membership ranging between 50,000 and 200,000. The unions in this size group accounted for 25 per cent of the total, and they also accounted for 25 per cent of all members. Finally, there were 25 unions—or 13 per cent of the total—with 200,000 or more members each. Yet this relatively small number of unions combined claimed 67 per cent of all organized workers in the United States.

For some time women have constituted a growing proportion of the labor force, but the American labor movement is predominantly made up of male workers. In 1960, women accounted for more than one third of total employment in the nation, but there were only 3.9 million women union members accounting for about 20 per cent of total union membership.

Another major trend in the labor force has been an increase in the proportion of white-collar workers. Most American union members, however, are blue-collar or manual workers. About 47 per cent of all employed workers in 1968 were in the white-collar category, while an estimated 3.2 million white-collar union members accounted for only 17 per cent of total union membership.

It is difficult to make an industrial classification of union membership since some unions cut across industry lines; they have members in two or more industries. The following table shows the approximate distribution of union membership in 1968 by broad industrial classification.

TABLE 1-1
Industrial Distribution of Union Membership, 1968

Industry Group	Number of unions[a]	Members (in thousands)	Percent of total
Manufacturing	103	9,868	45.6
Durable goods	182	5,998	26.4
Nondurable goods	155	3,658	18.2
Not Classifiable	36	212	1.0
Non-manufacturing	106	8,837	43.7
Mining and Quarrying	16	342	1.7
Contract Construction	26	2,541	12.6
Transportation	48	2,503	12.4
Service Industries	38	1,093	5.4
All Other	54	2,358	11.6
Government	59	2,155	10.7
Federal	57	1,351	6.7
State and Local	18	804	4.0

Source: U. S. Department of Labor, Bureau of Labor Statistics, *Directory of National and International Labor Unions in the United States, 1969*, Bulletin No. 1665 (1970), pp. 73–74.

[a] Figures in this column are not additive since some unions have members in more than one industrial classification.

The geographical distribution of union members is far from even. This is indicated by Map 1, which shows 1968 membership as a percentage of nonagricultural employment in each state. This distribution is based on reports submitted by 118 national and international unions, and BLS estimates for the remaining 71.

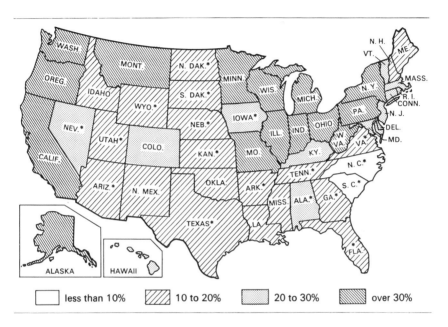

MAP 1.

AFL-CIO Membership as Percent of Nonagricultural Employment by State, 1968. *(Data from the U.S. Department of Labor, Bureau of Labor Statistics,* Directory of National and International Labor Unions in the United States, 1969, *Bulletin No. 1655 [1970], p. 76.)*

Unions have been least successful in organizing workers in the Southeast, and in a scattering of western and middle-western states with relatively large rural populations. With few exceptions, the states in which 20 per cent or more of the labor force belong to unions are highly industrialized, or, as in the case of Montana and West Virginia, are heavily dependent upon mining as a source of employment. In 1968, nineteen states had laws forbidding union shop agreements. These are the so-called "right-to-work" states. In all but three of these states, union members accounted for less than 20 per cent of all nonagricultural workers.

The Systematic Study of Labor Economics and Industrial Relations

The brief profile of American unions sketched in the preceding section tells us something about the present position of organized labor. But it is a statistical skeleton, and bare statistics can raise more questions than they answer. A cross-sectional analysis, for example, tells us nothing about the extent of organization in the past or about changes in union structure and objectives. These require at least a brief excursion into labor history, which is covered in Part III of the present book.

Unions have been more successful in organizing workers in manufacturing, mining, construction, and transportation than in other sectors of the economy. Why is this so? There is no universally accepted answer to this question. Since the early days of trade unions, however, scholars have speculated about the motives that lead some workers to organize and that keep others from doing so. There are a number of theories of the labor movement, and the more important of these, in the author's view, are examined in this text. Some authors have attempted to analyze various kinds of trade unionism; others to develop a unified explanation of this particular phenomenon of industrial society; and still others, to examine the question of union growth. What forces—economic, political, and social—contribute to rapid union growth at times and to little or no growth at others?

In a democracy, all of us live under the rule of law, but there is nothing static about the legal system. Indeed, the law has changed vastly since the reign of Hammurabi, and it will continue to change in the future. Labor law is a fairly new addition to jurisprudence in this country, but in recent decades it has become an important, if controversial, part of the legal system. An introduction to labor law is an integral part of a systematic study of trade unionism.

The essence of trade unionism is collective action, and collective bargaining today is a highly complex process. One who relies entirely upon news media for information about collective bargaining is likely to obtain a distorted image. Strikes and labor unrest are reported in detail, but peaceful collective bargaining is not regarded as newsworthy. One cannot hope to have an understanding of industrial relations, however, without some knowledge of the techniques of contract negotiations, contract administration, and dispute settlement. Like many other social processes, collective bargaining has been evolutionary. To understand this process, it is not enough to examine current practices independently; rather, they must be viewed in relation to changes that have occurred as unions have grown and as their position vis-à-vis management has altered.

There are some obvious questions which a student of labor economics and industrial relations will ask. What is labor's role in the production process? How are workers affected by technological change? How are wages determined? Do unions affect the wage level? What effect do they have on wage structure? Have unions changed the pattern of income distribution? The last four questions deal with the raw material of wage theory, a branch of economics with a long history. New theories have been advanced as our analytical tools have been refined, as new evidence for the testing of hypotheses has become available, and as the world has changed around us.

Economists also have developed theories of bargaining which examine the behavioral aspects of negotiations. Wage and bargaining theories do not, of course, provide definitive answers to the questions listed above. They have the virtue, however, of showing that simple answers—usually based upon personal predilections—are not likely to be convincing. In an introductory text many of the refinements of wage theory and of the theory of bargaining must be ignored, but enough can be said about them to show how the analytical tools of economics can be applied to problems of central interest to economists and policy makers alike.

An area of special interest to students of labor economics is the labor market. During the 1960s changes in public attitudes toward unemployment and other labor market problems were reflected in new manpower policies. The United States Employment Service had been in operation since the 1930s, but this federal-state agency played a limited and essentially passive role in the labor market. Local employment offices could provide unemployed workers with advice and guidance, but their basic function was to refer qualified workers to jobs listed with them by employers. Since enactment of the Manpower Development and Training Act in 1962, however, the Department of Labor, through its Manpower Administration, has played a more active role in the labor market. Like the USES, the Manpower Administration cannot create new jobs. But it has attempted to increase the employability of jobless workers through a variety of training and retraining programs.

It is not uncommon for textbooks on labor to begin with a discussion of "labor problems," a convention that has not been followed in this volume. But there certainly are labor problems, and they are not ignored in this book. There are the problems of labor-management disputes and of tensions that stop short of overt economic warfare. In recent years there has been a tendency for government to become involved in various ways in labor-management disputes. While such intervention has prevented some strikes, and has ended some others, rarely has *ad hoc* intervention managed to get to the root of the problem involved.

More general economic problems directly affect the behavior of union leaders and management in collective bargaining. One of the more troublesome complications has been the coexistence of relatively high levels of unemployment with inflation. Under the Nixon administration an effort was made to cope with the problem of inflation by controlling wages and prices. But in a market economy the administration of wages and prices by public bodies is never a simple process, and a system of partial controls can raise serious new problems of equity.

The "correct" answers to these and other labor problems will not be found in this or any other textbook. In a society made up of many groups with

diverse interests, no solutions to social and economic problems will completely satisfy everyone. The object of this book is to examine these problems
from different points of view, to consider alternative solutions and, wherever
possible, to assess the consequences of policies designed to deal with
specific problems.

Finally, the historical sections of this book show that major changes
have taken place in unions, in the collective bargaining process, in labor
laws, in both public attitudes and management reactions to trade unions.
Little imagination is required to realize that further changes are inevitable.
Only a prophet could foretell the exact nature of future change, and reliable
economic prophets are in short supply. Nevertheless, we know that the
future of institutional arrangements is determined to some extent by their
past. Institutions survive to the extent that they learn to cope with crises and
to adapt to change. American trade unions have shown that they can adjust
to a shifting social and economic milieu. Not only will they continue to adjust, but they also will help to shape the direction of future change.

The Economics
of Labor

2

The Labor Force and Labor Markets

This chapter deals with the labor force and with the markets in which workers and jobs are brought together. A market is a place where transactions occur; we go to a market to buy groceries, for example. But only in a few occupations, where the demand for labor fluctuates on a day-to-day basis, do workers go to a hiring hall to offer their labor services in exchange for money. Thus "the labor market" is an abstract concept, but one that should help you gain a better understanding of the complex world of work. Although this chapter deals with various kinds of labor markets, the discussion is not complete. Market analysis usually involves the relationship between prices and quantities exchanged. But we do not discuss wage determination, or the price of labor, in this chapter. This topic is sufficiently important to deserve a chapter of its own (Chapter 5).

The notions of labor supply and the demand for labor are covered in later sections of this chapter, but only in terms of broad aggregates. The next chapter is concerned with the demand for labor at the level of the firm, as well as with the relevant aspects of labor supply at that level. Chapter 4 follows with a survey of technological change and a look at the effects of technology on the work force and on the returns to labor. Thus, the present chapter and the three that follow make up a unit. Together they provide a reasonably detailed description and analysis of the abstraction we refer to as "the labor market."

Population and Labor Force

This section deals with some of the more prosaic and descriptive aspects of the labor force. Figure 2-1 summarizes population and labor force data for 1971. There were more than 207 million persons in the United States in 1970, and the noninstitutional population sixteen years of age and over came to

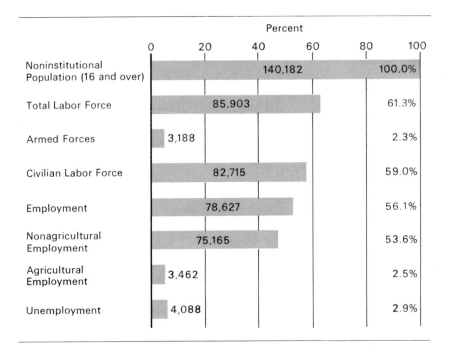

FIGURE 2–1.

Population and Labor Force, 1971. (*Source:* Economic Report of the President, *January 1972, p. 220.*)

more than 142 million. The noninstitutional population includes everyone not in hospitals, mental institutions, prisons, or other institutions that would keep them out of the labor force. The total labor force includes everyone who is working, full or part-time, and all those who are unemployed *and looking for work.* In 1971, the labor force included 61 per cent of the non-institutional population aged sixteen and over.

Almost 3 million persons, or 2 per cent of the noninstitutional population, were in the armed forces. The civilian labor force, the basis for most labor force analysis, included 84.1 million persons in 1971, or 59 per cent of the noninstitutional population. As Figure 2–1 shows, most of these were em-ployed, and most of those working had nonagricultural jobs. Figure 2–1 also shows one of the startling relationships found only in a "highly developed" economy. The agricultural sector employed about 3.4 million persons in 1971, or only 4 per cent of the civilian labor force. But in that year almost 5 million persons, or 5.9 per cent of the civilian labor force, were unemployed and actively seeking jobs.

The explanation of the relatively small number of persons in agricultural employment is fairly simple. Technological change and the accompanying gains in productivity have resulted in a sharp decline in agricultural labor requirements over the past thirty years. The explanation of the relatively high level of unemployment in a year characterized as one of "mild recession" is somewhat more complex. The causes of unemployment are discussed in considerable detail in Chapter 6.

Labor Supply

The amount of labor services available to a society at any given time depends upon a number of conditions. One of the more important conditions is the stage of the society's economic development, and this in turn is related to the state of its technology. Another closely related consideration is the level of *real income* in the society. In poor societies or "less developed countries," as they are now euphemistically called, the individual worker may not have much choice between work and leisure. The head of a typical household must work the entire day to provide a bare subsistence for himself and his family. His wife and children also may labor long hours to contribute to family income. In such a society there is little room for the exercise of choice between work and leisure.

In a modern industrial society, however, a worker can choose, at least to some extent, between work and leisure. This does not mean, of course, that the individual worker is free to decide how many hours a day or how many days a week he wishes to work. Once a worker has accepted a job he is expected to show up at a certain time and to work a prescribed number of hours during the day. But in a number of ways, including collective bargaining, workers have been able to indicate their collective preference for work or leisure. An individual may also elect to work on a part-time basis, or he may prefer to work more than full time at one job.[1] The total supply of labor services is influenced by the sum of these individual choices.

Alvin Toffler recently pointed out that: "In the United States, since the turn of the century alone, the society's measurable commitment to work has plummeted by nearly a third. This is a massive redeployment of the society's time and energy."[2]

The average work week in manufacturing at the turn of the century was sixty hours compared with an average of forty hours in 1970, and the average work week in the total private sector of the economy in 1970 was slightly in excess of thirty-seven hours. The nonmanufacturing average has probably declined less than the manufacturing average since 1900, but even here the drop has been substantial.

---

1. There were more than 4 million multiple jobholders in 1970, or 5.2 per cent of all employed persons. See Howard V. Hayghe and Kopp Michielotti, "Multiple Jobholders in 1970 and 1971," *Monthly Labor Review,* October 1971, p. 38.
2. Alvin Toffler, *Future Shock* (New York: Bantam Edition, 1971), p. 289.

Workers today spend less time each week on the job than their counterparts did at the turn of the century. They also spend more years in school and many retire earlier so they spend fewer years in the labor force. In 1900, only 6 per cent of the seventeen-year-old population had completed high school. By 1970, almost 90 per cent of all seventeen-year-olds were still in school, and 23 per cent of the population between twenty and twenty-four years of age had not yet entered the active labor force. There also has been a significant reduction in the retirement age. At the turn of the century there was no generally accepted "retirement age." With the advent of Social Security in the United States in the mid-1930s, sixty-five has become the standard retirement age, although many workers retire earlier than this. A 1961 amendment to the Social Security Act allows men to retire (with reduced benefits) at age sixty-two. And many collective bargaining agreements provide for special early retirement, particularly for older workers displaced by technological change or the closing of establishments.

Income and Leisure

The individual worker's choice between income and leisure may be analyzed within the framework of the theory of consumer behavior. This theory assumes that worker satisfaction depends on both income and leisure. (The satisfaction that he might obtain from his work is ignored in this analysis.) Since both income and leisure are desirable, the worker will maximize his utility by making the appropriate choice between them.

The trade-off between income and leisure is illustrated by Figure 2-2. On this diagram income from work is measured on the vertical axis, and leisure on the horizontal axis. An indifference curve relating the two variables is labeled I-I. The indifference curve is a useful analytical device for illustrating the process of choice. It is based on the assumption that the individual prefers more to less income, and also that he prefers more to less leisure, thus the curve must have a negative slope.[3]

The indifference curve between income and leisure is convex from the origin, or concave when viewed from above. The marginal rate of substitution of income for leisure shows the *relative* ease with which leisure may be substituted for income. It is measured by the expression $-\Delta Y/\Delta L$, where ΔY represents the amount of income the worker is willing to give up in order to enjoy a given increment of leisure, ΔL, without changing the level of his total satisfaction.

Figure 2-2 illustrates the *diminishing* marginal rate of substitution between wage income and leisure. If his income is high, a worker may be willing to accept a substantial cut in earned income in order to enjoy a relatively

---

3. For further discussion see Edwin Mansfield, *Microeconomics: Theory and Applications* (New York: W. W. Norton & Co., Inc., 1970), pp. 22–26.

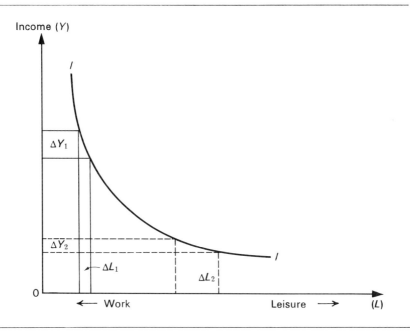

FIGURE 2–2.

The Trade-Off Between Income and Leisure.

modest increase in leisure. At a relatively high level of income, the marginal rate of substitution of leisure for income is greater than unity; that is, the absolute value of the ratio $-\Delta Y/\Delta L$ is greater than one. As we move down the curve, the value of the marginal rate of substitution declines.

At a low level of income, the absolute value of the marginal rate of substitution is less than unity; the worker will be willing to give up only a small amount of earned income in exchange for a substantial increase in leisure. If we assume that he is able to make very small adjustments in income and leisure and that he has no control over his rate of pay, the individual worker maximizes his utility—or performs the optimal amount of work from his point of view—when the marginal rate of substitution of income for leisure is equal to his wage rate.[4]

The preceding discussion illustrated the process of choice between income and leisure with a *fixed wage rate*. What happens, however, if the wage rate changes? Will the consumption model used above provide an answer to this question? According to conventional theory, consumer be-

4. For a formal proof, see James M. Henderson and Richard E. Quandt, *Microeconomic Theory* (New York: McGraw-Hill Book Co., Inc., 1958), p. 23.

havior is affected by changes in both prices and income. A change in relative prices, with income held constant, will lead to the substitution of one good for another. This is called the *substitution effect.* An increase in income, with relative prices held constant, will lead to an increase in the consumption of all goods which the consumer normally purchases, and this is known as the *income effect.* But an increase in wages poses a dilemma for the worker, which has been summarized by Parnes:[5]

> ... a rise in the wage rate increases the (opportunity) cost of leisure and tends to cause the worker to wish to supply more labor to the market. However, for any given amount of productive effort an increase in the wage rate also produces an increase in income which tends to cause the worker to wish to purchase more leisure, i.e., reduce hours in the labor market.

Under what circumstances will an increase in the wage rate cause a worker to supply more labor, and under what circumstances will he want to supply less? Figure 2-2 suggests that if a worker's earned income is already high he may respond to a wage increase by working less; a low-income worker will not necessarily respond in this way, however, if his wage rate is increased. He may choose to work as much as possible in order to maximize his income. The theory of consumer behavior provides no general rule for predicting the relative strengths of the income and substitution effects. The individual worker's decision could go either way as Lionel Robbins pointed out more than four decades ago.[6]

Labor Force Participation

Among the determinants of aggregate labor supply are the labor force participation rates of the subgroups that make up the noninstitutional population. One of the first economists to develop a model of labor force participation based upon the theory of consumer behavior was Jacob Mincer. Mincer's work has spurred a number of others to analyze the behavior of individual groups in the labor force classified on the basis of demographic characteristics. Mincer was also one of the first to use econometric techniques to analyze labor force participation. His work in this vein was followed by that of a number of other economists including Glen Cain, Thomas Dernburg, Kenneth Strand, William Bowen, T. Aldrich Finnegan, and Alfred Tella. This is not an exhaustive list of those who have dealt with this aspect of labor econometrics. It includes the economists who were particularly active in

5. Herbert S. Parnes, "Labor Force Participation and Labor Mobility," *A Review of Industrial Relations Research, Vol. I* (Madison, Wisconsin: Industrial Relations Research Association, 1970), p. 4.
6. Lionel Robbins, "On the Elasticity of Demand for Income in Terms of Effort," *Economica* June 1930, pp. 123–129.

this area of research during the early 1960s. An excellent summary of their work has been given by Parnes in the 1970 survey article already cited. The remainder of this section draws heavily on this excellent essay.

Mincer was critical of the basic income-leisure model because it assumes that time has only two alternative uses—work or leisure. The model fails to recognize that "there exists a range of activities constituting neither gainful employment nor pleasurable leisure."[7] As indicated in an earlier section, working time declines as an economy develops. But Gary Becker has pointed out that it is not always easy to distinguish between leisure and other forms of "non-work."[8] It is difficult at times to define "work" precisely, particularly in an age when many workers spend considerable time commuting to and from their jobs.

A second difficulty with the income-leisure model pointed out by Mincer is that this type of analysis relates to individual choices, whereas the family may be a more appropriate unit for the analysis of labor supply. The conventional model assumes that at a higher wage a worker may elect to substitute leisure for additional income. What may happen, in fact, is that at the higher wage rate the worker will continue to work as much as he did before, but his wife (or some other member of his family) will withdraw from the active labor force. Finally, Mincer has related his labor supply model to Friedman's permanent income hypothesis. According to this hypothesis, it is *long-run* levels of family income that determine present consumption expenditures. Temporary, or "transitory," departures from this level are adjusted for by either increased saving or withdrawals from saving. Similarly, transitory changes in income may lead to transitory labor force participation. If a family's income declines because the husband is temporarily laid off, his wife may enter the labor force. Such temporary labor force participation was labeled as "secondary attachment" to work by the late Richard Wilcock.[9]

One of the more comprehensive contributions to the "new labor economics" is Bowen and Finegan's *Economics and Labor Force Participation*.[10] This volume, which runs to almost 900 pages, summarizes several years of empirical research on labor force participation.

Bowen and Finegan seemed less interested in developing a labor force model based on conventional price theory than Mincer and others who followed Mincer's approach. Instead, they attempted to "explain" the labor

7. Richard Perlman, *Labor Theory* (New York: John Wiley & Sons, Inc., 1969), p. 13. See also Jacob Mincer, "Market Prices, Opportunity Costs, and Income Effects," in Carl F. Christ *et al.,* *Measurement in Economics* (Stanford, California: Stanford University Press, 1963), p. 51.

8. Gary S. Becker, "A Theory of the Allocation of Time," *The Economic Journal,* September 1965, p. 495.

9. See Richard C. Wilcock and Walter H. Franke, *Unwanted Workers* (Glencoe, Illinois: The Free Press, 1956), pp. 194–195.

10. William G. Bowen and T. Aldrich Finegan, *Economics and Labor Force Participation* (Princeton, N.J.: Princeton University Press, 1969).

force participation of various demographic subsets of the population by means of straightforward multiple regression analysis. They studied the relationships between labor force participation and approximately three dozen other variables, although not all of these relationships were statistically significant or necessarily meaningful. They found a positive relationship between labor force participation and earning power, as expected, and a negative relationship between labor force participation and nonlabor income. But labor force participation is not greatly influenced by changes in wage rates. Among workers with a primary attachment to the labor force (as opposed to those with a "secondary attachment"), it is not realistic to expect marginal adjustments in labor force participation in response to changing wage rates. This is not necessarily the case for "secondary" workers, however. The participation of women in the labor force, for example, is positively associated with levels of earnings. And this is particularly true in the case of married women. Another finding of the Bowen-Finegan study is that labor force participation rates—in general and for specific subgroups—are inversely related to unemployment rates. Labor force participation tends to be high where unemployment rates are low and vice versa.

Ever since the work of Woytinski in the 1930s, labor economists have been interested in the "additional worker" and "discouraged worker" hypotheses. The additional worker hypothesis states that during periods of economic decline and rising unemployment, the labor force will be increased by the entry of wives (and other family members) seeking to bolster family income when primary breadwinners are laid off. The discouraged worker hypothesis states that the labor force will shrink during periods of economic decline and increasing unemployment. Some workers will be discouraged by unsuccessful job searches and will withdraw from the labor force. This withdrawal may be temporary or, especially in the case of older workers, it may be permanent. Econometric studies by Tella, and by Dernburg and Strand, provide statistical support for *both* hypotheses. These studies used an employment-population ratio to estimate the responsiveness of the labor force to short-run changes in demand. After reviewing these studies, Mincer concluded that the procedure they followed overstated the sensitivity of the labor force to demand changes.[11] Using the unemployment rate in their analysis, instead of the employment-population ratio, Bowen and Finegan found a smaller "discouragement" effect than Dernburg and Strand.

The recent studies reviewed by Parnes, including the one by Bowen and Finegan, show that the labor force does respond to short-run changes in aggregate demand, and that this is largely the result of the movement of

---

11. Jacob Mincer, "Labor Force Participation and Unemployment: A Review of Recent Evidence," in Robert A. and Margaret S. Gordon (eds.), *Prosperity and Unemployment* (New York: John Wiley & Sons, Inc., 1966).

"secondary" workers into and out of the labor force. Secondary workers tend to respond to changes in family income, however, rather than to changes in wage rates. Labor force participation is also influenced by such demographic characteristics as color, marital status, health, education, and family size and composition. Black women have a higher labor force participation rate than white women. There is less difference in the case of white and black men, particularly when age, marital status, education, and nonlabor income are taken into account.

Marital status is an important determinant of labor force participation, not only for women but also for men. The family characteristic most closely related to labor force participation is the age composition of the family's children. Labor force participation is directly related to the level of educational attainment for practically all demographic subsets in the working population.

The Demand for Labor

The demand for labor is a *derived* demand; that is, it depends upon the demand for goods and services. Short-run fluctuations in the demand for goods and services are transmitted to labor markets, generally after a short time lag, and these lead to cyclical fluctuations in the demand for labor. As we saw in the last section, demand fluctuations result in changes in labor force participation, particularly among workers with a "secondary attachment" to the labor market.

In the long run, the demand for labor is affected by all the forces that alter the structure of an economic system. These include changes in consumer tastes and preferences, technological change, shifts in resource use, and changes in social and economic organization. As a result of these and other changes, the composition of the demand for labor changes over time. This is reflected by changes in the industry-mix of employment and similar changes in employment by occupation.

Employment Projections to 1980

The labor force in the United States has expanded steadily since colonial days as the nation's population has grown. The historical growth rate of the population is not expected to continue indefinitely, but rapid changes are not expected in the near future despite the recent drop in the birth rate. Thus the economy is expected to continue to grow throughout the 1970s at about the same rate it has shown in the recent past. Detailed projections of the labor force to 1980 have been made by the Bureau of Labor Statistics, and the results are summarized in Figures 2–3 and 2–4.

The projections of labor demand presented here are part of the work performed by the Interagency Economic Growth Project. This group consists of representatives of the Council of Economic Advisers, the Office of Management and Budget, the U.S. Department of Commerce, and the Bureau of Labor Statistics. Several alternative projections have been prepared. Those summarized in Figures 2-3 and 2-4 assume a 3 per cent unemployment rate in 1980, and a continued shift toward a "high service" economy. Another set of projections assumes a slightly higher unemployment rate in 1980, and a third set assumes more rapid growth of durable goods than the projections given in the text. The results of the different projections differ in detail, but the broad outlines are not changed.[12]

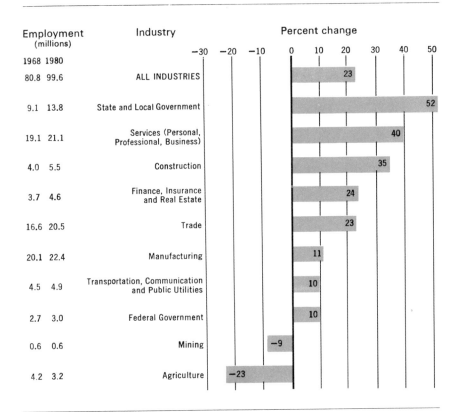

FIGURE 2–3.

Employment Projection to 1980 by Sector. *(Reproduced from the U.S. Department of Labor, Bureau of Labor Statistics, U.S. Manpower in the 1970s: Opportunity and Challenge [no date].)*

12. The details of the 1980 projections, which use 1968 as the base year, are given in *The U.S. Economy In 1980,* Bulletin 1672, U.S. Department of Labor, Bureau of Labor Statistics (1970). The 1968 data are themselves estimates that differ slightly from the final published figures.

The projections of labor requirements in 1980 were made in three steps. First, projections were made of the final demand for goods and services in 1980 in considerable industrial detail. The next step involved estimation of productivity trends, and of the effects which continued increases in productivity would have on the demand for labor by each industry and sector of the economy. The last step involved merging the projections of final demand and the productivity trends to obtain the employment projections.[13]

Total employment is expected to increase by almost one fourth between 1968 and 1980, and to reach almost 100 million in the target year. State and local government employment is expected to increase by more than one half over the 1968 level. The private sectors expected to grow most rapidly are the services, construction, finance (including insurance and real estate), and the wholesale and retail trade sectors. Manufacturing, which will still be the largest sector in 1980, is expected to grow at an average rate of less than 1 per cent per year. An even lower growth rate has been projected for communication, transportation, and the public utilities. Employment in federal government agencies is also expected to grow at less than 1 per cent per year. The sectors of declining employment—continuing long-term past trends—are mining and agriculture.

The trends summarized in Figure 2–3 show that the industry-mix of employment will continue to change during the 1970s as it has throughout the nation's history. Until 1948, more than half of all workers were employed in goods-producing industries. This is no longer true. And by 1980, the trades and services will employ about twice as many workers as those employed in the production of goods. Analysts in the Bureau of Labor Statistics expect that this will lead to greater job stability. This conclusion is based on the observation that employment in the trades and services tends to be affected less by fluctuations in the economy than does employment in manufacturing, mining, and construction.

The composition of the labor force will also continue to change. The proportion of women will rise, with married women accounting for the largest part of the increase. The labor force participation rate of married women, with husband present, has been rising steadily for several decades. The highest rate is for those who have no children at home under eighteen. Yet, while in 1948, for example, only 10 per cent of married women, with husband present and children under six years of age, were in the labor force, by 1970, this had increased to almost 30 per cent. In the words of the BLS analysts, this reflects "a major change in American life style."

Other changes in the composition of the labor force are due to age and

---

13. The Interagency Economic Growth Project uses an input-output model to make its detailed projections. This model takes into account all of the direct *and indirect* relationships among industries and sectors. It shows, in brief, how each sector of the economy depends on all other sectors. For a nontechnical discussion of this method see William H. Miernyk, *The Elements of Input-Output Analysis* (New York: Random House, 1965).

color. The most rapid increase during the 1960s was among young workers, including new entrants to the labor force aged sixteen to twenty-four. The most rapid increase during the 1970s will be among young adults in their prime working years of twenty-five to thirty-four.

The number of teenagers in the labor force increased by 43 per cent between 1960 and 1970. This increase came at a time when technological advances had reduced the demand for many kinds of relatively unskilled labor, and one consequence of these trends was a high level of youth unemployment throughout the 1960s. This age group in the labor force is expected to increase by only about 11 per cent between 1970 and 1980. And this demographic shift, coupled with efforts to provide jobs for young people, should reduce youth unemployment by the end of the decade.

However, one of the more glaring labor market problems of the 1960s was the high unemployment rate among black and other minority teenagers. Throughout the 1960s unemployment in the sixteen to nineteen age group was at least 12 per cent; but for black and other minority teenagers the rate fluctuated between 24 and 30 per cent. The problem of excessively high unemployment among black and other minority teenagers will not be solved by demographic trends. Although white teenagers in the labor force are expected to increase by only 9 per cent between 1969 and 1980, the number of black and other minority teenagers in the labor force is projected to grow by 43 per cent. Unless the demand for teenage workers increases substantially during the 1970s, unemployment rates for those in this age bracket will remain significantly higher than the average for all workers.

The Demand for Labor by Occupation

Total employment in this set of projections is about 5 per cent less than that given in Figure 2-3. This discrepancy is explained by the exclusion of self-employed and unpaid family workers from the occupational projections. Although this has an influence on several of the occupational categories, it is particularly significant in the case of farm workers.

Figure 2-4 shows that the occupational requirements of the United States are changing radically, and fairly rapidly. In 1968, for example, operatives, which include factory assembly workers and truck drivers, outnumbered professional and technical workers by 3.7 million or 36 per cent. In 1980, there will be more professional and technical workers than operatives. And clerical workers, who ranked second in 1968, will have moved into first place.

The rapid increase in the number of technical and professional workers is both a cause and a consequence of technological change. Also, as the economy becomes more complex, there is a corresponding growth in record-keeping. This accounts for the upsurge in clerical employment, which is expected to continue its rapid rate of growth throughout the 1970s.

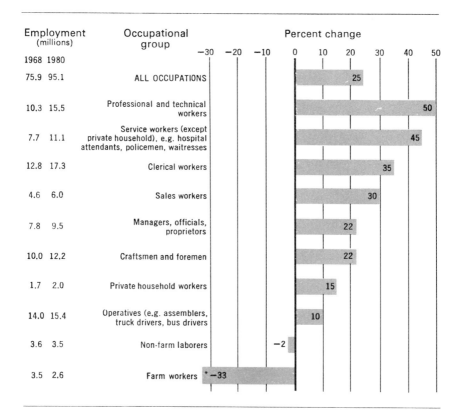

FIGURE 2-4.

Projections of the Demand for Labor to 1980 by Board Occupational Groups. (*Reproduced from the U.S. Department of Labor, Bureau of Labor Statistics,* U.S. Manpower in the 1970s: Opportunity and Challenge [*no date*].)

Total employment in agriculture has been projected to drop 23 per cent between 1968 and 1980 (see Figure 2-3). But there will be an even larger decline of 33 per cent in *hired* farm workers. This will continue a trend that goes back to the 1920s. The massive displacement of farm workers by mechanization and other improvements in productivity has had profound social and economic consequences. It has contributed to today's urban problems as former farm workers have gone to the cities in search of employment. Mechanization also has resulted in a reduction in the number of farms, and an increase in the average size of the remaining farms.

The family farm, which fifty years ago was still commonplace, is virtually a thing of the past. Today, farming is often referred to as "agribusiness." One consequence of this approach to farming has been a change in the relationship between workers and employers. This change is especially apparent in states such as California, where many farms are owned by corporations and operated by professional managers. The new agricultural milieu has produced one of the last frontiers of grass-roots labor organizing by Cesar Chavez and his United Farm Workers Union.

The future decline in the number of farm jobs will have much less impact on the economy than the large-scale decline of the past. Fewer persons will be involved. While individual adjustments will no doubt be as difficult as always to make, the economic impact will be smaller. In fact, the total number of farm workers who will be displaced throughout the economy during the 1970s will be smaller than the number who have migrated to New York, Los Angeles, and Chicago during the past decade.

The Wage Market and the Job Market

We noted in the introduction to this chapter that the "labor market" is an abstraction. But workers do exchange labor services for money wages. In this section we will examine the markets where such exchanges take place. We have already discussed one process of choice, where the alternatives are earned income and leisure. But as early as 1776, Adam Smith pointed out in *The Wealth of Nations* that workers are faced with other choices in the labor market. When choosing among jobs, Smith said, the worker will elect the job that will yield the greatest "net advantage" to himself. Some modern economists have been skeptical about this view of highly rational worker behavior, but it has been defended with considerable vigor by Simon Rottenberg.[14]

Up to now we have referred to *the* labor market. But this is an over-simplification. In the real world there are many kinds of labor markets; while all of these cannot be discussed, a useful classification developed by Clark Kerr will indicate some of the major differences.[15] As Kerr has pointed out, "two processes . . . are going on all the time in our economy: wage rates are changing and individuals are moving among jobs. The two processes may or may not be closely connected."[16] After distinguishing between "wage markets" in which wage rates are changing, and "job markets" in which individuals are moving among jobs, Kerr makes the following classification of wage and job markets:

1. *The Perfect Market.* This is the kind of market that forms the basis for much economic theorizing. It is made up of a large number of relatively small, and undifferentiated, buyers and sellers. There is

---

14. Simon Rottenberg, "On Choice in Labor Markets," *Industrial and Labor Relations Review, Vol. 9,* No. 2 (January 1956), pp. 183–199.

15. Clark Kerr, "Labor Markets: Their Character and Consequences," *American Economic Review,* Papers and Proceedings, Vol. *XL* (May 1950), pp. 278–291.

16. *Ibid.,* p. 278.

complete freedom of entry and exit, complete knowledge, and the absence of collusion. And while Kerr does not mention this, there would also have to be complete mobility of all resources and products within the market area. "Under the circumstances," Kerr notes, "the dichotomy of the wage market and the job market does not exist. Physical movement of workers and the wage setting process are inextricably interwoven. The single price prevails and the market is cleared."[17]

2. *The Neoclassical Market.* One need not be an economist to recognize that the perfect market described above is an abstraction; its conditions can never be completely met and are only rarely approximated. The neoclassical market recognizes the existence of "imperfections." The supply of skilled workers cannot be expanded suddenly because it takes time for a worker to acquire his skill. At the same time, unskilled wokers are at a disadvantage because they are available in abundance and their services are perishable. The neoclassical market also recognizes the existence of unions, but these are assumed to be "only sufficiently strong to offset market imperfections introduced by combinations, formal or informal, of employers."[18] Workers within each skill classification are presumed to be relatively homogeneous.

   In spite of the imperfections which it recognizes, the neoclassical model assumes that the market is what determines wages, and the allocation of resources approaches the optimum in the long run. Thus while neither the wage market nor the job market make the instantaneous adjustments assumed in the perfect market, they are still closely related; indeed, they remain inseparable.[19]

3. *The Natural Market.* In the neoclassical model it is assumed that wages will tend toward equality for workers in a given skill classification. But there is an abundance of evidence that in the real world this equality of wages is not found. A characteristic of actual labor markets is wage diversity rather than wage uniformity. During World War II, when the War Labor Board collected volumes of wage data, it was found that within local labor markets, especially where there was no collective bargaining, there was a wide dispersion of wage rates. Contrary to a widespread belief that wage differentials are offset by "fringe benefits," the latter were found to "reinforce rather than offset the rate inequalities."[20]

---

17. *Ibid.,* p. 279. Kerr cites a description of such a perfect labor market in J. R. Hicks, *The Theory of Wages* (New York: The Macmillan Company, 1935), pp. 4–5.

18. *Ibid.,* p. 280.

19. An outstanding economist in the neoclassical tradition was Alfred Marshall. See his *Principles of Economics,* 8th ed. (New York: The Macmillan Company, 1938).

20. Kerr, *op. cit.,* p. 280.

In the natural market, the typical worker has a very limited view of the market as a whole, and unless he is unemployed or just entering the labor force, he is not "actively in the market." The worker's knowledge of the labor market may be limited to his own plant or office and other jobs about which he has general information. Workers do not regularly weigh the advantages of the jobs they hold against other alternatives and employers are not constantly hiring and firing workers in an effort to find the greatest bargains in the labor market.

In the natural market there is a fairly clear distinction between the "wage market" and the "job market." Wages are not set entirely by the free influence of competitive forces, and they do not tend toward equality. Also, resources are not necessarily used to their best advantage.

4. *The Institutional Market.* The institutional market is one in which the policies of unions, employers, and the government have more to do with wage movements than free competitive forces. Indeed, the objective of policies developed by all three—unions, employers, and the government—is to limit the free operation of the forces of supply and demand. Under these circumstances the wage market and the job market operate in two separate orbits. Institutional policies, rather than the market, set the upper and lower limits of wages, and these clearly reduce the mobility of labor.

Uniform wages are often found for a given grade of workers in the institutional market, but this is because of the influence of institutions—notably unions—and to some extent government. It is not a result of the interaction of demand and supply. Demand and supply cannot be ignored, of course, but their influence is considerably curtailed by policies of unions, employers, and the government.

5. *The Managed Market.* The managed market, like the perfect market, does not exist in the real world. The objective of the managed market would be to tie wage setting and worker movement more closely together than they are in the natural or institutional market. This would be accompanied by the imposition of state controls of one kind or another, on wage setting or the allocation of labor, or perhaps both.

The long-run trend in the United States has been toward the institutional labor market, but collective bargaining and government intervention have not eliminated wage diversity. Where unions have an influence on wages there is a tendency toward uniformity within a craft, or for given grades of labor within an industry, but there is still a great deal of wage diversity among labor markets. Occupational wage surveys conducted by the Bureau of Labor Statistics show that for identical occupations there are substantial variations in wages from community to community.

Structured and Unstructured Labor Markets

Another useful way to view labor markets is to consider those which are *structured,* and those which are *unstructured* or "structureless."[21] Phelps has defined an unstructured labor market as one which "contains few, if any, established institutions by means of which people obtain market information, move into and out of jobs, qualify for advances in rank or pay, or identify themselves with any type of organization. . . ."[22]

According to Clark Kerr, some structure can be introduced into a labor market without institutional rules. This is so because some workers are more highly skilled than others; skilled crafts exist even without craft unions. But the degree of structure is increased as the labor market becomes institutionalized. In such markets institutional rules limit the movement of workers, affect hiring policies, and are often the deciding factor in wage determination.

Phelps has distinguished three main types of structured labor markets. First, there is the market for public employees, which is highly structured by legislation and administrative rules. The second type is the nonunion labor market in the large firm, where the rules are laid down by the personnel or industrial relations department. Finally, there is the labor market in which rules are negotiated by unions and formalized in the labor-management agreement.[23] Phelps has estimated that at least one third of the nation's workers are employed in unstructured labor markets.

Within the three broad types of structured labor markets there are many compartments, that is, many barriers to mobility. Each labor market is actually made up of an intricate network of submarkets. These submarkets can be considered as "noncompeting groups," to use a term originated by J. E. Cairnes many years ago, but not in the same sense that Cairnes used this term.[24]

Cairnes viewed the various socio-economic classes—unskilled manual workers, white-collar workers, and professional workers, for example—as noncompeting groups. But as Kerr has pointed out there are many other

---

21. See Clark Kerr, "The Balkanization of Labor Markets," *Labor Mobility and Economic Opportunity* (Cambridge, Massachusetts: The Technology Press of M.I.T.—John Wiley & Sons, Inc., 1954); and Orme W. Phelps, "A Structural Model of the U.S. Labor Market," *Industrial and Labor Relations Review, Vol. 10* (April 1957).

22. Phelps, "A Structural Model of the Labor Market," *Ibid.,* p. 406.

23. *Ibid.,* p. 407.

24. J. E. Cairnes, *Political Economy* (New York: Harper, 1874). See also Kerr, "Balkanization of Labor Markets," *op. cit.,* pp. 93–94.

barriers to mobility than the socio-economic status of workers. Differences in skill, the workers' lack of knowledge of the labor market, the individual preferences of employees, and the attitudes and policies of employers—plus the fact of space and the cost of travel—impose barriers to mobility which greatly cut down noncompeting groups in size.

Even within a single labor market, unskilled workers do not compete with skilled craftsmen, and skilled workers in one occupation do not compete with skilled workers in others. The result is an extremely complex interlacing of submarkets, each of which is governed by its own institutional rules, customs, legislation, or administrative procedures.

The geographic extent of submarkets also varies considerably. Skilled craftsmen, for example, often are not attached to any particular employer, and their movement need not be restricted to a particular community. A skilled carpenter, for example, might work part of the year in New York City and part in Miami, Florida. Similarly, a highly skilled auto mechanic may move around the country virtually at will. The operator of a spinning frame in a textile mill might find it difficult to locate another job, however, if he loses the one he has or if he quits voluntarily to search for other employment.

It is not easy to define the boundaries of labor markets or the submarkets within a given area. The labor market for some workers is national in scope while the mobility of some workers is highly restricted.[25] The extent of a market depends in part upon a worker's education and skills. Highly trained professionals are likely to find suitable employment in many different localities. Such workers are likely to be willing to move to another job which holds promise of being more interesting or which pays better. The same is true of highly skilled craftsmen, electronic technicians and glass blowers, for example.

Workers without skills—machine tenders, assemblers, clerks—find it much less easy to move about. The boundaries of their labor markets are likely to be restricted to an area within commuting distance of their homes. Age is also an important factor in the mobility of labor. In general, younger workers tend to be more mobile than their older counterparts in the labor force.[26]

One further characteristic should be noted about some types of structured labor markets. The skilled craftsmen, it has been pointed out, are able to move from employer to employer and many have no permanent attachment to a single employer throughout their work careers. But workers who are not members of a craft do not have the same degree of mobility, partly because of hiring practices which restrict the lateral movement of workers from company to company.

---

25. See Robert L. Raimon, "Interstate Migration and Wage Theory," *The Review of Economics and Statistics,* November 1962, pp. 428–438.

26. *Ibid.,* p. 429.

Many establishments—especially middle-sized and large concerns—recruit their work force through "hiring jobs." These jobs are generally open only to new entrants to the labor force. Even at the hiring level, new workers might be hired for a probationary period, but if they survive this—and perform effectively on the job—their job security increases with seniority. Promotion in such companies is from within. As workers retire, or leave the firm for other reasons, their places are filled by someone on a lower rung of the seniority ladder. It is quite rare in many companies for a worker to be brought in above the level of a hiring job.

In a broader sense, Kerr speaks of "ports of entry" in institutional labor markets.[27] It is through these ports of entry that workers enter a labor market, or are rejected and must turn elsewhere for employment. The typical port of entry outside the skilled crafts, is the "hiring job" in the large concern. There are also ports of entry to the skilled crafts. Some crafts insist upon a fairly long period of apprenticeship. Not all workers are willing to go through a long period of training even for the reward of fairly steady work at relatively high pay once the apprenticeship has been completed.

These are only some of the factors which stratify labor markets and break them up into smaller submarkets. They illustrate the point that when we talk about *the* labor market we are oversimplifying. Our economy is made up of a great network of labor markets, and the latter are further divided into submarkets of workers many of whom belong to essentially noncompeting groups.

Empirical Research on Labor Mobility

"Research on labor mobility," as Parnes has pointed out, "has as its principle objective evaluation of the allocative efficiency of labor markets."[28] There are various types of labor mobility, which are defined according to (a) job, (b) occupation, (c) industry, and (d) geographic location. Then, of course, some workers move in and out of the labor force at will. Labor market surveys indicate "that most job changes are 'complex,' i.e., that when a worker changes employers he more often than not either changes his occupation, his industry, or both."[29]

Evidence can be found for both relative stability and relative mobility within the labor force. In a typical year, as many as 10 per cent of all workers employed at any time during that year will change employers at least once. About one third of these will be multiple job changers who worked for more than one employer during that year. At the same time, Parnes refers to a study which showed that during the mid-1960s almost a fifth of all employed

---

27. Kerr, "Balkanization of Labor Markets," *op. cit.,* p. 101.

28. Herbert S. Parnes, "Labor Force Participation and Labor Mobility," *op. cit.,* p. 33.

29. *Ibid.,* p. 40.

workers had been with the same employer for more than fifteen years.[30] Like labor force participation, voluntary labor mobility is influenced by demographic characteristics. Younger workers change jobs more often than older workers, and younger workers without family attachment tend to be more mobile than those with family responsibilities. Men are more mobile than women, and in recent years Negro men have exhibited more mobility than white men. Professional and technical workers are less likely to change jobs in the course of a year than unskilled workers, but the highest rates of geographic mobility are exhibited by the best educated members of the labor force, who tend to be in the professional and technical category.

The process of job changing, which affects millions of workers and their families each year is not a simple one, and job changers do not necessarily behave as traditional theory says they will. After reviewing the labor market literature of the 1940s and 1950s, Parnes had the following to say[31]:

> Labor market studies of workers' attitudes and decisions about jobs have . . . tended to confirm the view that workers, far from being concerned exclusively —or even primarily—with "net economic advantage," have multiple and complex goals; that their "choices" are bounded by considerable degrees of ignorance of alternatives; and that the typical worker is a "satisficing" rather than a "maximizing" man. . . .

In a detailed report prepared for the Science Social Research Council in 1954, Parnes concluded that, ". . . to the extent that the market forces described by traditional theory are present, they operate with considerably attenuated vigor. The conflicting evidence is not among different studies, but within each. Regardless what emphasis a particular investigator has chosen to give in his summary and conclusions, there is in all studies evidence of both the presence and absence of the traditional economic forces."[32] After reviewing the labor market literature of the 1960s, Parnes concluded that there was no reason for him to substantially alter that view.

Much of the voluntary labor turnover in our economy is concentrated among young, short-service workers. When labor market conditions are favorable, a young worker might "shop around" for some time before settling down to a steady job. His ability to do this, of course, depends upon the state of balance in the labor market. If there is a high level of unemployment even the young worker will be less likely to quit his job—without an alterna-

---

30. *Ibid.*, p. 44.

31. Herbert S. Parnes, "The Labor Force and Labor Markets," H. G. Heniman, *et al., Employment Relations Research* (New York: Harper and Brothers, 1960), p. 30. For an alternative view see Rottenberg, *op. cit.* See also the comments by Lampman and Lester, and the replies by Rottenberg, on pp. 629–643 of the same.

32. Herbert S. Parnes, *Research on Labor Mobility* (New York: Social Science Research Council, 1954) cited in "Labor Force Participation and Labor Mobility," *op. cit.*, p. 66.

tive lined up—than he will if the labor market is fairly tight and the newspapers are filled with want ads. There are also drifters or floaters who never seem to stay with one job for any great length of time. As Sumner H. Slichter pointed out, a high turnover rate may be caused by many workers changing jobs occasionally, or by a small proportion of the work force changing jobs many times during the year.[33] Thus a large number of workers moving into and out of "hiring jobs" can lead to a relatively high turnover rate, but even then the majority of workers will not be changing jobs.

Research on the mobility of *involuntarily unemployed* workers indicates that they are less mobile than many economists appeared to believe in the past. Among the involuntarily unemployed are the highly mobile drifters who do not appear to be able to hold a job. They might perform well for a time but after a while they fail to meet work standards or refuse to accept plant discipline. When fired from a job such a worker will naturally move elsewhere in search of employment. But these workers are far from typical. Most workers are anxious to perform well and to advance at least within the limits of their capabilities.

Many capable workers are displaced from their jobs through the liquidation of a mill or factory, the shutdown of a mine, the depletion of resources or—in more recent times—by automation or other forms of technological change. The experience of these unemployed workers is of major interest since they constitute a much larger part of the unemployed than do the job drifters. Here also, empirical studies have raised doubts about earlier views of the operation of the labor market.

The typical view, until fairly recent times, was that involuntary unemployment resulting from the large-scale displacement of labor would result in one of two changes, or perhaps both in combination. First, it was assumed that as the level of unemployment in a labor market rose, wages would fall. This was supposed to attract new employers to the community to absorb the displaced workers and as unemployment declined wages would be bid up again. Another assumption was that the displaced workers would readily migrate to other areas where job opportunities were more plentiful. It was usually assumed that both types of movement would take place. Some workers would migrate, and some businesses would relocate to the communities with high-level unemployment, until equilibrium had been achieved again. Those who subscribed to such views accepted the classical or neoclassical versions of labor market behavior at face value.

But studies of displaced workers have revealed that many of them are highly immobile.[34] The studies show that a large proportion of the displaced

---

33. Sumner H. Slichter, *The Turnover of Factory Labor* (New York: D. Appleton and Company, 1919), pp. 10–44.

34. Myers and Shultz, *The Dynamics of a Labor Market* (New York: Prentice-Hall, Inc., 1951), and *Miernyk, Inter-Industry Labor Mobility* (Boston: Northeastern University, Bureau of Business and Economic Research, 1955).

workers do not move out of the community even in the absence of alternative jobs locally. As a result, some communities have had high-level unemployment for long periods—in some cases for a decade or more—following massive layoffs due to the liquidation of plants or the shutdown of mines.

The immobility of these workers is not the result of apathy or inertia. They want to work and many would gladly move if they felt they could find employment elsewhere. But when a plant is closed or a mine is shut down workers in all age groups are affected. The relatively young, short-service worker will move elsewhere in search of employment—especially if he is without family responsibilities—while those who are close to retirement age might make no effort to find new employment. But most workers affected by shutdowns of this kind fall somewhere between these extremes. They do not simply pack up and move—especially those who are middle-aged or older—because they are aware of the hiring practices which have become common in American industry. Many of them recognize that they are too old for the hiring jobs in large concerns, and those with family responsibilities might not be able to support their dependents on the pay they would earn in hiring jobs—even if these were available to them. They know that the "ports of entry" are closed to them. They remain in the community in the hope that job opportunities will improve, or they may commute to nearby communities in search of employment. Often such shutdowns occur during periods of recession, and the workers involved have little opportunity to find other kinds of employment until general economic conditions improve. Even then many of them are able to obtain only relatively unskilled jobs in one of the unstructured labor markets where there are no ports of entry, but where the pay is generally low and where there is little or no job security.

The Dual Labor Market

One of the newer concepts in labor-market theory is that of the dual labor market, divided into primary and secondary sectors. The primary sector, or primary market, "offers jobs which possess several of the following traits: high wages, good working conditions, employment stability and job stability, equity and due process in the administration of work rules, and chances for advancement."[35] The secondary market, or secondary sector, "has jobs which, relative to those in the primary sector, are decidedly less attractive. They tend to involve low wages, poor working conditions, considerable variability in

---

35. Michael Piore, "The Dual Labor Market: Theory and Implications," in David M. Gordon (ed.), *Problems in Political Economy: An Urban Perspective* (Lexington, Massachusetts: D.C. Heath and Company, 1971), p. 91. This section draws heavily on Piore's excellent paper. See also Peter B. Doeringer and Michael J. Piore, *Internal Labor Markets and Manpower Analysis* (Lexington, Mass.: D.C. Heath and Company, 1971), pp. 165–188.

employment, harsh and often arbitrary disciplines, and little opportunity to advance."[36]

By and large, the opportunities of workers below the poverty line are generally limited to jobs in the secondary sector. Piore and others who have analyzed the dual labor market believe that the dichotomy in job opportunities is the result of a number of complex factors. But the most important characteristic that distinguishes primary from secondary jobs "appears to be the behavioral requirements which [the former] impose upon the work force, particularly that of employment stability."[37] Workers confined to the secondary labor market are generally not kept from jobs in the primary market by real or tangible barriers. But workers employed in the primary market are expected to show up for work on time, minimize absenteeism, be properly dressed, and follow accepted modes of behavior in the job strata that make up the primary market.

The same characteristics do not apply to jobs in the secondary labor market. Employers who hire in this market tend to be more tolerant about lateness and absenteeism; they are much less concerned about the appearance and attitudes of their workers than employers in the primary market. Some of the work in the secondary market is casual and of short duration. Workers who have never held jobs outside the strata which make up the secondary market tend to develop behavioral characteristics and a life style compatible with the low-paying, often menial, and highly unstable jobs open to them.

Some workers in the secondary sector may actually be qualified to hold jobs in the primary labor market. But they may be rejected for primary jobs because their "superficial characteristics" are similar to those of secondary workers. This type of rejection may occur because employment decisions are typically based on readily discernible traits such as "race, demeanor, accent, educational attainment, test scores and the like."[38] Characteristics such as those listed above may be statistically correlated with job performance, but it does not follow that there is a *causal* relationship between job performance and "superficial characteristics." Workers excluded from the primary market on this basis are victims of what Piore has called *statistical discrimination.*

Discrimination, whether statistical or actual, affects the allocation of labor between the two sectors of the dual labor market. Economists who accept the dual labor market hypothesis feel that barriers between the two sectors result in a relative labor surplus in the secondary labor market, and a relative shortage in the primary. It follows that wages in secondary jobs will tend to be

---

36. Piore, *op. cit.*

37. *Ibid.*

38. *Ibid.*

depressed while wages in primary jobs tend to be higher than they would be in the absence of discrimination.

Discrimination is a necessary condition for the dual labor market to exist. The concept of discrimination employed by Piore in his general formulation of the dual labor market hypothesis is a general one; it is not specifically limited to racial discrimination. Other writers, however, have developed a variant of the dual labor market hypothesis based more strictly on racial dualism, and applied specifically to black ghettos.[39]

The dual labor market hypothesis seems highly plausible, and it has appealed to both orthodox economists—some of whom have incorporated it into traditional labor market theory—and to radical economists who have included it in their evolving body of doctrine. Piore has pointed out that the hypothesis is "consistent with autobiographical and sociological descriptions of urban ghetto life" in that it appears to apply to the black and Puerto Rican poor of Boston. "How far beyond these ghetto communities the applicability of the model extends is a moot question."[40] Efforts are being made to test the dual labor market hypothesis statistically, and early results of the statistical tests appear to support the hypothesis.[41]

Questions and Exercises

1. Product markets can generally be defined without ambiguity. Can the same be said of labor markets?
2. In 1970, about two thirds of the noninstitutional population aged sixteen and over was in the labor force. What major groups in this segment of the noninstitutional labor population are neither employed nor seeking work?
3. How would you define a society's labor supply?
4. A farmer selling wheat will offer more at a higher price than at a lower price. Is this true of a worker's offer of his labor services?
5. What are the specific assumptions that lie behind the theory of consumer behavior as it has been applied to the choice between income and leisure?
6. Define the marginal rate of substitution in terms of the choice between income and leisure. Describe the behavior of the marginal rate of substitution as you move from a high level of earned income to a low level of earned income. At what point is the individual worker "in equilibrium"—that is, what is the optimal amount of work from the individual's point of view?

---

39. For example, Harold M. Baron and Bennet Hymer, "The Dynamics of the Dual Labor Market," in Gordon, *idem.,* pp. 94–101.

40. Piore, *op. cit.,* p. 94.

41. See David M. Gordon, "Ghetto Employment Problems," in *51st Annual Report,* National Bureau of Economic Research, Inc. (September 1971), pp. 94–95.

7. Within the income-leisure model based on consumer behavior what dilemma is posed by an increase in the wage rate? Does the theory of consumer behavior provide a general rule for avoiding this dilemma?

8. What were some of the criticisms made by Mincer of the income-leisure model?

9. Bowen and Finegan found that labor force participation is not greatly influenced by changes in wage rates. Does this conclusion apply equally to workers with "primary" as well as with "secondary" labor market attachments?

10. What are the "additional worker" and the "discouraged worker" hypotheses?

11. According to Parnes, what is the major cause of variation in the labor force due to short-run changes in aggregate demand?

12. Why is the demand for labor a *derived* demand? What are some of the forces that influence the long-run demand for labor?

13. Which sectors of the economy are expected to show the largest gains in employment during the 1970s? Which broad sector will still be the major employer by 1980?

14. What major occupational shifts are expected to occur during the 1970s? Which groups of occupations will have the fastest growth rates, and which groups will have the slowest? Are any occupations expected to show an absolute decline during the 1970s?

15. On what basis, according to Adam Smith, will workers choose a job?

16. Clark Kerr has developed a taxonomy of labor markets. He defines these markets as: (1) perfect, (2) neoclassical, (3) natural, (4) institutional and (5) managed. What are the major characteristics of each?

17. What are the differences between "structured" and "unstructured" labor markets?

18. The behavior of labor markets is influenced to some extent by the mobility of labor. What are the various types of labor mobility? What did Parnes mean by the statement that most job changes are "complex?"

19. What is meant by the "dual labor market?" And what does Piore mean by "statistical discrimination?"

Suggested Readings

Books

Bowen, William G., and T. Aldrich Finegan. *The Economics of Labor Force Participation.* Princeton: Princeton University Press, 1969.

Doeringer, Peter B., and Michael J. Piore. *Internal Labor Markets and Manpower Analysis.* Lexington, Mass.: D. C. Heath and Company, 1971.

Fleisher, Belton M. *Labor Economics: Theory and Evidence.* Englewood Cliffs, N.J.: Prentice-Hall, Inc., 1970.

Gordon, David M. *Problems in Political Economy: An Urban Perspective.* Lexington, Mass.: D. C. Heath and Company, 1971.

Perlman, Richard. *Labor Theory.* New York: John Wiley & Sons, Inc., 1969.

Reynolds, Lloyd G. *The Structure of Labor Markets.* New York: Harper, 1951.

Wilcock, Richard C., and Walter H. Franke. *Unwanted Workers.* New York: The Free Press of Glencoe, 1963.

Articles

Barth, Peter F. "Unemployment and Labor Force Participation," *Southern Economic Journal,* January 1968, pp. 375–382.

Becker, Gary. "A Theory of the Allocation of Time," *Economic Journal,* September 1965, pp. 493–517.

Hayghe, Howard V., and Kopp Michielotti. "Multiple Job Holders in 1970 and 1971," *Monthly Labor Review,* October 1971, pp. 38–45.

Mincer, Jacob. "Market Prices, Opportunity Costs and Income Effects," in Carl F. Christ, *et al., Measurement in Economics.* Stanford, California: Stanford University Press, 1963.

Parnes, Herbert S. "Labor Force Participation and Labor Mobility," in Woodrow L. Ginsburg, *et al.,* (eds.), *A Review of Industrial Relations Research, Vol. I.* Madison, Wisconsin: Industrial Relations Research Association, 1970, pp. 1–78.

Robbins, Lionel. "On the Elasticity of Demand for Income in Terms of Effort," *Economica,* June 1930, pp. 123–129.

Scherer, Joseph. "Labor Force: Concepts, Measurement, and the Use of Data," *The Journal of Business of the University of Chicago, XXXI* (January 1958), pp. 38–62.

Strand, Kenneth, and Thomas Dernburg. "Cyclical Variation in Civilian Labor Force Participation," *Review of Economics and Statistics,* November 1964, pp. 378–391.

Tella, Alfred. "Labor Force Sensitivity to Employment by Age, Sex," *Industrial Relations,* February 1965, pp. 69–83.

Tella, Alfred. "The Relation of Labor Force to Employment," *Industrial and Labor Relations Review,* April 1964, pp. 454–469.

Ulman, Lloyd. "Labor Mobility and the Industrial Wage Structure in the Post-War United States," *Quarterly Journal of Economics,* February 1965, pp. 73–97.

Wilcock, Richard C. "The Secondary Labor Force and the Measurement of Unemployment," *The Measurement and Behavior of Unemployment.* National Bureau of Economic Research. Princeton, N.J.: Princeton University Press, 1957, pp. 167–210.

3

The Firm
and Its Work Force

This chapter is concerned with labor as an input in the production process. The focus is on labor as a physical input at the level of the firm. Moreover, the demand for labor is examined in terms of the theory of production without specific reference to the way in which wage rates are determined. The process of wage determination is discussed in Chapter 5.

Another issue discussed in this chapter is factor proportions and distributive shares. A relationship of particular interest in labor economics is the capital-labor ratio (K/L). This ratio is affected by technological change; thus, the question considered in the concluding section is: How do changes in the capital-labor ratio affect the share of total output going to labor?

The Firm's Production Function

Labor is a ubiquitous input. All firms, whether they produce goods or provide services, use labor as one of their inputs. In many cases labor is the largest physical input. But even in those cases where relatively little labor is used in relation to output, labor is the most critical input. This is true because labor is the only input that cannot be treated impersonally. When the owners of cement, shoes, wax, or copper tubing complete a transaction, they are not in the least concerned about the way in which these things are to be used. But the services of labor cannot be separated from the person selling them, and the worker will clearly want to have something to say about how his or her services are used. Later in the text, when we discuss collective bargaining, we will see that this process goes far beyond wage determination. Much collective bargaining is concerned with working conditions, including work rules that define how labor services are to be used. For the present, however, labor will be considered as an abstract physical input, and one that can be purchased in completely divisible quantities.

Labor as the Only Variable Input

Consider first the case where all of the factors of production except labor are fixed. In this case the firm's output will vary with its labor inputs only. This may be indicated symbolically as follows:

$$Q = f(L),$$

where Q represents the firm's output, and L represents labor input. This is a particularly simple example of a firm's *production function*.

How does output behave as increasing amounts of labor are used? This depends upon the nature of the firm's production process, but the general case with one variable input is illustrated by Figure 3–1.

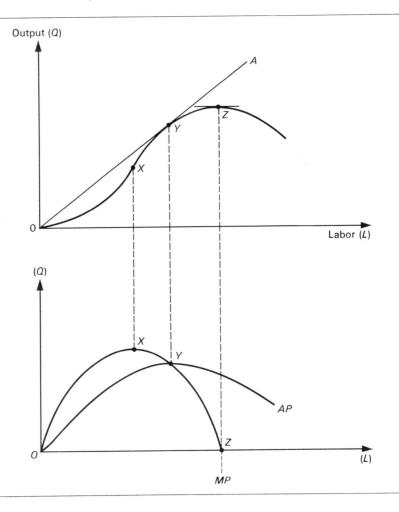

FIGURE 3–1.

Total, Average, and Marginal Product with Variable Labor Inputs.

The total product curve shown in the upper part of Figure 3-1 shows *alternative* levels of output associated with varying quantities of labor inputs. It illustrates, among other things, one of the time-honored "laws" of classical economics; namely, the law of diminishing returns. The assumptions on which this law is based are that (a) technology is constant, and (b) at least one input is held constant. More generally, the law of diminishing returns applies only in the case of variable proportions, that is, where it is possible to vary the proportions in which different inputs are used at different levels of output. In the case illustrated by Figure 3-1 we have assumed that all other inputs are constant and that labor is the only variable input. On the basis of these assumptions the marginal product of labor and the average product of labor may be derived directly from the production function.

The *marginal product* of labor is defined as the amount added to the firm's output with the addition of one unit of labor input. To obtain the smooth curves shown in Figure 3-1 we have assumed that labor can be varied in extremely small quantities. In empirical work, an effort is usually made to measure labor input in terms of man-hours.

The *average product* of labor is defined as total output divided by the quantity of labor inputs. Notice the relationships between the total product curve in the upper part of Figure 3-1, and the marginal and average product curves in the lower part of that diagram. Marginal product increases up to the point where the total product curve goes through a point of inflection, and after that marginal product declines. Marginal product becomes zero at a point where the slope of the total product curve is equal to zero, and if production continues beyond this point marginal product is negative. Since marginal product can be a negative quantity, the definition given earlier may be rephrased. The marginal product of labor is *the difference between* two successive levels of total output as a result of the addition of one more unit of labor input.

The average product curve rises and falls more slowly than the marginal product curve. It reaches a maximum at a point where a line drawn from the origin is tangent to the production function: point Y in Figure 3-1. Beyond this point, average product declines. Unlike marginal product the average product of labor can never become a negative quantity. Marginal product is the *change* in total output as one more unit of the variable input is added. And this change may be positive or negative as total output rises or falls. Average product is a physical quantity, however, and thus can never be less than zero.

The law of diminishing returns, as it relates to labor inputs, may be stated as follows: If all inputs except labor are held constant, output at first increases with increasing amounts of labor inputs, then continues to increase but at a declining rate, and finally, after a certain point, begins to fall below the peak level of output. This is illustrated by Figure 3-2, which combines the upper and lower portions of Figure 3-1.

Three phases of production have been marked off by vertical lines in

Figure 3-2. The reason for dividing the production function into phases is to show that some combinations of inputs are efficient while others are clearly inefficient.

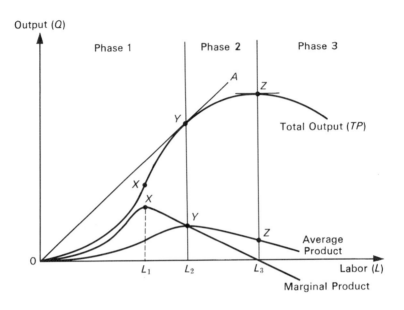

FIGURE 3–2.
The Three Phases of Production.

Phase 1 extends from the origin to the point at which the average product of labor is a maximum, or OL_2 in Figure 3-2. The marginal product of labor is increasing up to point OL_1 in Figure 3-2. Beyond this point—in the interval OL_1 to OL_2—the marginal product of labor is declining, but it is still greater than average product. Throughout the first phase the *percentage* increase in output is greater than the *percentage* increase in labor input. Phase 1 is thus called the range of *absolutely increasing returns.*

The second phase begins at the point where *average* product is a maximum, and ends at the point where *marginal* product becomes zero. In Figure 3-2 it is the interval from OL_2 to OL_3. Within this interval, both the average product and the marginal product of labor are falling, but the marginal product falls at a faster rate. In phase 2, the *percentage* increase in output is always less than the *percentage* increase in labor input. On the total product curve this is the range in which output increases at a decreasing rate. Thus phase 2 is the *region of diminishing returns.*

Phase 3 is the entire area to the right of point Z on the total product curve, or the entire region in which more than OL_3 units of labor would be employed. In this range total output is declining and the marginal product of labor becomes *negative*. This is the region of *absolutely diminishing returns*.

How are the phases of production related to the efficiency of the firm? A firm operating in phase 3 would not be using its inputs efficiently. The marginal product of labor is negative; each additional worker causes a *drop* in total output. To improve its efficiency position the firm would be forced to either reduce its labor input, or to increase other inputs such as land and capital to achieve an efficient combination.

There is a degree of symmetry between phase 3 and phase 1. The problem in phase 3 is that there is too much labor *relative to* the fixed inputs. The reverse situation is true in phase 1. Where there is not enough labor *relative to* the quantities of fixed inputs, the marginal product of one (or possibly more) of the fixed inputs will be negative. In other words, not enough labor is being used in relation to the quantity of fixed inputs employed.

The problem in both phases 1 and 3 is that of an improper *combination* of inputs. This problem is not encountered in phase 2. In this phase there is no excess of either the fixed inputs or the variable labor input. Hence, if the objective of the firm is to maximize profits, the firm will always operate in phase 2, the region of diminishing returns. The profit-maximizing firm is not free to operate anywhere within this range. But it is within phase 2 that the firm's equilibrium level of output is determined by the equality between marginal revenue and marginal cost.[1]

Production with Two Variable Inputs

The example of production with a single variable input is a useful way to describe the law of diminishing returns, one of the principles of economics that is frequently misunderstood. But this is not a situation encountered by many employers in practice. More frequently, the employer is concerned with the optimum or best combination of two or more variable inputs.

The analysis of more than two variable inputs cannot be handled geometrically, but even this difficulty can be circumvented by thinking in terms of two "bundles" of variable inputs. For example, labor may be one variable input and "capital" the other, if we assume that capital and all of the remaining inputs can be varied in fixed proportions.

Figure 3–3 illustrates the situation in which capital (K) and labor (L) are variable. These two variables are measured on the horizontal axes with an angle of 90° between them. Output (Q) is measured along the vertical axis.

---

1. *Marginal revenue* is the amount added to the firm's total revenue by the sale of one more unit of output; *marginal cost* is the amount added to the firm's total cost by buying one more unit of the variabie input.

Various *combinations* of capital and labor can be used to produce a given level of output. This production function may be written symbolically as $Q = g(K, L)$ which states that output depends upon the quantities of capital and labor used in the production process. If larger quantities of both inputs are used, total output will increase. On the three-dimensional diagram, total output is not a line; it is a surface that can best be pictured as a hill rising from the zero origin to a peak on the Q axis.

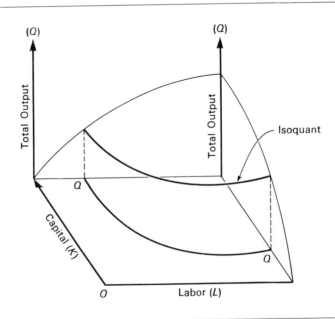

FIGURE 3–3.

Production Surface with Capital and Labor Inputs.

The three-dimensional diagram of Figure 3–3 can be translated into a more convenient two-dimensional graph. Since the quantity of output is measured by moving up or down the hill, a given level of output may be depicted by imagining a horizontal slice taken through the hill parallel to the capital and labor axes. The result is an *isoquant* or equal product curve.

If we imagine that isoquants are projected to the base of the hill—as shown for the single isoquant QQ in Figure 3–3—a number of isoquants can be considered simultaneously on a single graph. This is illustrated in Figure 3–4, which shows four isoquants or four different levels of output.

Each isoquant, as we move up the hill from Q_1 to Q_4, represents an increase in output due to the employment of larger quantities of capital and labor.

Any one of the isoquants of Figure 3–4 may be used to represent the

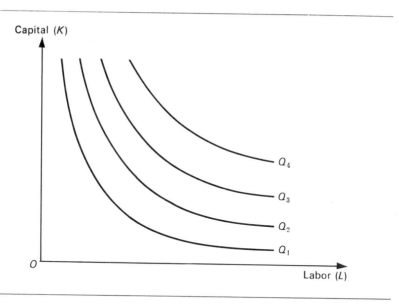

FIGURE 3–4.

Isoquants with Variable Proportions of Capital and Labor.

general case of *variable factor proportions.* This is where a *given* level of output can be produced by using more capital and less labor or, alternatively, the same level of output may be produced by using less capital and more labor. It is important to stress that it is the proportions of the two inputs that are variable. Within fairly narrow limits, factor proportions can be varied by increasing the quantity of one input while using another input more intensively. It will simplify matters, however, if we think of the case of variable proportions in terms of changing quantities of both inputs.

Under some conditions factor proportions are *not* variable. This is true of various manufacturing operations in the short run, and it is known as the case of fixed technical (or production) coefficients. A steel mill may be designed, for example, to use a single production process. It requires a certain number of workers, a certain quantity of capital, and specified inputs of coal, iron ore, limestone, electricity, chemicals, and other physical inputs, to produce 1 ton of steel. With constant technology, and fixed production coefficients, twice as much of each input will be required to produce 2 tons of steel.

The production function with fixed technical coefficients is linear and homogeneous. On a two-dimensional graph it is a straight line through the origin of the chart.[2] The isoquants are also straight lines with a 90° angle

---

2. It does not follow that all linear and homogeneous production functions have fixed coefficients. Some production functions with variable factor proportions (as in Figure 3–4) are also linear and homogeneous.

along the production function This type of production function is often referred to as a Leontief production function because it is the type on which his well-known input-output model is based. A Leontief production function and its isoquants are illustrated in Figure 3–5.

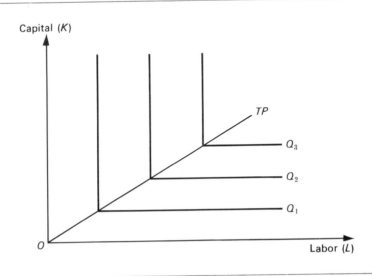

FIGURE 3–5.
Isoquants with Fixed Proportions of Capital and Labor.

The marginal product of capital is defined as the increase in output resulting from a unit increase in the quantity of capital, with labor held constant. Similarly, the marginal product of labor is defined as the increase in output resulting from a unit increase in labor, with capital held constant.[3]

The Marginal Rate of Substitution

When it is technically possible to substitute capital for labor, or vice versa, the isoquants will be convex when viewed from the origin. This is because of the declining marginal rate of substitution of labor for capital. The marginal rate of substitution of lábor for capital is defined as the marginal product of labor divided by the marginal product of capital. As an increasing amount of labor is substituted for capital, the marginal rate of substitution will decline. An increase in the quantity of labor employed with a fixed amount of capital

---

3. Symbolically, the marginal product of capital is $MPK = \partial Q/\partial K$, and the marginal product of labor is $MPL = \partial Q/\partial L$.

will result in a decline in the marginal product of labor. Because more labor and less capital is used, the marginal product of capital will increase. Since the marginal rate of substitution of labor for capital has been defined as the marginal product of labor divided by the marginal product of capital, if the numerator is a steadily declining number and the denominator a steadily increasing number, the quotient will be a declining number.[4]

The declining marginal rate of substitution—when substitution is technically feasible—limits the ease and rate at which one input may be substituted for another. This is illustrated in Figure 3-6.

Assume that a firm is producing a fixed amount of its product indicated by the isoquant. Suppose also that initially it is using OK_0 units of capital and

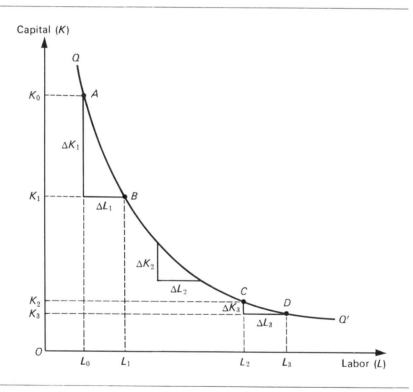

FIGURE 3-6.

The Marginal Rate of Substitution.

4. Symbolically, the marginal rate of substitution may be defined as follows. Total differentiation of the product function $Q = g(K,L)$ yields $dQ = (\partial g/\partial K)\, dK + (\partial g/\partial L)\, dL$. Output along any given isoquant is constant, so we may set $dQ = 0$; thus $(\partial g/\partial K)\, dK + (\partial g/\partial L)\, dL = 0$. The marginal rate of substitution, $-dL/dK$, is then $\partial g/\partial K \div \partial g/\partial L$.

OL_o units of labor. Now suppose that the firm decides to perform certain tasks handled by machines manually. The input of labor will be increased from OL_o to OL_1, and the input of capital will be reduced from OK_o to OK_1. The firm has moved along the isoquant from point A to point B; that is, it has held output constant. But the quantity of capital saved, represented by $-\Delta K_1$, is substantially larger than the amount of labor added (ΔL_1).

The firm is now using less capital and only slightly more labor than it did before to produce the same level of output. As Figure 3–6 shows, however, it will become increasingly difficult for the firm to substitute labor for capital. If the firm should move from point C to point D on the isoquant, for example, the saving in capital ($-\Delta K_3$) would be substantially smaller than the additional unit of labor (ΔL_3).

The substitution process is symmetrical so it works in reverse as well. The marginal rate of substitution of capital for labor is the marginal product of capital divided by the marginal product of labor. Everything that has been said above continues to hold if the substitution process is reversed. This can be seen again by reference to Figure 3–6. If the process of substitution had started at point D and proceeded to point A, successively larger inputs of capital would be required to offset unit reduction in labor inputs.

The Economic Region of Production

A firm that is attempting to maximize profits—or minimize costs—will always operate in the *economic region of production* illustrated by Figure 3–7.

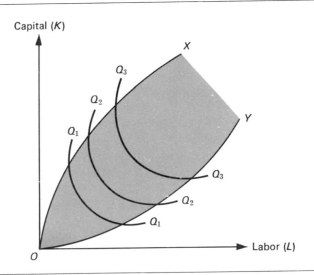

FIGURE 3–7.
The Economic Region of Production.

The economic region of production is bounded by the curved lines OX and OY. The area to the left of OX is equivalent to phase 1, in the one-variable case, and the area to the right is equivalent to phase 3. The firm may wish to increase its output by using more of both factors of production; that is, to increase output from Q_1 to Q_3. It could do this by maintaining a constant capital/labor ratio, or it could vary input proportions as discussed in the preceding section. Whatever it does in this respect, the firm will always remain in the shaded area. The reason for this is exactly the same as that given in the discussion of the three phases of production in the case where labor was the only variable input.

In the present case both capital and labor are variables. The curvature of each isoquant shows that if the firm operated in the area to the left of OX, the firm could reduce its capital input while holding labor constant, without changing the level of output. Similarly, the curvature of the isoquants to the right of OY shows that the firm could reduce its labor input while holding capital constant, without changing the level of output. Only within the shaded area would it be necessary to give up some capital if more labor were added, or to give up some labor if more capital were added, while maintaining a constant level of output.

It is not even necessary to take the prices of the two inputs into account to realize that the firm would not be in equilibrium if it operated outside the economic region of production. To reach a position of equilibrium the firm would use *less* capital or *less* labor. All that we need to assume is that the costs of labor and capital are greater than zero to conclude that the profit-maximizing (or cost-minimizing) firm will remain in the economic region of production.[5]

What Determines the Demand for Labor?

The theory of demand states that the rational consumer of a good or service will buy more at a lower than at a higher price. This is another way of stating that the conventional demand curve slopes downward to the right. The theory of demand also provides a rule for determining the number of units that will be demanded. This is the number at which the marginal utility of the product is equal to the price of that product. The same rule applies to the derived demand for labor if we substitute the marginal product of labor for the marginal utility of the rational consumer.

If labor is the only variable factor of production, the firm will continue to add units of labor until *the marginal product of labor is equal to the price of labor.* Symbolically, $MPL = P_l$, where P_l is the price of labor.[6]

---

5. For further discussion of the economic region of production, and a numerical illustration, see William H. Miernyk *Economics* (New York: Random House, 1971), pp. 176–177. See also Edwin Mansfield, *Microeconomics* (New York: W.W. Norton & Co. Inc., 1970), pp. 134–135.

6. The "price of labor" has been used instead of the *wage rate*, which is the term customarily used in marginal analysis, in order to include fringe benefits and any other component of *labor cost* not covered by the basic hourly earnings of employees.

Does this rule apply in the case of variable proportions? Actually it does, but it is now necessary to include all inputs in the formula. The following discussion concerns only two variable inputs, but the same rule applies no matter how many variable inputs are involved.

If we assume that the firm has no control over the prices of any of its inputs, the profit-maximizing firm will add each input until the ratios of marginal product to cost are equal for all inputs. Symbolically, when both capital and labor are variable, the optimal combination of inputs is found when $MPK/P_k = MPL/P_l$.

In words, the marginal product of capital divided by the price of capital is equal to the marginal product of labor divided by the price of labor.

What happens when the *relative* costs of inputs change? How would the firm react, for example, if the cost of capital remained unchanged while labor costs increased? Assuming that it is technically feasible to do so, the firm would substitute capital for labor. It would add additional units of capital until a new optimal combination of inputs had been reached; that is, when $MPK/MPL = P_k/P_l$. This expression (which is algebraically equivalent to the earlier statement of optimality), states that the marginal product of capital divided by the marginal product of labor is equal to the price of capital divided by the price of labor.

Physical and Revenue Products

Up to this point, labor inputs and the substitution of capital for labor have been discussed in terms of marginal *physical* products. It was necessary to introduce prices only to establish the equilibrium conditions that follow from changes in the relative quantities of capital and labor used in a production process. But the marginal products of each of the inputs must be valued before they can be compared with their costs.

In perfectly competitive markets this poses no problems since the *value of the marginal physical product* is equal to the firm's *marginal revenue product*. Under perfect competition all input and output prices are determined by the market. Thus average revenue or total revenue, divided by the number of units sold, is always equal to marginal revenue, which is the amount added to total revenue by the sale of one additional product. The marginal revenue product of the last worker hired is the amount received by the firm when it sells the additional output resulting from his employment. In equilibrium, this must be equal to the amount he is paid in wages and fringe benefits.

Under imperfect or monopolistic competition, average revenue *is not* equal to marginal revenue at different levels of output. With a downward sloping demand (average revenue) curve, the firm's marginal revenue curve has an even steeper downward slope. This leads to a discrepancy between the value of the marginal physical product and the firm's marginal revenue product. But it does not affect the optimizing rule that determines how much labor is to be employed by the firm. Whether it operates under perfect or monopolistic competition, the profit-maximizing firm will add labor until the marginal revenue product of labor is equal to the price (that is cost) of labor. If the firm uses less than this amount of labor, an additional worker will add more to revenue than to cost. Beyond the point on the output axis at which the marginal revenue product of labor is equal to its price (cost), the firm is employing too much labor. Each worker hired beyond this point is adding more to cost than to revenue. The profit-maximizing firm will thus be in equilibrium only when the marginal revenue product of labor (MRP_l) is equal to its price (P_l).

The Individual Supply of Labor

Alfred Marshall defined the price at which a given amount of product would be sold as its *demand price.* He defined the *supply price* of an input as the price that would result from *the exertion required to produce a given amount of a product.* The Marshallian notion of supply price is particularly appropriate when discussing the input of labor, since it is defined in terms of exertion.

The concept of a supply schedule—the quantities of any factor of production that will be made available at a set of different prices *at a given time*—applies only to perfectly competitive markets. In such markets, individual sellers have no control over the prices of either the inputs they purchase or the goods they sell. Similarly, the owners of factors of production have no control over the prices they receive. All prices are determined by the interplay of demand and supply in a free market. In general, supply schedules are assumed to have a positive slope. But economists sometimes make an exception in the case of the supply schedule of labor. They assume that as the supply price of labor increases, the quantity of labor services offered on the market will increase up to a point. Beyond that point, however, further increases in the supply price of labor would result in a *reduction* in the quantity of labor services offered. The reason for this was implicit in the discussion of the income-leisure model in Chapter 2. The backward bending supply schedule *assumes* that when wages rise above a certain level, a worker will begin to substitute leisure for additional increases in income. This situation is described by the backward bending labor supply schedule illustrated in Figure 3–8.

The labor supply schedule is relevant only to *earned* income. Figure 3–8 shows that if the earned income of a worker increased from Y_1 to Y_2, the quantity of labor services that he would offer would increase from OL_1 to OL_2. Within this range the worker's behavior is consistent with the conventional theory of supply. But if his earned income is increased to OY_3, the worker in this example will reduce his offer of labor services from OL_2 to OL_3.

How realistic is this model of worker behavior? We saw in the last chapter

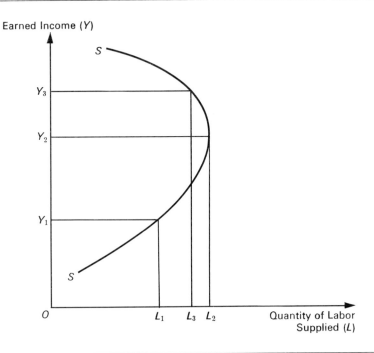

FIGURE 3–8.
Backward Bending Labor Supply Schedule.

that there has been a decline in the amount of labor services offered by the average worker since the turn of the century. This has been one of the long-run consequences of steady increases in productivity. Increases in productivity have been accompanied by a gradual reduction in the number of hours worked as well as by rising earned income. This suggests that an aggregate supply schedule for labor—if such a schedule could be imagined—might indeed be backward bending.[7] But does the individual worker have a backward bending supply schedule? The answer is that he may or may not.

Some workers have responded to a reduction in hours by finding a second job; that is, by "moonlighting." And it is not unusual when labor market conditions are tight for workers to supply overtime work at premium wages. But as Jacob Mincer has noted, the household rather than the individual may be the appropriate unit for the analysis of labor supply. An increase in a family's income may result in a decrease in the amount of labor supplied by the family,

---

7. An aggregate supply schedule would make sense only if *all* markets in the economy were perfectly competitive.

but it need not result in a reduction in the amount of labor supplied by the primary breadwinner.[8] It is possible, therefore, that the backward bending labor supply schedule may be a more realistic model of the labor supplied by a household than by an individual.

There is a rather general impression that the individual labor supply curve in underdeveloped countries is backward bending. This impression is the result of various case studies, which have found that workers not accustomed to industrial discipline often exert themselves only to the point of achieving a "satisfactory" level of earnings. They report for work more or less regularly until they have achieved the desired level of earnings, then do not show up on the job again until their earnings have been exhausted. Generalizations based on observed behavior of this kind may not be warranted, however.

The process of industrialization takes time. One reason for this is that workers without previous industrial experience do not immediately adapt themselves to the rigorous demands of factory jobs, even if those jobs consist mostly of tending machines. A detailed study of the industrialization of Puerto Rico has raised doubts about the willingness of workers to substitute leisure for higher earnings once they have become accustomed to industrial employment. Reynolds and Gregory feel that the Puerto Rican evidence runs strongly against the hypothesis of fixed income aspirations and a backward bending labor supply curve.[9]

Aggregate labor supply is fairly predictable, but individuals and households will respond differently to increases in their earned income. In some cases an increase in the wage rate will induce an additional offering of labor; in other cases an increase in earned income, particularly at the level of the household, will result in a reduction in the amount of labor offered. Neither the labor supply schedule that is positively sloped throughout, nor the one that is backward bending, appears to be general enough to apply to all cases.

Factor Proportions and Distributive Shares

The long-run decline in hours worked referred to earlier has been accompanied by a steady increase in real income per capita. This has been accomplished by technical change and the substitution of capital for labor.[10] A question of interest to all economists, but particularly to labor economists, is: How do changing factor proportions affect distributive shares? Some economists have taken the position that the relative shares going to capital

---

8. Herbert S. Parnes, "Labor Force Participation and Labor Mobility," *A Review of Industrial Relations Research, Vol. 1* (Madison, Wisconsin: Industrial Relations Research Association, 1970), p. 4.

9. Lloyd Reynolds and Peter Gregory, *Wages, Productivity, and Industrialization in Puerto Rico* (Homewood, Illinois: Richard D. Irwin, Inc., 1965), p. 301.

10. Robert M. Solow, "Technical Change and the Aggregate Production Function," *The Review of Economics and Statistics, XXXIX* (1957), pp. 312–320.

and labor have remained constant in spite of changes in factor proportions. Others have voiced skepticism about the constancy of relative shares.[11] Most of this discussion has been concerned with the distribution of broad income aggregates. The issue of aggregate income distribution is complicated by a number of purely statistical problems, including the problem of how to define "labor income" and the "returns to capital." For the present, however, we will limit discussion to distributive shares at the level of the firm, where the problem of aggregation does not arise.

The distribution of relative shares to capital and labor at the level of the firm may be analyzed in terms of the *marginal rate of substitution*. This is a measure of the relative ease with which capital can be substituted for labor, or vice versa. From the marginal rate of substitution it is possible to derive the *elasticity of substitution,* which determines the effects that substitution has on the relative shares received by each of the firm's inputs.

The inventor of the concept of the elasticity of substitution was J.R. Hicks. The concept first appeared in his *Theory of Wages* published in 1932. Thereafter followed a number of articles by various economists criticizing, defending, and modifying the notion of the elasticity of substitution as originally formulated by Hicks.[12] The concept is now one of the basic tools of economic analysis.

The formula for the elasticity of substitution is rather complex, because it expresses the ratio of the differentials that measure an increase or decrease in the marginal rate of substitution.[13] But it is possible to define the marginal

---

11. Robert Solow, "A Skeptical Note on the Constancy of Relative Shares," *American Economic Review*, September 1958, pp. 618–631.

12. J. R. Hicks, *The Theory of Wages,* 2nd ed. (London-Macmillan & Co. Ltd., 1963), pp. 286–303.

13. The elasticity of substitution, σ, is derived from the marginal rate of substitution as follows: Let r be the marginal rate of substitution; $g_k = \partial g/\partial K$, the marginal product of capital, and $g_l = \partial g/\partial KL$, the marginal product of labor, Then $r = -dL/dK = g_k/g_l$.

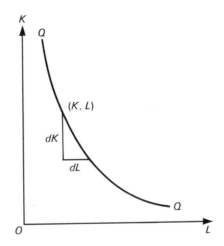

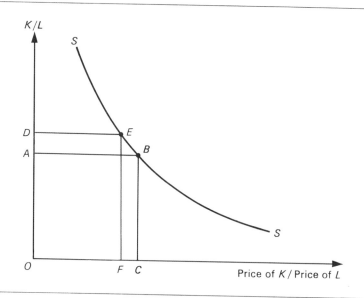

FIGURE 3-9.

Elasticity of Substitution.

rate of substitution without the use of complex algebra, and to illustrate the concept by a simple diagram first proposed by Abba Lerner. The Lerner diagram is given in Figure 3-9.

The ratio of capital to labor is given on the vertical axis, and the ratio of the *price* of capital to the *price* of labor is given on the horizontal axis. If the quantity of labor increases, and the quantity of capital remains unchanged, the ratio K/L will fall. But in a competitive market an increase in the supply of labor will cause the price of labor to decline, and with capital held constant the ratio of the price of capital to the price of labor will increase. Thus a curve connecting these two ratios will have a negative slope—it resembles the demand curve of conventional price theory. This curve, SS in Figure 3-9, is called a *substitution curve,* and the elasticity of this curve is the elasticity of substitution. The elasticity of substitution is a "pure" number; that is, it is independent of the units of measurement. Thus the ratio of capital

---

For any change from the point (K, L) on the isoquant, $d\,(L/K)$ is the increase in labor needed to reduce capital and maintain a constant product. Then $dr = d(g_l/g_k)$ is the corresponding change in r. The ratio of these differentials is the elasticity of substitution,

$$\sigma = \frac{(K/L)\,d\,(L/K)}{(l/r)\,dr}.$$

This derivation is based on that given in R.G.D. Allen, *Mathematical Analysis for Economists* (London: Macmillan & Co. Ltd., 1971), pp. 340–342.

to labor could be expressed in either physical or monetary terms. It simplifies matters, however, to think of the ratio in value rather than physical terms.

Assume that the ratio of capital to labor is initially such that the firm is operating at point B on the isoquant. Now assume that the ratio of the price of capital to the price of labor declines; to be specific, assume a decline in this ratio of 15 per cent. The ratio could decline because of a drop in the price of capital (a reduction in interest rates) or an increase in the price of labor (a wage increase) or a combination of the two changes. Whatever the cause, this change has resulted in a decline in the relative price of capital and an increase in the relative price of labor. Under these circumstances, a profit-maximizing firm operating in competitive markets for both its inputs and its product will substitute capital for labor. This will increase the ratio of capital to labor in the firm. Specifically, assume that the ratio increases by 20 per cent. What does this do to the *relative* shares received by the two factors of production?

Factor proportions are measured by the area under the substitution curve. And we may set the area under the curve at point B equal to unity (OABC = 1). After the change in factor proportions the firm will have shifted to point E on the substitution curve and the area under the curve is now given by ODEF. The area of this rectangle is larger than that given by the square under point B, since the increase in the factor ratio is greater than the decrease in the price ratio (to be specific $1.2 \times .85 = 1.02$ in this case).

Here the elasticity of substitution of capital for labor is *greater than 1*. We have assumed perfect competition in both factor and product markets, so the return to each factor will be equal to the value of its marginal product. Since the elasticity of substitution is greater than 1, the relative share going to capital will increase and the relative share going to labor will decrease.

If the elasticity of substitution is equal to 1 when a firm moves from one point of the substitution curve to another, the relative shares going to the two factors remain unchanged.

Finally, if movement along the substitution curve results in an elasticity of substitution that is less than 1 when capital is substituted for labor, the relative share going to capital will decline and the relative share going to labor will increase. This is the case that is supported most strongly by the empirical evidence.[14]

As previously noted, the elasticity of substitution was the subject of lively debate for some time after the concept was first developed by Hicks. It was criticized on a number of grounds, including the assumption of perfect competition, its limitation to the two-factor case, and the simplifying as-

---

14. See for example, K. J. Arrow, H. B. Chenery, B. S. Minhas, and R. M. Solow, "Capital-Labor Substitution and Economic Efficiency," *The Review of Economics and Statistics, XLIII* (August 1961), p. 230; and S. W. Black and H. H. Kelejian, "A Macro Model for the U.S. Labor Market," *Econometrica 38* (September 1970), p. 721, as well as the reference to other studies in footnote 15.

sumption that the firm makes a single product. Some of these criticisms were easily disposed of. It is always possible to talk in terms of two "bundles" of inputs, treating one factor of production as a single input and all others combined as the second input. The same can be done on the product market side. The concept was more vulnerable to the criticism that it assumed perfect competition in a world where many markets are characterized by monopolistic or imperfect competition.

Hicks has conceded that in the case of imperfect competition, which in its broadest sense includes the general case of increasing returns, his concept may not be applied as precisely as in the case of perfect competition. But he has been able to demonstrate that the same *tendencies* as those described for the case of perfect competition will also hold in the more general case of imperfect competition.[15]

The analytical tools discussed in this chapter are part of the general theories of production and distribution. Here they have been applied to the specific case of the labor market. As is true of all analytical tools of this type, they are based on simplifying assumptions. Among other things they assume the homogeneity of labor inputs, and if there is one thing we know about the labor market, it is that labor is anything but a homogeneous factor of production. It is always possible to get around this difficulty, either in theoretical analysis or in empirical research, by expressing labor inputs in terms of a basic unit of unskilled labor. Also, for analytical purposes it makes sense to work with man-hours rather than numbers of workers. This automatically adjusts for part-time members of the labor force, and for overtime work.

It is worth repeating a point made at the beginning of this chapter; namely, that labor is a unique factor of production. Labor service is the only input that cannot be separated from its owner, and the ways in which labor services are used are of vital concern to those who supply them. This chapter may leave the impression that labor can be treated as a "disembodied" input. Most of this book, however, is concerned with matters which show that this cannot be done.

Questions and Exercises

1. In what specific way does a transaction involving labor services differ from transactions involving commodities?
2. On a diagram, show the relationship between total product, marginal product, and average product, with labor as the variable input and all other inputs fixed.

---

15. Hicks, *The Theory of Wages, op. cit.,* pp. 292–303.

3. What is the law of diminishing returns? What assumptions must be met before this law applies?

4. How are the three phases of production (described by Figure 3-2) related to the efficiency of a firm's operations?

5. What is an isoquant? Illustrate graphically a set of isoquants for the case of variable factor proportions. Construct a second set of isoquants for a production process in which factor proportions are not variable in the short run.

6. Define the marginal rate of substitution. What happens to the marginal rate of substitution when an increasing quantity of labor is substituted for capital?

7. What is the "economic region of production" in the two-variable case? How does it compare with phase 2 in the case where labor is the only variable input?

8. What rule will the profit-maximizing manager of a firm follow when deciding how much labor to hire? More generally, what rule will this manager follow when deciding what proportion of two variable factors to use?

9. In perfectly competitive markets, what is the relationship between a firm's *marginal revenue product* and the value of that firm's marginal physical product? Does the same relationship hold in the case of imperfect or monopolistic competition?

10. What is the "supply price" of labor?

11. Illustrate diagrammatically a "backward bending" supply schedule for labor. What assumptions lie behind this analytical construct?

12. Is it possible to relate the backward bending supply curve of labor to the income-leisure diagram of Chapter 2?

13. What is the economic explanation of the long-term decline in hours worked?

14. Define the "elasticity of substitution" in terms of the K/L ratio and the ratio of the price of capital to the price of labor.

15. What will happen to the relative shares going to capital and labor if the elasticity of substitution is less than 1? What would happen if this measure were greater than 1?

16. What does the available empirical evidence suggest about the elasticity of subsitution and labor's relative share in total income?

Suggested Readings

Books

Cartter, Allan M. *Theory of Wages and Employment*. Homewood, Illinois: Richard D. Irwin, Inc., 1959.

Hicks, J. R. *The Theory of Wages* (2nd ed.). London: Macmillan & Co. Ltd., 1963.

Articles

Parnes, Herbert S. "Labor Force Participation and Labor Mobility," *A Review of Industrial Relations Research,* Vol. *I.* Madison, Wisconsin: Industrial Relations Research Association, 1970.

Solow, Robert M. "Technical Change and the Aggregate Production Function," *The Review of Economics and Statistics, XXXIX,* No. 3 (August 1957), pp. 312–320.

Solow, Robert M. "A Skeptical Note on the Constancy of Relative Shares," *American Economic Review,* September 1958, pp. 618–631.

Productivity
and Technological Change

The Meaning and Measurement of Productivity

One of the basic concepts of the theory of mechanics is *efficiency,* which is
defined as the ratio of the energy output to the energy input of a machine.
The corresponding concept in economics is *productivity,* defined as the
ratio of output to one or more of the inputs used in production. The object
of the measurement of productivity is to determine how efficiently resources
are being used.

The concept of productivity is important in economic analysis. The theory
of marginal productivity is an important part of the broader theory of distribution. But the concept of productivity is not only at the heart of distribution
theory; it is basic to our understanding of the process of economic growth,
and in recent years it has played an increasingly important part in discussions
of labor-management relations.

Economic growth is best measured in terms of increases in *real output
per capita.*[1] George J. Stigler put it well when he said[2]:

> We may, as a rule, view an increase in output per worker as evidence of
> economic progress whether it stems from improvements in labor or improve-
> ments in the cooperating resources. A general increase in output due to
> improvements in the productivity of labor is an unmixed blessing if it comes
> from better training, better minds and better physiques: we are in effect adding
> to the hands that run our economic system without—as the classical econo-
> mists sometimes believed necessary—adding to the mouths that consume its
> product. Similarly, increases in output per worker achieved by increasing

1. See W. W. Rostow, *The Stages of Economic Growth* (Cambridge: Cambridge University
Press, 1960), p. 34.

2. George J. Stigler, *Trends in Output and Employment* (New York: National Bureau of Economic
Research, Inc., 1947), p. 42.

the quantity or improving the quality of cooperating resources imply that we have extended our mastery over nature or over ignorance: we can live better without working harder.

The most widely used measure of productivity is *output per man-hour.* It is important to emphasize, however, that this is not a measure of labor efficiency. Rather, it is a simplifying statistical device used to express all inputs in terms of a single denominator—the man-hours involved in production. When output is measured in physical terms, and all inputs are expressed in terms of man-hours, a ratio may be derived to construct a productivity index. Some base period is selected and set equal to 100. Increases, or decreases, in productivity can be measured from this base.[3]

A more general measure of productivity is

$$\frac{\text{Output}}{\text{Input of Labor} + \text{Input of Other Resources}}$$

Generally, as a matter of convenience, the "other resources" (materials, capital equipment, management, etc.) are lumped together under the heading of "capital."[4]

The concepts described above are straightforward enough but the measurement of productivity is not simple. Thousands of man-hours of research and computation have gone into efforts by private and government agencies to measure productivity—for specific industries or sectors, or for the economy as a whole. But specialists in the measurement of productivity are far from satisfied with the results. The National Bureau of Economic Research, one of the outstanding private research organizations in the United States, has published a number of volumes dealing with the meaning and measurement of productivity.[5] The Bureau of Labor Statistics of the U.S. Department of Labor has a productivity division which is concerned with the continuous study and measurement of productivity. It has published indexes of real product per man-hour for the economy as a whole and specific indexes of productivity for a wide range of manufacturing and nonmanufacturing industries. "Because of serious difficulties in measuring the output of government which is neither priced nor reported in physical units, the broadest measure appropriate for productivity measurement is the real gross *private product.*"[6]

The productivity indexes published by the Bureau of Labor Statistics are

---

3. See John W. Kendrick, "Productivity, Costs and Prices: Concepts and Measurements," *Wages, Prices, Profits and Productivity* (New York: The American Assembly, Columbia University, 1959), pp. 38–39.

4. Stigler, *op. cit.,* p. 49.

5. Probably the most impressive of these is John W. Kendrick, *Productivity Trends In the United States* (Princeton, N.J.: Princeton Press, 1961). See also *Output, Input and Productivity Measurement* (Princeton, N.J.: Princeton University Press, 1961).

6. John W. Kendrick, "Productivity, Costs and Prices: Concepts and Measurements," *op. cit.,* p. 39.

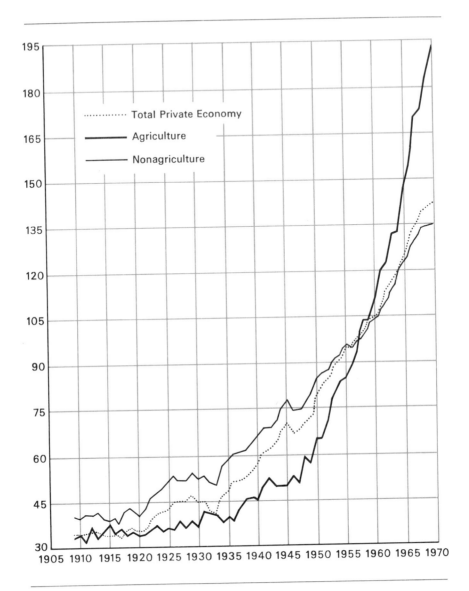

FIGURE 4–1.

Indexes of Real Product Per Man-Hour in the Total Private Economy, Agriculture, and Nonagriculture, 1909–1970. *(Data for 1909–1965 from U.S. Department of Commerce, Bureau of the Census, Long Term Economic Growth, 1860–1965, pp. 188–190.)*

expressed in terms of output per man-hour. Figure 4–1 shows trends in productivity, covering the period 1909–1970, for the total private economy and for the agricultural and nonagricultural sectors.

During this sixty-one year period, real output per man-hour in the total private economy increased about 310 per cent. Output per man-hour in agriculture began to increase more rapidly than the corresponding measure for the nonfarm sector during the 1930s, and there has been a particularly strong upsurge in farm productivity since 1947.

The measurement of changes in productivity from a common base requires careful interpretation. The word to emphasize in this connection is *changes* in productivity. As Ewan Clague, formerly Commissioner of Labor Statistics, has noted:[7]

> It is true that agriculture has forged far ahead since 1947, but this does not show that the *level* of productivity on farms is ahead of the level in nonfarm industry. On the contrary, the level of output per man-hour in agriculture has in the longer past been behind that of industry in general, and far behind that of many individual industries. What has happened recently is that agriculture is catching up with industry's productivity levels.

Improved management alone can lead to significant gains in output per man-hour even if other things remained unchanged. Similarly, if the health, stamina, training, and morale of the work-force—either in a specific industry or in the economy as a whole—improve significantly over time, output per man-hour will go up. But the greatest gains in productvity—and these often come in fairly short spurts over limited periods of time—result from the introduction of new and improved machinery. When power-driven looms replaced hand looms, for example, there was an increase in productivity although human effort was reduced.

When the early power looms were replaced by automatic looms, which could operate for hours without stopping, there was a further gain in productivity. And in recent years the introduction of high-speed "weaving machines" has resulted in further sharp gains in output per man-hour. This process has gone on in most manufacturing industries, although obviously not at the same rate.

Interindustry Variations in Productivity

Aggregate measures of productivity, such as those given in Figure 4–1, reflect trends in the economy as a whole. But there are wide variations in annual rates of change in output per man-hour among industries. During the 1960s these ranged from more than 10 per cent in petroleum pipelines to less than 1 per cent in footwear. A summary of trends in output per man-hour during the 1960s in twenty-nine industries studied by the Bureau of Labor Statistics is given in Figure 4–2.

---

7. Ewan Clague, "Interpreting Productivity Measurements and Their Application to Economic Problems," paper presented before the American Marketing Association-American Farm Economic Association, Washington, D.C., December 30, 1959 (mimeographed), p. 10.

FIGURE 4–2.

Growth in Output Per Man-Hour in Selected Industries, 1960–1970. (*From the U.S. Department of Labor, Bureau of Labor Statistics.*)

The rapid increase in productivity in petroleum pipelines was due to (a) the growing demand for petroleum products, (b) technical improvements and large capital investment in pipelines, and (c) a shift from other means of transport to pipelines.[8] The virtual absence of an increase in productivity in the footwear industry is a reflection of relatively stable demand conditions coupled with an absence of technological change.

According to economic theory, rapid increases in productivity should be accompanied by declining relative prices. And we should expect to find larger price increases in industries which register small gains in productivity. These expectations are supported by the available empirical evidence.

The scatter diagram (Figure 4–3) shows the expected relationship between large gains in output per man-hour and relatively small increases in prices. Indeed, in the case of household appliances, drugs, plastics, and other industries with exceptionally large productivity gains, there was an absolute decline in prices between 1958 and 1968.

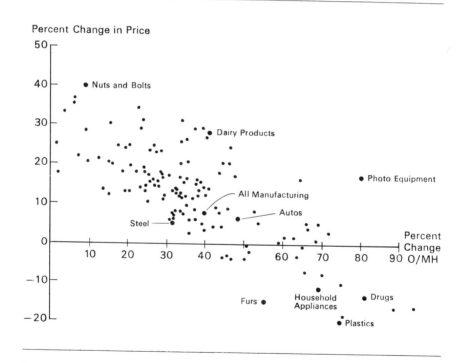

FIGURE 4–3.

Percent Change in Output Per Man-Hour and Prices in 139 Manufacturing Industries, 1958–1968. (*From the U.S. Department of Labor, Bureau of Labor Statistics.*)

8. Caroline S. Fehd, "Productivity in the Petroleum Pipelines Industry," *Monthly Labor Review,* April 1971, pp. 46–48.

Combining Labor and Capital Inputs

Until fairly recently, most productivity indexes were based upon labor inputs alone. In the economy as a whole and in a number of specific industries, labor is one of the major inputs. For this reason output per man-hour indexes are useful, at least as first approximations to the efficiency with which we are using our resources. But some economists feel that output per man-hour indexes alone are inadequate. The National Bureau of Economic Research, for example, has devoted considerable time and effort to the construction of productivity indexes based upon labor and capital inputs combined.

Scholars at the National Bureau feel that the omission of capital inputs lead to an upward bias in output per man-hour indexes. This is rather obviously the case in highly capital-intensive industries. But they feel that this is also true of measurements of productivity for the economy as a whole.[9] According to Fabricant, "indexes of productivity based on the comparison of output with the input of both labor and tangible capital are better measures of efficiency than those based on labor input or the capital input alone."[10]

Another criticism of output per man-hour indexes of productivity is that they treat all man-hour inputs as homogeneous. John W. Kendrick has computed output per man-hour indexes on an unweighted basis (similar to those prepared by the Bureau of Labor Statistics), but he has also developed *weighted* indexes of output per man-hour. For weighting purposes he has translated the compensation of labor into average hourly earnings. The logic of using the average hourly earnings as a weight for man-hours is that higher paid workers contribute more to productivity than lower paid ones.

Kendrick has computed similar unweighted and weighted indexes of capital productivity. The weights used in this case are rates of return on investment. This implies that capital which earns a high rate of return is being utilized more efficiently than that which earns relatively less.[11] The separate indexes have been combined into a general index of productivity based upon both capital and labor inputs. The results of these exhaustive studies, covering the period 1889 to 1957, are summarized in Table 4-1.

The unweighted index of output per man-hour shows the most rapid rate of increase. During the sixty-nine-year period, the unweighted index of physical output per man-hour showed an average annual increase of 2.4 per cent. When weighted in terms of hourly earnings the annual rate drops to 2 per cent. And when labor and capital inputs are combined, there is a further drop to 1.7 per cent. It is also interesting to note that all of the indexes show a slower rate of increase during the period 1889 to 1919. There was a notable acceleration in productivity during the years 1919 to 1957. This is shown

---

9. Solomon Fabricant, *Basic Facts on Productivity Change* (New York: National Bureau of Economic Research, Inc., Occasional paper 63, 1959), pp. 6–8.

10. *Ibid.*, p. 8.

11. Kendrick, *Productivity Trends in the United States*, pp. 32–35.

TABLE 4-1
Average Rates of Increase in Productivity, Private Domestic
Economy, 1889-1957 (annual percent of change)

	1889-1957	1889-1919	1919-1957
Physical output per man-hour *(unweighted)*	2.4	2.0	2.6
Physical output per man-hour *(weighted)*	2.0	1.6	2.3
Physical output per unit of tangible capital *(weighted)*	1.0	0.5	1.3
Physical output per unit of labor and capital combined *(weighted)*	1.7	1.3	2.1

Source: Solomon Fabricant. *Basic Facts on Productivity Change,* p. 10. Reprinted by permission of the National Bureau of Economic Research.

graphically in Figure 4-4. The scale along the left-hand side of this chart is a logarithmic or ratio scale on which equal vertical distances represent equal percentage changes. The index plotted at the top of Figure 4-4 has a considerably steeper slope than the one at the bottom. The index labeled "Output per Weighted Unit of Labor and Tangible Capital combined" shows only about 72 per cent as much increase as the "Output per Unweighted Man-Hour" index. This is what spokesmen for the National Bureau of Economic Research mean when they say that output per man-hour indexes have an "upward bias."

Representatives of the Bureau of Labor Statistics—which continues to publish indexes of output per man-hour—are aware of the criticism of these indexes which has been made by other agencies, notably the National Bureau of Economic Research. Ewan Clague, while Commissioner of Labor Statistics, commented on the debate over the measurement of productivity as follows[12]:

> We in the Bureau of Labor Statistics have, of course, examined the implications of the readjustment of the productivity index to allow for capital investment. We recognize clearly that productivity gains usually require capital investment, which becomes a cost that must be met in the long run. On the other hand, a measure of output per unit of total input is not necessarily the *one best* measure of productivity. We can repeat what we have said on many previous occasions, namely, that there is a whole family of productivity statistics, each with its own significance for certain purposes. The problem in connection with productivity statistics is not that any of them is right or wrong, but that each presents a certain picture of the economy. The real

12. Ewan Clague, "Productivity—What it is and How it is Measured," paper presented to the Chicago Association of Commerce and Industry, May 26, 1959 (mimeographed), pp. 16–17.

problem consists in determining the uses to which each of these should be put. A comparison of the United States rate of progress with the Soviet Union may require one statistic; a comparison with average hourly earnings may require quite a different statistic. And the development of a balanced rate of growth in the United States may require still another. It is for these reasons that it is most important for users of productivity statistics to know what they are using.

Whatever measure of productivity is used, the overall picture is one of greater efficiency in the use of resources in the long run. Indexes of output per man-hour show faster gains in productivity than those which combine labor and capital inputs. But as Figure 4–4 shows, whether indexes of labor productivity or total productivity are used, the long-run trend has been upward.

FIGURE 4–4.

Indexes of Productivity in the United States, 1889–1957: Estimates for the Private Domestic Economy. *(Reprinted by permission from Solomon Fabricant,* Basic Facts on Productivity Change, *Occasional Paper 63, National Bureau of Economic Research, Inc. [1959], p. 13.)*

Productivity and Earnings

Trends in output per man-hour and earnings, from 1947 through 1970, are given in Figure 4–5. Monetary earnings have been adjusted for changes in the consumer price index to obtain an index of "real" hourly earnings.

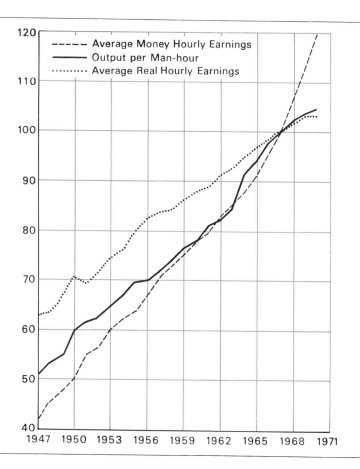

FIGURE 4–5.

Output Per Man-Hour and Average Real and Money Hourly Earnings, 1947–1970. (*Data from* Economic Report of the President, *February 1971, p. 236 and* Manpower Report of the President, *April 1971, p. 261.*)

At times, "real" earnings increase faster than output per man-hour, and at other times the reverse is true. But over a period as long as the one covered by Figure 4–5 the two indexes tend to move together. Throughout most of this period, money wages rose at a slightly faster rate than output per man-hour. But during the first half of the 1960s there was an upsurge in productivity with money wages lagging slightly behind. After the mid-1960s, however, money wages rose faster than output per man-hour, and "real" hourly earnings rose at a slower rate than productivity. But the long-run trend in "real" hourly earnings—which reflects changes in both output per man-hour and in consumer prices—has been steadily upward. During the twenty-three-year period covered by this chart, the "real" earnings of manufacturing workers in the United States increased almost 64 per cent.

Productivity and Collective Bargaining

In the early days of collective bargaining most negotiations dealt with wages, hours, and working conditions. Later, various kinds of "fringe benefits" were incorporated in labor-management agreements. The agreement signed by General Motors and the United Automobile Workers in May 1948 explicitly recognized the relationship between gains in productivity and wage increases. It provided for sharing the returns from increased productivity between capital and labor. Since then a number of collective bargaining agreements have included similar provisions. The GM-UAW agreement provided for an annual improvement factor—that is, an automatic increase in wages—based upon gains in productivity. The agreement stated[13]:

> The annual improvement factor provided herein recognizes that a continuing improvement in the standard of living of employees depends upon technological progress, better tools, methods, processes and equipment, and a cooperative attitude on the part of all parties in such progress. It further recognizes the principle that to produce more with the same amount of human effort is a sound economic and social objective.

The incorporation of annual improvement factors in labor-management agreements raises a number of questions. What measure of "annual improvement" should be used? As noted in earlier sections, different measures of productivity show different rates of change. Also, should the "annual improvement" be geared to changes in productivity in the plant, the company, the industry, or the economy as a whole?

We have already noted that there are wide variations in productivity increases among industries. There are also variations among the various sectors of the economy. Dunlop has said that "wage rates cannot be adjusted uniquely to increases in productivity in each occupation and plant and preserve for very long a balanced wage structure."[14] Even within a single plant there may be wide variations in productivity changes among depart-

---

13. Quoted by Ewan Clague in "Prices, Wages and Productivity," paper presented before the *Labor Relations and Arbitration Conference,* University of California, May 25, 1959 (mimeographed), p. 14.

14. J. T. Dunlop, "Productivity and the Wage Structure," *Income, Employment and Public Policy.* Essays in honor of Alvin H. Hansen (New York: W. W. Norton Company, Inc., 1948), p. 342.

ments. There are also interplant, interindustry, and intersector variations in productivity. It would scarcely be practicable to attempt to gear wage increases for a specific group of workers to increases in productivity in their department, plant, or industry. While annual improvement factors of the type originally negotiated by GM and the UAW have spread, they have not become a standard feature in labor-management agreements. Where they are used, there has been a tendency to gear automatic wage increases to average gains in productivity in the economy as a whole or—since agriculture is generally regarded as a special case—to increases in productivity in the nonfarm sector of the private domestic economy.

Union Attitudes Toward Productivity

One of the driving forces behind increases in productivity is technological change. And there was a time when workers were fearful of technology. During the early days of the Industrial Revolution in England, when skilled hand weavers were being displaced by machines, there was a violent reaction. Although the workers at this time were unorganized, a movement developed to halt the spread of machine production. The members of this movement were called Luddites, after a member of the group named Ned Ludd, and they attempted to safeguard the jobs of craftsmen by smashing the new machines. They accepted the "lump of labor" theory and felt that if machines did the work laborers would have to go unemployed. Needless to say, while their efforts led to serious social unrest in some British factory towns, they were unable to halt the march of technology.

Even in a much later age workers have been concerned with the possible effects of technological change upon employment. When unions consisted predominantly of skilled craftsmen, they tried at times to protect their jobs from the encroachment of machine production. Sumner Slichter has listed the following union policies toward the introduction of machinery[15]:

1. The policy of *obstruction* in which unions attempted to prevent the introduction of new machines into union shops.
2. The policy of *competition* under which organized workers made concessions to their employers in an effort to make them competitive with nonunion employers using machine methods.
3. The policy of *control* under which unions permit the introduction of machinery, but seek to control the men who operate the machines, and possibly the rate at which machinery is introduced.

15. Sumner H. Slichter, *Union Policies and Industrial Management* (Washington, D.C.: The Brookings Institution, 1941), p. 201. In a later study Slichter and his associates noted that some unions have actively encouraged technological change. See Sumner H. Slichter, James J. Healy, and E. Robert Livernash, *The Impact of Collective Bargaining on Management* (Washington, D.C.: The Brookings Institution, 1960), pp. 355–361.

Although a number of efforts were made to obstruct the introduction of machinery, or to compete with new machines, neither of these policies was successful. The march of technology seemed inexorable, and where unions attempted to obstruct it, the result was the destruction of the union rather than of the machines. The policy of control, however, has been somewhat more successful and, in its broadest sense, this policy is followed by some unions today.

Union attitudes toward productivity have changed since the rise of widespread industrial unionism in the United States. Individual workers might be concerned about the possible loss of employment due to technological change as in the past. But as industrial unions grew "they became preoccupied more with the responsibility of securing economic gains rather than fastening their controls on a specific job."[16] Some of the earlier craft unions attempted to maintain the demand for craftsmen by limiting output and the speed of work, by insisting upon time-consuming methods, and at times by regulating the number of men who could be assigned to a job.[17] But industrial unions not only accepted the inevitability of technological change; they also actively encouraged such change. The philosophy of the leaders of industrial unionism was that rapid gains in productivity would lead to higher per capita income; the latter, in turn, would stimulate demand. As the demand for goods and services increased, the demand for labor would also go up. The leaders of industrial unionism hoped that rapid industrial growth would lead both to steady improvement in real income and a tendency toward full employment.

The craft unions had lived through good times and bad. But during the early days of the A. F. of L. the notion was widespread that "good jobs"—and this meant jobs for skilled workers—were scarce. Hence union leaders felt that they were serving the best interests of their members when they engaged in restrictive practices and opposed technological change. The rapid growth of industrial unionism in the United States started midway through the worst depression this country has ever known. As industrial unions grew in size and strength they witnessed a slow rise in income and gains in employment. World War II convinced many leaders of industrial unionism that economic expansion was the best guarantee of steady improvement in the condition of organized labor. Thus the industrial unionist became strongly productivity conscious. Far from restricting output or opposing technological change, leaders of the industrial unions urged business to step up its rate of investment in order to increase its efficiency. This was not because of an altruistic interest in business; rather, it was because the leaders of industrial unionism hoped to capture a steady share of the gains resulting from increased productivity.

Even the productivity conscious industrial unions were concerned about

---

16. Solomon Barkin, "Trade-Union Attitudes and Their Effect Upon Productivity," *Industrial Productivity*, Industrial Relations Research Association, 1951, p. 110.

17. *Ibid.*, p. 111.

the potential impact upon specific workers—or groups of workers—when there were sudden changes in technology. While encouraging technological change, which would lead to gains in productivity, the unions wanted to be kept informed of impending change. And they wanted to have a say in the transfer of workers displaced by machines, the establishment of production standards when new processes were developed, and the negotiation of wage rates on new jobs.[18] Some unions negotiated provisions which permitted management to make technological improvements without consulting the union, but they reserved the right to file grievances if they felt that individual workers had been adversely affected, and these at times called for final determination of disputed issues by an impartial arbitrator. Other unions negotiated provisions calling for consultation prior to the installation of new machinery. The object again was not to restrain management, but to ensure that individual workers or groups of workers did not bear the entire cost of technological change.

At times some managements have complained that such rules—although seemingly innocuous—actually have restrained technological progress. In their opinion, management always takes a risk when a new machine is installed. The union contract permits the installation of new equipment, but the union retains its right to participate in the setting of rates and job standards and in the transfer of affected workers. Under these circumstances, those who subscribe to this point of view allege that management cannot be certain it will gain as a result of the change. The union response to this line of argument is that workers are entitled to a *share* of the gains resulting from increased productivity. If the job security of workers can be protected, through transfer and the maintenance of their old rates of pay, worker morale will be improved, and this in itself will be a stimulus to improvement in productivity.

Finally, some union spokesmen have recognized that upward pressure on labor costs has been an important stimulus to technological change. According to Barkin, "the sluggishness of management, which neither competition nor profit seeking seemed fully to overcome, is frequently partially corrected by the pressure from the recurrent demands for improvements in labor benefits."[19] Some might view this line of argument as an apology by trade unionists for their incessant demands for wage increases and expanded fringe benefits, but this view has been shared by many not connected with the trade union movement. Sumner H. Slichter, for example, frequently stated that trade unions provided an important stimulus to management to improve its operations, and that this led to gains in productivity. Others have noted that by pushing the economy toward full employment, unions have en-

---

18. See Philip Taft, "Organized Labor and Technical Change: A Backward Look," in Gerald G. Somers *et al.* (eds.), *Adjusting to Technological Change* (New York: Harper & Row, 1963), pp. 35–42.

19. Barkin, *op. cit.*, p. 22.

couraged more complete utilization of the existing labor supply, and this in itself leads to gains in productivity for the economy as a whole.[20]

Technological Change

Technological change has been defined as "the advance in knowledge relative to the industrial arts."[21] It is a prime mover of economic growth and explains to a large extent the increases in output per man-hour discussed in earlier sections. In a well-known study of technological change, which covered a period of forty years, Solow concluded that more than 87 per cent of the aggregate increase in output per man-hour could be attributed to technical change, and that the rest was attributable to the increased use of capital.[22]

Solow also has pointed out that while investment is a necessary condition for growth in productivity, it is not sufficient. Investment in tangible capital must be accompanied by continued investment in human capital.[23] As Solow's earlier study showed, it is not so much the quantity of capital used but its *quality*—that is, technical change—which results in increases in productivity. As machinery becomes more sophisticated, better educated and more highly trained workers are required to operate and maintain the machines. Furthermore, increases in productivity lead to higher income, and higher income results in increased spending on research and development, and the latter in turn begets further technical change. Much of the increased spending on research and development in recent years has been financed by the federal government.

Federal spending on research and development increased from less than $1 billion in 1946 to more than $17 billion in 1967. While there has been a slight decline since then, the level of spending remains high.

Most of the research supported by the federal government is carried out by private industrial firms. In 1970, for example, 58 per cent of federally funded research and development was carried out by private industry. An additional 23 per cent was conducted by federal agencies. Only 10 per cent of the funds went to universities and colleges. Universities administered an additional 5 per cent, which was actually carried out by federally funded research and development centers. The remaining 5 per cent was carried out by other nonprofit institutions and "all other" organizations.[24]

---

20. See, for example, Clark Kerr, "Productivity and Labour Relations," *Productivity and Progress* (Sidney, Australia: Angus and Robertson, 1957), p. 19.

21. Edwin Mansfield, *The Economics of Technological Change* (New York: W. W. Norton & Co., 1968), p. 8.

22. Robert M. Solow, "Technical Change and the Aggregate Production Function," *The Review of Economics and Statistics,* August 1957, p. 320.

23. Robert M. Solow, "Technical Progress, Capital Formation, and Economic Growth," *The American Economic Review,* May 1962, pp. 76–86.

24. National Science Foundation, *Federal Funds for Research, Development and Other Scientific Activities, NSF 70–38,* Vol. *XIX,* p. vi.

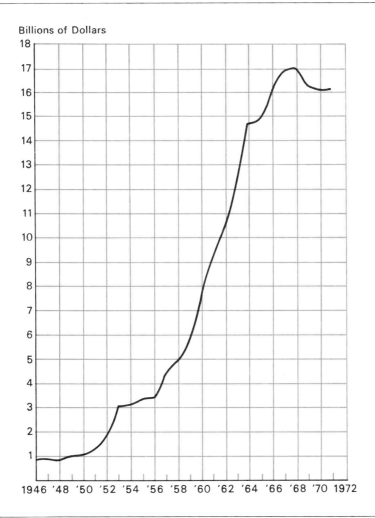

Billions of Dollars

1946 '48 '50 '52 '54 '56 '58 '60 '62 '64 '66 '68 '70 1972

FIGURE 4–6.

Federal Research and Development Expenditures, 1946–1971. *(Reproduced from the National Science Foundation,* Federal Funds for Research, Development, and Other Scientific Activities, *Fiscal Years 1969, 1970, and 1971, NSF 70–38, Vol. XIX, p. 2.)*

Automation

The advent of the electronic computer, shortly after the end of World War II, led to new methods of production which linked computers to machine tools and materials-handling devices. This method of production was referred to rather loosely as *automation.* Automation has been applied not only in factories, but also in offices and transportation systems. Many routine activities can be monitored by computers. Pipeline transmission is an example of an activity that can be handled to a large extent by computers, which is a major explanation of the rapid increase in output per man-hour in this industry, as discussed in an earlier section.

During the 1950s there was a spirited debate about the long-run consequences of automation. Some writers, including the distinguished M.I.T. mathematician Norbert Wiener, predicted dire consequences. Others, however, insisted that the new developments were nothing more than a continuation of the long-run trend of technological change. And some took the position that automation would have no adverse employment effects at all.

The massive depression which Norbert Wiener forecast has not materialized. But there can be no doubt that automation has had an employment impact. This impact has been on specific occupations and in specific industries, however, and as such, has not led to disruption of the economy as a whole.

Concern about the potential effects of automation led to the establishment of a National Commission on Technology Automation, and Economic Progress.[25] Chairman of the Commission was Howard R. Bowen, an economist, and it included a number of other economists, sociologists, labor leaders, businessmen, and specialists in industrial relations. The report of the Commission, entitled *Technology and the American Economy,* was issued in February 1966. It was accompanied by a set of six technical appendices totaling almost 1,800 pages. This is a landmark study, which examines technological change from a number of points of view.

It is difficult to summarize the Commission's report, because the report is itself a summary of the studies reported in the voluminous appendices. But the tone of the report is far from pessimistic. The Commission recognized that the occupational structure of the labor force would have to change—as it has been changing in the past—if new jobs were to be found for a steadily expanding work force in the face of continuing technological change.

The Commission concluded that there has been some increase in the rate of technological change, but that technological change was not primarily responsible for the relatively high levels of unemployment during the 1950s. It recommended a number of measures to adjust to future technological change, most of which emphasize the need for more education or training.

The Commission also saw an increase in public service employment as a means of providing jobs in useful community activities for the hard-core unemployed. Many of the Commission's recommendations are couched in general terms, but this recommendation is quite specific, suggesting that the government become "an employer of last resort" for those unable to find jobs

---

25. This Commission was established by Public Law 88–444, approved by Congress on August 5, 1964, and signed by the President on August 19, 1964.

otherwise. A first step in this direction was taken by Congress when it passed the Emergency Employment Act of 1971, signed by the President on July 12 of that year. While this is a modest program, which was expected to create no more than 150,000 jobs, supporters of the measure felt that it would demonstrate the viability of public service employment.[26]

Productivity and Unit Labor Costs

The manager of a firm is more interested in unit labor costs than in either productivity or rates of pay. These costs "reflect the interaction of hourly compensation and output per man-hour."[27] The trend in labor cost and non-

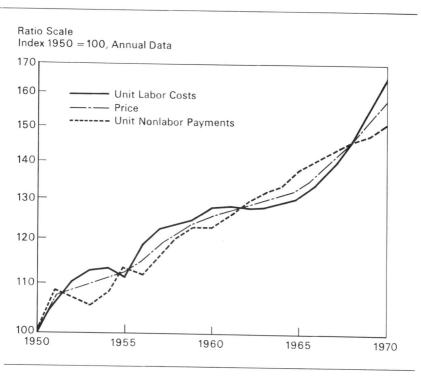

FIGURE 4-7.

Implicit Price Deflator, Unit Labor Costs, and Unit Nonlabor Payments, 1950–1970 (Private Economy).

26. For a detailed discussion of the Act and its expected consequences, see Everett Crawford, *Public Service Employment Programs*, Pamphlet No. 8 (Washington, D.C.: Center for Governmental Studies, August 1971).

27. Shelby W. Herman and Lawrence J. Fulco, "Changes in Productivity and Unit Labor Costs —A Yearly Review," *Monthly Labor Review*, May 1971, p. 5.

labor payments per unit of output in the private economy for the period 1950–1970 is shown in Figure 4–7.

The price index used is the "implicit price deflator" of national income accounting. Unlike the Consumer Price Index (CPI), which measures changes in the prices of goods and services purchased by "typical" urban worker families, the Implicit Price Deflator (IPD) measures price changes for the economy as a whole.

There were times during this twenty-year period when unit labor costs rose more rapidly than nonlabor payments, and other times when the reverse was true. Note that between 1960 and 1965 unit labor costs were nearly constant, but nonlabor payments registered an increase of more than 13 per cent. Between 1965 and 1970, however, nonlabor payments went up about 15 per cent, while unit labor costs registered an increase of 27 per cent. Most of the increase in the general price index during this five-year period was attributable to the sharp rise in unit labor costs.

Comparative Unit Labor Costs

The rapid increase in prices after 1965, coupled with a deteriorating international trade position, was primarily responsible for President Nixon's New Economic Program adopted in September 1971. How do recent trends in hourly compensation, output per man-hour, and unit labor costs in the United States compare with those of our more important trading partners? The answer is given in Table 4–2.

Throughout the 1960s, hourly compensation in the United States rose at a slower rate than that of the other ten countries listed in Table 4–2. But output per man-hour also rose more slowly in the United States than in the other countries. For example, hourly earnings in Japan increased at an annual rate of 13.4 per cent (compared with the U.S. increase of 4.6 per cent), while output per man-hour in Japan increased at an annual rate of 10.8 per cent (compared with a U.S. increase of 3.1 per cent). Thus unit labor costs in Japan registered an annual increase of 2.3 per cent, compared with the annual rise of 1.5 per cent in the United States. It is important to stress that Table 4–2 shows *rates of change* only. It does not in any way reflect the substantial differences in the *level* of unit labor costs between Japan and the United States.

During the first half of the 1960s the United States and Canada were the only countries listed in Table 4–2 to register a decrease in unit labor costs. In these two countries, annual increases in hourly compensation were less than annual increases in productivity. During the latter half of the decade, however, Canada registered the highest rate of increase in unit labor costs, followed by Germany and the United States, in that order. As in the case of Canada, the relative unit labor cost position of the United States improved between 1960 and 1965, but these gains were more than wiped out between 1965 and 1970.

TABLE 4-2
Rates of Change in Output Per Man-Hour, Hourly Compensation, and Unit Labor Costs, 1960–1970
(Average annual percent change)

Country[a]	Output per man-hour			Hourly compensation			Unit labor costs (U.S. dollar basis)		
	1960–70	1960–65	1965–70	1960–70	1960–65	1965–70	1960–70	1960–65	1965–70
United States	3.1	4.3	2.1	4.6	3.7	6.0	1.5	−0.7	3.9
Belgium	6.2	5.4	6.8	9.0	9.0	8.4	2.7	3.4	1.4
Canada	3.9	4.7	3.5	6.1	3.8	8.3	1.5	−3.0	5.1
France	5.8	5.0	6.0	8.8	9.0	9.5	2.1	3.8	0.6
Germany	5.9	6.5	5.3	8.9	9.7	8.7	3.5	3.9	4.7
Italy	6.4	6.8	5.1	10.3	13.6	9.1	3.7	6.3	3.8
Japan	10.8	8.5	14.2	13.4	13.1	15.1	2.3	4.3	0.8
Netherlands	6.7	5.1	8.5	11.4	11.0	11.1	4.7	6.4	2.5
Sweden	7.6	7.3	7.9	9.9	9.5	10.6	2.2	2.0	2.5
Switzerland	4.5	2.3	6.2	7.0	7.6	6.2	2.5	5.2	0
United Kingdom	3.7	3.7	3.6	7.0	6.2	7.6	1.4	2.4	−0.2

Source: *Monthly Labor Review*, August 1971, pp. 4–5.

[a] Percent change computed from least squares trend of logarithms of index numbers. Data relate to all employees in manufacturing, except in Switzerland where data relate to wage earners only.

Productivity and Hours of Work

Earlier in this chapter we noted that there was disagreement about the best way to measure gains in productivity, but whatever measure is employed, everyone is agreed that the long-run trend of productivity has been upward. A clear and forceful indicator of this is given by trends in hours worked and hourly earnings. The long-run trends for more than half a century are summarized in Table 4-3.

TABLE 4-3
Hours and Earnings of Production Workers in Manufacturing, 1909–1969

	1909	1959	Percent change 1909–59	1969	Percent change 1959–69	Percent change 1909–69
Average Weekly hours	51.0	40.3	− 21.0	40.6	+0.7	−20.4
Average hourly earnings	$0.19	$2.19b	+1,053	$3.19b	+45.0	+1,579
"Real" average hourly earnings (1967 = 100)a	$0.42	$1.57b	+273.8	$2.24b	+42.0	+433

Sources of data: U. S. Department of Commerce, Bureau of the Census, *Historical Statistics of the United States Colonial Times to 1957*, 1960, pp. 91, 126; *1960 Supplement to Economic Indicators*, U. S. Government Printing Office, 1960, pp. 43, 46, 81; *Economic Report of the President*, February 1971, p. 233.

a Straight-time average hourly earnings adjusted for changes in the consumer price index. The latter was estimated for 1909 from partial data.

b Excluding fringe benefits.

Twenty years before the beginning of this period, in 1890, the work week for *all* workers in manufacturing averaged sixty hours, but there had been a substantial drop by 1909. The decline continued slowly for the next two decades—as late as 1926, for example, the average work week in manufacturing was still slightly longer than fifty hours. But between 1909 and 1959, there was a reduction of 21 per cent in the average weekly hours of production workers in manufacturing. Meanwhile, average hourly earnings, without adjustment for price changes, showed more than a tenfold increase. A much more significant measure, of course, is the increase in "real" average hourly earnings, that is, changes in money earnings adjusted for changes in consumer prices. In terms of constant dollars, straight-time average hourly earnings increased almost 274 per cent during this fifty-one-year period. And it must be noted that the gains in hourly earnings over this period understate gains in the *total* returns to labor, since fringe benefits are excluded.[28]

28. Fringe benefits were virtually nonexistent in 1909 but were enjoyed, to varying degrees, by all manufacturing workers in 1959.

There was no further decline in average weekly hours between 1959 and 1969; indeed, there was a fractional increase. Although a number of firms — about 600 in mid-1971 — were experimenting with the four-day work week, average weekly hours have not been affected. In most of these companies, employees work four ten-hour days instead of five eight-hour days.[29] This indicates a preference for larger blocs of leisure time, and a willingness of workers to put in more working hours per day to achieve this goal.

Average hourly earnings have continued their steady climb, rising by 45 per cent between 1959 and 1969. Despite the continued price rise, increases in productivity led to a further gain of 42 per cent in "real" hourly earnings. The increase in "real" hourly earnings is not a measure of productivity gains in manufacturing. But real wages in manufacturing could not have increased without substantial increases in productivity, whether measured in terms of labor inputs or combined labor and capital inputs. Over an even longer period of time workers have enjoyed the fruits of increased productivity through a combination of greater leisure and increased earnings.

The decline in average weekly hours did not proceed continuously. The drop was rather slow from the 1890s until the Great Depression of the 1930s. There was a pronounced drop during the later years of the depression. The average work week was increased during World War II due to a combination of labor shortages and the demands of the war effort. Since 1946, however, there has been only a fractional decline in the average work week in manufacturing.

What forces were responsible for the reduction in hours? One of the goals of the early trade unions was a reduction in hours of work, and there is evidence that union pressures contributed substantially to the reduced work week between the 1890s and the 1930s. As Kerr has noted, shorter hours "would occur anyway over time with rising productivity; but schedules of hours of work are a convention of the labour market and it takes quite a shock, like a depression or union pressure, to get them changed. They are less likely to be changed in the normal course of events than are wages."[30]

The effects of legislation should also be noted. Since 1938, when the Fair Labor Standards Act was passed, employers have had to pay penalty rates for work in excess of the standard forty-hour week. Because they earn time and one-half for overtime, many workers are pleased if they have an opportunity to work more than forty hours a week — at least for relatively short periods of time. However, employers try to schedule production to avoid premium payments. As a consequence, since the end of World War II, the average work week in manufacturing has been fairly close to forty hours,

29. J. N. Hedges, "A Look at the 4-Day Workweek," *Monthly Labor Review,* October 1971, pp. 33–37. This article presents arguments for and against expansion of the four-day work week.
30. Kerr, "Productivity and Labour Relations," *op. cit.,* p. 18.

although specific companies, such as a number of those in the rubber industry, have adopted a shorter standard work week.

During the early 1960s there was some union pressure for further reduction in hours. Early in 1962, Local 3 of the International Brotherhood of Electrical Workers, located in New York City, negotiated a twenty-five-hour work week.[31] Other unions, such as the Retail, Wholesale, and Department Store Union, have negotiated more modest reductions in the standard work week. Still others have sought to reduce the amount of work on an annual basis by demanding longer vacations or in some cases more paid holidays. Indeed, some observers believe that in the future workers will prefer longer vacations and more paid holidays to a gradual reduction in working hours through a progressive shortening of the work day. As already noted, the average work week in manufacturing has dropped only fractionally since the end of World War II. But a recent Bureau of Labor Statistics study of fringe benefits showed that "the average full-time worker in 1960 had 155 more hours of paid leisure than a worker had in 1940. Of that total, 48 hours resulted from six days of paid vacation and 32 from four more days of paid holidays."[32]

It seems reasonable to expect that beyond some point further reduction in the average work week would become impracticable. While workers in the past obtained some of the gains of increased productivity in the form of a shorter workday and in a reduction of the work week from six to five days, it seems quite likely that in the future an equally significant measure will be the number of days worked per year as unions negotiate an increasing number of days off with pay.

What are the economic consequences of shorter hours? Earlier in this chapter it was stated that workers could not have enjoyed the gains in "real" income which they have received without corresponding increases in productivity. But to some extent increases in productivity were a *result* of shorter hours. When the standard work week was sixty hours excessive fatigue reduced the efficiency of a great many workers. Unless output is entirely paced by a machine, the output of workers is not uniform throughout the workday. The worker does not punch a time clock and immediately reach peak production if he has any control over the rate of output. During the early part of the workday there is some "warming up" time, and later in the day fatigue will impair his efficiency.

Thus, in many factories, when daily hours were cut from ten to eight, daily output per worker went up. In any work situation there is some "output

---

31. This contract set off a round of controversy. Even some union leaders appeared to object to such a drastic reduction in the work week. Some employer groups, never regarded as favorably inclined toward unions, denounced the move without reservation. It has been suggested that the members of this Local were less interested in more leisure than in having premium pay for "overtime" beginning after they had worked 25 rather than 40 hours in a week.

32. The results of this study were cited in *Business Week*, March 31, 1962, p. 83.

optimum" length of work period.[33] While precise measurement of the output optimum might be difficult—if not impossible—this theoretical construct has a counterpart in the real world. Neither daily nor weekly output per worker will be maximized if the workday is too short. On the other hand, if the workday is long enough to impair efficiency, average hourly output will also be reduced.[34] While the optimum output length of work period will vary from occupation to occupation, and industry to industry, it seems reasonable to suppose that beyond some point the workday cannot be shortened without adverse effects upon productivity. Since workers share in the benefits of rising productivity, they will not seek to shorten the workday or the work week to the point where total output will be reduced. The most probable course of events is that unions will continue to press for a combination of rising earnings and more leisure as productivity continues to increase. Except in isolated cases, however, it is not likely that they will press for substantial reductions in the work week, but will continue to negotiate more full days off with pay.

Questions and Exercises

1. How is the economic concept of "productivity" related to the idea of "efficiency" as the latter term is used in the theory of mechanics?

2. It has been said that the best measure of economic growth is *real output per capita*. What comment has Stigler made on this subject?

3. The most widely used measure of productivity is *output per man-hour*. How is it calculated? What is a more general measure of productivity?

4. Describe, in general terms, the long-run trends in productivity since 1905 in (a) agriculture, (b) the nonagricultural sector, and (c) the total private economy.

5. Contrast long-run trends in productivity in such activities as air transportation and petroleum pipelines on the one hand, and in such industries as cigarettes and footwear on the other. List some of the factors that in your opinion, influence wide variations in productivity among industries, including the industries mentioned above.

6. Is there a relationship between increases in output per man-hour and price increases on an industrial basis? If so, what is this relationship?

7. Contrast the long-run trends in productivity as measured by an index of

---

33. Clyde E. Dankert, "Shorter Hours—In Theory and Practice," *Industrial and Labor Relations Review,* April 1962, p. 307.

34. Some concern has been expressed that the four-day work week, where it is in effect, might impair the health and efficiency of workers. But it has also been pointed out that because of technical change work today demands less physical exertion than it did in an earlier day when the ten-hour day was common. See Hedges, *op. cit.,* p. 34.

unweighted physical output per man-hour, and an index of output per unit of weighted labor and capital inputs combined.

8. In the long run, how are average money earnings and real earnings related to output per man-hour?

9. According to Sumner Slichter, what policies were adopted by craft unions toward the introduction of new machines?

10. Were these attitudes shared by the newer industrial unions?

11. What is meant by "technological change"?

12. According to Robert Solow, what is the most important cause of increases in output per man-hour?

13. In what way has federal policy influenced technological change in the United States?

14. Give a concise and nontechnical definition of "automation."

15. What conclusion was reached by the Commission on Technology, Automation and Economic Progress about the rate of technological progress? What conclusion did the Commission reach about the effects of technological change on the relatively high unemployment rates of the 1950s?

16. What happened to unit labor costs in the United States between 1960 and 1965? Compare this result with the change that took place between 1965 and 1970.

17. How do changes in unit labor costs in the United States during the 1960s compare with similar changes taking place at that time in Japan and the countries of western Europe?

18. In general terms, describe what happened to average weekly hours and average hourly earnings in the United States between 1909 and 1969?

19. Discuss the probability of a further substantial decrease in average weekly hours during the coming decade.

Suggested Readings

Books and Pamphlets

American Assembly. *Wages, Prices, Profits and Productivity*. New York: Columbia University, June 1959.

Fabricant, Solomon. *Basic Facts on Productivity Change*. Occasional Paper 63. New York: National Bureau of Economic Research, Inc., 1959.

Mansfield, Edwin. *The Economics of Technological Change*. New York: W. W. Norton & Company, Inc., 1968.

National Commission on Technology, Automation, and Economic Progress. *Technology and the American Economy*. Washington, D.C.: U.S. Government Printing Office, February 1966.

Schmookler, Jacob. *Invention and Economic Growth*. Cambridge, Mass.: Harvard University Press, 1966.

Slichter, Sumner H. *Union Policies and Industrial Management*. Washington, D.C.: The Brookings Institution, 1941.

Slichter, Sumner H., James J. Healy, and E. Robert Livernash. *The Impact of Collective Bargaining on Management.* Washington, D.C.: The Brookings Institution, 1960.

Somers, Gerald G. *et al.* (eds.). *Adjusting to Technological Change.* New York: Harper & Row, 1963.

Articles

Barkin, Solomon. "Trade-Union Attitudes and Their Effects Upon Productivity," *Industrial Productivity.* Madison, Wisconsin: Industrial Relations Research Association, 1951, pp. 110–129.

Clague, Ewan. "Productivity—What It Is and How It Is Measured." Paper presented before the Chicago Association of Commerce and Industry, Chicago, Illinois, May 26, 1959. Mimeographed.

Dunlop, John T. "Productivity and the Wage Structure," *Income, Employment and Public Policy.* Essays in honor of Alvin H. Hansen. New York: W. W. Norton & Company, Inc., 1948, pp. 341–362.

Herman, S. W., and L. J. Fulco. "Changes in Productivity and Unit Labor Costs—A Yearly Review," *Monthly Labor Review,* May 1971, pp. 3–8.

Neef, Arthur. "Unit Labor Costs in Eleven Countries," *Monthly Labor Review,* August 1971, pp. 3–12.

5

Wage Determination: Theory and Policy

There is no topic of greater importance in labor economics than that of the returns to workers. The topic recurs frequently in various parts of this text. The present chapter deals with the theory of wages and the wage structure. The dynamic aspects of wage determination—with particular emphasis on the relationship between changes in wages, employment, and prices—are discussed in the next chapter. The theory of bargaining, which is concerned with the *process* of wage determination, is covered in Chapter 17. Wages represent only part of the returns to labor, and only part of the cost of labor. Various kinds of payments that come under the heading of "fringe benefits" are discussed in detail in Chapter 19.

In a review of the history of wage theory, John T. Dunlop suggested that it can be divided into three broad periods: (1) The *classical* period, extending into the 1870s, (2) a second period extending through the 1920s called the *neoclassical* period, and (3) the *contemporary* period.[1] There has been a revival of interest in neoclassical analysis in recent years, however, so the last two periods overlap to some extent.

Classical Wage Theory

During the classical period, one of the most widely-held views about wages was that of the *wage fund*. The classical period was one of rapid economic growth, no appreciable rise in real wages, and substantial differences in the level of real wages among countries. Although the Industrial Revolution was underway long before the end of the classical period, agriculture was still

---

1. John T. Dunlop, "The Task of Contemporary Wage Theory," in George W. Taylor and Frank C. Pierson (eds.), *New Concepts in Wage Determination* (New York: McGraw-Hill 1957), p. 117. See also his article with the same title in John T. Dunlop (ed.), *The Theory of Wage Determination* (London: Macmillan & Co. Ltd., 1957), p. 4.

the major occupation. Under these circumstances, in Dunlop's words: "The wage-fund apparatus seems congenial . . . as it still does to the broad features of many under-developed countries."[2]

In the short run, according to the classical formulation, the labor supply is fixed and the amount employers decide to spend on wages is also fixed. The sum of the individual amounts of all employers makes up the wage fund. The wage fund doctrine was not very sophisticated; it did not, for example, go into the complexities of variations in wage rates. According to this theory, if the average wage rate were set too high, some workers would have to remain unemployed, while if the average were too low, employers could not attract all the workers they needed. Hence, market forces would bring the average wage to the level that would just "clear the market." Employers in the aggregate would be able to attract as many workers as they needed and the wage rate would not be so high that some workers would be without jobs.

In the long run, however, the size of the wage fund could change. If the wage fund increased—and average wages rose—this would lead to an increase in population and thus to an increase in labor supply. The competition of workers for available jobs would then tend to depress the average level of wages again. In the long run, wages would tend toward the subsistence level. This was the essence of Ricardo's "iron law of wages," and of the Malthusian theory of population growth. The wage fund theory ignored the possibility that population *and* wages might rise together since it failed to take into account gains in productivity. As the sophistication of economists increased, and as they observed that the amount of a nation's total product which could be paid to labor did not remain fixed, the doctrine of the wage fund had to be scrapped. It was replaced during the neoclassical period by the more elegant marginal productivity theory.

Neoclassical Wage Theory

The marginal productivity theory of distribution cannot be credited to any single economist. Versions of it were developed independently by British economists Jevons, Wicksteed, and Marshall. Other versions were developed by western European economists such as Walras and Barone, and J. B. Clark in this country.[3] Originally, the marginal productivity theory was thought to apply only to economies that operated under conditions of perfect competition. By definition, this would exclude any economy in which trade unions have an effect upon wage determination.

But as late as 1932, J. R. Hicks, an eminent economic theorist wrote: "The same forces which determine wages in a free market are still present

---

2. Dunlop, in Taylor and Pierson, *New Concepts*, p. 118.

3. Allan M. Cartter, *Theory of Wages and Employment* (Homewood, Illinois: Richard D. Irwin, 1959), p. 11.

under regulation; they only work rather differently.... "[4] At the time Hicks wrote, unions were not strong in the United States, but they were an important economic force in Great Britain. Hicks was of the opinion, however, that in the aggregate, workers could not receive more than the total value of the marginal product of labor[5]:

> The only wage at which equilibrium is possible is a wage which equals the value of the marginal product of the labourers ... in this way the demand for labour of each employer is determined; and the total demand of all employers is determined from it by addition. Since in equilibrium it is necessary that the total demand should equal the total supply, the wage must be that which just enables the total number of labourers available to be employed. This must equal the value of the marginal product of the labourers available.

The theory of marginal productivity appeared at a time when the rate of population growth began to slow down as urbanization proceeded rapidly in western Europe and in this country. And it was at this time that there was a great upsurge in industrialization. There was a growing amount of government intervention through factory legislation. While the central interest of economists continued to be the theory of distribution, there was less interest in the question of how the total product was to be distributed among social classes than in the forces, which would determine returns to each of the factors of production. In a free market, it was assumed, each factor would receive a return proportional to its contribution to output—given the existing conditions of demand and supply. Until the Great Depression dispelled the illusion, it was generally supposed that the wage rate that would be equal to the marginal productivity of labor would also tend toward equilibrium; that is, the wage level would settle at a point where there would be no unemployment and where employers in the aggregate could obtain all the labor they needed.

As the theory of marginal productivity became more refined, it was pointed out that wages are not *determined* by labor's marginal product. It was argued only that once a wage rate was determined, marginal productivity would indicate how much labor would be employed at the prevailing wage.[6] Thus as Dunlop has pointed out, marginal productivity did not provide a complete theory of wages, "but only a statement of the demand side."[7]

---

4. J. R. Hicks, *The Theory of Wages* (London: Macmillan & Co. Ltd., 1932), p. vi. This view was reaffirmed by Hicks on pp. 318–319 of the second edition of his book, which was published in 1963.

5. *Ibid.,* p. 8.

6. Dunlop, in Taylor and Pierson, *New Concepts,* pp. 122–123, and Cartter, *Theory of Wages and Employment,* p. 23.

7. Dunlop, *op. cit.,* p. 122.

Wages in a Perfectly Competitive Labor Market

In a perfectly competitive market the following conditions must be met: (1) there must be a large number of buyers and sellers, so that no single individual or coalition of individuals can influence price, (2) the product or service sold must be homogeneous, (3) buyers must be very well informed about market conditions—technically, they should have "perfect" knowledge about the market—and, (4) there must be complete mobility of all factors of production and of all products.

Under these conditions, the hourly wage rate will be determined by the intersection of the demand and supply schedules for labor as illustrated in Figure 5–1 (a). The demand schedule slopes downward to the right, indicating

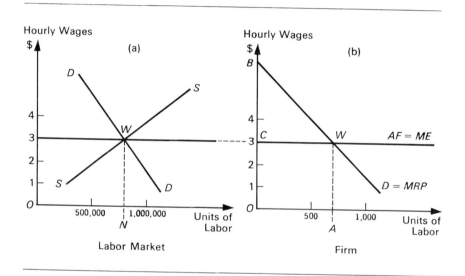

FIGURE 5–1.

Wages in a Purely Competitive Labor Market.

that at a lower wage employers will be ready to hire more workers in the specific occupational group involved. The supply schedule slopes upward to the right, which means that at a higher wage more workers will be attracted to this occupation. At a wage of *NW*, a total of *ON* workers will be employed. In the specific illustration of Figure 5–1 (a), 800,000 workers would be employed at a wage of $3.00 per hour.

In Chapter 3 we saw that a firm's demand for labor depends in part on its production function. We are now able to tie together the firm's demand for labor based on technical considerations, and the wage which the firm will have to pay in a perfectly competitive labor market. This is illustrated in

Figure 5–1 (b). The wage rate has been *determined by* demand and supply conditions in the competitive market, and the individual firm has no control over this wage. If it offered to pay even slightly more than $3.00 per hour, the firm would be overwhelmed by job applicants, and would be forced to cut back to the market rate. If the firm attempted to pay less than this amount, it would attract no workers at all. Thus the wage rate for a given class of workers in a competitive market is "given" to the firm. This is indicated by the horizontal average expenditure (AE) schedule of Figure 5–1 (b). Notice also that in the competitive case average expenditure, or the average wage, is equal to marginal expenditure or the firm's marginal wage.

The number of workers that the individual firm will be able to hire at the market-determined wage rate is determined by the firm's *marginal revenue product schedule.* The marginal revenue product of labor (MRP) is equal to the marginal physical product of labor (MPP) times the additional revenue derived from the output of one additional worker. This amount is known as labor's marginal revenue (MR).

In the example illustrated by Figure 5–1 (b), the marginal revenue product of labor is equal to the wage rate when 700 workers are employed by the firm. If the firm attempted to employ only 600 workers, the marginal revenue product of labor would be $3.50, and the firm would clearly gain by hiring additional workers at $3.00 per hour. If, on the other hand, the firm attempted to employ 800 workers, the marginal revenue product of labor would fall to $2.50. Since it would still have to pay $3.00 per hour, the firm would have to cut back employment. The firm is in equilibrium at the going wage rate when it employs 700 workers. This is the only level of employment at which the firm would maximize profits in a perfectly competitive labor market.

Wages Under Monopolistic Competition

We saw in the last section that if a firm operates under perfect competition, the marginal value product of labor is equal to the marginal revenue product of labor. The marginal value product of labor is defined as the marginal physical product of labor multiplied by the price of the product. As noted earlier, however, the marginal *revenue* product of labor is the marginal physical product of labor times the *additional revenue* derived from the sale of one more unit of output. In a perfectly competitive market the two are the same because the seller of the product has no control over price. Thus the individual firm will continue to expand its output under perfect competition until its marginal cost is equal to marginal revenue—that is, until the *total* cost of producing one more unit of output is equal to the revenue obtained from selling that additional unit of output.

There are some markets, however, in which the individual firm is able to exert some degree of control over price; it can sell more at a lower price or less at a higher price. Under these circumstances the profit-maximizing firm will again expand output until its marginal revenue equals its marginal cost, but there is an important difference between this case and the perfectly competitive case discussed in the last section. Under monopolistic or imperfect competition, the firm's marginal revenue will decline more rapidly than its average revenue. If the firm decides to expand its output by cutting price, it does not reduce the price on only the last unit of output sold. It must charge the same price for *all* units, whatever the level of output it chooses. But the firm can expand output only by reducing its selling price. This is reflected in the firm's marginal value product (*MVP*) and marginal revenue product (*MRP*) schedules for labor, as illustrated in Figure 5–2.

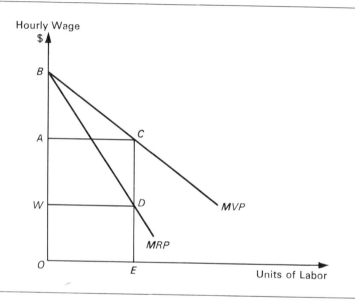

FIGURE 5–2.

Wages and Employment Under Monopolistic Competition.

In this example the firm would employ *OE* units of labor at a wage of *OW*, but the price the firm receives for its product would be given by *OA* (which is equal to *CE*). In this case, the total return to labor is given by the rectangle *OEDW*. The return to all other factors of production combined is given by the rectangle *ACDW*.

It is important to emphasize that the firm under discussion is assumed to have some control over the price of the product it sells, but it does not control wages. Wage rates are determined by demand and supply in the labor market, just as in the case of the perfectly competitive labor market described earlier. The only difference between this case and the competitive case is the divergence between marginal value product (*MVP*) and marginal revenue product (*MRP*) under monopolistic competition, and this follows from the firm's ability to control the price it charges for the product it sells.

What effect would a union have on employment if it were able to organize the workers in a competitive market? Since the firm's marginal revenue product schedule slopes downward to the right, and since the profit-maximizing firm will always equate the marginal revenue product of labor with its wage rate, the firm would be forced to employ fewer workers at the higher wage rate. This is illustrated in Figure 5–3, which shows that at a competitive wage of

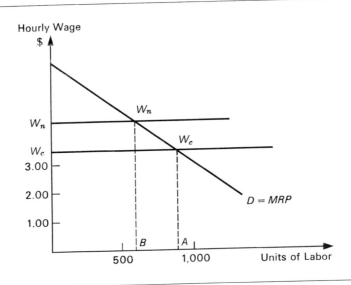

FIGURE 5–3.
Effects of a Negotiated Wage on Employment Under Competition.

$3.50 the firm would employ 900 workers. If a union were to negotiate a wage of $4.50, however, the firm would be able to employ only 600. Since all firms in the industry would behave in the same way, the result would be a leftward shift in the aggregate supply schedule of labor. The union could raise average wages in this occupation, but it could do so only by limiting the number of jobs to be filled.

The effect of a negotiated wage on unemployment would be the same under monopolistic competition, so long as the firm had no control over wages. This is indicated in Figure 5–4. At the competitive wage of OW_c, this firm would employ OA workers, and it would charge a price of OP_c for its product. If a union raised the wage that this firm had to pay to OW_n, it would cut back employment to OB workers, and raise the price of its product to OP_n. The firm

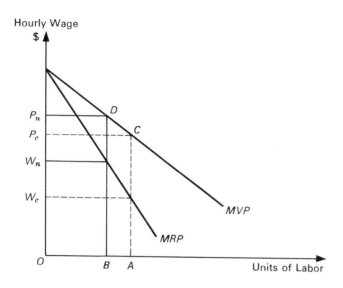

Hourly Wage

FIGURE 5–4.
Effect of a Negotiated Wage on Employment Under Monopolistic Competition.

could do this—whether or not its competitors were organized—so long as its MVP and MRP schedules remained unchanged. But as in the perfectly competitive case, the union could raise wages in this firm only if it were prepared to accept a smaller number of jobs.

The counterpart to monopolistic competition in the product market is monopsony in the labor market. Under this condition, an employer is able to hire more workers at a higher wage or fewer workers at a lower wage. A large employer in a relatively isolated labor market would typically have some degree of monopsonistic power. Under monopsony there is a divergence between the firm's average expenditure (AE) and marginal expenditure (ME) schedules. The reason for this is exactly the same as that which explains the divergence between the marginal value of product and marginal revenue product schedules under monopolistic competition. If the firm wishes to hire more workers it can do so only by paying a higher wage, and this wage must be paid to all workers hired at that level of output. And just as marginal revenue declines more rapidly than average revenue under monopolistic competition in the product market, marginal expenditure increases more rapidly than average expenditure under monopsony in the labor market. This situation is illustrated in Figure 5-5. In the absence of a union this firm would pay a wage of OW_m, or slightly more than $3.00 per hour. At this wage it would employ OA

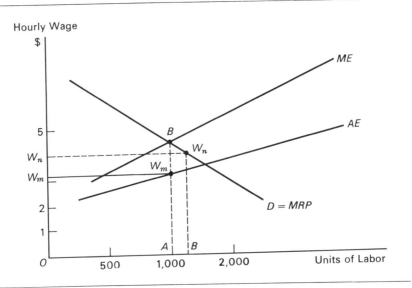

FIGURE 5–5.
Effect of a Negotiated Wage on Employment Under Monopsony.

or 1,000 workers. The number of workers is determined by the intersection of the marginal expenditure (*ME*) and marginal revenue product (*MRP*) schedules, and the competitive or free-market wage is found by dropping a perpendicular from this intersection at point *B* to the average expenditure schedule.

Assume next that a union organizes the workers in this community and negotiates a wage of OW_n or $4.00 per hour. The firm has now lost most of its monopsonistic power. It is no longer free to hire fewer workers at a lower wage. Indeed, since the firm has now lost control over the wage it can pay, it will behave in the same way as the competitive buyer of labor in Figure 5–1 (b). The number of workers it will hire will then be determined by the intersection of the firm's marginal revenue product (*MRP*) schedule and the "going" wage rate. This is indicated by OW_n, and at this level of wages the firm will employ OC workers, or slightly more than 1,200. Thus we have the seemingly paradoxical result of higher wages and more employment; but this result is entirely consistent with the profit-maximizing behavior of an employer who loses monopsonistic power through the organizing activities of a trade union.

The examples given illustrate two important points with respect to union wage policy. First, union wage policy will be influenced to some extent by its employment effects. Second, the employment effects of a negotiated wage increase will be influenced significantly by the market structure of the firm and industry involved.

The relationship between wages and market structure has been carefully analyzed in an important article by Martin Segal.[8] Segal distinguishes between local and national markets, and between competing and noncompeting industries. He concludes that unions would have the smallest impact on wages when organizing competitive industries whose firms sell in national markets. Unions dealing with local competitive industries would have more influence on wages than those organizing national competitive industries. But unions dealing with local competitive firms would have less influence on wages than those dealing with either local noncompetitive or national noncompetitive firms.

Segal's study has important implications both for union behavior and public policy. In their public pronouncements union leaders are often critical of the monopolistic power of big business, but if Segal's conclusions are valid (no one has challenged them as yet), unions may expect to meet with greater success when dealing with firms in noncompetitive than in competitive industries.

Contemporary Wage Theory

During the classical period, the question that concerned wage theorists was: How is the total product of the economy divided among social classes? During the neoclassical era, the emphasis was shifted to distribution among the factors of production. As Dunlop has noted, emphasis has now shifted to the general level of money wages, the level of real wages, and the structure of wage rates. The questions asked today are: How do unions affect wages? What effect do wage increases have on efficiency? Are wages determined more by economic forces or by the political considerations of union leaders? There are no precise answers to these questions, and there may never be. The fact that these questions are still asked, however, shows that they deal with important matters. The wage fund and marginal productivity theories provided simple answers, but both were based on simplifying assumptions. As we have learned more about wages, through the availability of a growing body of statistical data, the one fact which stands out starkly is the complexity of the wage structure. How does contemporary wage theory attempt to answer the questions raised above, given the observed diversity in wage rates and wage patterns?

From an economic point of view, a wage rate is a special kind of price. Thus a theory of wages is a specialized part of a more general theory of prices. The central concepts in price theory are demand and supply. As noted in earlier sections, however, the wage fund and the marginal produc-

---

8. Martin Segal, "The Relation Between Union Wage Impact and Market Structure," *The Quarterly Journal of Economics,* February 1964, pp. 96–114.

tivity theories failed to take into account the supply side of the price equation. In the earlier formulations the amount of labor supplied depended upon the labor force, and the labor force depended upon population growth. Wage rates were then determined by social custom or institutional rules. In Dunlop's words, ". . . the pivotal task of wage theory is to formulate an acceptable theory on the supply side."[9]

A further weakness of early wage theory was the emphasis on a single wage rate. Attention was centered on the wages of unskilled laborers. The wages of all other workers, it was argued, could then be translated into terms of this lowest common denominator. In the absence of statistical data against which to test wage hypotheses, this might not have been a bad first approximation. But the characteristic which stands out most in any empirical study of wages is *diversity* rather than uniformity. Contemporary analysts have concentrated on this aspect of wages in their efforts to provide a systematic explanation of *wage structure.*

Job Clusters and Wage Contours

In an effort to develop a manageable yet realistic framework for the explanation of wage structure, John T. Dunlop developed the concepts of "job clusters" and "wage contours."

A *job cluster* is defined as "a stable group of job classifications or work assignments within a firm (wage-determining unit) which are so linked together by (1) technology, (2) the administrative organization of the production process . . . or (3) social custom that they have common wage-making characteristics."[10] The wage rates for the jobs within a cluster are more closely related than are the rates outside the cluster.

Within a single firm or plant there may be a number of job clusters. Highly skilled machinists and pattern makers, for example, could constitute a job cluster in one type of plant; machine tenders or operatives might make up another cluster; and the plant maintenance workers might comprise a third.

Generally, each job cluster contains one or more *key rates.* The key rate might be regarded as the rate within a job cluster from which all other rates fan out. It could be the most typical rate in the cluster; it could be the highest; or it could be the lowest. The key rate is typically the critical rate in collective bargaining. In the short run, at least, the relationship of rates within a job cluster may be regarded as given. Thus, if a key rate is increased by ten cents an hour, proportionate increases would ordinarily be granted to workers paid at other rates within the job cluster.

Job clusters and key rates are part of the *internal* wage structure of an employment unit—the firm, a plant, or an office. But there is also a great deal

---

9. Dunlop, in Taylor and Pierson, *New Concepts,* p. 128.

10. *Ibid.,* p. 129.

of variation in wages from firm to firm, industry to industry, and locality to locality. When we step outside a single bargaining unit and view this array of wage rates we are observing the *external* wage structure.

The way in which the internal wage structure is established will be considered in a later section dealing with job evaluation. Now, however, we will consider the external wage structure in terms of the concept of the wage contour.

A *wage contour* is defined as "a stable group of wage-determining units (bargaining units, plants, or firms) which are so linked together by (1) similarity of product markets, (2) resort to similar sources for a labor force, or (3) common labor-market organization (custom) that they have common wage-making characteristics."[11]

The wage rates for given occupations in a particular firm are more closely related to the rates paid by some firms than to others. According to Dunlop a wage contour has three dimensions: (1) a particular group of occupations or job clusters, (2) a sector of industry, and (3) geographical location. Thus a given wage contour is defined in terms of both the product market and the labor market. The firms included in a specific contour may be located in a single labor market area within a specific region, or they may be scattered over the country as a whole. Finally, while the boundaries of some wage contours may be rather clearly defined, it is difficult if not impossible to discover the boundaries of others.

The wages of carpenters in a metropolitan area make up one type of wage contour. If the area is highly organized, as is true of most metropolitan areas, all carpenters doing a specific type of work may be earning the same rate of pay. This is so regardless of the size of the firms employing them. But the wages of carpenters vary significantly from one community to another even within the same region.[12] This is an example of a wage contour with a rather clearly defined boundary, that of the local labor market area. Other wage contours, however, can be nationwide. In the steel industry, for example, there has been a trend toward the equalization of wage rates by occupation without respect to locality. This is an example of an occupational-industrial wage contour that is independent of geographic location. As a final example, we might consider the wages of machinists who work in a wide variety of industries that blanket the industrialized section of the country. While the wages of machinists will not be identical from firm to firm, or from region to region, the wages of machinists are more similar to each other than to other wage rates. This is an example of an occupational wage contour. A wage

---

11. *Ibid.,* p. 131.

12. In January 1971, for example, the hourly earnings (basic hourly scale plus employer benefit payments) ranged from $5.15 in Portland, Maine, to $7.75 in Worcester, Massachusetts. This is a difference of $2.60, or slightly more than 50 per cent of the lower rate. (U.S. Department of Labor, Bureau of Labor Statistics, Regional Report No. 71-5, p. 5.)

contour is not specifically confined to a given industry or a given locality, but each wage contour is confined to some range of skills, occupations, or job clusters.

In the case of organized workers, each wage contour contains one or more *key settlements*. The key settlements in wage contour might be the key rates in the job clusters of the dominant firm in an industry. This firm might be outstanding because of the share of the market it commands or because of the firm's leadership in industrial relations.

The twin concepts of job clusters and wage contours are effective devices for explaining the *interdependence* of wages in modern industrial society. The focal point of the internal wage structure in each employment or bargaining unit is the key rate. And the key settlements within specific wage contours are interrelated. This does not mean that there is a tendency toward uniformity either in key rates or key settlements. But recognition of the existence of key rates and key settlements permits us to understand better the wide diversity of wage rates, while at the same time recognizing that individual wage rates are not determined in a vacuum but are related to one another. Both key rates and key settlements are affected by a host of economic forces.

Wage determination is the process of price-setting in the labor market. But wage contours cannot be divorced from the *product* market. Indeed, one of the most powerful forces affecting a specific wage contour is the nature of the product markets served by the firms in a given contour. In an industry where prices are administered—where there is an absence of price competition—key rates and key settlements might tend to be remarkably close together, if not actually uniform, regardless of the location of firms. In highly competitive industries such as cotton textiles, there have been remarkably persistent wage differentials from region to region. But within each region key rates or key settlements tend to be close to one another. In the latter case, the firms in each region make up the wage contour.

The concept of wage contours may be illustrated by referring to the union wage scales of selected truck drivers given in Table 5-1. Within the Chicago metropolitan area, the hourly rates of the highest-paid Teamsters were more than 80 per cent above those at the bottom of the wage scale. The differences are even greater when employer contributions to insurance and pension funds are included. Truck drivers delivering morning newspapers made a great deal more than truck drivers delivering merchandise for retail florists. The wages of the former make up one wage contour, whereas the wages of the latter make up another. Each contour is a reflection of the product market. Within the specific contour, the wage rates of competing firms tend to be close together, if not identical, but there are wide variations from contour to contour.

An earlier generation of economists would have dismissed such wage differentials as the result of "imperfections" in the marketplace. A nineteenth-century economist might have argued that if there were better knowledge,

TABLE 5-1
Union Wages and Employer Contributions to Insurers and Pension Funds for Selected Local Truck Drivers, Chicago, Illinois, July 1, 1970

Type of truck	Rate per hour[a]	Employer contribution to fund (cents per hr.)[a]		Total
		Insurance	Pension	
Construction dump truck, over 20 tons	$5.25	.15	.25	$5.65
Newspaper, morning	4.79	.15	.16	5.10
Coal, over 16 tons	4.66	.09	.10	4.85
Soft drink, less than 7 tons	4.65	.16	.11	4.92
Department store, bulk and parcel	4.35	na[b]	.27	4.62
Milk, steady routeman	4.28	.25	.34	4.87
Oil and gasoline	4.25	.17	.27	4.70
Refuse, private scavenger	4.25	.15	.10	4.50
Furniture, retail	4.23	.25	.20	4.78
Ice cream	4.14	.26	.27	4.68
Bakery	4.12	.20	.22	4.55
Beer, keg	4.09	.16	.32	4.58
Scrap iron and metal	4.00	.20	.20	4.40
Meat, under 3 tons	3.92	.19	.25	4.36
Armored car	3.88	na[b]	.25	4.13
Auto supply and accessory, less than 2 tons	3.60	.15	0	3.75
Tire	3.52	.15	0	3.67
Tobacco, candy, and cigarettes	3.34	.14	0	3.48
Nursery, landscaping—winch	3.04	0	0	3.04
Florist, retail, less than 2 tons	2.90	0	0	2.90

Source: U.S. Department of Labor, Bureau of Labor Statistics, *Union Wages and Hours: Local Truckdrivers and Helpers*, Bulletin 1708, (July 1, 1970), pp. 11–12.
[a] Rounded to nearest cent.
[b] Na—not available.

greater mobility, and an absence of institutional pressures on wages, such differences would eventually tend to disappear; but economists today recognize the prevalence of wide differences among product markets. Some product markets are vigorously price competitive, whereas in others, prices are administered. Some industries or lines of business are made up of many small firms with limited capital requirements; others are dominated by a few industrial giants, each of which is a multimillion dollar concern. The differences among product markets are not temporary. They are an integral part of our system of economic organization. Similarly, the differentials among wage contours are not transitory. They are not due to lack of knowledge, lack of mobility, or to other alleged "imperfections." They are a result of the blending of economic forces in labor markets and product markets, and while they are not fixed for all time, such differentials are remarkably persistent.

The Internal Wage Structure

Within a firm wage rates are associated with job clusters, each of which contains one or more key rates. But how are these key rates determined? The state of the labor market has a great deal to do with the determination of some key rates. Unskilled workers, for example, have generally been available in relatively ample numbers. And the forces of supply and demand have had a great deal to do with determining the wage rates of "common" labor. Custom, on the other hand, has been an important determinant of wages for highly skilled workers. Long apprenticeships have limited the supply of some craftsmen and, as a result, they have always earned relatively high wages.

Custom and institutional rules, including union rules, still play an important part in determining wages within a plant or a company. With the rise of industrial engineering, however, systematic techniques for the development of internal wage structures made their appearance. The application of these techniques is known as *job evaluation.*

Job Evaluation

There are four basic systems of job evaluation. In an introductory textbook we cannot go into the intricacies of any of these methods, but they can be described briefly.[13] The four basic systems are:

1. *The ranking method,* which compares job against job as a whole.
2. *The classification method,* which provides for established arbi-

---

13. For an excellent general discussion which provides further details, see Leonard R. Burgess, *Wage and Salary Administration in a Dynamic Economy* (New York: Harcourt, Brace & World, Inc., 1968), pp. 29–51. See also Solomon Barkin, "Wage Determination: Trick or Technique," in Joseph Shister (ed.), *Readings in Labor Economics and Industrial Relations,* 2nd ed. (Philadelphia: Lippincott, 1956), pp. 263–268.

trary job grades with definitions and requires all jobs to be slotted into these preestablished grades, as in the case of civil servants.

3. *The point system,* which provides for a comparison of the jobs against a given list of job factors (which may vary from ten to fifteen in number). Each job factor is assigned a number of point values.

4. *The factor comparison method,* which compares job against job on the basis of given job elements.[14]

The simplest type of job evaluation is the ranking method, under which no effort is made to measure specific factors involved in the job such as skill, responsibility, training, and experience, or such negative factors as job hazard or the unpleasantness of work. In a relatively small plant, for example, skilled craftsmen would be paid the highest wage, and the individual firm might have relatively little control over their rates. At the bottom of the scale, cleanup men and other unskilled workers might also have their wages determined by forces outside the plant. The availability of an ample supply of such workers might dictate the wage they are to receive. All other jobs will be ranked between these extremes, and the wages associated with each job might be determined by fairly rough rules of thumb.

The remaining three types of job evaluation, however, depend upon a more complicated process. The classification, or civil service, method is fairly well known.[15] Job grades are established on the basis of skill, education, responsibility, and other similar factors. Rate ranges are assigned to each of these classifications. A worker may move up the promotional ladder from one classification to another, each time starting at the bottom of the range and working his way to the top. The initial determination of the rate ranges might depend to a considerable extent upon market influences. The ranges could also be determined on the basis of wage surveys, which have played an important part in the development of internal wage structures in recent years. Again, however, no effort is made to assign specific weights to each of the factors associated with the job.

Under the point system and the factor comparison method, the various requirements associated with each job are arrayed. Weights are assigned to each of these factors. There is no single method of determining these weights, but once the weights are determined, a "wage curve" is developed and related to the weighted factors. The points assigned to each job are then added up. The jobs with the largest number of points are paid the rates at the top of the wage curve; those with the smallest number of points fall at the bottom of the curve.

In the early days of job evaluation some enthusiasts believed they had

---

14. *Ibid.*

15. It should be noted that this method is not limited in its application to civil service jobs.

discovered a "scientific" method of wage determination, which was independent of all subjective evaluations. Efforts to determine wages by quasi-mathematical or statistical methods were not warmly received by workers, however, and in recent years there have been few claims that job evaluation is a method for precisely determining the "right" wage rate for each job. Even the early enthusiasts recognized that they had to take market forces into account—as well as past practices—in arriving at a workable set of wage rates. As unions increased in power and began to play a more important part in wage determination, further adjustments had to be made in many job evaluation systems. While job evaluation is still widely used today, few claim that it is a "scientific" technique for wage determination.

Some Union Views of Job Evaluation

Union spokesmen have differing opinions about job evaluation. For example, Solomon Barkin, formerly a textile union staff official, feels that job evaluation has made several contributions to the process of collective bargaining. This is so, in his view, because job evaluation has stressed the need for a formal system of job rates instead of personal rates; it has reduced the number of different rates within a plant and it has provided a rational basis for differentiating rates for jobs. It has also reduced differences in wage rates by reason of sex, religion, race, or color. But some managements, in what Barkin considers to be "monopolistic and semi-monopolistic unorganized industries," have used job evaluation as a substitute for collective bargaining. Furthermore, some of the factors used in merit rating under such systems—cooperation and loyalty, for example—can be used to promote antiunion ends. Thus, Barkin concludes, the "job evaluation technique is a management tool."[16] He goes on to point out that unions have always favored a simple job rate structure with clearly defined job descriptions. In his opinion, however, these goals can be achieved in a much more satisfactory manner through collective bargaining than by means of formal job evaluation.

A contrary view has been expressed by William Gomberg, who at one time was associated with the International Ladies Garment Workers Union. Gomberg states that "the basic concepts of job evaluation were used by trade unionists long before these ideas were formalized into a systematic body of thought."[17] Workers, Gomberg believes, are "far more keenly interested in how much they receive compared to what some of their fellow workers in other occupations are receiving than in any absolute level of wages for the whole factory."[18] Thus job evaluation provides at least a rough measuring rod for

---

16. Barkin, *op. cit.,* p. 268.
17. William Gomberg, "A Collective Bargaining Approach to Job Evaluation," in Joseph Shister, *Readings in Labor Economics and Industrial Relations,* p. 268.
18. *Ibid.,* p. 269.

establishing rational relationships in rates of pay. Gomberg is as critical as Barkin of certain job evaluation techniques—notably the National Metal Trades Job Evaluation Plan—particularly if they are based upon *fixed* weights assigned to various factors. But on the whole, he believes, the problem which job evaluation presents to collective bargaining is "not so much how to fight it as a management tool, but rather how to reshape it into a more useful collective bargaining instrument."[19]

Much of the controversy surrounding job evaluation has diminished in recent years. As Livernash has pointed out, the way in which job evaluation is administered is of extreme importance. "If the management constructs the evaluation plan and brings the finished product to the union with an insistence upon accepting the placement of jobs virtually without criticism, the plan may well, if accepted, usher in a period of unrest and bitterness leading to its destruction."[20] But if management develops a job evaluation plan as a means of establishing a basic rate structure, and if it is willing to negotiate adjustments in the plan with the union, the technique can be introduced without leading to conflict. "Job evaluation does not necessarily create nor alleviate conflict, but there is no issue in job evaluation that cannot be resolved to the mutual satisfaction of both labor and management."[21]

The Internal Wage Structure and the Labor Market

Even in the absence of a union, few companies are in a position to establish an internal wage structure without reference to market influences. And where there is a union, job evaluation must take place within the framework of collective bargaining unless there is to be continuing strife and unrest. As Clark Kerr and Lloyd H. Fisher pointed out, "sound wage structures are subject to the forces of internal logic and of external environment *both at the same time.* . . ."[22] In the opinion of these authors, job evaluation programs which attempt to establish relative rates within a plant, independently of other considerations, do not go far enough. In their words[23]:

> A job description and job evaluation plan, where collective bargaining prevails, must coexist with the labor agreement. The two are related, not only (1) through the union security provisions of the contract as they influence the political situation of the union, and (2) through the grievance machinery

19. *Ibid.*

20. Edward R. Livernash, "Wage Administration and Production Standards," in W. S. Woytinsky and Associates, *Wages and Employment in the United States* (New York: Twentieth Century Fund, 1953), p. 338.

21. *Ibid.,* p. 339.

22. Clark Kerr and Lloyd H. Fisher, "Effective Environment and Administration of Job Evaluation," *Harvard Business Review* (May 1950), p. 77.

23. *Ibid.,* p. 86.

and its adequacy for handling the volume of cases normally incident to the introduction of a plan, but particularly (3) through the seniority clauses. A job evaluation plan sets up a wage structure, while seniority clauses affect the flow of employees through this structure. The two must be compatible.

The internal wage structure does not exist in a vacuum. Whether management alone determines what the wage rates for each job in a plant will be, or whether these are the result of bargaining between unions and management, the internal wage structure cannot be isolated from influences outside the plant or the company. While job evaluation can lead to an orderly system of wage rates the technique cannot be used without reference to external forces. Kerr and Fisher put it succinctly when they stated that: "A job evaluation plan must be devised and administered with one eye always on the market."[24]

Wage Incentives

Both job evaluation and collective bargaining tend to produce uniformity of rates for the same job in a given work environment. But workers may be paid either on an hourly basis or on the basis of some incentive plan. Where hourly rates are in effect—whether negotiated or unilaterally installed by management—the trend is toward uniformity of payment for the same kind of work. On assembly lines or in other machine-paced operations, the output of workers on identical jobs is the same. The worker must either keep up with the pace set by the machine or he cannot continue to hold his job. Under such circumstances hourly rates tend to be negotiated or—in the absence of unions—to be administered by management. There are other types of jobs in which the worker's daily output is determined by his skill, dexterity, and effort. In jobs of this kind, the worker is often paid by the piece or according to some other incentive plan. As Livernash has pointed out, incentive-pay methods are typically associated with "short-cycle, repetitive, standardized, worker-paced" operations.[25]

Typically, incentive-pay methods are based on a standard or "normal" daily output. The least efficient and ambitious worker in the plant is expected to produce a minimum number of units in the average working day and for this he will be paid a basic hourly wage. Workers who can produce more than the minimum standard, however, earn more for each unit of output. It is important under such circumstances that the work also meet basic production standards. This means that the output of each worker must be inspected, and unsatisfactory work returned to him to be redone without compensation. But

24. *Ibid.*, p. 91.
25. E. R. Livernash, "The Internal Wage Structure," in George W. Taylor and Frank C. Pierson (eds.), *New Concepts in Wage Determination* (New York: McGraw-Hill Book Co., Inc., 1957), p. 167.

the worker who is able to meet production standards satisfactorily can earn substantially more than the minimum daily wage in incentive-pay plants.

There are pressures, however, which hold the output of even the most efficient workers within limits. For example, an "eager beaver" in a plant might be able to produce twice as much as the minimum daily standard. But if he does this consistently, and particularly if he seems to do it with ease, the industrial engineers in the plant might begin to think that there is too great a spread between the output of the most efficient worker and the minimum standard. They might then restudy the job with a view to increasing the minimum daily standard without a corresponding increase in compensation. This is the essence of what unions refer to as the "speedup." Unions have consistently and vigorously opposed anything which they consider to be an effort to speed up the plant's operations without adding to worker income. Hence, social pressures operate to keep the spread between minimum daily standards and the maximum output of individual workers within what the workers consider to be reasonable limits; and these pressures operate whether or not there is a union in the plant.

The External Wage Structure

Actual determination of wage rates—or the internal wage structure—in a plant or company is far more complex than one would be led to believe by some of the earlier theories of wage determination. The factors that *determine* wages in a plant or company are many and complex. The output of some workers is fixed by the pace of the machines they operate, and in some work environments labor is not a completely variable input.[26] The output of others varies with worker skill and effort. In some cases the internal wage structure is installed and administered entirely by management. In others it is the result of collective bargaining. In still others it may be the joint product of formal job evaluation and collective bargaining.

Internal wage structures are far from simple yet there is an orderliness which shows that they are not determined randomly or by caprice. Dunlop's description of wage structures as depending upon key rates, wage contours, and key settlements, lacks the neatness and precision of the theory of marginal productivity. But it is an important step toward the explanation of diversity, as well as of regularities, in the wage structure. The notions of key rates, wage contours, and key settlements also provide a nexus between the internal wage structures of individual plants or companies and the external wage structure.

The internal wage structure of a plant or company, which at first glance might appear to be a disorderly maze of different wage rates, is the essence

---

26. See Walter Y. Oi, "Labor as a Quasi-Fixed Factor," *Journal of Political Economy, LXX* (December 1962).

of simplicity compared with the wage structure of the nation, a region, or of a single labor market area. The internal wage structure ranges from the top rates paid to highly skilled workers to relatively low rates for those who perform menial tasks. This can be explained in terms of market forces even if one conveniently chooses to ignore all other factors which impinge upon wages. Highly skilled workers may be in scarce supply while workers with no skills at all are relatively abundant. In a highly developed economy there is a considerable need for skilled workers, while unskilled workers are needed only for janitorial and similar tasks. This is a result of an increasing reliance upon machines, materials-handling devices, and various other forms of mechanical rather than human energy. Thus one should not be particularly surprised to discover that in the internal wage structure of a plant or company there is a grading of wages upward from unskilled to skilled jobs.

When we turn to the external wage structure, however, the diversity of rates is often bewildering. We find that skilled workers in some industries receive a great deal more than skilled workers in others, and that there are even significant variations in the rates paid to unskilled workers. At the extremes, the average hourly earnings of unskilled workers in "high pay" industries may be significantly greater than the average hourly earnings of semiskilled or even of skilled workers in "low-pay" industries.[27] How do we explain the diversity of wages so characteristic of the interindustry wage structure? This is a much easier question to ask than to answer. Many economists—both labor economists and general economists—have attempted to explain the variations in the interindustry wage structure, but the result has been one more of controversy than agreement.

One participant in the controversy, John T. Dunlop, has said[28]:

> The interindustry variations in wages over substantial periods are to be explained in terms of these factors: changes in productivity and output, the proportion of labor costs to total costs, the competitive conditions in the product market for the output of an industry, and the changing skill and occupational content of the workforce of an industry.

Significantly, Dunlop does not include unionization as one of the forces affecting interindustry wage structure. In a later study, however, Joseph Garbarino adds unionization to the factors earlier listed by Dunlop as affecting the interindustry wage structure.[29] Garbarino's conclusion received sup-

---

27. See Sumner H. Slichter, "Notes on the Structure of Wages," *The Review of Economics and Statistics* (February 1950), p. 83.

28. John Dunlop, "Productivity and the Wage Structure," in *Income, Employment and Public Policy*. Essays in honor of Alvin H. Hansen (New York: W. W. Norton & Co., 1948), p. 362.

29. Joseph Garbarino, "A Theory of Inter-Industry Wage Structure Variation," *Quarterly Journal of Economics*, May 1950, p. 305.

port from a study by Ross and Goldner.[30] Sawhney and Herrnstadt have recently demonstrated that the statistical measurement of interindustry wage variation depends to some extent on the measure of productivity used in the analysis. They conclude that *net value productivity* is superior to other productivity measures used in earlier studies of the interindustry wage structure.[31]

In a "structureless" labor market there is a tendency for wages to be the same. Not all unorganized labor markets are "structureless," however. A survey of unorganized workers in a metropolitan labor market revealed substantial variations. "The actual rates paid for similar work even within a given community tend to be rather persistently dispersed over a range larger than would be expected under competitive conditions."[32] The authors of this study feel that wages for nonunion workers are responsive to market forces. But the market they studied was far from "perfect" as this term is used in economic theory.

Conclusions

This chapter has distinguished between *internal* and *external* wage structures. It has also pointed out that labor markets are more complex than product markets. In a given product market, there is a tendency toward uniformity of prices after allowance is made for differences in quality among the various products that can be substituted for one another. The outstanding characteristic of wage rates, however, is their *diversity*. Within a plant or company that does not use incentive-pay methods, workers doing identical work will usually be paid at the same rate. Wages within a firm tend to be related to differences in skill levels.

The external rate structure is more complex. The average earnings of unskilled workers in some industries are higher than those of semiskilled or possibly even of some skilled workers in other industries. Wages are not related in a simple functional manner to one or a few easily observable factors.

The fact that there is such diversity in wage rates does not mean, however, that there is a lack of order in the labor market. Economists may not be in complete agreement about the relative importance of various factors causing interindustry wage variation, but they agree that wage rates are not the result of random causes. Various economic and institutional forces affect

30. Arthur M. Ross and William Goldner, "Forces Affecting the Inter-Industry Wage Structure," *Quarterly Journal of Economics,* May 1950, pp. 266–281.

31. Pawan K. Sawhney and Irwin L. Herrnstadt, "Interindustry Wage Structure Variation in Manufacturing," *Industrial and Labor Relations Review, 24* (April 1971), pp. 407–419.

32. George P. Shultz, Irwin L. Herrnstadt, and Elbridge S. Puckett, "Wage Determination in a Non-Union Labor Market," *Proceedings,* 10th Annual Meeting of the Industrial Relations Research Association, September 1957, p. 4.

wages in a variety of ways. Differences in net value productivity, the proportion of labor cost to total cost, competitive conditions in product markets, and skill (or occupational) requirements, all have a bearing upon the external wage structure.

Questions and Exercises

1. What did Dunlop mean by his statement that marginal productivity does not provide a "complete theory of wages" but only "a statement of the demand side"?

2. If a union organized all the workers in an industry made up of a large number of small firms—no one of which had any control over the price of the industry's product—what would be the employment effect of a negotiated wage increase? Compare this with the results of a negotiated wage increase in the case of a single *firm* that has some degree of control over price because it sells its product in a monopolistically competitive market. Finally, what is the effect of a negotiated wage increase on employment in a monopsonistic firm that has been organized by a union?

3. In June 1971, average hourly earnings of production workers in textile mills came to $2.56 while apparel workers earned $2.48. At the same time, workers in transportation equipment (which includes the automobile industry) earned $4.45 while those in primary metals (which includes steel) earned $4.18. Discuss these differences in terms of Martin Segal's analysis of the influence of unions on wages in local and national markets, and in competing or noncompeting industries.

4. Relate Dunlop's concepts of "job clusters" and "wage contours" to the parallel concepts of internal and external wage structures.

5. Are management schemes to rationalize the internal pay structure—such as job evaluation—compatible with union efforts to accomplish the same objective?

6. An outstanding characteristic of the interindustry wage structure is the diversity of wage rates among industries. What factors explain this variation, according to Dunlop? What additional factor was added by Garbarino?

7. Is there a difference between the perfectly competitive labor market of economic theory and a "structureless" labor market? What were the general findings of the survey conducted by Shultz and his associates of unorganized workers in a metropolitan labor market?

Suggested Readings

Books

Burgess, Leonard R. *Wage and Salary Administration in a Dynamic Economy.* New York: Harcourt Brace & World, Inc., 1968.

Dunlop, John T. (ed.). *The Theory of Wage Determination.* New York: St. Martin's Press, 1957.

Dunlop, John T. *Wage Determination Under Trade Unions.* New York: Augustus M. Kelley Inc., 1950.

Hicks, J. R. *The Theory of Wages.* London: MacMillan and Co. Ltd., 1932; 2nd ed., 1963.

Lewis, Harold G. *Unionism and Relative Wages in the United States.* Chicago: The University of Chicago Press, 1963.

Taylor, George W., and Frank C. Pierson (eds.). *New Concepts in Wage Determination.* New York: McGraw-Hill, 1957.

Articles

Barkin, Solomon. "Wage Determination: Trick or Technique," in Joseph Shister, (ed.), *Readings in Labor Economics and Industrial Relations,* 2nd ed. New York: J. B. Lippincott Co., 1956, pp. 263 ff.

Eckstein, Otto. "Money Wage Determination Revisited," *Review of Economic Studies,* 35 (April 1968), pp. 133–143.

Garbarino, Joseph. "The Theory of Interindustry Wage Structure Variation," *Quarterly Journal of Economics,* May 1950, pp. 282–305.

Gomberg, William. "The Collective Bargaining Approach to Job Evaluation," in Joseph Shister (ed.), *Readings in Labor Economics and Industrial Relations,* 2nd ed. New York: J. B. Lippincott Co., 1956, pp. 268 ff.

Livernash, E. Robert. "Wages and Benefits," in Woodrow L. Ginsburg, *et al.* (eds.), *A Review of Industrial Relations Research,* Vol. *I.* Madison, Wisconsin: Industrial Relations Research Association, 1970, pp. 79–144.

Reder, Melvin W. "Wage Determination in Theory and Practice," in Neil W. Chamberlain, *et al.* (eds.), *A Decade of Industrial Research Relations.* New York: Harper & Brothers, 1958, pp. 64–97.

Ross, Arthur M., and William Goldner. "Forces Affecting the Interindustry Wage Structure," *Quarterly Journal of Economics,* May 1950, pp. 254–281.

Shultz, George P., Irwin L. Herrnstadt, and Elbridge S. Puckett. "Wage Determination in a Non-Union Labor Market," *Proceedings,* Tenth Annual Meeting of the Industrial Relations Research Association, September 1957, pp. 1–13.

Slichter, Sumner H. "Notes on the Structure of Wages," *Review of Economics and Statistics,* February 1950, pp. 80–91.

II

Manpower Problems and Policies

Unemployment and Inflation

One of the major objectives of economic policy in the United States since the end of World War II may be summarized in a single phrase—full employment without inflation. "Full employment" does not mean that every member of society is working; it means a condition in which there are as many jobs and unfilled job openings as there are people at work or looking for work. Some dictionaries define inflation as a "substantial" increase in prices, but this is a highly subjective definition. A good working definition of inflation is a condition under which the *average* price level is increasing more rapidly than the average annual increase in productivity in the economy as a whole.

During the 1950s, the nation witnessed a decade of relative price stability and rising unemployment. Some economists attributed this rising unemployment to inadequate aggregate demand, and they prescribed monetary and fiscal measures to stimulate investment and consumption as the appropriate cure. Others attributed the rise in unemployment to structural changes in the economy, particularly those engendered by new technological developments, and advocated more active public intervention in the labor market. The debate between conventional macrotheorists and the "structuralists" receded into the background during the 1960s, however, particularly after 1965. As the Vietnam war was escalated unemployment fell and price indexes began to rise sharply. An issue of central concern to economists during this period was the relationship between changes in wages and prices, and changes in the unemployment rate. Finally, after 1970, the unemployment rate *and* the consumer price index both rose sharply. This resulted in the temporary wage-price freeze and the Nixon administration's New Economic Policy of 1971.

Employment and Unemployment Trends Since 1947

Trends in employment and unemployment since 1947 are summarized in Table 6-1. During this twenty-four-year period the civilian labor force increased by more than 24 million persons, or almost 42 per cent. During the

TABLE 6–1
Labor Force, Employment and Unemployment, 1947–1971
(Thousands of persons 16 years of age and over)

Year	Civilian labor force		Employment		Unemployment		
	Number	Annual percent change	Number	Annual percent change	Number	Annual percent change	Percent of civilian labor force
1947	59,350	—	57,039	—	2,311	—	3.9
1948	60,621	+2.1	58,344	+2.3	2,276	− 1.5	3.8
1949	61,286	+1.1	57,649	−1.2	3,637	+59.8	5.9
1950	62,208	+1.5	58,920	+2.2	3,288	− 9.6	5.3
1951	62,017	−0.3	59,962	+1.8	2,055	−37.5	3.3
1952	62,138	+0.2	60,254	+0.5	1,883	− 8.4	3.0
1953	63,015	+1.4	61,181	+1.5	1,834	− 2.6	2.9
1954	63,643	+1.0	60,110	−1.8	3,532	+92.6	5.5
1955	65,023	+2.2	62,171	+3.4	2,852	−19.3	4.4
1956	66,552	+2.4	63,802	+2.6	2,750	− 3.6	4.1
1957	66,929	+0.6	64,071	+0.4	2,859	+ 4.0	4.3
1958	67,639	+1.1	63,036	−1.6	4,602	+61.0	6.8
1959	68,369	+1.1	64,630	+2.5	3,740	−18.7	5.5
1960	69,628	+1.8	65,778	+1.8	3,852	+ 3.0	5.5
1961	70,459	+1.2	65,746	− .0	4,714	+22.4	6.7
1962	70,614	+0.2	66,702	+1.5	3,911	−17.0	5.5
1963	71,833	+1.7	67,762	+1.6	4,070	+ 4.0	5.7
1964	73,091	+1.8	69,305	+2.3	3,786	− 7.0	5.2
1965	74,455	+1.9	71,088	+2.6	3,366	−11.1	4.5
1966	75,770	+1.8	72,895	+2.5	2,875	−14.6	3.8
1967	77,347	+2.1	74,372	+2.0	2,975	+ 3.5	3.8
1968	78,737	+1.8	75,920	+2.1	2,817	− 5.3	3.6
1969	80,733	+2.5	77,902	+2.6	2,831	+ 0.5	3.5
1970	82,715	+2.5	78,627	+0.9	4,088	+44.4	4.9
1971	84,113	+1.7	79,120	+0.6	4,993	+22.1	5.9

Source: *Economic Report of the President,* January 1972, p. 220.

same period employment increased by more than 38 per cent. It is important to note the cyclical movements of employment and unemployment over this period as well. There were four clear-cut recessions during the period covered by Table 6–1, the first in 1949 and the last in 1961. In each of the recessions, employment dropped and the unemployment rate increased. There was also a "mini-recession" in 1970–71. From 1969 to 1971, there was a 1.6 per cent increase in employment, but the number of unemployed workers jumped by more than 76 per cent.

During the first two postwar recessions the consumer price index either declined slightly or held steady, but during the recessions of 1958 and 1961, prices continued to edge upward despite the rise in unemployment. The distinguishing feature of the mini-recession of 1970 is that increases in unemployment and in prices were both substantial.

Definitions and Measurement of Unemployment

The Monthly Report on the Labor Force

Information on the labor force, employment, and unemployment is collected each month by trained interviewers from the Bureau of the Census. The data obtained in each monthly survey are turned over to the Bureau of Labor Statistics for analysis and publication. The survey covers a carefully designed sample of about 50,000 households located in 449 areas, which in turn contain 863 counties and independent cities. All fifty states and the District of Columbia are covered by what is considered to be a representative cross section of the nation's labor-market areas. The population which the sample represents is the "civilian, non-institutional population" made up of persons sixteen years of age or older. This excludes all members of the armed forces and inmates of penal, medical, and similar institutions. Those persons in the sample who were "at work" or "with a job but not at work" during the survey week are counted as *employed*. From employed workers, information is collected about their occupation, the industry in which they work, and their hours of work. Data are collected on multiple job holders as well as those holding full-time or part-time jobs. Persons who worked at least 35 hours during the survey week are considered to be employed on a full-time basis; those who worked between one and 34 hours are classified as having part-time jobs.

Unemployed workers include those who did not work at all during the survey week but *who were looking for work*. Also counted as unemployed were those waiting either to return to a job from which they had been laid off or to report to a new job within the following thrity days (and who were not in school during the survey week). Finally, workers who were temporarily ill or who believed no jobs were available in their line of work in the community are included among the unemployed.

From this monthly sample national estimates are made by applying appropriate "blow-up" factors. The sample is a revolving one, that is, the same households are not included month after month, although a complete change is not attempted every month. The sample is selected in such a way as to give every household in the nation an equal opportunity to be included in the survey.

When the data have been collected by census enumerators, they are turned over to the Bureau of Labor Statistics for tabulation, analysis, and publication. The BLS publishes a measure of sampling variability known as the "standard error," which can be used to determine the upper and lower limits within which the "true" level of unemployment will fall on a probability basis. Without going into technical details, it may be noted that these limits are quite narrow. If, for example, in a specific month the BLS reports an unemployment estimate of 4 million, the chances are two out of three that the true figure lies somewhere between 3.9 million and 4.1 million. And the chances are 19 out of 20 that the true figure will fall between 3.8 million and

4.2 million.[1] Small month-to-month changes—40,000 to 50,000 for example—must be interpreted with caution. Such changes are within the limits of sampling variability and might not represent any change in the actual unemployment situation. The BLS is always careful to point this out, however. When the monthly survey of the labor force shows a small increase or decrease in unemployment—well within the limits of sampling variability—it is reported as "no change." The estimates prepared jointly by the Bureau of the Census and the Bureau of Labor Statistics have come under attack at times. But the integrity of the government agencies responsible for preparing the estimates of employment and unemployment has been staunchly upheld by professional statisticians, representatives of business, and the leaders of organized labor.[2]

The Taxonomy of Unemployment

Unemployment may be classified in a number of ways: (a) by degree (partial or total), (b) by volition (voluntary or involuntary), (c) by duration (short-term, long-term, and very long-term), and (d) by cause (seasonal, cyclical, frictional, structural, and so forth). There will always be some voluntary unemployment in a free-market economy, since there is a constant turnover of workers as some quit old jobs in search of new. Such unemployment is likely to be more prevalent during good times than bad, since a worker will not readily quit a job—even one he does not particularly like—at a time when other job opportunities are scarce. Some workers, especially married women in the labor force, are not interested in full-time, year-round jobs. At times they show up in the statistics as partially unemployed or temporarily unemployed workers.

Many kinds of short-term unemployment do not constitute a serious problem. But involuntary unemployment—especially if it is of relatively long duration—is a serious economic and social problem. The remainder of this chapter will be concerned almost entirely with involuntary unemployment, with particular emphasis on causes and proposed remedies.

Unemployment by Duration and Type

Any attempt to develop a simple cross-classification of unemployment by duration and type will run into difficulties. This is because the two are not mutually exclusive. Some kinds of unemployment are distinctly short-term but other kinds may be either short- or long-term. One cross-classification of unemployment by duration and type is given in Table 6–2. This classification will undoubtedly not be accepted by all economists, and the types of unem-

---

1. *Employment and Unemployment,* Hearings before the Subcommittee on Economic Statistics, Joint Economic Committee, Eighty-seventh Congress, December 18–20, 1961, p. 42.

2. For an extended discussion of this issue see *Measuring Employment and Unemployment,* Report of the President's Committee to Appraise Employment and Unemployment Statistics (Washington, D.C.: U.S. Government Printing Office, 1962.)

ployment listed in the left-hand column of this table do not exhaust all the possibilities. Some other kinds of unemployment are discussed below.[3]

TABLE 6–2
Types of Unemployment by Duration

	Short-term	Long-term or "Very long-term"
Casual	X	—
Seasonal	X	—
Frictional	X	—
Initial	X	X
Cyclical	X	X
Structural	X	X
Due to inadequate demand		X

The Department of Labor defines short-term unemployment as that lasting up to fifteen weeks. Long-term unemployment lasts from fifteen to twenty-six weeks. Unemployment of twenty-seven weeks or more is considered as "very long-term" unemployment. The various types of unemployment listed in Table 6–2 will be discussed briefly:

Casual

Some types of work are casual or intermittent. Various kinds of dock workers, for example, can only be employed when ships are available to be loaded or unloaded. The same applies to some kinds of construction workers and various other workers who cannot tell on a day-to-day basis when they will or will not be employed. Often such workers are employed on the basis of a roster; when their names come up through a process of rotation, they work on a given day. These workers are often unemployed for a few days at a stretch. But so long as they remain attached to a particular hiring hall or other agency that will call them to work when a job is available, they will not be included in the unemployment statistics. If, by chance, such a worker should be included in the monthly survey discussed above, he would be classified as "with a job but not at work." Some authors prefer to include casual unemployment under "hidden" or "disguised" unemployment, to be discussed below.

---

3. A Bureau of Labor Statistics publication lists 58 terms used to describe various kinds of unemployment. Many of these could be included under the seven types listed in Table 6–2, but some could not since they are not directly linked to duration. Furthermore, there is quite a bit of duplication involved in the BLS Glossary of Unemployment Terms, since the authors of this report have attempted to make it a comprehensive one. See Subcommittee on Economic Statistics of the Joint Economic Committee, *Unemployment: Terminology, Measurement and Analysis* (Washington, D.C.: U.S. Government Printing Office, 1961, pp. 15–22.)

Seasonal

Many types of employment are seasonal. Some shoe factories, for example, have two major "runs" a year; these usually come in the spring and the fall, and between the busy seasons some shoe workers may be unemployed for several weeks at a time. Workers in agriculture, food processing, some kinds of construction, and various service activities are often seasonally unemployed.

Frictional

Some workers are unemployed for short periods of time because their places of employment are temporarily closed down on a nonseasonal basis. There is also a considerable amount of *voluntary* unemployment which must be classified as frictional. There is always some turnover in the labor market as workers quit jobs to seek other employment. If a worker is "between jobs" and is included in the monthly survey of the labor force, he would necessarily be considered as frictionally unemployed. Some workers might also be temporarily unemployed because their place of employment is closed due to a labor dispute elsewhere. Employers cannot afford to keep these workers on the job if their major customers have been closed down by a strike.[4]

Initial

Some youngsters step right out of school into a job and might never experience involuntary unemployment. But others—and this is especially true of "dropouts"—experience several spells of unemployment before finding steady work. If this unemployment lasts only a few weeks it is short-term, but in many cases the new entrants to the labor force are unemployed for several months before finding steady work.

Cyclical

In a free-market economy certain types of business activity—notably manufacturing and construction—are highly cyclical. The upward and downward movements of industrial production and building activity—loosely referred to as the "business cycle"—are accompanied by similar fluctuations in employment. The effects of these fluctuations are felt by other sectors of the economy, but to a lesser extent. During the twenty five years from the end of World War II until 1970, for example, there were five recessions of varying intensity. During each of these recessions unemployment rose, and there was

---

4. There has been a considerable amount of controversy in some states over the question of whether or not striking workers should be considered as legally unemployed—at least after some period of time—and hence eligible for unemployment compensation.

a corresponding drop in unemployment as recovery got under way. Some indication of the intensity of each of the postwar cycles can be obtained by referring back to Table 6-1. Cyclical unemployment may be either of short or long duration. Not all workers are laid off or recalled at the same time. In many establishments workers with the lowest seniority are the first to go and the last to be recalled. Cyclical unemployment for such workers might definitely be long-term; it is if they are out of work fifteen weeks or longer. And some might fall in the "very long-term" category, if their spells of joblessness last more than twenty-six weeks. Even some relatively high seniority workers might be laid off during recessions. The chances are fairly good, however, that they will not be out of work long. If their layoff lasts less than fifteen weeks, they fall in the category of the short-term cyclically unemployed.

Some authors have argued that cyclical unemployment is aggravated by the entry of "secondary workers" into the labor market during periods of recession. The thesis is that when primary breadwinners are laid off and jobs are generally unavailable for male workers, some wives enter the labor market temporarily in search of employment. If their husbands were steadily employed they would not be seeking jobs, but they hope to find work of some kind to help tide their families over until the husbands are recalled to steady employment. This has been referred to as the "additional worker" hypothesis.[5]

Structural

Structural unemployment results from "once-for-all" changes in the economy. Structurally unemployed workers are not laid off; they are workers who have lost their jobs permanently. This might result from the relocation of a mill or factory, the closing of a mine or smelter, or a permanent cutback in the scale of operations of an enterprise. Some workers might also become redundant due to the introduction of automation or other forms of technological change.

Depletion of resources, shifts in demand, development of competitive products or processes, and competition from other countries are among the causes of structural unemployment. Some of the workers who lose their jobs due to these or other causes might be fortunate enough to find new employment within a relatively short time. Relatively young workers, particularly if they do not have family responsibilities, might move to other localities where job opportunities are more promising. And even where an industry is contracting, such as in the decline of the New England textile industry during the first half of the 1950s, there are some job openings due to normal turnover in the companies which remain in operation. Some workers who lose their

---

5. For a discussion, see Richard C. Wilcock, "The Secondary Labor Force and the Measurement of Unemployment," *The Measurement and Behavior of Unemployment,* National Bureau of Economic Research (Princeton, N.J.: Princeton University Press, 1957), p. 172.

jobs when a plant or mill is liquidated may thus find new employment in another plant or mill in the same industry. But if the industry as a whole is declining, there will not be enough jobs for all displaced workers. The workers who are middle-aged or older often find it difficult, if not impossible, to move to other localities. Even if they were able to move, they recognize that their age would be a barrier to reemployment. Such workers are likely to remain unemployed for long periods of time and some might never find continuous employment again; they are prematurely forced out of the labor force and the labor market.

Long-term structural unemployment is likely to be highly localized. It has been found, for example, in the declining textile areas of New England and the Middle Atlantic States. There has also been a considerable amount of structural unemployment in the coal-mining areas of Appalachia.

Unemployment Due to Inadequate Demand

Some economists have argued that there would be little or no long-term unemployment if the economy grew at a sufficiently rapid rate to sustain a high level of demand for goods and services. Since the demand for labor is derived from the demand for goods and services, those who subscribe to this view attribute much if not all of long-term unemployment to a slow rate of economic growth.

Other Types of Unemployment

"Hidden" Unemployment

A number of writers have referred to "concealed," "disguised," or "hidden" unemployment. These terms are not always used synonymously. But collectively they refer to the underutilization or unproductive use of labor in an economy. In some declining industries there are not enough jobs available for all the workers attached to the industry. In some locations, however, the available work is shared among a larger number of workers than would be needed to maintain operations through a system of "job rotation." Some workers may be employed for a week or two, then temporarily laid off while others take their places. And there are other cases where an enterprise operates only part of a week, with all of its work force idle the remainder of the time.

Another type of disguised or hidden unemployment is found in relatively poor agricultural areas. Some workers are able to eke out a bare subsistence on their farms, even if relatively inefficient methods are followed. Hidden unemployment is also found among displaced workers who are forced to withdraw from the labor force before they would normally retire. Workers who are only able to find part-time jobs when they would prefer full-time employment are considered by some authors to be among the hidden unemployed.

Some economists have argued that published rates understate the true level of unemployment at times when the number of jobless workers is rising. The argument is that some workers who have tried repeatedly to find jobs without success will become discouraged and leave the active labor force. This is known as the "discouraged worker" hypothesis. The Bureau of Labor Statistics estimated that 832,000 "discouraged" workers dropped out of the labor force during the first quarter of 1972 compared with 807,000 a year earlier.

The "Unemployables"

In any sizable labor market area some hard-to-place workers are considered to be basically unemployable. Workers with a history of mental illness often find it difficult to locate new jobs. Other workers find a lack of training or education, or language difficulties, to be barriers to employment, and some "emotionally handicapped" workers—even if they have not been treated for mental illness—find it difficult to obtain, or to retain, a job. Physically handicapped workers—even though perfectly capable of doing many kinds of work—might find the doors of employment offices closed to them.

In many cases age alone is a barrier to reemployment if a worker is displaced from an earlier job. Some workers may be "unemployable" only because of stratification in the labor market, however. It may be that appearance or other personal characteristics—rather than ability to perform specific tasks—is what keeps them out of the "primary labor market," as discussed in Chapter 2. It is significant that a great many "unemployable" workers found jobs and worked effectively during the World War II years of labor shortage. "Unemployability" appears to be a matter of degree; it depends as much upon conditions in the labor market as the characteristics of the workers who are rejected by employers when healthy, younger workers are available in the necessary numbers.

Employment and Unemployment as Economic Indicators

When viewed in isolation, neither total employment nor the unemployment rate may be accurate economic indicators. There are times when the unemployment rate increases, but the number of employed workers also rises. This can happen even after both measures have been adjusted for seasonal variation. The explanation is that at such times, there is a sharp increase in the number of new entrants to the labor force. If the number of job-seekers increases faster than the number who find jobs, the result is an increase in both components of the labor force.

The Duration of Unemployment

The average length of time that workers are unemployed—that is, the duration of unemployment—is one indicator of the severity of recessions. During the 1950s both total and long-term unemployment followed rising trends. Figure 6–1 shows the number of totally unemployed, and the long-term unemployed—defined as fifteen weeks or more—on a seasonally adjusted basis from 1953 through 1970. As recovery from the 1954 recession set in, unemployment dropped. But it remained well above the 1953 level until the beginning of the recession of 1958. Once again, the level of unemployment—and of long-term unemployment—remained higher than it had been before the recession even after the period of recovery was well under way. It was this rising trend that led to growing concern about "creeping unemployment" during the 1950s.

There was a reversal in the trend in unemployment after the recession of 1961, however. The brief recession of 1961 was followed by the longest period of sustained economic growth in recent history. The level of unemployment dropped steadily from 1961 through 1965, and the decline continued,

Thousands of Persons

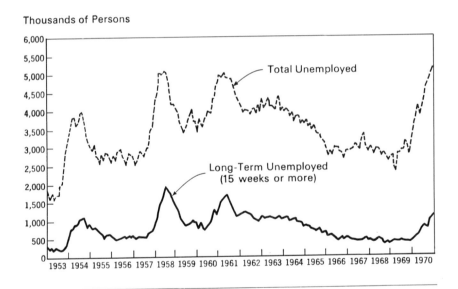

FIGURE 6–1.

Total and Long-Term Unemployment, Seasonally-Adjusted Monthly Data, 1953–1970. (*Data from Jane L. Meredith, "Long-Term Unemployment in the United States, Special Labor Force Report No. 17, Monthly Labor Review, June 1961, p. A–2, Table C; and* Economic Report of the President, *annual issues, 1961–1970.*)

although at a slower rate, into 1969. There was a similar drop in long-term unemployment from a peak of almost 1.7 million in 1961 to fewer than 400,000 in 1969.

Further details on the duration of unemployment are given in Figure 6-2. The chart shows that there was an increase in spells of unemployment of five weeks or less during the 1960s, while there were pronounced declines in long-term and very long-term unemployment. Not only did the unemployment rate decline from 6.7 per cent in 1961 to 3.5 per cent in 1969, but there was a pronounced shift during this decade from a rising to a declining proportion of long-term unemployment.

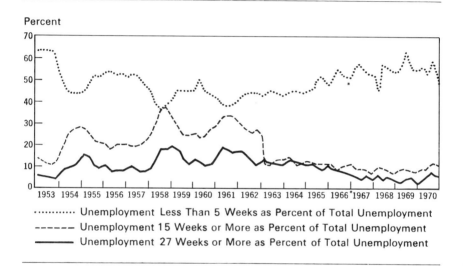

.... Unemployment Less Than 5 Weeks as Percent of Total Unemployment

------ Unemployment 15 Weeks or More as Percent of Total Unemployment

———— Unemployment 27 Weeks or More as Percent of Total Unemployment

FIGURE 6–2.

Seasonally-Adjusted Short- and Long-Term Unemployment, Quarterly Averages, 1953–1970. (Data from the U.S. Department of Labor, Bureau of Labor Statistics, Monthly Labor Review, monthly issues, 1953–1970.)

*New definition of labor force (sixteen years of age or older). Prior to 1967, data apply to the old definition of the noninstitutional population fourteen years of age or older.

Figures 6-1 and 6-2 show the levels of long-term unemployment in a given month and a given quarter, respectively. Another way to view long-term unemployment is to consider the total number of persons who have accumulated fifteen weeks of unemployment or more in a specific year. In 1968, slightly more than 2.4 million persons experienced fifteen weeks or more of unemployment. This represented a decline of more than 58 per cent from the 5.8 million persons who had experienced fifteen weeks or more of unemployment in 1961.

The incidence of long-term unemployment does not fall equally on various groups in the labor force. The probability of being included in the category of long-term unemployed is highest for nonfarm laborers, operatives, and craftsmen, and it is lowest for managerial, professional, and technical workers. Also, wage and salary workers in construction, agriculture, and mining are the most likely, and government workers the least likely, to accumulate fifteen weeks or more of unemployment.[6]

The Causes of Unemployment

Although a certain amount of oversimplification is involved, efforts to explain the rising trend of unemployment during the 1950s can be classified under two broad headings.

Inadequate Aggregate Demand

Those who accepted this theory, including Walter W. Heller, then Chairman of the Council of Economic Advisors, felt that "the unemployment rate has been quite high since mid-1957, because the rate of growth in final demand has been low relative to the actual and normal rates of growth and potential supply made possible by increases in capital stock, labor force, and productivity."[7]

The Structural Transformation Hypothesis

The authors of the Joint Economic Committee report on higher unemployment rates state that those who accept the structural transformation hypothesis maintain "that higher unemployment has been due not to inadequate final demand—and its concomitance in the labor market, and insufficient number of job opportunities—but rather, to technological changes which are currently reaching the American economy at an unusually rapid pace."[8]

The inadequate demand hypothesis given above describes one side of the debate about the causes of higher unemployment during the 1960s fairly well. But the "structural transformation hypothesis" as given in the Joint Economic Committee report is somewhat narrower than the explanation advanced by economists who felt that a lack of adequate demand by itself could not explain the rising trend of unemployment.

---

6. Edward J. O'Boyle, "America's Less Fortunate—the Long-Duration Unemployed," *Special Labor Force Report 118*, from the U.S. Department of Labor, Bureau of Labor Statistics, *Monthly Labor Review*, April 1970, pp. 35–43. See also Hyman B. Kaitz, "Analyzing the Length of Spells of Unemployment," *Monthly Labor Review*, November 1970, pp. 11–20.

7. Sub-Committee on Economic Statistics of the Joint Economic Committee, *Higher Unemployment Rates, 1957–60: Structural Transformation or Inadequate Demand* (Washington, D.C.: U.S. Government Printing Office, 1961), p. 6.

8. *Ibid.*, p. 6.

Perhaps the leading advocate of the structural change hypothesis was Charles C. Killingsworth, who attributed rising unemployment to *various* structural changes that had occurred in the American economy since the early 1950s. Among these, he included new technology and changing consumption patterns. He concluded that these changes had led to "a long-run decline in the demand for low-skilled, poorly educated workers and a long-run rise in the demand for high-skilled, well educated workers."[9] Other types of structural change not mentioned by Killingsworth, which almost certainly contributed to the rising unemployment of the 1950s, would include shifts in the location of industry, the depletion of resources, rising imports, and shifts in industrial demand—such as oil for coal, and synthetics for natural fibers.

The staff of the Joint Economic Committee had concluded that on balance the evidence supported the inadequate demand hypothesis.[10] But at least one member of the Committee, former Representative Thomas B. Curtis, dissented, stating that: "There are many other theories or possibilities that explain the rate of unemployment since 1957 beside the two theories posed."[11]

The debate about the causes of unemployment in the 1950s was not conducted in an academic vacuum; it had important policy implications. Those who supported the inadequate demand hypothesis argued that the cure for rising unemployment was more aggressive monetary and fiscal policy. They supported tax cuts to increase the rate of consumption and investment tax credits to stimulate investment. Most of those who accepted the structural transformation hypothesis argued that such conventional measures were necessary but not sufficient conditions to solve the problem of rising unemployment. In addition to policies that would stimulate consumption and investment, they advocated expanded government programs of education, training, and other forms of investment in human beings to bring about "the elimination of poverty."[12]

In a detailed and carefully reasoned analysis of the problem, Eleanor Gilpatrick concluded that rising unemployment during the 1950s was caused by both inadequate demand and structural change. Her study supported a broad range of programs that would be required to stimulate consumption and investment and to improve the operation of the labor market.[13] Although partisans on both sides of the debate may still be found, most economists would probably agree with the eclectic conclusion reached by Gilpatrick. More important, Congress refused to be trapped by the partisans. The leaders of Congress moved to stimulate aggregate demand by reducing personal income

---

9. Charles C. Killingsworth, "The Continuing Labor Market Twist," *Monthly Labor Review*, September 1968, p. 12.

10. *Higher Unemployment Rates*, 1957–60, pp. 78–79.

11. *Employment and Unemployment*, Report of the Subcommittee on Economic Statistics to the Joint Economic Committee, (Washington, D.C.: U.S. Government Printing office, 1962), p. 19.

12. Killingsworth, *op. cit.*, p. 12.

13. Eleanor G. Gilpatrick, *Structural Unemployment and Aggregate Demand* (Baltimore: The Johns Hopkins Press, 1966).

taxes and providing investment credits. At the same time Congress moved on a fairly broad front to develop a manpower policy designed to eliminate the problems emphasized by the "structuralists." These measures are discussed in considerable detail in Chapter 8.[14]

One result of the unemployment debate of the 1960s, and of the manpower programs that followed, was increased attention to the composition of unemployment. Unemployment rates vary widely among demographic groups. This is illustrated in Table 6-3, which shows the average relationships over a ten-year period (1959-1968) between selected demographic characteristics and two different unemployment rates.

TABLE 6-3
Average Relationships between unemployment rates for major age-sex-color groups at total unemployment rates of 3.7 and 4.7 percent, 1959-1968

Age-sex-color groups	3.7 percent	4.7 percent
All workers, 16 years and over	3.7	4.7
Men, 20 years and over	2.3	3.5
Women, 20 years and over	3.9	4.6
Teenagers, 16 to 19 years	12.9	14.3
Whites	3.3	4.2
Men, 20 years and over	2.1	3.1
Women, 20 years and over	3.4	4.2
Teenagers, 16 to 19 years	10.9	12.4
Negroes	7.1	8.9
Men, 20 years and over	4.4	7.0
Women, 20 years and over	6.6	7.9
Teenagers, 16 to 19 years	25.5	26.2

Source: Paul M. Ryscavage, "Impact of Higher Unemployment on Major Labor Force Groups," *Monthly Labor Review,* March 1970, pp. 21-25.

Unemployment rates for men twenty years and older have consistently been lower than the national average. The rates for women in the same age group are both closer to the national average and more stable than those for men. The highest unemployment rate—more than three times the national average—applies to teenagers.

When the unemployed are compared on the basis of color, similar dif-

14. For some recent views on the structuralist position, see Denis F. Johnston, "The Labor Market 'Twist', 1964-69," *Monthly Labor Review,* July 1971, pp. 26-36; Charles C. Killingsworth, "Full Employment and the New Economics," *Scottish Journal of Political Economy,* February 1969; and Killingsworth, "Facts and Fallacy in Labour Market Analysis," *Scottish Journal of Political Economy,* February 1970.

ferences are found. In general, unemployment rates for blacks are more than twice as high as the rates for the corresponding group of whites. The smallest difference is that between black and white women twenty years and older, but even here the black rate is almost twice as high as that for white women. The highest (and most stable) unemployment rate is for blacks between the ages of sixteen and nineteen. Even when the national unemployment rate is relatively low (3.7 per cent) more than one fourth of black teenagers in the labor force are unemployed and looking for work.

Unemployment rates also vary by region and on the basis of marital and family characteristics. Because of the large number of variables in these groupings, however, it is difficult to summarize differences. Details are published regularly, though, by the Bureau of Labor Statistics.[15]

The Minimum Wage and Youth Unemployment

One of the arguments advanced in support of the Fair Labor Standards Act (better known as the Wage-Hour Law), when it was passed in 1938, was that it would reduce unemployment. This was not because the law required employers to pay a minimum wage of twenty-five cents per hour to all workers involved in interstate commerce, but because of the overtime provision of the law. This provision required payment of "time and a half" for all hours in excess of forty per week. The intent of the law was to spread the available work by reducing the work week so that some of the unemployed would be pulled back into the active labor force.

The law has been amended a number of times since 1938, with the most recent amendment in 1966. The latest amendment for an increase in the minimum wage, to $1.60 per hour, was effective in February 1971. An exception was provided for agricultural workers on large farms, whose minimum remains at $1.30 per hour.

Although there have been several increases since 1938, the minimum wage has remained well below the average level of wages in the nation. There has been growing concern in recent years, however, that the federal minimum wage may contribute to the high level of teenage unemployment discussed earlier. One session of the 1970 meeting of the Industrial Relations Research Association was devoted to the topic "Youth Unemployment and Minimum Wages." Two of the papers reported on statistical studies of the relationship between unemployment and the federal minimum wage.

Thomas Gavett, Assistant Commissioner of the Bureau of Labor Statis-

---

15. See U.S. Department of Labor, Bureau of Labor Statistics Report 395, *Employment in Perspective: Regional Aspects of Unemployment, 1969–70* (no date); and Elizabeth Waldman, "Marital and Family Characteristics of the U.S. Labor Force," *Monthly Labor Review,* May 1970), pp. 18–27. Further statistical details are given in the reprint of this article as *Special Labor Force Report 120.*

tics, summarized a number of studies conducted by the Department of Labor and other organizations. He concluded[16]:

> Available studies do not provide adequate evidence that the Federal minimum wage has played an instrumental role in creating the problem (of youth unemployment) in the past. It is, of course, impossible to establish a negative conclusion. Certainly there are hints of adverse effects in the evidence, and certainly the *possibility* that there have been significant adverse effects upon the unemployment of teenagers remains.

At the same meeting Adie and Chapin of Ohio University reported on a detailed statistical study of the relationship between unemployment and minimum wages covering the period 1954 to 1965. They concluded that "the results of our study are unambiguous. Increases in the Federal minimum wage cause unemployment among teenagers; the effects tend to persist for considerable periods of time and seem to be strengthening as coverage is increased and as enforcement becomes more rigorous."[17]

The conclusions reached by Gavett, and by Adie and Chapin, clearly do not represent the last word on the effects of the federal minimum wage on youth unemployment. Much of the controversy surrounding this issue is concerned with statistical methods. It may not be possible to reach a definitive conclusion about the relationship between youth unemployment and the federal minimum wage on the basis of statistical studies. Meanwhile, about one out of four black teenagers, and more than 10 per cent of white teenagers, remain jobless on the average through good times and bad. It may be necessary to *assume* that some of this unemployment is caused by the minimum wage, and to permit some degree of flexibility—at least for a limited time—to see if this would reduce the unemployment rate among new or relatively new entrants to the labor market.

High-Level Unemployment

It has become axiomatic that the best way for an individual to avoid unemployment in the United States is to "get an education." As part of an effort to reduce teenage unemployment, the Department of Labor has sponsored a series of brief television announcements urging teenagers to finish high school. Those who have dropped out are urged to contact their local employment office to enroll in a training program. Education has never provided a guarantee that its recipients would find jobs and remain employed.

---

16. Thomas W. Gavett, "Youth Unemployment and Minimum Wages: An Overview," *Proceedings* of the Twenty-Third Annual Winter Meeting, Industrial Relations Research Association, December 1970, p. 116.

17. Douglas K. Adie and Gene L. Chapin, "Teenage Unemployment Effects of Federal Minimum Wages," in *ibid.*, p. 127.

But the correlation between education and employability in the United States is high. A phenomenon that has attracted a growing amount of attention since the late 1960s, however, has been increasing joblessness among scientists and engineers.

Reports on unemployment published by the U.S. Department of Labor, such as the Special Labor Force Reports issued by the Bureau of Labor Statistics, generally do not provide information about unemployment on a narrow occupational basis. Thus, information about the extent of unemployment among scientists and engineers is not available on a continuing basis, and much of the discussion of high-level unemployment has been based on fragmentary data and case studies. A National Science Foundation survey of more than a quarter million scientists indicated that 2.6 per cent were unemployed in May 1971, and that this compared with a rate of 1.5 per cent a year earlier. Respondents under the age of thirty reported a jobless rate of 5.3 per cent. The unemployment rate for women scientists was 52 per cent, whereas that for men was 2.3 per cent. About 45 per cent of the unemployed scientists reported that their last job had been supported in part by federal government funds.[18]

Companies that specialize in research and development rather than production tend to be concentrated in a relatively small number of areas. When these companies suffer a setback, unemployed scientists and engineers are also concentrated in a few areas. The unemployed scientists and engineers are thus quite visible, and their plight attracts a considerable amount of public attention.[19]

Much of the recent unemployment among scientists and engineers is due to changes in the pattern of government spending. The federal government cut back on research in the late 1960s, especially on research related to military and space activities. Even among those who agree that such changes are desirable, some have questioned the timing of the cutbacks. One commentator has argued that:[20]

> Government, as the biggest single customer for engineering, must attempt to plan more carefully and more farsightedly to avoid wasteful crash programs that lead to overhiring and painful subsequent mass firings. It should try to define national priorities and then attempt to estimate manpower needs, so that schools, and students can make rational plans. The professional societies ... should take a more active role in debating the nation's goals ...

---

18. The results of the NSF survey given in the text are from a summary presented in the *Wall Street Journal,* July 13, 1971.

19. See, for example, Berkeley Rice, "Down and Out Along Route 128," *New York Times Magazine,* November 1, 1970, pp. 28–29, 93–104; and "When the Brains Can't Get Work," *Business Week,* February 13, 1971, pp. 90–94.

20. Judson Gooding, "The Engineers are Redesigning Their Own Profession," *Fortune,* June, 1971, p. 146.

Unemployment In The United States And Abroad

During the 1950s, unemployment rates in Great Britain and in a number of western European countries were substantially lower than those in the United States.[21] Part of the explanation of low unemployment rates in Great Britain and most of western Europe was the high level of aggregate demand in these countries throughout that decade. This stemmed to some extent from the reconstruction of war-torn economies. But an important factor contributing to low unemployment rates abroad was the active manpower policies adopted by Great Britain, Sweden, and to a lesser extent the countries that made up the European Coal and Steel Community (Italy, France, West Germany, Belgium, The Netherlands, and Luxembourg). In Great Britain, special emphasis was placed on reducing unemployment in depressed areas by stimu-

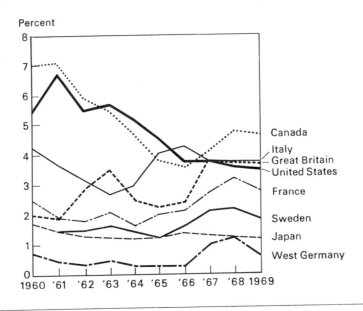

FIGURE 6–3.

Adjusted Unemployment Rates in Eight Industrial Countries, 1960–1969. (*Reprinted from the* Monthly Labor Review, *September 1970, p. 13.*)

21. For a discussion of some of the causes of these differences see Robert J. Myers, "Unemployment in Western Europe and the United States," in Arthur M. Ross (ed.), *Unemployment and the American Economy* (New York: John Wiley & Sons, Inc., 1964), pp. 172–186. For purposes of comparison, all rates have been adjusted to conform to the definition of unemployment used in the United States.

22. The British program has been discussed in a series of articles by the present author. See William H. Miernyk, "British and American Approaches to Structural Unemployment," *Industrial and Labor Relations Review*, October 1958, pp. 3–19; "Experience Under the British Local Em-

lating investment in these areas while discouraging new plant construction in prosperous areas.[22] In Sweden and the ECSC countries the emphasis was on training and retraining programs, and on efforts to increase the geographic mobility of unemployed workers.[23]

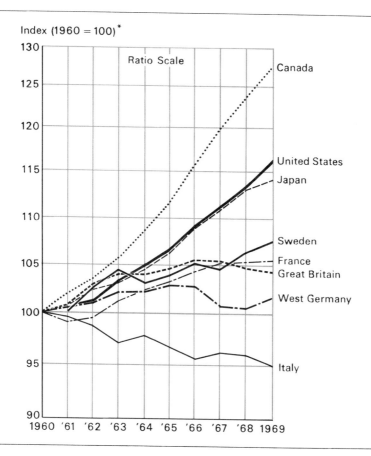

FIGURE 6–4.

Trends in the Civilian Labor Force in Eight Industrial Countries, 1960–1969. (*Reprinted from* Monthly Labor Review, *September 1970, p. 15.*)

*For Sweden, 1961=100.

ployment Acts of 1960 and 1963," *idem.,* October 1966, pp. 30–49, and "British Regional Development Policy," *Journal of Economic Issues,* September 1969, pp. 33–42.

23. These programs are discussed in *Studies in Unemployment,* Special Committee on Unemployment Problems, United States Senate, (Washington, D.C.: U.S. Government Printing Office, 1960), pp. 423–432. See also Fredric Meyers (ed.), *Area Redevelopment Policies in Britain and the Countries of the Common Market* (Washington, D.C.: U.S. Department of Commerce, Area Redevelopment Administration, 1965); and Margaret S. Gordon, *Retraining and Labor Market Adjustment in Western Europe* (Washington, D.C.: U.S. Department of Labor, Automation Research Monograph No. 4, 1965).

The unemployment rate in the United States dropped from almost 7 per cent in 1960 to less than 4 per cent in 1966. Meanwhile, unemployment rates rose in Britain, France, and Sweden, narrowing the gap between unemployment rates in the United States and other industrial countries, as illustrated in Figure 6–3.

The reduction in unemployment in the United States occurred at a time when the civilian labor force was growing faster than that of most other industrial countries (see Figure 6–4). This was a result of sustained growth in aggregate demand during the 1960s. But the adoption of a comprehensive manpower program during this decade also made an important contribution to reducing the U.S. unemployment rate.

In spite of the convergence in unemployment rates that occurred during the 1960s, the U.S. rate was still well above the rates of Sweden, Japan, and West Germany at the end of the decade. Japan and West Germany enjoyed substantial increases in industrial production during this decade. The low rate in Japan also reflects an important institutional and cultural difference between that country and other industrialized nations. Despite

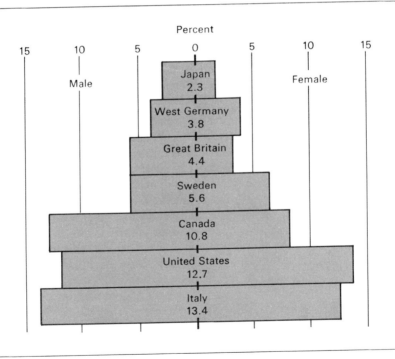

FIGURE 6–5.

Comparative Youth Unemployment Rates by Sex in Seven Countries, 1968. (*Reprinted from* Monthly Labor Review, *September 1970, p. 19.*)

the major cultural changes that have taken place in Japan since the end of World War II, there is still a great deal of paternalism in employer-employee relations. In many Japanese industries and occupations, when a worker is employed he is hired "for life." The employer has a moral obligation to keep his employee on the job, so unemployment is still a rare phenomenon in Japan.

Teenage unemployment rates in the United States and six other countries are compared in Figure 6-5. The low rate of teenage unemployment in Japan is due in part to the institutional framework mentioned above. The low rate in West Germany is the result of a virtual absence of unemployment in that country during a period of rapid economic growth. Although the general unemployment rate had gone up in Sweden and Great Britain by 1968—the year for which the comparison was made—teenage unemployment rates remained relatively low. This is undoubtedly due in large measure to the continuing active manpower policies of these countries.

The high rate of unemployment among American teenagers was discussed earlier. This is clearly one of the nation's more intractable labor market problems. As noted earlier, there is still a considerable amount of debate about the causes of teenage unemployment. And despite the success that has been achieved in reducing the total unemployment rate, little progress has been made in improving job opportunities for teenagers in the labor force. The U.S. Department of Labor is well aware of this situation, and the emphasis in labor market programs has been shifting to the teenage unemployed in recent years.

Wages, Prices, And Unemployment

Toward the end of the 1960s, the emphasis shifted in discussing labor market problems. A few economists, notably Charles Killingsworth, continued to stress the need for expanded and improved manpower programs.[24] But with the decline of unemployment in the 1960s and a rapidly rising consumer price index after 1965, the focus of discussion shifted to the wage-price-unemployment nexus.

The basic work on this problem is by A. W. Phillips, who presented his

---

24. Killingsworth has indicated his support for measures to stimulate aggregate demand, but he feels there is an urgent need for expansion of the manpower program. His most recent proposal is for a "large-scale public service employment program." This proposal, which has been supported by other labor economists, would train school and hospital aides, welfare field workers, and workers for various types of community employment. He feels that finding jobs for trained workers in the public sector would be one of the "lesser problems" of a public service employment program. See Charles C. Killingsworth, "Rising Unemployment: A 'Transitional' Problem?," Hearing of Senate Subcommittee on Employment, Manpower, and Poverty, *Manpower Development and Training Legislation 1970*, Part 3, pp. 1254–1267. See also, Melville J. Ulmer, "The Non-Answer to Nixonomics," *The New Republic* (December 11, 1971), pp. 19–21.

results in one of the more famous economic publications of recent times.[25]
After an intensive analysis, Phillips concluded that the statistical evidence
he had marshalled supported the hypothesis that "the rate of change of
money wage rates can be *explained by* the level of unemployment and the
rate of change of unemployment..."[26] He went on to say that "it seems
... that if aggregate demand were kept at a value which would maintain a
stable level of product prices the associated level of unemployment would
be a little under 2½ per cent. If, as is sometimes recommended, demand were
kept at a value which would maintain stable wage rates the associated level
of unemployment would be about 5½ per cent."[27] Phillips was careful to
emphasize the tentative nature of his conclusions. He also expressed a need
for further research into the interdependence of unemployment, wage rates,
prices, and productivity. That research has followed, and Phillips curves have
been constructed for many countries and even for regions within countries.
Not all economists who have studied the relationship between wages, prices,
and unemployment have been willing to conclude that the rate of change in
prices can be *explained by* the level of unemployment and the rate of change
of unemployment. Others, however, have accepted the conclusion that there
is a trade-off between the level of unemployment and the rate of price increases, with little or no qualification.

The Phillips curve hypothesis is closely related to analyses of the causes
of inflation. These have been classified by economists under two major heads:
(1) demand-pull and (2) cost-push. The demand-pull hypothesis states that
rising prices are caused by an excessive money supply. It is a case of too
much money chasing too few goods. Cost-push explanations of inflation
stress the wage-setting ability of trade unions and the administration of
prices by oligopolistic enterprises.

The literature on the Phillips curve and the causes of inflation is too
voluminous to permit a detailed summary in a textbook. Also, much of the
Phillips curve literature is too technical for inclusion in an introductory text.[28]
The following discussion of the Phillips curve avoids statistical technicality.

The relationship between annual percentage changes in the consumer
price index and the annual unemployment rate for the United States is given
in Figure 6-6, which covers the period 1945 through 1970. In his study,

---

25. A. W. Phillips, "The Relation Between Unemployment and the Rate of Change of Money
Wage Rates in the United Kingdom, 1861–1957," *Economica*, November 1958, pp. 283–299.

26. *Ibid.*, p. 299, emphasis added.

27. *Ibid.*

28. A good summary of some of the recent literature, as well as a lucid account of work on the
Phillips curve being conducted by economists in the Bureau of Labor Statistics, is given by
William R. Bailey and Arthur Sackley, "An Econometric Model of Worker Compensation
Changes," *Monthly Labor Review*, September 1970, pp. 32–38. See also A. G. Hines, "Trade
Unions and Wage Inflation in the United Kingdom 1893–1961," *Review of Economic Studies*,
October 1964, pp. 221–252.

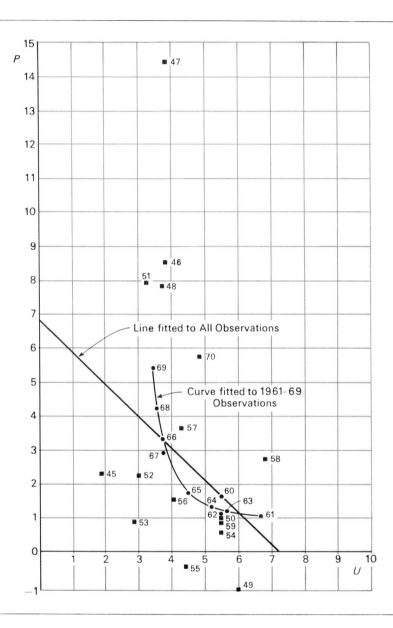

FIGURE 6–6.

The Relationship Between Annual Percentage Changes in the Consumer Price Index and the Unemployment Rate, 1945–1970. (*Reprinted from* Economic Report of the President, *February 1971, pp. 222, 249.*)

Phillips suggested that the relation between unemployment and the rate of change of wage rates is likely to be highly nonlinear.[29] Studies relating price changes to the unemployment rate (as in Figure 6-6) have also suggested a nonlinear relationship.[30]

A curve fitted to the price and unemployment data for the period 1961–1969 is indeed nonlinear, and it is an exceptionally good fit. It bears a strong family resemblance to the curve Phillips obtained for the period 1881–1913 in Great Britain, although the curve in the United States is shifted to the right. The *price*-unemployment curve for the United States during this brief period is a much tighter statistical fit than the Phillips curve relating wages and unemployment in Great Britain over a much longer period. When price changes and unemployment rates in the United States are considered for the entire period 1945–1970, however, there is no clearcut nonlinear relationship, and the statistical fit of the linear relationship is anything but good.[31]

The 1961–1969 cruve suggests that when unemployment is high—say above 6 per cent—a considerable reduction in unemployment can be achieved with a slight price increase. The curve also shows, however, that once the employment rate drops below 4 per cent, a further reduction in unemployment will be accompanied by rapid price increases.

The linear regression line fitted to the data for the entire period has a negative slope of approximately one. This implies a proportional trade-off between price increases and the unemployment rate. No one should take this regression line seriously, however, because it is a poor statistical fit, and some of the extreme observations can be explained by unusual events. The large price increases from 1946 through 1948 are explained primarily by the elimination of wartime price controls and the liquidation of pent-up wartime personal saving. This was clearly a period of rapid and fairly extreme demand-pull inflation. Similarly, the large price increase in 1951 may be explained primarily by stepped-up military spending at the outbreak of the Korean War.

It is now clear that a simple regression technique cannot satisfactorily explain a relationship as complex as the one that exists between wages, prices, and unemployment.[32] A simple regression curve does not necessarily

29. Phillips, *op. cit.*, p. 283.

30. One of the early studies to suggest such a nonlinear relationship for the United States was Paul Samuelson and Robert Solow, "Analytical Aspects of Anti-Inflation Policy," *American Economic Review,* May 1960, pp. 177–194.

31. A nonlinear curve of the form $\rho = \alpha U^{\beta}$, or $\log \rho = \log \alpha + \beta \log U$, was fitted to all the observations, but the result was not as good as the linear relationship shown in Figure 6-6, and it was not included on the chart to avoid further clutter.

32. See "The Unemployment-Inflation Problem," in *Studies by the Staff of the Cabinet Committee on Price Stability* (Washington, D.C.: U.S. Government Printing Office, 1969), pp. 125–150; and Daniel S. Hamermesh, "Wage Bargains, Threshold Effects and the Phillips Curve," *Quarterly Journal of Economics,* August 1970, pp. 501–517.

show causation; that is, high prices, do not necessarily "cause" unemployment, nor does the low unemployment rate necessarily "cause" a rapid increase in prices. Also, highly aggregated data, such as those used in some Phillips curve studies, fail to distinguish among the various types of unemployment examined earlier in this chapter. In the short run, at least, it is entirely possible to have a high level of *structural* unemployment which would have little or no direct connection with changes in wages or prices. If, on the other hand, a high level of unemployment were due almost entirely to inadequate demand, one would expect both prices and wages to be affected.

More recent studies have used multiple regression techniques which permit the introduction of more variables into the analysis. But these studies have not led to clear-cut support of the Phillips hypothesis.[33] Edwin Kuh, a distinguished econometrician, has recognized the intuitive and theoretical appeal of the Phillips hypothesis. He believes, however, that we need either "more powerful evidence of its actual, but hitherto obscured pervasive influence" or we need to find alternative explanations.[34] Kuh has pointed out that the unemployment level does not provide a satisfactory explanation of wage changes in the United States.[35] As an alternative, he has proposed what he calls a "productivity, distributed lag (PDL)" explanation. Kuh has constructed a multiple regression model in which one of the more important variables is labor productivity. Kuh's model gives better statistical results than a straightforward Phillips curve, but he is quick to point out that "the differences are not clearly decisive."[36] Unlike many econometricians, Kuh is not content to rest his case entirely on the results of statistical analysis. He feels there is a need for greater understanding of the institutional aspects of labor markets and their effects on wages and prices.[37]

Like the earlier debate about the causes of unemployment, the Phillips curve controversy has not been conducted in an academic vacuum. Policy makers are concerned with unemployment *and* inflation. But there is growing skepticism, even in relatively conservative quarters, about the necessity of an unemployment-inflation trade-off. Recently, a publication of the First National City Bank of New York stated that: "It is only a slight caricature of Mr. Phillips' world to say that it is one in which more unemployment can be purchased only at the price of more inflation. In fact, there are other—and better—ways to bring about lower unemployment."[38] Among the policies

---

33. See, for example, Bailey and Sackley, *op. cit.,* p. 37.

34. Edwin Kuh, "A Productivity Theory of Wage Levels—An Alternative to the Phillips Curve," *Review of Economic Studies,* October 1967, p. 358.

35. *Ibid.,* p. 334.

36. *Ibid.,* p. 358.

37. Cf. Hamermesh, *op. cit.*

38. "Has Mr. Phillips Thrown Policy Makers a Curve?" *Monthly Economic Letter,* First National City Bank, February 1971, p. 11.

suggested are the expansion of training programs to increase the supply of skilled workers, and modification of minimum wage laws to increase job opportunities for teenagers.

There has been criticism of what has come to be called the "stop-go" policy of dealing with inflation and unemployment, generally attributed to the Council of Economic Advisers. Essentially, this consists of measures that temporarily discourage production, and thus reduce real output, followed by other measures designed to stimulate rapid increases in output. Critics of the stop-go policy claim that it only temporarily reduces the rate of inflation, and is thus not an acceptable long-run solution.[39]

During the 1950s, when the unemployment rate crept steadily upward and price increases began to accelerate, it is understandable that concern would shift to the causes and control of inflation. In 1970, however, prices rose by almost 6 per cent, and the unemployment rate increased from 3.5 to almost 5 per cent. Prices and unemployment continued to rise during the first half of 1971. This situation clearly could not be handled analytically by the Phillips curve or any known alternative. It was also obvious that the stop-go policy had been unable to control either the forces of inflation or the causes of unemployment. After meeting with his chief economic advisors over a weekend in August 1971, President Nixon announced to the nation that in terms of economic policy, the United States was entering an entirely new ball game.

The Wage-Price Freeze and a National Incomes Policy

One of the central tenets of economic life in the United States, until very recent times, was that wages and prices should be determined without government interference. To contain the forces of inflation, wage and price controls were accepted during World War II. But this was a time when all citizens were called upon to accept some measure of sacrifice, and price and wage controls were regarded as a temporary if necessary expedient.

When controls were eliminated in 1945, consumer prices rose rapidly, and this increase continued until the first postwar recession during the 1950s. The American economy has been "inflation prone" since the end of World War II.

Concern about rising prices led the Council of Economic Advisers to advocate *voluntary* wage and price restraints in 1962. In their annual Economic Report to the President, the Council recommended that the annual increase in wage rates—including fringe benefits—be limited to the long-run trend in overall productivity increase. The Council also recommended that price increases, on the average, be limited to the overall trend in productivity

---

39. See, for example, Robert J. Gordon, "The Recent Acceleration of Inflation and Its Lessons for the Future," *Brookings Papers on Economic Activity, 1* (1970), p. 33.

increase.[40] Under the wage-price guideposts of 1962, annual increases in wages would have been limited to about 3.2 per cent.

The wage-price guideposts of 1962 made a great deal of economic sense. But all they amounted to was an exhortation by the President's Council of Economic Advisors to businessmen and labor leaders to exercise voluntary restraint. About all that the guideposts demonstrated was that such exhortations have little chance of success in a free-market economy.

Nothing further was attempted in the way of wage and price restraints until August 1971. In that month, President Nixon, acting on authority which Congress had earlier provided under the Economic Stabilization Act of 1970, imposed a 90-day wage-price freeze. The freeze was administered by the Office of Emergency Preparedness (OEP) under the general supervision of a Cost-of-Living Council. The three-month period was intended to give the Nixon Administration time to design and implement a longer-term program to regulate wage and price increases. This program, which went into operation on November 14, 1971, was referred to as Phase II. A fifteen-man, tri-partite Pay Board was appointed to provide guidelines for wage increases during Phase II.[41] A counterpart Price Commission of seven members was also set up to provide comparable guidelines for price increases. The Cost-of-Living Council, made up entirely of government officials, continued to provide general coordination and supervision.

The initial guidelines issued by the Pay Board called for annual wage increases of 5.5 per cent, a considerable jump over the 1962 guidelines. All large establishments (some 1,300 in number) were required to report prospective price increases to the Price Commission before putting them into effect. The initial goal of the Price Commission was to hold average annual price increases to 2.5 per cent.

The entire approach was one of administrative review of proposed wage and price increases. The effectiveness of such programs depends on the willingness of all parties involved to comply with approved increases. As this was being written, in late 1971, the program was too new to permit a definitive evaluation. The first wage increase approved by the Pay Board was a 16.8 per cent increase in the hourly compensation of bituminous coal miners, although the public members objected to an increase this much in excess of the guidelines. Some of the price increases approved by the Price Commission during the early days were also well in excess of the 2.5 per cent guideline. Basically, Phase II was an attempt to establish an *incomes policy* in the United States, at least on a temporary basis. Similar efforts have been made by Great Britain and a number of western European countries at various

---

40. *Economic Report of the President,* January 1962, pp. 185–190.

41. In March 1972, the three AFL-CIO members, and Leonard Woodcock of the independent United Auto Workers, resigned from the Pay Board. This left Frank Fitzsimmons of the Teamsters as the sole labor member.

times since the end of World War II. In general, incomes policies adopted by other countries have not been successful in stemming the rate of price inflation.[42] Annual increases in hourly earnings in manufacturing have not been much higher than those in the United States—in Western Germany they have been substantially lower. But annual price increases have been considerably higher in Great Britain and western Europe than in this country.[43] If the Pay Board and Price Commission are able to restrain the forces of inflation in the United States, they will have succeeded where similar efforts by other countries have failed.

Questions and Exercises

1. How is an employed worker defined in the Monthly Report on the Labor Force? Who is considered as an unemployed worker in this survey?

2. Assume that the economy is in a mild recession, and that the latest report on the labor force shows no change in the unemployment rate from March to April. In absolute terms, however, the report shows that the number of unemployed workers has declined by 5,000. Would you interpret this as evidence that recovery from the recession was under way?

3. Discuss trends in short- and long-term unemployment in the 1950s and 1960s. What public policies had a significant influence on these trends?

4. Summarize the major points made by both sides in the inadequate demand vs. structure debate over the causes of unemployment. How did Congress react to this debate?

5. On the basis of the average relationships that existed during the 1960s, about what would you expect the unemployment rate for black men twenty years and older to be compared with white men in the same age group? Make a similar comparison of the unemployment rates for white and black teenagers.

6. One of the objectives of the Fair Labor Standards Act when it was passed in 1938 was to spread available work among unemployed workers. This was to be accomplished by the overtime provision of the law. More recently, economists have been concerned about the effects of the minimum wage itself on teenage unemployment. What conclusion was reached by Gavett in his investigation of this question? How do his findings compare with those of the Adie-Chapin study?

7. Summarize trends in unemployment rates in the United States and other industrial countries during the 1960s. How would you explain the low unem-

---

42. See Lloyd Ulman and Robert J. Flanagan, *Wage Restraint: A Study of Incomes Policies in Western Europe* (Berkeley: University of California Press, 1971).

43. *Business Week*, November 13, 1971, p. 142.

ployment rates in Japan and West Germany, for example, and the relatively high rates in the United States?

8. What hypothesis was advanced by A. W. Phillips with respect to the relationship between unemployment and changes in wages?

9. Distinguish between the "demand-pull" and "cost-push" explanations of inflation.

10. Contrast the relationship between changes in the consumer price index and the unemployment rate in the United States during the period 1961–1969, and during the longer period 1947–1970. Discuss these relationships (as summarized in Figure 6-6) in terms both of the Phillips hypothesis and the critics of the Phillips hypothesis.

11. What were the "guideposts" advocated by the Council of Economic Advisers in 1962?

12. Describe briefly the administrative arrangement set up to direct Phase II of President Nixon's New Economic Program. What guidelines on wage and price increases were established at the beginning of Phase II?

13. What is meant by an "incomes policy"? Were the incomes policies adopted by Great Britain and various western European countries successful in stemming inflation during the 1960s?

Suggested Readings

Books

Fishman, Betty G., and Leo Fishman. *Employment, Unemployment, and Economic Growth.* New York: Thomas Y. Crowell Co., 1969.

Gilpatrick, Eleanor G. *Structural Unemployment and Aggregate Demand.* Baltimore: The Johns Hopkins Press, 1966.

President's Committee to Appraise Employment and Unemployment Statistics. *Measuring Employment and Unemployment.* Washington, D.C.: U.S. Government Printing Office, 1962.

Studies by the Staff of the Cabinet Committee on Price Stability. Washington, D.C.: U.S. Government Printing Office, January 1969.

Ulman, Lloyd, and Robert J. Flanagan. *Wage Restraint: A Study of Incomes Policies in Western Europe.* Berkeley: University of California Press, 1971.

Articles

Adie, Douglas K., and Gene L. Chapin. "Teenage Unemployment Effects of Federal Minimum Wages," *Proceedings,* Industrial Relations Research Association, 23rd Annual Meeting, December 1970, pp. 117–127.

Bailey, William R., and Arthur Sackley. "An Econometric Model of Workers Compensation Changes," *Monthly Labor Review,* September 1970, pp. 32–38.

Gavett, Thomas W. "Youth Unemployment and Minimum Wages: An Overview," *Proceedings,* Industrial Relations Research Association, 23rd Annual Meeting, December 1970, pp. 106–116.

Kaitz, Hyman B. "Analyzing the Length of Spells of Unemployment," *Monthly Labor Review* (November 1970), pp. 11–20.

Killingsworth, Charles C. "Rising Unemployment: A 'Transitional' Problem?" *Manpower Development and Training Legislation 1970*. Hearing of Senate Subcommittee on Employment, Manpower, and Poverty (Part 3), pp. 1254–1267.

Kuh, Edwin. "A Productivity Theory of Wage Levels—An Alternative to the Phillips Curve," *Review of Economic Studies, XXXIV* (4), No. 100 (October 1967), pp. 333–360.

Ryscavage, Paul M. "Impact of Higher Unemployment on Major Labor Force Groups," *Monthly Labor Review*, March 1970, pp. 21–25.

7

Income Distribution
and Job Opportunity

The discussion of unemployment in the last chapter was conducted largely within a labor market context. This chapter turns to other issues that are economic in character, but they are examined in a broader social context. These issues are (a) the distribution of income and (b) equality (or inequality) of job opportunity. The relatively high incomes of a majority of the population have not produced the social euphoria that might have been expected of the Age of Affluence. Instead, a considerable amount of restlessness and discontent prevail, especially among younger members of society.[1] It would be a gross oversimplification to attribute the recent discontent entirely to income and employment inequality; many other factors are involved. But it is no doubt entirely fair to state that the former are among the more important causes of social discontent. Furthermore, they are particularly relevant to the study of labor economics.

The issues of income inequality and inequality of job opportunity cannot be discussed extensively in a text that attempts to cover all the major areas of labor economics and industrial relations. This chapter does little more than catalogue the issues and indicate the nature of the social problems involved. The next chapter discusses recent changes in public policy which represent attempts by government to come to grips with the problems discussed here.

---

1. Daniel Bell's classic pamphlet, *Work and Its Discontents,* first published in 1956, was reissued by the League for Industrial Democracy in 1970. This is a critical study of the "cult of efficiency" in the industrial sector of American society. In an introduction to the new edition, the sociologist Louis Coser says: "The efficiency experts have now moved into the seats of power in Washington and this bodes ill for those of us who are concerned with the state of human welfare and creativity. What is possibly more perturbing, however, is that many intellectuals who in previous periods stood in the forefront of movements of industrial reform, have now seemingly lost any interest in the fate of the workers and in the world of work."

Social and Economic Systems

When Adam Smith published *The Wealth of Nations* in 1776, he advocated a policy of enlightened self-interest. This he believed would lead to the best of all possible worlds. Smith was critical of the restrictive practices that had emerged under the policy of Mercantilism; he argued that every man should be free to do the work he wants to do. Smith believed that if each individual could maximize his personal satisfaction, the satisfaction of society would also be maximized.

One of the things about Mercantilism that troubled Smith was its inefficiency; and an outstanding characteristic of the system he proposed would be its efficiency. The cult of efficiency, which is criticized by today's reformers, is built upon the foundation of classical economic theory. But the best of all worlds which Smith hoped for did not materialize. Factory workers gained little from the growth of industry and trade during the nineteenth century. Indeed, they may even have lost, because under the earlier and technologically more primitive cottage system, they enjoyed some degree of security, and this is something they did not have as factory workers.

Unequal income distribution and other inequities engendered by the factory system were accepted as necessary consequences of industrialism. In Great Britain, workers were forbidden to organize during the transition from a mercantile to an industrial system. Lawmakers were unwilling to take steps that might have had an adverse effect on efficiency. There were vocal critics of the system, of course, notably Karl Marx and other socialists. They urged workers to unite and overthrow their oppressors. But in countries that were developing a democratic tradition, workers were skeptical about dictatorship—including dictatorship of the proletariat—so the socialists attracted only a small following.

Although it was an unstable system, laissez-faire capitalism exhibited remarkable recuperative powers. While there were periodic depressions, the system was capable of generating its own recovery. Government involvement in the economy was minimal. The system broke down during the late 1920s, however, and this breakdown ultimately led to the Keynesian revolution in economic theory. The policy goal of those who adopted the new Keynesian view was full employment in a free society. The Keynesian system requires the government to take a more active role in economic affairs than in the past. Keynes talked about the "socialization of investment" rather than the socialization of the economy, however. He believed that full employment could be achieved by monetary and fiscal policy in a system that would retain the virtues of a market economy.

Acceptance of Keynesian economics came slowly in the United States. The Employment Act of 1946, which committed the government to a policy of maintaining a high and stable level of employment, was no doubt inspired by the Keynesian vision. But the major initial accomplishment of the Act was to establish the President's Council of Economic Advisers and the Joint

Economic Committee. Another twenty years would elapse before basic Keynesian principles were accepted by the federal government. Under the tutelage of Walter Heller, Chairman of the Council of Economic Advisers, President Kennedy accepted the notion of a full-employment budget. While this was widely regarded as an important philosophic break with the past, we saw in the last chapter that it did not solve the unemployment problem.

Personal Income Distribution

Before the 1930s little was known about income distribution in the United States. Even the most casual observer must have known that income was distributed unequally, but until the pioneering work of Simon Kuznets on national income accounting, there was no systematic collection and publication of data on the size distribution of personal income. Detailed data are published now on a regular basis by the U.S. Department of Commerce, and consistent time series are available back to 1929.

What Has Happened to Personal Income Distribution?

Inequality of income distribution in the United States diminished somewhat between 1929 and 1947, but there has been no significant change since the latter year. In 1929, an estimated 30 per cent of all consumer units had personal incomes of $2,000 per year or less. At the other extreme, about 6 per cent of all consumer units had incomes of $10,000 per year or more. By 1947, only 16 per cent of all consumer units had personal income of $2,000 or less, measured in constant (1963) dollars. Those receiving $10,000 or more (in constant dollars) had increased to 9 per cent of all consumer units.

The frequency distribution of personal income received by consumer units had changed remarkably in this eighteen–year period. It had become considerably flatter. This by itself does not indicate a change in the inequality of income distribution. But a direct comparison of the percentage distribution of income recipients, and the percentage distribution of the income they received, does show changes in inequality, if such changes occur. The simplest way to make such comparisons is by means of a Lorenz diagram, as illustrated in Figure 7-1.

In 1929, the lowest 40 per cent of all consumer units received 13 per cent of personal income, whereas the highest 20 per cent received 54 per cent. By 1947, the line of income distribution had shifted inward. The lowest 40 per cent then received 16 per cent of all income, whereas the share of income going to the highest 20 per cent had declined to 46 per cent. Since 1947, however, there has been no change in the shape of the Lorenz curve; the 1962 curve is identical with that for 1947. Census data and studies conducted by the Survey Research Center for the Federal Reserve Board show a slight decline in the share going to the top 5 per cent of families or spending

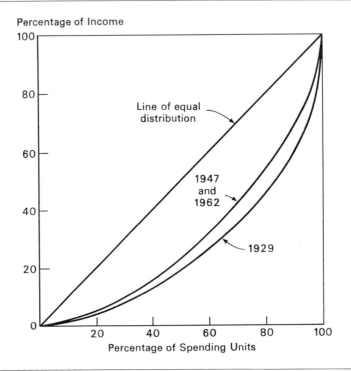

Percentage of Income

FIGURE 7–1.
Lorenz Curves of Income Distribution of Consumer Units, 1929, 1947, and 1962.
(*Reprinted by permission from Bernard F. Haley, "Changes in the Distribution of Income in the United States," in James G. Scoville [ed.],* Perspectives on Poverty and Income Distribution [*Lexington, Mass.: D. C. Heath and Company, 1971*], p. 18.)

units. But the same studies show no change in the share going to the bottom 5 per cent.[2]

Why was there a pronounced change in the size distribution of personal income between 1929 and 1947? Even more important, why has there been no apparent change since 1947?

The shift from a system that approximates *laissez-faire* capitalism to one that accepts a substantial amount of governmental intervention was accompanied by a change in society's attitude toward income distribution. Long before the 1930s, critics of unfettered competition considered the

2. Further details are given in Bernard F. Haley, "Changes in the Distribution of Income in the United States," in Jean Marchall and Bernard Duchros (eds.), *The Distribution of National Income* (New York: St. Martin's Press, Inc., 1968); reprinted in James G. Scoville, *Perspectives on Poverty and Income Distribution* (Lexington, Mass.: D. C. Heath and Company, 1971), pp. 17–40.

income inequality that it produced to be a violation of social justice. The socialists talked about complete equality. The Marxian postulate was that each member of society should contribute to the production process according to his ability, and that each would be rewarded according to his need. It does not follow that under socialism, there would be complete equality of income, but there would be a tendency toward equality.

The idea of strict equality of income distribution has had little appeal in nonsocialist societies concerned both with incentives to produce and distribution of the total product. In fact, even in the Soviet Union, which has practiced a variant of socialism longer than any other society, incentives are common and there is anything but equality of income distribution.

Writing toward the end of the nineteenth century, Vilfredo Pareto suggested the presence of a high degree of stability in income distribution both over time and among different kinds of social systems.[3] The notion that personal income distributions are relatively stable, which implies that they are independent of economic institutions, many economists have found repugnant. But while economists may not take kindly to "Pareto's law," they have not been able to provide an acceptable empirical refutation. This does not mean that Lorenz curves are identical from country to country. But there has been relatively little change in the shape of Lorenz curves—or of Gini concentration ratios—among the countries for which comparable data are available.[4]

We have already seen that between 1929 and 1947 a reduction in the inequality of income distribution occurred in the United States. How is this explained? It is widely believed that a progressive income tax redistributes income from the rich to the poor, and the income tax in the United States became more progressive during the 1930s than it had been before. But it has become no less progressive since 1947. Evidently, progressive income taxes have little to do with the inequality of income distribution.

Some other clues to the causes of income redistribution may be found by examining the sources of family personal income in 1929 and 1947. Such an examination shows that income from wages and salaries went up from 59.6 to 63.5 per cent. Transfer payments, meanwhile, increased from 1.7 to 6.3 per cent. During the same period, income from self-employment went up from 17.6 per cent to 19.1 per cent of family personal income. The only component to register a decline—and this was sizable—was property income. This share fell from 21.1 per cent in 1929 to 11.1 per cent in 1947.[5] Since low income groups are likely to benefit relatively more than high income groups

3. Vilfredo Pareto, Cours d'économie politique (Lausanne, 1897).

4. For illustrative Lorenz curves see "Income Distribution in Europe," in Scoville, op. cit., pp. 41–57. The Gini concentration ratio is calculated by dividing the area between the line of equal distribution and the Lorenz curve by the entire area under the diagonal line. Cf. Haley, op, cit., p. 19.

5. Haley, op. cit., p. 20.

from increases in wages and transfer payments, these changes help explain the reduction in inequality of income distribution that took place between 1929 and 1947.

Changes in Functional Distribution

An even longer-run comparison of the functional distribution of national income shows a similar shift. Comparisons have been made between the first decade of this century and the years extending from 1954 to 1963. Over this period of approximately fifty years, employee compensation increased from 55 to 70 per cent. Meanwhile, interest, rent, and corporate profits declined from 21.4 to 18.3 per cent. There was an even sharper drop in "entrepreneurial income," which declined from 23.6 to 11.8 per cent.[6]

The evidence is clear that there were substantial changes in functional distribution between the beginning of the century and the end of World War II. During this time labor's share of national income increased. This fact supports the hypothesis that the elasticity of substitution of capital for labor in the United States has been less than unity. In aggregate terms, the evidence suggests that it has been relatively easy to substitute capital for labor, and that one result of this substitution has been to increase labor's share of total output.

While labor's share was increasing, there was both a modest decline in the share of national income going to the owners of capital and a substantial drop in entrepreneurial income. The changes in functional distribution described above were accompanied by the structural changes in the American economy described in Chapter 2. The economy has become more capital-intensive. There has been a sharp decline in agricultural employment, as well as fundamental changes in the occupational composition of the nonfarm labor force. A majority of workers are now employed in service occupations rather than in the production of goods. There also has been a decline in self employment and a corresponding increase in the number and proportion of job-holders. These and other changes in economic structure help explain the observed shifts in functional distribution.

Although the American economy has continued to exhibit structural change, and although further shifts in functional distribution have occurred since the end of World War II, the size distribution of personal income in the United States has been remarkably constant. This has been true in spite of changes in attitudes that have been reflected in important changes in public policy. We have become a more egalitarian society in outlook than we were before 1929. But this change in attitudes has had no effect on the distribution of income in recent years. The changes in personal income distribution that

---

6. *Ibid.,* p. 33. The available data do not permit comparison of shifts *within* functional classes.

occurred between the 1930s and the end of World War II are largely explained by structural changes in the economy, the initial increase in transfer payments, and the shift from a deep and protracted depression to an economy of relatively full employment.

The War on Poverty

The elimination of poverty was announced as a national goal in the 1964 *Economic Report of the President.* The Council of Economic Advisers stated that there will always be some income inequality, but it does not follow in their view that the poor have always to be with us. The report pointed out that the anatomy of poverty is fairly complex. Following are some of the features of poverty in the United States listed by the Council:[7]

1. One fifth of all families are poor.
2. Although more than three fourths of the poor are white, almost half of all nonwhites live in poverty.
3. About two thirds of the heads of all poor families have only grade school educations.
4. Discrimination is an important cause of poverty.
5. Education increases the chances of escaping from poverty, but education does not remove all the effects of discrimination.
6. One third of all poor families are headed by a person over sixty-five.
7. Fifty-four per cent of the poor live in cities, 16 per cent on farms, and 30 per cent are rural, nonfarm residents.
8. Over 40 per cent of all farm families are poor, and over 80 per cent of all nonwhite farm families are poor.
9. Less than half of the poor live in the South, but a southerner's chance of being poor is roughly twice that of a person living in another part of the country.
10. One fourth of all poor families are headed by a woman, but nearly half of all families headed by a woman are poor.
11. The chances of a family being poor are increased substantially if several of the above characteristics apply.

To coordinate the war on poverty, the Office of Economic Opportunity was established in the executive branch of the federal government. This new agency was headed by Sargent Shriver, who had directed the highly success-

---

7. *Economic Report of the President* (Washington, D.C.: U.S. Government Printing Office, 1964), pp. 56–57.

ful Peace Corps. This is not the place for a detailed evaluation of either the strategy or the accomplishments of the Office of Economic Opportunity.[8] Only the broad outlines of the attack on poverty can be given here. These included the following measures, as summarized by the Council of Economic Advisers:[9]

1. *Accelerating economic growth.* An implicit assumption of this objective is that the American economy has not been growing fast enough. The Council called for a faster rate of growth in productivity. This in turn depends on science and technology, capital accumulation and investment—*including investment in human resources.*

2. *The elimination of discrimination.* The end of racial discrimination, the Council felt, would make it possible for many to break out of the poverty trap and to reduce the incidence of poverty in the groups discriminated against.

3. *Regional and urban development programs.* Special efforts were to be made to assist the poor in certain regions, such as Appalachia, with low per capita income and high unemployment rates. Although the initial plans were less specific about efforts to cope with urban problems, the Council recognized the concentration of poverty in urban slums and ghettos.

4. *Improving educational and employment opportunities.* The Council proposed various measures under this general heading, to improve the education of poor children, to increase the employability of the unemployed poor, and to upgrade the skills of workers who lacked the qualifications for advancement.

If there was a central theme to the war on poverty, it was the *improvement of opportunity.* Relatively little was said about such issues as motivation and ability. An implicit assumption underlying much of the early discussion is that all that the poor need to break out of the poverty trap is a *chance* to do so. This explains the emphasis on opportunity. Increasing employment opportunities for the poor was to be accomplished, in the main, by what we now refer to as *investment in human resources.* The concept of investment in human capital is discussed further in the next chapter. The remaining sec-

8. Such evaluations have been published elsewhere. For critical evaluations not only of the strategy of the war on poverty, but also of the exaggerated expectations of an early solution to the problem of poverty, see Daniel P. Moynihan, *Maximum Feasible Misunderstanding* (New York: The Free Press, 1969); and Roger H. Davidson and Sar A. Levitan, *Antipoverty Housekeeping: The Administration of the Economic Opportunity Act,* Institute of Labor and Industrial Relations (Ann Arbor and Detroit: The University of Michigan and Wayne State University, 1968). Several articles dealing with various aspects of the poverty problem and the war on poverty are presented in Scoville, *Perspectives on Poverty and Income Distribution.*

9. *Ibid.,* pp. 74–75.

tions of this chapter discuss some of the issues related to the goal of equality of employment opportunity.

Ability, Education, and Employment

The positive association between formal education and income is well known, since the statistical relationship between number of years of school completed and money income has been studied under a variety of conditions. Education does not guarantee a job, however, and it is by no means certain that the time or money invested in education will necessarily yield higher earning. Nor is there a constant rate of return to investment in education over time.

The problem of unemployed scientists and engineers discussed in the last chapter graphically illustrates that one may be highly trained and still be unable to find employment. If the aggregate supply of scientists and engineers at any given time is greater than the demand for these skills, some qualified persons will be without jobs. And it is not easy for a trained engineer or scientist with a doctorate in physics or chemistry to find employment outside his field of specialization. Many employers feel that highly trained workers may be looking for only temporary employment, although this may be the last thing the job applicant has in mind.

For some individuals interested only in maximizing their lifetime income, higher education may be a waste of time. A longitudinal study of gifted individuals by Lewis Terman and his associates at Stanford University showed that the highest incomes were earned by individuals who did not finish college, and the top income in this sample of persons with unusually high IQs was earned by a man who did not attend college at all. In the words of the Harvard psychologist, Richard Herrnstein, "if very high income is your goal, and you have a high I.Q. do not waste your time with formal education beyond high school."[10]

For most workers—undoubtedly the vast majority—there is a close relationship between *average* annual income and number of years of school completed. The average high school graduate can expect to earn at least 50 per cent more than the average worker who completed elementary school only. The average worker with four or more years of college will earn more than three times as much as the one who completed elementary school only. This evidence is sufficient to influence policy decisions. And it is the desire to improve job opportunities for minority workers that lies behind efforts to improve both the quality and duration of education for the disadvantaged.[11]

10. Richard Herrnstein, "I.Q," *The Atlantic Monthly*, September 1971, p. 53.

11. For further details on the relationship between income and education, see Herman P. Miller, "Annual and Lifetime Income in Relation to Education: 1939–1959," *American Economic Review,* December 1960. This article, with some details omitted, has been reprinted in Scoville, *op. cit.,* pp. 54–60.

Ability, Education, and Income

The relationship between education and income may be somewhat more tenuous than is often assumed, but this is not true of the relationship between intellectual ability and income. One reason may be that studies of the relationship between education and income ignore variability in "education," whereas studies of the relationship between intellectual ability and income focus sharply on variability.

Education is measured in terms of the number of years of school completed. But every teacher knows that some pupils or students learn more than others. It is a regrettable fact that by the proper selection of a major and a judicious selection of courses, a student who wishes to do so can "earn" a college degree without actually bothering to learn a great deal. Meanwhile, a highly motivated and intelligent student can learn much in high school and continue to learn beyond high school by independent study. The student who barely gets by in college may not do as well in economic terms as the highly motivated high-school graduate.

Economic rewards do not depend entirely on either intellectual ability or education. Additional factors, including motivation, determination, and other psychological characteristics which have not been measured to date, may have a major influence on an individual's economic success or failure. But the one characteristic that can be measured is intelligence. Psychologists may not be able to agree on what the word "intelligence" means, but the consensus is that whatever it is, it can be measured and expressed in terms of the familiar Intelligence Quotient or IQ.

It is a major understatement to point out that in recent years intelligence tests have become "controversial." At the center of this controversy is the question, is intelligence an inherited or an acquired trait? Or, more simply, in Herrnstein's terms, is intelligence determined by "nature or nurture?" The answer to this question has important policy implications. If, on the one hand, intelligence depends upon the environment—and if this characteristic is closely associated with economic success—programs designed to enhance intelligence by means of education, training, and other "investments in human capital" should in the long run reduce, if not eliminate, income disparities. This would be accomplished by increasing the earning power of groups that in the past have consistently made lower than *average* scores on intelligence tests. On the other hand, if intelligence is inherited, and if economic success depends upon intelligence, efforts to enhance the intelligence of those who have consistently scored low in intelligence tests will prove to be fruitless.

Recent discussions of the issues raised here have aroused highly emotional responses; this is because of the racial overtones involved. The same basic issues have been debated, quite literally, for centuries—only not within a racial context.

The recent controversy surfaced in 1965 when, in a speech at Howard University, President Johnson alluded to a report on the Negro-American family, which has since become widely known after its principal author as The Moynihan Report.[12]

The Moynihan Report ascribed many of the problems of the black community to the deterioration of the Negro family. Middle-class Negro families were described as highly stable, but lower-class Negro families were described as highly unstable and "approaching complete breakdown" in many urban centers. About one fourth of the black families were found to be headed by females, and among these families there was a high degree of dependency. The conclusion reached by the Moynihan Report was that legislation to end segregation in education and housing, and education designed to provide equal employment opportunities to all, would not solve the economic problems of American Negroes. Positive steps would have to be taken, according to this report, to "strengthen the Negro family."

The Moynihan Report traced the economic difficulties of low-income American Negroes to their cultural surroundings; that is, their environment. But several years later, in 1969, a University of California psychologist, Arthur R. Jensen, published an article in the *Harvard Educational Review* suggesting the possibility that blacks and whites might differ in *inherited* intelligence. The combination of the Moynihan Report and the Jensen article seemed to ensure that blacks have inhabited the worst of all possible worlds; they have been the victims of both cultural and genetic deprivation. As in the case of the Moynihan Report, Jensen's study contained a conclusion with important policy implications. It raised doubts about the value of compensatory education to narrow the gap between "minority" and "majority" pupils.

The most recent sally into this highly controversial area is the article on IQ by Richard Herrnstein. Herrnstein summarizes the points made earlier by Jensen, who had concluded "that the genetic factor is worth about 80 per cent and that only 20 per cent is left to everything else—the social, cultural, and physical environment, plus illness, prenatal factors, and what have you."[13] Herrnstein went on to say that: "Jensen's two papers leave little doubt about the hereditability of I.Q. among North American and Western European whites ... there is little dispute on this score ... It is the relation between hereditability and racial differences that raises the hackles."[14] But Herrnstein also makes the point that: "in general—not just for the racial issue—the question of nature and nurture *boils down to the study of variation.*"[15] The difference

---

12. For excerpts of the highlights of this report, see "The Negro-American Family (The Moynihan Report)," in John F. Kain (ed.), *Race and Poverty: The Economics of Discrimination* (Englewood Cliffs, N.J.: Prentice-Hall, Inc., 1969), pp. 38–44. For an even more concise summary, see the editor's introduction to Herrnstein, *op. cit.,* pp. 43–44.

13. *Op. cit.,* p. 56.

14. *Ibid.,* p. 56.

15. *Ibid.,* italics added.

between black and white IQs, which is on the order of about a 15-point spread, is a difference between averages. Individual blacks may have IQs as high—or higher—than individual whites. As Figure 7–2 shows, this depends on the amount of dispersion around the averages.

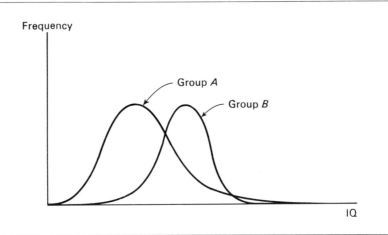

FIGURE 7–2.
Variability in Intelligence Between Two Hypothetical Groups.

Herrnstein discusses some of the implications of his conclusions. He believes that there is a long-run trend toward what he calls a "virtually hereditary meritocracy," and that technical and economic progress, along with political and social change, will increase the "hereditability" of intelligence.

What conclusions may be drawn from this brief excursion into one of the more controversial areas of psychology? In particular, if we assume that Herrnstein's conclusions have not been successfully challenged, how might they affect labor policy?

First, nothing that has been said suggests that our society will become stratified along *color* lines. In the future, as in the past, individuals with high and low IQs will be found among both blacks and whites.

Second, psychologists stress that while a high IQ may be a necessary condition for intellectual achievement, it is not sufficient. Other factors, notably motivation, have much to do with individual achievement. Success in the job market is not determined entirely by intelligence, but by a combination of intelligence and other personal characteristics. It may be necessary to ensure, however, that intelligence or aptitude tests are not used to erect artificial barriers to entry in various occupations. Formal educational attainment itself may be such a barrier. The Supreme Court has already ruled that the Civil Rights Act of 1964 makes it illegal to use tests that do not relate to qualifications to perform work. And the Court has ruled that requirements that workers pass high school equivalency tests, or that they possess high school diplomas, may be an unfair barrier to work.[16]

The Economics of Discrimination

Some of the difference in income between white and black families may be explained in terms of a combination of heredity and environment. But how do the earnings of black and white workers compare when other things are equal? Paul Siegel, a University of Michigan sociologist, answered this question by comparing the earnings of black and white workers in broad occupational categories at various levels of educational attainment. After taking into account what he called "compositional differences" with respect to regions, occupations, and educational attainment, he concluded that "about two-fifths of the difference in average earning between whites and non-whites is what it costs to be black."[17] He estimated that the cost of being a Negro, on the average, came to about $1,000 in 1960. In a brief introduction to this essay, Kain commented that: "Few birthrights come so high."

Numerous studies of the economics of discrimination have appeared in recent years. Two of the best known are those by Becker and Thurow.[18] Becker's model bears a resemblance to the Heckscher-Ohlin theory of international trade. He assumes two societies—one white and one Negro—with homogeneous factors of production, capital and labor, in each society. These societies do not exchange commodities, but they do exchange the factors used in producing commodities. And each society finds it advantageous to export its relatively abundant factor.

Employers behave as though hiring black workers imposes additional costs. These costs are measured by a "discrimination coefficient," that is, the wage differential at which it becomes a matter of indifference to the employer whether he hires a black or white worker. In a given job, a white and a black worker could have equal ability (and thus equal marginal productivities), but the black worker would be paid less than the white.

According to Thurow's model, white employers act as discriminating monopolists. They establish a hierarchy of jobs, and blacks are hired to fill the jobs felt to be "inferior" to those held by white workers.

---

16. This decision was handed down when thirteen black laborers at the Duke Power Company's Dan River Power Station at Draper, North Carolina, applied for jobs as coal miners and failed to pass the necessary qualifying tests. See the *New York Times,* March 9, 1971.

17. Paul M. Siegel, "On the Cost of Being a Negro," in John F. Kain (ed.), *Race and Poverty, op. cit.,* p. 67. For a graphic description of racial differences in annual income, see Arnold Strasser, "Differentials and Overlaps in Annual Earnings of Blacks and Whites," *Monthly Labor Review,* December 1971, pp. 16–26.

18. Gary S. Becker, *The Economics of Discrimination* (Chicago: The University of Chicago Press, 1957); and Lester C. Thurow, *Poverty and Discrimination* (Washington, D.C.: The Brookings Institution, 1969).

Both Becker and Thurow assume that white employers attempt to maximize their gains from discrimination. These employers attempt to allocate labor efficiently—so that the marginal physical productivities of equally qualified white and black workers will be equal—but black workers' wages are lower than their marginal productivity, and white workers are paid wages equal to their marginal productivity. Under these circumstances, by any acceptable definition, the black workers are being exploited.

Doeringer and Piore feel that the Becker and Thurow studies are "particularly congenial to economists," because they suggest that "the elimination of discrimination will increase competition. Such a step is generally thought to move toward a more efficient use of resources and hence a larger national income."[19] It follows that society as a whole would benefit from the elimination of discrimination and the exploitation of black workers.

More recently, Barbara Bergmann has analyzed the effect on white incomes of employment discrimination.[20] Her model is similar to Thurow's in that the allocation of workers follows a hierarchial order. In some occupations blacks are "underrepresented," whereas in others they are "overrepresented." Two occupations—service workers and nonfarm laborers—accounted for more than 80 per cent of the "overrepresentation" in 1960.[21]

Bergmann hypothesizes that black workers are crowded into a limited number of occupations. She assumes that black and white workers are perfect substitutes for each other and, using a constant elasticity of substitution production function, she estimates the income effects of discrimination. When expressed as annual equivalents, these differences ranged from $1,915 for workers with less than eight years of school to more than $5,000 for male workers who had completed sixteen or more years of school. For females, the differences ranged from $1,346 for those with less than eight years of school to slightly more than $1,000 for those with sixteen years or more of school.

Bergmann also calculated the income effects of the elimination of job discrimination, using estimates of the elasticity of substitution that ranged from .25 to 2.00. Her general finding is that:[22]

> for the great majority of whites the end of discrimination would have only a minor effect on rates of pay. Those whites in the lowest education bracket— those who had not achieved an elementary school education—would bear the brunt of the change. These white males might suffer losses on the order

---

19. Peter B. Doeringer and Michael J. Piore, *Internal Labor Markets and Manpower Analysis* (Lexington, Mass.: D. C. Heath and Company, 1971), pp. 135–136.

20. Barbara R. Bergmann, "The Effect on White Incomes of Discrimination in Employment," *Journal of Political Economy, 79* (March–April 1971), pp. 294–313.

21. *Ibid.,* p. 296.

22. *Ibid.,* p. 310.

of 10 per cent with losses running up to 20 per cent unlikely. While for white males the heavy damage will probably be restricted to those who did not achieve an eighth-grade education, for white females the damage would extend to all those who did not graduate from high school, and would be greater. The reason is probably the heavy concentration of Negro females in domestic work.

Bergmann feels that national income probably has not been affected by the inefficiencies resulting from discrimination. In her terms, discrimination can be described as a "zero-sum game between white and black workers."[23] Rearrangement of the work force to eliminate the overcrowding of blacks in certain occupations would increase the wages of workers who remained in those occupations. But increasing black representation in some occupations from which they have been excluded by discrimination would lead to lower relative wages in those occupations.

Unions and Job Discrimination

The economic models of discrimination just discussed assume, implicitly or explicitly, that job discrimination is entirely the work of employers. With a few outstanding exceptions, however, trade unions in the United States have contributed to the pattern of job discrimination against blacks and workers from other minority groups. Some unions have practiced segregation by maintaining Jim Crow locals. Others, moreover, have excluded Negroes from apprenticeship programs, thus effectively barring them from membership in skilled crafts, especially in the building trades.[24]

The status of minority workers is slowly changing. Barriers to job opportunity are falling, and black workers are now entering occupations from which they have been excluded in the past. Between 1960 and 1969, for example, the percentage of nonwhite workers, declined in all unskilled job categories and increased in the semiskilled, skilled, sales, and clerical categories. There was a shift in favor of nonwhites among managers, officials, proprietors, and technical and professional workers.[25] These gains are the result of antidiscrimination legislation, and of continued pressure by Negro organizations, especially the NAACP, to achieve equality of job

---

23. *Ibid.,* p. 311. A zero-sum game refers to any situation in which losses by some participants are exactly offset by the gains of other participants. A neighborhood poker game in which there is no "house cut" is an example of a zero-sum game.

24. See Ray Marshall, *The Negro and Organized Labor* (New York: John Wiley & Sons, Inc., 1965); and F. Ray Marshall and Vernon M. Briggs, Jr., *The Negro and Apprenticeship* (Baltimore: The Johns Hopkins Press, 1967). See also Thomas O'Hanlon, "The Case Against the Unions," *Fortune,* January 1968, pp. 170–190.

25. Charles E. Silberman, "Negro Economic Gains—Impressive but Precarious," *Fortune,* July 1970, p. 76.

opportunity for black workers. Progress has been slow, however, and spokesmen for the black community have expressed dissatisfaction with the rate of improvement.[26]

Discrimination on the Basis of Sex

One of the more dramatic changes in the labor market in recent decades has been the increased participation of women in the labor force. This has been especially true of married women with children.[27] To a large extent, men and women belong to noncompeting groups in the labor market. "Men work in occupations that employ very few women, and a significant fraction of women work in occupations that employ very few men."[28] This makes it difficult to compare the earnings of male and female workers. As Fuchs has noted: "The fact that men earn more than women is one of the best established and least satisfactorily explained aspects of American labor market behavior."[29] On the average, women earned about 40 per cent less than men in 1959. This differential was not affected appreciably by adjustment for color, years of school completed, age, and city size. When distance traveled to work, marital status, and class of worker were taken into account, the differential dropped to 34 per cent.

After a detailed statistical analysis of differences in male-female hourly earnings, Fuchs concluded that most of the differential "can be explained by the different *roles* assigned to men and women. Role differentiation, which begins in the cradle, affects the choice of occupation, labor force attachment, location of work, post-school investment, hours of work, and other variables that influence earnings." Fuchs conceded that role differentiation can result from discrimination. But he concluded that his study did not find evidence "that employer discrimination is a major direct influence upon male-female differentials in average hourly earnings."[30]

The existence of discrimination in the labor market is generally conceded. But the *measurement* of discrimination is not always easy. In the case of the male-female differential, the problem is compounded by occupational differences. This does not alter the fact, however, that women earn less.

Estimates for March 1970 show that about 5.6 million families—more than 10 per cent of the total—were headed by women. And the proportion of families headed by women has been increasing. Between 1960 and 1970,

---

26. See, for example, Herbert Hill, "Racial Inequality in Employment: The Patterns of Discrimination," in John F. Kain, *op. cit.,* pp. 78–88.

27. Elizabeth Waldman, "Marital and Family Characteristics of the U.S. Labor Force," *Special Labor Force Report 120,* reprinted from the *Monthly Labor Review,* May 1970, p. 20.

28. Victor R. Fuchs, "Differences in Hourly Earnings Between Men and Women," Reprint 2730, *Monthly Labor Review,* May 1970, p. 14.

29. *Ibid.,* p. 9.

30. *Ibid.,* p. 14.

the total number of families increased by 14 per cent. During this same period the number of families headed by women increased 24 per cent.[31] Women in general earn less than men, and many female family heads enter the labor market under a variety of handicaps, such as lack of training and the difficulty of arranging for adequate child care. This helps explain why 47 per cent of families headed by a female with children were below the poverty line in 1970.[32]

The problems discussed in this chapter are not new, although some of the details surrounding them are fairly recent knowledge. The details have been provided by studies stimulated by growing awareness and increasing discomfort that these problems exist in a society where the majority of families live in relative affluence. In the chapter that follows, we turn to the public policies that have been adopted in an effort to improve the economic opportunities of those who, thus far, have failed to share in this affluence.

Questions and Exercises

1. What happened to the inequality of income distribution in the United States between 1929 and 1947? What changes have occurred since the latter year?

2. Write a brief essay on the equality of income distribution. Include in your discussion the effects of income distribution on incentives, and the relationship between the income distributions and economic institutions of various societies.

3. What has happened to the relative share of income going to employees since the first decade of the present century? What other major shifts in functional distribution have occurred during this period?

4. Explain the long-run shifts in relative shares that have occurred in the United States in terms of the elasticity of substitution.

5. Have the changes in income distribution described in the text been accompanied by many significant changes in the structure of the American economy? If so, what are some of the major structural changes that have occurred?

6. What are some of the major characteristics of poverty in the United States in regard to age, sex, race, education, and place of residence?

7. What were the four broad measures proposed by the Council of Economic Advisers to eliminate poverty in the United States?

8. On the average, how much more can a typical high-school graduate

---

31. Robert L. Stein, "The Economic Status of Families Headed by Women," Reprint 2703, *Monthly Labor Review,* December 1970, p. 3.

32. *Ibid.,* p. 4.

expect to earn during his working life than the average worker who completed elementary school only? How much more will a worker with four or
more years of college earn, on the average, than a worker who has completed
elementary school only?

9. What were the principal conclusions of The Moynihan Report? What did
the studies by Jensen and Herrnstein have to say about the issue of "nature
and nurture" in the determination of intelligence? What conclusion may be
drawn from the debate over the causes of variation in intelligence with respect
to potential success in the job market?

10. After comparing the average earnings of whites and nonwhites and adjusting for "compositional differences," what did Paul Siegel conclude about
the cost of being black?

11. What does Becker mean by his "discrimination coefficient?"

12. According to Doeringer and Piore, what would be the result of the elimination of discrimination in the job market? What effect would this have on the
economy as a whole?

13. Barbara Bergmann feels that discrimination can be described as a "zero-
sum game between white and black workers." What does she mean by this?
Does she agree with the conclusion reached by Doeringer and Piore about
the income effects of an end to discrimination?

14. In general, do men and women compete for the same jobs? How does
Fuchs explain the difference in earnings between male and female workers?

Suggested Readings

Books

Becker, Gary S. The Economics of Discrimination. Chicago: The University of Chicago
    Press, 1957.
Doeringer, Peter B., and Michael J. Piore. Internal Labor Markets and Manpower Anal-
    ysis. Lexington, Mass.: D. C. Heath and Company, 1971.
Kain, John F. (ed.). Race and Poverty: The Economics of Discrimination. Englewood
    Cliffs, N.J.: Prentice-Hall, Inc., 1969.
Scoville, James G. (ed.). Perspectives on Poverty and Income Distribution. Lexington,
    Mass.: D. C. Heath and Company, 1971.
Thurow, Lester C. Poverty and Discrimination. Washington, D.C.: The Brookings In-
    stitution, 1969.

Articles

Bergmann, Barbara R. "The Effect on White Incomes of Discrimination in Employment,"
    Journal of Political Economy, 79 (March/April 1971), pp. 294-313.
Fuchs, Victor R. "Differences in Hourly Earnings Between Men and Women," Monthly
    Labor Review, May 1971, pp. 9-15.
Herrnstein, Richard. "I.Q.," The Atlantic Monthly, September 1971, pp. 43-64.
O'Hanlon, Thomas. "The Case Against the Unions," Fortune, January 1968, pp. 170-190.

Emergence
of a Manpower
Policy

The last two chapters described some of the problems that individuals encounter in the labor market. This chapter is concerned with the evolution of public policies intended to cope with these problems. As background for the discussion of manpower policy, we begin with a brief discussion of the concept of *human capital,* which has been defined by M. W. Reder[1] as follows:

> The basic idea of human capital is simple enough: like a machine, a human agent of production is produced by an application of productive resources to a pre-existing entity; in this case, "raw labor." The result of this particular application is a trained human agent—worker—whose enhanced productive capacity is manifested in a stream of services of enhanced value. Because the training process requires time to complete, and because its benefits derive over a considerable time period, the value of the resources used in training may be considered as *investment,* and the imputed increment in earning power that results from the training may be treated as its yield.

Investment in human capital is not limited to the resources devoted to the training of workers. Health expenditures may also be regarded as an investment if they lead to a more productive labor force.[2] Indeed, any type of expenditure—public or private—that enhances the value of the "stream of services" generated by a nation's work force may be regarded as an investment in human capital. And enhancement of the value of workers' services is

1. M. W. Reder, "Gary Becker's *Human Capital:* A Review Article," *The Journal of Human Resources, II* (Winter 1967), p. 97, italics added. Reder has described this book as a *locus classicus* of the conceptual analysis of investment in human capital.

2. See Burton A. Weisbrod, "Investing in Human Capital," *The Journal of Human Resources, I* (Summer 1966), pp. 5–21.

the prime objective of the programs that collectively make up the nation's "manpower policy."

What is meant by a "manpower policy"? This policy is not as easy to define as, say, monetary or fiscal policy, since it covers a broad spectrum of activities. An operational definition is given in a later section; and we will see that it distinguishes between "education" and "manpower programs." It is somewhat more difficult to make a meaningful distinction between these two at the conceptual level, however, since the line between educational and training expenditures may become a thin one, and these expenditures are only part of the nation's total investment in human capital.

The concluding section of this chapter describes recent legislation to outlaw discrimination in the labor market. We saw in the last chapter that some economists believe that the elimination of job discrimination will lead to an improved allocation of resources, and hence to a larger total national product. Bergmann argued, however, that gains to some Negro workers would be offset by losses to some white workers if the end of discrimination resulted in a considerable amount of job rearrangement. Whoever is right in this respect, it is important to bear in mind that legislation to ban discrimination in the job market is only part of broader legislation to end discrimination in education, housing, and the use of public facilities. It is hard to imagine that improved education, better health care, and more satisfactory housing will not enhance the "productive capacities" and the "stream of services" of those who have been denied these benefits in the past as the result of discrimination. Because of this, antidiscrimination legislation as it affects the job market has been considered as an integral part of the nation's manpower policy in this text.

Investment in Human Capital

There has been a burgeoning literature on investment in human capital in recent years.[3] But the concept of human capital is an old one, and the idea of investing in human beings can be found in the writings of such early economists as Sir William Petty and Adam Smith.[4]

The recent revival of interest in the returns to education, training, and other investment in human beings was stimulated by the work of Mincer, Becker, and T. W. Schultz.[5] Two general methods have been used to estimate

---

3. For an excellent if somewhat selective survey, see Jacob Mincer, "The Distribution of Labor Income: A Survey with Special Reference to the Human Capital Approach," *Journal of Economic Literature, VIII* (March 1970), pp. 1–26.

4. See B. F. Kiker, "The Historical Roots of the Concept of Human Capital," *The Journal of Political Economy, LXXIV* (October 1966), pp. 481–499.

5. See, for example, Jacob Mincer, "Investment in Human Capital and Personal Income Distribution," *Journal of Political Economy,* August 1958; T. W. Schultz, "Investment in Human Capital," *American Economic Review,* March 1961; and Gary S. Becker, *Human Capital* (New York: National Bureau of Economic Research, 1964).

the "value of human beings." These are (a) the cost-of-production method, which estimates the real costs, net of maintenance, incurred in "producing a human being" and (b) the capitalized earnings method, which estimates the present value of an individual's future income stream, either net or gross of maintenance.[6] The cost-of-production method provides an estimate of the "cost of producing an individual" up to a specified age, say, the age at which the individual is expected to finish school. The more widely used capitalized earnings method is used to estimate earnings at a given time as a function of the variables that are expected to influence those earnings. Some writers have related earnings to education (the "schooling model") while others have incorporated "experience" and other variables into a more general model.[7]

There are a number of reasons for treating human beings as "capital" and estimating their value in money terms. But the recent revival of interest in the human capital approach has coincided with a similar revival of interest in the problem of income distribution. In Mincer's words:[8] "The human capital approach is intimately related to the study of income distribution: costs and returns to investments in human capital are measured in the first instance by earnings differentials." Classical economic theory attempted to explain wage differentials in terms of either the compensatory principle or noncompeting groups. Adam Smith, who thought in terms of a perfectly competitive market, believed that wage differentials would tend to equalize the "net advantages and disadvantages" of various kinds of work. Other economists, including Mill and Cairnes, formulated the doctrine of noncompeting groups based on the assumption of an *absence* of labor mobility. The result of this immobility was a set of wage differentials based on social, legal, or cultural occupational stratifications.[9] Later economists were able to accept both concepts since Adam Smith was talking about competing workers—that is, workers in the same occupation—while the notion of noncompeting groups relates to workers in different occupations.

Studies of investment in human capital have been able to "explain" in a statistical sense some of the observed variations in income distribution. Some human capital models relate income to productivity, and productivity in turn is related to education or training. Statistical evidence shows that, in general, there is a positive relationship between formal education and earnings, but there is also a considerable amount of dispersion around the averages. Weisbrod and Kopeoff feel that a substantial part of this variation may be due to what they call "non-schooling variables," by which they mean

---

6. Kiker, *op. cit.,* p. 481.

7. Mincer, *op. cit.,* pp. 6–14. See also Giora Hanoch, "An Economic Analysis of Earnings and Schooling," *The Journal of Human Resources,* Summer 1967, pp. 310–329. A summary of returns in 1959, with breakdowns by race and region, is given on p. 313.

8. Jacob Mincer, "The Distribution of Labor Incomes," *op. cit.,* p. 1.

9. *Ibid.,* p. 3.

primarily ability and motivation.[10] Mincer suggests, however, that part of the statistical problem may be due to the use of *formal* schooling as the measure of investment. He points out, for example, that some of the differences between the earnings of male and female workers may be explained by human capital investment decisions. Females who expect to spend only part of their adult lives in the labor force may not be willing to invest in the training needed to enhance their productivity and increase their earnings. Male workers, on the other hand, may be more willing to invest in the vocational aspects of education, in particular, in on-the-job training. This increases the productivity of male workers and contributes to their average earnings.[11]

Much of the literature on investment in human beings deals with private investment, and frequently this investment is in formal education. Within the past decade, however, the federal government has spent large sums on training and retraining programs. These expenditures also represent investment in human capital, and the motivation for this collective investment is the same as that of individuals who invest in education in the hope of enhancing their skills and increasing their income. Indeed, whenever the government invests in programs designed to improve the skills and productivity of unemployed or other disadvantaged workers, it is making an investment in human capital with the expectation—or at least the hope—that the returns from the investment will be greater than the costs involved.

Manpower Programs

It will keep the discussion that follows in perspective if we define what is meant by the term "manpower programs." Federal concern with manpower problems is at least as old as the U.S. Department of Labor. But the programs discussed in this section are an outgrowth of the "new" unemployment problem discussed in Chapter 6. The manpower policy which emerged during the 1960s is an outgrowth of the structural inadequate-demand debate. While this debate may not have been settled to the satisfaction of academic economists, it had an important impact on Congress. One consequence was a wider recognition that labor markets do not function as smoothly as most product markets, and this led to the conclusion that positive steps had to be taken to improve the operation of labor markets.

The United States Employment Service (USES), established by the Social Security Act of 1935, cooperates with state agencies to provide a job placement service. One could argue that job placement is an essential part of an

---

10. Burton A. Weisbrod and Peter Kopeoff, "Monetary Returns to College Education, Student Ability, and College Quality," *The Review of Economics and Statistics,* L (November 1968), p. 497.

11. Mincer, *op. cit.,* p. 23. Private firms may also be reluctant to invest in the training of women on the assumption (valid or not) that their attachment to the firm's work force is more tenuous than that of male workers.

overall manpower program. But the employment service is not considered in the present chapter; it is discussed in Chapter 16, along with other legislation that deals with job security and labor standards. This is an admittedly arbitrary compartmentalization, but it has the virtue of maintaining consistency with present bureaucratic classifications. The programs discussed in this chapter are those classified by the Office of Manpower and Budget as Federal manpower programs:[12]

> These programs are intended to influence directly the skills and employment opportunities of persons in the work force, or those who desire to be in it but suffer from lack of vocational preparation or other barriers to employment. In general, they operate outside the normal educational process, enroll individuals for less than a year, provide skill training and job opportunities for nonprofessional jobs, and are targeted toward the disadvantaged portion of the population.

Manpower programs in operation today were started as efforts to retrain displaced workers. Initially, they had relatively little to do with "education," as this term is commonly used. This was partly due to jurisdictional disputes among federal agencies, but it was partly due to the limited objective of the first manpower program. It is somewhat harder to draw a fine line between training and educational programs today. Also, manpower policy now includes programs that are specifically concerned with the health and safety of workers. Manpower policy also encompasses legislation designed to protect workers against discrimination on the basis of age, color, creed, and sex. All of these programs may be considered as part of a policy of public investment in human capital.

Manpower Legislation

The conventional view of labor markets, one that may still be held by some economists, is that they operate essentially in the same way as product markets. But the labor market studies discussed in Chapter 2 indicate that this is not so. Labor markets tend to be much more "imperfect" than product markets. The objectives of manpower programs include those designed to overcome drags and frictions in labor markets by minimizing various kinds of labor immobilities, including occupational and geographical immobility.

The first manpower program, as this term is now used, was established by the Area Redevelopment Act of 1961. The Area Redevelopment Administration was primarily concerned with stimulating industrial and commercial investment in "depressed areas," that is, areas characterized by low income

---

12. *Manpower Report of the President* (Washington, D.C.: U.S. Government Printing Office, April 1971), p. 37. For a general discussion of labor market policy see E. Wight Bakke, *A Positive Labor Market Policy* (Columbus, Ohio: Charles E. Merrill Books, Inc., 1963).

and high levels of unemployment. The training programs established under this Act were not large. By April 1964, the Area Redevelopment Administration had invested $16.8 million in 657 training programs which enrolled 30,000 trainees. These programs served essentially as pilot schemes for the large-scale programs later established by the Manpower Development and Training Act of 1962 and the Economic Opportunity Act of 1964.[13]

Manpower programs are not limited to training or retraining. The 1971 *Manpower Report of the President*[14] indicates that authorized manpower activities include:

1. Recruitment, counseling, testing, placement, and followup services.
2. Classroom instruction in both remedial education and occupational skills.
3. Training on the job with both public and private employers, aided by manpower subsidies.
4. Job opportunities, including work experience and short-term employment for special age groups and the temporarily unemployed, and transitional public service employment at all levels of government.
5. Ancillary services like child-care assistance, relocation assistance, and minor health services.

The growth of federally assisted manpower programs since 1964 is summarized in Table 8-1. To support the activities listed in this table, annual federal spending on manpower programs increased from $142 million in 1964 to $1.4 billion in 1970, roughly a tenfold increase. The number of first-time enrollees increased from 278,000 in 1964 to an estimated 2.2 million in 1972, an eightfold increase.

There has been a shift in emphasis on different types of training during this period, with a decline in institutional training between 1965 and 1971, and a substantial increase in on-the-job training. Training programs, both institutional and on the job, are often considered to be the foundation of the nation's manpower program. In 1971, however, training programs accounted for about 18 per cent of all first-time enrollees. The largest single number of enrollees (442,000) were in the school and summer programs of the Neighborhood Youth Corps. These programs together accounted for 42 per cent of first-time enrollees. The characteristics of the various programs whose activities are not immediately apparent from their titles are described briefly below.

---

13. For further details see William H. Miernyk, "Area Redevelopment," in Joseph M. Becker (ed.), *In Aid of the Unemployed* (Baltimore: The Johns Hopkins Press, 1965), pp. 166–169.

14. *Manpower Report of the President*, April 1971, pp. xiii–xiv.

TABLE 8–1

First-Time Enrollments[a] in Federally Assisted Work and Training Programs, Fiscal Years 1964 and 1969–72 (in Thousands)

Program	1964	1969	1970	1971 (esti-mated)	1972 (esti-mated)
Total	278	1,745	1,819	2,027	2,194
Institutional training under the MDTA	69	135	130	130	
JOBS (federally financed) and other on-the-job training[b]	9	136	178	226	
Neighborhood Youth Corps:					
In school and summer		430	436	411	
Out of school		74	46	64	1,205[c]
Operation Mainstream		11	13	12	
Public Service Careers[d]		4	4	39	
Concentrated Employment Program		127	112	113	
Job Corps		53	43	45	
Work Incentive Program		81	93	125	187
Veterans programs	(e)	59	83	115	120
Vocational Rehabilitation	179	368	411	442	385
Other programs[f]	21	267	271	304	297

Source: Office of Management and Budget, "Special Analyses, Budget of the United States Government, Fiscal Year 1972," p. 138 (with a few minor revisions in 1970 data for programs administered by the Department of Labor); *Manpower Report of the President,* April 1971, p. 37.

[a] Generally larger than the number of training or work opportunities programed because turnover or short-term training results in more than one individual in a given enrollment opportunity. Persons served by more than one program are counted only once.

[b] Includes the MDTA-OJT program which ended with fiscal 1970 and the JOBS-Optional Program which began with fiscal 1971.

[c] Relates to the President's request in the 1972 budget for special revenue sharing for manpower training. No enrollments for categorical programs are estimated since, under the manpower reform proposal, states and local communities would be given the opportunity to determine how funds would be used.

[d] Enrollees in the Supplemental Training and Employment Program (STEP) segment of PSC are not included since they have previously been enrolled in one of the other manpower programs.

[e] Included with "other programs."

[f] Includes a wide variety of programs, some quite small—for example, Foster Grandparents and vocational training for Indians by the Department of the Interior. Data for some programs are estimated.

NOTE: Detail may not add to totals because of rounding.

Operation Mainstream This relatively small program was started by the Office of Economic Opportunity, but administrative responsibility for it was delegated to the Department of Labor in 1967. It is a program for chronically unemployed adults in rural areas and small towns. The focus of this program is not on training as such, since it was designed to provide work experience for those unable to find jobs because of age or lack of skills. A limited amount of basic education or skill training may be provided, however, to supplement the work experience. As Table 8-1 shows this program has remained relatively small with an estimated 12,000 first-time enrollees in 1971.[15]

New Careers This program has dual objectives: "to relieve shortages of personnel in numerous service activities and . . . to meet the needs of the unemployed and underemployed for meaningful jobs with career-ladder possibilities."[16] It was designed for adults with educational and other disadvantages in the job market. There is a basic difference between the New Careers program and Operation Mainstream, however, since the former is intended to provide specific training for paraprofessional jobs in such fields as health, education, welfare, neighborhood redevelopment, and safety. The program provides for a combination of classroom and on-the-job training, and the agencies providing the training guarantee employment upon its successful completion. This was the smallest of all manpower programs in 1970, with only four thousand first-time enrollees. The Department of Labor had projected, however, that the number of New Career enrollees would increase to 39,000 in 1971.

Concentrated Employment Program This program was started in 1967 to concentrate federal resources and manpower services in city slums and rural depressed areas. Overall responsibility for the management of each program was assigned to a single sponsor, usually the local Community Action Agency established by the Office of Economic Opportunity. Under this arrangement, local subcontractors provide training and supportive services. This program has attracted more than 100,000 enrollees annually. It has been plagued by a number of management deficiencies, however, probably as a result of some of the weaknesses of the Community Action Program described by Daniel Moynihan and others. An effort has been made to provide firmer guidelines to the local agencies involved, in the hope that this will lead to improvement in the management of the program.[17]

Neighborhood Youth Corps This is the primary manpower program established by the Office of Economic Opportunity. Between 1964 and 1971, it had enrolled an estimated 2 million young persons from low-income families, who were placed in various work activities. Enrollees in the Neighborhood Youth Corps live at home. Part-time jobs are found for those who remain in school, and training as well as placement are provided for school dropouts. An over-

---

15. *Manpower Report of the President*, January 1969, pp. 103–104.

16. *Ibid.*, p. 102.

17. For a general discussion of the problem, and of the efforts being made to cope with it, see *Manpower Report of the President*, April 1971, pp. 67–68.

whelming majority of the youth participating in this program have remained in school (see Table 8-1).

Job Corps   This has been one of the more controversial manpower programs. It is the only major residential program serving youth who have dropped out of school, who have the fewest educational and vocational skills, and who require a maximum amount of remedial training. Enrollees in the Job Corps typically come from home and social environments that have not encouraged an orderly transition from school to employment. In April 1969, about 30,000 young persons were in the Job Corps, but this number had dropped to about 22,000 by April 1971.

Work Incentive Program (WIN)   The intent of this program is "to move an estimated 1.1 million adults on welfare rolls to economic self-sufficiency through job training and employment. . . ."[18] The program is the result of a 1967 amendment to the Social Security Act. By the end of 1970, 260 WIN projects were operating in 53 states and other jurisdictions, and in that year 93,000 persons were enrolled in the program.

Jobs for Veterans Program   This is essentially, a public relations effort. Through television, radio, and press advertising, employers are urged to hire veterans. No separate program, however, except the familiar GI Bill, has been set up to train veterans or to provide jobs for them, and public employment offices have urged veterans to participate in other manpower programs.

The JOBS Program   The Job Opportunities in the Business Sector program is part of the federally financed on-the-job training program. It differs from the basic on-the-job (OJT) program in that it serves only disadvantaged workers. Originally limited to the nation's fifty largest urban areas, it has since been expanded to the country as a whole. A voluntary business organization, the National Alliance of Businessmen (NAB), was formed to help promote the program. Members of the Alliance have also provided jobs and training for hard-core unemployed workers. Cooperating employers have borne the extra cost of counseling, remedial education, and other services required for the successful completion of training. More will be said about this program in a later section.

One additional program, although not listed separately in Table 8-1, will be mentioned briefly at this point. This is the Trade Adjustment Assistance Program established by the Trade Expansion Act of 1962. This law was enacted to provide special assistance to workers displaced from their jobs by the reduction of trade barriers. The law was on the books for eight years, however, before any unemployed worker was certified as eligible for assist-

---

18. *Ibid.*, p. 52.

ance. In 1970, more than 16,000 workers were certified. The certified workers became eligible to receive cash readjustment and relocation allowances, in addition to the more conventional testing, counseling, skill training, and job placement services. The adjustment may be granted for as long as seventy-eight weeks if such time is required to complete a training program.[19]

Characteristics of Participants

The number of workers involved in federally assisted manpower programs was given in Table 8-1. The characteristics of 1970 enrollees are summarized in Table 8-2.

Most enrollees in institutional and on-the-job training programs are male, although 41 per cent of institutional trainees and 34 per cent of those in OJT were women. About one third of all trainees were black.

Several of the manpower programs launched by the Office of Economic Opportunity, particularly those geared to urban problem areas, have attracted mostly women. Similarly, the proportion of black enrollees ranged from 42 to 72 per cent of the total (excluding Operation Mainstream, which is roughly the counterpart for adults of the Neighborhood Youth Corps).

More than half of all trainees in the institutional and on-the-job training programs were between 22 and 45 years of age, and about 10 per cent were 45 years old or over. The Neighborhood Youth Corps and the Job Corps are, of course, entirely for young persons. But more than half of those in the Concentrated Employment Program were between 22 and 45 years of age, and 8 per cent were 45 or older.

In general, MDTA trainees had less education than those enrolled in OEO programs. Slightly more than one third of all MDTA trainees had completed nine to eleven years of school, while the percentage of those who had completed nine to eleven years in OEO programs ranged from 42 to 82 per cent.

Evaluation of Federally Assisted Manpower Programs

Manpower programs in the United States were evolving at about the same time that federal government agencies were going through a period of evaluation both from within and without. Benefit-cost analysis and program budgeting had been successfully applied to various Department of Defense activities. This success led President Johnson to ask for similar evaluations of all federal programs. Some of the early enthusiasm for the widespread application of benefit-cost analysis to government programs has subsided, but interest in evaluation, in some more general sense, remains high. Basically, all ap-

---

19. *Ibid.*, pp. 44–45.

TABLE 8-2
Characteristics of Enrollees in Federally Assisted Work and Training Programs, Fiscal Year 1970 (by percent)

Program	Women	Negro[a]	Age		Years of school completed		On public assistance[b]
			Under 22 years	45 years and over	8 or less	9 to 11	
Manpower Development and Training Act							
Institutional training	41	36	37	9	15	38	13
On-the-job training	34	30	35	11	17	36	6
Neighborhood Youth Corps							
In school and summer	50	42	100	0	17	82	32
Out of school	52	44	98	0	32	66	33
Operation Mainstream	29	25	4	51	52	28	18
New Careers	77	63	21	7	13	42	32
Concentrated Employment Program	42	67	41	8	20	45	12
JOBS (federally financed)	32	72	47	4	15	50	16
Work Incentive Program	71	43	23	6	24	44	100
Job Corps	26	61	100	0	37	56	31

Source: *Manpower Report of the President*, April 1971, p. 39.

a Substantially all the remaining enrollees were white except in Operation Mainstream, JOBS, and Job Corps. In these programs, 10 to 12 percent were American Indians, Eskimos, or Orientals.

b The definition of "public assistance" used in these figures varies somewhat among programs (e.g., it may or may not include receipt of food stamps and "in kind" benefits). In the NYC program, it may relate to enrollees' families as well as enrollees themselves.

proaches to the evaluation of social programs attempted to answer the question: Is this program worth what it costs? In more precise language, evaluation is an attempt to relate the benefits of the program to its costs.

The formal objective of a benefit-cost analysis is the benefit-cost ratio. This is calculated by first adding the annual benefits of the program over its useful life; then the sum of annual benefits is discounted to the present. This forms the numerator of the benefit-cost ratio. The next step is to add up annual costs, including all maintenance costs, of the program. The sum of the annual costs is then discounted to the present, and this forms the denominator of the ratio. The final step is to divide the discounted sum of benefits by the discounted sum of costs to obtain the benefit-cost ratio.

This is not a difficult procedure to follow when evaluating a construction project, for example, where the benefits and costs may be estimated quite closely. Even in cases of this kind, however, a problem is raised by the question: What discount rate should be used to calculate the benefit-cost ratio? If the discount rate used is lower than the "true" rate (which is, of course, unknown), benefits will be overstated relative to costs. But if the discount rate used is higher than the "true" rate, costs will be overstated relative to benefits. Thus, even in cases where benefits and costs are tangible, an element of uncertainty remains regarding the "true" relationship between discounted benefits and discounted costs.[20] This problem is compounded when benefit-cost analysis is applied to manpower programs where there are various intangibles (or "spillover effects"), and where there is insufficient experience to permit close estimates of either anticipated benefits or anticipated costs.[21]

The difficulties of evaluating social action programs—including manpower programs—have been emphasized by several writers who have attempted such evaluations. Cain and Hollister attribute these difficulties to the different attitudes of administrators and legislators on the one hand and the attitudes of scholars on the other.[22] Administrators and legislators, Cain and Hollister believe, prefer to make subjective judgments, whereas the academic scholars may demand standards of scientific rigor that cannot be met. They support the view recently advanced by Kenneth Arrow for the

---

20. For a lucid discussion of the problems of calculating benefit-cost ratios, see Joint Economic Committee, *Economic Analysis of Public Investment Decisions: Interest Rate Policy and Discounting Analysis* (Washington, D.C.: U.S. Government Printing Office, 1968). After reviewing the problems and considering a number of alternative methods of selecting a discount rate, the report concluded that: "While advocating the opportunity cost of displaced private spending as a correct conceptual basis for the Government discount rate, *the subcommittee does not presume to advocate a precise method for calculating this rate*" (pp. 13–14, italics added).

21. A nontechnical discussion of the basic principles—and some of the problems—of benefit-cost analysis may be found in E. J. Mishan, "The A B C of Cost-Benefit," *Lloyds Bank Review*, July 1971, pp. 12–25.

22. Glenn G. Cain and Robinson G. Hollister, "The Methodology of Evaluating Social Action Programs," in Arnold R. Weber, *et al.* (eds.), *Public-Private Manpower Policies* (Madison, Wisconsin: Industrial Relations Research Association, 1969), p. 7.

creation of a body of "rules of evidence" to be used in judging the effectiveness of social action programs. A systematic approach to evaluation would raise the standards of "what is admissible as evidence in a decision process," and would lessen the role of "hearsay" in this process.[23] In nontechnical terms, they argue that at present social action programs are considered to be "guilty until proven innocent," whereas they feel that a sounder approach would be to consider them "innocent until proven guilty."[24]

One author who is skeptical about the benefits of manpower programs is Burton Weisbrod.[25] He believes that government activities should be directed toward (1) greater allocative *efficiency,* (2) enhanced economic stability (less inflation and less unemployment), and (3) improved distributional *equity.* Weisbrod acknowledges the difficulty of estimating the benefits of particular manpower programs, but he feels that there is a tendency to overstate such benefits. This is true, in his view, because benefits are attributed to a single program, whereas they may be the result of a combination of programs. He recognizes that there may be "external benefits" which the private market fails to recognize. But he concludes that manpower programs, on balance, are not likely to produce benefits greater than costs with respect to either allocative efficiency or economic stability. He goes on to state that:[26]

> Even when manpower programs are not efficient, however, it does not follow that the programs are undesirable. For they have other virtues—particularly insofar as they have favorable income distribution consequences. They do not merely raise earnings, but they do so for a group deemed "deserving" —largely the poor and hard-core unemployed—and they do so in a manner that is socially preferred to transfer payment alternatives.

Measuring the Accomplishments of Manpower Programs

It may be difficult to evaluate manpower programs in terms of conventional benefit-cost analysis, but it is possible to measure some of the tangible accomplishments of these programs in terms of the employment of trainees. A summary of the record compiled by the training programs administered by the Manpower Development and Training Administration is given in Table 8-3. This table shows enrollments, completions, and post-training employment in 1963 and 1970, as well as the cumulative number of trainees involved over the entire period. The emphasis in 1963 was almost entirely on institutional

---

23. *Ibid.,* p. 29.

24. *Ibid.,* p. 30.

25. Burton A. Weisbrod, "Benefits of Manpower Programs: Theoretical and Methodological Issues," in G. E. Somers and W. T. Wood (eds.), *Cost-Benefit Analysis of Manpower Policies* (Madison, Wisconsin: University of Wisconsin Center for Studies in Vocational and Technical Education, 1969), pp. 3–15.

26. *Ibid.,* p. 15.

TABLE 8–3
Enrollments, Completions, and Post-training Employment for Institutional and On-the-Job Training Programs Under the MDTA, Fiscal Year 1963–70 (Numbers in Thousands)

	1963		1970		1963–70 Total	
	Number	Percent	Number	Percent	Number	Percent
Institutional Training						
Enrollments	32.0	93.8	130.0	58.9	978.4	67.4
Completions	19.2	60.0	85.0	65.4	651.7	66.6
Post-training employment	15.3	47.8	62.0	47.7	484.3	49.5
On-the-Job Training						
Enrollments	2.1	6.2	91.0	41.1	473.0	32.6
Completions	.9	42.9	62.0	68.1	335.5	70.9
Post-training employment	.8	38.0	53.3	58.6	289.1	61.1
Total						
Enrollments	34.1	100.0	221.0	100.0	1,451.4	100.0
Completions	20.1	58.9	147.0	66.5	987.2	68.0
Post-training employment	16.1	47.2	115.3	52.7	773.4	53.3

Source: *Manpower Report of the President,* April 1971, p. 302.

training, which accounted for almost 94 per cent of total enrollments. By 1970, however, enrollees in institutional training programs accounted for about 59 per cent of the total.

In 1963, about 59 per cent of all enrollees completed their training programs, and 47 per cent were employed at the completion of training. By 1970, the completion rate had increased to more than 66 per cent, and almost 57 per cent of all enrollees found jobs after completing their training. These numbers must be considered as minimal measures of the "success" of manpower programs. The employment numbers in Table 8–3 apply only to the enrollees who completed their training. Some trainees who failed to complete their programs did so because of a lack of motivation or ability, but others left the program to accept employment. It is possible to argue, of course, that those workers would have found employment in any event. This may be so, but it does not alter the fact that many trainees who dropped out of the program did so to accept jobs. This was particularly true during the early days of the Manpower Development and Training Act since, at that time, some well-qualified workers signed up for the training programs and were thus the more likely candidates for jobs when job openings materialized. As unemployment dropped during the 1960s, however, a larger proportion of enrollees were those who needed training in order to be qualified for gainful employment.

The Role of the Private Sector

Most transactions in the labor market take place without the intervention of a government agency. Workers find jobs by responding to advertisements, by direct application to firms known to be hiring, on the basis of referrals from friends and relatives, or through other informal channels. The local office of the United States Employment Service is responsible for the placement of a distinct minority of workers—in some cases as little as 2 per cent.[27]

The training of workers is also carried on predominantly by the private sector. Most production workers, whether employed in offices or factories, receive a certain amount of on-the-job training. As workers move up the ladder of promotion and seniority, they may be given additional training if this is required to fill more responsible and difficult jobs. Basically, all the activities carried out under the nation's manpower program are a regular part of the personnel and manpower program activities of private firms. Federal manpower programs were not designed to compete with these private activities. They were designed rather to assist hard-to-place workers. This includes all those who come under the general rubric of "the disadvantaged."

The JOBS program was described briefly in an earlier section. JOBS is the acronym for Job Opportunities in the Business Sector. As previously indicated, this is a joint effort by the Department of Labor and the National Alliance of Businessmen. Its objective was to upgrade present employees and fill their jobs with unskilled disadvantaged workers. Through its regional and city offices NAB enlisted the support of business establishments and obtained job pledges. The Department of Labor recruited suitable job applicants and contributed to the extra cost involved in employing individuals with special problems.

About 75 per cent of the workers hired under the JOBS programs were Negroes, and about 13 per cent had Spanish surnames. About half were under twenty-two years of age and only 4 per cent were over forty-five. All of the applicants had been unemployed for at least twenty-three weeks during the year before their enrollment in JOBS. It is interesting to note, however, that while these workers were classified by the Department of Labor as "greatly disadvantaged," they had completed an average of 10.3 years of school. Evidently, their greatest deficiency was not a lack of formal education. There

---

27. There is a voluminous literature showing the modest role played by the USES in job placement. For one of the more recent in a fairly long list of empirical labor market studies that support this conclusion, see Albert Rees and George P. Shultz, *Workers and Wages in an Urban Labor Market* (Chicago: The University of Chicago Press, 1970).

are many other obstacles to regular employment, including such handicaps as criminal records, dope addiction, unstable home environments or family situations, and the defeatism engendered by a lifetime of abject poverty and discrimination. Many of the workers who were enrolled in the JOBS program would have found it impossible to locate an entry job without special efforts on their behalf. They are what personnel departments describe as "high-risk" applicants.

About 80,000 workers had been hired under JOBS contracts with the Department of Labor by January 1970. But an additional 300,000 disadvantaged workers had been hired under this program without federal financial assistance. Initially, the program was limited to fifty major labor market areas, but it was expanded in 1970 to include the entire country. Although many of the workers included in the JOBS program had to be urged to accept the jobs found for them, and many are troubled by a variety of personal problems, about 53 per cent of all those hired through January 1970 were still on the job.[28]

Private enterprise has made other efforts to contribute to the employment of "unemployables." Working through such private organizations as U. S. Research and Development Corporation and MIND, Inc., private funds have been used to set up educational centers and training programs in new and existing enterprises. One of the best known results of this approach is the Watts Manufacturing Company, which was established in 1966, after the riots in the Watts District of Los Angeles, by Aerojet-General. Other large companies, such as AVCO and Control Data, have become involved in similar efforts. These cases are notable not only because they show a willingness on the part of large corporations to become involved in social issues, but also because of the innovative training methods that have been adopted. These go beyond conventional on-the-job training and include a substantial amount of remedial education.[29]

The Dual Labor Market and Manpower Policy

The dual labor market, discussed in Chapter 2, raises an important question about conventional manpower programs. Most training or retraining programs appear to be geared to employment in the primary labor market. Many of the early trainees who found jobs without difficulty probably were primary workers.

It is difficult, however, to prepare unemployed youth with secondary labor market characteristics for jobs in the primary labor market. This is not because of a lack of interest in employment on their part, but rather because of the attitudes of some young persons toward orientation and training pro-

---

28. *Manpower Report of the President,* March 1970, p. 62.
29. See Gilbert Burck, "A New Business for Business: Reclaiming Human Resources," *Fortune,* January 1968, pp. 158–161; 197–202.

grams. Such programs by their nature attempt to compensate for the "inadequacies" of the trainees. Many high-school dropouts—particularly those whose experience has been circumscribed by life in a ghetto—tend to develop hostile attitudes toward "straight" society. However much they may want jobs—and the evidence is that for most unemployed youth this is the objective—they view with distrust efforts to increase their employability by asking them to change the way they speak, dress, and wear their hair.[30] The problem is not only one of a lack of basic skills; these can be taught by conventional training methods, especially on-the-job training. Of greater significance is the clash between the life-style of some unemployed youth and the standards of employability set by the primary labor market. If the unemployment rate among ghetto youth is to be reduced, either these standards will have to be modified or more innovative orientation programs will have to be developed than those tried with little success in the past.

Combating Discrimination in the Labor Market

The Civil Rights Act of 1964 established the Equal Employment Opportunity Commission (EEOC), charged with the responsibility of ending discrimination in the labor market. The mandate of the Commission is broad; it extends beyond hiring and firing to wages, working conditions, and promotional opportunities. The Commission does not limit its activities to employers, but has jurisdiction over unions, employment agencies, and training sponsors as well. The Commission's responsibility extends to all minority groups.

The activities of the Equal Employment Opportunity Commission were initially limited to investigation, conciliation, and persuasion. Legislation giving the Commission power to issue cease-and-desist orders and to bring violators of these orders to court had been introduced in Congress regularly since the Civil Rights Act was passed, but these proposed amendments were voted down. As early as the fall of 1971, opposition to granting cease-and-desist power to the EEOC was weakening. *Business Week* magazine reported that: "Under new legislation—now expected to pass Congress easily—the EEOC will be transformed from an investigation and mediation body to a regulator with quasi-judicial procedures and legal power to compel companies to hire blacks, to reinstate fired employees, and to order payments of back pay."[31]

The Commission investigated cases where discrimination was alleged. When it had completed its investigation, it attempted to eliminate discrimi-

---

30. For an excellent discussion of the problem, written from the radical point of view, see David Wellman, "Putting-On the Poverty Program," in David M. Gordon (ed.), *Problems In Political Economy: An Urban Perspective* (Lexington, Mass.: D. C. Heath and Company, 1971), pp. 117–126. See also Jules Colin, "Private Industry and the Disadvantaged," *Idem.*, pp. 127–137.

31. *Business Week,* October 30, 1971, p. 33. See also "Equal Opportunities," *The New Republic,* October 30, 1971, p. 10.

natory practices, if these were found, by a process of conciliation. Although the Commission estimates that less than half of its conciliation efforts were successful, it felt that about 30,000 persons had been helped by its efforts through the year 1969.

One problem faced by the Commission was its growing case load. Starting in 1970, a short-cut procedure was adopted in an effort to reduce the backlog. This method consisted of efforts to settle cases immediately after an investigation and to issue a finding of fact without waiting for a formal decision by the Commission. Another innovation adopted in 1970 was the concentration of investigations in a single area. For this experiment the city of Houston was chosen because of its large Negro and Spanish-speaking population. The result was 179 charges of discrimination against 112 companies, unions, and apprenticeship programs. Another means used by the Commission to broaden its activities has been to provide financial assistance to local antidiscrimination agencies in an effort to help them enforce state and local laws.

Since March 1972, the EEOC has had the power to enforce its findings by taking offenders into the federal courts. Its jurisdiction was also broadened to include state and local government agencies and educational institutions. The 1972 amendments represent a major change in the government's attack on discrimination. But in the words of William H. Brown, Commission Chairman, "the full impact of the new law won't be felt for at least two or three years."[32]

Title VII of the Civil Rights Act of 1964 specifically prohibits discrimination on the basis of race, color, or national origin in programs receiving federal financial assistance. This section of the act is administered by the Office of Equal Employment Opportunity (OEEO) in the Department of Labor. All public or private establishments receiving federal financial assistance are required to publicize the fact that they are Equal Opportunity Employers, and violation of Title VII can lead to the loss of federal financing. Recently, OEEO investigated the federal-state employment service. Minority groups were found to be underrepresented in many state offices, and OEEO has been attempting to increase the proportion of minority group members in new hires.

The Office of Federal Contract Compliance (OFCC), also in the Department of Labor, is responsible for enforcement of Executive orders which prohibit discrimination on the basis of race, sex, creed, color, or national origin by any firm that has a contract of $10,000 or more from the federal government. Many of these contracts involve construction, and minority

---

32. *The Wall Street Journal*, April 25, 1972, p. 48.

33. See F. Ray Marshall and Vernon M. Briggs, Jr., *The Negro and Apprenticeship* (Baltimore, Maryland: The Johns Hopkins Press, 1967).

groups have been barred from many construction jobs in the past by apprenticeship programs.[33]

Efforts to increase the amount of minority hiring on federal construction projects have not been entirely successful. Originally, a tripartite voluntary approach involving unions, contractors, and minority community representatives was tried. But there was continued dissatisfaction among minority representatives with the slow progress resulting from this approach. In 1969, the Department of Labor, through OFCC, imposed specific minority hiring goals on federal contractors in Philadelphia. Similar goals were imposed in San Francisco, St. Louis, Atlanta, and, with some modifications, Chicago and Pittsburgh. But the "Philadelphia plan" encountered a bottleneck because OFCC "simply doesn't have the manpower to move into a significant number of cities fast enough to gather the extensive data needed to set the specific goals and timetables for such plans."[34] Instead of reverting to the tripartite arrangement, which Department of Labor officials conceded had not been working well, a new approach was proposed. Under this approach, unions and contractors would be expected to set and meet their own minority hiring goals. These goals, once established, would be enforced by the Office of Federal Contract Compliance. The major drawback to this approach is that it by-passes the community minority representatives.

Effectiveness of Antidiscrimination Programs

The Civil Rights Act of 1964 did not result in immediate changes in hiring practices. Viewed in its historical context, it is a revolutionary piece of legislation, but it is not always easy to maintain this perspective. Minority spokesmen and civil rights activists believe that progress under this Act has been much too slow. Some conservatives, on the other hand, tend to view the changes that followed as unduly rapid. In spite of special efforts to increase the number of minority youths in apprenticeships—efforts which include recruitment, special tutoring, and counseling—only an estimated 5,000 had been placed by 1969. By the end of the following year this number had been increased by 38 per cent. But because of the small base from which it was measured this meant only 1,900 new apprentices.[35] This is evidence of progress, but it is also evidence that change is occurring at a painfully slow pace.

Discrimination Against Women

Women account for a substantial and growing part of the labor force. About one out of three workers is a woman, and about 60 per cent of women workers are married. Most women—about two thirds—work less than full time, and

---

34. *Wall Street Journal,* September 7, 1971.
35. *Manpower Report of the President,* April 1971, p. 75.

they are heavily concentrated in a small number of occupations. On the average, they earn about 40 per cent less than men.[36]

The Fair Labor Standards Act was amended in 1963 to provide equal pay for equal work. But a survey conducted a year later showed that: "The principle adjustment that employers contemplated was a strict segregation of men's and women's work such as had long been characteristic of blue-collar and also to a marked extent, white-collar employment."[37] Title VII of the Civil Rights Act of 1964 prohibits discrimination on the basis of sex. Another survey conducted the following year showed that about one third of the companies contacted were making changes in personnel policy. These involved, to a large extent, changes in working conditions and fringe benefits. It also led to the elimination of some "male-only" jobs.[38]

The Equal Employment Opportunity Commission reported that complaints of discrimination based on sex increased between 1969 and 1970, when they accounted for about 20 per cent of all complaints received. Presumably, this increase in complaints will result in less discrimination if the Commission issues findings of fact to substantiate the complaints. The Wage and Hour Division of the Department of Labor, which administers the Equal Pay Act of 1963, reported that "women represented nearly all the claimants for the more than $25 million due through 1970 because of violations of the law."[39]

Eli Ginsberg, a leading student of womanpower, suggests that changes in women's education and training will be required if women are to be more fully integrated into the working life of the nation. He feels that elimination of discrimination in the labor market depends on the elimination of "latent discrimination in education and training."[40] His view is that policies directed specifically toward altering the position of women will be less effective than general policies that affect the level of economic activity, and the development and utilization of the entire work force. A report by *Business Week* (January 29, 1972) indicates, however, that several federal district courts have recently held that male-female wage differentials in retail sales violate the 1963 Equal Pay Act. If this view is upheld by the Supreme Court, it would eliminate what many women feel to be a discriminatory wage differential of long standing. Similar legal action could have the same impact on other occupations that employ large numbers of female workers.

---

36. For further details on women in the labor force, see the article by Eli Ginsberg, "Public Policies and Womanpower," in Arnold R. Weber, *et al.* (eds.), *Public–Private Manpower Policies* (Madison, Wisconsin: Industrial Relations Research Association, 1969), pp. 165–190.

37. *Ibid.*, p. 170.

38. *Ibid.*, p. 171.

39. *Manpower Report of the President,* April 1971, p. 76.

40. *Op. cit.*, p. 189.

Questions and Exercises

1. How did Reder define the concept of "human capital"?

2. When discussing *investment* in human capital, Reder referred to "the resources used in training." Is investment in human capital limited to the resources used in training workers? If not, what other types of expenditures might be regarded as "investment" in human capital?

3. Most discussions of antidiscrimination legislation are conducted in terms of social justice. In what way might expenditures on the enforcement of antidiscrimination legislation be considered an investment in human capital?

4. There are two general methods for estimating the "value of human beings." What are these methods?

5. "There is little or no relationship between investment in human capital and the study of income distribution." Do you agree or disagree with this statement? Why?

6. Statistical studies show a positive relationship between formal education and earnings, but with a considerable amount of dispersion around the averages. How do Weisbrod and Kopeoff explain much of this variation? What statistical problem in the measurement of investment in human beings is mentioned by Mincer?

7. According to Mincer, some of the differences between the earnings of male and female workers may be explained by human capital investment decisions. What are these decisions and how do they affect the income of male and female workers?

8. Is the concept of investment in human capital limited to the private sector of the economy? If not, what kinds of public investment in human capital are made?

9. How has the Office of Manpower and Budget defined federal manpower programs? What activities, in addition to training and retraining, are included in federal manpower programs?

10. What are the similarities and differences between the Neighborhood Youth Corps and the Job Corps?

11. What was the intent of the Work Incentive Program?

12. Describe the steps involved in the calculation of a benefit-cost ratio. In what ways does the discount rate used in the calculations affect the benefit-cost ratio?

13. Benefit-cost analysis has been used with considerable success for many years by government agencies involved in various kinds of construction projects. If benefit-cost analysis can be applied to construction projects, why should it not be applied with equal ease to manpower programs?

14. What suggestion has been made by Kenneth Arrow to increase the effectiveness of judging social action programs?

15. Burton Weisbrod feels that manpower programs have not been "efficient."

He feels, however, that they have other virtues. What are these virtues?

16. What is the JOBS program? What are some of the characteristics of workers who have been hired under the JOBS program?

17. What is the Equal Employment Opportunity Commission (EEOC), and how was it established?

18. If the EEOC investigates cases where discrimination is alleged and finds that it actually exists, what authority does the Commission have to eliminate the discriminatory practices?

19. What is the Office of Equal Employment Opportunity (OEEO) in the Department of Labor? How was this office established?

20. What is the Office of Federal Contract Compliance (OFCC), and what is its responsibility? Does the Civil Rights Act of 1964 prohibit discrimination only on the basis of race, creed or national origin?

21. Write a brief essay on the effectiveness of antidiscrimination legislation to date. How could its effectiveness be improved?

Suggested Readings

Books

Bakke, E. Wight. *A Positive Labor Market Policy*. Columbus, Ohio: Charles E. Merrill Books, Inc., 1963.

Becker, Gary S. *Human Capital*. New York: National Bureau of Economic Research, Columbia University Press, 1964.

Doeringer, Peter B. (ed.) *Programs to Employ the Disadvantaged*. Englewood Cliffs, N.J.: Prentice-Hall, Inc., 1969.

Investment in Human Beings. Papers presented at a conference called by the Universities–National Bureau Committee for Economic Research, *The Journal of Political Economy, LXX* (Supplement: October 1962). This supplement contains papers by Theodore W. Schultz, Gary S. Becker, Jacob Mincer, Larry A. Sjaastad, and George J. Stigler, Burton A. Weisbrod, Edward F. Denison, and Selma J. Mushkin.

Articles

Ginsberg, Eli. "Public Policies and Womanpower," in Arnold R. Weber, *et al.* (eds.), *Public–Private Manpower Policies*. Madison, Wisconsin: Industrial Relations Research Association, 1969, pp. 165–190.

Hanoch, Giora. "An Economic Analysis of Earnings and Schooling," *The Journal of Human Resources, II* (Summer 1967), pp. 310–329.

Joint Economic Committee. *Economic Analysis of Public Investment Decisions: Interest Rate Policy and Discounting Analysis*. Washington, D.C.: U.S. Government Printing Office, 1968.

Kiker, B. F. "The Historical Roots of the Concept of Human Capital," *The Journal of Political Economy, LXXIV* (October 1966), pp. 481–499.

Mangum, Garth L. "Manpower Research and Manpower Policy," *A Review of Industrial Relations Research, Vol. II*. Madison, Wisconsin: Industrial Relations Research Association, 1971, pp. 61–124.

McKay, Roberta B. "Job Training Programs in Urban Poverty Areas," *Monthly Labor Review,* August 1971, pp. 36–41. Also published with supplementary tables as Bureau of Labor Statistics Reprint 2755.

Mincer, Jacob. "The Distribution of Labor Incomes: A Survey with Special Reference to the Human Capital Approach," *Journal of Economic Literature, VIII* (March 1970), pp. 1–26.

Piore, Michael J. "On-the-Job Training in the Dual Labor Market: Public and Private Responsibility in On-the-Job Training of Disadvantaged Workers," in Arnold R. Weber, *et al.* (eds.), *Public–Private Manpower Policies.* Madison, Wisconsin: Industrial Relations Research Association, 1969, pp. 101–132.

Reder, M. W. "Gary Becker's *Human Capital:* A Review Article," *The Journal of Human Resources, II* (Winter 1967), pp. 97–104.

Schultz, Theodore W. "Investment in Human Capital," *American Economic Review, LI* (March 1961), p. 117.

History of
Trade Unions

Theories of the Labor Movement

Interest in worker organizations is almost as old as the institution of trade unionism. Various scholars have attempted to explain the reasons for the existence of unions and their impact—actual or potential—upon society. Their views, of course, have differed widely depending upon the author's predilections and social philosophies. Some have considered unions a threat to the economic system of their time, others as a benign influence. A few who have espoused the overthrow of capitalism—such as Karl Marx—have argued that unions can do little to improve the workers' status. According to this view, unions should be the vehicle for revolutionary economic and social change.

Early Views Of Unions

Adam Smith on Labor Organization

When Adam Smith published his monumental *The Wealth of Nations* (1776), the rudimentary forms of labor organizations were far different from the unions we know today. Smith pointed out, however, that wages depend upon an agreement between the worker and his master, "whose interests are by no means the same." This agreement, in his opinion, was the result of a continuous contest between the two parties. "Workmen," he wrote, "desire to get as much, the masters to give as little as possible. The former are disposed to combine in order to raise, the latter in order to lower the wages of labour." But in this contest, Smith pointed out, all the advantage was on the side of the masters since the law ". . . authorises or at least does not prohibit their combinations, while it prohibits those of the workmen."[1]

Any combination of workers designed to raise their wages was widely publicized and generally deprecated in Smith's day. But as the founder of

---

1. Adam Smith, *The Wealth of Nations,* Modern Library Edition (New York: Random House, Inc., 1937), p. 66.

modern economics pointed out, employers also combined to keep wages down and "to violate this combination is everywhere a most unpopular action, and a sort of reproach to a master among his neighbors and equals." The public, continued Smith, is not aware of employer combinations, however, since their discussions are held in secret.

At times, Smith wrote, employers agreed to depress the wage level. And this led to a "contrary defensive combination" of the workmen. Workers, however, sometimes combined without such provocation in an effort to raise the price of their labor. But whether the workers combined for offensive or defensive purposes, Smith pointed out, their combinations were always "abundantly heard of." The reason, he stated, is that "they have always recourse to the loudest clamour, and sometimes to the most shocking violence and outrage. They are desperate, and act with the folly and extravagance of desperate men, who must either starve, or frighten their masters into an immediate compliance with their demands."

Whenever there is an outbreak of labor unrest, however, the employers are just as clamorous as the workers, "and never cease to call aloud for the assistance of the civil magistrate, and the rigorous execution of these laws which have been enacted with so much severity against the combinations of servants, labourers, and journeymen."[2] Thus labor combinations were not highly successful in Adam Smith's day. The legal barriers to labor organization—which did not extend correspondingly to employers—effectively prevented concerted action on their part. Labor uprisings generally resulted in nothing more than the punishment or ruin of their ringleaders. As a result of the legal restrictions on workers, labor combinations could have no effect on wages in Smith's view. On the other hand, employers could not depress wages below the basic subsistence level if they hoped to maintain the necessary supply of labor.

Adam Smith was the great apostle of a policy of laissez faire. To him the ideal economy was one in which a free marketplace would determine the allocation of resources and the distribution of returns to workers, employers, landlords, and investors. He clearly condemned the unequal treatment of labor and employer organizations before the law, but he felt that market forces, in the long run, would determine the level of wages. Employers, even acting in combination, could not depress wages below the "natural" rate, nor could workers, even if they were permitted to combine, keep their wages above this level.

Karl Marx on Trade Unions

The policy of laissez faire did not, as its advocates claimed it would, lead to the best of all possible worlds. By the middle of the eighteenth century the industrial revolution was in full swing in Great Britain. The unfettered market-

---

2. *Ibid.,* p. 67.

place did not, however, lead to an equitable distribution of income. Manufacturers became enormously wealthy, but wages failed to rise and working conditions were generally deplorable. Marx attributed the conditions he saw to private ownership of the means of production. The only solution to this problem, in Marx's view, was the complete overthrow of capitalism and the substitution of communism.

Neither in the *Communist Manifesto,* which Marx wrote with Friedrich Engels in 1848, nor in *Capital,* his major work, did Marx discuss trade unions extensively. He was more than skeptical, however, that unions could accomplish anything for workers within the framework of capitalism—a position held by devout Marxists to the present day. Despite the rapid advances in production that the industrial revolution had produced and was producing, Marx argued that workers would be unable to raise their wages above the level of subsistence. Capitalists would insist on appropriating all returns from gains in productivity. Workers were aware of gains in productivity, Marx noted, but he concluded that any efforts on their part to share in these gains would be resisted. "The capitalist politely knocks on the head such pretensions as gross errors as to the nature of wage-labour," Marx wrote. "He cries out against this usurping attempt to lay taxes on the advance of industry, and he declares roundly that the productiveness of labour does not concern the labourer at all."[3] As long as workers felt that they could improve their conditions by combining into unions without overthrowing capitalism, Marx believed, they were deluding themselves. The full force of law and government was on the side of employers. Although a small minority, the latter controlled the nation's wealth. Workers could only improve their position by revolting against the capitalists and the governments which the capitalists controlled.

Marx did not oppose the formation of trade unions. Indeed, he conceded the necessity for worker organization. Even under capitalism, such organization would reduce somewhat the severe competition for available jobs engendered by the high level of unemployment, which he believed would always be present under capitalism. More important, Marx also thought in tactical terms; labor organizations, in his view, could spearhead the attack on capitalism. But unions could not be depended upon to revolt against their masters. Without proper leadership, from the Marxist point of view, workers would combine in an effort to improve their conditions under capitalism. Thus it would be necessary for communists to "educate" the leaders of trade unions so that, when the time was ripe, they would be prepared to dispossess the exploiters of labor and establish the "dictatorship of the proletariat."

Marx did not live to see the development of powerful, free trade unions in democratic countries. His followers, however, have continued to level attacks on the notion that satisfactory earnings and working conditions are

---

3. Karl Marx, *Capital,* Modern Library Edition (New York: Random House, Inc., 1906), pp. 610–611.

compatible with capitalism in any form. They have been contemptuous of "business unionism" and have labeled the leaders of free trade unions as willing tools of the greedy capitalists. Leaders of the free unions have returned Marxist insults in kind and have refused to listen to their blandishments. They point to the gains that unions have won through democratic means and insist that the Marxist conception of trade unionism is not only completely erroneous but also a snare and a delusion, which would cost workers their freedom if they were to follow the path of the Marxists.

James Thorold Rogers—An Early View of "Business Unionism"

When Adam Smith wrote about the economic effects of trade unions—or rather the lack of such effects—he did so largely in hypothetical terms, since labor combinations were forbidden by law. The British Combination Acts were repealed in 1824 and 1825, however, so that by the time Karl Marx wrote, unions were tolerated in Great Britain. But Marx denied categorically that unions would be able to improve the lot of the working man within the framework of capitalism—a belief consistent with his view that capitalism as a system was doomed to perish. When Thorold Rogers ventured a few remarks about unions in 1884, however, he presented an entirely different view. Most economists at that time considered any interference with the free operation of market forces as socially undesirable. But Rogers considered unions to be, on the whole, a benign influence. "A trade union conducted on legal and peaceful principles," he wrote, "by which I mean moral forces only, and with an entire abstention from violence, both in its inception and its administration, does not economically differ from any other joint stock partnership." He preferred the term "labour partnership" to trade union, and he pointed out that while successful businessmen were termed "merchant princes, pioneers of industry, creators of public wealth, benefactors of their country, and guarantors of its progress,"[4] labor leaders were denounced for trying to achieve the same thing as the successful businessman. In discussing unions, Rogers used the terminology of the business world and drew a parallel between the behavior of union leaders and businessmen.

Rogers was critical of John Stuart Mill for accepting the notion of a fixed wage fund. He also criticized Mill for arguing that an increase in wages must necessarily raise the cost of production and consumer prices. He argued that "in point of fact, if trade unions do or can raise wages, they may do so to the ultimate benefit of producers and consumers." This would follow, Rogers argued, if a trade union could reduce the number of competing capitalists and improve efficiency in a given market. Unions could also successfully raise wages, he further argued, if in their dealings with employers they would reduce the number of middlemen who he felt "do mischief instead of service, are

---

4. James Thorold Rogers, *Six Centuries of Work and Wages* (London: Swan Sonnenschein and Co., Ltd., 1903), p. 400.

parasites, and not, in any sense, producers."[5] Rogers clearly had little love for the middleman, and felt that such intermediaries between trade and production did more to destroy producers' profits than union efforts to raise wages.

In a sense, Rogers developed a reverse notion of Galbraith's concept of "countervailing power."[6] Galbraith argued that the countervailing power of unions was induced by the growth of original power on the product side of the market. Rogers suggested that the growth of unions would lead to fewer but larger producers in a given market and have the further effect of cutting into the ranks of middlemen, a development which he considered would be altogether beneficial.

Rogers was critical of some union tactics. He believed that strikes could seldom be successful, although he considered them to be analogous to speculative purchases by sellers who hoped to control the market by reducing supply. He condemned union violence as "indefensible and suicidal." But even undesirable union behavior he attributed in part to the position that the early unions occupied under British law. Rogers wrote after repeal of the Combination Acts and noted that unions were no longer forbidden by law. But the union, he went on, "was not, indeed, under the protection of laws; and I conceive that much of the savagery which for a long time characterized the conduct of trade unions was due to the outlawry under which those wholesome institutions were placed."[7]

In addition to supporting the early trade union movement as such, Thorold Rogers was one of the early advocates of labor-management cooperation. He considered unions to be socially desirable institutions, which would help improve the efficiency of capitalism and thus be beneficial to workers, producers, and consumers alike. An unparalleled optimist, Rogers also hoped that the growth of an international trade union movement would diminish the warlike instincts of governments. "I confess that I look forward to the international union of labour partnerships as the best prospect the world has of coercing those hateful instincts of governments, all alike, irresponsible and indifferent, by which nations are perpetually armed against each other, to the infinite detriment, loss and demoralization of all."[8]

Traditional Trade Union Theory

The term "traditional analysis" was applied by Clark Kerr and Abraham Siegel to the writings of a number of scholars who dealt with the question of trade unionism. These writers are classified on the basis of their *approach* to the discussion of unions; Kerr and Siegel do not suggest that they reach

---

5. *Ibid.*, pp. 402–403.

6. John Kenneth Galbraith, *American Capitalism*, rev. ed. (Boston: Houghton Mifflin Company, 1956), pp. 114–117.

7. Rogers, *op, cit.,* p. 439.

8. *Ibid.*, p. 402.

similar conclusions about the nature of trade unions or their effect upon society.[9] The ideas of some of the leading "traditional theorists" are discussed in this section.

Sidney and Beatrice Webb

Sidney and Beatrice Webb (1859–1947; 1858–1943)—later Lord and Lady Passfield—were among the founders of Fabian socialism. They are usually included among the relatively small number of "institutional" economists who have made important contributions to economic thought. Fabian socialism is the evolutionary approach to social reform which eventually led to a system of democratic socialism in Great Britain. Institutional economics is less easy to define. Essentially it is descriptive rather than theoretical, and institutional analysis is built around careful study of the various organizations that play an important role in the life of society at any given time. Among other things, the Fabian Society favored the strengthening of trade unions. Unlike Marxists, who believe that trade unions can play a useful role if they spearhead a revolution designed to establish the dictatorship of the proletariat, the Fabians believe that trade unions can improve wages, hours, and working conditions by democratic collective action. As John Dunlop has shown, however, the Webbs did not have a fully rounded theory of the labor movement.[10] They did not concern themselves with the reasons for the emergence of trade unions or with patterns of union development. But they made important contributions to our understanding of trade union government, and were among the pioneers of labor history.

The Webbs were critical of classical economists, such as Nassau Senior, who stressed the social benefits of vigorous competition. They recognized that aggressive price competition often led to substandard wages. In their view one of the most important objectives of a trade union was that of guarding its members from the evil effects of unrestricted competition.

To the Webbs, a trade union was "a continuous association of wage earners for the purpose of maintaining or improving the conditions of their working lives."[11] Unions, the Webbs believed, were not a passing phenomenon in the historical sweep of forces. They felt that labor organizations are essential to the preservation of democratic society.

Broadly speaking, the Webbs believed that unions could pursue one of

---

9. Clark Kerr and Abraham Siegel, "The Structuring of the Labor Force in Industrial Society: New Dimensions and New Questions," *Industrial and Labor Relations Review, 8*, No. 2 (January 1955), pp. 151–168.

10. John T. Dunlop, "The Development of Labor Organization: A Theoretical Framework," in Richard A. Lester and Joseph Shister (eds.), *Insights Into Labor Issues* (New York: The Macmillan Company, 1948), p. 168.

11. Sidney and Beatrice Webb, *History of Trade Unionism* (New York: Longmans, Green & Co., 1920 ed.), p. 1; quoted by Dunlop, *ibid.*, p. 166.

two courses of action to improve conditions for their members. The first was to pursue a policy of restrictionism; that is, to control the supply of labor. The second was to work toward the establishment of minimum wage and working standards for the entire work force. The Webbs were critical of unions that tried to restrict labor supply in order to raise wages, however. They strongly favored union efforts to establish a "Common Rule" based on the notion of a "living wage" for all workers. Such minimum standards would be achieved, according to the Webbs, through collective bargaining, political action, and through establishment of schemes of mutual insurance.

Through collective bargaining, unions would seek to raise wages and press for a gradual extension of fringe benefits. The Webbs were convinced that the establishment of a Common Rule would be beneficial not detrimental to industry. Once minimum standards for labor were established, they believed, employers would seek to increase productivity through technological progress. If this followed, all of society would benefit.

It is somewhat surprising, in view of their socialist predilections, that the Webbs would advocate mutual insurance schemes for the payment of sick benefits and unemployment compensation. Such schemes are administered by governments today through programs of social security. Unions support such programs and are spared the problems of administration that mutual insurance plans would have involved.

The Webbs were critical of the autocratic attitudes of employers in their day. In their view the spread of trade unionism would lead to more democratic relations in industry. They anticipated to some extent what Sumner Slichter was later to refer to as a system of "industrial jurisprudence."[12]

The Webbs did much to provide intellectual support for the trade unions, which were emerging in Great Britain at the time they wrote. Public resistance to union growth was strong, and the doctrines of the classical economists went largely undisputed. There was still widespread acceptance of the notion of a fixed "wage fund" and it was argued that if unions "artificially" raised wages there could be only one consequence—unemployment. The Webbs recognized the argument that if trade unions made headway in a particular sector of the economy only, there could be a flight of capital to nonunion sectors, which would lead to unemployment.

But they countered this argument by insisting that trade union pressure would lead to improved technology, and that both workers and society would gain from effective trade union action.[13] They also acknowledged that there were upper limits to which unions could push wages at a given time without causing employers either to go out of business or to relocate their establish-

---

12. Sumner H. Slichter, *Union Policies and Industrial Management* (Washington, D.C.: The Brookings Institution, 1941), p. 1.

13. Sidney and Beatrice Webb, *Industrial Democracy* (New York: Longmans, Green and Co., 1897), pp. 615–616.

ments. However, they thought that there were lower limits to wages below which workers would desert particular employers and seek jobs elsewhere. Within these limits unions could have an effect upon the wage level. In this respect, the Webbs' theory of wage determination under trade unions was remarkably close to the notions of certain modern wage theorists.

Robert F. Hoxie and Functional Unionism

Robert Hoxie (1868–1916), who had been a student of the iconoclastic Thorstein Veblen, was interested in both the structure and functions of unions. He regarded unions as only one of the institutions devised by men—acting collectively—to alter their environment. Workers faced with common problems reacted by banding together to form a union, which would serve their specific needs. This led him to question monocausal explanations of the rise of trade unions and to advance his own notion of unions as functional types.[14] He distinguished four major types of unions, each designed to serve a different function.

Business unionism, according to Hoxie, is the type which develops among skilled craftsmen. Their specific interest is in improving wages, hours, and working conditions for their own membership. They tend to be conservative and to rely primarily on collective bargaining for the achievement of their goals. Hoxie's description of business unions applied to many of those in the AF of L at the time he wrote.

Some workers are not interested in immediate economic gains, however. These tend to band together in *uplift unions.* Such unions support movements for broad social reform. They often align themselves with radical reform groups in search of a panacea for the ills of society. Those attracted to such unions are easily swayed by rhetoric, and their goals are not narrow but broadly inclusive. Uplift unionists have been inclined to think in terms of producers and consumers cooperatives, radical schemes of monetary reform, and elimination of the wage system of payment. There were some elements in the Knights of Labor with a strong uplift tinge. But as Millis and Montgomery have pointed out, uplift unionism has rarely found much of a following in the United States.[15]

Revolutionary unionism, as the name implies, is dedicated to the overthrow of capitalism. It is the kind of unionism advocated by Marxists. The ideology of the International Workers of the World was also revolutionary. This type of unionism has been strongly condemned by American labor leaders, and it has made relatively little headway in other nations of the Western world.

Predatory unions, according to Hoxie, are entirely nonideological. Their

---

14. Robert F. Hoxie, *Trade Unionism in the United States* (New York: D. Appleton-Century, Inc., 1917), Chapter 1.

15. Harry A. Millis and Royal E. Montgomery, *Organized Labor* (New York: McGraw-Hill Book Co., Inc., 1945), pp. 33–45.

members are interested in obtaining "more here and now," and they are not particular about the means used to obtain this end. The leaders of predatory unions are often corrupt and some have close ties with the underworld. The McClellan Committee's investigation, conducted during the late 1950s, revealed the presence of some predatory unionism in the United States. It also revealed that there were some employers who raised no objections to dealing with predatory unions.

In discussing the structure and function of trade unions, Hoxie was reluctant to generalize. But in his discussion of collective bargaining, he reached a rather sweeping conclusion[16]:

> Collective bargaining and arbitration . . . are steps toward full labor control. They are an entering wedge toward industrial democracy and abolition of the profit system. Recognition of the union is the first step, since individual bargaining gives the worker no voice. This, then, is the important thing—not the lack of a principle of justice. Collective bargaining is not an instrument of peace, primarily, it is a step in the process of control. Indeed, the significant thing about unionism is the development of a process of control. This is the larger aspect of unionism and in this sense collective bargaining is a solution of the labor problem.

Tannenbaum's View of the Union as a Response to the Challenge of the Factory System

To Frank Tannenbaum (1893–1969), the trade union was more than an economic institution. During medieval times, for example, the skilled artisan belonged to a guild. While the guilds were not forerunners of trade unionism— they were more nearly akin to business organizations—the worker identified himself with his organization. This sense of belonging disappeared with the rise of Mercantilism and the cottage system of production. It was completely destroyed by the Industrial Revolution, which created a class of wage workers.

The rise of trade unions in modern times, according to Tannenbaum, is the result of the worker's need to feel a strong identification with his job. The factory system poses a threat to the worker's security. It is large and impersonal, and the worker as an individual can do little to protect his own interests. Workers react collectively by joining forces to gain as much security as possible in an essentially insecure world.[17] But it is not just economic security that the worker seeks. In the modern world, workers "belong to nothing real, nothing greater than their own impersonal pecuniary interests."[18] The trade

---

16. Hoxie, *op. cit.,* in Joseph Shister, *Readings in Labor Economics and Industrial Relations,* 2nd ed. (New York: J. P. Lippincott Co., 1956), p. 178.

17. Frank Tannenbaum, *The Labor Movement, Its Conservative Functions and Social Consequences* (New York: G. P. Putman Sons, 1921), p. 32; cf. John T. Dunlop, *op. cit.,* p. 166.

18. Frank Tannenbaum, *A Philosophy of Labor* (New York: Alfred A. Knopf, 1951), p. 53.

union provides the worker not only with greater security than he could expect as an individual under the factory system, but also with a nexus between his job and his source of income. Whether he realizes it or not, a worker who joins a trade union is trying to fulfill his need for a sense of belonging.

Tannenbaum feels that trade union values are not unlike those of management. The individual worker joins the union to protect himself against the vagaries of the market. But often management also seeks to avoid the consequences of unrestrained competition by entering into collusive arrangements. Both trade union leaders and businessmen are responding to acquisitive instincts when they seek to strengthen their security and add to their income. Thus "trade unionism is often monopolistic, restrictive, arbitrary, often at war within itself, costly, and in contradiction of all theories of a free unrestricted market. So is the corporation."[19]

If there is a strong similarity between the trade union and the business organization, what is the most likely outcome of the contact between these two institutions? In his earlier views, at least, Tannenbaum felt that the trade union would ultimately lead to a radical transformation of our economic system. He felt that trade unions would eventually create a system of "industrial democracy," which would displace the existing capitalistic system.

John R. Commons: Trade Unions as Part of "Collective Democracy"

John R. Commons (1862–1945) was one of the small group of "institutional" economists who made important contributions to American economic thought. A prodigious scholar, he directed publication of the eleven-volume *Documentary History of American Industrial Society* (1910-1911). With his associates, he published the first two volumes of *History of Labor in the United States* in 1918. The remaining two volumes were published in 1935 by his associates, D. D. Lescohier, Elizabeth Brandeis, Selig Perlman, and Philip Taft.

Commons believed that the trade union could not be analyzed in isolation. The origin, development, and impact of trade unionism could only be understood within the broader framework of general history, including political history. He was not alarmed by the tendency he saw toward group organization. The rise of a single powerful pressure group would be cause for alarm. But collective action on one side of the market faced by similar action on the other side is part of what Commons referred to as "collective democracy."[20]

To Commons, American trade unionism was not a protest against the factory system.[21] "Whatever may have been its origin in other countries, the labor

---

19. Frank Tannenbaum, "The Social Function of Trade Unionism," *The Political Science Quarterly*, June 1947, p. 176, quoted by Paul Sultan, *Labor Economics* (New York: Henry Holt and Co., 1957), p. 214.

20. In this respect his ideas are similar to some advanced by John K. Galbraith in *American Capitalism* (Boston: Houghton Mifflin Company, 1956).

21. Contrast this view with that of Tannenbaum discussed in the preceding section.

movement in America did not spring from factory conditions. It rose as a protest against the merchant-capitalist system."[22]

Commons was the first major labor historian to point out the obstacles to union growth in the United States. The labor force was made up of immigrants from many countries. Workers had difficulty in communicating, not only because of language barriers, but also because of differences in their cultural backgrounds. The fluidity of the labor force and universal male suffrage prevented the formation of the rigid class lines found in Europe. And as industrialism developed in the United States, the mass production system led to a dilution of labor skills.

Competitive pressures, however, eventually forced workers with common interests to form trade unions. Commons was not alarmed by the interference with market forces that trade unions were bound to produce. He disagreed quite strongly with those economic theorists who felt that unrestrained markets would produce ideal equilibrium solutions to economic problems. This disagreement, incidentally, went back to his days as a graduate student, when it had caused him considerable trouble in courses dealing with orthodox economic theory. Instead of searching for ideal solutions based on the concept of an atomistic society, Commons believed that economists should recognize the collective nature of human behavior in a group society. Within this framework, he saw the trade union representing the interests of the working man. He felt that unions and business organizations would be able to accommodate their differences and to work out areas of agreement which would permit both to survive.

John R. Commons has had wide influence on labor economists and specialists in industrial relations, whether or not they have accepted all of his views. He was a prodigious worker and left an important heritage of books and scholarly articles. Some of his students, such as Edwin Witte, Sumner Slichter, and Selig Perlman, not only continued the Commons tradition but also made important contributions of their own to the field of labor economics.

Selig Perlman and "Job-Conscious" Unionism

Selig Perlman (1888–1959), a protégé of John R. Commons, had a long and distinguished career at the University of Wisconsin. He collaborated closely with Commons, and in his *History of Trade Unionism in the United States,* published in 1922, provided a great deal of detail about the early days of American trade unionism. Later, in *A Theory of the Labor Movement,* he developed his concept of job-conscious unionism based upon the argument that there is a continuous scarcity of job opportunities. He explained the delayed development of a trade union movement in the United States by a lag on the part of

---

22. *A Documentary History of American Industrial Society,* Vol. V, p. 23, quoted by Dunlop, *op. cit.,* p. 165.

workers in recognizing that good jobs are scarce. Once this was recognized, however, job-conscious craftsmen banded together to stake out a property right on the jobs available to them.

Stable trade unionism could not develop, Perlman believed, until the worker recognized that he stood to gain as an individual through the union's administration of job opportunities for the group as a whole. A union cannot become strong until "it has educated the members to put the integrity of the collective 'job territory' above the security of their individual job tenure."[23] Thus the union may at times demand sacrifices from individual members, and the latter cannot stop to count too closely the costs involved to themselves.

Perlman anticipated the rise of industrial unionism. As technological change broke down the partitions between various grades of labor in an industry, it would lead to a broadening of the "job territory." When this happens, Perlman said, "the now expanded job-territory will sooner or later be taken over by an *industrial* union or by an *amalgamated* union bordering upon the industrial type."[24] The new industrial unions, Perlman believed, would display the same kind of solidarity as had the earlier craft unions.

Perlman felt that the trade union movement in the United States is affected by three groups of influences. These are (1) the "resistance power of capitalism," based upon the confidence of employers in their ability to satisfy customers and workers alike; (2) the role of the intellectual, who typically underestimates the resistance power of capitalism and overestimates the desire of workers to alter the system, and (3) the "manualist" sentiment of workers which leads to their concern about the scarcity of job opportunities. All of these influences are important, but Perlman seemed to attach the greatest importance to job consciousness. He also recognized that the control of job territories was not simple.[25]

> Many are the influences affecting union job control: the legal status of unionism, the policies of the government, a favorable public opinion, and others. Thus every union soon discovers that the integrity of its "job-territory" like the integrity of the geographic territory of a nation, is inextricably dependent on numerous side relationships.

The Nature of Trade Unions

The theories discussed in the preceding section were formulated at a time when unions were relatively weak and predominantly of the craft variety. The authors of the early theories were concerned with the answers to one or more of the following questions:[26]

---

23. Selig Perlman, *A Theory of the Labor Movement* (New York: The Macmillan Company, 1928), p. 273.

24. *Ibid.*, p. 275.

25. *Ibid.*, p. 276.

26. John T. Dunlop, *op. cit.*, pp. 164–165.

1. How is one to account for the origin or emergence of labor organizations?
2. What explains the pattern of growth and development of labor organizations?
3. What are the ultimate goals of the labor movement?
4. Why do individual workers join labor organizations?

Dunlop points out a number of similarities in the trade union theories described briefly in the last section; but there are also sharp differences. A particularly sharp cleavage is that between the writers (such as the Webbs and Commons) who explain the rise of trade unions in terms of *economic developments,* and those (such as Hoxie and Perlman) who emphasize worker attitudes or psychology. This cleavage, in Dunlop's view, "represents a fundamental failure in the formulation of 'theories of the labor movement.' " In his opinion, four *interrelated* factors must be considered in exploring the development of trade unions: (1) technology, (2) market structures and the character of competition, (3) community institutions of control, and (4) ideas and beliefs. Instead of seeking a single or a few causes of union development, Dunlop believes that the rise of the labor movement must be viewed in the context of its *total* environment. It is his view that labor organization emerges "among employees who have strategic market or technological positions." The organizations of workers in strategic positions then become "growth cones," which facilitate the organization of workers in less strategic positions.[27]

Dunlop's thesis that trade unions spread from a strategic nucleus is particularly applicable to the emergence of a labor movement prior to the Wagner Act. "Organization by ballot rather than by the picket line places much less emphasis upon strategic employees in the technological and market scene."[28] Thus he feels that his theory is a less satisfactory explanation of the rise of industrial unionism in the United States for the period following the advent of the CIO.

Are Trade Unions Basically "Economic" or "Political" Organizations?

In an important book entitled *Wage Determination Under Trade Unions,* first published in 1944,[29] John T. Dunlop examined the ways in which trade unions affect wage levels and the wage structure within the framework of economic theory. Dunlop did not, however, insist that wage determination could be explained entirely in economic terms. "The fundamental tenet of the following pages," he stated in the introduction, "is that modes of behavior that are

---

27. *Ibid.,* pp. 174–180.

28. *Ibid.,* p. 183.

29. All references here are to the second edition of John Dunlop, *Wage Determination Under Trade Unions* (New York: Augustus M. Kelley, Inc., 1950).

broader than economic theory contribute materially to the understanding of wage determination."[30] But he did develop an economic model of a trade union, and he examined bargaining power under varying degrees of competition and monopoly both in labor markets and product markets.

A few years after Dunlop's book appeared, Arthur M. Ross published his *Trade Union Wage Policy*,[31] in which he stated that "many of the most interesting questions concerning union behavior cannot be answered by any strictly economic analysis. . . ."[32] He then went on to assert that among all the participants in economic life, "the trade union is probably the least fitted to purely economic analysis." After considering the various criteria used by labor and management in wage negotiations, and the pressures to which those responsible for wage determination are subjected, Ross concluded that "a trade union is a *political* agency operating in an economic environment." He did not intend, however, to analyze union behavior exclusively in political terms. This, he asserted, would be just as unsatisfactory as an explanation based entirely upon economic analysis. Ross explicitly recognized the interdependence between political and economic influences. On balance, however, he appeared to grant primacy to the political process. "The economic environment is important to the unions at the second remove: because it generates political pressures which have to be reckoned with by the union leader."[33]

In the preface to the 1950 edition of *Wage Determination Under Trade Unions,* Dunlop replied that "the thesis must be rejected that wage determination under collective bargaining is to be explained most fundamentally or fruitfully in terms of a political process."[34] This is so, in Dunlop's view,[35] because:

1. Emphasis upon the political process reflects the experience of newer unions in which there have been factional struggles.
2. Those who stress political wage setting are preoccupied with the short run, and largely ignore more persistent factors.
3. The political approach underestimates the knowledge labor leaders have of technology and the "economic facts" of an industry.
4. Emphasis upon political wage setting leads to excessive concern with internal union and management affairs and neglects "the stubborn facts of the external world."

---

30. *Ibid.,* p. 5.
31. Arthur M. Ross, *Trade Union Wage Policy* (Berkeley and Los Angeles: University of California Press, 1948).
32. *Ibid.,* p. 4.
33. *Ibid.,* pp. 7–14.
34. Dunlop, *Wage Determination, op. cit.,* p. iii.
35. *Ibid.,* pp. iii–iv.

It is worth repeating that neither Dunlop nor Ross insisted that union behavior could be explained *only* in economic or political terms. Dunlop chose to emphasize the economic aspects of wage determination under trade unions while acknowledging that noneconomic factors must also be considered. Ross, for his part, conceded that economic factors cannot be ignored in explaining union behavior, but emphasized the political pressures to which union leaders are subjected. Economic factors are important, Ross admits, but largely because they will have an influence on those political pressures.

Theories of Trade Union Growth

Labor theorists and labor historians have long been interested in the process of union growth. John R. Commons, for example, associated fluctuations in union growth with business cycles. He claimed that during periods of prosperity there was union growth, and that during depressions the labor movement contracted.[36] This appears to have been the pattern during the early days of American trade unionism. Commons based his conclusions on rather scanty statistical data. Indeed, until 1936, with the publication of Leo Wolman's *Ebb and Flow in Trade Unionism,*[37] there was no consistent series of union membership figures covering a long time period, and Wolman's data go back only to 1897. These have now been supplemented by figures collected annually by the U.S. Department of Labor. And while there are some weaknesses in the data, it is possible to project a statistical picture of union growth covering a period of more than seventy years. Figure 9–1 shows the trend in membership of American unions from 1930 through 1968.[38] Most of the growth, of course, has occurred since 1935.

The labor force has also increased substantially since 1930, however. Thus a measure of "real" membership must make allowances for the growth of employment and the labor force. This can be done by expressing union membership as a percentage of either nonagricultural employment or the total labor force (see Figure 9–2).

Once fairly reliable statistical data on trade union membership were available, a number of scholars began to analyze the figures. It is not surprising that they did not all reach the same conclusions. Indeed, there has been a lively debate about union growth.[39] Virtually everyone agrees that union

---

36. See John R. Commons, *A Documentary History of American Industrial Society, Vol. V* (Glendale, California: Arthur H. Clark Co., 1910–11), p. 19.

37. Leo Wolman, *Ebb and Flow in Trade Unionism* (New York: National Bureau of Economic Research, 1936).

38. For the period 1897–1930, see Irving Bernstein, "The Growth of American Unions," *American Economic Review,* June 1954, pp. 303–307.

39. The precision of union membership figures has also been the subject of considerable controversy. For an excellent analysis of some of the weaknesses of union membership figures, see Albert Epstein, "Union Records as Statistical Sources," 108th Annual Meeting, American Statistical Association, December 29, 1948.

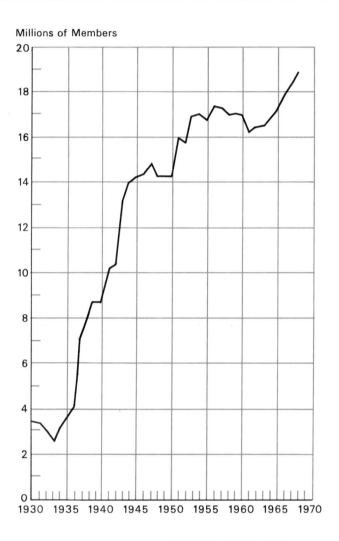

FIGURE 9–1.

Membership of National and International Unions, 1930–1968. Totals exclude Canadian membership but include members in other areas outside the United States. Members of AFL-CIO directly-affiliated local unions are also included. For the years 1948–1952, midpoints of membership estimates, which were expressed as ranges, were used. (*Reprinted from the U.S. Department of Labor, Bureau of Labor Statistics, Directory of National and International Labor Unions in the United States, 1969, Bulletin No. 1665 [1970], p. 66.)*

growth has not been steady. There have been times when union membership has grown rapidly, and other times when the rate of growth has slowed down or when union membership has declined. But there seems to be relatively little agreement about the causes of such fluctuations in the growth of union membership.

It will be recalled that John R. Commons felt that union growth was closely related to the business cycle; that membership increased during good times and declined during depressions. Others have related it to the business cycle, but have come to different conclusions.

Wars and Depressions as Causes of Union Growth

In a rather sketchy discussion of short-term fluctuations in union growth, John T. Dunlop identified seven major periods of rapid union expansion between 1827 and 1945.[40] He divided these seven periods into two groups: (1) wartime periods, and (2) periods of fundamental unrest. He noted that unions grew during the Civil War, the Spanish-American War, and the two World Wars. Union expansion during wartime, in Dunlop's view, is explained by labor market developments. Labor shortages and rising prices stimulate union membership.

The remaining three periods of union growth in Dunlop's schema coincided with the low points of major depressions. He feels that at the bottom of depressions, worker dissatisfaction rises to a crest and workers respond by joining unions.

Irving Bernstein, who has made extensive statistical studies of union growth, has also concluded that "in the short run membership has expanded sharply as a consequence of wars and very severe depressions. Unions, in other words, have been the beneficiaries of disaster."[41]

A Critique of the Disaster Theory

The short-run variations in union growth advanced by Dunlop and Bernstein have come under sharp criticism from Julius Rezler. Rezler points out, for example, that Bernstein attributes union growth early in this century to the depression of 1893, whereas Dunlop relates it to the Spanish-American War. In Rezler's opinion, however, "the growth was initiated by a twenty-four months' expansion of business activity starting in June 1897 and augmented by an exceptionally friendly attitude of Americans toward unionism." He also disagrees that World War I itself led to growth, and attributes growth during

---

40. Dunlop, "The Development of Labor Organization," in Lester and Shister, *Insights into Labor Issues*, p. 190.

41. Irving Bernstein, "The Growth of American Unions," *American Economic Review*, June 1954, p. 317.

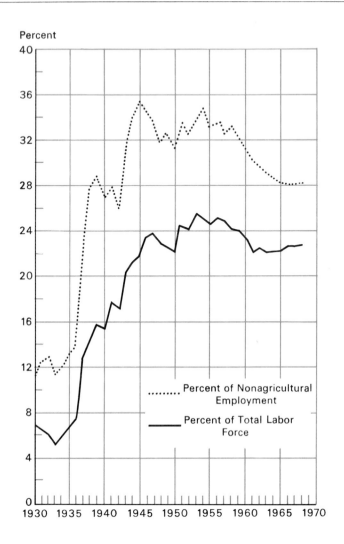

FIGURE 9–2.

Union membership as a Percent of Total Labor Force and of Employees in Nonagricultural Establishments, 1930–1968 (excluding Canadian members). (*Reprinted from the U.S. Department of Labor, Bureau of Labor Statistics,* Directory of National and International Labor Unions in the United States, 1969. *Bulletin No. 1665 [1970], p. 67.*)

this period to "the friendly attitude of the Federal Government toward union-ism."[42] He supports this argument by pointing out that union membership continued to grow *after* World War I when, presumably, the conditions favorable to union growth during wartime no longer existed.

The Role of Inertia in Union Growth

Horace B. Davis has argued that, whatever causes an upsurge or decline in union membership, there is considerable inertia once the movement has started. Davis is of the opinion that while union membership fluctuates, the waves of membership "are not closely synchronized with those of the business cycle."[43] By and large, however, Davis's[44] theory would tend to support the Dunlop thesis, although there might be some differences of opinion on timing:

> A major wave of growth, if not brought on by a war, will nearly always be found to have been preceded by an accumulation of wage-earners' grievances, as during a major depression, while the accumulation of employer resistances during the wave of growth is a factor in the ensuing period of absolute or relative decline.

Multicausal Theories of Union Growth

There has been considerable debate about short-run fluctuations in union membership. When one examines various theories of long-term union growth, however, there seems to be considerable agreement that many causes are involved. For example, whereas Davis relates waves of union growth to wars and depressions, he also takes into account the effects of union leadership, the growth of industrialism, and technological change, particularly as the latter leads to the displacement of labor. Dunlop has mentioned the influences of technology, market structures and the character of competition, community institutions, and ideas and beliefs. And in a final summation, Rezler has mentioned ten major factors affecting union growth, which include variations in business activity, changes in the composition of the labor force, technology, union leadership, the legal framework, the structure of union organization, and the value system of society.[45] Bernstein has also concluded that long-run growth cannot be explained in terms of a single cause, and that single explanations are "only sporadically helpful" in explaining short-

---

42. Julius Rezler, *Union Growth Reconsidered: A Critical Analysis of Recent Growth Theories* (New York: The Kossuth Foundation, Inc., 1961), pp. 4–8.

43. Horace B. Davis, "The Theory of Union Growth," *Quarterly Journal of Economics,* August 1941, pp. 611–637; reprinted in Francis S. Doody, (ed.), *Readings in Labor Economics* (Reading, Mass.: Addison-Wesley Press Inc., 1950). Page references are to this volume.

44. *Ibid.,* p. 22.

45. Rezler, *op. cit.,* p. 16.

term fluctuations. Among the primary forces that have shaped long-term growth, he includes expansion of the labor force, growing social acceptability of unionism, increasing homogeneity in the working class, and the extension of collective bargaining provisions for union security.[46]

Econometric Models of Union Growth

The most recent attempts to "explain" variations in the rate of trade union growth have made use of econometric models. A fairly elaborate single-equation model was constructed by Ashenfelter and Pencavel.[47] In this model, trade union growth is related to (a) price changes, (b) *changes* in employment in the unionized sectors of the economy, (c) the *proportion* of employment in the organized sectors of the economy,[48] (d) cyclical unemployment, and (e) the percentage of Democratic Congressmen.[49]

The empirical results of the Ashenfelter-Pencavel study support their basic hypothesis that workers join unions by weighing expected benefits against expected costs. Union growth, they found, is not particularly sensitive to either the cyclical or the political variables in their model. But the union membership coefficient supports the hypothesis that "further growth of unions is hampered by their own size."[50]

Ashenfelter and Pencavel are aware of the measurement errors in published union membership figures, so despite the fact that their equations resulted in good "statistical fits," they make no exaggerated claims for their model. They feel that it "does provide a relatively accurate and *compact* [but not] an exact description of the historical progress of trade union membership."[51]

A much simpler model was developed by Mancke, who was critical of the earlier effort by Ashenfelter and Pencavel.[52] In Mancke's model, trade union

---

46. Bernstein, *op. cit.*, p. 317.

47. Orley Ashenfelter and John H. Pencavel, "American Trade Union Growth: 1900–1960," *The Quarterly Journal of Economics, LXXII* (August 1969), pp. 434–448. Four separate equations were tested, but there are no major differences among them in terms of "goodness of fit." An earlier study by A. G. Hines should be mentioned at this point, although it will not be discussed in the text. Hines examined the hypothesis that money wage rate variation can be explained in terms of union "pushfulness," and his statistical findings support the hypothesis. See his paper, "Trade Unions and Wage Inflation in the United Kingdom, 1893–1961," *The Review of Economic Studies, XXXI* (October 1964), pp. 221–252.

48. This term was included to measure what Hines called "the diminishing response to a given intensity of recruiting effort" as trade union membership increases. See Hines, *op. cit.*, p. 229.

49. This term was used as a proxy measure of public attitudes toward trade unions on the assumption that Democratic members of Congress have a higher degree of "pro-labor sentiment" than Republicans.

50. Ashenfelter and Pencavel, *op. cit.*, p. 444.

51. *Ibid.*, p. 447.

52. R. D. Mancke, "American Trade Union Growth, 1900–1960: A Comment," *The Quarterly Journal of Economics, LXXXV* (February 1971), pp. 187–193.

growth is said to depend upon (a) union membership in an earlier period, (b) the national unemployment rate, and (c) four "dummy" variables, which were intended to reflect political forces, especially enforcement of the National Labor Relations Act of 1935. The only substantive conclusion reached by Mancke was that the coefficients of his dummy variables confirmed his hypothesis that "enforcement of the Wagner Act immediately led to a large and permanent jump" in union membership.[53] This is a conclusion that would occasion little surprise among labor economists or labor historians.

Ashenfelter and Pencavel had noted that spurts of union growth often have been attributed to periods of "social unrest," but in their view there is no need to "resort to such an *ad hoc* device to explain American union growth. . . ."[54] They feel that it can be explained by a single behavioral equation. Mancke's specific criticism of the Ashenfelter-Pencavel model is that it, in turn, "is not free of *ad hoc* devices."[55] But Mancke made liberal use of dummy variables in his equation, and one reason for the use of such variables is to account for *ad hoc* events that cause discrete breaks in economic time series. It may be difficult to develop econometric models of trade union growth that are entirely free of *ad hoc* devices. The process of union growth may be too complex to be described by a single equation that fails to take into account unique political, social, and economic events that impinge upon union membership.

Econometric models may be incompletely specified; that is, they may not include all of the variables that have an important influence on the growth of unions. The models discussed above, for example, do not specifically take into account the effects of change in occupational structure on union membership; these effects will be discussed in Chapter 11. A recent study by Leo Troy suggests that structural changes may be quite significant.[56] Labor historians list other factors of a political and sociological character that they feel cannot be ignored in the analysis of trade union growth, and it would be difficult to quantify some of these factors.[57] Certain other forces have affected membership in specific unions, not to mention various legal and institutional changes that have no doubt influenced total union membership.[58]

The above comments are not meant to suggest that there is no place for econometrics in the analysis of trade union growth. To the extent that econ-

53. *Ibid.,* p. 193. In other words, the coefficients of the dummy variables confirm the hypothesis that led to their inclusion in the equation in the first place.

54. Ashenfelter and Pencavel, *op. cit.,* p. 434.

55. Mancke, *op. cit.,* p. 187.

56. Leo Troy, "Trade Union Growth in a Changing Economy," *Monthly Labor Review,* September 1969, pp. 3–7.

57. Albert A. Blum, "Why Unions Grow," *Labor History, 9,* No. 1 (1968), pp. 39–72.

58. Some of these are discussed in Woodrow Ginsburg, "Review of Literature on Union Growth, Government and Structure—1955-1969," in Woodrow L. Ginsburg, *et al.* (eds.), *A Review of Industrial Relations Research, Vol. I* (Madison, Wisconsin: Industrial Relations Research Association, 1970), pp. 207–260.

ometric models provide new insights, or develop approximate weights for some of the major determinants of union growth, they serve as useful supplements to studies based on more conventional and less quantitative methods of historical analysis. It is not likely, however, that the new method will replace the older ones.

The Union Stagnation Debate

Although considerable debate has developed regarding the causes of union growth, especially in respect to short-term fluctuations in growth, an even livelier debate about the prospects of future growth has been in progress. A number of economists and historians have been involved in this discussion, but the major ideas have been developed by two of the outstanding antagonists—Irving Bernstein and Daniel Bell.

The Stagnation Thesis

The stagnation thesis was first advanced by Daniel Bell in *Fortune* magazine, April 1953. It was elaborated the following year, after it had been criticized by Bernstein.[59]

The basis of Bell's argument is "that because something once grew in a specific way in the past, there is no guarantee, logically or empirically, that it will develop in the same manner, or respond to the same stimuli, in the future."[60] Bell argued that in the past, unions had grown by *eruption, extension,* and *enforcement.* The most important of these, in Bell's view, is *eruption.*

An eruption in union membership occurs, as it did in the latter half of the 1930s, when some factor or combination of factors leads to a large-scale willingness on the part of workers to join unions. There was clearly an eruption of membership after 1935, the year in which the Wagner Act was passed and the AFL-CIO split occurred.

The extension of union membership occurs after the initial breakthrough, when some of the hold-out firms are brought into line, and unorganized workers begin to feel that they could benefit from unionism. There can also be an extension of union membership during wartime, when government agencies adopt a benign attitude toward unions, and employer resistance is diminished by cost-plus contracts and the necessity of meeting production schedules.

The phase of enforcement occurs when unions have become strong enough to negotiate union security provisions, such as those calling for the closed shop or union shop. This course of action tends to bring all workers in

---

59. *Proceedings of the 7th Annual Meeting of Industrial Relations Research Association,* December 28–30, 1954, pp. 231–236.

60. *Ibid.,* p. 231.

a bargaining unit into the union, whether or not they would willingly join as individuals.

After this brief description of union growth in the past, Bell considered the effect of these forces on future growth. He concluded that the prospects for further growth were dim. He could see no reason why there might be another eruption similar to that of the late 1930s. The problem of union growth, in his view, is primarily one of *extension*. And here, he insisted, unions would encounter difficulties. In manufacturing, with the notable exception of the textile and chemical industries, most industries were between 80 and 100 per cent organized at the time he wrote. The same was true in mining and rail transportation. These are the areas of successful union penetration, and they have been largely saturated, according to Bell's thesis. Also, there is a high degree of organization in large enterprises, and it is easier for a union to sign up members in a single large firm than in many scattered small establishments. There had been little growth of trade unionism among supervisory and white-collar workers.

The only areas in which there can be large-scale union growth in the future will be the so-called "white-collar" trade and service occupations; yet in these occupations, Bell feels, unions will make little headway. For one thing "in office and financial institutions unionism has failed to take hold because its language and actions are cast in the mold of the industrial worker and unions have failed to find a language appropriate to white collar workers."[61] Also, many workers in such establishments are relatively young women who do not expect to remain in the labor force permanently.

In addition, Bell felt that management had learned a great deal since the eruption of union membership in the 1930s. It had developed personnel practices and granted benefits to workers which made unionism relatively unattractive to them. He also felt that government policy was less conducive to union growth after World War II than it had been during the 1930s. While Bell did not pretend to make a projection into the indefinite future, he concluded after examination of these factors that the tide of unionism in the United States had reached a high-water mark. In the immediate future, he concluded, there would be no significant growth in trade unionism.

Bernstein's Critique of the Stagnation Thesis

Shortly after Bell's initial article appeared in *Fortune*, Irving Bernstein wrote that the stagnation thesis had "only surface plausibility."[62] This was so, he argued, because despite Bell's gloomy prognosis unions had in fact continued to grow. In a later article, which included union membership figures

---

61. *Ibid.*, p. 235.
62. Irving Bernstein, "The Growth of American Unions," *American Economic Review*, June 1954, p. 301.

through 1959, with his own estimates for 1960, Bernstein insisted that American trade unionism was continuing to exhibit growth. He distinguished between short-term and long-term growth, and repeated the points he had made in his earlier article. Short-term growth tends to come in sharp spurts following wars and depressions. But long-term growth, in Bernstein's view, is due to expansion of the labor force, the increasing social acceptability of unionism, the growing homogeneity of the working class, and the extension of union security provisions in labor-management agreements.[63] Bernstein's figures, which have been subject to some criticism, show a slow growth of union membership through 1960. But his measure of "real" membership, that is, union membership as a per cent of the civilian labor force, shows a modest but fairly sustained decline since 1953.

Figure 9–2 shows that "real" membership reached a peak at about 25 per cent of the total labor force in 1953. There was a decline until 1961, and then a slow rise through 1968. In the latter year, "real" union membership amounted to about 23 per cent of the labor force. Figure 9–1 shows, however, that there was a fairly sharp rise in actual union membership after 1961, and that total membership in national and international unions reached an all-time peak of nearly 19 million members in 1968. In part this gain in membership was due to the continued growth of old, established unions such as the Teamsters; but it was also due to the growth of some of the newer "white-collar" unions, particularly those which organize government employees. These changes in the structure of American trade unions are discussed in some detail in Chapter II.

Questions and Exercises

1. What conclusion did Adam Smith reach about the ability of unions to raise wages in the long run? Did he believe that employers, acting singly or in combination, would be able to depress wages in the long run?
2. Did Karl Marx view the trade union as an effective vehicle for improving the conditions of workers under capitalism? What role did he see trade unions playing in the eventual overthrow of capitalism?
3. James Thorold Rogers has been identified as the author of an early view of "business unionism." What does this mean?
4. Sidney and Beatrice Webb believed that unions could pursue one of two courses of action to improve the conditions of their members. What are these courses of action? In your view, is there any reason why unions could not follow both plans?

---

63. Irving Bernstein, "The Growth of American Unions, 1945–1960," *Labor History,* Spring 1961, pp. 131–132.

5. Describe Hoxie's concept of "functional unionism." How did he classify unions under this heading?

6. Frank Tannenbaum wrote that unions were more than "economic institutions." What other role, according to Tannenbaum, does the trade union play?

7. What did John R. Commons mean by "collective democracy"? Is it true that he viewed the rise of powerful pressure groups in a democratic society with considerable alarm?

8. Define Selig Perlman's concept of "job-conscious unionism." Perlman felt that the trade union movement in the United States was affected by three strong influences. What are these influences, and how have they affected organized labor, according to Perlman?

9. Write a brief essay on "trade unions as economic or political institutions," drawing on the ideas advanced by John T. Dunlop and Arthur M. Ross.

10. Briefly discuss the influence of wars and depressions on union growth. Contrast the views of Dunlop, Bernstein, and Rezler on this issue.

11. What are some of the primary forces, according to Bernstein, that have shaped long-run trends in the growth of American unions?

12. In their econometric model of trade union growth, Ashenfelter and Pencavel used (i) the proportion of employment in the organized sectors of the economy and (ii) the percentage of Democratic Congressmen, as two of their variables. Why were these variables included in the model?

13. What conclusion did Ashenfelter and Pencavel reach about the effects of cyclical and political variables on trade union growth? Did they feel that membership growth is helped or hindered by the "size of unions"?

14. Why was Mancke critical of the Ashenfelter-Pencavel model? Do you feel that his criticism was justified?

15. What is the stagnation thesis, and who advanced this notion?

16. Summarize Bernstein's critique of the stagnation thesis. What were Bernstein's views about the long-run prospects for trade union growth?

17. In your opinion, do the data since 1951 support or deny the stagnation hypothesis of trade union growth?

Suggested Readings

Books

Barkin, Solomon. *The Decline of the Labor Movement.* Santa Barbara, California: The Fund for the Republic, Inc., 1961.

Commons, John R. *A Documentary History of American Industrial Society,* eleven volumes. Glendale, California: Arthur H. Clark Company, 1910–11.

Commons, John R., and Associates. *History of Labor in the United States,* four volumes. New York: The Macmillan Company, 1918–32.

Fuchs, Victor. *The Service Economy.* New York: National Bureau of Economic Research, 1968.

Miernyk, William H. *Trade Unions in the Age of Affluence.* New York: Random House, 1962.

Millis, Harry A., and Royal E. Montgomery. *Organized Labor.* New York: McGraw-Hill Book Co., Inc., 1945.

Perlman, Selig. *The Theory of the Labor Movement.* New York: The Macmillan Company, 1928.

Rezler, Julius. *Union Growth Reconsidered.* New York: The Kossuth Foundation, Inc., 1961.

Ross, Arthur M. *Trade Union Wage Policy.* Berkeley and Los Angeles: University of California Press, 1948.

Webb, Sidney and Beatrice. *History of Trade Unionism.* New York: Longmans, Green and Co., 1897.

Articles

Ashenfelter, Orley, and John H. Pencavel. "American Trade Union Growth: 1900–1960," *The Quarterly Journal of Economics LXXII* (August 1969), pp. 434–448.

Bernstein, Irving. "The Growth of American Unions," *American Economic Review, XLIV* (June 1954), pp. 301–318.

Bernstein, Irving. "The Growth of American Unions, 1945–1960," *Labor History, 2,* No. 2 (Spring 1960), pp. 131–157.

Blum, Albert A. "Why Unions Grow," *Labor History, 9,* No. 1 (1968), pp. 39–72.

Ginsburg, Woodrow W. "Review of Literature on Union Growth, Government and Structure—1959–1969," in Woodrow L. Ginsburg, *et al.* (eds.), *A Review of Industrial Relations Research, Vol 1.* Madison, Wisconsin: Industrial Relations Research Association, 1970.

Colonial Times to the AF of L

General histories of the United States touch only briefly on the trade-union movement. Because unions have had an impact on our political and economic lives only in fairly recent times, few students are likely to be well informed about the obscure beginnings of trade unionism in the United States. Labor unions existed in the early days of our history, however, although a labor movement as such did not get started in the United States until the second quarter of the nineteenth century.

The Early Experience of American Unions

The broad outlines of labor history are sketched in this and the following chapters. In this compressed treatment only the highlights can be touched upon, but it is hoped that this will provide a framework for later discussions of trade union policy, labor law, the structure and government of unions, and collective bargaining.

Early Labor Organization in the United States

The first labor organizations formed in this country bore little resemblance to a modern trade union. In colonial America there were organizations, strongly reminiscent of the medieval guilds, which included both masters and journeymen, but there were others, typically charitable and benefit societies, which consisted of journeymen alone. Both types of organizations consisted of workers in the skilled trades only. One of the earliest of these organizations was the Carpenters Society of Philadelphia, which was established in 1724. This organization engaged in both charitable activities and bargaining. Among other things, it maintained a secret wage scale, imposing fines on its members for disclosing the list of wages to nonmembers.[1]

---

1. Norman Ware, *Labor in Modern Industrial Society* (Lexington, Mass.: D. C. Heath and Company, 1935), p. 27.

Similar organizations were established by journeymen printers, shoe-makers, tailors, hatters, bricklayers, and coopers. Many of these, first established as charitable societies, gradually became involved in a form of bargaining, although in those days this was typically limited to the establishment of a "price list" or scale of wages. There was some effort, however, to exert control over apprentices in order to protect the job security of the journeymen, but there was no counterpart in those days to modern collective bargaining agreements.

The first labor organizations in this country were not exceptionally stable. The colonial period was one of great flux. One day a man might be a journeyman in one of the skilled trades, and the next an independent businessman. The skilled worker did not consider himself part of a wage-earner class. There were cases where master and journeyman cooperated to by-pass the "merchant capitalist," a middleman who performed the function of today's retail store.

Toward the end of the eighteenth century, however, organizations were formed that bore a stronger resemblance to today's trade unions. They were made up entirely of wage earners, and their objective was solely that of improving the economic condition of employees. The Federal Society of Journeymen Cordwainers was such an organization. It was established in 1794 by the Philadelphia shoemakers and survived until 1806. Similar societies were established by the carpenters and shoemakers of Boston in 1793 and 1794. The printers of New York also organized in the latter year.

Although some of these organizations lasted for a number of years, their members still did not consider themselves to be part of a working class. While they practiced their trades, however, they felt the need for mutual protection both from merchant capitalists and employers. They sought to negotiate joint agreements with the masters and in a few cases even demanded a closed shop. To achieve their ends they used the weapon of the strike. There are records of strikes for the ten-hour day, for the closed shop, and even some instances of sympathy strikes. The first labor dispute of a modern character was evidently conducted by the Philadelphia printers, who went on strike for a minimum wage of six dollars a week. The union was sufficiently well organized to pay strike benefits at that time.[2]

The early unions did not go unchallenged. A number of militant employer associations were formed specifically to deal with organized workers. Some agreed to negotiate with the unions, but by and large they set out to destroy the unions by recruiting nonunion workers and by turning to the courts for protection from what they considered to be "labor conspiracies." The courts were sympathetic. Between 1806 and 1815, there were at least six conspiracy cases, and in four of these, organized workers were found guilty of conspiring

---

2. Harry A. Millis and Royal E. Montgomery, *Organized Labor* (New York: McGraw-Hill Book Co., Inc., 1945), p. 21.

to injure their employers. One of the verdicts also concluded that labor organizations were adverse to the best interests of the community.

But it was not so much employer opposition or the courts which limited the growth of early American trade unions; economic instability was their greatest enemy. They could not achieve sufficient strength to withstand the shocks of the short but severe depressions commonplace at that time. For example, following the end of the Napoleonic Wars, there was a severe and prolonged depression which reached its depth in 1820. Few of the early labor organizations were able to survive this economic onslaught.

The Beginning of a Labor Movement

The existence of trade unions in a handful of skilled trades does not constitute a labor movement. This comes into being only when wage earners develop a feeling of solidarity which extends beyond the members of a single occupation. This feeling did not exist among the early charitable and benefit societies that were eliminated by the depression of 1820. The revival following the depression was spirited but short-lived. By the middle of the 1820s, the nation was again in the grip of an industrial depression. Discontent was more widespread than ever before, and it found expression in increased political activity, which culminated, in 1828, in the election of Andrew Jackson as President— an event which signalized the rise of the "Common Man."

Jacksonian democracy was the result of more than industrial depression. The average citizen and wage earner had many grievances.[3]

> Economic and political inequality between citizens of different classes, the length of the work day, imprisonment for debt, absence of mechanics' lien laws, . . . the Pennsylvania compulsory militia system under which the wealthy could avoid service, lack of free public education, . . . governmental favoritism toward the banks and other corporations, the issue of banknote currency of unstable purchasing power and the monopoly of credit maintained by the banks. . . .

These were among the complaints of Jackson's supporters in his campaign against the "aristocrats" of New England and Virginia.

There was general agreement that all of the problems of the Common Man were not solved by the introduction of Jacksonian democracy, but there was less agreement about how reforms should be achieved. Some thought the answer lay in the direction of agrarian reform; a few were intrigued by Robert Dale Owen's proposal of "public guardianship"; and others believed that the wage earner would receive equitable treatment only if workers organized for political action. Property qualifications for voting had been removed in most states by 1821. The first American Labor Party was organized in

---

3. Millis and Montgomery, *ibid.*, pp. 24–25.

Philadelphia in May 1828, and a second workingman's party was organized in New York the following year. These parties were not led by laborers, however, but by reformers or small businessmen. The platforms of the labor parties demanded the ten-hour day, the abolition of imprisonment for debt, an end to prison contract labor, enactment of mechanics' lien laws, abolition of discriminatory militia systems, curbs on licensed monopolies (especially banks), and universal education. The labor parties in the United States did not survive, however. They were gradually absorbed by the two major parties, with some segments splintering off into small factions like the "Loco-Focos" or the "Equal Rights" group.

The reform organizations were so badly divided that they accomplished little. However, during this era of agitation, trade unionism was revived again. This time the individual organizations of skilled craftsmen did not operate in a vacuum. We can trace the beginning of a labor *movement* in the United States to the late 1820s. For example, in 1827, the Philadelphia Mechanics Union of Trade Associations was formed. This is believed to be the first coordinated movement of several trade unions to accomplish a common objective. It grew out of a strike by workers in the Philadelphia building trades for the ten-hour day. The ten-hour movement also sparked formation of The New England Association of Farmers, Mechanics and Other Workmen which, as the name suggests, was somewhat broader than a trade union. It was both a political and an economic organization. Some of the leaders of the new labor movement also supported the labor parties that had been formed, but the association between the unions and the political organizations was not close. The unions were more intent upon achieving job security than political power.

The First Attempts at Federation

Some of the unions organized during the early days of Jacksonian democracy were able to survive for a number of years. They resembled modern trade unions more than any of the organizations formed before the 1820s. From 1832 to 1837, partly due to the expansion of state banks and the circulation of irredeemable currency, the cost of living surged upward. The number of local trade unions began to increase rapidly as workers made an effort to protect their real income by seeking higher wages. By 1833, it is estimated that there were twenty-nine unions in New York, twenty-one in Philadelphia, and seventeen in Baltimore. Skilled craftsmen in a number of other eastern cities were also organized. In addition to higher wages, most of these unions demanded the ten-hour day, control of apprenticeship, and the closed shop.

More important, the individual unions did not try to carry on alone. The individual societies combined into what were then called "trades' unions"— later to be designated city centrals. And local unions in the various trades began to form national organizations. Finally, in March 1834, the National

Trades Union was formed—the first federated labor body in the United States. It was headed by Eli Moore, who was also a labor candidate for Congress. But from the beginning, all efforts to turn the National Trades Union into a political movement were effectively squelched. For the next two years the trade union movement in the United States grew and gained in strength. A number of conventions were held by the national unions, and viable trade unionism appeared to have come to the United States. Then came the panic of 1837, one of the worst financial disasters in our history, and during the depression which followed this panic, virtually every labor organization in the nation was wiped out.

For the next decade the American economy was in the grip of a severe depression. Reform of the unstable monetary system was slow in coming. Wage earners, farmers, and small businessmen were all victims of the deflationary pressures strongly at work during this decade. Workers had organized during an earlier period of inflation to protect their real earnings, but they seemed incapable of concerted action during a period of widespread unemployment.

Following the crash of 1837, a number of reform movements were started or revived. The brand of socialism advocated by Robert Owen (and practiced at New Harmony in the mid-1820s) was revived by his son, Robert Dale Owen and the latter's associate, Frances Wright. The disciples of Fourier advocated his program of Association. Both groups were critical of the waste and inefficiency which they claimed stemmed from the competitive system. There were also demands for producers' and consumers' cooperatives, and for agrarian reform. All of these movements gained adherents during the "hot air forties," but they failed to attract wage earners in significant numbers. Indeed, most labor historians are of the opinion that these and other reform movements impeded the growth of job-conscious unionism during this decade of economic stagnation in the United States.

The Emergence of Stable Trade Unionism

As the economy emerged from the depression in the late 1840s, trade unionism again appeared on the American scene. The experience of the 1840s indicated quite clearly that wage earners in this country were not interested in humanitarian schemes designed to alter the structure of American society. But as business conditions improved, and as prices began to rise again, a number of national trade unions were formed. The National Typographical Union was established in 1852—the first national union to survive to the present day. It was followed in 1854 by the Hat Finishers, in 1855 by the Journeyman Stonecutters Association, and in 1856 by the United Cigar Makers, a union destined to play an important part in subsequent trade union history. Two other national unions, the Ironmoulders, and the Machinists and Blacksmiths, were established in 1859.

The long depression following the panic of 1837 was followed by an equally long period of prosperity. This was a period of rapid population growth, rising prices, and of growing industrialization—all of which contributed to an increase in trade union membership. In addition, the rapid expansion of a network of rails led to broadened markets. Indeed, the growth of the railroad system was one of those innovations, like the subsequent growth of the automobile industry, which had far-reaching economic ramifications. Under these conditions, the trade union movement grew steadily, if not spectacularly. But trade unionism in the United States was far from strong enough to withstand the impact of a severe depression, and such a depression struck again in 1857. During this depression most of the weaker unions in the nation were again wiped out.

Most of the unions which survived the crash of 1857 disappeared soon after the outbreak of the Civil War. But by 1863, wartime conditions were stimulating economic growth. The cost of living rose sharply and there was a labor shortage. These conditions have generally provided a stimulus to union growth in the United States.

The trade unionism that emerged during the Civil War followed the pattern established before the crash of 1857. Local unions were formed in the skilled trades, and these were combined into city centrals or trades' assemblies. As these grew in number, national unions were formed. The growth of unions continued after the Civil War ended. Before the end of the 1860s, there were about thirty national unions in existence. Some of the unions formed during the Civil War and the post-Civil War period have survived to the present day. The Brotherhood of Locomotive Engineers was founded in 1863. The conductors organized in 1868, and the Brotherhood of Firemen and Enginemen was founded in 1873. The unions that grew during this period were pragmatic craft organizations primarily interested in bargaining. As had been true of earlier unions, many joined in the movement for a shorter workday, but there was at least some modest flirtation with more radical reform schemes.

The post-Civil War period was similar to the 1830s and 1840s in terms of general confusion and lack of direction in the American economic system. It was a time of rapid growth in the manufacturing sector, and a period of increased concentration of ownership and control. Broadened markets had stimulated competition, and many businessmen sought to evade the uncertainties of aggressive price competition through collusion or consolidation. Agriculture also grew rapidly and, after the Homestead Acts were passed, land prices soared while farm production increased and farm prices fell. The real wages of industrial workers thus went up, but the plight of the farmers again stimulated a host of agrarian reform movements. It was during this time that Henry George advanced his proposal for the Single Tax to appropriate unearned increments in land. The existing unions steered clear of this and other reform movements during the 1860s.

Another severe panic occurred in 1873, followed again by a sustained depression. By this time, however, some of the national trade unions were suffi-ciently strong to withstand a depression of some duration. During the depres-sion of the 1870s, some labor support for Greenbackism was visible, along with a heightened interest in consumer's cooperation. Despite their flirtation with reform movements, however, most unions continued to emphasize bargaining, and considerable collective bargaining, as we know it today, was practiced in occupations where unions had achieved a measure of strength.

There were a number of strikes during the 1870s, some quite violent. Much of the violence, however, was initiated by a terrorist organization known as the Molly Maguires, which Millis and Montgomery[4] have called "a kind of labor Ku Klux Klan." Never a large group, the Molly Maguires

> terrorized the community with a success entirely disproportionate to their strength and numbers. . . . Between 1871 and 1879 the Pennsylvania coal strikes gravitated, to a considerable extent, into the hands of the Molly Mag-uires, and several of the Mollys, in turn gravitated into the hands of the Pink-erton Detectives.

Few of the strikes during this period succeeded, however. The courts came to the aid of employers and granted injunctions liberally. Where physical vio-lence occurred or threatened, Federal troops were used to settle industrial disputes.

A second attempt at national federation had been started before the panic of 1873. The National Labor Union was founded in 1866. This was a federa-tion of trade unions, but it had strong political overtones. Organizationally, it had a rather loose structure, composed of city centrals, national trade unions, and individual local unions. It also included in its membership some reform organizations, which ranged all the way from anarchists to women suffragists, and included a few socialist groups. When the first convention was held in 1866, unemployment was a major problem, and the federation urged legisla-tive enactment of the eight-hour day. Partly as the result of this agitation, the eight-hour day for federal employees was established in 1868. However, the general eight-hour movement failed, as did many other objectives of the Na-tional Labor Union and its member organizations.

There was some support in the National Labor Union for producers coop-eratives. Indeed, the national shoemakers union—the Order of the Knights of St. Crispin—had as one of its objectives the ultimate self-employment of its members. The Ironmoulders, led by William H. Sylvis, went beyond the mere advocacy of producers cooperatives and set up at least ten cooperative foundries after losing strikes in 1867 and 1868. None of these survived for any length of time. A number of other trades also attempted producers coopera-tives with an equal lack of success. The flirtation with such radical reform

---

4. Millis and Montgomery, *Ibid.,* p. 49.

movements undoubtedly contributed to the relatively short life of the National Labor Union.

The trade unions formed during the 1860s bore a close resemblance to today's craft unions. At the local level, skilled workers in a common trade— carpenters, ironmoulders, and the members of the railroad Brotherhoods, for example—banded together to protect their job security and earnings. This was done both through control of apprenticeship and the establishment of wage lists. In a number of skilled trades, as local unions multiplied, national organizations were formed. This was partly a consequence of the extension of market areas, which had led some craft union leaders to believe that it was necessary to broaden their geographic jurisdictions. With the improvement of transportation facilities, as the nation's railroad network expanded, local unions often could not stand alone against employers. If they went on strike, products or workers could be imported from other communities. Local unions provided the funds for national treasuries through per capita taxes. This permitted the national office to support local unions in strike activities and to exert some control over competition from other areas when a local union went on strike.

The national union could also try to establish wage and other standards extending beyond a single community. Under these circumstances, a growing amount of power and authority gravitated into the hands of the national union leaders. Local union leaders often did not relinquish authority readily. But in time, as organization in specific crafts spread, the locus of power in American trade unionism gradually shifted from the local to the national union.

Early attempts at federation, with the formation of the National Trades Union (1834) and the National Labor Union (1866), had failed.But even when the second of these federations collapsed, many of the national unions survived.

The Knights of Labor

A new development in 1869 was to lead to one of the more turbulent eras in the history of American trade unionism. In that year, the Knights of Labor was founded. The purpose of this organization was to establish "One Big Union." Even when they had banded into federations, leaders of the national craft unions had jealously guarded their power and prerogatives. The emergence of a new "federation," in which power was to be centralized at the top, set the stage for a period of internecine warfare in the American labor movement.

The founder of the Knights of Labor was Uriah Stephens, who as a young man had been trained for the Baptist ministry. Although the original nucleus of the Knights of Labor consisted of seven tailors, Stephens had come to the conclusion that craft unionism was not the right approach to organization, because of what he considered to be its divisive effects on the labor movement.

He wanted to bring together into a single organization all workers, including farmers, without regard to occupation, nationality, sex, or creed.

The Knights of Labor was initially a secret society. During most of the tenure of Uriah Stephens as Grand Master Workman the organization grew slowly, although it continued to expand even after the crash of 1873. Many workers, who might otherwise have joined, stayed out of the organization, however, because of the vow of secrecy that each member had to swear. Catholic workers, for example, were unwilling to join a secret society. When Terrence V. Powderly became Grand Master Workman in 1879, he eliminated the secret vow. Up to that time Cardinal Gibbons had opposed the Knights of Labor, not only because of the vow but also because he believed the group had socialistic tendencies. Powderly convinced him that this was not so, and the Cardinal's opposition ended. Following this, Catholic workers felt free to join the Order, and its membership grew more rapidly. For example, on October 1, 1879, there were slightly more than 9,000 workers in the Order. By July 1, 1883, this number had increased to almost 52,000.

The most powerful impetus to the growth of the Knights of Labor came in 1885. There was a strike that year against a wage cut on the Wabash and the Missouri, Kansas, and Texas railroads, both of which were controlled by Jay Gould, one of the more powerful financiers in the nation at that time. The railroad shopmen went out first and were supported by the running crafts. At the Moberly, Missouri shops, layoffs were interpreted as a lockout, and the Knights of Labor threatened to call a general strike on all Gould railways. Because he was engaged in the manipulation of his railroad stocks at that time, Gould felt he could not afford a strike. Not only did he capitulate to the demands of the striking workers, but he firmly avowed his belief in trade unions. Following this, there was a virtual stampede into the Knights of Labor. Membership in 1885 stood at slightly more than 111,000. The following year it leaped to almost 730,000 and was a power that had to be reckoned with by employers in many industries and areas. After this upsurge, membership in the Knights of Labor declined, at first gradually, then precipitously. By 1890, membership was down to an estimated 100,000, and the Knights of Labor clearly was on the way out.

Conflict Between the Knights and the National Unions

Why did the Knights of Labor fail to survive? Essentially, the answer is that the notion of "One Big Union" came into conflict with the various national unions of skilled craftsmen. The Knights had wanted to organize everyone, excluding lawyers, bankers, gamblers, stockbrokers, and saloon keepers. But workers were not to be organized along occupational lines. Obviously, in an organization of any size, there must be some hierarchical arrangement, and this was recognized by the Knights. The organization which was planned was quite simple. At the top was the National Assembly. Below this were District Assemblies made up of Local Assemblies. The Local Assemblies could consist of existing local unions, most of which were made up of skilled craftsmen. But the leaders of the Knights did not intend that all Local Assemblies be limited to the members of a single craft. Some could follow industrial lines, and others could be mixed.

Relatively few District Assemblies actually came into existence. The first was established in Philadelphia, in 1873, consisting of about eighty locals. A second was planned for the anthracite coal region, but was never actually formed. The third assembly covered locals in western Pennsylvania. Basically, the leaders of the Knights wanted the District Assemblies to be geographical in character—not limited to a specific craft or industry. However, some of the District Assemblies were made up almost entirely of workers in a specific industry and geographic area. Finally, following the upsurge in membership in 1886, National Assemblies were authorized. But this authorization came after the Knights of Labor had passed its apogee and was on the way down.

Throughout the period of rapid growth of the Knights of Labor, there was a running battle between the leaders of the national craft unions and those dedicated to the notion of "One Big Union." In part, the rapid growth of the Knights of Labor from 1883 to 1886 was facilitated by the absorption of local unions already in existence. Some of these locals found themselves torn between two loyalties. If they belonged to a national union, the officers of the national wanted to direct their bargaining and other activities. There was no place for the national union in the Knights of Labor table of organization, although it could accomodate locals of skilled craftsmen. Also, the leaders of the Knights wanted to have the final say on all union matters.

This conflict was apparent from the outset, and as early as 1881 the national unions—with support from some disaffected members of the Knights of Labor—had established the Federation of Organized Trades and Labor Unions of the United States and Canada. This organization was originally set up, among other reasons, to engage in political action, but it soon became embroiled in the growing controversy between the leaders of the Knights and the national unions. Throughout this controversy there were workers who belonged to both a national union and the Knights of Labor, but these workers could not give their complete loyalty to either.

The growing friction came to a head in 1886. On May 18 of that year a conference was held between the leaders of the Knights and the national unions, which was expected to lead to a "treaty of peace." It was agreed that the Knights were not to attract local unions without the consent of national headquarters. The charter of any local joining the Knights without this consent was to be revoked. At the same time the Knights proposed an exchange of cards, which would have permitted the continuation of dual membership. This was unanimously rejected by the leaders of the national unions. Little came out of this conference, and at their convention of 1886, the leaders of the Knights ordered all members of the Cigarmakers Union—one of the more powerful craft unions—to resign from their union. The conflict was now in the open. In December, 1886, at Columbus, Ohio, a convention of national unions was held. Although only about half of the national unions then in existence, plus a few city centrals, were represented, the American Federation of Labor was formed at this convention. All national unions were urged to join, and the break with the Knights was complete.

After 1886, the membership of unions affiliated with the American Federation of Labor began to grow slowly, and membership in the Knights of Labor began to decline. The decline was accelerated when the Knights called a number of strikes which they lost. Continued resistance within the Knights to the formation of National Assemblies along craft or occupational lines also contributed to its eventual demise. Craft unions began to leave the Knights *en bloc* and to reaffiliate with nationals in the AF of L. The Knights of Labor was never formally disbanded, but after 1890, this organization was no longer a significant part of the American labor movement.

The Formative Period of the AF of L

When the AF of L was founded in 1886, its constituent national unions had a total membership of roughly 175,000, about one fourth the membership of the Knights of Labor. Membership in the Knights declined sharply after 1886, while the number of workers in the AF of L increased slowly. It was not until the turn of the century that the AF of L could claim more members than the Knights of Labor had signed up at peak strength. However, membership in the AF of L continued to grow slowly.

Further efforts were made to conciliate the differences between the declining Knights of Labor and the slowly growing AF of L. As late as 1888, the Knights proposed a mutual recognition of membership cards, which would have permitted a worker to belong to both a trade union and the Order. But at the same negotiations, leaders of the AF of L proposed that the Knights revoke all charters of trade districts, and thus become a purely benevolent, educational, and humanitarian order. Under such conditions, leaders of the AF of L averred, they were quite willing to have union members also belong to the Knights of Labor, but they completely rejected the notion that a worker who belonged only to the Knights was a union man. The practical effect of this was to keep members of the Knights who did not belong to one of the national trade unions out of closed shops.

The unions which banded together to form the AF of L, and those which subsequently joined, were organized along craft lines, and their membership consisted of skilled workers.[5] By the time the AF of L was formed, the center

5. There were two major exceptions; the United Mine Workers and the Brewery Workers—both industrial unions—enrolled all workers under their jurisdictions without regard to skill or occupational classifications.

of power in the craft unions had gravitated to their national headquarters. In setting up the AF of L, the leaders of the craft unions made sure that this power would not be surrendered to the offices of the Federation. The national union leaders also agreed that there would be only one legitimate union in each occupation or industry. These agreements formed the two basic principles upon which the AF of L was founded.

The Principle of Autonomy

The American Federation of Labor, it was hoped, would be the spokesman for all organized workers on some matters. But partly because of their prior experience with the Knights, and partly because of the structure of the unions that initially formed the Federation, it was agreed that there would be no interference from the outside with the activities of each of the individual national unions.

This meant that each national union would be free to determine which workers it would attempt to organize, the dues to be paid by each member, the tactics to be employed in organization, and the formulation of bargaining demands. Each of the craft unions was to be free to make its own plans with respect to its members. The Federation could take a stand on issues of *public* policy, but it was not to tamper with the internal affairs of its constituent unions.

The Principle of Exclusive Jurisdiction

The second of the major principles upon which the AF of L was founded called for one legitimate union in each trade. The great fear of the leaders of the national unions—and of the AF of L—throughout the era under discussion was that of "dual" unionism, that is, more than one union competing for membership within a single occupation.

This principle was at variance with that adopted by unions in other parts of the world. The British trade unions at that time, for example, held to the notion that no union had the exclusive right to organize any given group of workers. In the United States, while the craft unions that predominated by the end of the nineteenth century were anxious to limit their members to skilled tradesmen, they were equally anxious to avoid the splintering of these tradesmen into various competing groups. During the early stage of the development of the AF of L, the principle of exclusive jurisdiction posed relatively few problems. But later, as the complexity of economic life increased, it was to lead to a considerable number of jurisdictional disputes.

Somewhat surprisingly, the principle of exclusive jurisdiction worked well during the early years of the AF of L. Dual unionism could not be entirely suppressed. There were, for example, dual unions in the clothing and shoe industries. Elsewhere, however, dual unionism failed to survive.

It was originally thought that one of the functions to be performed by the Federation would be the prevention of jurisdictional disputes. But it was not clear exactly how this was to be accomplished if the Federation was to be kept weak—and this was something the leaders of the national unions insisted upon.

There were a few cases, after the turn of the century, in which the AF of L intervened to settle jurisdictional controversies by recommending amalgamation. This approach was most successful when the disputants consisted of one strong and one weak union. The leaders of a weak union could readily see that it would be the better part of valor to merge with their stronger brethren. But there were also cases of disagreement between two strong unions, when neither was willing to accept the AF of L's jurisdictional award. In a case decided in 1903, for example, the AF of L ruled that the Operating Engineers were to have jurisdiction over all members of this craft wherever employed. Most other unions went along with this, but the Brewery Workers refused to give up their operating engineers who, incidentally, did not want to leave this union. Four years later, despite repeated gestures by the AF of L, the Brewers were still adamant. The AF of L then revoked the charter of the Brewery Workers. The Brewers had many friends in the labor movement, however, and when the AF of L met in convention that year the delegates ordered the restoration of the Brewery Workers' charter. They went beyond this to amend the AF of L constitution, relieving the Executive Council of its right to revoke charters, which henceforth could be done only by a two-thirds majority of delegates to the annual convention.

There were other difficulties with jurisdictional awards between pairs of strong unions, such as the Teamsters vs. the Brewery Workers, and the Carpenters vs. Machinists, when both unions were represented on the Executive Council. Some of the AF of L's jurisdictional awards led to mergers. Some involving pairs of strong unions were never really settled. Others led to the withdrawal of unions from the Federation. Those who seceded were usually relatively weak unions. Of the fifty unions that withdrew from the AF of L prior to 1933, for example, only a dozen were to survive their secession. This is at least a rough measure of the success the relatively weak AF of L had in enforcing the principle of exclusive jurisdiction.

No Political Involvement

The two basic principles of what some have termed "the AF of L settlement" were autonomy and exclusive jurisdiction. A further assumption upon which the AF of L operated was that American trade unions would have to rely upon economic power to achieve their ends. The American trade union movement was to avoid political alliances or entanglements. It must be remembered that by the time the AF of L was formed, there was a fairly long history of labor organization in the United States, and that some of the earlier organizations had been basically reformist in character.

The leaders of the AF of L made it clear that they had no intention of overthrowing the capitalistic system. The leaders of the craft unions wanted to improve the economic lot of their members. This was to be done by tightly sewing up each craft or trade so that strictly economic pressures—such as strikes and boycotts—could be brought to bear on recalcitrant employers who resisted their demands. The approach of AF of L leaders was entirely pragmatic. The kind of unionism they forged was called "business unionism" by their critics both in this country and abroad. This term, which was used contemptuously by Socialists and others who condemned the AF of L approach, was an appropriate one. Trade unions, their leaders insisted, were designed to get "more here and now" for their members. They were not to be concerned with ultimate goals and lofty aspirations. They were to achieve their stated goals by a show of their own economic muscle, not by relying upon political action.

This did not mean that trade union members were to ignore politics. It did mean, as the first president of the AF of L succinctly put it, that American trade unions would "reward their friends and punish their enemies" without respect to party affiliation.

The Founders of the AF of L

Who were the men that formed the first successful federation of national trade unions in the United States? Among the most active leaders of the movement were Adolph Strasser, P. J. McGuire, W. H. Foster, and Samuel Gompers. Strasser, who had emigrated to the United States from Germany, was president of the Cigarmakers Union, a powerful craft union in its day. P. J. McGuire was the founder and leader of the Brotherhood of Carpenters and Joiners, which was also a power in the late nineteenth-century labor movement. But the man who undoubtedly did more than anyone else to hold the new organization together was Samuel Gompers, formerly a vice president of the Cigarmakers Union. Perhaps the most important step taken at the Columbus convention where the AF of L was organized was the election of Gompers as president of the new Federation (at a salary of $1,000 per year). From that time on, Samuel Gompers devoted his life to the AF of L. He aspired to no public office and refused to use his position in later years to add to his own income. He was totally devoted to the trade union cause.

Both Strasser and Gompers had been reared in the tradition of German Socialism. They continued their study of this doctrine while they practiced their craft in New York. To ease the monotony of their tasks, the cigarmakers would designate one of their group to read aloud while the remainder worked. Each member would make a contribution to make up for the wages lost by the reader. Gompers, who was considered to have a pleasant and resonant voice, was often designated as the reader. He would read aloud from Karl Marx's *Das Kapital* or from other Socialist literature of the day.

Strasser and Gompers recognized that socialism had little appeal for the average American worker, who was job-conscious but not class-conscious. Indeed, many workers hoped to remain at their jobs only long enough to accumulate a stake, which would permit them to go into business for themselves or to move west in search of land. Though well grounded in socialist theory, both Strasser and Gompers rejected it as a guide to the American labor movement. Although Strasser and Gompers continued to have an interest in the welfare of all workers, they felt that there was only one formula which could lead to trade union success in the United States. This was the organization of skilled workers along craft lines in national unions that would manage their own internal affairs. Their objectives were to be achieved through economic strength rather than political action. The basic goal was the immediate improvement of wages, hours, and working conditions.

The craft unionists were anxious to be accepted by the society in which they operated, and they went to great pains to emphasize that they had no plans for the transformation of that society. This is illustrated by an excerpt from the testimony of Strasser before the U.S. Senate Committee on Education and Labor during a hearing held in 1883. The chairman of the committee had asked Mr. Strasser what ultimate ends were sought by trade unions. In reply, Strasser said: "We have no ultimate ends. We are going on from day to day. We are fighting only for immediate objects—objects that can be realized in a few years." Somewhat later, the chairman said, ". . . you are a little sensitive lest it should be thought you are a mere theorizer." To which Strasser replied: "Well, we say in our constitution that we are opposed to theorists, and I have to represent the organization here. We are all practical men."[6]

More than three decades later, Samuel Gompers was to reiterate these views. He stressed that the AF of L was guided by the lessons of history; that it was bound to no theory of social reform, and that it sought only the immediate improvement of the economic conditions of workingmen. The founders of the AF of L were thoroughly familiar with earlier unsuccessful attempts to establish even a moderately radical form of trade unionism in the United States. They were convinced that a successful trade union movement in this country had to be essentially conservative in its aims.

Gompers became president of the AF of L in 1886, and was to continue in this office, with the exception of a single year (1894–1895), until his death in 1925. He guided the AF of L through its formative period during the years after the turn of the century when employer resistance hardened, and later, when opposition from dissidents within some of the unions threatened to alter the fundamental character of American trade unionism by urging the adoption of a socialist program.

A decade after the AF of L had been formed, its leaders could feel that

---

6. J. B. S. Hardman, *American Labor Dynamics* (New York: Harcourt, Brace and Co., Inc., 1928), p. 99.

they had found the formula for a stable and successful brand of American trade unionism. The intervening years had not been easy. In 1892, for example, the Association of Iron and Steel Workers led a strike against the Carnegie Homestead Plant. It was a bitter strike, conducted with much violence, and the union was utterly defeated. By this time the Carnegie Corporation was the dominant firm in the steel industry, and when it broke off relations with the union, other companies in the Pittsburgh area followed suit.

The following year saw the nation once again plunged into a severe financial panic, but fortunately for the AF of L the depression which followed was relatively short. The next year, 1894, was also a bad one for the trade-union movement. In that year the American Railway Union, led by Eugene V. Debs, went on strike against the Pullman Company. This union, which was making an effort to unite all railroad workers into a single organization, was not affiliated with the AF of L, but there was some pressure within the Federation for support of the Pullman strike. Gompers urged all AF of L affiliates to stand clear of the strike, which eventually collapsed when President Cleveland sent federal troops to Chicago, (ostensibly to protect the U.S. mails but effectively to break the strike).

The violence of the Homestead and Pullman strikes, which led some to consider that it was necessary for the government to intervene in the latter dispute, caused many citizens to view the growing labor movement with alarm. Some of the public alarm died down, however, as economic conditions improved and the craft unions adhered fairly closely to the new brand of business unionism.

The Victory of Craft Unionism

The relative success of the older unions which had formed the AF of L, and their ability to survive the crash of 1893, stimulated the formation of an increasing number of new craft unions. Between 1897 and 1904, for example, the number of national and international unions affiliated with the AF of L rose from 58 to 120. This number was to decline during the following decade, partly as a result of union mergers, but also due to the liquidation of a few of the weaker unions.

After 1904, there was continued growth, although it was quite slow. From 1897 to 1904, the number of union members in the United States increased from 447,000 to slightly more than 2 million. By 1914, however, this figure had increased to only 2.7 million. Much of the growth that occurred after 1904 was concentrated in a few of the stronger unions; the most rapid growth was in the building trades, transportation, communications, and mining. In 1914, the unions in these industry groups accounted for 55 per cent of total union membership in the United States. Thus, craft unionism was limited to relatively few lines of economic activity. Most manufacturing industry was predominantly unorganized, and the same was true of virtually all service activities. The craft form of organization appeared to be particularly suitable in building construction and transportation. The major union in the coal industry, however, was organized along industrial lines. It was one of two unions in the country that had succeeded in establishing and maintaining this form of organization.

Emergence of the Labor-Management Agreement

By the late 1890s, one of the goals of the craft unions was well along the road to realization. This was the signing of labor-management agreements, which were the result of negotiations between union leaders and employers. Although there was no legal compulsion to do so at that time, a growing number of employers had "recognized" unions.

In 1890 an agreement was negotiated in the glass container industry, and in 1891 the National Union of Ironmoulders and the Stove Founders Defense Association signed an agreement which has often been characterized as the precursor of the modern labor-management agreement. The bituminous coal miners succeeded in negotiating an agreement in 1897, and the following year the anthracite miners also reached agreement with the operators. Organized printers signed a contract with an association of employers in 1898. Agreements between some of the building craft unions and employers, and also between the operating crafts and the railroads, had been signed as early as 1880, but these were exceptions, not the rule. By the turn of the century, however, a growing number of employers entered into agreements with unions representing craftsmen in their employ. When a trade union had achieved sufficient strength to negotiate a signed agreement with an employer—or better still with a group of employers—it had "arrived." The negotiated trade agreement was, of course, the hallmark of successful business unionism.

The IWW—A New Threat of Radical Unionism

Everything considered, the period from 1897 to 1904 was a good one for the AF of L. These were years of prosperity and rapid growth for the trade unions, which experienced almost a fourfold increase in seven years. The craft unions were not without their problems, however, and during the decade following 1904 their problems were to multiply. Part of their troubles were due to the establishment of a rival labor organization in 1905—an organization which had an impact far out of proportion to its numerical strength.

The early growth of the craft unions was largely concentrated in the urban East where the building trades were important, and where there was a large number of railroad and other transport workers. The Miners, who were organized along industrial lines, were also highly successful in the East. But farther west, in the hard-rock mining communities and the scattered coal towns of the Mountain States, the threat of dual unionism had been raised as early as

1898, when the American Labor Union was established as a rival to the AF of L. This grew out of an earlier organization known as the Western Federation of Miners, which initially sought to organize only hard-rock miners and smelter employees.

The leaders of the American Labor Union were extremely militant, and they sought to broaden the scope of their organization to include all laborers in one big union. In June 1905, this group met with representatives of the Socialist Labor and Trade Alliance, and with leaders of a few dissident AF of L locals. A scattering of intellectuals, members of various socialist parties, and some disgruntled trade unionists also attended this convention, which was held in Chicago. The only features that bound the delegates together were their militancy and revolutionary outlook.

Out of this assembly grew the Industrial Workers of the World, a revolutionary organization which was the complete antithesis of the conservative, job-conscious AF of L. Several of the more colorful radical leaders of the day played leading roles at this meeting, including "Wild Bill" Haywood, of the Western Federation of Miners; Mother Jones, an organizer for the United Mine Workers; Daniel DeLeon, leader of the revolutionary Socialist Labor Party; and Eugene Debs, who headed the more moderate Socialist Party. But while these and other leaders of the IWW could agree on the revolutionary ends of the new organization, they were far from agreed on the means. They wanted to abolish the wage system, but could not agree whether this would be accomplished best through political action or by more direct measures. Almost from the start, there were serious differences of opinion between the intellectual revolutionaries and the somewhat more pragmatic leaders of the miners. Within a few years, the Western Federation of Miners withdrew from the new organization it had helped create, to become once again a relatively conservative trade union.

The leaders of the IWW were exuberant in their revolutionary zeal. Organizers would move into a mining community and urge the local miners to go on strike. They were ruthless in their treatment of employers and were not in the least averse to violence. After reaching a "settlement," the organizers would move on. After a time, without the leadership needed to hold them together, the miners were often persuaded to go back to their former terms of employment. Thus, while the IWW created considerable stir throughout the West, its long-run achievements were negligible.

During the early days, when the IWW limited its activities to the mining areas of the West, the leaders of the AF of L were not seriously concerned, although they always opposed dual unionism. In 1912, however, the IWW began to move into some of the industrial centers of the East, such as Lawrence, Massachusetts, and Paterson, New Jersey, where it led bitter strikes whose scars were not eradicated for many years. The Paterson strike was a failure, and the IWW left no lasting establishment in Lawrence. Following this unsuccessful incursion into the industrial Northeast, membership in the IWW declined sharply. Indeed, it has been estimated that total membership in the "Wobblies" never reached 60,000. However, the short-term impact of this turbulent and radical organization was far out of proportion to the number of card-carrying members it was able to sign up. The decline, which started when the IWW failed to achieve lasting trade agreements, was hastened when its leaders opposed American entry into World War I.

Leaders of the AF of L became alarmed by the activities of the IWW, particularly after its brief foray into the East. Employers, and those sympathetic to the employers' point of view, used the record of the IWW as a propaganda tool to combat the conservative AF of L unions. The AF of L's leaders reacted by becoming even more conservative. Samuel Gompers and other leaders of the AF of L, missed no opportunities to publicize the pragmatic, nonrevolutionary basis of craft unionism. They not only denounced the dual unionism of the IWW, but condemned its revolutionary goals and violent tactics. There is little evidence that these denunciations won the applause of many employers, or of the community at large, however. By the time the IWW had started its campaign, employers, including many who recognized the conservatism of the AF of L, were organizing to resist the spread of unionism, especially in manufacturing.

Growing Job Consciousness

One obstacle to the formation of lasting trade unionism during the nineteenth century was the mobility of workers. There was a steady stream of immigrants, many of whom would stop in urban areas only long enough to accumulate sufficient savings to permit them to move westward. After the turn of the century, however, although the number of immigrants continued to rise, opportunities for self-employment and land ownership diminished. This strengthened the job consciousness of craft unionists who felt that they had to protect themselves from the competition of the new immigrants; at first by limiting their organization to the skilled trades, but eventually by urging that restrictions be imposed upon the flow of immigrants into the nation. Partly because of technological developments, employers were not at first willing to go along with such restrictions.

The trend toward fewer and larger industrial units had started long before the advent of the AF of L. It was accelerated during the first quarter of the twentieth century by the development of mass production techniques. As the size of plants increased, employers found that they could break skilled jobs into their component parts so that the work could be performed by semiskilled or, in some cases, unskilled laborers. In building trades, transportation, and mining, there was little opportunity to do this, and these were the sectors in which trade unionism grew. The assembly line technique was spreading throughout the manufacturing sector, however, especially in the heavy industries. This development effectively barred the entry of craft unions, which limited their membership to the skilled trades.

Some employers actively recruited immigrants for the semiskilled and unskilled jobs in their plants. In plants that could be departmentalized, the departments were staffed by workers of different national origins. This practice was followed in some of the gigantic textile mills of New England, for example, where the selection of workers for different departments was not left to chance. Many of the immigrants brought with them their antipathies toward other ethnic groups. They continued to speak their native language and to follow many of their native customs after coming to this country. This was not discouraged by employers, since it was an effective bar to communication and since it precluded solidarity among all the workers in the plant. Unions raised no objections to these practices; indeed, they made no overtures toward the growing number of semiskilled and unskilled workers in manufacturing.

Coupled with growing employer opposition and the side effects of the activities of the IWW, this self-limitation to the skilled trades contributed to slow union growth from 1904 until our entry into World War I. In 1904, total union membership in the United States amounted to 6.4 per cent of the civilian labor force. In 1916, on the eve of our entry into World War I, this proportion had increased to only 6.9 per cent.

Trade Unionism During World War I

Most of the trade unions founded before the formation of the AF of L were unable to withstand economic adversity. Recurring financial panics often spelled their ruin, and the initial effects of the Civil War on unions were disastrous. By the time we were preparing to enter World War I, however, there had been vast changes. By that time federated craft unions had been able to survive for three decades. While their membership had increased only slowly, there were relatively few years of actual decline. A growing number of employers had been forced to recognize unions, and this had been achieved without legal sanctions. Public acceptance of trade unionism was far from a reality, but at the same time public hostility had clearly diminished. There had been organized attacks by employers in some areas, and the well-publicized activities of the IWW had no doubt contributed to the slow rate of union growth. But in spite of these obstacles, trade unions had expanded. A labor movement had been firmly established in the United States.

An important deterrent to rapid union growth throughout the life of the AF of L was the structural rigidity of federated craft unions. The growing number of unskilled and semiskilled workers in manufacturing was largely ignored by the unions in the AF of L. The building trades, transportation, and mining were the strongholds of organized labor. The great manufacturing enterprises of the nation had resisted trade unionism, and the craft unions were not flexible enough to override the opposition of the manufacturers.

Wartime Union Growth

From the turn of the century until the beginning of World War I, total union membership in the United States about tripled, but this growth was from a relatively small base. There was a strong upsurge in union membership during the war and the immediate postwar period, however. The number of workers belonging to unions almost doubled between 1916 and 1920, when there were more than 5 million union members in the nation. At that time they accounted for 12 per cent of the civilian labor force.

There were various reasons for this rapid growth. As thousands of young men entered military service, labor shortages developed. At the peak of the war effort, more than 5 million men had been drawn from the civilian labor force into the service. Also, the supply of labor had been sharply curtailed by growing restrictions on immigration.

The leaders of the AF of L supported the war effort. The generally conservative views of union leaders encouraged some employers to seek their wartime support, and also encouraged some employers to enter into agreements with them. Government operation of the railroads and government administration of some other sectors of the economy provided a further stimulus to union growth, since the administrative agencies adopted policies which, by and large, encouraged union membership. Employers faced with an unprecedented demand for their products were reluctant to run the risk of strikes or other labor disturbances. They were also more agreeable to union demands for higher wages than they had been in the past. This no doubt resulted less from altruistic or patriotic motives than from the innovation of the cost-plus contract. Higher costs meant a larger "plus" and thus higher profits.

The growth of union membership was not widespread. As might be expected, most of it occurred in industries such as the metal-working, machinery, shipbuilding, and garment industries, those most closely associated with the war effort. It has been estimated that about three fourths of all union growth between 1915 and 1920 was concentrated in these industries.[7] Thus, growth was largely limited to existing craft unions.

Unions after the Armistice

Although there was a brief business recession shortly after announcement of the Armistice of November, 1918, union membership continued to grow. There were large gains in total membership both in 1919 and 1920. The drop in business activity was very brief, and the labor market remained tight until demobilization was completed. Also, the demand for American products remained at a high level while the war-torn economies of the European combatants

---

7. Leo Wolman, *Ebb and Flow in Trade Unionism* (New York: National Bureau of Economic Research, 1936), p. 28.

were being restored. Due to favorable economic conditions, and partly no doubt due to inertia, unions continued to sign up new members. For a time it seemed as though broadly based trade unionism might be realized in the United States, but the immediate postwar prosperity was relatively short-lived. The economy took a downward plunge in 1920, and this marked an end to the growth of federated craft unionism in the United States.

Trade Unions During The 1920s

Union Membership in the Twenties

After five years of steady and rapid growth, union membership began to decline in 1920. This decline continued in every year but one until 1934. It would be going too far to say that the institution of trade unionism had been widely accepted during World War I. But active resistance to unionism was at a minimum when the overriding concern of the nation was the defeat of Germany. The postwar reaction to the inevitable dislocations of war came slowly, but when it came, it did so with a vengeance.

World War I had involved America in a large-scale international venture for the first time. By the end of 1919, however, it was clear that the mood of international cooperation had passed. The forces of isolationism were victorious in Congress, and they succeeded in keeping us out of the League of Nations. On the domestic scene there was a resurgence of conservatism. The successful Bolshevik Revolution in Russia added to the alarm of those who, without looking carefully into the matter, suspected all trade unions of radical leanings. There were, to be sure, a few radical political parties in the nation— including the Communist Labor and the Communist parties. Competent scholars have estimated, however, that the membership of all the radical parties lumped together at that time would account for scarcely one tenth of 1 per cent of the nation's adult population. There was great concern about the "Red Menace," however. Anything that appeared to threaten the "return to normalcy" was often linked in the public mind with the threat of revolution, and the press rarely did anything to disabuse the public of this notion.

The Postwar "Strike Wave"

During World War I and the immediate post-Armistice period, there was little strike activity. Late in 1919, however, there were a few widely publicized strikes. These were cited by opponents of trade unionism as examples of the growing threat unions posed to the American way of life. The Boston Police Strike, which began in September 1919, provided a great deal of propaganda for those preaching the alleged threat of trade unionism to the American system.

The Boston police had a number of grievances. Their minimum pay was less than $100 per month, and out of this the officers had to buy their own uniforms. Following the lead of the nation's craftsmen, the Boston police organized a union and affiliated with the AF of L. They did this despite an injunction from Police Commissioner Curtis not to affiliate with an outside organization. Charges were brought against a number of officers known to be union members and, following a hearing on police union activities, nineteen officers were suspended by the Commissioner. The remainder of the force then threatened to strike. The mayor of Boston appointed a committee to settle the dispute, and this committee suggested a compromise. Commissioner Curtis refused to consider a compromise settlement, however, and on September 9, a large proportion of the force failed to show up for evening roll call. The press quickly announced that Boston was almost entirely without police protection. The city's hoodlums—recognizing an unparalleled opportunity when they saw one—thereupon had a field day. Windows were smashed; stores were looted; and there were numerous incidents of violence. The mayor asked Governor Calvin Coolidge for assistance from the National Guard, and on the following day this was provided. A call was also issued for volunteer police. Both the Guardsmen and the volunteers were inexperienced, however, and the city remained in a state of virtual anarchy.

The Boston Central Labor Union briefly considered calling a general strike in support of the policemen's demands, but recognizing that public opinion was overwhelmingly against the police strike, the trade union leaders decided against this action. Commissioner Curtis then began to deal with the strike on his own terms. He discharged the nineteen officers who had been suspended, and he began to recruit a new force. Samuel Gompers protested to Governor Coolidge, who then issued the dictum that there was "no right to strike against the public safety by anybody, anywhere, anytime." This clearly spelled the end of the Boston Police Strike. It also made Coolidge a national figure, and undoubtedly played an important part in his subsequent election as vice president.

Although local in character, the Boston Police Strike attracted national attention. To the public it seemed that this was only the beginning of a wave of strike activity. Shortly after the beginning of the Boston Police Strike, there was a large-scale walkout in the steel industry involving several hundred thousand workers. Although subsequent investigation revealed that the steel workers had a number of genuine grievances, steel management quickly labeled the strike as Communist inspired. One of the leaders of the strike was William Z. Foster—at that time a Syndicalist—who subsequently became a leader of the American Communist Party.

There was little mention of the real issues involved in press accounts of the steel strike. At that time the standard shift in the steel industry was twelve hours, and when a worker changed shifts he was on the job for twenty-four consecutive hours without rest. The pay of steel workers was low, and working conditions were often deplorable. These factors seemed much less important to the newspapers than the fact that Foster was seeking to organize the workers along industrial lines. Steel management—led by Elbert H. Gary of U.S. Steel—refused to have any dealings with union spokesmen, and the strike eventually collapsed. Even before the steel strike had ended, however, there was a major strike in the coal fields, which added to the public alarm. The miners had an industrial union, and some of their spokesmen had advocated nationalization of all coal mines. This seemed to clinch the case for those who equated unionism with radicalism.

There were growing demands that the government "do something" to halt the wave of "labor terrorism." Attorney General A. Mitchell Palmer, whose name had been prominently associated with the "Red Scare" following World War I, was quick to respond to what he considered the pressure of public opinion. President Wilson, by then too ill to keep in touch with daily affairs, was not aware of what was going on and could not restrain his Attorney General. The day before the coal strike was scheduled to begin, Mr. Palmer secured an injunction from a federal court enjoining the leaders of the miners' union from doing anything to further the strike. In spite of the injunction, almost 400,000 coal miners walked out of the pits. Their leaders, however, could not participate in the strike without running the risk of criminal contempt of court, and the strike collapsed.

There can be no doubt that by the beginning of the 1920s, the public had grown increasingly fearful about trade unionism. There were other factors, however, which contributed to the decline of the federated craft unions in the United States. These included important shifts in the composition of the work force as the result of growing mass production, a new and energetic "open shop" campaign, and general prosperity which, however, concealed a substantial amount of unemployment—much of it concentrated in the skilled crafts that had been highly organized by AF of L unions.

The American Plan

In the early 1920s, anti-red hysteria and a number of major strikes made it relatively easy for certain employers to openly attack trade unions. "Yellow-dog" contracts, which bound workers not to join a union as a condition of employment, were widely used by employers to combat what they termed the "un-American" institution of trade unionism. The main attack was on the closed shop. Under this form of the agreement, employers hired union members only and obtained workers from union hiring halls rather than going directly into the labor market. A housing shortage after World War I was attributed by some to the high wages of construction workers and the allegedly restrictive practices of building trade unions. The slow pace of construction cut sharply into the ranks of the construction unions. In three years, according to Wolman's estimates, membership in construction unions dropped by almost 100,000 from the peak of nearly 900,000 which had been reached in 1920.[8]

A substantial number of employers proclaimed their acceptance of the principle of trade unionism, but many of them argued that unions should not be "outside" organizations. According to this employer-sponsored approach, unions should be restricted to the workers of a single company; they should free themselves from the clutches of "dues hungry outsiders." In a number of industries this appeal was successful. Local unions broke away from their national organizations and became "company unions." The term "company union" eventually came to have a definite connotation. It meant a company-*dominated* union, which engaged in little if any collective bargaining.

Why did workers in some industries break away from the national unions that contributed to their collective strength? Some employers were rather outspoken about their preference for company unions. And they could point out that growing unemployment in some areas would make it relatively easy for them to recruit nonunion workers. Also, many workers fortunate enough to remain steadily employed, accepted the arguments that the United States had reached a state of permanent prosperity, and that their ability to share in this depended upon labor-management "cooperation."

This prosperity was not reflected in a rising wage level. One sector of the economy that failed to share in the new prosperity of the twenties was agriculture. Farm prices fell, so that the real earnings of industrial workers went up. Increasingly aggressive competition in the textile and garment industries also led to reduced prices for clothing. Industrial workers were able to obtain the necessities of life on better terms than they had in the past. Under such circumstances there was little pressure for wage increases, and indeed the AF of L unions were often unable to forestall wage cuts.

Finally, the 1920s will be remembered as a decade of unrestrained speculation. Many workers were induced to share in the promised riches of the stock market by purchasing shares in the companies which employed them. Since these workers became capitalists, although rather small ones, they could be convinced that their best interests were tied to the fortunes of the company. Many workers took a somewhat dim view of the unions, which allegedly were hampering managerial efficiency and curtailing company earnings. Such workers could easily be induced to switch from a bona fide trade union to a company union.

The Acceleration of Mass Production

Another factor that contributed to the decline of craft unions during the 1920s was the rapid spread of mass-production techniques. The automobile industry began to grow rapidly during this decade and, as the demand for automobiles

---

8. *Ibid.,* p. 30.

increased, manufacturers turned to assembly line methods. These techniques spread to other industries engaged in continuous production, such as steel. Jobs in the mass-production industries were carefully engineered to reduce them to the lowest skills. Some jobs, which had formerly been performed by skilled craftsmen, were broken into components; each of the operations could then be handled by semiskilled, or at times unskilled, workers after brief on-the-job training.

The AF of L responded by stepping up its organizational activities in steel, the nation's largest industry in terms of value of output, and in the automobile industry. But the craft unionism of the AF of L did not accommodate itself to the growing number of unskilled and semiskilled workers in these industries. There was also an effort to organize the rapidly expanding southern textile industry, and to bring within the AF of L the growing number of women workers in industry in general. All of these organizing campaigns ended in failure.

The AF of L could not cope with the new era of prosperity. Its leaders refused to adapt the rigid structure of their craft unions, which might have permitted a greater amount of organization in the mass-production industries. Instead of becoming more militant, the union leaders tried to adapt to their changing environment by becoming more conservative. Even more than in the past, they preached the gospel of "business unionism." Wages, they urged, should be tied to increasing productivity, and they promised that organized labor would cooperate with management to increase overall efficiency. But these pleas, directed both to the unorganized workers and to management, fell on deaf ears. The blandishments of "bread and butter" unionism had little appeal for the employed industrial workers whose real wages were rising. This made it relatively easy for employers to resist sporadic attempts by unions to organize the unorganized. By 1929, the total number of union members in the country had dropped to 3.4 million. This represented a decline of about 33 per cent from 1920, despite the fact that the nation's labor force had grown during this period.

Then came the financial crash of October 1929, which rocked the foundations of American capitalism. The new era of "permanent" prosperity had come to an end. Unrestrained speculation had greatly inflated the book value of stocks, and the dizzying upward spiral of equity prices stopped abruptly, then plunged downward. Within a matter of months, unemployment was widespread. Much of it was concentrated among the unorganized workers in mass-production industries. To a lesser extent it also affected the nation's skilled craftsmen. Union membership continued to decline after 1929, as unemployment spread throughout the nation. By 1933, total membership had dropped below the 3 million mark, and fewer than 6 per cent of the nation's civilian workers belonged to trade unions. In numerical terms, trade unionism in the United States was weaker than at any time since 1917.

Questions and Exercises

1. In what ways did the labor organizations of the Colonial period resemble modern trade unions, and in what ways did they differ from these unions?

2. Although unions existed before the 1820s, it has been said that a labor *movement* in the United States started during this decade. How would you define a "labor movement"?

3. The National Trades Union, founded in 1834, avoided political issues and in other ways resembled later—and more successful—labor federations. Yet, in 1837, the National Trades Union ceased to exist as an organization. What was the cause of its collapse?

4. What is unique about the National Typographical Union, which was established in 1852?

5. Describe the development of labor organizations during the Civil War. Did trade unions continue to grow immediately after the end of the Civil War?

6. The second national labor federation—The National Labor Union—was founded in 1866. Like its predecessor, the National Trades Union, this federation lasted only a few years. What contributed to the collapse of this organization? Did the national trade unions organized during the 1860s also go out of existence when the federation disappeared?

7. Describe the organizational structure of the Knights of Labor founded in 1869. Compare the structure of the Knights of Labor with earlier labor federations in the United States.

8. What caused membership in the Knights of Labor to increase substantially after 1885?

9. What was the basis of conflict between the Knights of Labor and the national unions of skilled craftsmen? What organization was formed by the disaffected national unions in 1881? As a result of this new organization, there was a showdown between the leaders of the Knights and the leaders of the national unions. What was the outcome of this confrontation in 1886?

10. What are the two basic principles on which the AF of L was founded?

11. How did the AF of L attempt to settle jurisdictional controversies between its constituent national unions? How successful were these attempts, and under what conditions was the AF of L approach successful?

12. What was the attitude of AF of L leaders toward involvement in political matters?

13. Who were the major founders of the AF of L? What was their basic philosophy with respect to trade union organization and the function of unions?

14. Have unions been able to negotiate labor-management agreements throughout their history in the United States? What did the negotiation of agreements mean to unions in terms of the acceptance of trade unionism as an institution?

15. Briefly describe the events that led to organization of the International

Workers of the World. What philosophy was espoused by the leaders of this organization?

16. Describe the reaction of AF of L leaders to the formation of the IWW.

17. What is meant by "job consciousness," and how did it affect the development of stable trade unions?

18. How did entry of the United States into World War I affect the IWW and the AF of L? What effect did the war have on union membership? How do you account for this effect?

19. Write a brief essay describing the events and conditions that contributed to the decline in membership of AF of L unions during the 1920s.

20. What was the "American Plan"? Describe the reaction of AF of L leaders to this plan.

Suggested Readings

Books

Bernstein, Irving. *A History of the American Worker, 1920–1933, The Lean Years.* Boston: Houghton Mifflin Co., 1960.

Commons, John R., and Associates. *History of Labor in the United States, Vols. I–IV.* New York: The Macmillan Company, 1918–1935.

Gompers, Samuel. *Seventy Years of Life and Labor.* New York: E. P. Dutton and Co., 1925.

Lorwin, Lewis. *The American Federation of Labor.* Washington, D.C.: The Brookings Institution, 1933.

Millis, Harry A., and Royal E. Montgomery. *Organized Labor.* New York: McGraw-Hill Book Co., Inc., 1945.

Perlman, Selig. *History of Trade Unionism in the United States.* New York: The Macmillan Company, 1937.

Wolman, Leo. *Ebb and Flow in Trade Unionism.* New York: The National Bureau of Economic Research, Inc., 1936.

Articles

Gulick, Charles A., and Melvin K. Bers. "Insight and Illusion in Perlman's Theory of the Labor Movement," *Industrial and Labor Relations Review, 6,* No. 4 (July 1953), pp. 510–531.

Laslett, John M. "Socialism and the American Labor Movement: Some New Reflections," *Labor History, I,* No. 2 (Spring 1967), pp. 136–155.

Levinson, David. "Perlman's Theory and the Marginal Utility Theory," *Industrial and Labor Relations Review, 20,* No. 4 (July 1967), pp. 665–666.

The American Labor Movement Comes of Age

The stock market crash of 1929 ushered in the longest and deepest depression in American history. It was some time after the crash, however, before it was widely recognized that this depression was different from those our economic system had successfully weathered in the past. After the first precipitous drop in economic activity in the fall of 1929, there was a slower decline that continued until 1933. During much of this period many businessmen and economists confidently predicted that there would be an upturn, but the upturn did not come.

The political campaign of 1932 dealt largely with the depression and with means of combating it. The New Deal government was swept into office by an alarmed electorate which looked to the federal government to get the economic machine back on the track. The first measures taken by the new government were largely of an emergency nature. During the early days of the New Deal there was little thought of fundamental reform of the economic system; it was only after the depression had persisted for a number of years that lasting reforms were initiated. Among these reforms were some which had a profound effect on union growth and on the role that unions were to play in our economic system. The first New Deal legislation to deal specifically with the trade union issue was a jerry-built law, passed in 1933, known as the National Industrial Recovery Act.

The National Industrial Recovery Act was the result of a somewhat frantic effort by Congress to attack the depression on a broad front. Its major purpose was to stimulate a revival of the economy. But Section 7(a) of the Act stipulated that workers had the right to organize unions and to bargain collectively through representatives of their own choosing without fear of employer interference, restraint, or coercion. Many employers, however, refused to take this section of the law seriously, since they were advised by their attorneys that it would be declared unconstitutional. Also, the Act failed to

distinguish clearly between employer-dominated company unions and independent labor organizations. As a consequence, while there was considerable union growth between 1933 and 1935—when the NIRA was declared
unconstitutional—most of this was in company unions. It has been estimated that membership in company unions amounted to about 1.3 million in
1932, and that the number of workers in such organizations increased to
approximately 2.5 million by 1935.[1] By 1935, the members of company unions
amounted to about 60 per cent of the number in independent trade unions.

About three fifths of all company unions were formed between 1933 and
1935. Although much of the membership in independent unions was concentrated in the nation's smaller industrial plants, company unions were formed
in some of the nation's larger enterprises. The liberal senators and congressmen who had insisted upon including Section 7(a) in the NIRA were concerned about the growth of employer-dominated company unions and the
failure of independent unions to make headway under the law. There was
relatively little dismay in Congress when the Supreme Court ruled that this
entire piece of hastily constructed legislation was unconstitutional.

Two subsequent developments were to have a profound effect upon the
trade union movement. These were enactment of the National Labor Relations
Act—better known as the Wagner Act—and a split in the AF of L, which was
to lead to the subsequent formation of a new federation, the Congress of
Industrial Organizations.

The National Labor Relations Act of 1935

Some of the detailed provisions of the Wagner Act will be discussed in a later
chapter, which deals with public policy toward trade unions. But it would be
difficult to understand trade union development in the United States during
the latter half of the 1930s without specific reference to this law.

The Wagner Act, unlike the earlier NIRA, dealt only with the matter of
trade union organization, and it was far more carefully thought out than the
law which had been declared unconstitutional. Two provisions of the law in
particular, Sections 7 and 8, guaranteed that if workers in a company wished
to form an independent union they were free to do so. For example, Section 7
declared that: "Employees shall have the right to self-organization, to form,
join, or assist labor organizations, to bargain collectively through representatives of their own choosing, and to engage in concerted activities, for the
purpose of collective bargaining or other mutual aid or protection." For the
first time in our history the complete legality of trade unions was established
by this section of the Wagner Act.

Equally important, Section 8 outlawed company-dominated unions. This

---

1. Millis and Montgomery, *Organized Labor* (New York: McGraw-Hill Book Co., Inc., 1945), p. 194.

section prohibited employers from dominating or interfering with the formation or administration of any labor organization. Employers were also prohibited from contributing financial or other support to any labor organization. Another provision of this section prohibited discrimination against workers for union activity. And finally, the provision which put teeth into the law was one that made it an unfair labor practice for an employer "to refuse to bargain collectively with the representatives of his employees. . . ." It is important to stress that the National Labor Relations Act did not *compel* an employer to enter into a union agreement; all that the employer was compelled to do was to meet and negotiate with representatives of his employees chosen by them for collective bargaining purposes.

To administer the Wagner Act, Congress provided for a three man National Labor Relations Board. The Board had the assistance of a sizeable staff of investigators, including field examiners, attorneys, and review officers operating through regional offices, who helped them administer and enforce the law.

At first, many employers thought that the Wagner Act would go the way of the earlier NIRA—that it would be declared unconstitutional. This issue was not decided until 1937 in *NLRB v. Jones & Laughlin Steel Corp.,* when the Supreme Court upheld the constitutionality of the Act. Trade union leaders were jubilant; henceforth, there could be no question about the legality of trade unions, and employers could no longer avoid meeting and negotiating with trade union leaders if a majority of their employees voted for union representation.

Union membership started to grow again in 1935, and it grew rapidly and steadily until the end of World War II. There can be no doubt that the Wagner Act was a powerful stimulus to union growth. It is difficult to assess the effects of this Act in isolation, however, since another event occurred in 1935 that permitted unions to penetrate the mass-production industries which had heretofore successfully resisted organization. This was the split in the AF of L, which led to a new federation of industrial unions, the result of a long-smoldering debate that had gone on among the top leaders of the Federation for many years.

The AF of L Split and the Formation of the CIO

Even before the Wagner Act was passed, a faction within the American Federation of Labor had been urging structural reform to permit organization of the vast number of workers in mass-production industries who were not eligible for membership in the existing craft unions. But the principle of craft unionism was so firmly imbedded in the thinking of those who controlled the AF of L that the radical change needed to organize workers along industrial lines was not seriously considered. At the 1933 convention of the AF of L, a conference was authorized to study the problem of organizing the unorganized. In January of the following year this conference proposed the establishment of "federal unions" to be affiliated directly with the AF of L in those industries where craft unions had made no progress. The language of the proposal was somewhat equivocal, however, on the issue of craft vs. industrial unions.

At the 1934 convention the issue was discussed intensively and debated heatedly. Once again the Executive Council of the AF of L reiterated the urgent necessity of organizing workers in the automotive, cement, aluminum, and steel industries. But the leaders of craft unions, jealously guarding their prerogatives, would not yield on the issue of structural change. Workers in the mass-production industries, according to the resolution passed, would be organized into federal unions. It was assumed that these workers would be channeled into the appropriate craft unions at a later time. There were some efforts during the following year to put this plan into practice, but it met with limited success. Meanwhile, those leaders in the AF of L who urged unrestricted industrial unionism, were becoming increasingly dissatisfied. The issue finally came to a head at the Atlantic City Convention of 1935.

At Atlantic City, a minority of the Committee on Resolutions submitted a report which bluntly called for the establishment of industrial unionism. After bitter debate, the convention voted by a substantial margin to reject the report. However, even before the convention was adjourned, those who supported industrial unionism held an informal conference and agreed to keep in touch with each other on this issue. On November 10, 1935, shortly after the AF of L convention had ended, the officers of eight unions, representing slightly more than 900,000 workers, met to form the Committee for Industrial Organization. Although this was initially a somewhat loose organization, its avowed purpose was the organization of workers in mass-production industries, without regard to craft jurisdiction. Shortly afterwards, six other unions joined the original eight in the CIO.

In a program adopted at the November 10 meeting, the leaders of the new committee stated that they had no intention of forming a "dual" federation, and indicated that they would continue to work within the AF of L. But in January 1936, the Executive Council of the AF of L expressed concern about the new organization and suggested that it be immediately dissolved. The organizers of the Committee refused to comply, and the member unions of the CIO were suspended from the AF of L in July. Later that year, at the AF of L convention, the Executive Council's suspension order was overwhelmingly accepted, partly because the rebellious industrial unions were not represented. Although the Committee did not become a permanent organization until two years later—at which time it changed its name to the Congress of Industrial Organizations—the American labor movement was definitely split in 1936.

The unions which had left the AF of L then began a sustained drive to organize workers in the clothing, printing, textile, and hat industries, as well as in glass, steel, autos, rubber, and electrical machinery. They moved into oil fields and refineries and into the nation's shipyards. Spearheading the drive for industrial unionism was John L. Lewis, President of the United Mine Workers of America. His union required no structural reorganization, since it had always been organized along industrial lines.

In each industry, special organizing committees were set up, which eventually became national or international unions. The organizing committees met stiff resistance. They moved into industries which had long resisted union organization, except among some of the more highly skilled craftsmen. There was considerable violence and bloodshed. This often alarmed many citizens who recognized that the advocates of industrial unionism were less conservative than the leaders of the AF of L. The public was further led to believe by press reports that the leaders of the vigorous organizing committees were Communists, or at least "fellow travelers."

The radicalism of the early CIO leaders was greatly exaggerated, however. Some of the organizing committees made use of young Communists during the early days of their forays into open shop industries. But with very few exceptions, the leaders of the CIO organizing committees accepted the American economic system quite as fully as their AF of L counterparts. Once they had successfully penetrated the industries they set out to organize, the CIO conducted a successful purge of Communists in strategic positions. Some of the tactics employed—such as the "sit down" strikes in the automobile industry—added to the public alarm. But once the major firms in the mass-production industries had recognized the new unions, the latter settled down to the tactics that had been employed by earlier trade unions.

The AF of L unions did not simply sit by and watch the progress of the new industrial CIO unions. The earlier philosophy of "voluntarism," which had relied on the grass-roots formation of unions by workers with a common skill, was largely scrapped by the AF of L, which stepped up its own organizing activities. Many of the principles to which the AF of L leaders had clung before the split were gradually ignored as the craft unions that remained in the older Federation stepped up their organizing activities to match the gains of the CIO unions. There can be little doubt that the formation of a new and competing federation did much to revitalize the AF of L. Under the stimulus of competition from the industrial unions, and aided by the sanctions provided by the Wagner Act, the AF of L unions conducted a strenuous campaign to add to their membership. In spite of the fact that the economy remained depressed with widespread unemployment, when World War II broke out, total union membership in the United States had reached an all-time peak of 8.6 million.

Trade Union Growth During World War II

World War II provided a powerful impetus to union growth. When the attack on Pearl Harbor suddenly plunged the nation into a full-scale world conflict, labor-management differences were subordinated to the broader goal of military success. There was a tremendous amount of slack in the economy when Pearl Harbor was attacked, but the rapid mobilization of millions of young men, coupled with an all-out production effort, quickly eliminated unemployment. Labor shortages developed, particularly in strategic industries, and labor and management cooperated to meet the wartime emergencies. Federal agencies were set up to control wages and prices, and the War Labor Board was established to handle labor-management disputes which might affect the war effort. Technically, the status quo was to be maintained with respect to union organization. Wartime regulations were supposedly designed to neither encourage nor discourage union membership. The device adopted to maintain this state of affairs was known as the "maintenance-of-membership" agreement. Such agreements required that workers who were union members at the time the agreement went into effect had to maintain their membership as a condition of employment. The object was to prevent workers who had been union members from leaving their unions in a tight labor market, but these agreements were not supposed to force new workers entering the labor market to join unions. However, the sharp upsurge in employment during a time when employers offered little resistance to trade unions led to a rapid rise in membership. By 1945, when World War II ended, there were about 12.7 million union members in the nation, and they accounted for almost 23 per cent of the civilian labor force. World War II consolidated the gains that had been initiated by the twin forces of the Wagner Act and the AF of L-CIO split in 1935.

The Postwar Reaction to Trade Unions—the Taft-Hartley Act

American trade unions emerged from World War II as a powerful force in our society. Unions had participated wholeheartedly in the war effort, and opposition to trade unions was negligible during the war. But following World War II— as had been the case after the first World War—a wave of conservatism swept the country. While some of the excesses that had followed World War I were avoided, there was mounting alarm over the tactics of trade unions during the postwar period. A conservative Congress enacted a new law governing labor-management relations, which many believed to be less one-sided than the earlier Wagner Act—the Labor-Management Relations Act of 1947, better known as the Taft-Hartley Act. This law retained the basic provisions of Sections 7 and 8 of the Wagner Act, which protected the rights of workers to organize unions, and required management to meet and negotiate with union representatives where a majority of workers voted for representation. But in addition, it specified a series of unfair labor practices for unions and eliminated some of the restrictions on management's ability to express its opinion of unions, so long as such expression contained no threats of reprisal or coercion.[2]

---

2. Further details of the Taft-Hartley Act will be discussed in Chapter 15.

During the hearings preceding enactment of the Taft-Hartley Act, union spokesmen refused to make any concessions. They insisted that the Wagner Act was entirely satisfactory and that no changes were required. Spokesmen for organized business groups argued to the contrary, however, and in the climate of the times their views prevailed. Once the law was enacted it was denounced as a "slave labor" act by union leaders, and some predicted that this was only the first step in a broader onslaught on the American trade union movement. The so-called "right to work" provision of the Taft-Hartley Act was particularly objectionable to union leaders. It permitted those states which chose to do so to outlaw the union shop, under which workers are required to join the union after accepting a job. They felt that this would make it more difficult for unions to organize the unorganized in those areas, such as the South, where unions had made little headway.

The rate of union growth slowed down after 1947, but the extent to which this was due to the Taft-Hartley Act alone is debatable. There were undoubtedly other factors which contributed to the declining rate of union growth, but these were largely ignored by union spokesmen, who continued to demand total repeal of the new Labor-Management Relations Act. During subsequent election campaigns, union political activity was stepped up. Representative Hartley was defeated when he ran for office again, and the unions worked hard to defeat Senator Taft when he came up for re-election in Ohio, but without success.

Some union leaders undoubtedly feared a loss of membership, similar to that of the 1920s, under the Taft-Hartley Act. But this did not happen. Although unions had already succeeded in organizing a large proportion of the nation's manufacturing workers—with the notable exception of textiles, chemicals, and a few smaller industries—total membership in trade unions continued to rise. The growth rate was much slower than it had been in the past, however. For several years union leaders continued to press for repeal of the Taft-Hartley Act, but when the likelihood of this became increasingly remote, they settled for the removal of certain objectionable features—such as elimination of the noncommunist affidavit formerly required of unions wishing to use the machinery of the National Labor Relations Board.

The AF of L–CIO Merger

Slowly union leaders came to recognize that their position in our society had changed. They were no longer regarded as the underdogs; their power was now recognized even by legislators and others basically sympathetic to the trade union cause. Partly because of the changing climate of public opinion and partly because of the decline in the rate of union growth, the leaders of the AF of L and CIO began to reexamine their respective positions and to consider the prospect of merging into a single federation. Some union leaders believed that the fragmentation of union power resulting from the split in the House of Labor in the 1930s was not serving the best interests of the American labor movement. They began to hold preliminary discussions to consider the prospects of reuniting the two federations.

Even before World War II, there had been some preliminary—if highly tentative—discussions about the feasibility of a reunified labor movement. While these early efforts were unsuccessful, they were renewed from time to time even during the war years. By the end of the 1940s, it became apparent that the chances for a successful merger were increasing. One of the obstacles to reunion was removed when the CIO expelled some of its unions, which had been charged with Communist domination. Meanwhile, the issue of craft vs. industrial unions had diminished in importance. While the AF of L was still broadly characterized as a federation of craft unions and the CIO as a federation of industrial unions, some of the differences had disappeared. During the period of active rivalry between the two federations, some of the AF of L unions had modified their structures to such an extent that they came to resemble industrial unions. The leaders of the two federations began to suggest that the differences which divided them were less important than the threat of outside opposition to a divided labor movement.

Leaders of the AF of L and the CIO began to work together on political and legislative matters. From the beginning, the CIO had played an active part in political affairs, and leaders of the AF of L gradually abandoned their opposition to political action. The Korean War during the early 1950s brought the two federations closer together, when their leaders worked jointly to develop an emergency defense program. A further step toward unity was taken in 1953 when a "no-raiding" agreement was negotiated by the two federations and ratified by their conventions.

The movement toward a merger gained impetus in 1954 following the establishment of "unity committees" by each of the federations. The basic agreement to merge was reached as early as October 1954, but the details of the proposed merger—including the jurisdictions of competing unions in the two federations—were not worked out at that time.

The executive boards of the AF of L and the CIO approved the terms of the merger in February 1955. Their last conventions were held on December 1 and 2 of that year. These conventions approved the merger agreement and an "implementation agreement," which was designed to bring the two federations together without formally dissolving either organization. A constitution for the merged federation was also approved at these conventions.

The American Federation of Labor and Congress of Industrial Organizations (AFL-CIO) was founded on December 5, 1955. At the first convention George Meany, who had led the AF of L into the merger, was elected president. Walter Reuther stepped down from the presidency of the CIO to become a vice president and head of the Industrial Union Department of the new federation. Under the constitution of the AFL-CIO, the president, the secretary-treasurer, and the vice presidents make up the thirty-five man Executive Council which governs the federation between its biennial conventions.

Under the terms of the merger, state and local bodies were required to combine within two years. The affiliated unions of the former AF of L and CIO were also encouraged to combine in those circumstances where a single national union seemed appropriate. But such mergers were not made mandatory by the new federation. Conflicts between competing unions were also to be settled on a voluntary basis.

Both sides had made genuine concessions in arriving at the merger agreement. The new federation is a conglomerate of unions organized predominantly along craft lines, alongside others which have organized workers without respect to occupation. It is significant of the changes that had taken place in the older federation that more than half of the affiliates of the new Industrial Union Department had formerly belonged to the AF of L. As members of a common parent body, the affiliated unions agreed to continue to abide by the earlier no-raiding agreement and a few signed mutual assistance pacts. Long before the merger, the AF of L had departed from its earlier position of avoiding political action to establish Labor's League for Political Education, a counterpart to the CIO's Political Action Committee. In the merged federation these activities came together under the Committee on Political Education (COPE).

The rivalry between AF of L and CIO unions during the twenty years of their separate existence no doubt contributed to the growth of total union membership. The AF of L, which had been unwilling to change its structure prior to the split, was forced to depart from earlier practices when the CIO began its explosive growth. The split settled the question of how to go about organizing the mass-production industries. Once a large proportion of workers in manufacturing had been organized, however, the going became more difficult for both federations. By the middle of the 1950s, their leaders were convinced that they had more to gain than to lose from the merger.

Cracks in the House of Labor

The AFL-CIO merger did not change the locus of power in the American trade union movement; this remained in the hands of national union leaders. Most of the time federation and national union policies have not come into open conflict, but there have been exceptions.

John L. Lewis, the egregious leader of the United Mine Workers, had been a prime mover in the AF of L split, and was one of the major architects of the new Congress of Industrial Organization. By 1942, however, Lewis had become disaffected with the CIO and led the miners out of the Federation. Lewis returned the UMW to the AF of L in 1946, but his stay there was brief. He moved the miners out of the AF of L again in 1948, and the UMW has remained an independent union since then.[3]

---

3. Lewis continued as head of the United Mine Workers until 1960, when he retired at the age of 80. He was president emeritus of the UMW until his death in 1969. For a lucid account of the role played by Lewis in the formation of the CIO, see Irving Bernstein, *A History of the American Worker, 1933–1941, The Turbulent Years* (Boston: Houghton Mifflin Company, 1970), *passim.*

The first break in the AFL-CIO came shortly after its merger. Early in 1957, a Senate committee was established to investigate the internal affairs of unions under the chairmanship of Senator McClellan of Arkansas. This investigation, and the law that resulted from it, are discussed in Chapter 15. One immediate result, however, was expulsion of the Teamsters Union, which had been charged by the AFL-CIO Executive Council with corrupt practices.[4] The Bakers Union and the general officers of the United Textile Workers also were expelled on the same grounds, but the Teamsters accounted for more than 9 per cent of total union membership in 1958, and expulsion of this union meant a substantial loss of federation membership.

The only major union to leave the Federation voluntarily since the merger was the United Auto Workers. Technically, the UAW was suspended by the Executive Council in May 1968, for failure to pay dues. But on July 1 of that year, Walter Reuther and three other officials of the UAW sent a letter to the AFL-CIO "formally disaffiliating" from the Federation.

Some writers have interpreted the split between the UAW and the Federation as a power struggle between Reuther and George Meany, president of the Federation since the merger.[5] This is an oversimplified explanation of the split, however. Reuther, who died in a plane crash on May 9, 1970, at the age of 62, was one of the more charismatic labor leaders this country has produced. He was involved in both the United Auto Workers and the CIO from their inception and, unlike many other labor leaders, he remained concerned about the problems of the poor and the oppressed long after the strength of his own union was assured. Reuther felt that many union leaders had become complacent about social and economic problems, and his departure from the Federation was a protest against this complacency.[6]

Shortly after the UAW left the Federation, Reuther and Frank E. Fitzsimmons, acting president of the Teamsters, formed the Alliance for Labor Action (ALA). The initial agreement was reached in July 1968, and this Alliance held its founding convention in May 1969. Reuther announced that the purpose of formation of the ALA was to "revitalize" the labor movement. It was denounced by leaders of the AFL-CIO, however, as a "dual organization rival to the AFL-CIO." The Chemical Workers Union affiliated with the

---

4. At that time the Teamsters Union was led by James R. Hoffa, who subsequently was sentenced to a thirteen-year prison term after being convicted of jury tampering. Hoffa received a presidential pardon, late in 1971, after five years in prison, evidently with the understanding that he was to have nothing further to do with the Teamsters Union. Dave Beck, Hoffa's predecessor as president of the Teamsters also had ended his career as a labor leader in prison as a result of the McClellan investigation. For a brief account of the McClellan investigation and its aftermath, see William H. Miernyk, Trade Unions in the Age of Affluence (New York: Random House, 1962), pp. 71–72.

5. See, for example, Frank Cormier and William J. Eaton, Reuther (Englewood Cliffs, N.J.: Prentice-Hall, Inc., 1970).

6. See the review of Cormier and Eaton's book on Reuther by Jack Barbash, Monthly Labor Review, March 1971, p. 80.

ALA in August 1969, and was expelled from the AFL-CIO in October of that year for this action.

One can only speculate about the effect of Reuther's death on the Alliance for Labor Action. The Chemical Workers Union, with 90,000 members, left the ALA and returned to the AFL-CIO in 1971. Also, early in 1971, the United Auto Workers and the International Association of Machinists (AFL-CIO) signed a "no raiding" agreement. There was speculation at the time that the UAW, under its new president Leonard Woodcock, might consider a reconciliation with the Federation. When Hoffa resigned, and Fitzsimmons was sworn in as the new president of the Teamsters in July 1971, there was a renewed possibility that the Teamsters might return to the AFL-CIO. Meany had announced long before that the Teamsters would be welcome to return to the Federation any time after a new president had been elected to replace Hoffa.

There have been cracks in the House of Labor since the new federation was founded at the end of 1955, but the AFL-CIO was able to survive the departure of the nation's two largest national unions. It seems evident that the Federation is built on a more solid foundation than many believed to be the case at the time of the merger.

The Merger of National Unions

The AFL-CIO split in 1935 is the classic example of "dual unionism" in American labor history. One consequence was the development of new unions whose jurisdictions in some cases overlapped those of the older AF of L unions. The merger of the two federations was expected to set a precedent for affiliated unions organizing in the same jurisdiction. At the 1965 convention of the AFL-CIO, however, President Meany expressed disappointment with the slow pace of union mergers.

Between the end of 1955, when the AFL-CIO merger occurred, and February 1971, there were thirty six mergers of national unions. The thirty six mergers resulted from the combination of seventy-seven unions, however, since in some cases two or more unions were involved.[7] One example of a multiple merger was the formation of the United Transportation Union on January 1, 1969 by the merger of four railway operating unions. Also, early in 1971, one independent and four AFL-CIO postal unions merged to form the American Postal Workers Union (AFL-CIO). This merger may have been hastened by reorganization of the postal system. In 1970, under the Postal Reform Act, Congress had replaced the federal postal system by a quasi-governmental organization. Under the Act, the Postal Workers Union bargains directly with the new organization rather than attempting to achieve better wages and improved working conditions through federal legislation.

---

7. Lucretia M. Dewey, "Union Merger Pace Quickens," *Monthly Labor Review*, June 1971, p. 63.

It is likely that the merger movement will continue. In some cases relatively small unions will merge with larger organizations to gain added strength at the bargaining table. On January 1, 1971, for example, the United Stone and Allied Products Workers of America, with about 20,000 members, merged with the 1.2 million-member United Steelworkers of America.

The Changing Structure of Unionism

Membership in the first stable unions in the United States was limited to skilled craftsmen. Only after the CIO had been formed in 1935 was there extensive organization of production workers in manufacturing. During the 1950s, there was a lull in union growth since by this time most of the nation's large manufacturing concerns were organized, and there was also a high degree of unionism among workers employed in transportation, construction, and mining. We saw in Chapter 9 that the "stagnationists" of this period were not optimistic about organized labor's chances of unionizing white-collar workers. And most new entrants to the labor force in recent years have been professional, technical, clerical, secretarial and other workers in the "white-collar" or "nongoods" sectors of the economy.

To what extent may the revival of union growth since the early 1960s be attributed to the successful organization of white-collar workers? There is some evidence that white-collar workers may now be less averse to joining unions than they have been in the past, because of what they consider to be a change in their status in an increasingly impersonal world of work.[8]

Table 11-1 shows the size and growth rates of most of the nation's larger unions between 1958 and 1968.[9] It is important to note that 1958 was a year of economic recession, whereas 1968 marked the end of the longest sustained boom in recent American economic history. Thus, not all of the increase in membership during this period may be regarded as actual union "growth." Some of the increase represents *cyclical* rather than long-term change. In general, manufacturing workers are more susceptible to cyclical unemployment than workers in the trades and services. But even in the trades and services part of the increase in union membership is undoubtedly the result of cyclical rather than secular or long-term forces.

Inspection of Table 11-1 shows that much of the increase in union membership since the early 1960s has been in the "traditional" unions, that is, unions representing workers in construction, manufacturing, transportation, and mining. Notice, however, that membership in the Retail Clerks increased about 80 per cent, and that membership in the Postal Clerks rose 66 per cent.

---

8. Judson Gooding, "The Fraying White Collar," *Fortune*, December 1970, pp. 78–81; 108 ff.

9. Some large unions, such as the United Mine Workers and the Railroad Trainmen, are not included in the table because they did not report their membership figures to the Bureau of Labor Statistics.

TABLE 11-1
Increases in Membership, 1958–1968, in Unions having 100,000 or more Members in Both Years

Unions	1958 Members		1968 Members		Difference 1958–1968	
	Number	Per cent of Total	Number	Per cent of Total	Absolute Change	Per cent Change
Teamsters	1,418,246	9.9	1,755,025	10.7	336,779	23.7
Auto Workers	1,027,000	7.1	1,472,696	9.0	445,696	43.4
Steelworkers	960,000	6.7	1,120,000	6.8	160,000	16.7
Electrical (IBEW)	750,000	5.2	897,114	5.5	147,114	19.6
Laborers	476,598	3.3	553,102	3.4	76,504	16.1
Retail Clerks	305,000	2.1	552,000	3.4	247,000	81.0
Meat Cutters	325,304	2.3	500,000	3.0	174,696	53.7
Hotel and Restaurant	436,315	3.0	459,053	2.8	22,738	5.2
Garment, Ladies	442,901	3.1	455,022	2.8	12,121	2.7
Service, Employees	260,000	1.8	389,000	2.4	129,000	39.2
Clothing Workers	376,000	2.6	386,000	2.3	10,000	2.6
State, County	200,000	1.4	364,486	2.2	164,486	8.2
Communication Workers	255,365	1.8	357,000	2.2	101,635	39.8
Engineers, Operating	280,000	1.9	350,000	2.1	70,000	25.0
Electrical (IUE)	278,281	1.9	324,352	2.0	46,071	16.5
Plumbers	255,800	1.8	297,023	1.8	41,223	16.1
Musicians	262,882	1.8	283,155	1.7	20,273	7.7
Rubber Workers	158,570	1.1	203,000	1.2	44,430	28.0
Painters	184,502	1.3	200,000	1.2	15,498	8.4
Pulp, Sulphite	165,000	1.1	182,795	1.1	17,795	10.8
Retail, Wholesale	160,000	1.1	175,000	1.1	15,000	9.4
Iron Workers	152,389	0.9	167,928	1.0	15,539	10.2
Electrical (UE)	160,000	1.1	167,000	1.0	7,000	4.4
Postal Clerks	100,000	0.7	166,000	1.0	66,000	66.0
Bricklayers	159,126	1.1	160,000	1.0	874	0.5
Paper Makers	135,000	0.9	144,682	0.9	9,682	7.2
Boilermakers	132,356	0.9	140,000	0.8	7,644	5.8
Printing, Pressmen	110,500	0.8	126,000	0.8	15,500	14.0
Typographical Unions	110,449	0.8	123,310	0.7	12,861	11.6

Source: U.S. Department of Labor, Bureau of Labor Statistics, *Directory of National and International Labor Unions In the United States*, Bulletin 1267 (1959) and Bulletin 1665 (1970).

These are the two highest *rates* of increase listed in the table. This suggests that there may be substance to the view that white-collar workers—including government employees—are becoming more amenable to organization.

TABLE 11-2
Decline in Membership, 1958–1968, in Unions having 100,000 or more Members in Both Years

| Unions | 1958 Members | | 1968 Members | | Difference 1958–1968 | |
	Number	Per Cent of Total	Number	Per Cent of Total	Absolute Change	Per Cent Change
Machinists	992,689	6.9	903,015	5.5	−89,674	− 9.0
Carpenters	835,000	5.8	793,000	4.8	−42,000	− 5.0
Railway Clerks	360,899	2.5	280,000	1.7	−80,899	−22.4
Textile Workers	197,200	1.4	183,000	1.1	−14,200	− 7.2
Oil, Chemical	180,175	1.2	173,185	1.1	− 6,990	− 3.9
Maintenance of Way	183,000	1.3	125,000	0.7	−58,000	−31.7
Railway Carmen	156,900	1.1	117,386	0.7	−39,514	−25.2

Source: U.S. Department of Labor, Bureau of Labor Statistics, *Directory of National and International Labor Unions in the United States,* Bulletin 1267 (1959) and Bulletin 1665 (1970).

Table 11-2 shows the *decline* in union membership in seven large national unions between 1958 and 1968. This decline occurred in spite of the fact that 1958 was a year of recession and 1968, a year of prosperity. This suggests that the long-term decline indicated in Table 11-2 may have been cushioned somewhat by cyclical influences. Three of the unions represent railroad workers, and the decline of membership in these unions is a reflection of the long-term drop in employment on American railroads. The decline of membership in other unions, however, is no doubt largely the result of technological change, which has reduced labor requirements in the industries represented by these unions. Other forces undoubtedly have contributed to the decline in membership in the Carpenters Union. Building construction is a volatile economic activity, and some of the "decline" in union membership among carpenters may have been cyclical.[10]

Table 11-3 shows increases in the membership of seven unions with fewer than 100,000 members in 1958 but more than this number in 1968. It also shows the decline in membership in four unions that had more than 100,000 members in 1958 but fewer than this number at the end of the period.

One of the unions in the upper part of Table 11-3 requires special men-

10. One technological change that has affected employment in the building trades, however, has been the rapid increase in construction and occupancy of mobile homes in recent years. On this see Allan H. Young *et al.,* "Residential Capital in the United States, 1925–1970," *Survey of Current Business, 51* (November 1971), pp. 16–27.

TABLE 11-3

Change in Membership, 1958–68, in Unions with fewer than 100,000 Members in either 1958 or 1968

Unions	1958 Members		1968 Members	
	Number	Per Cent of Total	Number	Per Cent of Total
Government (AFGE)	—	—	294,725	1.8
District 50, Allied and Technical (Independent)	—	—	232,000	1.4
Teachers	—	—	165,000	1.0
Sheet Metal	—	—	140,000	0.8
Transit Union	—	—	134,000	0.8
Fire Fighters	—	—	132,634	0.8
Chemical (Independent)	—	—	103,780	0.6
Packing House	157,690	1.1	—	—
Transport Workers	135,000	0.9	—	—
Street, Electric Railway	124,637	0.9	—	—
Mine, Mill (Independent)	100,000	0.7	—	—

Source: U.S. Department of Labor Statistics, *Directory of National and International Labor Unions in the United States*, Bulletin 1267 (1959) and Bulletin 1665 (1970).

tion, since it does not necessarily represent membership growth. When John L. Lewis was president of the United Mine Workers he formed District 50 as a "catch-all" union of nonminers organized by the UMW. District 50, a sizeable union in itself, broke away from the UMW in 1958, and is shown as an independent union in 1968.[11]

Three of the unions that had passed the 100,000 member mark by 1968 represent government employees. Indeed, by 1968, the American Federation of Government Employees had almost 300,000 members. Membership in the Teachers and Fire Fighters unions also had increased enough to include them among the nation's "large" unions. Although unions composed of government employees are still small, when compared with such unions as the Teamsters and Auto Workers, they have experienced rapid growth in recent years. This has raised a number of new issues concerning collective bargaining with public employees.[12] There also have been changes in public attitudes toward

---

11. At their 1971 convention, leaders of the International Union of District 50, Allied and Technical Workers of the United States and Canada, had planned to vote on a proposed merger with the Steelworkers. The officers of the union were enjoined by court order from holding an election on this issue. A few days later, however, the injunction was modified to permit the union to make plans for a referendum to determine whether or not rank and file members wished to merge with the Steelworkers. Apparently, members of District 50 have no interest in returning to the UMW.

12. These issues are discussed in Chapter 19. For a survey of some of the effects of the organization of government employees see a series of articles in the *Monthly Labor Review*, July 1970, also issued as BLS Reprint 2679. See also Orley Ashenfelter, "The Effect of Unionization on Wages in the Public Sector: The Case of Fire Fighters," *Industrial and Labor Relations Review*, 24, No. 2 (January 1971), pp. 191–202.

the organization of government employees and even toward strikes conducted by civil servants. Early in 1971, for example, most of New York City's 25,000 patrolmen began a work stoppage. Only a skeleton force of about 6,500 officers and patrolmen remained on duty until the strike ended on January 20. But this strike did not produce the chaotic conditions that accompanied the Boston Police Strike of the early 1920s discussed in the last chapter. This is not to say that either the unions or the agencies with which they deal have fully adjusted to the organization of public employees. But the *idea* of collective action by public employees, at all levels of government, is widely accepted today.

The trade union movement as a whole is only now beginning to adjust to an economy dominated by white-collar employees.[13] The structural changes in the economy that have reversed the proportions of white-collar and blue-collar workers in recent years will continue. A growing proportion of the labor force will be employed in professional, technical, trade, and service activities, and in state and local government. This is bound to affect the structure and composition of future trade-union membership. Undoubtedly, it also will have a profound influence on the future of collective bargaining.

The Organization of Professional Workers

Professional unionism has proceeded more slowly in the United States than in other democratic societies.[14] Efforts have been made at various times to organize scientists and engineers; some have been successful, while others have failed. A few professional unions have enjoyed a period of temporary success followed by decline. The Engineers and Scientists of America, for example, achieved some success during the 1950s. But partly because of the attitude that "professionalism and unionism are incompatible," the union lost strength and was dissolved in 1960.[15] In 1969, the Seattle Professional Engineering Employees Association (SPEEA), consisting of 13,000 Boeing employees, joined the Council of Engineering and Scientific Organization (CESO). In another merger, the Professional Air Traffic Controllers Organization (PATCO) joined the Marine Engineers Beneficial Association (MEBA). Other professional associations have joined the MEBA, which no longer limits membership to marine engineers. The merger of relatively small, independent professional associations could strengthen the foundation of professional unionism in the United States.

One area of union activity that has attracted considerable attention in recent years is the organization of college professors. A study by Joseph

---

13. See Leo Troy, "Trade Union Growth in a Changing Economy," *Monthly Labor Review*, September 1969, pp. 3–7.

14. See the symposium on "Professional and White-Collar Unionism: An International Comparison," in *Industrial Relations, 5* (October 1965), pp. 37–141.

15. Miernyk, *op. cit.,* pp. 34–36.

Garbarino, of the University of California, shows that 133 of the nation's 2,500 colleges and universities had recognized unions as bargaining agents.[16] Some writers feel that unionism will spread rapidly among college faculties. One reason for this expectation is growing concern among young faculty members about job security in a tightening labor market.[17]

Most of the organization of professors to date has been limited to community colleges and other relatively new institutions.[18] The average age of faculty members at such institutions is relatively low, and there is a lack of opposition from faculty members with more seniority. It may be more difficult to organize the faculties of older and more conventional educational institutions.

The organization of professional workers is probably most advanced in Sweden, and analysis of the Swedish experience may shed some light on prospects for the future organization of professionals in the United States.[19] According to Kassalow, while there may be no direct relationship between the growth of professional employment and professional unionism, "this seems to have been the case in many instances."[20] As the number of professional and technical workers increases, their work comes under an increasing amount of administrative control. A corollary of this is a decline—real or imagined—in the individual status of the professional worker. Egalitarian policies that tend to reduce differences in the education and income of professional and nonprofessional workers may also diminish the status of professionals. In Sweden, professional workers—doctors, engineers, and even some clergymen—have reacted by forming collective bargaining associations.[21] It is possible that if the tendencies observed in Sweden become more pronounced in the United States, one result will be an increase in professional unionism.

The Organization of Farm Workers

The forgotten men and women of the American labor movement have been the nation's hired farm workers. In the past, the small size of farms and the migratory character of much of the farm work force, made it difficult to organize farm workers. The number of hired farm workers also has been reduced by technological progress to a relatively small fraction of the labor force. In

---

16. Cited in M. A. Farber, "Professors' Unions are Growing," *New York Times,* November 14, 1971.

17. See Myron Lieberman, "Professors Unite!" in *Harper's Magazine,* October 1971, pp. 61–70; and "Unions Woo the College Faculties," *Business Week,* May 1, 1971, pp. 69–74.

18. A few older institutions, such as City University in New York, are also organized and engage in active collective bargaining.

19. Everett M. Kassalow, "Professional Unionism in Sweden," *Industrial Relations, 8* (February 1969), p. 120.

20. *Ibid.,* p. 119.

21. *Ibid.,* pp. 124–126.

many states the hired agricultural work force is too small and widely scattered for effectual organization. The agricultural sector of California, however, includes a number of large farms, and the size of the farm work force in this state provided an opportunity for the organization of farm workers.

The United Farm Workers Organizing Committee was established as an indigenous organization under the leadership of Cesar Chavez. The Committee received only a modest amount of financial aid from organized labor and, until recent years, no more than token moral support from the rest of the community. The year 1970 was a turning point for the Committee, however. In April 1970, the Committee signed an agreement with five grape growers in the Coachella Valley of California. And on July 29, 1970, a strike that had lasted for almost five years was ended when the Committee signed an agreement with twenty-six grape growers, representing 35 per cent of their industry, in the San Joaquin Valley.

On August 30, 1970, the Committee signed an agreement with International Harvest Inc., the largest lettuce grower in the Salinas Valley. In the same month a "no raiding" agreement was signed by the Teamsters and the UFWOC. Under this agreement the Teamsters were to represent processing and cannery workers, and the United Farm Workers Organizing Committee was to bargain for field workers.[22]

In February 1972, the UFWOC became the United Farm Workers of California and was accepted by the executive council of the AFL-CIO as a full-fledged union. The following month, Chavez won his first major bargaining victory outside California. Following two months of relatively amicable negotiations, the union signed a three-year agreement with the foods division of the Coca-Cola Company, covering 1,200 farm workers in Florida.

The recent successes of the UFW do not mean that resistance to the organization of farm workers has collapsed. At least fifteen state legislatures have considered proposals to restrict agricultural organization. One of them, Arizona, passed a law which went into effect August 13, 1972. If it is allowed to stand, this law will prohibit organizing activities on growers' properties and strikes at harvest time. It also will outlaw secondary boycotts and limit primary boycotts to specific employers. The Arizona law has been challenged by the union, but as long as it stands on the books it will seriously hamper the further organization of farm workers in that state.

---

22. This did not mean that the UFWOC's problems with the Teamsters were completely solved. In Februrary 1971, the Committee filed a $10 million damage suit against the Teamsters and Bud Antle, Inc., a major lettuce producer, charging a "sham contract" that interfered with the "legitimate organization" of Antle's agricultural workers.

Questions and Exercises

1. Section 7(a) of the National Industrial Recovery Act of 1933 stipulated that workers had the right to organize unions and to bargain collectively through representatives of their own choosing. Although this act was declared unconstitutional in 1935, there was a substantial increase in union membership between 1933 and 1935. Does this mean that the NIRA provided a stimulus to organization by the AF of L?

2. After the NIRA was declared unconstitutional, Congress passed the National Labor Relations Act—also known as the Wagner Act—in 1935. How did this Act differ from the NIRA, and what influence did it have on union organization?

3. What was the basic issue that led to establishment of the Committee for Industrial Organization in 1935? How was this committee formed?

4. What is the difference between a craft and an industrial union?

5. Describe briefly the reaction of AF of L unions to the organizing campaign initiated by the CIO.

6. What happened to trade union membership during World War II? What was a "maintenance-of-membership" agreement?

7. The Labor-Management Relations Act of 1947—better known as the Taft-Hartley Act—was passed in 1947. What did this law have to say about the right of workers to organize and engage in collective bargaining? What changes in the Wagner Act were made by the Taft-Hartley Act?

8. Describe the events that led to the merger of the AF of L and the CIO.

9. What provision was made in the new AFL-CIO for the industrial unions that are now part of the Federation?

10. Contrast the attitudes of the former AF of L and CIO with respect to union political activity. What arrangement was made for political activity in the AFL-CIO?

11. Why were the Teamsters expelled from the AFL-CIO? Under what circumstances did the United Auto Workers leave the Federation? What action was taken by Walter Reuther and Frank Fitzsimmons when these two unions left the Federation?

12. Some writers have implied that the departure of the UAW from the AFL-CIO was the result of a "power struggle" between Walter Reuther and George Meany. Is this a generally accepted explanation of the break?

13. What was the reaction of the leadership of the AFL-CIO to formation of the Alliance for Labor Action? Does it seem likely to you that the ALA will grow in size and strength until it rivals the AFL-CIO?

14. Were there any significant changes in the structure and composition of American trade unions during the 1960s?

15. Some of the nation's largest unions, such as the Teamsters, Auto Workers, and Steelworkers, showed substantial increases in membership in 1968 com-

pared with 1958. Is this evidence of a revival of trade union growth in the manufacturing sector?

16. There was a decline in membership in a number of unions between 1958 and 1968. What was the principal cause of this decline?

17. What types of unions showed the most rapid *rate* of growth between 1958 and 1968?

18. Under the terms of the merger agreement, what action was to be taken by national unions with overlapping jurisdictions?

19. Indicate briefly the nature and extent of mergers among national trade unions since 1955.

20. Describe the nature and extent of professional unionism in the United States. Contrast the experience of professional unions in the United States and Sweden. What can you say about the future prospects of professional unionism in the United States on the basis of the Swedish experience?

21. For a number of years the United Farm Workers Organizing Committee appeared to be making little headway. What events occurred in 1970 which suggest that this organization may have arrived as a representative of hired farm workers?

Suggested Readings

Books

Bernstein, Irving. *A History of the American Worker, 1933–1941, The Turbulent Years.* Boston: Houghton Mifflin Company, 1970.

Galenson, Walter. *The CIO Challenge to the AFL.* Cambridge, Mass.: Harvard University Press, 1960.

Millis, Harry A., and Royal E. Montgomery. *Organized Labor.* New York: McGraw-Hill Book Co., Inc., 1945.

Articles

Dewey, Lucretia M. "Union Merger Pace Quickens," *Monthly Labor Review*, June 1971, pp. 63–70.

Gooding, Judson. "The Fraying White Collar," *Fortune*, December 1970, pp. 79–81; 108 ff.

Kassalow, Everett M. "Professional Unionism in Sweden," *Industrial Relations, 8* (February 1969), pp. 119–134.

Symposium on "Professional and White-Collar Unionism: An International Comparison," *Industrial Relations, 5* (October 1965), pp. 37–141.

Ulman, Lloyd. "The Development of Trades and Labor Unions" and "Unionism and Collective Bargaining in the Modern Period," Chapters 13 and 14 in Seymour E. Harris, *American Economic History.* New York: McGraw-Hill Book Co., Inc., 1961, pp. 366–482.

Trade Union Structure and Government: Public Policies Toward Unions

12

Trade Union Structure and Government

Most trade unions in the United States belong to the AFL-CIO, which claimed a membership of 15.6 million in 1968. The organizational structure of the Federation seems complex, but for an organization of this size it is fairly streamlined. The Federation is made up of 126 national and international unions and a relatively small number of local unions that are affiliated directly with the AFL-CIO. It will be convenient to consider first the structure of the Federation, which is shown in Figure 12-1, then that of the national or international unions. There are also state and local bodies which perform specific functions, and these will be discussed separately.

The Structure Of The AFL–CIO

The highest governing body of the Federation is the *Convention,* which meets every two years to determine basic policies. There are also provisions in the constitution for special conventions, which can be called at any time to consider specific problems.

Each national or international union is entitled to send delegates to the convention. The number of delegates is determined by the per capita tax of 10 cents a month per member paid by the national or international unions. Other organizations affiliated with the AFL-CIO are entitled to one delegate each.

The Executive Council

Since the convention meets at two-year intervals, it is necessary to have a governing body to deal with issues and problems which arise between conventions. The Executive Council consists of the Federation's president, the secretary-treasurer, and thirty-three vice presidents. All members of the

261

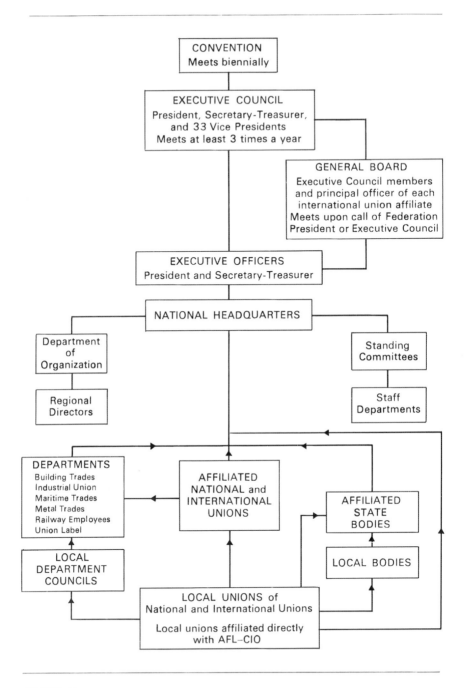

FIGURE 12–1.

Structure of the AFL-CIO. (*Reprinted from the U.S. Department of Labor, Bureau of Labor Statistics,* Directory of National and Inernational Labor Unions in the United States, 1969, *Bulletin No. 1665 [1970].*)

Executive Council are elected by majority vote at the convention. The Council is required to meet at least three times a year, and it may meet at more frequent intervals if the need arises.

The Executive Officers

Although it is up to the Executive Council to see that policies voted by the convention are carried out, an organization as large as the AFL-CIO must have a headquarters and executive officers to deal with day-to-day problems. The elected executive officers who are responsible for the regular supervision of affairs of the Federation are the president and secretary-treasurer. Currently, the president is George Meany, and the secretary-treasurer is Lane Kirkland.

The president appoints a number of *Standing Committees,* which deal with such matters as economic policy, ethical practices, legislation, public relations, civil rights, and a wide variety of other matters. The standing committees report to the executive officers of the Federation, and they may be given a wide range of assignments.

The *General Board,* consisting of the Executive Council, one principal officer of each national or international union, and one officer representing each affiliated department, meets upon call of the Federation President or the Executive Council.

The national or international unions are divided into trade and industrial departments. The most important department is the Industrial Union Department, made up largely of unions formerly affiliated with the CIO. There are other departments for unions in the building trades, the metal trades, maritime employees, and railway employees. The sixth department—the Union Label Department—was established to promote consumer interest in union-made products and union services by urging the purchase of only those which bear the union label.

The Government Employes Council, formed in 1945, brings together union leaders and government employees to prepare legislative programs. In 1970, it included thirty-three AFL-CIO unions. Finally, the Council of Unions for Scientific, Professional and Cultural Employees (SPACE) was organized in 1967. Its goal is to encourage the members of scientific, cultural, and professional organizations to become union members.

The Federation Staff

A body as large as the AFL-CIO requires the services of a large number of specialists such as accountants, lawyers, and public relations personnel. The staff of the Federation is divided into sixteen departments with each department head responsible to the executive officers of the Federation. There are staff specialists who deal with such routine matters as accounting, purchasing, and library affairs. Other staff specialists are concerned with civil rights, community services, education, international affairs, and legislation.

Organizational matters, political education, public relations, and the publication of union magazines and papers are also part of the Federation's headquarters structure. The Federation maintains a substantial research staff, which serves the executive officers and assists others on the headquarters staff in their relations with unions, employers, the government, and the public. The AFL-CIO also maintains specialists in the field of social security both to assist union members in routine matters and to work with legislative and other groups in the AFL-CIO in proposing changes in legislation.

Affiliated Organizations

In addition to the trade and industrial departments to which many of the national or international unions belong, the structural organization of the AFL-CIO includes state and city central bodies and local department councils.

There is a state central body—usually called the AFL-CIO State Council —in each of the fifty states and in Puerto Rico. The state bodies are made up of representatives of the local unions in each state. Their principal function is to advance the statewide interests of organized labor and to represent trade unions on state legislative matters. The state central bodies do not report directly to the officers or Executive Council of the AFL-CIO. They are tied in with the trade and industrial departments through the local unions which they represent. Each state body has its own elected officers, some of whom function on a full-time basis but some of whom also hold office in a national or international union.

At the bottom of the structural pyramid are almost 900 local central bodies, which have been formed at the community level by the local unions directly affiliated with the AFL-CIO or through a national or international union. These organizations deal primarily with local civic and community problems or with other matters strictly of a local nature. There are also more than 900 local department councils made up of representatives of the local unions, which are affiliated both with a national or international union and with one of the trade and industrial departments. As is true of the local central bodies, the local department councils deal primarily with community matters of concern to the members of the unions they represent.

The National and International Unions

It will be recalled that one of the conflicts between the Knights of Labor and the trade unions was over the question of where decision-making authority should be located. The Knights wanted "one big union" with the headquarters making all major decisions. But the trade unions at that time wanted to be the guardians of their own destinies, and the latter philosophy won out in this struggle. From the beginning of the AF of L, the locus of trade union power has moved steadily toward the national union headquarters. There is, of course, some variation among national unions. There are unions in which the locals have a great deal to say about collective bargaining and other matters, but it is a fair generalization to say that more often decision-making authority resides with the national union officers. From the beginning of the AF of L, the federation has had little, if anything, to say about collective bargaining or other matters directly affecting the members of a national or international union. This is consistent with the principle of autonomy—one of the basic principles on which the AF of L was founded.

Each national union has its elected officers, its executive boards or councils, and staff specialists to advise the officers, to prepare union publications, and to deal with other matters of a technical or specialized nature. The headquarters staff of national or international unions varies greatly in size and degree of specialization. Some of the smaller national unions operate with very little staff assistance. But the larger unions—such as the United Auto Workers and the Steelworkers—have fairly large staff setups.

Some of the larger national unions are organized along regional lines. The regional representatives are generally staff men directly responsible to the national union president, and their function is to assist locals in the administration of agreements and in the solution of day-to-day problems as they arise. They also provide liaison between the local unions in a particular part of the country and national headquarters.

A further link between the local unions and national headquarters— often working through a regional organization—is the business agent or the international representative. These are the field officers of the national union who work with locals in a relatively small area to see that contracts are being administered properly, that dues are transmitted to the national headquarters, and in some cases that grievances are settled which are not of sufficient gravity to be referred to a higher level in the union organization.

To some extent the structure of the national union perpetuates the centralization of power in the national headquarters. The president of a national union will try to surround himself with staff members who are loyal to him and who are in broad agreement with his basic views on collective bargaining and other union matters. These staff members handle the national union's publicity and they also deal with the local unions which make up the national organization. The job security of staff members depends upon the way they perform. They are employees of the national union, not elected union officials. The national president will see to it that any staff member who does not go along with the national union's (that is, the president's) policies will not hold his position long.

This is not to imply that the presidents of national unions are dictators.

Some come very close, but others are closely attuned to the desires of the rank and file. Even with the support of a strong and loyal staff, an unpopular national union president can be voted out of office. There are sporadic instances of rank and file revolt, although it is rare indeed for the president of a national union to be turned out of office. This is not because the president has an iron grip on his members, but generally because the rank and file—while not necessarily approving of every action of the president—are generally satisfied with the union's policies and with the union's accomplishments for its members.

The Local Union

The broad base upon which American trade union organization rests is made up of thousands of local unions. Some are craft locals made up of members of a particular occupational group with a strong common bond. Such locals do not deal with a single employer; indeed, the members of the local may move from employer to employer as one job is finished and other jobs open up. Other locals belong to industrial unions. Their membership is far more heterogeneous. The locals of some industrial unions may also deal with several employers, but some of the larger locals—in the steel and auto industries, for example—may be made up of the employees of a single concern.

    The officers of the local union are unpaid, and there is far more turnover of local union officers than at any other level of the trade union organization. At the very bottom of the trade union hierarchy—but of critical importance to the success of the administration of labor-management agreements—are the shop stewards. A local which deals with a number of small companies will generally have a shop steward in each company. It is his duty to see that the terms of the agreement are respected, to accept grievances from workers, and wherever possible to settle these on the spot. In some industrial union locals that deal with a single employer, there will be a number of shop stewards assigned to various departments in a plant. A good shop steward can do much to minimize grievances. If his working relationship with management is good, the shop steward can keep minor grievances from becoming major issues, and he can do this while protecting the rights of the workers he represents, without antagonizing the foremen with whom shop stewards usually deal. A contentious shop steward, however, can turn an amicable relationship into one marked by excessive petty bickering over minor details.

    In 1970, the AFL-CIO reported approximately 64,000 local unions belonging to national or international unions. In many communities, most locals affiliated with the AFL-CIO belong to the local central labor organization. The same locals are likely to be represented on the state central labor bodies, and some of them will also belong to local department councils.

    The greatest variation in the trade union movement comes at the local union level. Some local unions are well organized and are very active while others do very little. Their officers collect dues and transmit the appropriate amounts, per capita, to national union headquarters. Shop stewards process routine grievances, and the affairs of the local are handled in a generally lackadaisical manner. Meetings, when they are held are poorly attended, and there is little rank and file enthusiasm for trade union activities in general. But there are other locals in which the membership is active and often militant. In the United Auto Workers, for example, some locals wield considerable influence. The wishes of the rank and file get a respectful hearing at national headquarters, and the local officers may take an active part in the collective bargaining process.

By and large, however, the affairs of local unions are managed by a handful of "activists." This is not because the organization involved is a trade union, since the same is true of many other kinds of organizations which engage in political, economic, social, religious, or other activities. Trade unions are sometimes singled out for criticism because the rank and file do not take a more active interest in their affairs, yet if the critics were to take a careful look at other organizations, they would find that much the same is true. The typical union member is content to let the officers of the local, and the paid officers of his national union, handle affairs so long as things are going satisfactorily. When crises arise—as they do from time to time—the rank and file can generally be counted on to take an active interest in union matters until the problem that precipitated the crisis is settled to their satisfaction.

Independent National Unions

Not all national or international unions are affiliated with the AFL-CIO. The largest union in the country—the Teamsters—has been an independent union since it was expelled from the AFL-CIO following the investigation of the McClellan Committee. A number of smaller national unions were expelled from the CIO prior to the McClellan investigation because of the left-wing tendencies of their leaders. These unions, such as the Mine, Mill, and Smelter Workers, and the United Electrical Workers, have operated as independent national unions since that time. Chapter 11 indicated that since the end of 1947, the United Mine Workers has been an independent union, and that the United Auto Workers became an independent union in 1968.

The structure of an independent national or international union is very similar to that of the national unions that make up the AFL-CIO. Because the center of power in American trade unionism is found in the national union headquarters, the operations of most independent national unions seem not to have been impaired by their lack of affiliation with the AFL-CIO. Some of the independent national unions have lost membership in recent years because of the left-wing stigma attached to their leaders. When the United Electrical Workers was expelled from the CIO, for example, a rival union was formed within the federation known as the International Union of Electrical Workers

(IUE), which soon attracted a majority of the workers in the electrical machinery industry. Since the ouster of the UE and the formation of the IUE, there has been "dual unionism" in this industry.

Local Independent Unions

One type of labor organization remains to be discussed. It should be noted that this segment of the American labor movement has led to controversy among labor economists, some of whom doubt that all of the organizations involved may be considered as bona fide trade unions. These are the local independent unions, those labor organizations whose members are employed in a single plant or company and who are not affiliated with any national union or with the AFL-CIO. Local independent unions are also considered to be free of employer control or domination, directly or indirectly.[1] Troy distinguishes between local independent unions and company unions. The latter are considered to be company-*dominated* unions, and these have been illegal since the Wagner Act was passed.

Not everyone would agree with Troy's distinction. Professor Philip Taft, for example, acknowledges that many local independent unions function as bona fide labor organizations while others do not. "Many independents," he writes, "cannot be regarded normally as part of the labor movement ... "[2] In his opinion, many local independent unions "are either employer dominated or influenced by racket organizations whose chief aim is the victimization of the workers they organize."[3]

Troy has developed a series of "tests of legitimacy" and feels that most local independent unions pass this test—that they are legitimate trade unions and part of the American labor movement. Professor Taft, however, questions some of the criteria developed by Troy and argues that since company-dominated unions are illegal per se, all local independent unions must give the *appearance* of bona fide trade unions. It is important to emphasize that both Troy and Taft agree that some local independent unions are entirely legitimate and are accepted by the rest of the American labor movement as such. They disagree on the number of such organizations that should be considered as legitimate trade unions.

Information about local independent unions is less complete than that available for national or international unions. The Bureau of Labor Statistics has conducted two surveys, however, about the membership of the former. In both years, membership in local independent unions accounted for about 2.6

---

1. Leo Troy, "Local Independent Unions in the American Labor Movement," *Industrial and Labor Relations Review,* April 1961, p. 331.

2. "Local Independent Unions in the American Labor Movement," *Industrial and Labor Relations Review,* October 1961, p. 105.

3. *Ibid.,* p. 102.

per cent of total union membership in the United States. Between 1961 and 1967 the number of independent locals declined, but the survivors reported an increase in membership. In 1961, the BLS survey covered 1,277 locals, which reported total membership of 452,000. The number of independent locals covered in 1967 dropped to 884, but reported membership increased to 475,000.[4]

The Size and Composition of Trade Unions

In 1968, there were 189 national or international unions with headquarters in the United States, of which 126 were affiliated with the AFL-CIO. Thirteen of these unions accounted for more than half of all organized workers in the United States. This concentration of membership in a few large unions has long been characteristic of the American trade union movement. Two of the unions in the top ten, the Teamsters and the United Automobile Workers, are independents; all of the others are affiliated with the AFL-CIO.[5]

The size distribution of American unions in 1960 is summarized in Table 12-1. The distribution, in finer detail, is shown graphically in Figure 12-2. The curved line is the actual distribution of unions and union membership. The "line of equal distribution" shows the distribution as it would be if all unions had the same number of members.

TABLE 12-1
Distribution of Unions and Members by Size of Union, 1968

Number of Members Reported	Unions		Membership	
	Number	Per Cent	Number (thousands)	Per Cent
400,000 or more	11	5.9	9,460	46.8
200,000 to 400.000	14	7.4	4,171	20.6
50,000 to 200,000	47	24.9	4,977	24.6
10,000 to 50,000	53	28.0	1,433	7.1
Under 10,000	64	33.9	168	0.8

Source: U.S. Department of Labor, Bureau of Labor Statistics, *Directory of National and International Labor Unions in the United States, 1968,* Bulletin No. 1665 (1970), p. 69.

Figure 12-2 shows that 67 per cent of all union members—excluding those in local independent unions—belong to 13 per cent of the nation's unions. Thirty-eight per cent of all unions account for 92 per cent of total membership. Slightly more than one fourth of all unions, excluding the local indepen-

---

4. U.S. Department of Labor, Bureau of Labor Statistics, *Unaffiliated Intrastate and Single-Employer Unions, 1967,* Bulletin No. 1640 (November 1969), p. 1.

5. This does not include the United Mine Workers—also an independent union—since the UMW did not report membership to the BLS in 1968.

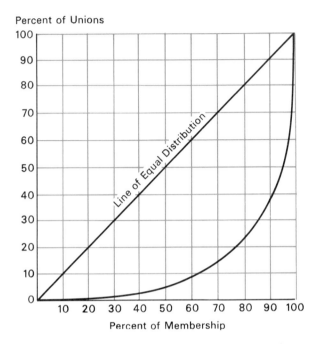

FIGURE 12–2.

Size Distribution of Unions, 1960. (*Data from U.S. Department of Labor, Bureau of Labor Statistics,* Directory of National and International Labor Unions in the United States, 1969, *Bulletin No. 1665 [1970]*.)

dents, have fewer than 5,000 members each. Collectively, these small unions include less than 1 per cent of total membership. The organizations that have done much to shape the "image" of trade unionism in America are the giants— the Teamsters, Steelworkers, Autoworkers, Machinists and Carpenters. At the other end of the spectrum are dozens of small unions representing workers in a wide variety of industries and occupations, yet the public rarely hears of these organizations or of their activities.

Trade union members are predominantly male. In 1968, it was estimated that about 20 per cent of all union members were women. Only about one out of seven women in the labor force belonged to a trade union. The highest ratios of women union members were in the garment and apparel industries; other unions with substantial female membership are in the communications, electrical, and transportation equipment industries, and in retail trade and service occupations.

Most union members are production workers. The U.S. Department of Labor has estimated that only about 3.2 million union members were in so-called white-collar occupations in 1968. White-collar workers accounted for almost 16 per cent of all union members in 1968, compared with about 12 per cent in 1958. Although two thirds of the white-collar unionists belong to one fourth of the nation's unions, there has been a tendency toward less concentration, or more dispersion, throughout the labor movement.

The Industrial Distribution of Membership

Less than half (45.6 per cent) of all union members in 1968 were employed in manufacturing industry. Trade unionists in nonmanufacturing activities accounted for 43.7 per cent of the total in the same year. The remaining 10.7 per cent were in federal, state, or local government employment. Two major nonmanufacturing activities—contract construction and transportation—accounted for 25 per cent of all union members in 1968. The trade and service sectors combined included about 16 per cent of total union membership. Elsewhere in nonmanufacturing—excluding mining and quarrying, which are highly organized—union organization is not widespread.

The degree of organization in manufacturing varies widely. The metal working industries—steel, autos, transportation equipment, for example—are heavily organized. Some nondurable goods industries, such as the garment and apparel trades, are fairly well organized; but in others, such as textiles and chemicals, unions have not been able to sign up a majority of workers in the industry.

The Government of Trade Unions

Before the rapid growth of unions in the mid-1930s, there was relatively little public interest in the ways in which trade unions were administered. Union membership was not widespread. As Sumner H. Slichter put it, "...some pioneer trade unionists who battled valiantly to build unions before the days of the Wagner Act...were brought up to regard unions as private clubs."[6] Today, however, unions are regarded by some as quasi-public institutions since, where union shop agreements obtain, a worker must remain a union member in good standing as a condition of employment. As early as 1947, Slichter estimated that 11 million jobs could be held only by men who remained in good standing in their unions.[7] Because the livelihood of so many union members is tied directly to their standing in a union, the ways in which unions are governed have come under close scrutiny. A number of scholars have made careful investigations of trade union government, but the results of these studies are not always easy to interpret.

---

6. Sumner H. Slichter, *The Challenge of Industrial Relations* (Ithaca, New York: Cornell University Press, 1947), p. 123.

7. *Ibid.*, p. 101.

Are trade unions democratic organizations? If not, is there some way they can be made to function in a democratic manner? Or is there any reason to expect that democracy will flourish in trade unions? None of these questions can be answered by a simple *yes* or *no*. It is generally agreed that in some respects unions should be democratic. They should not practice discrimination, for example, and the rank and file members should be protected from arbitrary disciplinary action by union officers. But beyond this, some scholars feel, it is futile to expect unions to function in the manner of the old New England town meeting. Following a careful study of trade union government, C. Peter McGrath concluded that American labor unions have become businesslike organizations. The successful union, in his view, is essentially nondemocratic. "However unpleasant the reality, democracy is as inappropriate within the international headquarters of the UAW as it is in the front office of General Motors."[8] Moreover, McGrath did not single out the UAW and General Motors for criticism; he believes that this conclusion applies widely throughout American labor and business organizations.

Others have pointed out that while we insist upon democracy in government we do not expect all the organizations to which we belong to function in a democratic manner. Even college professors would resist having classroom matters decided by popular vote. Those who demand simple answers to even the most complex problems will find little comfort in the conclusions regarding union democracy reached by scholars who have made meticulous studies of trade union government and administration. There are wide variations in union policies. Yet, in spite of this, some generalizations can be made about trade union government.

Union Admission Policies

Most unions admit properly qualified workers without regard to race, creed, or politics, and relatively few exclude members through excessive initiation fees. But apprenticeship rules may be effective barriers to persons seeking membership in some unions and, in a few cases, "fraternal" approval of all applicants for membership can be used for discriminatory purposes. Some unions, for example, exclude women. Slichter pointed out that a number of national unions had excluded Negroes through constitutional provisions or through union rituals; others discriminated against Negroes by establishing separate "Jim Crow" locals.[9] Even before the Civil Rights Act of 1964, however, some unions had become concerned about the problem of racial discrimination and were taking steps to eliminate it. After the Civil Rights bill became law, there were increasing pressures on other unions to put an end to discriminatory practices.

There have been times when union locals have restricted the entry of new

---

8. C. Peter McGrath, "Democracy in Overalls: Futile Quest for Union Democracy," *Industrial and Labor Relations Review, 12*, No. 4 (July 1959), p. 525.

9. Slichter, *op. cit.*, pp. 102–103.

members for economic purposes. Some locals have an informal rule, for example, that new members will not be admitted while members in good standing are involuntarily unemployed. National union officers generally oppose such practices, however, particularly in areas where there are nonunion shops. Once refused admission—for any reason—a worker will rarely regard unions with a kindly eye. Even if there were absolutely no restrictions on membership—if the doors were wide open to all—the issue of union democracy would not be completely settled, since there would still be problems involving the election of officers, the determination of basic policies, and the thorny problem of union discipline. Perhaps it is as unreasonable to expect a union with hundreds of thousands of members to follow strictly democratic procedures as it is to expect the executives of a large corporation to poll all stockholders before company decisions are made.

The Determination and Execution of Union Policies

In a study of seventy international unions, with a combined membership of almost 16 million, Leo Bromwich found that "all the unions in the sample designate the convention as the supreme body of the organization . . ."[10] But who selects delegates to the conventions? Who appoints convention committees? And who presides over the convention? The fact that grass-roots organizations are represented at a national convention does not in itself guarantee that democracy is at work.

The selection of delegates is of crucial importance, since in most cases the officers of the union are elected by the convention.[11] Most union constitutions specify the intervals at which conventions are to be held. Generally, conventions are held every two years, although some unions hold conventions only at five-year intervals. There have been times when conventions have been skipped entirely; during one period, for example, the Tobacco Workers allowed thirty-nine years to elapse between conventions.[12]

The selection of delegates is of critical importance if all factions in a national or international union are to be represented at the convention. As Bromwich[13] points out:

> Most of the rules for representation in the convention are clear, quantitative, and precise. They permit little opportunity for sharp practices or crafty pre-convention maneuvers. The differences which exist among the various unions

10. Leo Bromwich, *Union Constitutions* (New York: The Fund for the Republic, 1959), p. 38.

11. One of the few notable exceptions is the International Typographical Union, where national officers are elected by popular vote. This union is unique in a number of other respects, however, including its two-party system, which generally results in lively pre-election contests for office. For an excellent and detailed discussion of this union, see Seymour Martin Lipset, Martin Trow, and James Coleman, *Union Democracy* (Garden City, New York: Doubleday and Co., Inc., 1962).

12. Slichter, *The Challenge of Industrial Relations,* p. 104.

13. Bromwich, *Union Constitutions,* pp. 10–11.

largely reflect varied approaches to the problem of reconciling the interests of larger locals with those of the smaller ones in the distribution of convention power.

More than a third of the unions Bromwich studied have a graduated scale of representation which tends to favor smaller locals. The United Auto Workers constitution provides a typical example: it specifies that each local union shall have 1 delegate for 200 members or less, 1 additional delegate for the next 300, and an added delegate for each additional 800 members.

Most constitutions also contain rules for the election of delegates to national conventions. Some of these rules are precise, while others are quite vague. Some call for nominations at one time and elections at a later date, with prior notification of all members; others set a date for elections and do not provide for prior nominations. Still other constitutions state that delegates are to be elected, without specifying how, when, or where, and some have no provisions at all for the election of convention delegates. The constitution of the United Textile Workers, for example, requires only that each delegate establish his claim to a seat at the convention by credentials duly signed by the president and secretary of the local union.

The Convention Committees

The selection of delegates by democratic procedures does not guarantee democracy in a trade union. The various committees which run conventions can, if they wish, exert considerable control over procedures. Credential committees, for example, play an important part in settling disputed elections. Resolutions committees typically transmit policy statements from locals to the convention and can determine the priority of issues to be discussed, thus controlling the direction of the convention. Appeals committees handle grievances against local union officers. Convention committees, in brief, wield considerable power in determining what is to be discussed and when it is to reach the floor for discussion. In his survey of union constitutions, Bromwich found that "in the majority of cases, control of the committees is in the hands of the union president, and there is no real rank-and-file check on his power. In 49 of the 70 unions, the committees are simply appointed by the president. In another 11, the executive board has this job . . ."[14] Since he controls the convention committees, the union president is in an excellent position to manipulate the convention if he wishes to do so.

There is a lack of precision in union constitutions about the ways in which resolutions are to be handled. Generally, an officer of the national or international union is assigned the task of listing resolutions prior to the convention, but he is usually permitted considerable discretion in deciding how this is to

---

14. *Ibid.*, p. 13.

be done. An even greater shortcoming in some union constitutions is the absence of specific and unambiguous rules for reporting out resolutions. The resolutions committee appears to have considerable power to decide what is and what is not to be reported out.

Once resolutions have reached the floor of the convention, debate is generally conducted according to established rules, and decisions are made by majority vote. There are a few exceptions to this general rule. Some unions require a two-thirds majority for passage of a resolution. By and large, however, if resolutions reach the floor, they are decided by a simple majority of the delegates.

It must be emphasized that the existence of procedural weaknesses in some union constitutions with respect to convention procedures does not mean that union officers and convention committees abuse their power. All that can be said is that in many national and international unions the opportunity for such abuses exists.

Union constitutions can, of course, be amended, but the rules for constitutional amendments again range from the precise and detailed to the ambiguous. Some unions permit the conventions themselves to alter the constitution, whereas others call for discussion of proposed amendments at the convention, with a final decision to be made by a referendum. There is again no evidence of widespread rigging of constitutional amendments in national or international unions. The possibility exists, however, for unscrupulous officers to do so in some unions, if they are so inclined.

The Union Officers

Basic union policies are determined by conventions, but the execution of these policies is in the hands of union officers. Theoretically, the executive board is charged with the responsibility of executing policy, and the president, as chief executive officer, is subject to the board. In practice, however, the powers granted to national or international union presidents are very broad, while the powers granted to executive boards tend to be much more diffuse. The union president handles decisions on a day-to-day basis, whereas executive boards meet only at stated intervals or at the call of the president.

In typical cases, the union president has authority to appoint or suspend staff members and other employees. He also may exercise considerable control over union funds and may have the authority to approve or disapprove of strikes by locals.

Important grievances may also be handled by the president or by other national officers selected by the president. He also typically selects national representatives who provide liaison between the national union, regional headquarters, and the locals. Most national union presidents exercise considerable control over conventions, over the appointment of staff members and union employees, over union funds, and over union publications. The typical union president surrounds himself with able staff assistants who keep him informed of conditions in the industry or industries with which he must deal; help him in making important policy decisions; and regularly keep his views exposed to the rank and file. The capable union leader—and most of them have demonstrated their capability—thus becomes a knowledgeable professional. Once in a position of power, the union president is difficult to dislodge. There have been notable instances in the Teamsters and Steelworkers, for example, of sizeable rank-and-file revolts, but these are rarely successful. The president has the weight of national headquarters on his side, and it is difficult for dissident members to air their views beyond a specific local.

This does not mean that the president can be indifferent to the wishes of the rank and file. He must be able to "deliver the goods" to the satisfaction of most members. Machinery does exist for the removal of presidents if a majority of the rank and file wish to make a change, but there have been few cases where national or international presidents have been voted out of office. Once at the helm, the chief executive officers of national unions typically remain in control until death or retirement.

Election and Recall

A minority of national unions provide for the election of officers by a referendum vote. The outstanding example is the International Typographical Union, which has become famous for its two-party system, ensuring that the members can change officers annually if they wish to do so.

In the ITU, members announce their candidacy for office in the union's *Journal*. Each local nominates one candidate for each office from the published list; the five candidates for each office with the largest number of local union votes become eligible for election. All candidates are required to publish both their reasons for seeking office and arguments in support of their candidacy, in the union's periodical. Elections are conducted annually with appropriate safeguards at the polls.

Other unions use the referendum method, but none has worked out such precise procedures as those followed by the ITU. A majority of unions—more than three fourths of those studied by Bromwich, for example—elect officers at conventions.

Nominating procedures are far from precise in most union constitutions, and some specify no rules at all. Most unions which elect officers at conventions do not provide for nomination and election at separate times, and few provide for the supervision of elections by representatives of candidates or by a neutral body.

In most unions, election procedures give an advantage to those in office. This does not mean that union elections are rigged; but a president whose position is in jeopardy is in a position to make the decisions on the timing of nominations and elections. He will undoubtedly see that little time elapses between the two. Since his views are usually well known to the rank and file, an extended period between nominations and elections could give the opposition time to consolidate its forces.

In some of the older unions, which formerly belonged to the AF of L, the president has the power to remove any international officer, and there is no appeal from his decision. Where there are provisions for appeal, it is generally made to the executive board which, in the typical union, is controlled by the president.

Among the industrial unions formerly belonging to the CIO, the presidents are not allowed to remove international officers without appeal. Yet in some of these unions the executive board has the authority to suspend international officers, and there are no provisions for appeal. Where the president or executive boards have authority to suspend officers, this authority is not limited to specific causes. The same broad authority is generally given to officers or executive boards to revoke the charters of local unions.[15]

The ability to control elections and the power to suspend officers makes it difficult for dissidents in a union to gain support for their positions. This is not entirely accidental. One thing trade union leaders stress in their speeches and articles is the need for *union*. Workers, they maintain, must present a united front if the union is to realize gains for the rank and file. Unions are not debating societies, and if their leaders often develop the attitude that "papa knows best," this is often justified. Few rank and file members are in a position to see union problems in the same broad setting as their national or international officers.

A few unions—although a distinct minority—provide for control over officers through recall provisions. Generally, a single local may initiate a recall petition. If a specified percentage of locals support the petition, the officer whose recall is being demanded is required to answer the charges. A rival candidate is selected to run against the accused officer, and a referendum vote is held to determine if he is to be removed. Only a minority of nationals or internationals provide for recall. In practice, it has not been used at all, but this does not mean that it could not be used. Some unions retain at least the right to get rid of national or international officers if they fail to act in the interests of the rank and file.

Disciplining Union Members

It has been said that the issue of union government that attracts the greatest attention and arouses the most fear is union discipline.[16] The question of union discipline is not a simple one. On the one hand, unions must protect them-

---

15. Slichter, *op. cit.,* pp. 108–109.

16. See Philip Taft, *The Structure and Government of Labor Unions* (Cambridge, Mass.: Harvard University Press, 1954), p. 243.

selves against agents of employers or outside political groups intent upon sowing the seeds of dissension among the rank and file. On the other, if unions are to make more than a show of democracy, members who are disciplined must have some protection against the arbitrary action of union officers.

A number of union constitutions permit members to be disciplined for rather vague offenses. These include "slandering an officer," "creating dissension," "undermining the union or working against its interests," "action which is dishonorable or might injure the labor movement," and "circulating written material dealing with trade union business without permission of the general executive board."[17] What protection does the individual union member have against disciplinary action for such vague and nebulous offenses? Most unions provide for appeal procedures of one kind or another. But the critical question is: How effective are these procedures?

Bromwich feels that "there are a significant number of unions which do not set forth careful disciplinary procedures."[18] The major weakness is in the selection of review boards. In his survey Bromwich found that twenty-six unions, with a membership of more than 5.5 million, called for establishment of a review board by the local executive board. In eight other cases such boards are appointed by presidents of the local unions. It is not likely, however, if the member has been disciplined for criticizing local union leaders, that his review board will be entirely unbiased.

Other unions provide for the election of trial or review boards by the membership of the local, or the local meeting itself becomes a trial board. Such provisions, it would appear, should lead to the impartial judgment of workers subject to local union discipline. But even some unions noted for their democratic and responsible practices do not have clear-cut provisions for the unbiased review of disciplinary cases. A few unions, however, have developed procedures for guaranteeing a fair trial to members subject to union discipline. The outstanding examples are those developed by the International Typographical Union, the United Automobile Workers, and the Upholsterers.

The ITU constitution provides for a democratically elected trial committee to hear disciplinary cases. If the decision goes against the union member, he has the right of appeal. The first appeal is to the international executive council, but there are provisions for further appeals to the convention and ultimately to the courts. In the case of international officers, discipline is administered by a trial board made up of the presidents of the five largest locals, and the decision of this board can be appealed to the next convention. The disciplinary procedures of the United Automobile Workers roughly parallel those of the ITU. But the UAW has gone a step further by providing

---

17. Sumner H. Slichter, op. cit., pp. 110–111, quoted from Philip Taft "Judicial Procedures in Labor Unions," Quarterly Journal of Economics, May 1945, pp. 370–385.

18. Bromwich, op. cit., p. 33.

for an "outside" review board made up of seven well-known public figures who have no connection with the union. The Upholsterers Union provides for a similar independent public review system.

In all cases, a disciplined union member may have ultimate recourse to the courts. Yet in cases where disciplinary measures are upheld by outside review boards, it is highly unlikely that an aggrieved member would take his case to court.

Some students of trade union government have argued that except in the ITU, the UAW, and the Upholsterers, the rights of disciplined union members are not strongly protected. On the other hand, Professor Philip Taft, who has made exhaustive studies of trade union government, points out that even in unions noted for their autocratic government, such as the United Mine Workers, there have been many appeals against discipline. He feels that "rights of members and their protection in the union seem, on the whole, adequate."[19] Clark Kerr has also said that "a good deal more democracy exists in unions than . . . outside observation would indicate.[20]

Unions cannot function as simple "town meeting democracies" without endangering their cohesiveness. There undoubtedly have been instances where individual union members have not received the full justice to which they are entitled, but in the overwhelming majority of cases disciplined members have had an opportunity for review of their cases. Despite the fact that in many local unions review boards cannot always be considered unbiased, there is always ultimate recourse to the courts. As Professor Taft has observed, much of the concern about union discipline is without foundation. The issue has undoubtedly been greatly overplayed. A few instances of abuse do not form an adequate basis for criticizing union disciplinary procedures as a whole.

The AFL–CIO Ethical Practices Codes

Leaders of the American labor movement have recognized that as trade unions have matured, opportunities have developed for unscrupulous union officers to capitalize on their positions of power to their personal advantage and to the detriment of the labor movement as a whole. In response to this, the AFL-CIO, at its 1955 convention and through subsequent action by the Executive Council, set up six codes of ethical practices as guides to its member unions. These codes deal with the following issues:

I. Local union charters
II. Health and welfare funds
III. Racketeers, crooks, Communists, and Fascists

---

19. Taft, *op. cit.*, p. 245.

20. Clark Kerr, *Unions and Union Leaders of Their Own Choosing* (New York: The Fund for the Republic, December 1957), p. 10.

    IV. Investments and business interests of union officials
    V. Financial practices and proprietary activities of unions
    VI. Union democratic processes

The first code was directed primarily against "paper locals." Such locals have been established by racketeers, in collusion with employers, to forestall the organization of legitimate unions. In the language of the AFL-CIO, racketeers have also used such charters as "hunting licenses" to invade the jurisdictions of other national unions. To prevent these practices, Code I specifies that national unions should issue local charters only upon "application by a group of bona fide employees eligible for membership in the union within the jurisdiction covered by the charter."[21]

The second code specifies that no union official is to receive fees or salaries from funds established for health, welfare, or retirement programs, nor should the union official have "any compromising personal ties" with agencies—such as insurance carriers or brokers—who do business with the welfare plan. This code also calls for auditing and full disclosure of welfare funds, and for the selection of insurance carriers through competitive bids. Unions are urged to remove violators of the code from office.

The third code urges all affiliated unions to prevent racketeers, crooks, Communists, Fascists, or representatives of other totalitarian agencies, from holding office. The fourth attempts to prevent conflicts of interests, such as would arise if a union official had a substantial interest in the firms of employers with which he deals. The fifth code urges all unions affiliated with the AFL-CIO to follow sound accounting practices. There are specific provisions covering union purchases, loans and investments, and contracts for the purchase or sale of goods or services that could lead to the benefit of a union officer.

The final code in the series urges that each member of affiliated unions be given the right to full and free participation in union self-government and fair treatment in the application of union rules and law. There are specific provisions dealing with union conventions, the election of officers, and the conduct of meetings.

It should be noted that many of the provisions of the ethical practices codes are also covered by the Landrum-Griffin Act, passed September 14, 1959. The last of the codes was adopted by the AFL-CIO Executive Council on May 23, 1957. Thus some time before Congress provided legal measures for the control of internal union affairs, the AFL-CIO had noted that there were problems in some of its affiliated unions and had set up standards for dealing with these problems, which it hoped all unions would meet.

---

21. Sar A. Levitan (ed.), *Government Regulation of Internal Union Affairs Affecting the Rights of Members,* Selected readings prepared for the Subcommittee on Labor, Committee on Labor and Public Welfare, U.S. Senate, 85th Congress, Second Session (Washington, D.C.: U.S. Government Printing Office, 1958), p. 151.

Labor Corruption and Racketeering

The vast majority of American unions are led by men whose honesty and integrity are above question. Members of the community might not always approve of either their objectives or their methods. And there are times when union leaders appear to place the welfare of their members above that of the community as a whole. As Philip Taft has pointed out, however, "such conduct does not indicate venality or corruption even though it might not be, from the point of view of many, socially desirable."[22]

There have been instances of the corruption of union leaders, the infiltration of bona fide unions by racketeers, and the establishment of bogus local unions by racketeers intent upon the victimization of businessmen and the public. Some union leaders have not been able to resist the abuse of power. They are not unique in this respect. The crooked politician, the embezzling financier, and the shady or dishonest businessman are not—unhappily—unknown in our society. This is not to suggest that because corruption is found elsewhere it can be tolerated in the labor movement. The honest citizen will oppose corruption wherever it is found. There has been particular indignation about labor corruption, however, because of the idealistic foundation upon which trade unionism rests. Revelations of labor corruption evoke much the same reaction as that which follows the exposure of malfeasance in public office.

Labor corruption, in the minority of unions where it is found, runs the gamut from outright criminal activities—such as embezzlement of union funds and the acceptance of bribes or kickbacks—to what many might regard as simply "sharp" business practices. The latter include collusive agreements with employers to create monopolies and the acceptance of loans from employers. Such loans are generally made on terms favorable to the labor leader, since the employer who lends money to a labor leader, at a lower rate of return than he could obtain elsewhere, is looking for some other form of payment. This might come in the form of a substandard contract or "sweetheart" agreement. Pay-offs also have been made to corrupt union leaders as "insurance" against organizing campaigns, strikes, or other legitimate union activities.

The growth of union health and welfare funds provided a lush field for the enrichment of a few ingenious but dishonest labor leaders. Insurance policies, with high premiums and skimpy benefits, have been placed with friends of the labor leader in return for a consideration. Union funds have been invested in enterprises in which labor leaders have had an interest—sometimes as silent partners. Such investments usually have not been the kind that an honest investment counselor would recommend.

There have been a few instances in the past where labor leaders have

---

22. Philip Taft, *Corruption and Racketeering in the Labor Movement* (Ithaca, New York: New York State School of Industrial and Labor Relations, Bulletin 38 (February 1958), p. 1.

sought alliances with racketeers to protect their organizing activities. They found, however, that once established such alliances were not easy to break off, and some unions ended up by becoming the prey of underworld elements whose "protection" they had earlier sought. A more frequent phenomenon, however, has been the invasion of legitimate unions by thugs and gangsters. Following repeal of the 18th Amendment, and the loss of revenue from bootlegging, some underworld elements in Chicago moved into the labor-management field. The waterfront unions in New York were long under the domination of racketeers who victimized employees and employers alike.[23] Extortion, pilferage, murder, and other criminal activities, on a scale that probably will never be fully known, were the result of domination of the New York waterfront by underworld elements.

As Philip Taft has noted, corruption and racketeering are not new to the American labor movement. More than half a century ago Congress appointed the United States Industrial Commisison to investigate labor problems. This Commission found evidence of extortion in the Chicago building trades. Shortly after this investigation there were revelations of illicit activities on the part of labor leaders such as Sam Parks of the New York building trades, Skinny Madden of the Chicago Steamfitters, and Robert P. Brindell of the New York Dock and Pier Carpenters' union.[24]

It is significant that the members of some unions have continued to support labor leaders even after their corrupt activities have been exposed. Sam Parks, for example, was re-elected to his office as head of the Housesmiths' Union of New York while serving a term in Sing Sing for arranging collusive agreements and selling strike insurance.[25] This has always puzzled outside observers but it is a reflection of the mores of our society. If corrupt labor leaders have continued to "deliver the goods" for the rank and file, the latter have appeared to be unwilling to pass judgment on the morals of their officers.

The most widely publicized revelations of labor corruption resulted from the investigation of the Senate Select Committee on Improper Activities in the Labor or Management Field—the McClellan Committee. This investigation extended over a period of almost three years. One result was the Landrum-Griffin Act of 1959. In 1956, the Ethical Practices Committee of the AFL-CIO had recommended to the Executive Council that the Allied Industrial Workers, the Laundry Workers and the Distillery Workers should "show cause" why they should not be expelled because of corrupt influences in the administration of welfare funds. And at the December 1957 convention, the Teamsters, the Bakery Workers, and the Laundry Workers were expelled on charges of domination by corrupt influences. Thus the leaders of the AFL-CIO were

---

23. *Ibid.,* pp. 12–13.
24. *Ibid.,* pp. 4–9.
25. *Ibid.,* p. 6.

taking steps to renovate the House of Labor just as the McClellan Committee hearings were getting underway.

The McClellan Committee hearings ran to many thousands of pages, and only some of the major findings can be given here. Further details can be obtained from the Committee's interim reports.[26] A dramatic account of the complete investigation is given in Robert F. Kennedy's *The Enemy Within*.[27]

The Committee found evidence of corruption in a number of unions, including the Hotel and Restaurant Workers, the Sheet Metal Workers, the Mail Deliverers, the Bakery and Confectionery Workers, two locals of the Amalgamated Meat Cutters and Butcher Workmen of North America, and the United Textile Workers.[55] But the union and official most intensively investigated were the International Brotherhood of Teamsters and its president, James R. Hoffa. The *Second Interim Report* of the McClellan Committee listed 19 topics covered by the inquiry involving the Teamsters, Hoffa, and other officers of the union, and one section of this report dealt entirely with alleged malfeasance in the administration of Teamster insurance plans. As pointed out in the last chapter, Hoffa was eventually convicted of jury tampering, and served five years of a thirteen-year sentence before receiving a pardon.

Dave Beck, president of the Teamsters at the start of the McClellan hearings, and a powerful and respected man before his exposure, was completely destroyed as a labor leader by the investigation. He was subsequently convicted by a federal court of income tax evasion. The Teamsters elected Hoffa to succeed Beck. Both Hoffa and the Teamsters were under a cloud of suspicion at the time of his election, but under a consent decree, he was permitted to take office, and a board of monitors was appointed by the court to supervise his and the union's activities. Hoffa refused to accept the monitors' recommendations, however, and there is little evidence that they inhibited his activities in any way.

Following the McClellan Committee investigation, a number of labor officials were indicted by federal courts on charges ranging from perjury to extortion and embezzlement. A few were convicted, while others were acquitted, usually because of insufficient evidence to support the charges against them.

Leaders of the AFL-CIO and of the many unions untouched by scandal were disturbed, perhaps more than anyone else, by the revelations of corruption in a handful of unions.[29] They realized that the entire labor movement

---

26. For excerpts of the *First Interim Report* (March 1958), see *Monthly Labor Review,* May 1958, pp. 518–520. Somewhat more extensive excerpts of the *Second Interim Report* (August 1959) are given in *Monthly Labor Review,* September 1959, pp. 981–991.

27. Robert F. Kennedy, *The Enemy Within* (New York: Harper and Brothers, 1960); also published in paperback edition (New York: Popular Library, 1960). Page references are to the latter edition.

28. The United Textile Workers, a relatively small union, should not be confused with the Textile Workers Union of America, which has not been touched by scandal.

29. Kennedy, *op. cit.,* p. 204.

would suffer from guilt by association, at least in the eyes of some. This was cogently expressed by a group of foreign labor officials, members of a mission from the International Labour Office: "Even though the inquiries of the Mc-Clellan Committee only covered a tiny minority of the unions operating in the United States, and even though the proved facts only relate to a very small number of cases, some mud has nevertheless stuck to the American trade union movement as a whole.[30]

The McClellan Committee hearing dealt largely with corruption and racketeering in the labor movement. But the Landrum-Griffin Act—an outgrowth of the McClellan investigation—attempts to deal with two distinct issues: one of these is union corruption and racketeering, and the other is the lack of union democracy. Few would question the social desirability of legislation aimed at the elimination of labor corruption and racketeering. However, in the Landrum-Griffin Act, Congress assumed that union democracy can be legislated. Many union officials, and some observers outside the labor movement, have serious doubts that this is so.

Voluntary vs. Legislative Control of Internal Union Affairs

Two broad issues of union government have been discussed in this chapter. One deals with internal union affairs: the control of corruption and the establishment of sound procedures for the administration of union financial affairs. The matter of "conflict of interest" is also involved in this connection. The other issue is that of trade union democracy.

One would expect almost unanimous agreement that all means, whether voluntary or legislative, should be used to ensure that union affairs are conducted honestly, with appropriate auditing and disclosure, and that union officials should not allow themselves to get into compromising positions where their integrity as union leaders is open to question. The only dissenters from this point of view would be the crooks or racketeers against whom the Ethical Practices Codes and some provisions of the Landrum-Griffin Act are aimed. It is not likely that every vestige of corruption can be eliminated, but every effort should be made to do so. Trade unions are not private clubs. In many ways they are quasi-public institutions. Some union leaders might bridle at public regulation of internal union affairs; however, the honest union official has nothing to fear. If regulation makes it more difficult for crooks and racketeers to subvert trade unions to their own selfish ends, the entire labor movement will gain.[31]

On the issue of union democracy, however, the matter is much less simple. There is considerable disagreement about the extent of democracy

---

30. *The Trade Union Situation in the United States,* Report of a Mission from the International Labour Office (Geneva: ILO, 1960), p. 89.

31. Many union officials have indicated their satisfaction with the reporting and disclosure sections of the Landrum-Griffin Act. See the *New York Times,* November 18, 1962; and George Strauss, "The Shifting Power Balance in the Plant," *Industrial Relations,* May 1962, p. 73.

in trade unions, part of which stems from a lack of agreement on the meaning of democracy. Sumner Slichter pointed out, for example, that it is not easy to answer the question: Are unions democratic? If democracy means rank and file participation, unions might not be considered very democratic. Professional leaders decide most policy matters at the national level, yet Slichter distinguished between rank and file participation and *influence*. He felt that the influence of rank and file members is great—far out of proportion to their participation. Although there is little competition for offices at the national level, the leaders must be responsive to the wishes of the rank and file. Union constitutions generally contain provisions for turning out officers if the rank and file should become disaffected.

On specific matters—such as voting rights, union discipline and appeal procedures, the selection of convention delegates, and so on—there is wide variation among unions. Many labor scholars feel that there is considerable room for improvement in a number of national and international unions. But how is this improvement to be achieved? Can it be legislated? Jack Barbash, who has had a long career both as a trade union staff official and as an educator, feels that: "It is a serious mistake to work on the theory that union democracy can be instituted through legislation where it does not now exist."[32] This does not mean that Barbash is opposed to all legislation regulating union affairs. His view on union democracy, quoted above, was written before the Landrum-Griffin Act was passed and, at that time, he indicated his support for certain kinds of labor legislation—specifically of the disclosure type—which would ensure responsibility in the handling of union funds. But when it comes to such matters as union elections and protection of the rights of individual members, Barbash is inclined to place the "greatest reliance on the preservation and strengthening of the democratic processes of the labor movement on the labor movement itself."[33]

Many unions have gone to great lengths in their efforts to increase rank and file participation in union affairs. By and large these efforts have been unsuccessful. Only a minority of rank and file members will give up part of their leisure time to attend union meetings. This is not a matter of indifference; rather it indicates that the rank and file are generally satisfied with the way local and national union officers are conducting union affairs. Slichter's comment [34] on this is revealing:

> If one asks whether unions give their members what they want, the proper answer is that for most unions the question is irrelevant. The great majority of the members do not have much opportunity or desire to consider and discuss alternative policies. Hence they are not to be regarded as making a choice. The proper question to ask is: "Do the members like what they get?" The answer to that question is usually: "Yes."

---

32. Jack Barbash, "Union Democracy," in Levitan, *Government Regulation of Internal Union Affairs Affecting the Rights of Members*, p. 135.
33. *Ibid.*, p. 137.
34. Slichter, *op. cit.*, p. 114.

Questions and Exercises

1. What is the highest governing body of the AFL-CIO? What role does the Executive Council play in the Federation? Who are the members of the Executive Council?

2. Describe the role of the Departments in the AFL-CIO. How do state councils and local central bodies fit into the structure of the AFL-CIO?

3. Describe the structure of a typical national or international union. It is often said that the locus of power in the American trade union movement is in the headquarters of national unions. Why is this so? What role is played by local unions in the AFL-CIO structure?

4. Under what conditions did the Teamsters Union leave the AFL-CIO? Are there any basic differences in the structure and operation of independent national unions and national unions that belong to the AFL-CIO?

5. What distinction has been made by Leo Troy between local independent unions and company unions? How extensive are local independent unions? Has membership in local independent unions increased relative to total union membership in the United States?

6. Describe in general terms the size distribution of American trade unions.

7. White-collar workers accounted for an estimated 16 per cent of total union membership in 1968. Has the proportion of white-collar unionists been increasing or decreasing?

8. Describe briefly the industrial distribution of trade union membership in the United States, and relate this to the distribution of employment discussed in Chapter 2.

9. What conclusion was reached by C. Peter McGrath in his study of democracy in trade unions?

10. The supreme body of all labor unions in the United States is the convention. Because of this, methods of selecting delegates to the convention may reflect the responsiveness of the union to its members' wishes. According to Bromwich, what can be said about the rules governing conventions? Are convention committees able to exercise any control over convention procedures?

11. Write a brief essay on the office of national union president. Among other things, discuss the ways in which union presidents are elected, their tenure of office, and their relationship to staff and other union officials.

12. Describe the procedure by which the president of the International Typographical Union is elected. Is this procedure typical of most national unions?

13. In general, is it true that union constitutions clearly set forth disciplinary procedures? In most unions, what provisions are made for the establishment of review boards to handle disciplinary cases? Is there anything unique about the review arrangements that have been established by the International Typographical Union, the United Automobile Workers, and the Upholsterers Union?

14. What are the AFL-CIO ethical practices codes? Why were these codes adopted?

15. Why was the McClellan Committee established, and what were some of the results of this committee's investigation? What did the McClellan investigation show about the extent of corruption and racketeering in the American trade union movement?

16. Briefly discuss the issue of voluntary vs. legislative control of internal union affairs.

Suggested Readings

Books

Estey, Marten S. et al. Regulating Union Government. New York: Harper and Row, 1964.

Kerr, Clark. Unions and Union Leaders of Their Own Choosing. New York: The Fund for the Republic, 1957.

Lipset, Seymour Martin. et al. Union Democracy. Glencoe, Illinois: The Free Press, 1956; paperback edition, Garden City, New York: Anchor Books, Doubleday and Co., 1962.

Miller, Robert W., Frederick A. Zeller, and Glenn W. Miller. The Practice of Local Union Leadership. Columbus, Ohio: The Ohio State University Press, 1965.

Slichter, Sumner H. The Challenge of Industrial Relations. Ithaca, New York: Cornell University Press, 1947.

Taft, Philip. Corruption and Racketeering in the Labor Movement. Bulletin 38. Ithaca, New York: New York State School of Industrial and Labor Relations, 1958.

Taft, Philip. The Structure and Government of Labor Unions. Cambridge, Mass.: Harvard University Press, 1954.

Articles

Ginsburg, Woodrow. "Review of Literature on Union Growth, Government and Structure—1955–1969," in Woodrow L. Ginsburg et al., A Review of Industrial Relations Research, Vol. I. Madison, Wisconsin: Industrial Relations Research Association, 1970.

McGrath, C. Peter. "Democracy in Overalls: The Futile Quest for Union Democracy," Industrial and Labor Relations Review, 12 (July 1959), pp. 503–525.

Taft, Philip. "Local Independent Unions in the American Labor Movement," Industrial and Labor Relations Review, 15, No. 1 (October 1961), pp. 102–106, and "Reply" by Leo Troy, pp. 106–110.

Troy, Leo. "Local Independent Unions in the American Labor Movement," Industrial and Labor Relations Review, 14, No. 3 (April 1961), pp. 331–349.

13

Trade Union Philosophy and Objectives

Earlier chapters discussed the rise of the American labor movement and the structure and government of trade unions. Before turning to a discussion of labor law, and the various issues involved in collective bargaining, it might be well to look at the broad objectives of trade unions. What are the goals of American unions? How do they seek to accomplish their objectives? Has the basic philosophy of the American labor movement changed over time, and if so in what direction? How do trade union attitudes in the United States compare with those found in the democracies of Western Europe? These questions cannot be answered in fine detail within the scope of this chapter, but a broad framework can be developed, which should contribute to a better understanding of the collective bargaining process.

The Distinctive Ideology of American Labor Unions

Trade unions in the United States differ in a number of ways from their counterparts in other democratic countries. The character of the labor movement in each country has been determined to a large extent by the environment in which stable trade unionism emerged. The trade unions which finally took root in the United States, after almost a century of experimentation, were of the pragmatic variety referred to as "business unions." While there were numerous radical and reform ideas in the United States during the nineteenth century, none was able to attract a large following. The leaders of the early AF of L recognized the failure of reform groups to appeal to the American imagination—including that of the workingman—and out of this developed the formula which led to the growth of craft unionism in this country. Until fairly recent times, conditions in Europe were quite different from those in the United States, and these conditions led to a distinctly different type of labor movement.

What are some of the characteristics of western European society that helped shape a kind of trade unionism quite different from the one we are familiar with in this country? Because of the feudal background of most western European countries, there was, until recent times, a great deal of social stratification. In the United States, by way of contrast, there has been considerably more social mobility. Thus workers in western Europe felt themselves to be part of a working class from which there was little hope of escape, short of emigration. Property qualifications for voting also kept most workmen from active political participation. The standard of living in most western European countries was also well below that of the United States; there was no opportunity to escape to an open frontier, and there was little opportunity to become an independent businessman.

Because of class consciousness, lack of political participation, and limited mobility, European workers became strongly ideological.[1] Workers did not join trade unions simply to improve their economic status. There was a close connection between trade unions and political parties, and a worker's political ideology would determine the union of his choice. Thus workers employed in a single plant might belong to different unions. They were not bound together by job consciousness. Indeed, workers at the same bench might often be divided by a wide ideological gap. Each political party—the Socialists, Communists, Anarchists, Social Democrats, and various religious parties—had its own trade union. A worker might move from job to job, or even change occupations, without changing his union affiliation. Ideological conflicts among the various political parties of western Europe often prevented workers from forming a united front when seeking concessions from employers. Thus the trade union movement in many western European countries remained fragmented. In terms of numerical strength, union growth might have appeared impressive, but European unions were able to accomplish much less for their members, in terms of wages, hours, and working conditions, than their numerically weaker American counterparts.

The founders of the AF of L saw the weakness of such fragmentation, and insisted that a common *job interest* would bind workers together effectively. While union membership grew slowly in the United States during the early years of the AF of L the workers who joined unions were able to win solid gains. Meanwhile their European counterparts were less interested in collective bargaining than in political maneuvering, and by dissipating their energies along broad fronts, they made limited gains in any direction.

There was little kinship between American and European leaders, especially before World War II. European labor leaders were critical of their American counterparts. They spoke scornfully of business unionism in the United States and were critical of American labor leaders for their lack of

---

1. Morris Weisz, "Labor Ideology and Practice in Europe and the U.S.," *Monthly Labor Review,* March 1958, pp. 265–269.

ideology. At the same time, trade-union leaders in America were often openly scornful of the failure of European trade unions to improve the economic lot of their members.

The failure of politically oriented European unions to make substantial progress, despite their numerical strength, helped solidify the conviction of the leaders of the AF of L that their form of union organization was superior. It is quite possible that the relative weakness of European unions was due more to *fragmentation* than to political orientation. But the founders of stable trade unionism in America were convinced that political alliances of any kind were dangerous. The only way to get ahead, in their minds, was through a show of economic strength.

The Left-Wing Challenge

The principle of no political entanglements in the American labor movement did not go entirely unchallenged. Until our entry into World War I, a highly vocal and well-organized group within the AF of L insisted that business unionism was not the ultimate answer to the problems of American labor. This group insisted that organized labor would eventually have to wrest control of the economy from the owners of property. Various socialist groups at different times tried to gain control of the AF of L, but like their European brethren, the socialists in this country could not unite under a common banner.

The Socialist Labor Party

One of the splinter groups, which was impatient with the stated goals of the AF of L, was the Socialist Labor Party founded in 1876. When Daniel De Leon became the leader of this party in 1889, he was determined that the party would slowly take over the growing AF of L. At one time De Leon was a teacher of mathematics, and later of international law, but he gave up his academic career to lead the Socialist Labor Party and to carry on an unremitting attack against Samuel Gompers and other leaders of the AF of L.

The Socialists managed to gain control of the Central Labor Federation of New York and petitioned for a charter in the AF of L. But at the 1890 convention this was refused. Following this, the Socialists attempted to "bore from within." Following their rejection at the 1890 convention, the Socialists gained some strength in the ranks of organized labor. Their propaganda campaign was aided by the depression of the early 1890s and the failure of the AF of L to grow under adverse economic conditions. The Socialist minority in the craft unions agitated strongly for political action and urged the Federation to adopt a program for the nationalization of industry. Their campaign came to a head at the Denver convention of 1894. Because of widespread unemployment and general political unrest, a majority of the unions represented at the convention had endorsed the Socialist program.

A number of planks in the convention's platform that year had a Socialist tinge. For a time it appeared that the AF of L was about to depart from its policy of no political involvement, in a very extreme way. The most controversial part of the program was Plank 10, which called for "collective ownership by the people of all the means of production and distribution." Acceptance of this plank would have meant repudiation of business unionism and adoption of an outright Socialist program.

The debate over Plank 10 raged for five days, and was finally defeated only after a number of parliamentary maneuvers by the anti-Socialists at the convention. This they accomplished by introducing a number of palpably ridiculous amendments to Plank 10, which in the general confusion the delegates voted down. Another motion calling for independent political action by the Federation was defeated by a relatively close vote. The advocates of business unionism won. However, it was close and the Socialists continued to carry on their criticism of the job-conscious craft unionism of the AF of L until their program fell apart after our entry into World War I. After the Denver convention, however, there was a split in the ranks of the Socialist Labor Party. While both groups continued to denounce AF of L leaders, they could not again unite in a common attack.

Meanwhile, two new socialist movements were started in the Middle West, one led by Eugene V. Debs and the other by Victor Berger. Eventually these two groups came together and united with a splinter group, which had left the Socialist Labor Party. In 1901, they met to form the Socialist Party of America which, among other things, declared its intention of organizing the workers of America—and those in sympathy with the working class—with the ultimate objective of collective ownership of the means of production. The new Socialist Party was less doctrinaire than the De Leon group had been, but it was rejected as completely by the AF of L as had been the earlier more radical group. Efforts to bore from within were continued, although the socialists were not again to become the threat they had been in 1894.

When World War I broke out in Europe, the leaders of socialism in the United States joined their counterparts in Europe in denouncing the war effort. They urged workers in all countries to refuse to bear arms and thus sought to abort the war in its early stages. But this was not a popular cause in the countries then at war, and it soon became unpopular in the United States. While socialist parties and socialist trade unions became active in Europe after the end of World War I, membership in the various socialist parties in this country dwindled to the point where they became ineffective even as protest groups.

The Victory of Voluntarism

The philosophy adopted by the AF of L after the defeat of the socialist threat has been called "voluntarism." This was the notion that workers should rely exclusively on trade unions to promote their interests as wage earners. No positive aid from the government was to be sought or accepted; as a matter of fact, government assistance was to be rejected.[2]

The advocates of voluntarism wanted no help from government, not even in the form of social legislation. The only concession they would make was to support legislation that would have guaranteed both the rights of workers to organize and the protection of trade unions from outside interference. They also favored legislative enactment of the eight-hour day. But as late as 1931, the AF of L Convention refused to endorse legislation which would have provided unemployment insurance. Prior to this, the AF of L had supported various forms of legislation, but most of it was of a negative character. The Federation supported legislation to restrict immigration, and other legislation designed to remove legal impediments to organization and effective strike action. The third type of legislation the Federation supported was that which eventually provided standards for the employment of women and children.[3]

By 1954, however, the year before the merger with the CIO, the AF of L had clearly departed from its earlier philosophy of voluntarism. At that convention the Federation adopted a ten-point program for government action, which included a declaration that the "resumption of full production and full employment is the overriding objective of national policy."[4] As Douty pointed out, while the Federation had "not lost faith in the value of collective bargaining for improving the worker's lot, it [had] elevated government, and hence politics, to something approaching an equal role."

Trade Unions and Political Action

The philosophy of voluntarism in the American labor movement had disappeared long before the 1954 convention of the AF of L. Even before the advent of the CIO, the AF of L had made a few minor concessions, such as supporting unemployment insurance. But the real break with the past, marked by active trade union participation in politics, came after the CIO had become a going organization.

During the early days following the AFL-CIO split, the AF of L leaders continued to insist upon the necessity of keeping out of partisan politics. The CIO also claimed in principle that it would support all candidates for political office whose views it favored, but in practice most of these candidates turned out to be members of the Democratic Party. There were times, indeed, during the early years of the split, when the two federations openly supported opposing candidates, especially in primary elections.

---

2. David J. Saposs, "Voluntarism in the American Labor Movement," *Monthly Labor Review,* September 1954. See also Michael Rogin, "Voluntarism: The Political Functions of an Antipolitical Doctrine," *Industrial and Labor Relations Review,* July 1962, pp. 521–535.

3. See H. M. Douty, "The Seventy-Third Convention of the AFL," *Monthly Labor Review,* November 1954.

4. *Ibid.*

For a brief time after 1936, leaders of unions in both federations cooperated to form Labor's Non-Partisan League, which supported the candidacy of President Roosevelt for re-election. But by 1938, AF of L leaders had left the League and some denounced it strongly. On the other hand, by 1944, the CIO had made it clear that it intended to continue to play an active part in political campaigns, and in that year it established its Political Action Committee (PAC). The PAC worked hard to support candidates of its choice.

The AF of L did not follow the CIO's lead until after the Taft-Hartley Act was passed in 1947. Among other things, this law restricted the political activity of labor unions by prohibiting the use of union funds for political contributions. This act forced the AF of L to set up an organization structurally independent of the federation if it wished to make political contributions. The result was Labor's League for Political Education (LLPE). Both Labor's League for Political Education and the Political Action Committee obtained their funds by direct contribution from union members instead of from general union funds. It is somewhat ironical that the Taft-Hartley Act, which sought to restrict the activities of unions in a number of ways, actually stimulated labor participation in political action. The CIO had already been committed to a program of political education, but the AF of L set up its political arm only after the Taft-Hartley Act had forced the federation to take a stand on participation in political campaigns.[5]

Following the AFL-CIO merger in 1955, the merged federation established a new political arm, the Committee on Political Education (COPE). While there were some difficulties in establishing the Committee, as there had been in working out other details of the merger, they were eventually ironed out, and the trade-union movement in the United States has continued to participate actively in political campaigns.

What are the political goals of trade unions? Would the nation's union leaders like to gain political control of the country? At times it has been asserted that the ultimate goal of union leaders is the establishment of a Labor Party, either through the capture of the Democratic Party or the establishment of a new and independent political force. However, there is no evidence to support this contention. Indeed, there is considerable evidence to the contrary. Union leaders have repeatedly insisted that they have no intention of changing established political relationships. They actively support candidates who tend to be sympathetic toward trade union views.

Union leaders would like to see certain objectives realized, such as greater stability of employment and more rapid economic growth, with workers sharing in the gains of increased productivity. But union leaders insist that they will seek these goals by supporting candidates in the two major political parties. Most often they have supported "liberal" members of the Democratic party, but this has not been universally true. Some union leaders have been

5. See Edwin L. Witte, "The New Federation and Political Action," *Industrial and Labor Relations Review,* April 1956, pp. 409–414.

outspoken in their support of Republicans. While unions are much more active in political affairs than they were a quarter of a century ago, they have departed much less from Samuel Gompers's dictum of "reward your friends and punish your enemies" than many critics of trade unions would have us believe.

It is worth recalling that the rapid growth of trade unions came at a time when a liberal administration and a liberal Congress were pushing through a number of social and economic reforms. Most union leaders actively supported these reforms and were openly associated with the liberal cause. But some students of organized labor feel that as unions have prospered, their leaders have tended to become increasingly conservative. Indeed, it would be surprising if the outlook of labor leaders did not change as the environment in which they operated has been altered. As Neil Chamberlain has pointed out, the dominant theme of trade unionism during the nineteenth century was that of reform of the wage system.[6] With the rise of the AF of L, the trade union movement tried to find its place in a political system which it accepted. Events of the 1930s led to explosive growth and the rise of a number of militant and politically oriented labor leaders. However, as the trade union movement has grown in size and has become more secure in its position, much of this militancy has been replaced by complacency.[7]

From Militancy to Maturity

In what ways have trade unions changed? And what are some of the causes of changes in the philosophy of union leaders? Some aspects of this question were examined by Will Herberg.[8] Herberg began his analysis by noting the dual nature of modern trade unions: on the one hand, businesslike service organizations, and on the other, vehicles for expressing the needs of workers for social recognition and democratic self-determination. In Herberg's view, the dual nature of unions leads to a fundamental conflict of purpose and orientation. As service organizations, modern unions require efficient administrations similar to those of business enterprises. This leads, according to Herberg, to the development of union bureaucracy and a corresponding weakening of union democracy. Yet democratic self-expression is the essence of a successful mass movement.

In the early days of trade unionism, according to the Herberg thesis, the "idealistic, democratic, emancipatory aspect is dominant."[9] But as unions grew and became firmly entrenched in our political-economic system, the service aspect of unionism overwhelmed the earlier idealistic orientation.

---

6. Neil W. Chamberlain, *Labor* (New York: McGraw-Hill Book Co., Inc., 1950), p. 52.

7. *Ibid.*

8. Will Herberg, "Bureaucracy and Democracy in Labor Unions," reprinted from *Antioch Review,* Fall 1943, in Joseph Shister (ed.), *Readings in Labor Economics and Industrial Relations,* 2nd ed. (New York: J. B. Lippincott Co., 1956), pp. 114–122.

9. *Ibid.,* p. 115.

The very size of unions and the need for the development of an efficient administrative setup made it impossible for the "grass-roots" democracy of early trade unionism to survive. Moreover, the founders of trade unionism—crusaders motivated by a desire for reform—were eventually displaced by paid professionals. This development, in Herberg's view, was inevitable, but it might have been speeded up by the search for power on the part of some labor leaders.

What Herberg has described is a shift in the locus of power from local to national unions as the American trade-union movement passed through successive stages in its development. This shift has been noted in earlier chapters, but the point to be stressed here is the change in the *outlook* of labor leaders as this evolution has progressed.

A later study by Richard Lester carries Herberg's analysis a great deal further.[10] Lester pointed out that during the period of rapid union growth, the leaders of the labor movement were motivated by a "missionary spirit." The zest for organization was not limited to professional union leaders; it was shared by many rank and file members who worked hard during the organizing campaigns following 1935. There was also a great deal of rivalry during the time when the AF of L and the CIO were competing for members, and this contributed somewhat to the militant attitudes of union leaders at that time.

But missionary zeal is hard to maintain. As unions became large organizations, their leaders had to devote an increasing proportion of their time to the problems of administration. Sizeable staffs were recruited and the work of staff members had to be supervised. After a union has succeeded in organizing a substantial proportion of an industry, or a specific occupational group, the outlook of its leaders is bound to change. They are less concerned with organizing the unorganized workers than with administering the organization they have helped create. This often leads to changes in behavior both at the bargaining table and in other respects. In general, unions become less vigorous and much less militant. Union leaders are anxious to demonstrate their responsibility, and this leads to a moderation of demands in collective bargaining—particularly after the major goals of the unions have been achieved. During the formative stages of a union—when its future is far from secure—its leaders will naturally be greatly concerned with the survival of the organization. However, as unions achieve a degree of stability there is growing interest in the *mutual survival* of the union and of the employers with which it deals.[11]

Some writers who have noted the gradual shift in the philosophy and

---

10. Richard A. Lester, *As Unions Mature* (Princeton, N.J.: Princeton University Press, 1958). See also Solomon Barkin, *The Decline of the Labor Movement* (Santa Barbara, California: The Fund for the Republic, Inc., 1961).

11. See E. Wight Bakke, *Mutual Survival: the Goal of Unions and Management* (New Haven: Yale University Labor and Management Center, 1946), pp. 17–18.

outlook of union leaders have adopted a mildly critical tone. They imply that union leaders have become soft and, as a consequence, the labor movement has lost its dynamism. But others feel that such changes are to be expected. It is hard to maintain enthusiasm at fever pitch for any cause unless there are recurring crises to be faced. Once the larger unions had become established and had reached many of their announced goals, the nature of their problems changed. And as the problems they dealt with changed, the behavior patterns of union leaders also were altered. It is hard to see how it could have been otherwise in some of the larger craft and industrial unions. Given the structure of the American labor movement, these unions do not go outside their industry or occupational groups in search of members after they have achieved considerable success in organizing the workers within their jurisdictions.

There are some who look back to the period of union militancy with nostalgia. But others, such as Bakke, have noted that there is a delicate balance in the relationship between powerful unions and powerful management. If either side concentrates on individual survival, and does so by attacking the other side vigorously, Bakke believes that the result will be disastrous to both parties. In Bakke's view: "The result of failure to work out the means of *mutual survival* will not be the elimination of one by the other, but the elimination of both as free institutions by public regimentation."[12]

Attitudes of the Rank and File

A great deal has been written about the changing attitudes of labor leaders as trade unions have matured. This is not surprising. Union leaders are relatively few in number and their behavior can be analyzed from the outside, that is, by examining their demands at the bargaining table and by reading their speeches and other publications. It is not necessary to ask union leaders how they feel about certain issues and how these feelings have changed over time. Their attitudes are a matter of public record. It is much more difficult to get at the attitudes of union members, yet there can be little doubt that these also have changed as unions have grown in size and strength.

The apathy of American union members has often been noted and commented upon. However, during the early days when a union is being formed there must be at least a hard core of "activists" willing to do much of the hard work associated with organization. For unions to win organizational elections, at least a majority in the bargaining unit must give the union their active support. Even during this phase, however, American union members appear to be basically nonideological. As the position of the union becomes secure, most of the rank and file are inclined to leave union affairs in the hands of their paid leaders. They are also likely to become less interested in the political blandishments of their leaders as expressed in union publications.

---

12. *Ibid.*, p. 82.

The interdependence of political and trade union action, a dominant characteristic of European trade unionism, is clearly lacking in the United States. Trade union members often demonstrate a strong independence in their political behavior, while at the same time remaining staunchly loyal to their unions. The presidential campaigns of 1952 and 1956 illustrate this. In both campaigns, most trade unions strongly supported Adlai Stevenson, but it is evident that many union members cast their votes for Dwight Eisenhower. It is undoubtedly a fair generalization that most rank-and-file union members in the United States have always been nonideological. There are frequent references to the "labor vote," but the evidence strongly suggests that there is much less bloc voting among union members than is popularly believed.

Some union leaders continue to support candidates of their choice, and the Committee on Political Education is active before elections, but there are fewer claims by labor leaders that they will deliver votes. Politicians continue to seek the support of organized labor, but the ties between political and labor leaders are not as close as they were in the days of Franklin D. Roosevelt. When President Nixon appeared before the AFL-CIO convention in 1971, his remarks were given only a lukewarm reception. Moreover, after the convention, Meany announced that he planned to help defeat the President in the next election. There was no evidence, however, that this caused great consternation among Republican political strategists.

Rank-and-File Attitudes Toward Employers

Richard Lester has noted that as unions have moved into positions of security, demands at the bargaining table have been moderated. There might have been inflammatory speeches during organizing campaigns, in which employers were described in very unflattering terms, but once unions have achieved recognition and union security, relations between union leaders and employers become at least polite if not completely amicable.

How do the rank and file view their employers? If unions are to succeed, the members must have some degree of allegiance to the union. Does this mean that they have little or no allegiance to their employer? Although there has been relatively little research on these important questions, studies to date indicate that support of a union does not mean hostility toward an employer. The most comprehensive research on this issue has been conducted by Father Theodore V. Purcell of Loyola University, who concluded that the vast majority of workers in the situation he studied had *dual* allegiance to their union and their employer.[13] This study revealed that nearly three-fourths of

---

13. Theodore V. Purcell, "Dual Allegiance to Company and Union—Packing House Workers, A Swift-UPWA Study in a Crisis Situation, 1949–1950," *Personnel Psychology*, March 1954, pp. 48–58. A more extended treatment of the research summarized in this article is given in his book *The Worker Speaks His Mind on Company and Union* (Cambridge, Mass.: Harvard University Press, 1954).

the workers in a large meat-packing plant felt a sense of allegiance to *both* their employer and their union. An even larger proportion (88 per cent) of the shop stewards—the lowest rung of union officialdom—indicated their loyalty to both company and union.

Another study conducted by the Institute of Labor and Industrial Relations at the University of Illinois led to similar findings. It showed that "men feeling positive allegiance to the company feel similarly about their union."[14] Professor Stagner believes that "it is virtually certain that disputes between company and union will arise, but it is not clear that such disputes must be accompanied by hostility, or must lead to the extermination of one side or the other."[15]

The studies of rank and file attitudes toward union and management have been cross-sectional studies; that is, they have revealed worker attitudes at a particular time. Unfortunately, data are not available to show the changes in these attitudes from the beginning of a union-management relationship, or an organizing campaign, to a later period, when the union is well established and the collective bargaining relationship has been stabilized. However, workers would not join a union unless they felt somehow that their employers were not doing as much for them as they should, and in many cases they no doubt feel a strong sense of grievance against the management. There must be, in brief, some degree of worker dissatisfaction before a union can be organized. If wages, hours, and working conditions improve after a union has organized a company, many of the earlier causes of dissatisfaction will be removed.

It is entirely possible—although this conjecture cannot be supported by empirical evidence—that the successful organization of a company by a union can lead to a stronger sense of allegiance to the company than was felt in preunion days. This is unquestionably the case where unions and management have worked out a system of cooperation acceptable to both parties. Some arrangements of this kind will be discussed in a later chapter, and the evidence in the cases to be examined supports the view given above.

Trade Unions and the New Left

How did union leaders and, as far as can be determined, the rank and file react to the revival of radicalism during the late 1960s? It is impossible to explore all the dimensions of radical thought during this period in a general survey of labor economics and industrial relations. But a few key issues—and labor's response to these issues—can be considered. In light of what was said earlier in this chapter, however, it is important to add the caveat that there is no unique "labor position" on the issues to be discussed, just as there is no clear-

---

14. Ross Stagner, "Dual Allegiance as a Problem in Modern Society," *Personnel Psychology,* March 1954, p. 46.

15. *Ibid.,* pp. 46–47.

cut labor vote. But if there was no unanimity, on some issues there was a consensus. Laboı leaders met other issues with an eloquent silence.

What are the issues that united the radicals? The outstanding ones include the Vietnam War, racial discrimination, urban blight and decay, environmental deterioration, and the persistence of poverty in a generally affluent society. Radicals believe that these problems stem from deep-seated imperfections in the present economic and social system. Their proposed solution is to revolutionize the system, although there has been relatively little talk of violent revolution. Also, unlike those who joined or flirted with the Communist Party during the 1930s, latter-day radicals have not suggested that the new system be modeled after that of the Soviet Union. Those who belong to the new radical movement are aware of a strongly entrenched bureaucracy in the USSR, and they know that the economic gains achieved by the Soviet Union have not produced corresponding gains in civil or individual liberties.

Few American labor leaders have been outspoken critics of the Vietnam War. Indeed, some, including George Meany, have been strong supporters of the military and their allies in Congress and the Administration. Again, with a few notable exceptions, labor leaders have not been in the front rank of those who have battled against racial discrimination. The same can be said about the attitudes of most labor leaders toward problems of urban blight, environmental deterioration, and the persistence of poverty. Indeed, whenever they feel that proposals for reform might endanger jobs of their members, trade union leaders can be counted on to side with those who oppose reform. An illustration of this is the attitude of labor leaders toward liberalized international trade policies, which they feel will result in a loss of employment among their members.[16]

On occasion, disenchanted liberals have called for a new coalition of the poor, the black militants, the "New Left," and "the labor movement."[17] Such a coalition formed the basis of the "New Populism" espoused by Senator Fred Harris of Oklahoma during his short-lived campaign for the presidency in 1971. Proposals of this kind assume a commonality of interest between trade unions and critics of the American economic and social system. But this appears to be a complete misconception of the attitudes and aspirations of most American trade union leaders, as well as of the rank and file.[18] It is strange that this view of a radical core in the American labor movement per-

---

16. See *A Trade Policy for America, An AFL-CIO Program,* based on testimony by AFL-CIO president George Meany before the Subcommittee on International Trade of the Senate Finance Committee, May 18, 1971.

17. See, for example, James MacGregor Burns, *Uncommon Sense* (New York: Harper & Row, 1972).

18. Those who became radicals in an earlier period, and who are familiar with the history of American trade unions, recognize the conservatism of American union leaders and their followers. See, for example, Michael Harrington, *The Accidental Century* (Baltimore: Penguin Books, Inc., 1965), pp. 124; 135.

sists. The well-publicized clashes between New York construction workers and antiwar demonstrators apparently did little to alter this view. Although Archie Bunker, of the television series "All in the Family," may be a caricature of the modern "hard hat" trade unionist, he comes closer to expressing the views on many social issues of the "typical" trade union member than do the spokesmen for radical causes. The business unionism created by Samuel Gompers and his followers—many of whom came from socialist backgrounds —has firmly established its conservative credentials. It is not likely that many labor leaders, or a substantial part of the rank and file, will be found in the forefront of any movement to revolutionize the existing social and economic order.

American Labor and the ICFTU

By the end of the nineteenth century some form of trade unionism had been established in most of the industrial nations of the world. After a number of tentative earlier efforts, the International Federation of Trade Unions (IFTU) was formed by representatives of the world's major trade union movements in 1913. The AF of L joined the new international federation and remained a member until the organization was dissolved by World War I. When the international federation was reactivated in 1919, however, the AF of L refused to resume membership. The IFTU was disrupted for a second time by World War II and was replaced during the postwar period by the World Federation of Trade Unions (WFTU). Again, the AF of L refused to become a member, but after the Congress of Industrial Organization was established it joined the WFTU.

The WFTU was unable to survive ideological conflicts between communist and noncommunist unions. And in December 1949, the International Confederation of Free Trade Unions (ICFTU) was formed by noncommunist and anticommunist unions. At the time of its founding the ICFTU consisted of 67 labor organizations from 51 countries representing 48 million members. The number of countries represented reached a peak of 106 in 1962.[19]

As early as the 1965 congress of the ICFTU, AFL-CIO president George Meany had been highly critical of the international federation.[20] The uneasy relationship between the ICFTU and the AFL-CIO came to an end in 1969 when the AFL-CIO disaffiliated. Although there may have been other reasons for this disaffiliation, the immediate cause was a dispute between AFL-CIO leaders and the ICFTU over a request by the United Auto Workers—who had left the AFL-CIO the year before—to become a member of ICFTU.[21]

---

19. John P. Windmuller, "Cohesion and Disunity in the ICFTU: the 1965 Amsterdam Congress," *Industrial and Labor Relations Review, 19,* No. 3 (April 1966), p. 355.

20. Meany's attitude is not always easy to understand, but in response to a reporter's question about how long he felt the ICFTU had been going downhill, Meany answered, "since December 1949." This is the date the international federation was founded. See Windmuller, *ibid.,* p. 353.

21. John P. Windmuller, "Internationalism in Eclipse: The ICFTU After Two Decades," *Industrial and Labor Relations Review, 23,* No. 4 (July 1970), p. 510.

The loss of the AFL-CIO, the ICFTU's largest affiliate, was a serious blow to an international organization that had never been strong either financially or in terms of leadership. The officers of noncommunist unions throughout most of the world evidently feel the need for an international forum where labor leaders representing workers who belong to diverse cultures can meet to exchange views and discuss problems of mutual interest. AFL-CIO officials have indicated by their behavior, however, that they do not share this need.

Conclusions

The outlook of union leaders has changed as trade unions have moved through successive stages of development. The early attempts at reform unionism did not win a large following. The narrow preoccupation of the early craft unions was not conducive to growth. The explosive growth of the 1930s led to great deal of militancy; yet as unions have matured there is evidence of growing complacency and conservatism.

Rank and file union members have shown a considerable amount of independence in their political behavior. The scanty evidence available indicates quite strongly that union members do not regard their employers with hostility, but feel a sense of allegiance to both their employers and their union.

Modern trade unions have departed from the earlier AF of L principle of no political involvement. While the political activities of trade unions have been stepped up in recent years, there is no evidence to support the view that American union leaders seek political power as such. Indeed, despite the establishment of structurally independent political organizations, American trade unions have continued to rely on economic strength to achieve their goals. Political action in American unions remains a relatively small part of their total activity. They are, as they have been virtually from the outset, institutions for the conduct of collective bargaining.

American union leaders, with very few exceptions, have not become involved in the antiwar and antidiscrimination movement of the late 1960s and early 1970s. They have had relatively little to say about the problems of environmental deterioration and persistent poverty. American union leaders also have not been highly internationalistic in their outlook. This has been true not only in terms of domestic economic policy, but also with respect to membership in international labor organizations. Although they helped set up the International Confederation of Free Trade Unions in 1949, leaders of the AFL-CIO disaffiliated from the Confederation in 1969 after a dispute over the admission of the United Auto Workers to the ICFTU.

Questions and Exercises

1. In what way is the ideology of American trade unions distinctive, and how was this ideology formed?
2. Contrast the characteristics of western European and American trade

unions. Describe briefly the left-wing challenge to the AF of L during the early 1890s.

3. What is meant by the philosophy of "voluntarism," which appeared to guide the AF of L after the defeat of the socialist threat?

4. In what way did formation of the CIO affect the attitude of AF of L leaders toward involvement in political action? What has the AFL-CIO done about political action since the merger in 1955?

5. Describe briefly Herberg's hypothesis of the relationship between bureaucracy and democracy in trade unions.

6. According to Lester, what changes have occurred in the American trade union movement between the period of rapid growth following the AF of L split of 1935 and more recent times?

7. What is meant by the concept of "mutual survival"?

8. What did Purcell find about the attitudes of rank-and-file workers toward their union and their employer in his study of a large meat-packing company?

9. How did most trade union leaders react to the revival of radicalism in the United States during the late 1960s?

10. Describe briefly the participation of American trade unions in international labor organizations. What does this suggest, in your opinion, about the attitudes of American labor leaders toward involvement in international organizations?

Suggested Readings

Books

Bakke, E. Wight. *Mutual Survival: the Goal of Unions and Management.* New Haven: Yale University Labor and Management Center, 1946.

Howe, Irving (ed.), "The World of the Blue Collar Worker," special issue of *Dissent* (Winter 1972).

Jacobs, Paul. *Old Before Its Time: Collective Bargaining at 28.* Santa Barbara, California: Center for the Study of Democratic Institutions, 1963.

Lester, Richard A. *As Unions Mature, an Analysis of the Evolution of American Unionism.* Princeton, N.J.: Princeton University Press, 1958.

Purcell, Theodore V., S. J. *The Worker Speaks His Mind on Company and Union.* Cambridge, Mass.: Harvard University Press, 1954.

Articles

Barbash, Jack. "American Unionism: From Protests to Growing Concern," *Journal of Economic Issues, II,* No. 1 (March 1968), pp. 45–59.

Herberg, Will. "Bureaucracy and Democracy in Labor Unions," *Antioch Review,* Vol. 3 (Fall 1943); reprinted in Joseph Shister (ed.), *Readings in Labor Economics and Industrial Relations,* 2nd ed. New York: J. B. Lippincott Company, 1956.

Rogin, Michael. "Voluntarism: The Political Functions of an Antipolitical Doctrine," *Industrial and Labor Relations Review, 15,* No. 4 (July 1962), pp. 521–535.

Weisz, Morris. "Labor Ideology and Practice in Europe and the U.S.," *Monthly Labor Review*, U.S. Department of Labor, Bureau of Labor Statistics, March 1958.

Windmuller, John P. "Cohesion and Disunity in the ICFTU: the 1965 Amsterdam Congress," *Industrial and Labor Relations Review, 19*, No. 3 (April 1966), pp. 348–367.

Windmuller, John P. "Internationalism in Eclipse: The ICFTU After Two Decades," *Industrial and Labor Relations Review, 23*, No. 4 (July 1970), pp. 510–527.

Labor Law: From Repression to Encouragement of Unions

In this chapter and the two that follow we consider the evolution of labor law in the United States. It may be helpful to list the stages through which public policy toward trade unions has passed. These are:[1]

1. A period of repression during which unions were denied the right of legal existence.
2. A stage of sufferance, in which unions were tolerated, however grudgingly, but in which union activities were severely limited.
3. A period of nonintervention during which a few of the major restrictions on union behavior were curtailed.
4. Full legal recognition, and a period of encouragement and assistance by government.
5. A stage of growing control over union activities in which, however, the full legal rights of unions have been protected.

Our discussion will go beyond the laws and court decisions that deal directly with trade unions. There is a considerable body of legislation, most of it dating from the 1930s, that deals with labor standards and the provision of a minimum of protection against the vicissitudes of life in a modern industrial society. The laws which provide this protection are often referred to collectively as *social legislation* to distinguish them from the labor laws which, in one way or another, have affected or now affect trade unions.

From Repression to Nonintervention

Common Law and Statutory Law

There are a number of ways that systems of law can be classified. For present purposes, however, it will be sufficient to distinguish between *common* law and *statutory* law.

---

1. The first four stages are based upon a similar classification by Ludwig Teller in *A Labor Policy for America* (New York: Baker, Voorhis and Co., Inc., 1945), pp. 3–5.

Laws that are specifically enacted by the Congress and by state legislatures are known as statute laws. Much of our law, however, is known as common law—part of our Anglo-Saxon heritage—which consists of the gradual accumulation of court decisions.

Statute laws typically are the result of political pressures. Such laws generally represent a change either in earlier statute law or in the common law. Common law also changes over time, however. Many court decisions are based upon earlier judicial precedent. From time to time, however, a court will make a path-breaking decision, which departs from earlier precedent, and which might be cited subsequently as precedent for later decisions.

The Period of Union Repression

The first unions in the United States did not find the political and economic climate particularly hospitable. The British doctrine of laissez faire, enunciated by Adam Smith in 1776, was largely accepted in this country by the beginning of the nineteenth century. One of the strongest unions in existence at that time consisted of a group of Philadelphia shoemakers producing high-grade boots and shoes largely made of cordovan leather. The journeymen cordwainers, or employees in the shoe shops, had organized a club. Eventually they got around to drawing up a schedule of rates, which they presented to their employers, the master cordwainers. The journeymen's demands came at a time when the Philadelphia shop owners were trying to depress prices to compete with shoemakers in other cities for the expanding markets of the country. The journeymen demanded that the masters meet their schedule "or else." The masters accepted the latter alternative.

The masters immediately took the case to court. The journeymen were charged with "contriving, and intending unjustly and oppressively, to increase and augment the prices and rates usually paid and allowed to them and other artificers," and with preventing "by threats, menaces, and other unlawful means," others from working as cordwainers for wages below the rates they had set. Basically, the journeymen cordwainers were charged with engaging in a criminal conspiracy. And criminal conspiracies were at variance with the British common law, which had been adopted virtually intact in this country.

The counsel for the defense argued bravely that the British common law conflicted with the goals of the Revolution, but the judge who heard the case, Recorder Levy, was not impressed. The Recorder, it seems quite clear, was determined to defend the best interests of businessmen and property owners in Philadelphia. An obvious disciple of Adam Smith, he castigated the journeyman cordwainers for interfering with the natural forces of supply and demand. There could be no objection, he said, to an individual workman's demand for a higher wage. But in a widely quoted passage he concluded that: "A combination of workmen to raise their wages may be considered in a two-fold point of view: one is to benefit themselves . . . the other is to injure those who do not join their society. The rule of law condemns both." The redoubtable Recorder made it abundantly clear that society could not tolerate conspiracies of workmen whose goal was to disturb the equilibrium of wages set by the forces of a free market.

The precedent set in the *Philadelphia Cordwainers* case of 1806 was widely followed for the next three decades. Similar restrictions were not placed on the combination of capital. In other cases that reached the courts during this time, judges decided that combinations of businessmen were permissible, since this would permit them to engage in ventures "too weighty for an individual."[2] The courts continued to decide, however, that if workers organized to raise wages they were guilty of criminal conspiracy. And the New York legislature obligingly passed a conspiracy law which, though vaguely worded, could be cited by the courts in conspiracy cases.

The workers of the day did not accept the conspiracy doctrine with equanimity. Public resentment against what many people considered to be the unfair treatment of wage workers was growing. In some cases juries refused to convict workers charged with conspiracy, and the press was critical of judges who hewed closely to the conspiracy doctrine.

Commonwealth v. Hunt: The End of the Conspiracy Doctrine

The upshot of the growing resentment against conspiracy decisions came in 1842 in a decision handed down by Chief Justice Shaw of the Massachusetts Supreme Court. Shaw had no strong sympathy for labor organizations. But he knew that Massachusetts employers were becoming increasingly concerned about the reactions of workers—not always peaceful—when they were called criminals for attempting to better their wages. The textile and shoe industries were beginning to expand rapidly at that time in the Bay State, and the employers wished to avoid worker unrest. There were political implications in *Commonwealth v. Hunt* as well, since industrialists were then seeking tariff protection to guard the nation's "infant industries."

This case again involved a group of shoemakers, a craft which seemed to have a penchant for organizing and even for calling strikes despite the legal climate of the day. The workers involved had been convicted of conspiracy by a lower court. Chief Justice Shaw did not attack the conspiracy doctrine head-on. Instead, in a neat bit of judicial toe-dancing he sidestepped the issue, concluding that the organization of workers as such could not be considered as socially undesirable.[3] Indeed, his decision went so far as to deny that a closed shop, an arrangement under which union workers only were hired, could be considered illegal.

While Justice Shaw did not actually abolish the doctrine of criminal conspiracy, his decision established an important precedent, and there were no subsequent decisions in which unions as such were held to be conspiracies.

---

2. Charles O. Gregory, *Labor and the Law* (New York: W. W. Norton & Co., Inc., 1946), pp. 22–26.

3. *Ibid.,* p. 29.

Union Restraint Through Use of Injunctions

For the remainder of the nineteenth century there were no path-breaking cases comparable to the *Philadelphia Cordwainers* case, which started a train of conspiracy decisions, and *Commonwealth v. Hunt,* which effectively ended the conspiracy doctrine. This is not to say that there were no labor cases; in fact, there were many involving specific strikes and union efforts to restrain employers from having work done off the premises, and some cases were comparable to modern jurisdictional disputes. These cases were concerned with specific issues, however, and did not result in decisions that were precedent setting. This does not mean that the nation's judges regarded unions as benign institutions. Indeed, well before the end of the nineteenth century a new legal weapon had been forged, which effectively restrained trade union activity—this was the device of the restraining order or injunction.

The first labor injunction appears to have been issued by an equity court handling a railroad bankruptcy case. A receiver was appointed to take over the road, and one of his first problems was that of a threatened strike. The strike was forestalled, however, when the judge involved issued a restraining order, and as a by-product discovered a powerful device for restraining labor disputes.

Injunctions are issued by equity courts, as distinguished from courts of law. The same judge might sit on an equity court and a court of law, but he follows different rules in the two cases. Both in Great Britain and the United States, equity courts evolved to deal with cases where money damages would not solve the problem at issue. In an equity case the judge will issue an order either to do something or refrain from doing something, and in labor disputes it was such negative orders that became important. If a union were enjoined from performing a specific act—and went ahead with the act anyway—its leaders could be held in contempt of court. Their punishment under the criminal law could then include imprisonment. This was indeed an effective device for calming down the obstreperous labor leader who might threaten to do damage to property by calling a strike. Following the initial use of an injunction in the 1880s, similar orders were willingly issued by numerous equity courts. The initial purpose of the injunction was to protect property, but many able scholars feel that the injunction was severely abused. One of the strongest critics of the unrestrained use of labor injunction was Justice Felix Frankfurter, then a law professor at Harvard.[4]

Injunctions were generally granted upon request, and many courts failed to look into the legality or illegality of the action they were restraining. Even many conservatives early in the present century were strongly critical of the courts for the way in which they granted injunctions against organized labor. Samuel Gompers and many other union leaders thought that the Clayton Act

---

4. Felix Frankfurter and Nathan Greene, *The Labor Injunction* (New York: The Macmillan Company, 1930).

of 1914 outlawed the use of the injunction, but subsequent events showed them to be wrong. It was not until the Norris-LaGuardia Act of 1932 that effective restraints were imposed upon courts in issuing labor injunctions.

Unions and Antitrust Laws

The Sherman Act of 1890

Between the Civil War and the 1880s, there was a marked transformation in the ownership and control of American industry. In many industries, there was a decline in the number of independent establishments, and an increase in the size of those which remained. This was often brought about through mergers and other forms of consolidation, and by the 1880s, a number of markets were largely controlled by one or a few firms. New corporations were set up to hold the stock of formerly competing establishments "in trust." Their objective was to restrain price competition and to ensure profits for the operating corporations which had turned over a controlling share of their voting stock to the trust.

A considerable hue and cry about the activities of the trusts was raised in the press. In the campaign of 1888, both the Democrats and the Republicans solemnly professed their opposition to monopolistic practices. When the Republicans won, President Harrison asked Congress to enact the antimonopoly plank in the Republican platform. Several bills were introduced, one by Senator Sherman of Ohio. Congress displayed only minor interest in the proposed legislation, which was enacted with little dissent and signed by the President on July 2, 1890.

The Sherman Act is an unusually short and simple piece of federal legislation. Its major provisions are covered by the first two sections of the Act. Section 1 states that "every contract, combination in the form of trust or otherwise, or conspiracy, in restraint of trade or commerce among the several States or with foreign nations, is hereby declared to be illegal." The second section simply states that any person who monopolizes or attempts to monopolize trade or commerce shall be guilty of a misdemeanor. During the early years of the law, violations were punishable by fines up to $5,000, maximum imprisonment of one year, or both. The law also contained a provision—which later had an important bearing upon a case involving a trade union—which permitted persons injured by illegal restraint to sue for triple damages. Whether or not the Congress that enacted the Sherman Act intended to apply to trade unions, has long been a matter of controversy. In 1890, however, the courts evidently did not regard the bargaining functions of unions as restraints of trade. For the first eighteen years that the Sherman Act was in existence—while there was much argument about the intentions of Congress—the law was not applied to unions as such. The debate was settled, for a time at least, in 1908, in the case of *Loewe v. Lawlor,* better known as the Danbury

Hatters' case. In this case the Supreme Court stated that Congress had intended that the Act apply to unions as well as to business combinations. "The Court then proceeded to do so, applying the act adversely to a union in a way that didn't seem sensible and thereafter refusing to apply it in many ways that would have made sense."[5]

The union involved in this case was relatively strong. It had organized most of the large felt hat manufacturers in the country, but the few unorganized companies made life difficult for the union by engaging in aggressive price competition. One of the oustanding recalcitrants, from the union's point of view, was the Loewe Hat Company of Danbury, Connecticut. Despite the union's best efforts, including a series of local strikes, Loewe's remained unorganized. The union thereafter imposed a nationwide boycott on Loewe hats. Following a slump in orders, Loewe brought suit against the union under the Sherman Act, and the court awarded the company triple damages of more than half a million dollars.

This came as a severe shock not only to the organized hatters, but also to the leaders of the AF of L. Recognizing that the Supreme Court had read into the Sherman Act a provision which allowed it to be applied against unions, the leaders of the AF of L departed from their long-established principle of no political involvement and campaigned actively for legislation that would specifically declare the immunity of trade unions to the antitrust law.

The Clayton Act of 1914

The union's campaign appeared to bear fruit when a new Congress under President Wilson passed the Clayton Act. The new law, an amendment to the Sherman Act, was intended to clarify, among other things, the status of unions under the nation's antitrust laws. Section 6 stated that

> the labor of a human being is not a commodity or article of commerce. Nothing contained in the antitrust laws shall be construed to forbid the existence and operation of labor, agricultural or horticultural organizations . . . or to forbid or restrain individual members of such organizations from lawfully carrying out the legitimate objects thereof; nor shall such organizations, or the members thereof, be held or construed to be illegal combinations or conspiracies in restraint of trade, under the antitrust laws.

Section 20 went on to state that

> no restraining order or injunction shall be granted by any court in the United States, or a judge or the judges thereof, in any case between an employer and employees . . . involving, or growing out of, a dispute concerning terms or conditions of employment . . .

---

5. Gregory, *op. cit.,* p. 206.

Had Section 20 stopped at this point, the most effective antiunion weapon of the time might have been nullified. But it went on to hedge this initial statement with a number of conditions under which injunctions could be issued.

Samuel Gompers hailed the Clayton Act as "Labor's Magna Carta," but his jubilation was premature. In reply to Section 6, many judges stated that no one had ever supposed that labor was a commodity or article of commerce. And there was a great deal of latitude in the language of Section 20, which permitted them to grant injunctions as freely after the Clayton Act as they had before. Thus the Clayton Act did not give unions relief from the dreaded injunction. The authors of the Clayton Act carefully refrained from stating that unions were specifically immune from prosecution under the antitrust laws. There was still room for considerable judicial leeway in this respect. This was demonstrated in two cases involving a single labor-management incident.

The Judicial Control of Union Activities

In 1914, the year of the Clayton Act, the Coronado Coal Company of Arkansas, which had signed agreements with the United Mine Workers of America, decided to terminate its contracts. To do this, the company closed down a number of unionized mines and announced that they would open them on a nonunion basis. The workers at one of the Coronado Company's mines went on strike in an effort to force the company to reverse this decision. The strike was bitter and violent, and the mine itself was virtually destroyed by fire and dynamite. The company brought suit under the Sherman Act, claiming damages of $740,000. After long litigation in the lower federal courts the case reached the Supreme Court, which handed down its decision in what is now known as the *first Coronado* case in June 1922, almost eight years after the strike had occurred. The Court denied the damages which the company sought on the grounds that the company had not been able to prove that the union intended to restrain commerce within the meaning of the Sherman Act. But this was not the end of the Coronado case.

The case was reopened when a disgruntled union official offered to testify for the company. In the *second Coronado* case this witness testified that the union had intended to keep the company's coal "from getting into the market," an objective which should have seemed rather obvious to the court at the first trial. With this "new evidence," the court ruled that the union was guilty of violating the Sherman Act, and conceivably would have awarded triple damages if the union had not effected a settlement out of court. In the first Coronado case the Court ruled that a labor organization engaged in a strike did not come under the Sherman Act, and this appeared to reverse the *Danbury Hatters* decision—although boycott was an issue in the first case, a strike in the second. But in the second Coronado case the court ruled, as in *Loewe v. Lawlor,* that the union was subject to the terms of the Sherman Act.

The second Coronado case showed that unions were not exempt from the potent triple-damage provision of the Sherman Act. Moreover, in a case decided in 1921, the court made it quite clear that unions were not exempt from injunctions. This case, involving the Duplex Printing Press Company of Michigan and the International Association of Machinists, contained many elements similar to the *Danbury Hatters* case. Only four companies made presses of the kind sold by the Duplex Company. Three of them were organized, but Duplex was not. The other three companies notified the union that unless Duplex could be organized and their labor costs brought into line, they would break off relations with the union. The IAM called a strike at the Duplex plant, but only a handful of workers responded. They then instituted a secondary boycott in an effort to hamper the sale of Duplex presses. Union members were ordered not to install or repair Duplex presses, and the union took other steps to hamper the company's sales.[6] The company responded by seeking an injunction, and despite the Clayton Act, the injunction was granted. It was this decision which made it clear that Gompers's enthusiastic response to the Clayton Act was not justified.

A similar decision was reached by the Court in the *Bedford Cut Stone* case of 1927. This case came about when union stonecutters refused to handle nonunion limestone coming from Indiana, which led to a virtual end of out-of-state shipments. The Court once again restrained the union from continuing its boycott.

In other cases, the courts continued to invoke the antitrust laws to restrain union action. Some of these, such as the Brims case, decided in 1926, involved agreements between unions and employers to protect each other's interests and thus exclude outsiders from specific markets. The latter decisions, most legal scholars agree, were fully justified by the Sherman and Clayton Acts. Even Justice Brandeis, who had dissented in the Bedford case, concurred with the decision in the Brims case. But long after the Clayton Act was passed, the status of unions under the antitrust laws remained ambiguous. Whatever the intent of Congress had been—and the Act is sufficiently vague to permit differences of opinion about this—the courts continued to exercise considerable control over labor-management relations.

Within the framework of antitrust legislation, the courts hampered union progress after 1914. This was done by granting injunctions against unions when they attempted to use the secondary boycott as an organizational tactic. There was also the continued threat of the triple damages provision of the Sherman Act if unions appeared to be acting in restraint of trade. Another way in which the courts supported employer efforts to ward off union organization was by upholding the legality of "yellow dog contracts."

The term "yellow dog contract" was union inspired. It was applied to agreements exacted from workers that, as a condition of employment, they

---

6. For a lucid and concise discussion of the secondary boycott, see Albert Rees, *The Economics of Trade Unions* (Chicago: The University of Chicago Press, 1962), pp. 43–46.

would not join a union.[7] There were various kinds of "yellow dog contracts," some oral and some written. Until 1917, such agreements were not considered to be enforceable in the equity courts, but a decision rendered that year changed this.

The case involved the West Virginia Mine of the Hitchman Coal Company and the United Mine Workers. The mine had been organized, but relations between the union and management had never been good. Finally, a strike was called. The management held out until individual workers sought reemployment. This was granted upon the condition that they would not join the union so long as they were employed by The Hitchman Company.

Organizers from the United Mine Workers began to obtain promises from individual workers that they would join the union, however. The plan was to line up enough union workers to strike the mine again. Management learned of this, and obtained an injunction against all organizational activity. The case was carried to the Circuit Court of Appeals, and then to the Supreme Court. In *Hitchman Coal Company v. Mitchell* (1917), the Supreme Court ruled that the union was engaged in an effort to induce breach of contract, and that it had been appropriate for the lower court to issue an injunction. Thus the enforceability of "yellow dog contracts" was upheld by the highest court of the land.

Limiting the Judicial Control of Labor-Management Relations

For a time, after the first *Coronado* case, it appeared that the courts were taking a somewhat more lenient attitude toward the activities of trade unions. But this notion was dispelled by the second *Coronado* decision. The courts, relying partly on the antitrust laws and partly on common law, continued to issue restraining orders. The law was still used to repress union activities under a wide variety of circumstances. But the relief from blanket injunctions, which the unions thought they were going to receive from the Clayton Act, finally was granted when Congress passed the Norris-LaGuardia Act in 1932. This law ushered in a brief period of virtual nonintervention by the government in labor matters. It should be noted that it was put on the books *before* the New Deal Administration and a liberal Congress were swept into office in the election of 1932.

The Norris-LaGuardia Act

One of the purposes of this law, which is sometimes referred to as the anti-injunction act, was to limit the jurisdiction of courts sitting in equity cases. It will be recalled that it was equity courts which granted injunctions, and typically they did so without hearings or investigation, upon the complaint of

---

7. See Millis and Montgomery, *Organized Labor* (New York: McGraw-Hill Book Co., Inc., 1945), pp. 512–513.

an aggrieved employer. The Norris-LaGuardia Act did not prohibit courts from granting injunctions. What it did was to spell out in considerable detail the conditions under which injunctions could be granted and only "after hearing the testimony of witnesses in open court (with opportunity for cross-examination) in support of the allegations of a complaint made under oath, and testimony in opposition thereto, if offered . . ." After such hearings, an injunction could be granted if:

1. Unlawful acts had been threatened, or would be committed unless restrained, or had been committed and would be continued unless restrained.
2. Such acts could then be held to be enjoinable on the ground that substantial and irreparable injury to the complainant's property would follow.
3. The court was satisfied that failure to grant injunctive relief would lead to greater injury to the complainant than would be inflicted upon the defendant by the injunction.
4. The complainant also was able to demonstrate effectively that he had no adequate remedy at law and that "the public officers charged with the duty to protect complainant's property are unable or unwilling to furnish adequate protection."

Under emergency conditions a court would be able to issue a temporary restraining order upon the sworn testimony of the complainant, but it could be effective for no more than five days. If such an emergency injunction should be issued, the complainant was required to be prepared to compensate those enjoined for any "damage caused by the improvident or erroneous issuance of such order or injunction."

The Act also listed specific conditions under which courts could not issue temporary or permanent injunctions. Broadly speaking, injunctions could not be granted while workers were conducting a peaceful strike. Also, workers could not be prevented from publicizing the issues involved in a dispute, provided their message did not involve fraud or violence.

The Norris-LaGuardia Act also put an end to "yellow dog contracts," declaring that they were not enforceable by law. This removed one of the barriers to union activity that had been widely used at various "growing points" of union organization in the past.

The new law did not explicitly sanction the use of secondary boycotts. But Section (a) of the Act was sufficiently general to permit both primary and secondary boycotts if a union could demonstrate an economic interest in such actions. The qualification that an economic interest had to be shown excluded secondary *sympathetic* boycotts from this interpretation. The law was not entirely clear on the matter of secondary *consumption* boycotts. But Section 4 (e) permitted unions to publicize any labor dispute. By inference, at least, this permitted unions to seek public support for their position without fear of an injunction, provided they could demonstrate an economic interest in a dispute. This appeared to be sufficient for the courts to sanction consumption boycotts in some later cases.

Section 2 of the Norris-LaGuardia Act is a declaration of public policy in labor controversies. This section points out that the government had authorized property owners to organize corporations and other forms of association.

But the individual worker, the Act pointed out, is "commonly helpless to exercise actual liberty of contract and to protect his freedom of labor, and thereby to obtain acceptable terms and conditions of employment." The worker should be free to refuse to join a union. But "it is necessary that he have full freedom of association, self-organization, and designation of representatives of his own choosing, to negotiate the terms and conditions of his employment, and that he shall be free from the interference, restraint, or coercion of employers."

This statement of policy, embodied in statute law, indicated a marked change in the status of organized labor in the United States. In more emphatic terms than those used in the Clayton Act, the law made it clear that workers had the right to organize into unions and to select bargaining representatives of their own choosing. This was a far cry from the days when unions were considered as conspiracies. There was one major loophole in the law, from organized labor's point of view, since, while Congress had specifically declared that workers had the *right* to form unions, nothing was said about the *obligation* of management to recognize these unions or to bargain with their chosen representatives. After the Norris-LaGuardia Act, however, it could no longer be said that unions were the victims of judicial repression. Public policy toward labor organizations by this time had clearly moved into the stage of nonintervention. There was nothing in the Act to provide a positive stimulus to union growth, but unions were allowed to enter the "self help" stage of their development.

A New Judicial View of Unions and the Antitrust Laws

Organized labor had achieved one of its goals, with respect to the antitrust laws, when the Norris-LaGuardia Act was passed. This was the end of the dreaded blanket labor injunction. But the labor injunction, it will be recalled, had not originated in antitrust law. It was the somewhat accidental discovery of the equity courts. The danger of prosecution under the Sherman Act still existed if unions could be found guilty of acting to restrain trade. The lessons of the *Danbury Hatters'* case and the second *Coronado* case were not lost upon the nation's labor leaders. They recognized that an unfavorable court ruling could still lead to punitive triple damages. The unions were still not out of the woods as far as the antitrust laws were concerned. A firm ruling was needed on the status of organized labor under the antitrust laws. This was finally achieved in the case of *United States v. Hutchison*, decided in 1941.

The *Hutchison* case involved a jurisdictional dispute between the Carpenters Union and the International Association of Machinists over which one was to install and dismantle machinery in the Anheuser-Busch plant in St. Louis. The job had been awarded to the IAM, and the Carpenters not only called a strike at that plant but refused to permit their members to work on Anheuser-Busch property. Finally, through a publicity campaign, the Carpenters Union called upon its members and friends to refrain from buying or selling Anheuser-Busch beer.

Although by this time the Supreme Court was favorably inclined toward organized labor, the Hutchison case led to a split decision with three justices dissenting. The Hutchison case involved a secondary boycott of the kind that had led to an adverse ruling, from the union point of view, in the *Danbury Hatters'* case. The Court ruled that because of the Norris-LaGuardia Act, such union behavior was no longer enjoinable. As might be expected following a split decision, legal scholars have differed in their interpretations of the *Hutchison* decision. Some feel that Congress did not intend to prevent courts from enjoining secondary consumption boycotts. Justice Roberts pointed out in his dissent that while the Norris-LaGuardia Act forbade the use of injunctions, there remained the triple damages and criminal prosecution provisions of the Sherman Act. Some lawyers agreed with Justice Roberts that the Anheuser-Busch Company should have had an opportunity to recover damages suffered as a result of the boycott. Others felt that the Supreme Court acted according to the strict letter of the law.

Although the *Hutchison* decision provided lawyers with ample ammunition for further debate, it appeared to settle the issue of the status of trade unions under the antitrust laws. Since the *Hutchison* case, it appears that "a union, acting in its own self-interest and not in combination with non-labor groups, is immune from antitrust legislation. If, on the other hand, a union combines with non-labor groups to monopolize, it is no longer immune."[8] Also, subsequent decisions indicate that unions are subject to the antitrust laws if their activities do not occur within the setting of a labor dispute or in situations where the employer-employee relationship is not involved. Thus, as Douglass Brown has pointed out, when unions become involved in the *product* market, they are on the same footing as any other group and are subject to the antitrust laws. But antitrust legislation does not apply to union activities in the *labor* market. This is a widely accepted view among economists and lawyers today, but it should be hastily added that there are many who dissent from it. Some critics of the *Hutchison* decision do not believe that union action should be entirely unrestrained. They suggest that cases involving secondary boycotts and problems that might arise out of jurisdictional disputes should be handled by legislation dealing specifically with these issues rather than under the antitrust laws.

---

8. Douglass V. Brown, "Labor and the Antitrust Laws," *American Bar Association Proceedings,* August 1955, p. 23.

Government Encouragement of Trade Unions

The Norris-LaGuardia Act of 1932 resulted in a brief period of nonintervention in labor-management affairs. Prior to that, public policy toward trade unions had been one of repression. This was due to an absence of protective labor legislation, and the judicial interpretation of existing law which permitted unrestrained use of the labor injunction. The Norris-LaGuardia Act was the first law to provide unions with a measure of security. The Act did not give them protection against a variety of tactics used by employers to forestall union organization, but for the first time they were given equality under the law. This description of labor policy through 1932 applies to unions in general. Long before the Norris-LaGuardia Act, however, Congress had granted legislative protection to a limited group of workers—namely, the nation's railroad employees.

The Erdman Act of 1898

The objective of the Erdman Act was to encourage and promote interstate commerce. To accomplish this goal, the members of Congress reasoned, it would be necessary to reduce labor disputes on the nation's railroads. The Erdman Act was to a large extent an outgrowth of the *Pullman* strike of 1894. That strike started when employees of the Pullman Company tried to force management to recognize their union; eventually, the strike spread to the railroads themselves. It was broken by a blanket injunction prohibiting virtually any activity by the union, and it resulted in the jailing of Eugene V. Debs, a well-known Socialist labor leader. There was a great deal of bitterness among the nation's railroad workers following the Pullman strike, and Congress attempted through the Erdman Act to minimize this discontent and to encourage stable labor-management relations on the nation's railroads.

The most important provision of the Erdman Act was Section 10, which, in essence, outlawed "yellow dog contracts" for railroad employees, and made it a misdemeanor for railway employers to threaten workers with loss of employment or to discriminate against any employee because of membership in a labor organization. The law also provided for mediation and arbitration of railroad labor-management disputes.

The Erdman Act no doubt made it somewhat easier for the nation's operating crafts to strengthen their unions. There was nothing in the law to preclude the formation of company-dominated unions, however, and it did not effectively ban the various methods used by antiunion employers to prevent the organization of workers or to break strikes where unions existed. There was nothing in the Erdman Act requiring employers to recognize railroad unions and to bargain with their elected representatives. Thus the law was much less effective than later railway labor legislation.

The weakness of the Erdman Act was due to the failure of Congress to incorporate in this law any provisions for enforcement. In the absence of enforcement machinery, it was up to the courts to see that the law was obeyed.

At a time when most judges had strong antiunion predilections, it is not at all surprising that employers won out in most of the court proceedings under the Erdman Act.

Between 1898 and 1926, unions representing the railroad operating crafts grew in numbers and strength. But it is probably fair to say that this happened in spite of the Erdman Act rather than because of it. In 1926, however, Congress took further steps to reduce labor conflict on the nation's railroads. In that year it passed the Railway Labor Act, which some writers considered to be a "model" piece of labor legislation.

The Railway Labor Act of 1926

One of the major provisions of the Act was contained in Section 2. This section provided for the settlement of railway labor-management disputes by representatives of the two parties who were to be selected "in such manner as may be provided in their corporate organization or unincorporated associations, or by other means of collective action, without interference, influence, or coercion exercised by either party over the self-organization or designation of representatives by the other." In an early test case, a railroad attempted to win court approval of its preference for dealing with a company-dominated union rather than one of the independent Brotherhoods. In cases decided before the Railway Labor Act was passed, the courts had supported this position. But in the *Texas and New Orleans Railway* case, the Supreme Court unanimously ruled that railway employees had a right to organize and bargain through representatives *of their own choice* without interference or coercion by their employers. In effect, this meant that if the workers chose to be represented by an independent union, the companies could not insist upon bargaining with a company-dominated union.

In spite of this decision, there was considerable employer interference with union activities. In 1934, Congress passed several important amendments to the 1926 law, which made it increasingly difficult for employers to avoid dealing with independent unions. One amendment established the National Mediation Board to administer the Railway Labor Act. This board was authorized to conduct elections to determine which union was to represent the workers. The union receiving a majority of votes was certified as the lawful representative of railroad workers, and employers were compelled to bargain with the union thus certified.

As noted earlier, the Railway Labor Act was hailed by some writers as a "model" labor law. This favorable judgment was based on the small number of railway labor-management disputes from the early thirties until World War II, a period characterized by widespread labor strife in manufacturing industry as the new CIO unions swung into their organizing campaigns. But the railroads were already well organized by the beginning of this period. There was "an absence of great organizing drives and new unionism on the railroads at a time when industry generally was involved in the difficult task of adjusting to unionism for the first time."[9]

Critics of the Railway Labor Act feel that it is too highly structured and that the parties have been all too willing to allow federal boards to settle disputes rather than resolving them through the bargaining process. An even more stinging criticism, however, is that, especially after the 1934 amendment, the Railroad Brotherhoods used their political power to effect more favorable settlements than those recommended by emergency boards. This was particularly true during World War II and the immediate postwar period.[10]

The National Industrial Recovery Act of 1933

The National Industrial Recovery Act was an attempt by the first New Deal Congress to enact legislation that would speed recovery from the Great Depression. In many ways it was a jerry-built law, and there was relatively little mourning when it was declared unconstitutional by the Supreme Court two years later. But one provision of the NIRA was to play an important part in subsequent legislation for the encouragement of union growth. This was Section 7(a), which required

> that employees shall have the right to organize and bargain collectively through representatives of their own choosing, and shall be free from the interference, restraint, or coercion of employers of labor, or their agents, in the designation of such representatives, or in self-organization or in other concerted activities for the purpose of collective bargaining. . . .

The law went on to specify that no worker or no one seeking employment would be required as a condition of employment to join a company union. It also specified that employers had to pay stated minimum wages, and it established maximum hours and other conditions of employment which were prescribed by the various codes of this Act.

The NIRA was enacted in 1933, and it was followed by a spurt in union membership. The number of union members increased by almost one third between 1933 and 1935, when the NIRA was held to be unconstitutional.

The National Labor Relations Act of 1935

Congress responded to the Supreme Court's ruling which outlawed the NIRA by passing the National Labor Relations Act of 1935, better known as the Wagner Act after its principal author. This law was limited to labor-manage-

---

9. Gordon F. Bloom and Herbert R. Northrup, *Economics of Labor and Industrial Relations* (Philadelphia: The Blakiston Company, 1950), p. 627.

10. See Herbert R. Northrup, "The Railway Labor Act and Railway Labor Disputes in Wartime," *American Economic Review*, June 1946, pp. 324–343. Other criticism of the Railway Labor Act, as well as proposed new legislation to handle emergency transportation disputes, is discussed in Chapter 15.

ment relations, and it contained much more stringent provisions than the broader law which the court had overruled.

Many employers were led to believe that the Wagner Act would go the way of the NIRA, but this did not happen. A series of court cases culminated in the *Jones and Laughlin* decisions of 1937, when the Supreme Court upheld the constitutionality of the National Labor Relations Act. The Wagner Act then became the law of the land in labor-management relations whenever interstate commerce was involved.

Section 7(a) of the Wagner Act was a counterpart of Section 7(a) of the defunct NIRA. It specified that "employees shall have the right to self-organization, to form, join, or assist labor organizations, to bargain collectively through representatives of their own choosing, and to engage in concerted activities, for the purpose of collective bargaining or other mutual aid or protection."

The Wagner Act, however, went far beyond the NIRA. In Section 8, it specified a list of unfair labor practices for employers, which made it unlawful for an employer to "interfere with, restrain, or coerce employees in the exercise of the rights guaranteed in Section 7." Employers were also forbidden to "dominate or interfere with the formation or administration of any labor organization or contribute financial or other support to it. . . . " It became unlawful for employers to discriminate against union members in employment or discharge workers because of union activity. Finally, it became unfair labor practice for the employer to "refuse to bargain collectively with the representatives of his employees. . . . "

This was the strongest piece of labor-management legislation enacted by Congress. Its intent was clearly that of encouraging the growth of independent trade unions. To administer the law, the Wagner Act set up the National Labor Relations Board to determine union representation by conducting elections. The union receiving a majority vote was certified as the bargaining agent, and employers were required to bargain collectively with that union.

Not all employers gave in easily. The court dockets were crowded with cases involving the National Labor Relations Board and recalcitrant employers who sought to avoid one or more provisions of the Act. But the courts continued to rule that employers would have to recognize the principles of this Act, and as case after case was decided its coverage was broadened. The *Jones and Laughlin* case had made it clear that the law applied to manufacturing industry. As other cases were decided, mining, newspaper offices, the telegraph service, the lumber industry, department stores, and chain stores were brought within the purview of the law. The courts took a liberal view of what constituted interstate commerce, and applied the law to many businesses formerly considered to be "local" in character, despite the fact that they operated across state lines. Within a few years it became clear that virtually all workers except agricultural laborers and domestic servants—who were specifically excluded—came under the protection of the National Labor Relations Act or the Railway Labor Act, provided the businesses involved were not completely local in character.

As noted in Chapter 9, there was a virtual explosion of trade union membership in the United States after 1935, but this was not due entirely to the Wagner Act. The split between the AF of L and the CIO came in that year. The formation of the CIO was followed by massive organizational drives in the nation's mass-production industries. With a divided labor movement, in which some unions sought to organize along craft lines and others to bring within their ranks all workers in an industry, the question of which type of union was to represent a company's workers became of paramount importance. The AF of L unions insisted that they had an historical right to organize on the basis of a common skill, while the CIO unions split off from the parent organization because they wanted to ignore occupational lines.

The National Labor Relations Board was faced with a thorny problem. How was it to determine what the appropriate bargaining unit should be? If the members of a specific occupational group were permitted to choose their union, those in the more highly skilled occupations would be inclined to vote for a craft union. If, on the other hand, the Board should insist that all workers in a specific company vote for a single union, it would appear to be favoring the CIO approach. In practice, the Board took a number of factors into account, including the prior history of collective bargaining, management practices in making wage adjustments, and the numerical importance of particular occupational groups.

Following a court decision involving the *Globe Machine and Stamping Company,* in 1937, the Board applied the "Globe doctrine" in deciding on bargaining units. This doctrine permits the members of a craft group to vote for union representation as a body. While the Board made an effort to avoid interpretation of the "Globe doctrine," a number of scholars feel that it tended to favor the AF of L unions over the CIO.

The question of the appropriate bargaining unit has continued to be a troublesome one, and it was not completely ended when the AF of L and CIO merged into a new federation. For some time after the Wagner Act was passed, the Board was accused of favoring industrial unions. But following the *Globe* case, the charge was more often made that the Board was favorably inclined toward craft unions. Once the great surge of organization in the mass-production industries had ended, the growth of the AF of L unions began to outpace that of the CIO. But this could have been due to a number of factors, such as different growth rates in various occupations and industries, and a less doctrinaire attitude on the part of the AF of L leaders toward organization along strictly craft lines. Whatever the effects of the Wagner Act on the growth rate of the AF of L versus CIO unions, there is no question that this law provided a powerful stimulus to overall union growth. It was soon followed by another law designed to prevent employer interference with labor disputes.

The Anti-Strikebreaker Law of 1936

This law, frequently referred to as the Byrnes Act, made it a felony to "transport in interstate commerce any person employed for the purpose of interfering by force or threats with: (a) peaceful picketing during any labor dispute affecting wages, hours, or working conditions, or (b) exercise of employee rights of self-organization or collective bargaining." The law is not aimed at the common carriers by which such strikebreakers might be transported, but at those persons who "willfully transport" or cause them to be transported for the purposes of breaking a strike. The Department of Justice is charged with the prosecution of violators, who are subject to fines up to $5,000, imprisonment up to two years, or both.

Labor Legislation During World War II

By the end of the 1930s, legislation favorable to trade unionism, coupled with the AF of L-CIO split, had led to a prodigious growth of union membership in the United States. Total membership more than doubled between 1935 and 1939. As the new unions gained in power, they redoubled their efforts to organize workers in those industries which continued to resist union penetration. There was a great deal of strike activity, and the press seemed more than willing to give it front-page billing. Conservative elements in Congress felt that unions had been given too much encouragement, and there were efforts to rescind the public policy that encouraged union organization and the practice of collective bargaining. In June of 1940, the House of Representatives passed the Smith Amendments to the Wagner Act, which would have accomplished this objective, but the Senate failed to take action and the House bill died as the 76th Congress adjourned.

Strike activity remained at a high level as the national economy was tooled up for the defense effort. And early in 1941, President Roosevelt, whose sympathy for the trade union movement had been made apparent, publicly condemned the jurisdictional disputes that were interfering with defense activity. In March 1941, the President established the National Defense Mediation Board by executive order, and charged it with the responsibility of minimizing industrial conflict. Some unions—especially those affiliated with the CIO—took a dim view of the newly established Board and charged that it was an effort to slow down their organizational activities. But with the German attack on Russia in 1941, and the growing belief that our entry into the war was inevitable, much of this opposition was dissipated. After this, the National Defense Mediation Board was able to settle a great many labor disputes.

Then came Pearl Harbor. On January 12, 1942, the President signed Executive Order No. 9017 establishing the National War Labor Board. Originally the Board was made up of four union representatives, four employer representatives, and four representatives of the public; later, in 1944, the number of public members was increased to eight.

Shortly after our entry into the war, unions voluntarily made a no-strike pledge, but there was plenty of work for the War Labor Board to do. The most important issues it faced were those dealing with union security and wages. To restrict the output of consumer goods, so that resources could be devoted to the war effort, the government had instituted a policy of price controls and rationing. An inevitable corollary was that wages would also be subject to control. And one of the duties of the War Labor Board was to see that the line was held on wages, although the Board was also given the right to make adjustments to correct inequities and to eliminate substandard rates.

Despite the efforts of the Office of Price Administration, prices rose about 10 per cent between 1941 and 1942. Following this, prices continued to rise slowly through 1945. The War Labor Board could not ignore these price increases and, in a decision involving the International Harvester Company, it proposed reasonable protection of real wage levels negotiated through collective bargaining. In practice, the Board permitted fairly large increases to be granted in the lower wage brackets and restrained increases in higher brackets. There was some confusion about the base from which wages were to be raised, however. This led to adoption of the "Little Steel Formula" in July of 1942.[11] Under this formula, real hourly earnings were to be maintained at the January 1941 base. Wage increases were to be limited to 15 per cent, the amount by which prices had gone up between January 1941 and July 1942. The Board was still permitted to eliminate inequities and substandard rates, however.

As the war progressed, there were growing pressures on the Board to grant further wage increases, and these were not resisted by employers, especially those who were faced with a serious labor shortage. Following an order issued by the Director of Economic Stabilization in May 1943, the Board was given authority to make further adjustments to bring low rates up to the minimum going rate in specific labor market areas. The Board was further authorized to set up a series of wage-rate brackets for particular occupational groups in each labor market area. This permitted some further maneuvering within the "little steel" formula, and wage increases were granted perhaps more liberally than the Director of Economic Stabilization had anticipated.

The problem of holding the line on wages was one of two major problems that confronted the War Labor Board from the beginning. The other was the issue of union security. Union security involves the type of agreement that has been negotiated by labor and management. The tightest form of union security is the closed shop, under which union members only are hired, typically through a union hiring hall. Next comes the union shop, a provision specifying that all employees in a given concern must join a union within a certain

---

11. The formula was based on decisions involving the Bethlehem, Republic, Youngstown Sheet and Tube, and Inland Steel Companies, sometimes referred to as the "little steel" companies to distinguish them from the nation's larger producers.

number of days after accepting employment with the company. Following this is the "open" shop—which union leaders regard as no security at all—under which, technically, both union and nonunion workers are to be given similar treatment.

Theoretically, the War Labor Board was charged with maintaining the status quo on union security; it was not supposed to either encourage or discourage the two parties in their efforts to arrive at an agreement. But a compromise of some sort seemed inevitable, and this was developed early in the Board's life through awards of "maintenance of membership" provisions. Under a maintenance of membership provision, a worker who had belonged to a union as of a given date was required to maintain his membership in that union as a condition of employment. But newly hired workers would not be required to join the union, and the union was not to coerce any employee into joining. This led to a number of difficulties, however. In a case decided in August 1942, a new formula was announced, which provided for maintenance of membership provisions after a fifteen-day waiting period, during which workers could withdraw from the union if they wished to do so. The maintenance of membership provision was based on the theory that by adopting no-strike pledges, unions had given up their most powerful weapon for achieving both union security and wage increases. To stabilize labor-management relations, therefore, the Board announced that maintenance of membership awards were both equitable and essential, and the Board continued to follow this policy throughout the period of hostilities.

Although it was the announced public policy that the government would attempt to maintain the status quo insofar as labor-management relations were concerned, the wartime handling of union security provisions did nothing to discourage union membership. And there was a further increase in membership of roughly 30 per cent between 1941 and 1945.

Management, of course, made little effort to stem the rising tide of union membership, and there is evidence that some managements were more than willing to go along with the wage increases permitted within the bracket system established by the War Labor Board. This was not because management had suddenly recognized the benefits of trade unionism, but was rather a consequence of the tight labor market. With some 12 million men between the ages of eighteen and thirty-five under arms, the problem of unemployment that had lingered throughout the Great Depression evaporated and was replaced by one of labor shortages. Thus many companies, which had displayed a marked coolness toward trade unionism before World War II, were willing to accept a limited form of union security, and did little if anything to discourage their workers from joining a union, if they wished to do so.

Between 1935 and 1940, public policy in the United States encouraged the growth of trade unions. While it might be going too far to say that wartime policies provided a further spur to the growth of union membership, it seems clear that nothing was done to discourage union growth. The unions, for their part, behaved admirably during the wartime emergency. There were a few strikes, to be sure. By and large, however, unions observed the no-strike pledge and worked mightily to further the war effort.

By the end of World War II, trade unions in the United States claimed over 12½ million members. The labor movement had become a mighty colossus. Union demands during the war had been moderate, and labor-management relations—under the guidance of the War Labor Board and the National Labor Relations Board—were relatively stable and peaceful. All was not sweetness and light, however. Some union leaders grumbled at wage restraints, and some employers were resentful at having to deal with union leaders at all. Their differences could be temporarily subordinated to the common goal of winning the war, but these differences set the stage for an eruption of labor-management disturbances once the war had ended and the economy had begun rapidly to shift back to a peacetime basis.

Questions and Exercises

1. Describe briefly the five stages into which public policy toward trade unions may be divided.
2. What legal precedent was set in the *Philadelphia Cordwainers* case of 1806? What decision was reached in *Commonwealth v. Hunt* (1842), and how did this decision affect the precedent set in the *Philadelphia Cordwainers* case?
3. What is an injunction, and what type of court issues injunctions? How were legal injunctions used to interfere with trade union activity?
4. Describe briefly the conditions and events that led to the Sherman Act of 1890. Did Congress intend that this act apply to trade unions?
5. What decision was reached by the Supreme Court in *Loewe v. Lawlor* (1908), better known as the Danbury Hatters' case?
6. What did the Clayton Act of 1914 have to say about the use of injunctions in labor disputes? What effect did this have on the granting of injunctions by the courts?
7. Were injunctions granted in labor-management disputes after the Clayton Act was passed? What decisions were reached in the *Duplex Printing, Bedford Cut Stone,* and *Hitchman Coal* cases?
8. Describe briefly the major provisions of the Norris-LaGuardia Act of 1932. In addition to the provisions dealing with injunctions, what did the Norris-LaGuardia Act have to say about "yellow dog" contracts?
9. Contrast the decisions that were reached in the *Danbury Hatters'* and second *Coronado* cases, on the one hand, and the *Hutchison* case of 1941, on the other.
10. What were the basic provisions of the Erdman Act of 1898?

11. Describe briefly the major provisions of the Railway Labor Act of 1926.

12. Section (a) of the National Recovery Act of 1933 required that "employees shall have the right to organize and bargain collectively through representatives of their own choosing." How was this provision of the NIRA related to the National Labor Relations Act of 1935?

13. What were the major provisions of the National Labor Relations Act, or Wagner Act, of 1935?

14. After the split between the AF of L and the CIO in 1935, how did the National Labor Relations Board decide on the appropriate jurisdictions for union elections? What did the court decide in the *Globe* case of 1937?

15. What were the major provisions of the Anti-Strikebreaker Law of 1936?

16. In 1942, President Roosevelt established the National War Labor Board by executive order. What was the purpose of this board, and what were the results of the board's activities?

17. What compromise was reached by the War Labor Board with respect to union security? What actually happened to union membership between 1941 and 1945?

Suggested Readings

Books

Gregory, Charles O. *Labor and the Law.* New York: W. W. Norton and Co., (second revised edition, 1961).

Millis, Harry A., and Royal E. Montgomery. *Organized Labor.* New York: McGraw-Hill Book Co., Inc., 1945.

Shister, Joseph, *et al.* (eds.). *Public Policy and Collective Bargaining.* New York: Harper & Row, 1962.

Articles

Brichner, Dale J. "Labor and Anti-Trust Action," *Industrial and Labor Relations Review, 13,* No. 2 (January 1960), pp. 245–253.

Brown, Douglass V. "Labor and the Antitrust Laws," *American Bar Association Proceedings,* August 1955, pp. 23–29.

15

Labor Law: The Regulation of Union Activities

The Emergence of Restrictive Labor Legislation

The word restrictive in the heading of this section is intended to be descriptive rather than deprecating. An unbiased observer has to admit that the Wagner Act was "pro-labor." The intent of the law was to foster the growth of unions, and it contained few limitations on union behavior. By listing a series of unfair labor practices, however, the Wagner Act clearly placed a number of restraints on management.

The Wagner Act was widely accepted by the public when it was passed. That was a time when union members accounted for less than 7 per cent of the nation's civilian labor force. By the end of World War II, however, unions included almost 25 per cent of the civilian work force, and their status had changed markedly during a decade of protection under the Wagner Act.

The War Labor Disputes Act of 1943

The first restrictive labor law was passed at a time when both labor and management had agreed to avoid labor disputes in order to prevent interruption of wartime production. This was the War Labor Disputes Act, better known as the Smith-Connally Act, passed in June 1943 over President Roosevelt's veto. The law was designed to prevent interference with the war effort. It empowered the President to seize an essential facility threatened by a shutdown. The law required a thirty-day notice before the start of any strike that would interrupt war production. At the end of this period the National Labor Relations Board was to conduct a secret election to determine if the workers involved wished to go ahead with the strike. Penalties were also provided for anyone attempting to instigate a strike in a seized plant or other defense facility. In addition, the Act outlawed political contributions by unions in any national election. Inadvertently, this provision may have been added to the political influence of the CIO. After passage of the Smith-Connally Act, the CIO established its Political Action Committee (PAC), which raised funds from contributions rather than from union dues.

In practice, the Smith-Connally Act had little effect. If a union wished to strike, it simply gave notice, and at the end of the thirty-day waiting period its members would overwhelmingly support the union position. About all that the law accomplished was to add to the already heavy load of the National Labor Relations Board, which had to supervise the elections. In some ways the law may have been helpful to unions, although this was not the intent of its authors. Most employers were anxious to avoid seizure. Within the limits of the wage and price stabilization programs, which both parties were expected to respect, the threat of seizure might have made them somewhat more amenable to union demands. There was also a basic incongruity in the law, which permitted both seizure and strikes under certain circumstances. The objective of seizure is to prevent strikes, yet the law permitted strikes after a waiting period and an election. Union officials justifiably grumbled about the vagueness of the law, which could have made them innocent victims of militant employers or dissident minorities within their own organization. Fortunately, as wartime legislation, the Act expired six months after the formal cessation of hostilities.

Readjustment to a Peacetime Economy

Even in the Congress that passed the Wagner Act, there had been a vocal antiunion minority that continued to press for a return to restrictive labor legislation. The amount of labor strife between 1935 and the outbreak of World War II alarmed many citizens, and the number of congressmen and senators who viewed unions as a threat to established society grew. Under the emotional stress of wartime conditions, they were unable to convince a majority in Congress that union power had to be curbed to protect the war effort. Although the Smith-Connally Act was ineffective, it indicated the beginning of a change in public opinion toward unions, which subsequently was to have an effect on public policy. The long days of New Deal and Fair Deal control of Congress ended as the Republican Party seated a majority in the 80th Congress. Since the postwar strikes produced a considerable amount of public resentment, legislation to impose restrictions upon union behavior was high on the agenda when the new Congress convened.

The first law to impose restraints upon union practices dealt with a relatively small and specific group. This was the Unlawful Practices in Radio Broadcasting Act of 1946 sometimes referred to as the Lea Act, but more generally as the "Anti-Petrillo" Act.[1] This Act prohibits certain types of

---

1. James C. Petrillo was president of the American Federation of Musicians at the time this Act was passed, and it was this union that was the target of the Lea Act.

coercive labor practices in the entertainment industry. There had been instances where unions had compelled radio stations to employ workers who were not needed and to restrict the use of recorded programs. The Lea Act outlawed such activities, and made it a criminal offense for anyone to use or threaten to use force or violence to compel a radio station to hire extra workers or to pay for services that were not performed. The Act also outlawed the use of pressure to restrict the use of recordings and transcriptions. While highly restricted in coverage, and not entirely successful in achieving its intent, this Act marked a break with the prewar policy of encouraging union growth without restraints upon union behavior.

The Taft-Hartley Act

The major change in the nation's public policy toward trade unions came when the Labor-Management Relations Act of 1947 was passed. This Act is better known by the names of its two principal sponsors, Senator Taft and Representative Hartley.

During the extensive hearings held while the Taft-Hartley bill was being debated, management witnesses testified that the Wagner Act restricted their behavior without placing corresponding restraints upon union leaders. Union leaders also appeared before Congressional committees to discuss the bill, but they insisted there was no need to change the terms of the Wagner Act. Some legislators and others sympathetic to the trade union movement urged union leaders to make some concessions, since it was impossible to deny that the Wagner Act was one-sided in character. The union leaders were adamant. The Wagner Act, in their view, was all the labor legislation this country needed. It is evident, however, that union leaders misjudged the temper of the times. Congress passed the Taft-Hartley bill, which was then sent to President Truman for his signature. The President vetoed the bill, but Congress overrode the veto and the Taft-Hartley bill became law.

The Taft-Hartley Act contains the provisions essential for the protection of trade unions found in the Wagner Act. It guarantees the right of workers to organize and bargain collectively. It also gives workers the right to refrain from all union activities. It places certain limits on the activities of employers, but it also restricts some of the activities of labor organizations.

The new law, as was true of the Wagner Act, is administered by the National Labor Relations Board. The Taft-Hartley Act does not apply to workers covered by the Railway Labor Act, nor to agricultural laborers, domestic servants, government employees, independent contractors, or employees of nonprofit hospitals. Supervisors are also excluded from the terms of the Act. Section 7 of the Taft-Hartley Act is largely a carry-over from Section 7(a) of the Wagner Act, with the added proviso that workers shall have the right to refrain from any or all union activities unless the union and management have negotiated a union shop agreement. This is an agreement specifying that each member of a bargaining unit must become and remain a union member—typically after a brief waiting period—as a condition of employment.[2]

Unfair Labor Practices for Employers

The Taft-Hartley Act, as was true of its predecessor, lists unfair labor practices for employers. There are six general types of unfair practices which employers are forbidden to engage in:

1. *Interference, restraint, or coercion of employees in the exercise of rights as guaranteed by Section 7.* For example, employers are forbidden to threaten employees with the loss of jobs or benefits if they should join a union, or to threaten to close down a plant if a union should succeed in organizing it. Under the terms of this unfair labor practice, employers are forbidden to question employees about their union activities or membership, if this will tend to restrain or coerce the workers. Also, employers cannot spy on union meetings or grant increases deliberately timed to defeat the self-organization of workers.

2. *Illegal assistance or domination of a labor organization.* Employers are forbidden to take an active part in organizing a union or a committee to represent their workers; to bring pressure upon their employees to join a particular union; or to indicate favoritism if two or more unions are seeking to represent their employees. This is a continuation of the earlier ban on company-dominated unions, and also an effort to prevent an employer from favoring a particular outside union.

3. *Discrimination in employment for union activities.* Any form of discrimination in hiring or tenure of employment, or the terms or conditions of employment, which would tend to encourage or discourage membership in any labor organization, is prohibited by the Taft-Hartley Act. One result of this provision is that the "closed shop" was outlawed. The closed shop is a form of union security under which only those workers who already belong to a union can be hired by an employer.[3] Unions and employers are permitted to negotiate union shop agreements, however, under which employees may be required to join the union within thirty days of their

---

2. The union shop must be distinguished from the *closed* shop. Under the latter form of union security, a worker must be a union member *before* being hired. In the past this generally meant that employers with closed shop agreements obtained workers through a union hiring hall.

3. In practice, many employers in a number of industries continued to obtain workers through union hiring halls. This was especially true in industries (such as construction and longshoring) where employment tends to be casual or intermittent.

employment. In building and construction, employees may be required to join after seven days. Types of discrimination forbidden by this section of the law include: demoting or discharging a worker for urging others to join or organize a union; refusing to reinstate an employee because he took part in a lawful strike; refusing to hire a qualified applicant because he belongs to a union, or because he belongs to one union rather than another. Employers are not, of course, prevented from firing, transferring, or laying off workers for economic or disciplinary reasons.

4. *Discrimination for participation in NLRB proceedings.* The law specifically makes it an unfair labor practice for an employer to fire a worker because he has filed charges or given testimony under the terms of the Taft-Hartley Act.

5. *Refusal to bargain in good faith.* Examples of unfair labor practices forbidden by this section include: granting wage increases without consulting union representatives; granting larger wage increases than the amount offered to union representatives; refusal to put an agreement with employees' representatives into writing; and refusing to deal with the representatives of employees because the latter are on strike.

6. *"Hot Cargo" agreements.* Employers were forbidden by the Taft-Hartley Act to make an agreement to stop handling another employer's products or to stop doing business with any other person. Certain exceptions were made to this provision in the case of subcontractors in the construction industry and jobbers in the apparel and clothing industries.

Unfair Labor Practices for Unions

The basic rights of workers to belong to unions have been protected by the Taft-Hartley Act. Further, employers are prevented from discriminating against union members. As under the Wagner Act, they must also bargain with the freely chosen representatives of their workers after the National Labor Relations Board has certified a union as the employees' bargaining representative. The Taft-Hartley Act also specifies a series of unfair labor practices for unions, which are covered under eight broad headings:

1. *Restraint or coercion.* This provision states that it "shall not forbid the right of a labor organization to prescribe its own rules with respect to the acquisition or retention of membership." But unions are forbidden to restrain or coerce employees in the selection of bargaining representatives, or of no representatives at all, except after a union shop provision has been negotiated. For example, unions are forbidden to engage in mass picketing that would

physically bar nonstriking employees from entering a plant. Acts of force or violence on the picket line or in connection with strikes; threats to do bodily injury to nonstriking workers; or threats to employees that they will lose their jobs unless they support the union's activities are also outlawed by the Act.

2. *Attempts to cause discrimination for union activities.* Under this provision, for example, a union cannot force an employer to fire a worker who has urged a change in the union's method of selecting shop stewards. Nor can the union enter into an agreement requiring the employer to hire only those persons "satisfactory" to the union.

3. *Refusal to bargain in good faith.* This is a counterpart to the provision relating to employers. For example, union officials cannot refuse to make written contracts of reasonable duration, and they cannot insist upon the inclusion of an illegal provision (such as a closed shop) in an agreement.

4. *Secondary boycotts and certain types of strikes and picketing.* One of the more complex provisions of the Taft-Hartley Act attempted to control various forms of union activity against employers not directly engaged in a dispute with the union. Under its terms, the Board has found that it is illegal for a union to picket the plant of an employer who continues to deal with a company with which the union has a dispute. It is also illegal to picket an entire construction project because one of the subcontractors on the project employs nonunion workers. The Board has also ruled that a union official who contacted members in a retail market to tell them that a wholesaler had been placed on the union's "unfair list" was guilty of an unfair labor practice. It is *not* an unfair labor practice, however, for a union to picket the plant of an employer with whom it has a direct dispute, even though such picketing might discourage other workers from entering the plant. This section does ban "sympathy" strikes or boycotts to force recognition of an uncertified union, however. It also prohibits strikes over jurisdictional disputes, or disputes involving work assignments.

The problem of secondary union pressure is a complicated one, and the Taft-Hartley Act did not settle it.[4] Some unions continued to refuse to handle "hot cargoes," that is, the products of an employer with whom the union had a dispute. The Board upheld this action in some cases. The picketing of trucks at a neutral site

---

4. For discussion of some of the issues involved, with reference to a number of cases, see Charles H. Tower, "A Perspective on Secondary Boycotts," reprinted from *Labor Law Journal,* October 1951, in George P. Shultz and John R. Coleman, *Labor Problems: Cases and Readings* (New York: McGraw-Hill Book Co., Inc., 1953), pp. 424–434.

was upheld in some cases, while in others it was considered a violation of the Taft-Hartley Act. The reasoning behind these decisions is not easy to follow. This is an indication that the language of the Act was not sufficiently precise to give the Board a clear mandate on how to deal with a variety of secondary union activities.

The NLRB was given authority to decide jurisdictional disputes by the Taft-Hartley Act. The unions involved in such a dispute are given ten days to reach a settlement following the filing of a charge. If they do not do so the Board steps in to make the decision for them. To avoid this provision of the Act, some unions, such as those in the building trades, have set up private machinery to make jurisdictional awards. This typically involves an outside "umpire," whose decisions are final and binding and, in recent years, has led to a drop in the number of jurisdictional disputes—an indirect but generally welcomed consequence of the Taft-Hartley Act.

5. *Charging excessive or discriminatory initiation fees.* In determining what constitutes a discriminatory initiation fee the Board considers practices and customs of labor organizations in the particular industry, and the wages currently paid to employees affected. The Board found, for example, that it was an unfair labor practice when a union charged old employees—who failed to join the union before a union-shop agreement took effect—a fee of fifteen dollars while charging employees hired after that date only five dollars.

6. *"Featherbedding."* The Taft-Hartley Act declared it an unfair labor practice for unions to cause or attempt to cause an employer to pay for services not performed or not to be performed. This was an attempt by the framers of the Act to eliminate "featherbedding" by legislative fiat, but it has had little practical effect upon union policies. The Act mistakenly assumed that "make work" rules are easily identified, and that they could be abolished by declaring them to be unfair labor practices.

Some kinds of "make work" can be identified. The practice of setting "bogus type" or "dead horse" in some branches of the printing trades is a clear-cut example of what Paul Jacobs has called "un-work."[5] This is work performed and paid for, but which serves no useful purpose. Other types of work rules have been labeled as "featherbedding," however, when it is far from clear

---

5. Paul Jacobs, *Dead Horse and the Featherbird* (Santa Barbara, California: Center for the Study of Democratic Institutions, 1962), p. 4.

that they have been imposed by a union solely for the purpose of maintaining its members' income or to avoid unemployment. Whether or not a specific rule is designed to make work calls for detailed and specific analysis, but as Norman Simler has pointed out, there are cases where even careful observation cannot provide a definite answer.[6]

The Taft-Hartley Act attempted to deal with one of the most complex issues in collective bargaining by the simple declaration that "featherbedding" is an unfair labor practice. Thus the Act had little effect upon existing work rules. As will be noted in a later chapter, work rules have become a central issue in collective bargaining in recent years. But where changes have been made, they have been due to negotiations, arbitration awards, or the recommendations of fact-finding boards.

7. *Recognition and organizational picketing.* Under the Taft-Hartley Act a union cannot picket an employer in an effort to force him to bargain with the union (unless the union has been certified by the National Labor Relations Board as the representative of the firm's employees), if that employer has already lawfully recognized another union under the terms of the Taft-Hartley Act. The union also cannot picket the employer if there has been a valid representation election within the last twelve months. This provision does not, however, prevent informational picketing, that is, advising the public that the employer does not employ members of a union, unless the effects of such informational picketing would be to prevent the delivery of goods to or by the firm, or the performance of services in the firm. Unions are permitted, under the terms of this provision, to picket an employer who has no labor agreement at all, if the purpose of their picketing is simply to discourage customers from patronizing the firm.

8. *"Hot cargo" and subcontracting agreements.* It is an unfair labor practice for any union and employer to make an agreement (written or implied) under which the employer would agree not to handle, use, sell, transport, or otherwise deal in the products of any other employer, or to cease doing business with any other person. This is a counterpart of the unfair labor practice for employers, which makes specific exceptions in the case of subcontracting in the construction industry, or relations with jobbers or subcontractors in the apparel and clothing industries. As noted earlier,

---

6. Norman J. Simler, "The Economics of Featherbedding," *Industrial and Labor Relations Review,* October 1962, p. 119. See also Morris A. Horowitz, *Manpower Utilization in the Railroad Industry* (Boston: Northeastern University, Bureau of Business and Economic Research, 1960).

the Board has not always held refusal by other unions to handle "hot cargoes" to be illegal. It has held, however, that if a union refuses to handle certain products as part of an organizational drive, rather than to protect existing levels of pay, it is in violation of the "hot cargo" ban.[7]

The "Free Speech" Provision

One of the provisions of the Wagner Act that was most bitterly criticized by employers was that which, in their view at least, limited employers' freedom of speech. The law stated that employers could not "interfere with, restrain, or coerce employees" in exercising their rights to self-organization. The interpretation of this provision was, of course, somewhat tricky. What might be considered coercion by one person might simply be accepted as an expression of opinion by another. It must have been recognized at the outset that there would have to be considerable latitude in the interpretation of this provision, but it remained a hotly debated one. The Supreme Court expressed its opinion on this provision in the case of *NLRB v. Virginia Electric and Power Company* in 1941.

In that case the court said:

Neither the Act nor the Board's order here enjoin the employer from expressing its view on labor policies or problems, nor is penalty imposed upon it because of any utterances it has made. The sanctions of the Act are imposed not in punishment of the employer but for the protection of the employees. The employer in this case is as free now as ever to take any side it may choose on this controversial issue.

The court made it clear that the employer was free to express his opinions about trade unions. But the decision went on to assert that "certain *conduct,* though evidenced in part by speech, may amount in connection with other circumstances to coercion within the meaning of the Act."[8] It was the conduct of the employer, in the court's view, and not simply his opinions, which might be considered as coercive. However, the line between speech and action is not always a simple one to draw, and the court concluded that "if the *total activities* of an employer restrains or coerces his employees in their free choice, then those employees are entitled to the protection of the Act and . . . pressure exerted vocally by the employer may no more be disregarded than pressure exerted in other ways."[9]

Although in subsequent opinions, the courts continued to insist that the Wagner Act did not interfere with the employer's basic constitutional right of

---

7. *Sheet Metal Workers, Locals 150 and 99 and Associated Pipe and Fittings Manufacturers,* 170 National Labor Relations Board No. 116 (March 26, 1968).

8. *National Labor Relations Board v. Virginia Electric and Power Company,* 314 U.S. 469 (1941), italics added.

9. *Ibid.,* italics added.

freedom of speech, the charge was regularly made that this was the case. The Taft-Hartley Act attempted to clarify this thorny issue in Section 8(c):

> The expression of any views, argument, or opinion, or the dissemination thereof, whether in written, printed, graphic, or visual form, shall not constitute or be evidence of an unfair labor practice under any of the provisions of this Act, if such expression contains no threat of reprisal or force or promise of benefit.

In interpreting this provision of the Taft-Hartley Act, the National Labor Relations Board has held that the section applies only to unfair labor practice cases and not to conduct affecting elections. The Board has ruled, for example, that Section 8(c) does not cover cases where employers threaten workers with the loss of benefits in the event a union wins an organizational election.

This provision has also been used to restrain unions. The Board has held that picket signs claiming that an employer is "unfair," when making an effort to induce his workers to engage in a secondary boycott, is a violation of Section 8(c). Moreover, statements by union officials to employees that the latter would lose their jobs if a union won an organizational election have also been ruled as a violation of the "free speech" provision of the Taft-Hartley Act.

Changing or Terminating a Contract

The Taft-Hartley Act provides for four basic steps when a contract is renegotiated. If either party desires to change or to terminate its existing agreement, it must: (1) serve written notice at least sixty days before the termination date; (2) offer to meet with the other party to discuss a new contract; (3) if agreement is not reached within thirty days, notify the Federal Mediation and Conciliation Service that a dispute exists, and (4) maintain the status quo on all terms and conditions of the existing contract until sixty days after notice is given or until the contract expires, whichever occurs later. Any worker who goes on strike during the sixty-day waiting period automatically loses his status as an employee under the terms of the Act.

These rather formal arrangements were designed to reduce the number of strikes, but they have been of relatively little consequence. They assume that an element of surprise is important in changing a contract, and that if this can be eliminated the chances of a peaceful settlement will be improved. There seems to be little support for this assumption, however, and the formal steps required to terminate or change a contract have had no apparent effect upon collective bargaining behavior.

State Right-to-Work Laws

There is one provision of the Taft-Hartley Act which unions have criticized bitterly. This provision permits unions and employers to reach union shop agreements except in states where such agreements are forbidden by state law. It is somewhat unusual, since it is not customary for Congress to permit state laws to take precedence over federal law. At the time the Act was passed, some union spokesmen said that the inclusion of this provision was an open invitation to states where unions were relatively weak to pass laws prohibiting this form of union security. They were quite right. By the end of 1965, nineteen states had general "right-to-work" laws, and one other— Louisiana—had a right-to-work law that affected agricultural and certain processing workers only.[10] The geographical distribution of these states is shown on Map 2. It is interesting to compare this map with Map 1 (p. 5), which shows the distribution of union membership on a geographical basis. With the exception of Nevada, union membership amounts to 20 per cent or less of nonagricultural employment in the right-to-work states.

Most of the southern states adopted such legislation as did some of the more sparsely populated and relatively nonindustrial states in the Mountain

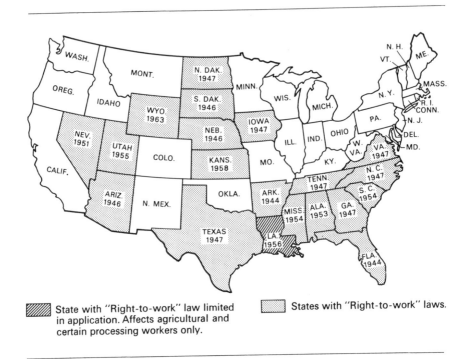

⬛ State with "Right-to-work" law limited in application. Affects agricultural and certain processing workers only.

⬜ States with "Right-to-work" laws.

MAP 2.

State "Right To Work" Laws, Showing Year Adopted. (*Reprinted from the U.S. Department of Labor, Bureau of Labor Standards,* State Right-to-Work Laws, *Bulletin No. 204 [May 1959], facing p. 1; and* Business Week, *February 16, 1963, p. 56.*)

10. Indiana had a right-to-work law from 1957 until 1965. Also, under a 1951 amendment to the Railway Labor Act, union shops are permitted for railroad workers even in right-to-work states.

West and the middle-western Farm Belt. States in which industry and mining are of considerable economic significance, and in which unions wield considerable political power, have refused to enact such legislation.

State right-to-work laws also prohibit "maintenance of membership" agreements, widely negotiated during World War II, requiring those workers who belong to a union at the beginning of a contract period to remain members during the life of the contract. The latter provision is of relatively little consequence since maintenance of membership agreements were largely a wartime expedient.

The closed shop was banned everywhere by the Taft-Hartley Act. In practice, the ban has had little effect. There was not much change in hiring arrangements in previous closed shops. Enactment of state right-to-work laws may have had some effect on union membership, however. The loss of a union shop agreement, even if union recognition is maintained, will cause some workers to drop out of a union. Not all workers covered by union shop agreements are ardent union supporters. Given the opportunity, some will prefer to "ride the gravy train," particularly if they feel reasonably sure that a majority will continue to vote for the union. This gives them the protection of union standards without having to pay union dues. On balance, however, the right-to-work laws probably have not been as damaging to unions as some employers might have wished, or as some union spokesmen insist they have been. On the other hand, the available evidence indicates that right-to-work laws have not had a significant effect on the economic growth or industrial development of the states that have adopted them.[11]

Some unions responded to the union shop prohibition in right-to-work states by negotiating, or attempting to negotiate, "agency shop" contracts. An agency shop agreement requires those workers in the bargaining unit who refuse to join the union to pay a fee in lieu of union dues. Where such a provision can be negotiated, the union might suffer a loss of membership, but it can at least maintain its financial strength. It can also be argued by proponents of the agency shop that such an agreement meets the criticism of compulsory union membership.

Unions have made relatively little headway with the agency shop, however.[12] Indeed, eleven of the state right-to-work laws specifically prohibit the payment of union dues as a condition of employment.[13] And in other states, Arizona and Florida, for example, the courts have ruled that the agency shop violates state right-to-work laws.

---

11. Neil A. and Catherine A. Palomba, "Right-to-Work Laws: A Suggested Economic Rationale," *The Journal of Law and Economics,* Vol. *XIV* (October 1971), pp. 475–483.

12. Paul E. Sultan, "The Union Security Issue," in Joseph Shister, *et al.* (eds.), *Public Policy and Collective Bargaining* (New York: Harper & Row, 1962), p. 99.

13. *Ibid.,* p. 106. Nebraska became the eleventh right-to-work state to prohibit the denial of employment because of refusal to pay a fee, through a 1961 amendment to its law. See U.S. Department of Labor, *Annual Digest of State and Federal Labor Legislation, 1961–1962,* Bureau of Labor Standards Bulletin 253 (Washington, D.C.: U.S. Government Printing Office, 1963), p. 88.

The Taft-Hartley Act in Emergency Disputes

Emergency disputes are defined as those that might jeopardize national health or safety. The Taft-Hartley Act attempted to avert such disputes by setting up a number of steps which unions and employers are required to follow.

If the President believes that a threatened or actual strike (or lockout) will constitute a national emergency, the following steps can be taken:

1. He can appoint a board of inquiry to prepare a written report on the facts of the dispute, but which board does not have authority to make recommendations.
2. After reviewing the report, the President can direct the Attorney General to seek an injunction to prevent the strike or lockout.
3. If the court which was asked to grant the injunction agrees that the national health or safety will be threatened by a strike, it can issue the injunction.

If the issues are still unsettled at the end of a sixty-day waiting period, the board of inquiry is asked to make another report on the status of the dispute and the positions of the parties, which is to include a statement of the employer's "last offer of settlement." Within fifteen days after this report is submitted, the National Labor Relations Board is directed to hold a secret election on the employer's "final offer of settlement." As a final step, within five days after this election, the Attorney General is directed to seek discharge of the injunction, and the court is directed to lift the injunction.

The basic assumption behind the emergency dispute proceedings under the Taft-Hartley Act is that if unions and managements are forced to go through a "cooling-off" period they might reconsider their actions and call off an existing or proposed dispute. A number of writers have been critical of this assumption. It is their contention that neither union leaders nor management decide to initiate a strike or lockout in the heat of anger, and that cooling-off periods are not the appropriate remedy. There is evidence that this machinery has not been effective in averting strikes that might constitute "national emergencies." Between 1947, when the Taft-Hartley Act was passed, and 1953, twelve labor-management disputes were judged to be of an emergency nature. In five of these cases, strikes occurred after the last provisions of the law were invoked, and in the three cases where an election was held on the employer's "final offer," it was rejected. In the words of Sumner Slichter, this record "cannot be regarded as a 'good batting average' for the law."[14]

A widely publicized application of the emergency procedures of the

---

14. Sumner H. Slichter, "Revision of the Taft-Hartley Act," *Quarterly Journal of Economics,* May 1953, p. 170.

Taft-Hartley Act was in the steel strike of 1959. However, the use of the injunction and an enforced cooling-off period had little to do with the ultimate settlement of a serious strike—in terms of man-days of idleness. The basic issue involved was that of work rules. Management insisted that it needed greater freedom to make work assignments if it was to grant "noninflationary" wage increases. The union denied that existing work rules interfered with technological progress, and pointed to the industry's excellent record of productivity gains in support of this position. Other issues were involved but they were of secondary importance.

After prolonged negotiations, which made little headway, more than half a million steelworkers went on strike on July 14, 1959. Industry stockpiles of steel were high, since the strike came after more than a year of recovery from the 1958 recession. The strike had been in progress for 116 days before the emergency provisions of the Taft-Hartley Act were invoked. A fact-finding board was appointed on October 9, and issued its report on October 19. On the same day President Eisenhower requested a district court at Pittsburgh to issue an injunction. This decision was the President's, since the board had no authority to make recommendations. The union asked for and obtained a stay on the injunction, arguing that in view of the substantial amount of steel in inventory, the defense program was not affected. This request was carried to a Circuit Court of Appeals and thence to the Supreme Court. On November 7, the latter upheld the District Court decision, and the injunction went into effect. The striking workers were ordered by the union to return to their jobs.

The steel companies made their "final offer of settlement" on November 15, but it was never voted on. A number of informal polls of steelworkers had indicated that they would reject the offer; the strike could have been resumed in January of 1960. Negotiations continued during the cooling-off period, however, and agreement on all major economic issues was reached on January 4, 1960. Vice President Nixon and Secretary of Labor Mitchell had participated in the discussions prior to the settlement. This, in the union's view, permitted the steel industry to save face: "What the companies were reluctant to offer voluntarily, they were ready to do if requested by a high officer of the government."[15]

The union achieved virtually all its demands, and the work rules provision in the earlier agreement remained unchanged. It was agreed that a joint committee, headed by a neutral chairman, would be appointed to study the issue and to make recommendations. But the union had won the major point leading to this protracted and costly strike.

The 1959 steel strike offered further evidence that the Taft-Hartley Act does not contain adequate provisions for the settlement of so-called "emergency disputes." There is considerable agreement that the steel industry has

---

15. *The 1959 Steel Strike,* The United Steelworkers of America, International Affairs Department (no date), p. 56.

a "high emergency potential."[16] But it is doubtful that the 1959 situation was a critical one. The union contended that the defense program was not affected and that the companies might have reached an earlier settlement if the injunction had not been granted. Economic pressures, rather than government intervention, would have brought about the settlement. This method, in the view of a number of authorities, has much to commend it in a free society.[17]

The Taft-Hartley Act can only postpone a strike that might imperil the nation's health and safety. One suggestion to improve the Act's effectiveness would be to permit the board of inquiry to make recommendations for a settlement. The President could then be authorized to put these into effect for a stated period. This would put pressure upon both sides to reach a settlement through collective bargaining.[18] Another suggestion calls for "flexibility and uncertainty" in the handling of emergency disputes. In essence, this means asking Congress to work out a solution to the particular problems involved. Since the parties would not know what action Congress might take, they would be under pressure to settle their differences through negotiations.[19]

More recent evaluations of the emergency strike provisions of the Taft-Hartley Act—which have now been in effect for a quarter of a century—suggest a continued lack of satisfaction with the law's procedures. They indicate "... disagreement over both *the nature of the problem* of emergency disputes and the most appropriate procedures for dealing with it."[20] Methods of dealing with emergency disputes in this country and abroad range from conciliation to government seizure.[21] All have been suggested by various writers as the appropriate way to deal with emergency disputes in the United States. A detailed survey of the recent literature on the problem of emergency disputes led Aaron and Meyer to conclude that there is no "single answer" or "final solution."[22]

The Railway Labor Act Revisited

The emergency dispute procedures of the Railway Labor Act have come under scrutiny along with those of the Taft-Hartley Act. Charles Killingsworth has commented that when he was a graduate student in the 1930s "the Rail-

---

16. See Irving Bernstein, et al. (eds.), *Emergency Disputes and National Policy* (New York: Harper and Brothers, 1955), pp. 16; 27 ff.

17. See, for example, Clyde W. Summers, "A Summary Evaluation of the Taft-Hartley Act," *Industrial and Labor Relations Review,* April 1958, p. 412.

18. Sumner H. Slichter, *op. cit.,* pp. 178–179.

19. Arthur J. Goldberg and Jack Barbash, "Labor Looks at the National Emergency Provisions," in Bernstein *et al., op. cit.,* pp. 114–120.

20. Benjamin Aaron and Paul Seth Meyer, "Public Policy and Labor-Management Relations," in Benjamin Aaron *et al.,* (eds.), *A Review of Industrial Relations Research, Vol. II* (Madison, Wisconsin: Industrial Relations Research Association, 1971), p. 41, italics added.

21. See Stuart Rothman, "National Emergency Disputes under the LMRA and the RLA," *Labor Law Journal, 15* (April 1964), p. 201.

22. Aaron and Meyer, *op. cit.,* p. 45.

way Labor Act was widely regarded as a triumphant success—a model of the right way to handle labor disputes which affected the public interest..." Today, there is fairly general agreement—at least among those generally regarded as neutral experts—that the Railway Labor Act has become a model of the *wrong* way to handle emergency disputes.[23]

The October 1971 issue of the *Industrial and Labor Relations Review* was largely devoted to the subject of "Labor Relations in Transportation." In general, the articles in this symposium support Killingsworth's view that the RLA has not provided effective procedures for handling emergency disputes on the nation's railroads and airlines. Since the end of World War II, most disputes handled under the Railway Labor Act remained unsettled after all of the law's procedures had been exhausted. As a consequence, the disputes have been settled either by the president or by Congress. In 1971, for example, when four rail unions threatened to strike, a presidential emergency board was appointed. This board recommended a 37 per cent wage increase over a three-year period in exchange for union concessions on work rules. The unions refused this offer and went on strike on December 10, 1971. Congress then intervened and ordered the striking workers back to their jobs after awarding them a 13.5 per cent immediate wage increase. The work rule issue was not, of course, settled. As Kilgour has pointed out, this method of averting a strike amounts to compulsory arbitration.[24]

Several bills were introduced in the 92nd Congress to amend the Railway Labor Act.[25] Although none of the bills became law, one—the Emergency Public Interest Protection bill—was expected to be reintroduced in 1972. This bill would eliminate the emergency procedures of the Railway Labor Act and provide a new set of procedures—covering railroads, airlines, trucking, and shipping—to be added to the Taft-Hartley Act. The new law would provide for mediation to be followed by the appointment of a neutral panel, presumably by the president, which would select one of the "final offers" made by either labor or management. The final offer selected would be made binding on both parties. The proposed procedure is clearly a form of compulsory arbitration, something that has been steadfastly opposed by both labor and management in this country. But since both parties would know that *one* of their offers would be selected, the procedure would provide an incentive for them to bring the two offers as close together as possible. One longstanding criticism of the Railway Labor Act is that it has weakened the incentive to bargain. Whatever else might be said about the proposed Emergency Public Interest Protection Bill, it would provide a strong incentive for the two parties to reach a settlement by means of bargaining.

---

23. Charles Killingsworth, "Emergency Disputes and Public Policy," *Monthly Labor Review*, August 1971, p. 42.

24. John G. Kilgour, "Alternatives to the Railway Labor Act: An Appraisal," *Industrial and Labor Relations Review*, 25 (October 1971), p. 76.

25. For discussion of a number of these bills, see Jacob J. Kaufman, "Procedures v. Collective Bargaining in Railroad Labor Disputes," *Ibid.*, pp. 53–70.

Herbert Northrup, one of the first economists to challenge the reputation of the Railway Labor Act as "model" legislation, agrees that the proposed bill is designed to discourage third-party intervention, but he feels that a better approach is to prevent strikes by injunction, then to encourage settlement by taxing union dues and company revenues until the parties reach an agreement. In his view, "labor and management should be penalized for not settling rather than rewarded by government action when they fail to come to terms."[26]

Other Union Reactions to the Taft-Hartley Act

Union leaders, as noted earlier, unanimously opposed the Taft-Hartley bill while it was being debated. When the law was passed it was roundly denounced by many union leaders as a "slave labor" law. Some predicted that it would mean an end to the growth of trade unions. An objective appraisal of the law cannot avoid the conclusion that it is restrictive on certain types of union behavior, and it is certainly a far cry from the earlier Wagner Act in terms of its treatment of the two parties in labor-management relations. But despite its restrictive features, the Taft-Hartley Act did not spell the end of union growth.

During the first few years that the Taft-Hartley Act was on the books, union membership failed to increase. There was even a modest decline between 1947, the year the Act was passed, and 1950. This was followed by a spurt in union membership which lasted until 1953, and there was a further moderate increase between 1955 and 1956. The most recent surge of union growth has come since 1961. Whether or not union membership would have increased more rapidly in the absence of the law is something that has been debated. A number of influences have acted on union growth in recent years. The provision that permits states to enact right-to-work laws is probably the one that could affect union growth most. Enforced union membership through union security provisions has contributed to union growth in the past. But unions had met with limited success in most states with right-to-work laws even before Taft-Hartley.

It seems clear that the failure of unions to grow since the mid-1950s is due to a number of factors. This point is conceded by some writers with a pro-labor point of view. Solomon Barkin, who was associated with one of the nation's larger industrial unions for many years, feels that the Taft-Hartley Act and other restrictive labor laws have impeded union growth. But he points to a number of other influences, which have contributed to declining union membership.[27] These include worker satisfaction with social conditions, the sullied image of trade unions due to the exposure of corruption by the McClellan

---

26. Herbert R. Northrup, "The Railway Labor Act: A Critical Reappraisal," *Industrial and Labor Relations Review, 25* (October 1971), p. 31.

27. Solomon Barkin, *The Decline of the Labor Movement* (Santa Barbara, California: Center for the Study of Democratic Institutions, 1961).

Committee, and the apathy of workers. Apathetic union leadership, structural difficulties in some cases, inadequate union organizing staffs, and the use of obsolete organizing techniques are also included by Barkin in his list of impediments to union growth.

For a number of years after the Taft-Hartley Act was passed, union leaders vowed to fight for its total repeal. In the first Congressional election following enactment of the law, Representative Hartley, one of the co-authors of the Act, was defeated. Union activity during the election was credited in part for his failure to return to Congress. Despite their best efforts, however, unions could not unseat Senator Taft. Even in subsequent Congresses, with substantial Democratic majorities, unions could not generate sufficient pressure to bring about repeal of the law. Once they recognized that repeal was highly improbable, some union leaders began to agitate for major revisions, but even these more limited efforts have been largely unsuccessful. There have been amendments of a relatively minor nature, but the Taft-Hartley Act, with only a few modest changes, remains the basic law of labor-management relations in the United States.

The failure of unions to dislodge the Taft-Hartley Act does not mean that there is general satisfaction with this legislation. Union leaders continue to regard the spirit of the Act as basically hostile toward trade unionism, while some employer spokesmen are equally critical because in their view it did not go "far enough." A symposium of papers prepared by economists, lawyers, and other specialists in the field of labor-management relations, ten years after passage of the Taft-Hartley Act, suggests that the law had failed to completely satisfy all parties concerned. Some contributors pointed out what they considered to be the weaknesses of the Act, but most of them appeared to agree with one contributor,[28] who stated that:

> Ten years of experience under the Taft-Hartley Act have made one point crystal clear: It is certainly not a 'slave labor law' and it has certainly not destroyed trade unionism and collective bargaining. In terms of both economic and non-economic gains, trade unionism has flourished in the last decade as never before. While union membership has not grown as rapidly as it would have in the absence of Taft-Hartley, it has nevertheless risen by over three million—which is hardly symptomatic of a labor movement in the process of disintegration.

Legislation restricting certain trade union practices did not end with the Taft-Hartley Act. The philosophy behind this Act was that unions had become powerful institutions—that they were no longer the underdogs which the earlier Wagner Act had sought to support. It was also noted after the end of World War II that unions had become the guardians of substantial treasuries. They had been restricted during the war years from pressing for wage in-

---

28. Joseph Shister, "The Impact of the Taft-Hartley Act on Union Strength and Collective Bargaining," *Industrial and Labor Relations Review,* April 1958, p. 350.

creases, but had been permitted to bargain for various kinds of "fringe bene-fits," since deferred payments would not disturb wage stability. Partly as a consequence of this, the larger unions negotiated welfare and pension plans to which employers contributed. As these funds grew, there was growing public concern about their administration, and in 1958, Congress enacted a law requiring unions to follow certain reporting practices in the handling of these funds.

Welfare and Pension Plans Disclosure Act of 1958

This law is described as a "disclosure statute" rather than as a regulatory measure. It makes it a duty of the administrator of every employee welfare and pension plan—with certain specific exceptions noted below—to publish a description of the plan together with an annual report. It applies in all cases covered by federal statutes, which means that more than one state must be involved. Exemptions include (1) plans that cover twenty-five or fewer em-ployees; (2) plans administered by government agencies; (3) plans directly connected with workmen's compensation or unemployment compensation disability insurance laws; and (4) plans involving nonprofit charitable, re-ligious, or educational organizations.

The plans and annual reports must be available for examination in the main office of the organization by a participant or beneficiary, and two copies of each must be filed with the Secretary of Labor, where they are available for public inspection.

Although the provisions of this Act are not unduly stringent, calling only for public disclosure of funds that many consider to be of a quasi-public nature, there was still some resentment about the law; it seemed to carry the implication that not all unions were competent enough or honest enough to handle such funds. It should be noted, however, that the Act was passed by Congress only after prior investigation had revealed a limited number of cases of misuse of union welfare and pension funds.

The Labor-Management Reporting and Disclosure Act of 1959

In January 1957, a Select Committee was appointed by the U.S. Senate to investigate corrupt influences in labor-management relations. For a year and a half, the investigation of the American labor-management scene by the McClellan Committee dominated the nation's headlines. Many of the public hearings were televised, and millions of viewers who might have paid only cursory attention to newspaper accounts observed the behavior of various trade union leaders as they testified before the Committee.[29] The investigation culminated in the Labor-Management Reporting and Disclosure Act of 1959, usually referred to as the Landrum-Griffin Act or the LMRDA.

---

29. For a readable account of the events leading to the establishment of the Committee, as well as a concise summary of its activities, see Robert F. Kennedy, *The Enemy Within* (New York: Harper and Brothers, 1960).

In its declaration of findings, Congress stated that "there have been a number of instances of breach of trust, corruption, disregard of the rights of individual employees, and other failures to observe high standards of responsibility and ethical conduct. . ."[30] In attempting to cope with these problems the authors of the Landrum-Griffin Act were dealing with two broad issues: democracy in the labor movement, and corruption and racketeering in trade unions.

The Seven Titles of the Landrum-Griffin Act

The provisions of the Act are covered by seven rather detailed titles:

A bill of rights for union members Title I specifies that every union member is entitled to equal rights and privileges. Union members, under this section of the law, are guaranteed freedom of speech and assembly. They are protected against increased dues and initiation fees, except when approved by a majority vote by a secret ballot, and individual members are given the right to sue a union, if aggrieved. The law does specify that the union member must "exhaust reasonable hearing procedures" within the union before going to court. A four-month time limit is placed on the union review of his case. The union member is also protected against improper disciplinary action; he cannot be expelled (except for nonpayment of dues) until specifically charged in writing with a violation of union rules. He must also be given time to prepare his defense and be given a "full and fair hearing."

Union reporting The reporting provisions of the Landrum-Griffin Act are covered by Title II. Each union must file a copy of its constitution and bylaws with the Secretary of Labor. It must submit a report covering initiation fees, dues, qualifications and restrictions on membership, benefit plans, and disciplinary procedures. An annual report of the union's assets and liabilities must also be filed with the Secretary of Labor.

Every union officer is required to file a detailed annual report of any personal financial dealings he might have had with employers of the members of his union. This is obviously an effort to discourage unscrupulous union leaders from selling out the rank and file. Employers must also report financial transactions with unions, except for the routine transactions between banks or other financial institutions and the labor organizations or officers included among their clients.

Title II of the Landrum-Griffin Act also repealed the sections of the Taft-Hartley Act dealing with the filing of fiscal information and eliminated the requirement that union officers take an oath swearing they are not members of the Communist Party.

Trusteeships Union trusteeships were originally designed to permit national or international unions to control improperly managed local unions. There

---

30. Public Law 86-257, 86th Congress, September 14, 1959, p. 1.

have been cases, however, of the abuse of trusteeships by national or international union officers. Trusteeships have been arbitrarily imposed by such officers to thwart local autonomy or to gain control over local funds.

Under Title III of the LMRDA, trusteeships may be established only under the constitutional provisions and bylaws of a national or international union, and for the sole purpose of correcting corruption or financial malpractice. A union which has imposed a trusteeship over one of its locals must report this information to the Secretary of Labor and must continue to report on the status of the trusteeship twice a year until the affairs of the local have been turned back to its own officers.

Elections   Congress has tried to ensure the democratic operation of unions through Title IV of the Landrum-Griffin Act. This calls for elections at the national or international level at least every five years. At the local level, elections must be held at least every three years. The law goes on to specify in some detail how such elections are to be conducted. Union funds, or employer contributions, cannot be used to promote the candidacy of any person. Notices must be mailed to each member in good standing at least fifteen days before an election, and each member in good standing is entitled to one vote. Complaints of improper election procedures must be investigated by the Secretary of Labor. If he finds the complaint to be justified, the Secretary can bring civil suit against the union; if the court agrees that the election was improperly conducted, it will be nullified. A new election will then be held under the supervision of the Secretary of Labor.

Financial safeguards   Title V provides stringent penalities for any union officer or employee found guilty of misuse of union funds. It requires the bonding of all union officers and employees and imposes limitations upon loans of union funds. This section prohibits members of the Communist Party or convicted felons from holding union office for a period of five years following the termination of party membership or release from prison. It also strengthens the provisions of the Taft-Hartley Act designed to prevent various kinds of payments by employers to union officers.

Miscellaneous provisions   Title VI of the LMRDA is a catch-all dealing with a variety of matters. The most significant section is that dealing with "extortionate picketing," which is outlawed by this Act. Fines up to $10,000 and imprisonment up to 20 years are provided for persons convicted of picketing for the purpose of personal profit or enrichment. Most of the other sections under this title deal with administrative procedures. One section, however, makes it unlawful for a union to expel a member for attempting to exercise his rights under the Act.

Amendments to the Taft-Hartley Act   In the view of one authority on labor law, the first six titles of the Landrum-Griffin Act constitute all that the sponsors of the bill had in mind as a result of the McClellan Committee investigation.

In his view the remainder of the Act—Title VII—"proved to be a miscellany of uncoordinated, halfbaked, and politically contrived amendments to the 1947 NLRA."[31] It attempted to settle the issue of federal versus state jurisdiction in marginal cases, and it amended the Taft-Hartley Act to permit those economic strikers not entitled to reinstatement to vote in elections conducted by the National Labor Relations Board for a period of one year from the beginning of a strike.

The most important sections under this title, however, are those which attempt to close the loopholes in the secondary boycott provisions of the Taft-Hartley Act. The Landrum-Griffin Act is more specific than Taft-Hartley in its ban on "hot cargo" agreements. The law declares it to be an unfair labor practice for a union to force an employer into such an agreement. As in the Taft-Hartley Act, exemptions are provided for subcontractors in the constructon and in the apparel and clothing industries. Further limitations on secondary picketing are also implied by this part of the law, and organizational and recognition picketing are declared to be unfair in certain situations.

Most of Title VII was the result of an attempt to tighten up the provisions of the Taft-Hartley Act dealing with secondary pressures, including the matter of "hot cargo" clauses. One section, however, amended the Taft-Hartley Act to permit modified hiring hall agreements in the construction industry. The closed shop is still outlawed—although in fact it has continued to operate in many parts of the country. But a modified form of union security is now permitted, which is a tacit recognition by Congress that hiring halls serve a useful purpose in labor markets characterized by intermittent employment with workers attached to an industry or occupation rather than to specific employers. The Landrum-Griffin Act is careful to specify, however, that the modified hiring hall arrangement is not to conflict in any way with the state right-to-work laws permitted by the Taft-Hartley Act.

The Impact of Landrum-Griffin on Union Behavior

The Landrum-Griffin Act was an outgrowth of the McClellan investigation, which revealed that a few unions had been tainted by corruption. Implicit in a number of its provisions is the assumption that union abuses can be traced to a lack of union democracy. Indeed, one sympathetic interpreter of the law has stated that: "A major purpose of the [act] is to insure that labor organizations are democratically controlled . . . the entire structure of the act emphasizes democratic self-correction rather than governmental action."[32]

Some unions have modified their election and disciplinary procedures since the Act was passed, and it is a fair inference that the law provided the

---

31. Charles O. Gregory, *Labor and the Law*, 2nd rev. ed. with 1961 supplement (New York: W. W. Norton and Co., 1961), p. 576.
32. John L. Holcombe, "Union Democracy and the LMRDA," *Labor Law Journal*, July 1961, p. 597.

stimulus for these changes.[33] During its first two years the Bureau of Labor Management Reports investigated nearly 600 cases of alleged election violations. Many of the violations were of a technical nature. Most of these cases were closed following investigation and voluntary compliance by the union with the corrective action ordered. In only a handful of cases has it been necessary for the Bureau to institute court action.[34] It is apparent that steps have been taken to implement the technical election provisions of the Act. The effects of the Act on the *outcomes* of union elections are not easy to determine, and some doubts have been expressed about the effectiveness of the LMRDA in those cases where compliance has not been voluntary.

One critic of the Act feels that the courts "have been reluctant to discard the doctrine of noninterference in the internal affairs of 'voluntary' organizations."[35] The legislative history of the law indicates clearly that there was no intent to require unions to modify admission requirements. Unions with restrictive membership provisions have not been affected by the law, and many would argue that such unions can scarcely be considered to be democratic.

It is evident that Congress considered the problem of union democracy "to be one of protecting members from autocratic officers."[36] There are obvious examples of unions dominated by strongly entrenched leaders, and there is no evidence that the LMRDA has changed this. Moreover, the framers of the Act did not include provisions to protect some union officers from others. The officers of unions were conceived of as a tightly-knit group acting in concert which, it should be noted, is far from the case in a number of unions.

The notion that the rank and file must be protected from autocratic officers was also given expression in the provision that individual members have the right to sue a union for improper disciplinary action. However, the member must exhaust all internal remedies before turning to the courts. An even more serious limitation is that if a member brings suit against a union under the "bill of rights" sections of the Act there are no provisions for the payment of his court costs if his suit is successful. It has been suggested that this is one reason why so few cases of this kind have reached the courts.[37] Few workers are in a position to finance litigation, particularly if it is to be carried to Courts of Appeal.

Collective Bargaining with Public Employees

There have been few changes in public policy toward bargaining in the private sector since the Landrum-Griffin Act of 1959. Indeed, since Landrum-Griffin was primarily concerned with the internal affairs of unions, it had only

---

33. *Ibid.*, p. 599, and David A. Swankin, "Influence of the LMRDA on Constitutional Discipline Provisions," *Monthly Labor Review*, May 1963, pp. 491–492.
34. Holcombe, *op. cit.*, pp. 600–601.
35. Linda Rosenberg, "Interpretive Problems of Title I of the Labor-Management Reporting and Disclosure Act," *Industrial and Labor Relations Review*, April 1963, p. 405.
36. *Ibid.*, p. 409.
37. *Ibid.*, p. 427.

a minimum impact on bargaining.[38] The Landrum-Griffin Act did tighten up some of the Taft-Hartley provisions dealing with secondary boycotts. But in the words of one observer, "unions will manage to live with the closed secondary boycott loopholes, as they have since 1947."[39]

There is a marked contrast between the relative constancy of public policy toward bargaining in the private sector since 1959, and the changes that have occurred in attitudes toward bargaining with public employees. Before 1962, there was virtually no bargaining with federal public employees. Personnel practices were decided by the Civil Service Commission, while wages and fringe benefits were determined by Congress. The first break came in January 1962, when President Kennedy issued Executive Order 10988. Although Congress continued to determine wages and fringe benefits after this order, "changes in working conditions and codification of existing local practices became proper subjects for determination by collective bargaining."[40]

The introduction of collective bargaining into the federal service produced few immediate changes. Indeed, it led one author to conclude that it resulted in an "impasse on impasses."[41] This was Hart's way of summarizing what he considered to be a conflict between the basic philosophies of the Department of Labor (the "Labor approach") and the Civil Service Commission (the "Commission approach") toward bona fide collective bargaining by federal government employees. In Hart's view, the Department of Labor was more strongly inclined toward genuine collective bargaining between unions and government agencies than the Civil Service Commission.

The thesis advanced by Hart was criticized vigorousiy by John W. Macy, Jr., Chairman of the United States Civil Service Commission.[42] Macy denied that Civil Service Commission officials resented creation of the Federal Employee-Management Cooperation Program—an outgrowth of Executive Order 10988—and pointed out that the Commission participated in the background work and preparation of this Executive Order.[43] Hart has cited evidence, however, that organized labor was not entirely happy with the small strikes toward collective bargaining made by the executive order; he quotes George Meany to the effect that "certain departments of the Government

---

38. The Aaron and Meyer essay on public policy and labor-management relations cited earlier, for example, is devoted almost entirely to NLRB decisions, and to court review of those decisions. *Op. cit.,* pp. 9–36.

39. Boaz Siegel, "The Impact of the Labor-Management Reporting and Disclosure Act of 1959 on Collective Bargaining," *Labor Law Journal,* July 1960, p. 589.

40. James L. Stern, "Collective Bargaining Trends and Patterns," in Aaron, Meyer, *et al., A Review of Industrial Relations Research,* Vol. II (Madison, Wisconsin: Industrial Relations Research Association, 1971), pp. 132–133.

41. Wilson R. Hart, "The Impasse in Labor Relations in the Federal Civil Service," *Industrial and Labor Relations Review, 19,* No. 2 (January 1966), p. 189.

42. John W. Macy, Jr., "The Federal Employee-Management Cooperation Program," *Industrial and Labor Relations Review, 19,* No. 4 (July 1966), pp. 549–561.

43. *Ibid.,* p. 561.

do not agree whole-heartedly with the President's intent in promulgating an Order to give Federal employees representation rights."[44]

The next step in the evolution of bargaining with federal public employees came in October 1969, when President Nixon issued Executive Order 11491, which became effective on January 1, 1970.[45] The new executive order established a Federal Labor Relations Council, consisting of the chairman of the Civil Service Commission, the Secretary of Labor, an official of the Executive Office of the President, and others to be designated by the President. It provides for the recognition of qualified labor organizations, the negotiation of agreements relating to personnel policies and practices, the negotiation of disputes, and the use of the Federal Mediation and Conciliation Service to assist the parties in reaching agreement.

In spite of the extended coverage of the new Executive Order as compared with its predecessor, there is relatively little scope for actual collective bargaining in the federal government. There is one exception to this statement. The Postal Reorganization Act of 1970 provided a separate labor relations system for postal workers. The scope of bargaining between the postal workers and the new quasi-governmental postal agency was broadened to include wages, and the National Labor Relations Board has jurisdiction over this bargaining.[46] Postal workers' agreements do not provide for union security, so that individual postal workers need not join a union. Also, compulsory arbitration has been substituted for strikes as a means of resolving deadlocks. But in other respects, postal workers' agreements are similar to a typical agreement in the private sector.[47]

Collective bargaining will undoubtedly become a more important aspect of federal public employment in the future than it has been up to the present. By the end of 1970, the Civil Service Commission reported that more than 1.5 million workers—or 58 per cent of civilian employees of the executive branch of the government—belonged to unions. There were more than 3,000 exclusive bargaining units, and in more than half of them union-management agreements had been negotiated.[48]

The behavior of federal public employees is still highly limited when

---

44. Hart, *op. cit.,* p. 176.

45. The complete Executive Order, as well as a highly detailed comparison, section by section, between this Order and its predecessor, Executive Order 10988 are given in *Labor-Management Relations in Federal Service, Report and Recommendations, Executive Order No. 11491* (Washington, D.C.: U.S. Government Printing Office, October 29, 1969).

46. Stern, *op. cit.,* p. 134.

47. *Ibid.*

48. *Ibid.,* p. 133. There is some disagreement about the extent of union membership of federal employees. Goldberg has reported that in 1971 there were 1.41 million federal employees who belonged to unions, and that they accounted for 52 per cent of federal employment. See Joseph P. Goldberg, "Public Employee Developments in 1971," *Monthly Labor Review,* January 1972, p. 56. The difference in these estimates, while large, does not change any of the conclusions about collective bargaining by federal public employees.

compared with the activities permitted by workers in the private sector. In two separate court cases, the United Federation of Postal Clerks and the National Association of Letter Carriers challenged the existing ban on strikes by federal employees. They contended that the right to strike is a fundamental right protected by the Constitution. The Federal district court replied, however, that "the Federal employees' constitutional right to strike is not violated, simply because it does not exist. No Federal statute has given the employees such a right."[49] The court went on to point out that while the Taft-Hartley Act gives workers in the private sector the right of association and the right to strike, it specifically withholds the right to strike from federal and other public employees.

There have been pronounced changes in labor-management relations in federal government employment during the past dozen years, and there have been equally rapid changes at the state and local level. In some states, there is now relatively little difference between the private sector and some parts of the public sector, so far as collective bargaining is concerned.

The first law authorizing collective bargaining by state or municipal employees was passed by Wisconsin in 1959.[50] At the end of 1970, according to Goldberg, "40 States had legislation authorizing some form of union activity by public employees, while eight had no legislation and two prohibited such activity."[51] By the end of 1971, according to Goldberg, there were 2.67 million organized state and local employees, and they accounted for 28 per cent of state and local employment. It is difficult to summarize the details of state labor legislation as it relates to public employees, because of wide variation in provisions among the states. In some states, compulsory arbitration of public employee disputes is required, whereas in others, public employees are allowed to strike, if necessary, to reach agreement with their employers. A study by the Bureau of Labor Statistics shows that public employee strikes increased from 15 in 1958 to 254 in 1968. There was a further increase in public employee strikes to 411 in the following year.[52] Teachers have exhibited a greater propensity to strike than other public employees, followed by sanitation, hospital, and health service workers. On a geographic basis, strike activity by public employees has been most prevalent in the Northeast.[53]

Conclusions

The Taft-Hartley Act was designed to "equalize" the rights, duties, and obligations of unions and employers. When the Wagner Act was passed, unions were weak and many members of Congress felt that union growth

---

49. "Ban on Federal Strikes," *Monthly Labor Review*, July 1971, p. 60.

50. Stern, *op. cit.*, p. 135.

51. Goldberg, *op. cit.*, p. 63.

52. *Work Stoppages in Government 1958–1968*, BLS Report No. 348 (1970); and Stern, *op. cit.*, p. 141.

53. Stern, *op. cit.*, pp. 141–142.

should be encouraged to offset the power of large corporate employers. But as unions grew in numbers and in strength, there was mounting concern about the power they wielded. Unions fought passage of the Taft-Hartley Act, and many union leaders continue to denounce it to this day. Some unions have been particularly critical of state "right-to-work" laws—a by-product of the Taft-Hartley Act—and some union officers claim that the "freedom of speech" provision has added to their difficulties. It is not easy, of course, to decide what is and what is not coercion and intimidation. Whether they like it or not, however, union leaders have learned to live under the Taft-Hartley Act.

The Landrum-Griffin Act deals with the internal affairs of trade unions. It was the result of a lengthy investigation revealing that some union officers had sadly abused their positions of trust, and that some unions either through membership apathy or dictatorial control at the top were not operating in a democratic manner. The Landrum-Griffin Act was designed to require a certain amount of public disclosure of union practices and public accounting of union funds. There are provisions with the obvious intent of making unions "more democratic." There has been little objection to these provisions, but there is also little evidence to date that unions have become more democratic as a result of the law.

It has often been observed that most organizations to which American citizens belong are run by a handful of members. There are "activists" in all sorts of organizations—religious, fraternal, political, and social. These are the members who attend all meetings and who speak up on all issues; it is largely from their ranks that officers are elected. The degree of participation varies considerably among organizations, but in most organizations a majority of the members are content to let others make the decisions. This seems to be especially true of trade unions, whose members often have the attitude that their officers are paid to take care of union affairs, and so long as the officers "deliver the goods," most rank and file members are not active participants in union affairs. As Sumner Slichter pointed out, however, this is more often an expression of satisfaction with the state of affairs than of dissatisfaction. Many union leaders have exhorted their members to attend meetings more often and to take a more active interest in union matters, but the rank and file have been largely unresponsive. They continue to leave union decisions in the hands of their officers and the minority of activists who regularly attend union meetings.

The most dramatic changes in the American labor movement during the past dozen years have involved public employees at the federal, state, and local levels. At the federal level this has not been due to new legislation, but rather to executive orders issued by Presidents Kennedy and Nixon. Postal workers are now able to negotiate wages as well as working conditions, although the wages of other federal employees are not at this time subject to negotiation. Recent court decisions have reaffirmed that federal public employees do not have the right to strike.

There have been equally rapid developments in collective bargaining at the state and local levels. Four fifths of all states allow some form of collective bargaining, and in some states workers are allowed to strike, if this is necessary to achieve their objectives. Differences between public and private bargaining in these states are not large. While it is hazardous to predict the future course of labor legislation, it is highly likely that the momentum of the past decade will be maintained and that a growing proportion of public employees will be involved in collective bargaining.

Questions and Exercises

1. In what sense may the labor legislation enacted since the end of World War II be described as "restrictive"?
2. What was the objective of the Smith-Connally Act, and did it achieve this objective?
3. In what major ways did the Taft-Hartley Act amend the earlier Wagner Act? Were any of the basic provisions of the Wagner Act carried over to the Taft-Hartley Act?
4. What is the "hot cargo" provision of the Taft-Hartley Act? Has the NLRB always held union refusal to handle "hot cargos" to be illegal?
5. Briefly describe the extent and nature of state right-to-work laws. What does the available evidence show about the effects of right-to-work laws on state industrial development?
6. Describe the emergency disputes procedures of the Taft-Hartley Act. What did the 1959 steel strike show about the adequacy of these provisions?
7. The Railway Labor Act was long described as "model" labor legislation. Is this view of the law widely held today? How have all of the emergency railroad disputes since the end of World War II been settled?
8. What device was included in the Emergency Public Interest Protection bill to ensure that labor and management would be able to reach an agreement? What alternative was proposed by Herbert Northrup? Why did he suggest this alternative?
9. Describe the Welfare and Pension Plans Disclosure Act of 1958. Is this a regulatory measure?
10. Describe in general terms the major provisions of the Labor-Management Reporting and Disclosure Act of 1959 (the Landrum-Griffin Act). To what extent does this act deal with internal union affairs, and to what extent does it apply to collective bargaining activities?
11. One of the hypotheses behind the McClellan Committee investigation was that trade unions are not democratic institutions. Has the Landrum-Griffin Act succeeded in making most unions more democratic?
12. Before 1962, personnel matters were decided by the Civil Service Com-

mission, and the wages and fringe benefits of federal employees were determined by Congress. What changes were made by Executive Order 10988 issued that year?

13. What provisions were established by President Nixon's Executive Order 11491 with respect to the settlement of disputes? Do federal employees have the right to strike?

14. Are federal employees more or less extensively organized than state and local government employees? Do public employees have the right to organize in all fifty states?

15. Describe, briefly, trends in collective bargaining by state and municipal employees since 1959. Are there circumstances under which state or municipal employees have the right to strike?

Suggested Readings

Books

Barkin, Solomon, *The Decline of the Labor Movement,* Santa Barbara, California: Center for the Study of Democratic Institutions (1961).

Jacobs, Paul, *Dead Horse and the Featherbird,* Santa Barbara, California: Center for the Study of Democratic Institutions (1962).

The Taft-Hartley Act After Ten Years: A Symposium, Industrial and Labor Relations Review, Vol. II (April 1958).

Articles

Aaron, Benjamin, and Paul Seth Meyer. "Public Policy and Labor-Management Relations," in Aaron, Meyer, *et al., A Review of Industrial Relations Research, Vol. II.* Madison, Wisconsin: Industrial Relations Research Association, 1971, pp. 1–60.

Goldberg, Joseph P. "Public Employee Developments in 1971," *Monthly Labor Review,* January 1972, pp. 55–66.

Kilgour, John G. "Alternatives to the Railway Labor Act: An Appraisal," *Industrial and Labor Relations Review, 25,* No. 1 (October 1971), pp. 71–84.

Killingsworth, Charles C. "Emergency Disputes and Public Policy," *Monthly Labor Review,* August 1971, pp. 42–48.

Macy, John W., Jr. "The Federal Employee-Management Cooperation Program," *Industrial and Labor Relations Review, 19,* No. 4 (July 1966), pp. 549–561.

Northrup, Herbert R. "The Railway Labor Act: A Critical Reappraisal," *Industrial and Labor Relations Review, 25,* No. 1 (October 1971), pp. 3–31.

Palomba, Neil A., and Catherine A. Palomba. "Right-to-Work Laws: A Suggested Economic Rationale," *The Journal of Law and Economics, XIV* (October 1971), pp. 475–483.

Rhemus, Charles M. "Railway Labor Act Modifications: Helpful or Harmful," *Industrial and Labor Relations Review, 25,* No. 1 (October 1971), pp. 85–94.

Stern, James L. "Collective Bargaining Trends and Patterns," in Aaron, Meyer, *et al., A Review of Industrial Relations Research, Vol. II.* Madison, Wisconsin: Industrial Relations Research Association, 1971, pp. 125–182.

16

Social Security and Labor Standards

During the Roosevelt and Truman administrations, a number of laws were passed to provide workers with a minimum of protection against the vicissitudes of the marketplace and the problems associated with aging in an industrial society. Other laws were passed to provide for minimum labor standards. A number of federal agencies were established to administer these programs. While some conservatives have been critical of social legislation, it has won widespread public acceptance. Unions have generally supported such legislation wholeheartedly and have often urged that it be expanded. Conservatives, and even some moderates, have recommended caution in the expansion of social legislation, but they have not suggested that we turn back the clock; that we try to return to an age when each man was required to provide for all of his needs or to turn to private charity in the event of unforeseen hardships.

Setting Labor Standards on Public Contracts

The first federal law to establish basic labor standards was the Davis-Bacon Act of 1931. This Act is limited in scope; it covers direct federal construction projects, including the repair or alteration of public facilities, on all contracts of more than $2,000. The Secretary of Labor determines wage rates to be paid in a locality, usually the prevailing union rates in the area. Workers paid less than the established wages may file a claim with the Comptroller General, who is authorized to withhold funds from the contractor to settle such claims. If contract funds are insufficient, individual workers may sue the contractor for the difference under The Miller Act of 1935.

Violators of the Davis-Bacon Act may not be awarded further government contracts for three years, and existing contracts are cancelled with the contractor obligated to bear any extra costs incurred. Under a series of laws starting with the Housing Act of 1937, construction workers on federally aided housing, highway, school, hospital, and airport programs are covered by provisions similar to those in the Davis-Bacon Act.

The Walsh-Healey Public Contracts Act of 1936 is broader than the Davis-Bacon Act but is still limited in scope. It has been amended several times, and the following provisions are those that have applied since the latest amendment was made in 1958. The Public Contracts Act sets basic labor standards for all work performed on United States government contracts amounting to $10,000 or more. The Secretary of Labor determines the prevailing minimum wage in an industry, and all workers employed on government contracts must be paid this wage or more. Industry minima are generally set by the Secretary after a public hearing.

The Walsh-Healey Act also sets basic hours of work. The standard work day is eight hours and the standard work week is forty hours. Overtime is permitted but must be paid at the rate of time and one half. The law prohibits child labor (boys under sixteen and girls under eighteen) and forbids the use of convict labor. It also regulates conditions under which work may be performed on government contracts. Work cannot be done under conditions that are unsanitary, hazardous, or otherwise dangerous to the health or safety of employees. The law also prohibits home work, that is, all work under a government contract must be performed on the premises of the manufacturer.

Every government contractor must display a copy of the Public Contracts Act in special poster form. Contractors are also required to maintain special records, which may be inspected by representatives of the Wage and Hour and Public Contracts Divisions of the U.S. Department of Labor. There are certain exemptions under the Walsh-Healey Act; for example, some contracts involving transportation by common carrier, utility services, perishable agricultural products, rentals, or seasonal services are exempt from the provisions of the law. In any case where it can be shown that the operation of the Act will impair the conduct of government business, the Secretary of Labor is authorized to make exceptions. Exceptions to the minimum wages are also permitted in the case of learners or apprentices, and under certain circumstances, in the case of handicapped workers.

If a contractor violates any term of the Walsh-Healey Act, his contract may be cancelled with any additional costs involved charged to the contractor. Any firm convicted of violating the Act may not be granted a governmental contract for at least three years following the original breach of contract. Since 1952, court review of alleged violations is permitted.

Following the 1952 amendment to the Walsh-Healey Act, the Secretary's freedom to set industrywide minima was challenged in *Mitchell v. Covington Mills*. A district court ruled that the minima on a specific contract could apply only to a given locality. This decision was reversed by a court of appeals, however, and the Supreme Court upheld the latter decision in 1956. This reaffirmed the principle that the Secretary of Labor can set industrywide minima in cases where competition is nationwide.

The President's Committee on Government Contracts, established by executive order, requires all contracting agencies dealing with the federal government to provide employment without regard to race, religion, color, or national origin.

The Fair Labor Standards Act of 1938

This act, often referred to as the wage and hour law, was passed in June 1938. Like the Walsh-Healey Act it has been amended several times, and the following description is based on the most recent amendments.

The federal wage-hour law is administered by the Administrator of Wage and Hour and Public Contracts Divisions of the U.S. Department of Labor. It is much broader than the Walsh-Healey Act, since it establishes minimum wages, overtime provisions, and child-labor standards which apply to all employees engaged in interstate commerce.

The law provides for minimum wages which are uniform throughout the United States, with exceptions in the case of Puerto Rico, the Virgin Islands, and American Samoa, where lower rates may be sent by special industry committees representing labor, management, and the public. Workers must be paid at time and one half for all work in excess of forty hours during a given work week. A minimum age of sixteen is established for general employment while in hazardous occupations, the minimum age is eighteen years. For certain occupations, where work is performed outside of school hours, the minimum age is fourteen. The Act applies to all workers covered by the interstate commerce clause, whether employed in a factory, office, or at home. As in the case of the Walsh-Healey Act, exceptions may be made in the case of learners, messengers, apprentices, and handicapped workers.

There is also a "white-collar" exemption in the case of executive, administrative, or professional personnel. Local retailing activities and "outside salesmen" are exempted. Numerous other workers, including seamen, taxicab and bus drivers, employees of small newspapers, small lumbering concerns, small telephone exchanges, and fishing or fish processing concerns, are not covered by the law.

Most of the exemptions apply to workers who earn more than the statutory minimum wage but whose jobs often require them to work more than eight hours on certain days and perhaps more than forty hours in a certain week. The exemptions represent an attempt by Congress to avoid fitting all workers into a legal strait jacket. The objective of the law is to eliminate substandard wages, particularly in areas where workers have few alternative job opportunities. A single employer in an area—a monopsonist in the terminology of economics—could easily exploit his workers in the absence of legal protection. While such employers might not be numerous, Congress wished to protect workers from downward wage pressure in such circumstances.

Generally speaking, all work in excess of forty hours in a given work week must be paid at one and one half times the regular hourly rate. Special provisions are made in the case of workers employed at piece rates and workers who do two or more kinds of work at different hourly or piece rates. Where the nature of jobs requires irregular hours, Section 7(b) of the Act permits payment to be made on the basis of contract arrangements.

Some workers are paid partly "in kind," which generally means board, room, or both. Under such circumstances, an employer may deduct the "reasonable cost" of furnishing his workers board, lodging, or other facilities, but he is not expected to make a profit on such services. The law does not require that workers receive the statutory minimum "free and clear." If, for example, workers agree to the deduction of union dues or charitable contributions, these may be made under the terms of the Act even if the result is that take-home pay drops below the statutory minimum.

The law also prohibits "oppressive" child labor; that is, employment of workers between the ages of fourteen and sixteen in most occupations; workers must be at least eighteen if the jobs involved are particularly hazardous or detrimental to health. The Act specifically lists a fairly large number of such jobs in mining, manufacturing, lumbering, and other occupations where the operation of machinery is involved. Exemptions to the entire law are made in the case of youngsters in school doing nonhazardous part-time work.

The Equal Pay Act of 1963 applies to every employer covered by the Fair Labor Standards Act. It requires employers to pay equal wages to men and women doing equal work on jobs that require equal skill, effort, and responsibility. It does not prohibit lower wages to one sex if the differential is based on seniority, a merit system, piece rates, or "on any other factor other than sex."

Unlike the Walsh-Healey Act, the Fair Labor Standards Act permits home work in certain industries such as jewelry and some parts of the apparel and garment industries. But the same provisions which apply to factory work also apply to home work under these conditions.

There are no particular reporting provisions under the Fair Labor Standards Act, and employers are not required to keep any specified set of records. The law does require each employer to keep reliable records which clearly reflect the wages, hours, and other conditions and practices of employment in his establishment.

In case of violations, employees may sue for the amounts by which they have been underpaid, or upon the request of workers, the Secretary of Labor may bring suit against an employer to recover the amounts of underpayment. The government may also bring action on its own initiative against any person who willfully violates the Fair Labor Standards Act, if there is evidence of such violation. If convicted, the employer may be fined up to $10,000, and for a second conviction may be imprisoned for as much as six months. The Secretary of Labor may also seek injunctions in federal district courts to restrain employers from violating the Act. The law prohibits discharge of or discrimination against workers who have filed complaints or participated in other proceedings under the Act.

The Fair Labor Standards Act has been a controversial piece of labor legislation since its enactment. Although numerous Department of Labor Studies have shown that only a small minority of employers have been affected each time the minima have been raised, there is a general hue and cry when Congress proposes to further increase the prevailing minimum. In general, the statutory minimum is well below the prevailing hourly wages of workers in most business establishments in most areas. As noted earlier, the law was designed to protect those workers who do not have alternative employment opportunities, and to prevent the fairly rare unscrupulous employer from depressing wages to substandard levels in areas where there might be considerable unemployment. Staunch conservatives, however, have generally been critical of the Fair Labor Standards Act on the grounds that it is an interference with the free market. Except when the minimum is being revised upward, however, the Fair Labor Standards Act is quite widely accepted as part of a broader policy designed to provide minimum standards of hours and earnings for all workers covered by the law.

The most recent amendment was in 1966, providing for an increase in the minimum to $1.60 per hour, effective February 1971. An exception was made for agricultural workers on large farms, whose minimum wage remains at $1.30 per hour. A 1963 amendment had broadened the coverage of the Act to include slightly more than 3½ million workers, mostly in retail and service establishments, who formerly were excluded from its provisions. The Act interprets "interstate commerce" quite liberally, and it covers employees who are only *indirectly* engaged in interstate or foreign commerce. But there are still many workers—those employed in strictly *intra*state activities—who are not covered by the law. Most states have laws providing for minima—generally lower than the federal minimum—covering these workers.

The Social Security Act of 1935

This is one of the most comprehensive pieces of social legislation to come out of the New Deal. It provides for nationwide systems of social insurance to protect wage earners and their families against the unexpected loss of income due to unemployment, and also provides a system of payments upon retirement or the disability or death of the family breadwinner. Programs covering old age, disability, and survivors insurance—all operated through a federal system—are administered by the Social Security Administration. Unemployment insurance, to be discussed in the next section, is a joint federal-state program administered by a separate agency. Since 1965, when Medicare was enacted, all persons eligible for social security benefits have automatically been eligible for hospital insurance at age 65. Some individuals not eligible for social security cash benefits may still be eligible for hospital insurance under Medicare. And since 1970, medical assistance payments for low-income individuals and families, and for the needy blind and disabled, have been made under the Medicaid program, administered by the states under HEW guidelines. Grants are also provided to the states for maternal and child-health services and other child-welfare programs, including services for crippled children, to supplement state and local public and private funds used for such purposes. The administrative setup of the social security program is illustrated in Figure 16-I.

Old-age and Survivors Insurance

This is a nationwide social insurance program which provides pensions to retired or disabled workers. Retirement benefits are determined by the age at which retirement begins and the individual's average yearly earnings after 1950; disability benefits are determined by the worker's average yearly earnings between 1950 and the time he became disabled. Wives of retired workers are also entitled to payments, depending upon the wife's age and the worker's average annual earnings.

The Social Security Act has been amended a number of times since it was first passed in 1935. Originally, for example, retirement benefits could be claimed only at age 65; in 1956, however, women became eligible for retirement payments at age 62. The law was amended again in 1961 to permit men to retire at this age. Benefit payments are scaled down, of course, if covered workers choose to retire before reaching the age of 65. A worker is entitled to his full social security payment, after retirement at age 65, if he earns no more than $1,200 a year, and he is entitled to full benefits after age 72 regardless of earnings.

Benefits are paid to all persons, or to their dependents and survivors, who have become insured by working in covered employment. Federal Government employees who have their own retirement program are not covered by the law. Almost all other workers are covered, including the self-employed, if they choose to come under the terms of the Act.

A worker becomes eligible for social security by being employed a certain number of covered quarters. A covered quarter is defined as a calendar quarter after 1936 in which the employee received at least $50 in wages or at least $100 of self-employment income. Once a worker has earned credits for forty quarters in covered employment he is fully insured for life, and his dependents are then entitled to survivors insurance in the event of his death. There are three kinds of benefits: retirement, disability, and survivor.

Retirement Benefits

Payment is not automatic. When a worker reaches retirement age and wishes to collect his social security, he must file a claim for benefits at the nearest social security office. There are currently 850 district offices through which claims may be filed or, if necessary, the worker can apply directly to the Washington office.

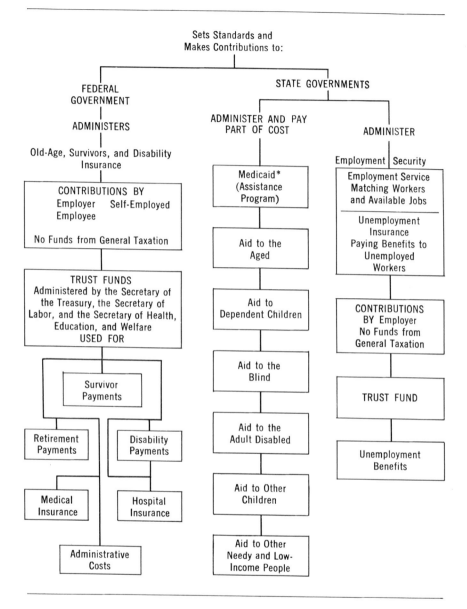

FIGURE 16–1.

How the Social Security Law Works. (*From Social Security Administration publications.*)

*Medicaid is not administered by the Social Security Administration, but by state governments, with financial assistance from the federal government and under guidelines established by the Department of Health, Education, and Welfare.

Survivor Benefits

Survivor benefits may be claimed by the widow of an insured wage earner. At the time of death, the widow of the fully insured worker receives a lump sum payment, which may be equal to three times his monthly benefit but may not be more than $255. If the widow is under 62, she is entitled to a monthly payment equal to three fourths of the primary insurance amount. If she has one child under 18, she is entitled to an additional benefit of the same amount, and benefits of one half the primary insurance amount for other children under 18. If the insured worker does not leave a widow or children, dependent parents of retirement age are entitled to benefits.

Disability Insurance Benefits

A new type of protection became available to workers and self-employed persons as the result of a 1956 amendment to the Social Security Act. This provides protection against the loss of earnings as the result of disability. After a waiting period of six months, a totally disabled worker who is both fully and currently insured becomes eligible for payments. He must have been employed at least half of the forty quarters prior to his disability. Applicants for disability payments are first referred to the state rehabilitation agency. If the worker refuses rehabilitation services he is not eligible for payments. If he participates in the rehabilitation program, however, he is eligible for benefits, which continue for a year after he is re-employed if he begins to do gainful work again.

The latest schedules of monthly payments for retirement, disability, and survivors insurance are given in Tables 16–1 and 16–2. If a man elects to retire at 62 instead of 65 his monthly payment is reduced 20 per cent. His wife's payment starting at age 62 will be one fourth less than the amount she would receive starting at 65. The table also shows that payments under survivors insurance depend upon the insured worker's average earnings. Supplements are provided for widows under 62 with children.

Who Bears the Cost of Social Security?

Wage earners and their employers share the cost of old-age disability and survivors insurance by paying special taxes. Self-employed persons pay a tax on the basis of net earnings reported on their income tax forms. Taxes are now paid on wages up to $9,000 per year. The schedule of tax rates, showing increases since 1961, is given in Table 16–3.

Every employer is required to give each worker a receipt for the social security tax deducted, once yearly or if, and when, the worker leaves his job. Each covered worker has a social security number and the Social Security Administration maintains a separate account for every individual covered.

TABLE 16-1
Monthly Retirement and Disability Insurance Payments

Average Yearly Earnings After 1950[a]	Retirement Benefit at 65 or Later, or Disability Benefit	Retirement Benefit for Worker, Starting at Age 62	Wife of Retired Worker Starting at Age	
			62	65 or older
$ 923 or less	$ 70.40	$ 56.40	$ 26.40	$ 35.20
1,800	111.90	89.60	42.00	56.00
3,000	145.60	116.50	54.60	72.80
4,200	177.70	142.20	66.70	88.90
5,400	208.80	167.10	78.30	104.40
6,600	240.30	192.30	90.20	120.20
7,800	275.80	220.70	103.50	137.90
9,000	295.40	236.30	110.80	147.70

[a] Generally, average earnings are figured over the period from 1951 until the worker reaches retirement age, becomes disabled, or dies. Up to five years of low earnings or no earnings can be excluded. The maximum earnings creditable for social security are $3,600 for 1951 to 1954; $4,200 for 1955 to 1958; $4,800 for 1959 to 1965; and $6,600 for 1966 to 1967. The maximum creditable for 1968 to 1971 is $7,800, and beginning in 1972, $9,000; but average earnings usually cannot reach these amounts until later. Because of this, the benefits shown in the last column on the right generally will not be payable until later. When a person is entitled to more than one benefit, the amount actually payable is limited to the larger of the benefits.

Source: Data for Tables 16-1, 16-2, and 16-3 from the U.S. Department of Health, Education, and Welfare, Social Security Administration.

TABLE 16-2
Monthly Survivors Insurance Payments

Average Yearly Earnings After 1950*	Widow, Widower, 62 or Over or 1 Aged Parent Alone	Widow Under 62 and One Child	Widow Under 62 and Two Children
$923 or less	$ 70.40	$105.60	$105.60
1,800	92.40	167.90	167.90
3,000	120.20	218.40	222.90
4,200	146.70	266.60	308.90
5,400	172.30	313.20	389.90
6,600	198.30	360.60	435.20
7,800	227.60	413.80	482.70
9,000	243.80	443.20	517.00

*See note to Table 16-1.

TABLE 16-3
Schedule of Social Security Tax Rates

Years	Employers Per cent	Employees Per cent	Self-Employed Per cent
1961	3.0	3.0	4.5
1962	3.13	3.13	4.7
1963–65	3.63	3.63	5.4
1966–67	4.13	4.13	6.2
1968–70	4.63	4.63	6.9
1971–72	5.2	5.2	7.5
1973–75	5.65	5.65	7.65
1976–79	5.85	5.85	7.7
1980–86	5.95	5.95	7.8
1987 and after	6.05	6.05	7.9

The Social Security program is the largest system of insurance in the United States. The number of beneficiaries has increased rapidly since 1940, as indicated in Figure 16-2, and this growth will continue as more covered workers reach retirement age. The Social Security Act was resisted by conservatives in Congress, but now the law has found widespread acceptance. Some insurance companies were fearful before the law was passed that the Act might interfere with the private insurance business. However, the benefits paid under the law are relatively modest, and insurance companies have urged workers to supplement their retirement and survivors insurance with private plans. The Social Security program is designed to provide a *minimum* of protection for survivors of fully covered workers, and a *minimum* of retirement income for those workers who are fully insured when they leave the active labor force.

Medicare and Medicaid

The most recent major amendment to the Social Security Act was made in 1965 when the Medicare program was adopted. A companion program called Medicaid, started by the Medical Service Administration in the Department of

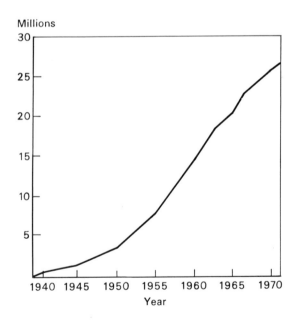

FIGURE 16-2.

Social Security Beneficiaries, 1940–1971. (*From Social Security Administration publications.*)

Health, Education, and Welfare, became effective in 1970. Medicare is a hospital *insurance* program with its own trust fund, while Medicaid is an *assistance* program supported by federal, state, and local taxes. As a federal program, coverage under Medicare is uniform. But since Medicaid is a joint federal-state program, there is variation in coverage from state to state. In some states, for example, Medicaid is limited to those eligible for public assistance, while in other states coverage extends to everyone on public assistance, plus others who belong to low-income groups. By mid-1971, all states except Arizona and Alaska had adopted some form of Medicaid.

The hospital insurance program of Medicare, automatically covers all social security beneficiaries aged 65 and over and all inpatient hospital bills except for the first $60 in each benefit period of 60 days. Voluntary medical insurance pays 80 per cent of all "reasonable" medical costs, except for the first $50 in each calendar year. The hospital program is financed by monthly payroll contributions, while the voluntary medical program is financed by monthly premiums paid by each insured person, each payment being matched by the federal government. At the end of 1971, the monthly premium was $5.60. At that time more than 20 million persons were covered by hospital insurance, while more than 19 million had signed up for medical insurance.

Persons on public assistance, or otherwise eligible for Medicaid, may also receive payment for the deductible portions of Medicare hospital and medical insurance. In some states Medicaid coverage is extensive; in others it is minimal. The federal contribution to this program varies from 50 per cent in high-income states to 83 per cent in low-income states. In 1970, about 17 million persons received some form of assistance under Medicaid.

Unemployment Compensation

During the Depression of the 1930s unemployment was widespread and protracted. In 1932 and 1933 about one-fourth of the civilian labor force was jobless; and at no time between 1931 and 1940 did unemployment drop below 14 per cent of the civilian work force. When Congress passed the Social Security Act of 1935 it provided for a joint federal-state system of unemployment insurance. This system was merged with the United States Employment Service, established in 1933 by the Wagner-Peyser Act. The federal government's participation in these programs is under the administration of the Bureau of Employment Security of the United States Department of Labor's Manpower administration. Each state has a cooperating Division of Employment Security which carries out the state's responsibilities and supervises administration of the programs at the local level. The two programs, the employment service and unemployment insurance, are handled by different departments in the state agency, but there is close coordination between them. The objective of the overall program is to place workers who lose their jobs in new employment. But if this cannot be done immediately, workers are entitled to unemployment compensation.

The unemployment compensation program has had an interesting side effect, which undoubtedly was not anticipated by members of Congress when the law was passed. There have been five recessions in the American economy since the end of World War II. During each of these recessions, industrial production has dropped, and this has generally been accompanied by a decline in construction activity. When the level of unemployment rises, the Employment Service cannot find jobs for many of the unemployed; there simply are not that many job vacancies during recession periods. These workers then become eligible for unemployment compensation, which permits them to maintain consumption spending at higher levels than would be the case if they had to rely on savings alone. Thus millions of dollars are pumped into the economic system from unemployment insurance funds, and this helps sustain the level of consumption in the face of a drop in production. After a time, inventory accumulations—an important cause of downturns—begin to be depleted. Factory production is stepped up again, and building activity picks up once more.

The unemployment insurance program has become one of the most important, if not the most important, of the "built-in stabilizers" that have helped reverse each of the postwar recessions within a relatively short time and have started a new cycle of recovery. The American economy is undoubtedly much more stable, in terms of employment and production, than it would be in the absence of a system of comprehensive unemployment compensation.

The United States Employment Service

The United States Employment Service, in cooperation with state agencies, attempts to find jobs for all applicants. It also supervises state programs to see that they conform to the federal laws. It provides state agencies with technical assistance and supervises the program of referring labor from one area to another. To a limited extent it serves as a nationwide clearinghouse, which attempts to match idle workers with vacant jobs.

Unemployed workers may obtain information about job opportunities, both in their own communities and elsewhere, at one of 1,800 full-time or 2,000 part-time local offices. Employers who have job vacancies may list these with the local office, and the local office staff attempts to refer the best qualified applicants to the vacant jobs.

The local offices provide counselling and testing services, and they attempt to find jobs for new entrants to the labor force, older workers, the physically handicapped, and minority workers. Special services to veterans were also provided as part of the Servicemen's Readjustment Act of 1944.

The Bureau of Employment Security regularly publishes labor market information in a monthly bulletin. The state employment offices cooperate with local economic development organizations and with other groups interested in stimulating economic activity in their respective states and communities.

The public employment service has been only moderately successful in its efforts to establish a nationwide clearinghouse for unemployed workers. This is not because of a lack of effort or initiative on the part of the administrators of this agency. There are thousands of private employment agencies in the United States which also seek to find jobs for unemployed workers on a fee basis. Many of the private agencies view the public employment service as a subsidized competitor; and the existence of private agencies has made it somewhat more difficult for the public employment service to develop a unified program of job placement.

Many employers feel that the best qualified workers will be obtained through private employment agencies. Larger establishments typically maintain their own employment offices, where they accept job applicants "off the street" and hire only those whom they consider the best qualified. Some employers thus feel that marginal workers who always find it difficult to obtain employment will turn to the public employment service. On a statistical basis this cannot be so. During recessions, when hundreds of thousands of workers become unemployed, practically all those eligible for unemployment compensation will register with the local unemployment office. If there are job vacancies to which the unemployed workers can be referred, they must accept suitable employment or be denied compensation. Thus not all workers referred by the Employment Service are marginal. Many are able, efficient, and highly desirable workers, but not all the latter are searching for new and permanent jobs.

Many workers who are cyclically unemployed expect to be called back to their old jobs. They might accept employment with other employers on a temporary basis, but when their original employers call them back, they will generally return to their own jobs where they have built up seniority and other fringe-benefit rights. This poses a continuing problem. Employers are often aware that the workers who come to them during recessions will return to their regular employers, except on the somewhat rare occasions when the job openings they have filled are superior to their regular jobs. This has contributed somewhat to the employer's "image" of the Employment Service as an agency attempting to place marginal workers.

The efforts of local employment offices to find jobs for handicapped persons, older workers, and members of minority groups have also made some employers shy away from the public employment services. To a large extent, however, this image is the result of widespread public misunderstanding about the nature of job applicants referred by the public employment service. As a general rule, the local employment office will refer the best qualified applicant for each job vacancy. An effort is made, however, to avoid discrimination on the basis of sex, age, color, creed, or national origin. Each month thousands of well-qualified workers are placed in productive employment through the efforts of the public employment service. As more and more employers find that they can obtain good workers through the local employment office, the effectiveness of the public employment service may be expected to increase. The state agencies can be particularly effective in helping new entrants to the labor force find jobs for which they are qualified. Through programs of testing and counselling, those entering the labor force for the first time can be helped to find the jobs for which they are best suited. This will not mean the end of private employment agencies. Many unemployed workers will continue to register with private agencies, and many employers will continue to use their services. There is room for both types of placement services in a large and diversified economy in which the task of matching qualified workers and job openings appears to be of increasing importance.

The Unemployment Compensation Program

One outgrowth of the Social Security Act of 1935 was a comprehensive system of unemployment insurance based on a joint federal-state program. Each one of the fifty states has enacted an unemployment compensation law. All state laws must meet certain federal standards established by the Social Security and Federal Unemployment Tax Acts.

Basically, unemployment insurance is designed to tide workers over periods of temporary unemployment. Compensation is not granted automatically to all unemployed workers. Before an unemployed worker can receive unemployment compensation, he must have been employed on a job covered under his state's unemployment insurance law for a specified period. He must also be able and willing to work, and his unemployment must be entirely involuntary.

Federal minimum standards have been established by the federal laws upon which the joint federal-state programs are based. If these standards are met, the federal government pays the costs of administering the state unemployment insurance laws and permits employers to credit state contributions against the federal tax imposed by the Federal Unemployment Tax Act.

When a worker is laid off temporarily, or loses his job through no fault of his own, he reports to his local employment security office. There he files a claim for unemployment compensation. This does not begin immediately, but if he cannot be placed in another suitable job, payments begin after a brief waiting period. As long as he is unemployed—and drawing compensation—the worker must report to his local employment office regularly, usually every week. He will continue to draw compensation until he returns to his old job, until suitable new employment is found for him, or until he exhausts his benefit rights.

If the unemployed worker is referred to a job, he must be willing to investigate it. If he refuses a job, and the local employment service considers it "suitable" employment, he may be disqualified for further compensation. The worker has the right of appeal, however, and his case will be considered by a board of review. If the board upholds the local office's determination, further compensation will be denied. If the board disagrees that the job was "suitable," his compensation will be restored.

There is wide variation in state unemployment insurance laws. Maximum weekly benefit amounts differ from state to state and this is also true of the maximum weeks an unemployed worker can draw benefits. The amount of wages or employment during a base period required to qualify for benefits also varies from state to state. In some states only those workers employed by firms with four or more employees during twenty weeks of the year are covered. In other states, however, the law covers firms with a single employee. Some workers are generally excluded from state unemployment compensation programs. These include (a) railroad workers who are covered by the Federal Railroad Unemployment Insurance Act, (b) agricultural workers, (c) domestic workers, (d) state and municipal workers, and (e) casual laborers. Until 1972, employees of nonprofit corporations were not covered by state unemployment compensation programs. The major impact of this extended coverage was expected to be felt by about 6,500 hospitals employing an estimated 2.2 million workers. Unlike private industry, however, hospitals may either pay a tax and participate in a state program or administer their own programs and pay unemployment compensation claims directly.

In general, a worker will be disqualified for state employment compensation if he quits his job voluntarily without good cause, or if he was discharged for misconduct in connection with his work. In most states, compensation is not granted if the worker is out of a job because of a labor dispute in his plant. As indicated above, he will be refused compensation if he is not willing to accept an offer of suitable alternative employment.

There are provisions to protect the benefit rights of workers, however. For example, a worker cannot be denied unemployment insurance benefits if he refuses to accept new work because the job is open due to a labor dispute, or if as a condition of accepting a job he must resign from or refrain from joining a bona fide trade union. To be considered "suitable" the new job must also provide wages, hours, and conditions of work substantially similar to those which he enjoyed in his previous employment. Special provisions have been made to provide partial unemployment benefits to workers whose wages and hours have been substantially reduced as the result of a cutback in the normal work week.

The employment service has improved the operation of the labor market. And unemployment compensation has helped stabilize the economy. As we saw in Chapter 6, however, this does not mean that the nation's unemployment problem has been solved. The employment service cannot create jobs; it can only direct idle workers to reported job vacancies. Unemployment compensation has been effective only in mitigating the effects of relatively short-term unemployment.

A 1954 amendment to the Social Security Act established an unemployment insurance program for federal civilian employees, providing the same terms and coverage as if they were covered by a state law. A further amendment in 1958 extended this protection to members of the armed forces. Anyone separated from the service since 1958 may be entitled to unemployment compensation if he is unable to find suitable employment.

Financing Unemployment Compensation

Social Security taxes are levied equally on employers and employees. In general, this is not true of unemployment compensation taxes. Except in three states (Alabama, Alaska, and New Jersey), unemployment compensation funds are built up from taxes levied on employers only. Under the Federal Unemployment Tax Act, which is part of the Internal Revenue Code, all employers of four or more workers must pay an unemployment insurance tax based on the first $4,200 earned by a worker in a calendar year. Individual states may increase the tax base, and Alaska, Hawaii, and Minnesota have done so.

Unemployment tax rates vary from state to state. They are influenced by variations in unemployment among the states and by differences in state laws. At the end of 1971, for example, the *maximum* tax rate varied from a high of 6.6 per cent of covered payrolls in Michigan to a low of 2.7 per cent in eleven states. Minimum rates also vary, as do year-to-year changes, depending upon economic conditions within the state. Some states provide more liberal benefit payments than others, and the duration of benefits also varies from state to state. At the beginning of 1972, maximum weekly benefits—exclusive of allowances for dependents—ranged from a low of $47 in Montana and South Dakota to $86 in Connecticut. The maximum duration of benefits varied from 26 weeks in the vast majority of states to 36 weeks in Utah.

Most states provide for some form of *experience rating*. Under this system of tax assessment, an employer's tax depends upon the extent to which he has been able to stabilize employment. Experience rating schemes have been criticized by some writers. Employers in stable activities, such as the trades and services, might enjoy low rates through no effort on their part. Other employers pay high rates because of the vagaries of the marketplace, despite their efforts to stabilize employment. Thus experience rating might not be a fair method of allocating the social costs of unemployment.[1]

The Railroad Unemployment Insurance Act

This act, administered by the Railroad Retirement Board, provides unemployment compensation and sickness benefits to qualified railroad workers under a uniform nationwide system. The fund from which payments are made is based on a payroll tax on all carriers. The amount of the tax varies from one

---

1. See Charles A. Myers, "Experience Rating in Unemployment Compensation," *American Economic Review,* June 1945, pp. 353–354.

half to 3 per cent of wages, depending upon the balance in the fund. The Act contains qualifications similar to those applying to the federal-state unemployment insurance program. For example, a railroad worker will not be paid unemployment benefits if he is out of work because of a strike that violates the Railway Labor Act or the rules and practices of his union. He will also not be paid benefits if he leaves his work voluntarily, without good cause, or fails to comply with instructions from the Board to apply for work or to report to an unemployment office.

State Workmen's Compensation Laws

All states now have laws providing for payments to workers for injuries on the job or for illness directly related to work. The earliest state laws go back to 1911, much earlier than the other forms of social legislation discussed in this chapter. As is true of unemployment compensation legislation, there is much variation among the states.[2] Workmen's compensation laws are either compulsory or elective. In states which have compulsory legislation, every employer subject to the state act is required to arrange for compensation for workers who are disabled as a result of an accident or injury. In states with elective laws, the employer is not required to participate in the workmen's compensation program. But if he chooses not to participate, the employer places himself in legal jeopardy. In the latter case, an injured employee may obtain compensation only by suing for damages. More than half of all state laws are compulsory.

In states where employers are required to participate in the workmen's compensation program, or in those states where the law permits them to do so, covered employers must either obtain insurance or provide proof that they can carry their own risks. The latter is known as self-insurance. Self-insurance programs require approval by the state agency administering workmen's compensation and generally require the posting of a bond to guarantee that payments can be made.

Some states require employers to insure through a state fund, whereas others permit private companies to compete with the state program. The latter states also permit qualified employers to establish their own funds. Generally speaking, workmen's compensation laws provide payments for all work-connected injuries or illnesses, so long as these are not due to the willful misconduct or gross negligence of the worker. Compensation is generally based upon a percentage of weekly wages, and this varies considerably from state to state. This is also true of the terms and periods of payment and of qualifications for complete coverage. In general, workmen's compensation ceases when the worker is fully recovered and is able to return to his job or to seek new employment. There are also varying provisions among the

---

2. See Monroe Berkowitz and John F. Burton, Jr., "The Income-Maintenance Objective in Workmen's Compensation," *Industrial and Labor Relations Review, 24* (October 1970), pp. 18–23.

states for payments to workers who are partly disabled as a result of job-connected injuries or illnesses.

Federal legislation has been enacted to provide workmen's compensation for specific classes of workers. The Longshoremen and Harbor Worker's Compensation Act of 1927 covers practically all maritime workers except masters or members of the crew of a vessel. The principal workers covered are longshoremen and ship repairmen, while working on board a vessel. This law provides benefits to workers for accidental injuries on the job, and for occupational diseases arising out of their employment. Compensation is based on the average weekly wage of the insured worker. If a worker is totally disabled, either temporarily or permanently, he will be paid benefits at the rate of two thirds his weekly wage up to a maximum of $70 a week, with an aggregate maximum of $24,000 for permanent partial disability. For total disability, benefits up to $70 per week are paid for life; and burial expenses, up to a maximum of $400, are provided for workers who lose their lives in connection with their employment. Although there are limits on the amount a worker can receive in the form of partial disability payments, all necessary medical costs are covered by this law, and the employer is required to arrange for medical care. There is no limit either on the cost or period of treatment. In 1941, the Defense Base Act extended the Longshoremen and Harbor Worker's Compensation Act to the employees of all private employers on defense bases and to all employees on public works outside the continental United States.

Child Labor Laws and Other Measures to Protect Labor Standards

Various laws at both the state and federal levels prohibit child labor, regulate industrial home work, and limit the hours of work for women. As early as 1853, seven states had laws limiting the hours of work for children. It was not until 1917, however, that a federal child labor law was passed, and the Supreme Court declared this law to be unconstitutional in less than a year. Further efforts to enact federal legislation stimulated the states to take action, and today every state has a child labor law. In 1938, the Fair Labor Standards Act established minimum ages for employment in industries engaged in interstate commerce, and the constitutionality of this law was upheld.

Industrial home work is not a serious problem in the United States today, although this could not have been said a generation ago. There are still a few industries which engage in this practice to some extent, however, and twenty-one states have laws that either prohibit or regulate industrial home work. Finally, forty-three states and the District of Columbia have laws regulating the hours of work for women. Some of these also require rest periods. In twenty-one states and Puerto Rico, there are laws which either prohibit night work or regulate the conditions under which women may work after specified evening hours.

Vocational Training and Rehabilitation

Programs conducted under the Manpower Administration, an outgrowth of the Manpower Development and Training Act of 1962, were discussed in Chapter 8. A number of other agencies at both the federal and state levels deal with some aspects of job training and worker education. At the federal level, these activities come under the Bureau of Apprenticeship and Training, the Rehabilitation Services Administration, and the Division of Vocational and Technical Education of the U.S. Office of Education. There are counterpart agencies within the states which deal with job training, education, and rehabilitation.

The Bureau of Apprenticeship and Training of the U.S. Department of Labor was established to aid in the training of wage earners. Its purpose is to improve the opportunities for promotion through a program of training for workers in industry. A Federal Committee on Apprenticeship, made up of representatives of employers, labor, and the government, has been established to help the Bureau attain its objectives.

Basically, the Bureau sets up standards for approved apprenticeship programs. These provide for schedules of work processes, organized instruction under proper supervision, and a progressively rising wage schedule as the apprentice completes his training. In cooperation with other bureaus of the Department of Labor, the Bureau of Apprenticeship and Training tries to anticipate occupational changes and to stimulate the training of workers in those occupations which it expects to be in short supply. The Bureau is also responsible for on-the-job training programs conducted under the Manpower Development and Training Act.

The Division of Vocational and Technical Education of the U.S. Office of Education promotes vocational education and training under a federal-state-local plan. The plan is the result of the Smith-Hughes and George-Bardon Acts which provide about $60 million annually to the states for vocational training. Funds are distributed on the basis of population and may be used for almost any purpose, including research, that will stimulate vocational training.

Local schools carry out the programs under state supervision, and the latter must be approved by the U.S. Office of Education. Grants are available to provide full-time preemployment training for youngsters preparing to enter the labor market, and evening classes are conducted for apprentices and others over sixteen years of age. The Vocational Education Act of 1963 provided for expansion of this program to include new vocational-educational schools—as well as regional, as opposed to local, facilities—and new work-study programs for vocational students.

The Rehabilitation Services Administration, in the Department of Health, Education, and Welfare, provides services to civilian men and women of working age whose ability to obtain employment or to hold a job has been impaired through a mental or physical handicap, regardless of cause. Services include medical, surgical, and psychiatric therapy. This agency also provides vocational counselling and training, financial aid during the period of reha- bilitation, and job placement. Some of these services are conditioned upon the economic circumstances of the applicant. The objective is to return to useful employment workers who would be unable to hold a job without such training and medical treatment.

Services are also provided to management for the retraining of injured workers. The basic program goes back to 1920, but a 1954 amendment to the law increased appropriations to permit states to step up their rehabilitation activities. This amendment also provided grants to institutions which train therapists, social workers, psychologists, rehabilitation counsellors, and others who can participate in the program. Another law passed in 1954—the Medical Facilities Survey and Construction Act—provides federal grants for the construction of rehabilitation facilities such as chronic disease hospitals, nursing homes, and diagnostic and treatment centers.

While such programs of vocational training and rehabilitation are gener- ally not widely publicized, they serve a useful purpose. Not every worker can be trained to become a skilled worker, and not every disabled worker can be helped—through rehabilitation and therapy—to hold a productive job. But those who can be helped benefit enormously both in an economic and psychological sense. As part of its broad scheme of providing a minimum of security to the vast majority of workers, the federal government has not over- looked those who, as the result of an occupational injury or work-connected illness, would find it most difficult to obtain new employment.

Conclusions

Over the past four decades a fairly comprehensive system of social insurance has been built up in the United States. Some conservatives have opposed this trend and claim that it has led to a "welfare state." One of their major ob- jections is that social security in the United States is compulsory. Another complaint is that protection against the vicissitudes of the market is likely to encourage indolence and malingering among workers. Critics of social insurance are not numerous, however, and few seriously suggest that our present system be scrapped. Such criticism can serve a useful purpose if it leads to more effective administration of the programs that make up our system of social security.

No doubt there are abuses of unemployment compensation.[3] Some workers may draw benefits illegally, but this usually involves the collusion of

---

3. See Leonard P. Adams, *Public Attitudes Toward Unemployment Insurance: A Historical Account with Special Reference to Alleged Abuses* (Kalamazoo, Michigan: The W. E. Upjohn Institute for Employment Research, 1971).

an employer. Similarly, individuals may draw workmen's compensation to which they are not entitled by faking injuries. In any society, some will be out "to beat the system." But it would scarcely make sense to gear social policy to the behavior of a lazy or dishonest minority. The answer to these problems lies in improved administration and in stiffer penalties for those who draw social insurance benefits illegally.

The adequacy of benefits under the various social security programs is one of those thorny problems which cannot be resolved to everyone's satisfaction since, as Richard Lester has noted, "adequacy is a relative matter."[4] There are more technical problems, involving the impact of social insurance on worker mobility, the effects on interstate competition of widely varying state programs, the financing of social insurance under conditions of rising prices, and the shifting and incidence of taxes levied under social insurance schemes. Discussion of these would go beyond the scope of an introductory volume. They are mentioned to indicate the dynamic nature of social insurance. Any suggestion that we have found final answers to these problems would be misleading.

It might be well, however, to conclude this discussion by attempting to place the American program in perspective. The United States has not been a pioneer in social legislation. Indeed, it has been suggested by a number of writers that we lag about a generation behind Great Britain and the democratic countries of Western Europe, whose social insurance programs are far more comprehensive than ours. American workers enjoy higher wages and, in general, more liberal fringe benefits than workers in other countries. At the same time, they are more susceptible to the threat of unemployment. While substantial progress has been made in providing worker security, our basic philosophy has been one of insuring a *minimum* of security for the aged, the disabled, the unemployed, and the surviving members of families who lose their primary breadwinners.

Questions and Exercises

1. What are the basic provisions of the Davis-Bacon Act of 1931? The Davis-Bacon Act is limited to federal construction projects. Has the concept behind this Act been extended to other types of federally aided projects?

2. Describe the basic provisions of the Walsh-Healey Public Contracts Act of 1936. The Secretary of Labor's freedom to set industrywide minima was challenged in *Mitchell v. Covington Mills.* What was the outcome of this case, and what is the Secretary's present authority to set industrywide minima?

---

4. Richard A. Lester, *The Economics of Unemployment Compensation* (Princeton, N.J.: Princeton University Industrial Relations Section, 1962), p. 25.

3. Describe the basic provisions of the Fair Labor Standards Act of 1938. How was this act amended by the Equal Pay Act of 1963?

4. Does the Social Security Act of 1935 apply only to workers directly engaged in interstate or foreign commerce? Describe, in general terms, the program of old-age and survivors insurance and the program of retirement benefits under the Social Security Act. How is the social security program financed?

5. What provisions are made for the survivors of covered workers, or covered workers who become disabled? What is required for a worker to be "fully insured" under the Social Security Act?

6. Briefly describe the Medicare and Medicaid programs.

7. What federal agency administers the unemployment insurance program started by the Social Security Act of 1935? How is the unemployment compensation program related to the United States Employment Service?

8. Why is unemployment compensation sometimes referred to as a "built-in stabilizer"?

9. Describe the organization and functions of the United States Employment Service.

10. What is the basic objective of unemployment compensation? Are all workers in the United States eligible to receive unemployment compensation if they become involuntarily unemployed?

11. How is the unemployment compensation program funded? Do all employers in the nation pay the same tax rate? What is meant by "merit rating"? Is this generally regarded as a suitable method for determining the appropriate unemployment compensation tax rate?

12. Are civilian employees of the federal government covered by unemployment insurance? Are former members of the armed services entitled to unemployment compensation?

13. Describe in general terms state workmen's compensation laws. In states with workmen's compensation laws, are all employers required to carry workmen's compensation insurance?

14. What activities are conducted by the Bureau of Apprenticeship and Training, the Rehabilitation Services Administration, and the Division of Vocational and Technical Education? Which agency supervises on-the-job training programs conducted under the Manpower Development and Training Act?

15. Can the United States accurately be characterized as a pioneer in the development of social legislation?

Suggested Readings

Books

Adams, Leonard P. *Public Attitudes Toward Unemployment Insurance: A Historical Account with Special Reference to Alleged Abuses.* Kalamazoo, Michigan: The W. E. Upjohn Institute for Employment Research, 1971.

Becker, Joseph M., S.J. *The Adequacy of the Benefit Amount in Unemployment Insurance.* Kalamazoo, Michigan: The W. E. Upjohn Institute for Employment Research, 1961.

Lester, Richard A. *The Economics of Unemployment Compensation.* Princeton, N.J.: Princeton University Industrial Relations Section, 1962.

Our Developing Social Security System: The First Twenty-Five Years (a symposium), *Industrial and Labor Relations Review,* Vol. *14* (October 1960).

Scoville, James G., *Perspectives on Poverty and Income Distribution,* Lexington, Mass., D. C. Heath and Company (1971).

Worker Security in a Changing Economy (a symposium), *Monthly Labor Review,* Vol. *86* (June 1963).

Articles

Berkowitz, Monroe, and John F. Burton, Jr. "The Income-Maintenance Objective of Workmen's Compensation," *Industrial and Labor Relations Review, 24* (October 1970), pp. 14–31.

Burns, Eveline M. "Social Insurance in Evolution," *American Economic Review, XXXIV* (March 1944), pp. 199–211; reprinted in Francis S. Doody (ed.), *Readings in Labor Economics.* Reading, Mass.: Addison-Wesley Press, 1950, pp. 455–467.

V

Collective Bargaining

17

The Negotiation
of Labor-Management
Agreements

Trade unions in the United States have relied largely on collective bargaining rather than political action for achieving their goals. What is the nature of the collective bargaining process? What issues are negotiated by unions and management? Have there been significant changes in collective bargaining as the trade union movement has matured? These and a number of other questions concerning collective bargaining will be considered in this and the following four chapters.

Collective bargaining was practiced, at least in isolated cases, long before the AF of L was founded. "Although a name had not yet been found for union-management negotiation the practice of collective bargaining was already evident by the middle of the nineteenth century."[1] Moreover, in Jensen's opinion, "the beginnings of collective bargaining reveal it as a process conceived in the best heritage of our democratic traditions. It is founded not in radicalism or necessarily in militance, but in the desire to be conciliatory, fair, and businesslike."[2]

The objective of collective bargaining is a labor-management agreement. Equally important is the day-to-day administration of this agreement. But a sound agreement provides for most situations likely to come up before it expires, and instances of labor disputes when an agreement is in existence are fairly rare. "Wildcat strikes"—those which occur during the life of an agreement—occur only infrequently and are frowned on by unions and management alike.

What is the nature of the collective bargaining agreement? It is generally

---

1. Vernon H. Jensen, "Notes on the Beginning of Collective Bargaining," *Industrial and Labor Relations Review,* Vol. 9 (January 1956), p. 232.

2. *Ibid.,* p. 234.

referred to in the press, and in popular discussions, as a *contract*. It is mis-leading, however, to think of a labor-management agreement as a counter-part of the typical business contract. If business contracts are not lived up to by the parties signing them, the aggrieved party has recourse to the courts; in fact, a substantial body of contract law has evolved to settle such business disputes. There are a few instances in which unions and managements have made their agreement into a legal contract, usually by having one party make a nominal payment to the other. But these are not typical of the vast majority of labor-management agreements in the United States.

In an effort to sharpen the distinction between business contracts and labor-management agreements, some writers have resorted to various analo-gies. The labor-management agreement is sometimes compared with inter-national treaties. The treaty, it is hoped, is something that the nations signing it can live with. If for some reason they cannot, diplomatic relations between the countries are ruptured, and it is possible that a third country might even enter the picture and try to settle differences between the disputants. If the two countries cannot settle their differences, even with the aid of a third party, the result might be open warfare. Analogous behavior can often be found between unions and management.

Another analogy sometimes used is that of the marriage agreement. This is clearly not the same thing as a business contract. If two businessmen sign a contract and one of the parties fails to live up to its terms, the case usually ends up in the courts. Once the judge has made a settlement it is not likely that the two parties will do business again. But disagreements can also arise in the happiest of marriages. It is not usual, however, for a husband who has become upset with his wife to threaten to haul her into court unless she mends her ways. And a wife displeased with the behavior of her husband does not as a rule try to reform him by threatening a lawsuit. Differences of opinion have to be ironed out if the two parties are to live together. The marriage can break up and the two parties go their ways just as the businessmen who had a dispute over a property contract. But the important thing is that every minor disagree-ment in a marriage does not lead to its dissolution. The two parties must learn to settle their grievances and live together afterwards. It is this which is stressed by the writers who use the analogy of the marriage agreement in trying to explain collective bargaining. There are disputes between unions and management; there can be much table pounding, shouting, threats, and abuse. But once the storm and fury is over and the issue has been settled, the two parties must be able to live together and work together in reasonable harmony if the goals of the union and management are to be realized.

The Content of Labor-Management Agreements

The earliest agreements on record were nothing more than lists of wages to be paid to the various occupational groups covered. Today, however, there is tremendous variation in labor-management agreements. Some are relatively brief documents consisting of a few pages, while others are lengthy documents, usually presented in the form of printed booklets.

The language of an agreement is important. A good agreement tends to avoid legalistic jargon and yet it must be carefully worded lest the misinterpretation of a phrase lead to a dispute completely unforeseen by either the union or management. Perhaps the best way to illustrate the coverage of an agreement is to consider a single hypothetical example. It must be remembered, however, that while such an example may be reasonably "typical," no two agreements are exactly alike in scope and coverage.

Recognition and Specification of Bargaining Units

Most agreements begin by specifying that the company recognizes the union as the sole representative of its workers within the bargaining unit covered by the agreement. In some cases the bargaining unit will be an occupational group, in others it will be the plant, and in others the entire company. There are companies which have agreements with more than one union—in some cases with several. Each agreement, therefore, must carefully specify the workers covered.

Form of Union Security

If the union has been able to negotiate a union shop agreement, the terms under which all workers in the bargaining unit are to become members will be spelled out. A typical union shop agreement indicates that the company is free to employ whomever it wishes, but all workers, as a condition of employment, must become members of the union, generally within a period of thirty days. Some agreements also specify that the company will deduct union dues from the paycheck of each union member. This is known as the "check off." Some unions, however, prefer to collect dues directly from the workers, and in this case the contract contains no checkoff provision.

The Rights and Duties of Employers

Most agreements contain provisions indicating the rights of employers. A typical provision will show that the employer has the right to determine what and how much is to be produced, and where production is to take place. Some agreements are quite specific that the union will have nothing to say about the company's activities in the product market.

Wages

This is usually the most important provision of a collective bargaining agreement. If there is to be a wage increase, the agreement specifies the amount. In some cases wages are not negotiated on an annual basis, but an agreement is reached to increase wages by a specified amount or percentage at different stages. In some cases deferred increases are spelled out in the agreement. Some agreements contain provisions for wage reopening during the contract period. This means that all other provisions are to be unchanged during the life of the agreement, but if—as of a given date—either party wishes to do so, the wage provision will be reopened for negotiation.

Some agreements also contain provisions for revision of existing rates on particular jobs. Such revision is usually associated with a change in work method or work load often as the result of a technological change. The wage section of a typical collective bargaining agreement may also contain provisions dealing with reporting time, shift premiums, equal pay for women doing the same work as men, the rates applicable when employees are transferred from one job to another, and payment for waiting time or travel time. In some industries and occupations wages are specified on an hourly basis; in others there are piece rate systems. Agreements in such cases typically contain provisions dealing with basic piece rates and incentive pay.

A number of agreements provide for cost-of-living adjustments in wages as prices change. Such "escalator" clauses usually indicate that basic wages will be increased (or decreased) at stated intervals, depending upon the changes that have taken place in the Consumer Price Index published monthly by the Bureau of Labor Statistics.

Hours of Work and Overtime Pay

The basic workday and work week are generally spelled out in a labor-management agreement. Under the Fair Labor Standards Act, there must be premium pay for overtime work. But in a specific case, the basic work week might be less than the forty-hour standard established by law. In such cases, the agreement will contain provisions for overtime pay. There will also be agreement on holiday pay. And some agreements indicate that workers are to be paid when absent from the job to perform civic duties, such as jury duty.

Vacation Pay

Most agreements specify the number of days of paid vacation to which workers are entitled. Vacation pay is generally a function of length of service. As a worker gains increasing seniority with the company, he will be entitled to a longer paid vacation.

Technological Change

This is often one of the more complex provisions in a labor-management agreement. Most agreements specify that management has the right to make technological changes such as the installation of new and better machinery or basic changes in production methods. Many agreements, however, contain a provision that the union must be consulted before such changes are made. The union is generally interested in the effects of the change on employment and wage rates. If workers are to be displaced by the change, the agreement often contains provisions for the orderly reassignment of the displaced workers to new jobs. It is not unusual for the agreement to specify that reassigned workers will not suffer a reduction in earnings while learning a new occupation. This problem is also covered by another set of provisions dealing with seniority, to be discussed below.

Severance Pay

Some agreements provide for lump-sum payments to workers who lose their jobs because of a plant shut down, technological change, or the curtailment of activities that will displace some workers permanently. Severance pay usually depends upon the length of service with the company.

The Grievance Procedure

It would be impossible in most cases for those who draft a labor-management agreement to foresee all of the possible problems that might come up during its life. Thus a quasi-judicial procedure must be established to protect the individual worker. If during the life of an agreement a worker feels that he has been the victim of unjust treatment in one way or another, he may file a grievance. The details of grievance procedure will be discussed in a later chapter since this is one of the more important parts of a successful labor-management agreement. It provides the "safety valve" which insures that the broad provisions of the agreement will be met by both parties, while still allowing for the careful treatment of individual cases.

Arbitration

The final stage of most grievance arrangements is arbitration. Since there are a number of ways in which arbitration can be handled, all of which will be discussed in a later chapter, each labor-management agreement must specify how arbitration is to take place. Most agreements which contain an arbitration clause indicate that the decision of the arbitrator will be final and binding on both parties.

Seniority

The seniority section in a typical labor-management agreement is likely to be both comprehensive and complex. It will usually specify seniority districts and seniority lists. Some agreements call for probationary periods, and almost all indicate the relationship between seniority, layoffs, and recalls. The seniority section of the agreement also contains provisions dealing with promotions, transfers, leaves of absence, and the termination of seniority and employment. In some agreements, provisions are made for "super" seniority. This usually applies to shop stewards or other union officials.

Fringe Benefit Provisions

Fringe benefits deal with such matters as group life, accident, and health insurance; supplementary unemployment insurance; pension and other retirement programs.

Discharge Cases

Companies usually reserve the right to discharge a worker for "cause." This will vary greatly from case to case. Usually an agreement specifies that a worker can be discharged for insubordination, shirking on the job, or violating safety rules. Workers can also be discharged, in most cases, for excessive absenteeism, drunkenness, fighting, or otherwise violating the company rules which the union has agreed to observe. The worker who feels he has been unjustly discharged almost always has the right to appeal through the grievance procedure.

Miscellaneous Provisions

Many agreements contain provisions dealing with such matters as the use of bulletin boards, the company's policy with respect to military service, the payment of shop stewards for performing union duties on company time, and a wide variety of other matters, some of them relatively minor in character. Most agreements conclude with a statement spelling out the terms of the agreement.

Criteria Used in Wage Negotiations

Labor-management agreements cover a wide variety of issues, many of which have nothing to do with wages. But wages, hours, and conditions of employment are still basic. Hours and conditions of employment can be dealt with in a relatively straightforward manner. This is not to imply that there cannot be disputes, particularly over hours. Shorter hours may be demanded by unions that have been losing members; in an effort to bolster their membership, they seek to share the work available in an industry or occupation. While this demand can cause considerable disagreement, the issue itself is not complex. The union will demand a reduction in hours and the company may be unwilling to grant a reduction without a corresponding drop in pay. The issue will then be settled by a show of economic strength.

The negotiation of wages is a fairly complicated matter. As a general principle, unions want to win wage increases for their members. Yet different unions will use different arguments in seeking wage increases, and the same union might employ different arguments under varying conditions. In the following section we consider briefly some of the major criteria used by unions seeking wage increases and some of the criteria used by management in resisting wage increases.

Criteria Used by Unions in Seeking Wage Increases

The actual reason why a given union seeks a specified wage increase is not always easy to determine. At times, rivalry among union leaders influences their wage demands. We can only speculate about such matters, however. The actual reasons may or may not coincide with the criteria used in wage negotiations. A number of years ago, Sumner Slichter discussed some of the criteria used in negotiating wage changes. We will consider briefly the following: (1) changes in the cost of living, (2) maintenance of take-home pay in the face of reduction of hours, (3) changes in productivity, (4) the ability of the employer to pay, (5) the effects of higher or lower wages upon purchasing power and employment, and (6) wages paid in other industries or places.[3]

Unions with built-in escalator clauses do not need to seek wage increases as a result of rising prices, but most labor-management agreements do not contain such clauses. During a period of rising prices, unions often indicate that *part of* a wage increase which they are seeking is to compensate for the loss of purchasing power due to rising prices. This is not the only reason that unions seek wage increases, even when prices are going up. But if the Consumer Price Index has gone up by a significant amount during the life of an agreement, the union is almost certain to emphasize this fact when negotiating basic wages for the next agreement.

Union leaders often have been criticized for using the cost-of-living criterion in seeking wage increases. Editorial writers, for example, point out that such wage increases will be self-defeating since employers will only raise their prices again following a wage boost. If all unions seek wage increases on these grounds there will be a general rise in the price level, and nonunion firms will have to follow the lead of those dealing with unions if they are to avoid labor difficulties in their own concerns. It has been argued that workers would gain far more if instead of seeking wage increases to compensate for higher prices they could work toward the reduction of prices. Then, not only would organized workers gain but all consumers would be better off.

Some union leaders have conceded that this would indeed be the case. But as they have pointed out, unions are not able to negotiate prices with

---

3. See Sumner H. Slichter, *Basic Criteria Used in Wage Negotiations* (The Chicago Association of Commerce and Industry, 1947), pp. 8–9.

employers since price setting is generally an employer prerogative. In the absence of any control over prices, they argue, union leaders must seek higher wages if their members are not to suffer a drop in real income during a period of rising prices.

Improvements in Productivity

Technological change—a broad term used to describe improvements in products and production processes—has been the major force contributing to rising real per capita income in the United States. Union leaders argue that the nation's workers should share in the fruits of technological progress, and they have frequently supported demands for wage increases by pointing to changes in productivity.

The use of this criterion is tied to the broader issue of income distribution. The way in which gains from productivity should be shared among workers, the owners of capital, and consumers, is a matter of continuing controversy. The issues involved are not simple. A few of the major questions to consider are noted as follows: Which measure of productivity should the union use in seeking a wage increase? Should it be the increase in productivity in the company with which the union is bargaining? If so, should all workers get proportionate increases? Would industrywide—or even economywide—averages be more appropriate? To what extent have increases in productivity been due to the greater efficiency of workers, and to what extent are they the result of better management or equipment? As Slichter has shown, the consequences of wage increases geared to productivity changes depend to some extent upon the causes of productivity gains.[4]

Ability to Pay

Unions have frequently supported demands for wage increases by the ability of employers to grant these increases. If profits in an industry are high compared with other industries—or within the same industry compared with earlier time periods—union leaders have argued that wage increases could be granted without price increases, or at least without proportional price increases. In some cases it has almost seemed that union and management were bargaining over profits rather than wages. Union leaders in this country have repeatedly asserted that they are not opposed to the profit system. However, they contend that companies should not earn "excessive" profits, and when profits are at a relatively high level, this criterion is frequently used in support of demands for wage increases.

---

4. *Ibid.*, pp. 22–24.

Effects of Wage Increases upon Consumer Purchasing Power and Employment

At times, union leaders have tried to justify demands for wage increases by asserting that higher wages are needed to maintain or increase the purchasing power of consumers. The same argument is often used when the level of unemployment is relatively high. If consumers had more money to spend, union leaders maintain, the demand for services and goods would be increased, and this in turn would permit businesses to expand output and consequently increase their demand for labor.

Wages Paid in Other Industries or Places

Unions sometimes support demands for wage increases by referring to the higher wages paid by other industries, or to higher wages in the same industry in other areas. The average level of wages varies considerably from region to region in the United States. And there is a surprising amount of wage diversity even within a local labor market area. Industry and area wage averages are affected to some extent by differences in product-mix and in industry-mix. It would be surprising if there were not considerable diversity in average wages from place to place, even within a given industry, since the various companies which make up an industry differ from each other in a number of ways. In general, however, unions have sought to achieve uniformity of wages within industries, at least for similar occupations. And in regions where wages are low, unions have argued that the average level should be more nearly in line with the averages prevailing in relatively high-wage areas.

The criteria used by unions in seeking wage increases are not entirely independent, and a given union will not rely on the same criteria all the time. Conditions in the economy as a whole, as well as in specific industries and occupations, will frequently determine the basis upon which unions seek wage increases. Unions have sometimes been accused of a lack of consistency in arguing for higher wages, but since economic conditions change over time, the union will use the arguments that seem most compelling at the time it is asking for a wage increase. While each criterion when considered by itself may be debatable—else there would be no need to bargain over wages—union leaders could scarcely be expected to use the same arguments in support of wage increases time after time, in view of changes in economic conditions between bargaining sessions.

Criteria Used by Employers in Resisting Wage Demands

Several of the criteria used by unions in seeking wage increases are also used by management in resisting such demands. Obviously, however, management looks at the other side of the coin in formulating its arguments.

Increases in the Cost of Living

When unions ask for wage increases because the Consumer Price Index has been rising, management often objects on the grounds that wage increases will lead to further price increases, with no net gain for union members. Management accepts, in brief, the "cost-push" theory of inflation. And at the bargaining table management often claims that it must keep the consumer in mind—that in resisting the union's demands for wage increases, it is not only thinking of the good of the company, but of the good of society as well. Needless to say, members of the "general public," that is, those not involved in the labor dispute, often feel sympathetic toward this position, especially during a period of rising prices, and this criterion has been used by management quite frequently in recent years to resist demands for wage increases.

Changes in Productivity

Management often points out that increases in productivity are not the result of greater labor effort but stem from improved products and production processes. If these gains are to be sustained, management argues, a substantial part of the company earnings will have to be plowed back into new equipment. In most cases, management is willing to concede that workers should share in gains resulting from productivity increases. The issue boils down to the *amount* of increases that should go to the workers of a particular company. There are a few cases—the United Auto Workers-General Motors agreement is an outstanding example—where an "annual improvement factor" is computed. This forms the basis of wage increases due to productivity gains. It is assumed that some of the gains from productivity will go to consumers and some to stockholders, and that some will be used to improve plant and equipment in the company.

Inability to Pay

Just as unions frequently seek wage increases because they claim the company is *able* to pay, management often resists the wage increase on the grounds that it is *unable* to pay higher wages and to continue to operate at the level of profits needed to remain in business.

Effects of Wages on Costs and Employment

While unions use the "purchasing power" argument in support of wage demands, management looks at the cost side of the picture in resisting these demands. It is frequently claimed by management that if higher wages are granted, the increase in cost will lead to a drop in employment. The economic model used in support of this argument is a highly simplified one, which ignores many of the dynamic changes that occur in the real world. Yet conservative groups in particular have warned unions that persistent demands for wage increases will only result in labor's "pricing itself out of the market." In specific bargaining situations, management will use the same argument insisting that if it grants the wage increase demanded, it can do so only by sacrificing jobs.

Wages Paid in Other Industries or Places

While unions generally press for wage uniformity, management generally objects to this criterion. Company spokesmen will point out that they cannot be concerned with wages in other industries or other areas—that they can only look at their own books in making wage decisions. Some company spokesmen have accused union leaders of trying to "whipsaw" the wage level; that is, they claim that unions are not actually interested in wage uniformity, but only in pushing wages up as far and as fast as they can. Spokesmen for a specific company might argue, for example, that the union wants to push its wages above the average and then use this to bring wages in other concerns "into line" with the higher wages it had initially negotiated.

The Threat of Foreign Competition

A criterion used in recent years by companies faced with increasing competition from abroad is a variant of the "ability to pay" criterion. Management has argued that if unions insist on pushing up the wage level, a greater share of the market will be taken over by foreign producers, and that this must ultimately lead to the displacement of American workers.

Objectively, one cannot argue that either side is right or wrong in its choice of criteria. Bargaining implies give and take. Each side must be expected to muster the arguments that it feels will be most convincing, and each side will try to appeal to a wider audience than sits around the bargaining table. The negotiation of major agreements in basic industries is generally preceded by a considerable amount of publicity issued by both parties. The publicity campaigns are stepped up if negotiations break down and a strike results. Each side tries to sway public opinion in support of its point of view, in the hope that this will help break down the resistance of the other party at the bargaining table. It is difficult to assess the effectiveness of these publicity campaigns. It is possible that publicity makes settlement more difficult at times since, if one or both of the parties announce publicly that there will be no retreat from a fixed position, it is more difficult to make concessions without losing face.

In a free society, the public statement or argument either supporting or resisting wage demands is no doubt all to the good. The public is, after all, interested in the outcome; and those not associated with the dispute might be interested in evaluating the arguments of both sides. Collective bargaining would undoubtedly proceed more smoothly, however, if neither side insisted that it would *never* back down on a specific issue. Something obviously has to give if a deadlock is to be broken, and nothing appears to be gained from such adamant statements—which are typically followed by the kinds of compromises needed to end a labor dispute.

Bargaining Theory: Bilateral Monopoly and Risk Evaluation

Earlier sections of this chapter described the content of typical labor-management agreements and listed some of the criteria used by labor and management to support demands for wage increases or to justify resistance to those demands.[5] The remainder of this chapter is concerned with the *process* of collective bargaining, and this process is examined in terms of a number of bargaining theories. Bargaining theories generally are limited to analysis of wage negotiations, and this analysis is conducted in highly abstract terms. Actual collective bargaining is a highly complicated process; any attempt to reduce the process to terms that apply to most if not all situations necessarily requires a high degree of abstraction.

Bargaining theories are presented here neither because they "explain" what goes on in negotiation sessions, nor because they have been highly successful in *predicting* the outcomes of labor and management negotiations. They are discussed here because, in spite of their abstract character, bargaining theories may provide insights into the complicated process of collective bargaining.

Some bargaining theories make extensive use of mathematical notation. This has been eliminated in the survey that follows. Also, only the highlights of the better known bargaining theories are presented here. Readers interested in further details should consult the original sources listed at the end of this chapter.

Hicks's Theory of Negotiations

One of the earliest formal bargaining theories was developed by J. R. Hicks.[6] He had as one of his objectives to show that wages determined by collective bargaining would not differ from those determined by the market (following the marginal productivity principles discussed in Chapter 5 of this text). Actually, Hicks's theory was concerned more with industrial disputes than with wage determination *per se*. He argued that a union would be willing to go on strike to increase wages—up to a point. Similarly, an employer would be

---

5. Collective bargaining deals with much more than wages, of course, and nonwage issues in bargaining are discussed in detail in Chapter 19.

6. J. R. Hicks, *The Theory of Wages* (London: Macmillan & Co. Ltd., 1932).

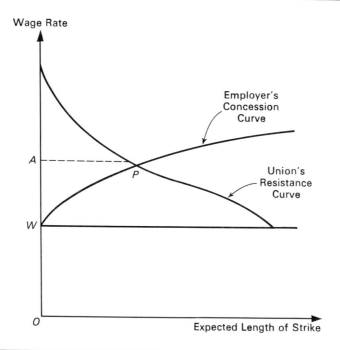

FIGURE 17–1.

Hicks's Theory of Industrial Disputes. (*Reprinted by permission from J. R. Hicks,* The Theory of Wages *[London: The Macmillan Company, Ltd., 1932], p. 143.*)

willing to accept a strike rather than grant a wage increase above some given level—again up to a point. Hicks's theory of industrial disputes is summarized in Figure 17–1.

Hicks constructs a schedule for the union and the employer, setting wage rates against various expected strike lengths. As shown in Figure 17–1, the union's resistance curve drops sharply for an expected strike of moderate length, indicating that above a certain wage rate the union is not willing to take a long strike. Below that rate, however, the union's resistance curve drops much more slowly, indicating that workers are willing to strike for an extended period of time rather than accept a wage less than *OW* in Figure 17–1. Similarly, the employer's concession curve rises rapidly to point *P* on Figure 17–1, and more slowly beyond that point. The point *P*—at the wage *OA*—indicates the highest wage the union can obtain through skillful negotiation.[7]

7. *Ibid.,* p. 143.

In an extensive review of *The Theory of Wages*, Gerald F. Shove dismissed Hicks's theory of industrial disputes rather summarily. He felt that it added little of anything to earlier views on the subject expressed by Pigou and Zeuthen. He also felt that interpretation of the employer's concession curve and the union's resistance curve was hazy and did not actually yield the conclusions that Hicks drew from them.[8]

Another British economist, G. L. S. Shackle, criticized Hicks's assumption that the union's resistance curve slopes continuously downward to the right. This would indicate that the lower the wage rate, the longer a union would be willing to stay out on strike. Shackle presented a modification of Hicks's diagram, which is shown in Figure 17–2.

The union's *inducement curve,* as Shackle termed it, slopes *upward* to

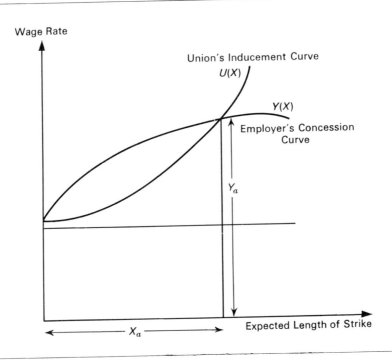

FIGURE 17–2.

Shackle's Modification of Hicks's Diagram. (*Reprinted by permission from G. L. S. Shackle, "The Nature of the Bargaining Process," in John T. Dunlop [ed.], The Theory of Wage Determiation [London: Macmillan and Company, Ltd., 1957], p. 302.*)

8. Shove's review first appeared in *The Economic Journal* in September 1933 and was reprinted in full in the second edition of *The Theory of Wages*, published in 1963. *Op. cit.*, pp. 49–267.

the right. This indicates that the union will accept a longer strike the higher the wage rate it seeks. Shackle's diagram shows that an employer would be willing to grant a wage of Ya rather than accept a strike longer than Xa. According to both Hicks and Shackle, if the two parties knew the shapes of each other's schedules, agreement on wages would be reached at the point of intersection. Given such knowledge, there would be no strike. Industrial disputes occur, however, because unions and employers do not know the shapes of the inducement and concession (or resistance and concession) curves.

Some recent bargaining theorists, working with more sophisticated models, have tended to be highly critical of Hicks's simplified theory of industrial disputes. But McKersie and Walton, who have written a book on the theory of labor negotiations, to be discussed later, feel that Hicks made an important contribution. In fact, they find his diagram useful in illustrating some points of their own theory.[9]

Fellner's Theory of Bilateral Monopoly

A highly abstract treatment of collective bargaining was developed by William Fellner in his celebrated article, "Prices and Wages Under Bilateral Monopoly."[10] A complete treatment of his theory requires the use of somewhat advanced economic concepts, but the essence of his argument, and his major conclusion, can be given in simplified form.

The basic postulate of Fellner's theory[11] is that under collective bargaining, labor-management relations typically contain elements of bilateral monopoly:

> Labor representatives have some monopoly power because the trade agreements set the conditions on which labor may be employed by an enterprise or by a group of enterprises; and managements frequently have some monopsony because employment by other enterprises is not typically a *perfect* substitute for the given employment, as viewed from the standpoint of the worker.

A monopsony is the counterpart on the buyer's side of the market of a monopoly on the seller's side.

Fellner also assumes that the union makes a choice between higher or lower wages on the one hand and more or less employment on the other. Figure 17-3 illustrates the situation where a union wants to achieve the

---

9. Robert B. McKersie and Richard E. Walton, "A Theory of Bargaining," *Industrial and Labor Relations Review, 19* (April 1956), pp. 414–424.

10. William Fellner, "Prices and Wages Under Bilateral Monopoly," *Quarterly Journal of Economics* (August 1947), pp. 503–532.

11. William Fellner, *Competition Among the Few* (New York: Alfred A. Knopf, 1949), p. 252.

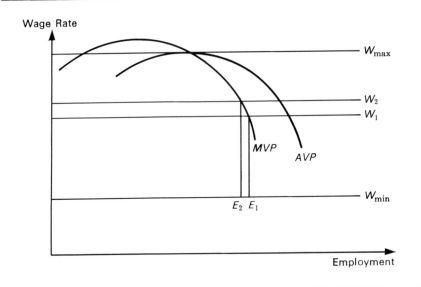

FIGURE 17–3.
Relationship Between Wages and Employment at Maximum Wage Rates.

highest wage rate it can get, regardless of the number of workers that can be employed at this wage.

There is an upper limit (W_{max}) above which wages cannot go and similarly there is a lower limit (W_{min}) below which they cannot fall in this particular bargaining situation. The upper limit is set by the top of the average value of product curve (AVP). If wages were pushed above this level the firm would go out of business. The lower limit is determined by other employment opportunities for this firm's workers, or it could be the minimum wage established by government order.

Between the upper and lower limits, the actual wage will be determined by the relative bargaining power of the employer and the union. For example, if the company's bargaining power is relatively strong, the best wage the union might be able to obtain is indicated by W_1. And the intersection of this wage line with the marginal value of product curve (MVP) shows the quantity of employment at that wage (E_1). If, however, the union has considerable bargaining power, it might push wages up to W_2, and in this case employment would drop back to E_2. The situation described above assumes that the union negotiators are able to choose *freely* between the wage levels they can negotiate and the number of workers who will be employed at each wage level. But this would be true only in somewhat unusual circumstances. A

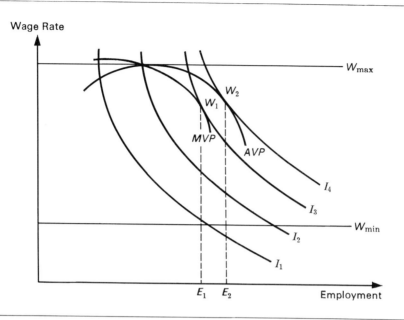

FIGURE 17–4.
Indifference Map of Relationship Between Wages and Employment.

powerful union leader could convince his members that those who remained employed would be better off with higher wages and lower employment as perfect substitutes. But most union leaders would have to recognize that wages and employment are *imperfect* substitutes. This situation is illustrated by Figure 17–4.

The lines marked I_1, I_2, and so on, are called *indifference curves*. The family of these curves makes up an indifference *map*. Each of these curves describes the relationship between wages and employment that would be acceptable to the rank and file under different circumstances. Again we see that there are maximum and minimum levels within which the negotiated wage must fall. And in this case, because of the shape of the indifference curves, the highest wage the union could negotiate would be given by the point of tangency between the marginal value product curve (*MVP*), and the highest indifference curve touching the *MVP*. In Figure 17–4 this is shown by the point W_1. The number of workers employed at that wage is shown by E_1 on the horizontal axis. This case assumes that the union is in a position to bargain over wages only and to accept the level of employment that will be forthcoming at that wage.

It is also conceivable, however, that a union could negotiate an agreement which specified *both* a wage level and a certain amount of employment. This would be called an "all-or-none contract." Under these circumstances, the maximum bargaining power of the union would be at the intersection of the average value of product curve (AVP), and the union's indifference curve tangent to AVP. In Figure 17-4, this wage is shown by W_2, and the volume of employment associated with that wage is given by E_2 on the horizontal axis. This shows that if the union is in a position to negotiate an all-or-none contract, it can achieve both higher wages and greater employment than if it is able to bargain over wages only.

Within the upper and lower limits he has described, Fellner concludes that the actual wage rate to be negotiated will be *indeterminate*, that is, it will depend upon the relative bargaining power of the two parties. Moreover, this bargaining power will depend in part upon the ability of each party to correctly estimate the reactions of the other.

Assuming that each party starts from his own end of the bargaining range (W_{max} for the union and W_{min} for the employer), Fellner draws the following conclusions: The willingness of one party to move away from his end of the range depends upon the probability that the other party will *not* move. Hence,

1. If each party overestimates the willingness of the other to move, there will be a stalemate—a strike will result.
2. If each party underestimates the willingness of the other to move, an agreement will be reached. This agreement will be favorable to the party whose willingness to move was *most* underestimated.
3. If one party estimates the other's willingness to move correctly, an agreement will be reached regardless of whether the estimate of the other is correct. In both cases (2) and (3) an agreement will be reached without a breakdown in negotiations. What this agreement will be cannot be determined until the bargaining is over, and it depends largely upon the ability of one party or the other to correctly assess reactions to its proposals and its moves.[12]

Fellner's theory stands in marked contrast to that of Hicks, primarily because it is limited to the case of bilateral monopoly, but also because of his general conclusion that within a specified range, the actual negotiated wage rate will be indeterminate. Although Fellner's theory is based on a set of restrictive assumptions, some economists feel it is useful because it shows that it is difficult if not impossible to predict the actual outcome of wage negotiations.

---

12. Fellner, *op. cit.,* pp. 530–532. For further discussion of this type of bargaining theory, see Allan Cartter, *Theory of Wages and Employment* (Homewood, Illinois: Richard D. Irwin, Inc., 1959), especially pages 87–115.

Pen's "General" Theory of Bargaining

Most economists tend to be skeptical of theories that claim to be perfectly "general." A completely general theory is one that would apply to all cases and at all times. Critics of such theorizing point out that as economic and social conditions change, earlier efforts to describe economic processes in abstract terms become outmoded. One must admire an author who is undaunted by such difficulties, however. Pen's theory is developed almost entirely in mathematical terms, and some of its full flavor is lost in the brief summary that follows.[13]

Pen was critical of Hicks's theory, and also of Zeuthen's theory, mentioned by Hicks's critic Gerald Shove, because these theories lead to *determinate* solutions without (according to Pen) showing *why* the equilibrium solutions should be reached. He is equally critical of other authors, such as Fellner, who conclude that bargaining solutions must be *indeterminate*.

Pen assumes that each party will derive a certain amount of satisfaction if bargaining results in a certain wage rate. He refers to this satisfaction as *ophelimity*, a term suggested by Vilfredo Pareto as a substitute for *utility*. According to Pen's theory, each party wants to maximize its ophelimity. If the wage demanded by a union is greater than that which management is willing to grant, there is a "bargaining problem."

One interesting feature of Pen's theory is the recognition that psychological factors are involved in the bargaining process. He refers to these factors as the ludic elements behind each party's ophelimity.[14] The "will to win" in any kind of contest; the fear of "losing face;" or the desire to improve one's status are examples of what Pen means by *ludic* elements.

Recognizing that a form of satisfaction is to be maximized and that noneconomic as well as economic elements are involved in this satisfaction, the bargaining problem, in Pen's view, becomes a problem of bargaining *power*. The next question is: what determines bargaining power?

A basic element in the power struggle is the *mutual dependence* of the two parties. This establishes upper and lower limits to the wage that can be reached through negotiations. The upper limit is called management's net contract ophelimity, and the lower limit is the union's net contract ophelimity. The negotiated wage must fall within these limits. Up to this point, evidently, there is considerable similarity between the bargaining theories of Pen and Fellner.

Pen goes on, however, to introduce a *risk valuation function,* which is a

---

13. Pen's basic theory was given in J. Pen, "A General Theory of Bargaining," *American Economic Review,* March 1952, pp. 24–42. More complete details are given in his book *The Wage Rate Under Collective Bargaining,* trans. T. S. Preston (Cambridge, Mass.: Harvard University Press, 1959).

14. The word *ludic* is derived from the Latin *ludere,* to play a game.

measure of the satisfaction (or dissatisfaction) derived by either party from the fact that a risk is involved in collective bargaining. If either side is too unyielding in its demands, a strike is likely to result. How far can each side push the other without inducing actual conflict? To answer this question Pen introduces what he calls the *correspection function*—a term borrowed from an earlier treatment of bargaining by Schumpeter—which relates the net contract ophelimity of *management* and the risk valuation of the *union.* Somewhere along this function the two parties will arrive at a final wage agreement.

Since all of the relationships in this theory may be treated as mathematical functions, Pen views the bargaining process as a series of efforts by each of the two parties to shift the other's functions. Each side starts with a satisfaction that it wishes to maximize. Management must keep in mind its cost and profit situation, and how changes in the wage level will affect its balance sheet. The union must consider the morale of its members. The possibility of a conflict—with the costs that this will involve—must be kept in mind by both parties. Pen implies that each party might begin negotiations with somewhat exaggerated claims, recognizing that a certain amount of "horse-trading" will be involved before a solution is reached.

Pen concedes that it is impossible to measure the ophelimities and risk valuations involved. Thus his theory cannot be tested empirically. But he feels that his theory indicates the factors that determine the outcome of negotiations, and while these factors cannot be measured, at least at present, "they make the result of the bargaining determinate. . . . "[15]

Zeuthen and Shackle on Bargaining

F. Zeuthen was the first to use the risk evaluation approach to a theory of bargaining.[16] Zeuthen reasoned that bargaining is a process under which each side compares possible advantages and disadvantages at each step of the proceedings. The advantages are the economic gains that would accrue to either party as a result of a favorable settlement; the disadvantages result from the possibility of a breakdown in bargaining that would mean a strike. Agreement will be reached, according to Zeuthen, when the maximum risks of the two parties are equal.

G. L. S. Shackle developed a theory of bargaining strategies based on probabilities. These probabilities he refers to as "potential surprise."[17]

---

15. Pen, *op. cit.,* p. 39.

16. F. Zeuthen, *Problems of Monopoly and Economic Warfare* (London: G. Routledge & Sons, 1930). See also his *Economic Theory and Method* (Cambridge, Mass.: Harvard University Press, 1955), especially the chapter on "Economic Warfare," pp. 286 ff.; and Edward Saraydar, "Zeuthen's Theory of Bargaining: A Note," *Econometrica, 33* (October 1965), pp. 802–813.

17. G. L. S. Shackle, *Expectations in Economics* (Cambridge: Cambridge University Press, 1949), pp. 101 ff.

Shackle assumes that the values of potential surprise can be compared by means of indifference maps similar to those used by Fellner. Given their respective indifference maps, two parties can make rational choices among the strategies available to them. Shackle concludes that if each party's preference system includes a risk evaluation (which he calls a *focus-value*), the result of negotiations "is determinate: it is conceptually knowable in advance, if we are fully informed about the gambler-preference system of each bargainer. . . ."[18]

The Theory of Games and Bargaining Theory

The theory of games deals with involved situations such as might be encountered by the military, in which the strategy on one side of a conflict must take into account the most probable counter moves of the opposition.[19] Game theory is much too complex to be treated in detail in this book, but some of its elements can be illustrated by borrowing from an example developed by J. D. Williams in his lucid and entertaining introduction to game theory, *The Compleat Strategyst.*[20]

The example concerns two campers, a man and his wife, planning a trip into the mountains. The husband likes high altitudes, whereas his wife is partial to lower elevations. The mountains are crisscrossed by a network of roads, four running north and south, and four running east and west. All of the roads go through peaks and valleys. The husband would prefer to camp on one of the peaks and his wife in one of the valleys; the problem is how to find a campsite high enough to satisfy the husband and low enough to satisfy the wife. To simplify the problem they agree to camp at a junction where one of the north-south roads crosses one of the east-west roads. The problem can be solved by setting up a table of altitudes at each of the intersections. This is called a *payoff matrix,* and the hypothetical table developed by Williams is shown below.

The husband's strategy will be to read across each row and pick that row with the *highest* minimum (this is called the *maximin*). The wife's strategy will be to read down each column and pick the one with the *lowest* maximum (this is called the *minimax*). In the simple contrived example, it will be noted that the husband will select Row 3 and the wife Column 2. Fortunately for the success of this camping trip, and the continued harmony of the hypo-

---

18. *Ibid.,* p. 108.

19. The basic work, which has led to a new and highly technical literature on problems of strategy in various contexts, is John Von Neumann and Oskar Morgenstern, *Theory of Games and Economic Behavior* (Princeton, N. J.: Princeton University Press, 1944; New York: John Wiley & Sons, Inc., Science Editions, 1964).

20. J. D. Williams, *The Compleat Strategyst,* A RAND Publication, (New York: McGraw-Hill, 1954), pp. 24–27. This example has been used with permission of the Rand Corporation and McGraw-Hill.

MATRIX A

Wife
▼

	1	2	3	4
1	7	2	5	1
2	2	2	3	4
3	5	3	4	4
4	3	2	1	6

Husband ▶ (row 3)

thetical marriage, two of the roads will intersect at an altitude of three thousand feet—the lowest altitude that the husband would be willing to accept and the highest that his wife will agree to. Such a fortunate intersection in the theory of games is known as a *saddle point,* and the common value at this intersection is known as the *value of the game.*[21]

Not every payoff matrix will yield the neat solution given above. For example, if we interchange the numbers in Row 3-Column 2 and Row 4-Column 3 we will get the new matrix given below. If we go through the same procedure, that is, inspect each row to find its minimum and select the greatest of these, then go down each column to find its maximum and select the one with the smallest of these, we will find that there are two intersections

MATRIX B

Wife
▼

	1	2	3	4
1	7	2	5	1
2	2	2	3	4
3	5	1	4	4
4	3	2	3	6

Husband ▶ (row 3)

21. *Ibid.,* pp. 27–66.

(Row 2-Column 2 and Row 4-Column 2). But both of these will be at a lower altitude than the husband is willing to accept, and they will also be less than the highest altitude that the wife is willing to accept. This would not be a satisfactory solution to either, and they would probably call off the camping trip.

This very brief and highly simplified excursion into game theory suggests that this analytical framework could be applied to collective bargaining. If in the example above we substitute the union for the husband's position, and management for the wife's position, and assume that their strategies deal with wages, we would obtain the same results. The union wants to get the highest wage possible and management the lowest. *Thus if we assume that there is a payoff matrix,* the union would select the row with the highest minimum; management would select the column with the lowest maximum. This would be the saddle-point solution to the problem.

Carl Stevens has attempted to develop a theory of collective bargaining within the game-theory framework. He does not suggest that there would be a single payoff matrix, but rather a series of these, which he refers to as the *game-variant sequence.* There might be one matrix that applies while negotiations are going on up to a strike deadline, for example, and another that applies after this deadline has passed. Moreover, one of the parties might not *try* to reach a solution before the strike has occurred, hoping to alter the conditions inside the matrix during the strike.

In commenting on the effort by Stevens to apply game theory to collective bargaining, D. W. Irwin questions that game theory "is sufficiently developed to cope with the infinite varieties of actual negotiations."[22] In an earlier article, Stevens himself had suggested that "the game-theory format is essentially inappropriate to the analysis of negotiation ..." because a solution in game theory depends on a known or arbitrarily assumed payoff matrix. The objective of the exchange of information during negotiations "is to change the negotiators' perception of the values comprising the payoff matrix."[23]

No one has seriously suggested that the two parties to negotiations could sit down and construct an actual matrix with appropriate numbers in each of the cells, and then juggle these numbers until a saddle-point solution is reached. But one object of theory is to gain a better understanding of complex situations. The game-theory approach, *with its emphasis on strategy,* may lead to an improved understanding of the collective bargaining process.

---

22. *Proceedings,* 13th Annual Meeting, Industrial Relations Research Association, 1960, p. 159.

23. Carl M. Stevens, "On the Theory of Negotiation," *Quarterly Journal of Economics,* February 1958, pp. 96–97. In his book *Strategy and Collective Bargaining Negotiation* (New York: McGraw-Hill Book Co., Inc., 1953), Stevens makes only limited reference to the concept of a payoff matrix; see, however, pages 79–82, 89–90; and Appendix II.

Other Game-Theoretic Studies of Bargaining

Following publication of the *Theory of Games and Economic Behavior,* game-theoretic models were developed by Nash, Harsanyi, Raiffa, Cross, and others.[24] All of these game-theoretic analyses differ in detail, but they have some common characteristics. Only Nash's theory will be discussed here, since it has been described by Cross as the "most precise" of the theories in this class.

Nash assumes that there is a "utility frontier," which is known to both of the bargaining parties. This is illustrated in Figure 17–5. It has the shape of the typical production-possibility frontier known to all students of introductory economics. In this diagram the union's utility is shown on the vertical axis, and management's utility on the horizontal. Early on in the bargaining process the union may try to hold out for a wage that would place it at U_1 on the utility frontier. Management, meanwhile, may be holding out at point M_1 on the same utility frontier. At this stage of bargaining the two parties are far apart, but through negotiations—with the threat of a strike or lockout in the background—they will move toward an eventual settlement, which is indicated by S in

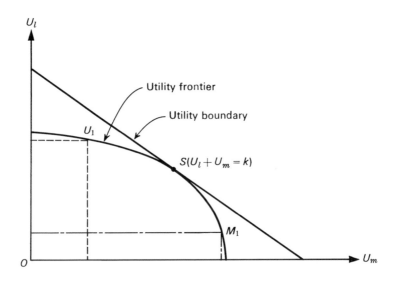

FIGURE 17–5.

Nash's Game-Theoretic Bargaining Solution.

24. See Robert L. Bishop, "Game-Theoretic Analyses of Bargaining," *The Quarterly Journal of Economics, LXXVII* (November 1963), pp. 559–602; and John G. Cross, "A Theory of the Bargaining Process," *The American Economic Review, LV* (March 1965), pp. 67–94.

Figure 17–5. This is the point at which the "utility boundary" is tangent to the utility frontier. The utility boundary is a straight line with a negative slope. At point S, the utility of labor plus the utility of management is equal to k; moreover, $U_l + U_m = k/2$. The negotiated solution is at the mid-point of the straight-line utility boundary.[25]

Wagner's Unified Bargaining Theory

Harvey Wagner examined the three major approaches to bargaining theory: (1) bilateral monopoly, (2) risk evaluation, and (3) the theory of games.[26] He developed an interesting variation of the bilateral monopoly theory, in which he stresses the uncertainty involved. This uncertainty stems from the implicit knowledge each party has about the strategy that the other party will adopt. Wagner does not appear to be greatly impressed by the risk evaluation approach followed by Zeuthen, Pen, and others. In his view, these theories assume knowledge of certain quantities that could not be known until the bargaining process had been completed.

Wagner also developed a bargaining theory using the game-theory framework. His theory is of the "non-zero sum" type, that is, losses to management when an agreement is reached are not necessarily equal to the union's gains. He also assumed that collective bargaining is a "non-cooperative game." This type of game assumes that there is no direct communication between the parties. Each side decides upon a strategy, then informs an "umpire" of its choice. The umpire in turn informs each side of the result of the two strategies adopted. An interesting feature of this theory is the conclusion that under certain circumstances the parties might not *want* to reach agreement, but might prefer a strike. Earlier theories of bargaining showed the conditions under which labor and management would reach agreement. Wagner shows both the case where the parties will reach agreement, and the case where a strike will remain indeterminate, except in the case where an "umpire" would be involved as a go-between in the bargaining process; that is, a bargaining situation where a mediator or conciliator is called in to help the two parties reach an agreement.

A Behavioral Theory of Bargaining

Walton and McKersie incorporated behavioral concepts into earlier bargaining theories that rely essentially on economic concepts. Their book is not limited to labor negotiations, but is intended to encompass social negotia-

---

25. For a discussion of the formal assumptions underlying this theory, and a proof of the solution illustrated by Figure 17–5, see Cross, *op. cit.,* pp. 68–69.

26. Harvey M. Wagner, "A Unified Treatment of Bargaining Theory," *Southern Economic Journal, XXIII* (April 1957), pp. 380–397. See also the debate between J. C. Harsanyi and Wagner in the April 1957 issue of the same journal.

tions in general.[27] They describe a number of bargaining models and, in each case, attempt a synthesis of economic and behavioral analyses. Unlike the game-theoretic and earlier models, the Walton-McKersie approach is non-mathematical. It is thus much easier to understand than the more rigorous analyses of the game theorists. At the same time, it is more difficult to summarize the conclusions reached by Walton and McKersie. They believe, however, that negotiators attempt to minimize disutility rather than maximizing utility, as the game-theoretic models assume.[28] As Strauss has noted, Walton and McKersie go beyond the discussion of strategy and tactics to include attitudes and the relationships between bargaining agents and their constituents. Their work may be criticized, Strauss believes, "as being badly written, oversimple, and as ignoring important relevant research. Nevertheless, as the first of its kind it filled an obvious need."[29]

Evaluating Bargaining Theories

This chapter has described a number of different approaches to bargaining theory, and the work of a number of different individuals in this field. The specific theories mentioned are only a sample of a larger number that could have been mentioned. What can be said about progress in this highly specialized area of research? "Unfortunately . . . if the views of the theorists about the models of their colleagues are to be believed, we have not made great strides."[30] It is not uncommon for scholars to be highly critical of competing or opposing ideas. But the literature of bargaining theory appears to contain a disproportionate number of harsh judgments about the inadequacies of *other* bargaining theories.

One of the more durable bargaining models is the early and relatively simple one developed by Hicks. In the second edition of the *Theory of Wages,* Hicks tended to deprecate his own earlier work, publishing in full Shove's critical review. Others, however, take a more favorable view of this model and—despite its simplicity—feel that it can be incorporated in more recent contributions.[31]

---

27. Richard E. Walton and Robert B. McKersie, *A Behavioral Theory of Labor Negotiations* (New York: McGraw-Hill Book Co., Inc., 1965).

28. See James L. Stern, "Collective Bargaining Trends and Patterns," in *A Review of Industrial Relations Research,* Vol. *II* (Madison, Wisconsin: Industrial Relations Research Association, 1971), p. 166.

29. George Strauss, "Organizational Behavior and Personnel Relations," in *A Review of Industrial Relations Research, Vol. I* (Madison, Wisconsin: Industrial Relations Research Association, 1970), p. 175.

30. Stern, *op. cit.,* p. 166.

31. See, for example, Robert B. McKersie and Richard E. Walton, "The Theory of Bargaining," *Industrial and Labor Relations Review, 19* (April 1966), pp. 414–424. See, however, the critical comments on the Hicks-McKersie-Walton model by Bevars DuPre Mabry, *idem.,* pp. 424–435. For another synthesis including Hicks's model, see Robert L. Bishop, "A Zeuthen-Hicks Theory of Bargaining," *Econometrica, 32* (July 1964), pp. 410–417.

It is easy to criticize bargaining theories for their lack of "realism." But as Mabry[32] has pointed out in his reply to the criticism of McKersie and Walton,

> Of course, my theory is a simplification of the real world. . . as all theories must be, at least initially, if they are to be conceptually tractable. My theory is also tautological, as all theories must be (even those of geometry), in the sense that their conclusions are implied in their assumptions. . . What they mean to say, I think, is that my theory is not empirically *relevant*. If the conclusion follows logically from the assumptions, a theory is valid regardless of whether or not it is relevant to the events of the real world.

How useful are the theories of collective bargaining discussed above? Because some bargaining theories use concepts that have no measurable counterpart in the real world, the nontheorist is likely to be critical of the high degree of abstraction involved. But this is not a justifiable criticism of the theories as such. All theories deal with abstractions. Perhaps the only relevant question is: are they useful? If they help us understand the bargaining process by focusing attention on some aspects that might otherwise be ignored, the answer will be affirmative. But there are some who judge the usefulness of a theory solely in terms of its ability to predict outcomes. In this respect, we are far short of the mark; no theory has been developed to date which permits us to predict in advance the outcome of a particular bargaining situation. This is so even if we consider the wage bargain only, and in the real world collective bargaining deals with many issues other than wages.

Collective Bargaining as a System of "Industrial Jurisprudence"

Slichter noted that collective bargaining has two principal aspects. First, it is a method of pricemaking, that is, of arriving at wage rates. Second, it is "a method of introducing civil rights into industry. . . of requiring that management be conducted by rule rather than by arbitrary decision." By developing the institution of the state, we have developed a body of law and procedures for administering laws. "Similarly, laboring men, through unions, formulate policies to which they give expression in the form of shop rules and practices . . . When labor and management deal with labor relations analytically and systematically . . . it is proper to refer to this system as *industrial jurisprudence*."[33]

The most complex theory of collective bargaining developed to date deals only with its first aspect—wage determination. In the earliest days of collective bargaining this was no doubt the major issue. But as unions have grown and become an increasingly important part of our political and eco-

---

32. Mabry, *op. cit.*, p. 425.

33. Sumner H. Slichter, *Union Policies and Industrial Management* (Washington, D.C.: The Brookings Institution, 1941), p. 1, italics added.

nomic lives, collective bargaining has expanded to deal with many issues other than the determination of wage rates. It is true that many fringe benefits involve a cost to the employer and a return to union members, current or deferred, and matters such as these can be subsumed under the general heading of wages. But unions and management bargain about other matters, which cannot be related so directly to costs or returns. For this reason, even the most "general" theory of collective bargaining would be in fact only a partial theory.

In Chapter 19, some of the major nonwage aspects of collective bargaining will be considered, including issues that involve labor costs and returns to the workers as well as some questions that deal largely with "industrial jurisprudence." The latter involves the joint negotiation of work rules and practices. It is what Slichter referred to as the introduction of civil rights into industry.

Questions and Exercises

1. Labor-management agreements are frequently referred to as contracts. What is the difference between a labor-management agreement and the typical business contract? In what way is a labor-management agreement similar to an international treaty? Some writers have compared labor-management agreements to marriage agreements. Do you think this is a useful comparison?

2. Describe the content of a typical labor-management agreement. Is there any relationship between grievance procedures and arbitration?

3. What are some of the criteria used by unions in seeking wage increases?

4. What criteria are frequently used by employers in resisting wage demands?

5. What are the three general types of bargaining theories?

6. Briefly describe Hicks's theory of negotiations. What was Shackle's basic criticism of Hicks's theory?

7. Describe Fellner's theory of bargaining under bilateral monopoly. What conclusions did Fellner reach about the wage rate under bilateral monopoly?

8. Pen criticized Hicks's theory because it led to a determinate solution. What was Pen's attitude toward the conclusions reached by Fellner about the wage rate under bilateral monopoly?

9. Does Pen's bargaining theory rely entirely on economic concepts? If not, what other concepts does it include?

10. The bargaining problem in Pen's view, is one of bargaining *power*. What determines bargaining power, according to Pen?

11. What contributions were made to bargaining theory by Zeuthen and Shackle?

12. Briefly describe the theory of games, and show how it may be applied to bargaining situations.

13. In an early article, Carl Stevens concluded that the game-theory format is essentially inappropriate to the analysis of negotiation. Why did he reach this conclusion? In his later work, Stevens did make use of game theory to analyze collective bargaining. What variant of game theory did he introduce?

14. Briefly describe Nash's game-theoretic bargaining solution.

15. Why did Wagner refer to his contribution as a "unified" theory of bargaining?

16. What innovation in bargaining theory was introduced by Walton and McKersie?

17. Write a brief essay evaluating the theory of bargaining.

18. What did Sumner Slichter mean when he referred to collective bargaining as a "system of industrial jurisprudence"?

Suggested Readings

Books

Cartter, Allan M. *Theory of Wages and Employment.* Homewood, Illinois: Richard D. Irwin, Inc., 1959.

Hicks, J. R. *The Theory of Wages.* London: Macmillan & Co. Ltd., 1932; second edition, 1963.

Slichter, Sumner H., James J. Healey, and E. Robert Livernash. *The Impact of Collective Bargaining on Management.* Washington, D.C.: The Brookings Institution, 1960.

Slichter, Sumner H. *Union Policies and Industrial Management.* Washington, D.C.: The Brookings Institution, 1941.

Stevens, Carl M. *Strategy and Collective Bargaining Negotiations.* New York: McGraw-Hill Book Co., Inc., 1963.

Walton, Richard E., and Robert B. McKersie. *A Behavioral Theory of Labor Negotiations.* New York: McGraw-Hill Book Co., Inc., 1965.

Articles

Bishop, Robert L. "Game Theoretic Analyses of Bargaining," *Quarterly Journal of Economics, LXXVII* (November 1963), pp. 449–602.

Cheng, Pao Lun. "Wage Negotiation and Bargaining Power," *Industrial and Labor Relations Review, 21* (January 1968), pp. 163–182.

Compini, Bruno. "The Value of Time in Bargaining Negotiations: Some Experimental Evidence," *The American Economic Review, VIII* (June 1968), pp. 374–393.

Fellner, William. "Prices and Wages Under Bilateral Monopoly," *Quarterly Journal of Economics, LXI* (August 1947), pp. 503–532.

Mabry, Bevars DuPre. "The Pure Theory of Bargaining," *Industrial and Labor Relations Review, 18* (July 1965), pp. 479–502.

Nash, J. P. "The Bargaining Problem," *Econometrica, 18* (April 1950), pp. 155–162.

Pen, J. "A General Theory of Bargaining," *The American Economic Review, XLII* (March 1952), pp. 24–42.

Stern, James L. "Collective Bargaining Trends and Patterns," in Benjamin Aaron, Paul S. Meyer, *et al., A Review of Industrial Relations Research, Vol. II.* Madison, Wisconsin: Industrial Relations Research Association, 1971, pp. 125–182.

Stages of
Collective Bargaining

Collective bargaining in the United States has been an evolutionary process. The legal requirement forcing businessmen to bargain with trade unions, under certain circumstances, came as a shock to many of them. It is not surprising that they were less than happy with this development and that they approached the bargaining table prepared to do battle with the representatives of their workers. As John A. Stephens, vice president of industrial relations in the U.S. Steel Corporation in 1955, put it:

> We have made substantial progress since the early years of our union relationship. Those early years were difficult. I don't mean that the present are not difficult, too, but we do have improved relationships. We then learned, and continue now to learn, that man has an almost infinite capacity for disagreement and that decency, good will, and understanding cannot be induced by law or discipline alone. The relationship some years ago was, of course, new on both sides. Adjusting to it required time, patience, tolerance, integrity of character. . . .[1]

Economic historians have often found it convenient to analyze economic change in terms of stages, and it is equally convenient to analyze the development of collective bargaining in the United States in the same way. It must be pointed out, however, that not all relationships go through the stages to be described in the following section, and individual collective bargaining relationships do not always move in the same direction. At times there is retrogression when it appears that the two parties have lost ground in their efforts to live and work together. By and large, however, collective bargaining relationships tend to move along the same path—from an early stage of resistance to a later state of acceptance.

---

1. John A. Stephens, "Evolution of Labor Relations in U.S. Steel" in Neil W. Chamberlain, *Source Book on Labor* (New York: McGraw-Hill Book Co., Inc., 1958), p. 50.

The Stages of Collective Bargaining

Open Warfare

Before 1935, many companies resisted trade unionism by any means at their disposal. Some firms maintained their own police forces, and members of these forces did not object to manhandling union organizers if they came on or near the premises. In the steel, coal, and automobile industries, for example, there were numerous instances of violence; this was played up at times in the press as class warfare. While this designation was less than accurate, it was a form of warfare.

The use of physical force did not disappear entirely after 1935, although given the temper of the times, it became less widespread. Today, more than thirty-five years after the Wagner Act became law, some companies continue to resist organization. Physical violence is still used occasionally to restrain union organizers, but more often management relies on subtler techniques. There are cases where other elements in the community — the local police, the press, and even in some cases, the ministry— have allied to discourage union organization in a community. Employers in some small communities which are just beginning to industrialize often maintain a discreet silence, since they know that the local press, other businessmen in the community, and various community leaders will effectively discourage the activities of union organizers. And they know that overaction on their part would be a violation of the Taft-Hartley Act, which could lead to lengthy litigation and eventually to an organization election.[2]

Union leaders recognize such opposition as a form of warfare, and carefully plan their campaigns to break opposition to the union. They avoid violence and concentrate on a form of psychological warfare in their efforts to sign up a majority of the members of a company or plant before requesting a National Labor Relations Board election.[3]

The stage of open warfare, which has been marked at times by bitter resistance to unionism in unorganized companies, can be brief, or it can last a long time. But where opposition to organization has been total on management's part, the scars of this stage of the relationship can last a long time, even after a company has been successfully organized.

---

2. For a carefully documented account of tactics used by antiunion employers see: *Almost Unbelievable ... The Story of an Industry, the Union and the Law* (New York: Textile Workers Union of America, 1961).

3. An exception should be noted in the case of the small handful of unions which have been associated with racketeers. They have often used "goon squads" of strong-arm men to bring both recalcitrant workers and employers into line. See Robert F. Kennedy, *The Enemy Within* (New York: Harper and Brothers, 1960).

Grudging Recognition

Under the law, if a majority of workers in a bargaining unit vote to be represented by a union, management must recognize the union and bargain collectively with its representatives. But especially in cases where recognition has followed a long period of warfare between the union and management, the early relationship is likely to be a strained one to say the very least. Management will make it clear that it did not want to recognize the union but was forced to do so. Bargaining during this stage of the relationship is often quite hectic. There is much table pounding, much talk of prerogatives and legal obligations. If the management has fought hard to keep a union out of the plant or company, it is not likely to give in gracefully once recognition has been forced upon it by a majority vote. There is often a feeling of resentment against the workers who voted for the union, and there is even greater resentment against the "outsiders"—the representatives of the national or international union—with whom management must deal. An interesting example by Shultz and Coleman, of this stage of collective bargaining, involves an actual bargaining relationship between a company, which is given the fictitious name of the Lennox Corporation, and the union with which it dealt.[4]

In the Lennox Case, management objected to the union because it allegedly introduced a leveling influence into the work group and deprived management of the flexibility it needed to run the business. In addition, it was charged that the union leaders were personally difficult to get along with and that they insisted upon introducing extraneous issues into plant-level bargaining. In this case the top management of the company felt that the collective bargaining relationship would not survive—that the union was not there to stay. The only reason the union won elections in the company's five plants, top management believed, was that lower management was not effectively practicing the personnel policy laid down at the top. Its objective was to hold the union at bay until such time as new supervisors could be trained to implement what top management firmly believed was a sound personnel policy, which would eventually wean workers away from their loyalty to the union.

Under such conditions a collective bargaining relationship cannot stand on solid ground; it is similar to an armed truce. During this stage of the relationship, the union must engage in hard bargaining to retain the loyalty of the workers it has signed up. And management's antiunion position is generally played up by union leaders to bolster the solidarity of the rank and file. It is made perfectly clear to the workers involved that the company is out to "get" the union, and that if this happens the workers will once again be at a complete disadvantage. It is also pointed out that union activists will be

---

4. "Holding the Union at Bay: The Lennox Case," in George P. Shultz and John R. Coleman *Labor Problems: Cases and Readings* (New York: McGraw-Hill Book Co., Inc., 1953), pp. 125–133.

subject to retribution if the union is driven out of the plant. The stage of grudging recognition is essentially unstable. Either the union will be able to convince management that it is there to stay, and that management had better adopt a reasonable attitude toward it, or the management view will prevail and workers can be convinced that it is in their best interests to vote for decertification at the next NLRB election. More often than not, union leaders are able to convince management that the union is not going to be dislodged, and the relationship moves on to the next stage.

Accommodation or Willing Recognition

During the period of grudging recognition there is likely to be a feeling of ill will on both sides of the bargaining table. But anger is an emotion that is difficult to sustain. Either there will be a blowup and the relationship will fall apart, or the ill feeling will gradually subside and the two parties will begin to work together on a more amicable basis. This is partly due to changes in personal relationships. Gradually management recognizes that it can work with the union. As the leadership of the local union begins to feel more secure, some of the early antagonism toward management will begin to disappear. Collective bargaining becomes a process of give and take. There is a greater amount of information sharing; the parties become somewhat less adamant in their bargaining positions; and the general process of accommodation begins to take place. The settlement of grievances may become more informal and flexible than during the earlier stage of grudging recognition and earlier personal animosities may disappear.[5]

Many bargaining relationships no doubt do not go beyond the stage of accommodation. But at this stage the two parties have learned to work and live together. Management no longer seeks to alienate the loyalty of workers to their union. The union gives up its attack on management *per se* and concentrates on issues and problems. At this stage of development, collective bargaining has become stabilized. There can be strong differences of opinion, and even occasional strikes, but the relationship is one that is likely to endure. There can still be a great deal of hard bargaining under such conditions. But the two parties want to reach agreement; they are no longer interested in attempting to destroy each other. The periods of warfare and armed truce are over and both labor and management are interested in finding a formula that will lead to their mutual survival.[6]

---

5. For an example of accommodation, see Frederick H. Harbison and King Carr, *Causes of Industrial Peace Under Collective Bargaining: The Libbey-Owens-Ford Glass Company and the Federation of Glass, Ceramic, and Silica Sand Workers of America* (Washington: National Planning Association, 1948); partly reprinted in Shultz and Coleman, *op. cit.,* pp. 133–150.
6. See E. Wight Bakke, *Mutual Survival: The Goal of Unions and Management* (New Haven: Yale University Labor and Management Center, 1946).

Acceptance

Many labor-management relationships do not go beyond the stage of accommodation or willing recognition. In other cases management comes to accept the union completely. There is a difference between recognition and acceptance, although it is partly one of degree. A collective bargaining relationship reaches the stage of acceptance when a company would not be willing to give up its relationship with the union even if it had an opportunity to do so. To the uninitiated this might seem highly improbable. Even if a relationship is of the best, it might be argued, wouldn't management still prefer to avoid dealing with a union? The answer to this question will often be *yes.* But there are other cases in which it is *no.*

Once the leaders of a union feel that they themselves and the union have been completely accepted by management, the whole collective bargaining relationship is changed. It is no longer a contest. Both sides recognize that they stand to gain from working together. The day-to-day relationship between shop stewards and foremen is an easy one. Problems are often settled informally, and there may be considerable consultation between union and management representatives.

Union leaders, secure in their position, can develop an interest in the efficiency of the company. The union can help maintain discipline; absenteeism, tardiness, and careless work habits can be discouraged by local union leaders. There is no reason at this stage of a relationship for carrying on an unremitting attack on management. Instead, the union can point out to rank and file workers that everyone stands to gain if the overall productivity of the company can be improved.

By the time management has accepted unionism, negotiations and day-to-day administration of the labor-management agreement are in the hands of professionals. The management of national union affairs has long been in the hands of full-time elected officials and their appointed staff assistants. Professional advice and assistance is always available to local union officers, most of whom continue to work at their regular occupations. On the management side, labor relations are now handled by specialized management personnel, many with training in industrial relations.[7] In a mature relationship, representatives of the two parties handle many matters on an informal basis.[8]

---

7. For a discussion of the early development of the industrial relations function in American management, see Charles A. Myers and John J. Turnbull, "Line and Staff in Industrial Relations," *Harvard Business Review,* July-August 1956, pp. 113–124. Recent developments are discussed in George Strauss, "Human Relations—1968 Style," *Industrial Relations, 7* (May 1968), pp. 262–276. See also Lyman W. Porter, "Personnel Management: A Review of the Recent Psychological Literature," *Annual Review of Psychology, 17* (1966), pp. 395–422.

8. A description of contemporary negotiations, and a contrast with those of an earlier day, are given by Jack Barbash, "American Unionism: From Protest to Growing Concern," *Journal of Economic Issues, II* (March 1968), pp. 46–49.

Complete acceptance of a union does not mean the end of hard bargaining. What it does mean is that both sides argue from the conviction that what they demand—or are willing to give—will serve the best interests of all concerned. Acceptance of the union does not mean, as some have implied, the "sharing" of management.[9] Management continues to run the company and the union to represent its workers. Union leaders and management will not always see eye to eye. It is possible for negotiations to break down and strikes to result even where the union is fully accepted. But when the stage of acceptance has been achieved, such strikes are conducted without acrimony or bitterness. Once the issues have been resolved, the two parties are able to resume their relationship on the former basis.

It is likely that a considerable number of collective bargaining relationships in the United States have reached the stage of acceptance. This is, of course, a highly stable kind of relationship. Once an agreement has been reached, management knows that the union will make every effort to live up to the terms of the contract; and the security of the union is reflected in good work habits, high worker morale, and little or no bickering over relatively unimportant issues.

Union-Management Cooperation

Acceptance of the union is undoubtedly the terminal stage in most labor-management relationships in the United States. There are a number of cases of union-management cooperation, however, which go beyond the stage of acceptance. In this section, union-management cooperation will be discussed in general terms. In the next section, one particular approach to cooperation will be discussed in greater detail.

Union-management cooperation is not entirely new in collective bargaining.[10] There is evidence that cooperative arrangements have been spreading, although slowly. Union-management cooperation exists wherever the two parties work *jointly* on one or more phases of the labor-management relationship. In some cases this might simply be the joint determination of piece rates. At the other extreme, however, joint committees might be established to discuss all problems relating to production, sales, and distribution.

In some cases, union-management cooperation is accompanied by profit sharing, but this is not a necessary condition for cooperation to exist. The

---

9. Union leaders expect to participate in decisions affecting employment, but most of them have rejected the notion of "shared power" in *total* management functions. See Adolf Sturmthal, "Workers' Participation in Management: A Review of United States Experience," *Bulletin No. 6, Country Studies Series* (Geneva: International Institute for Labour Studies, 1969), pp. 4; 36.

10. For a discussion of several experiments in union-management cooperation during the 1920s and 1930s, see Sumner H. Slichter, *Union Policies and Industrial Management* (Washington, D.C.: The Brookings Institution, 1941), pp. 393–571.

difference between the stage of acceptance and the stage of cooperation can now be made somewhat more explicit.

During the stage of acceptance, collective bargaining proceeds along traditional lines. The union formulates a set of demands and management formulates a set of counter proposals. Then an agreement is negotiated. There is considerable give and take at the bargaining table with each side recognizing the good faith of the other. And the day-to-day administration of the agreement, once it is signed, can be highly informal and flexible. But the identity of management and the identity of the union are clearly maintained. The relationship is friendly, and there is a strong spirit of cooperation on both sides. However, there is no *formal* arrangement for the two parties to settle issues or to approach problems on a *joint* basis. Once joint committees are set up, the relationship has moved into the stage of union-management cooperation. The objective of such joint action is to increase the efficiency of the company. As Joseph Shister has put it: "Union-management cooperation will be said to exist when the union and the management in question, through joint action, attempt to reduce the unit costs of production."[11] Shister points out that union-management cooperation should not be confused with industrial peace. Cooperation cannot exist without industrial peace, but industrial peace can and does exist without joint action by labor and management to improve efficiency.

In general, union-management cooperation is an outgrowth of adversity. The company involved finds itself in a difficult competitive situation, which can be due to a number of factors: poor management in the past, the growth of new forms of competition, or the impact of a sudden recession, for example. If union leaders and management are on good terms when adversity strikes, it is not unusual for them to discuss the situation. Out of such discussions have grown a number of formal plans for cooperation.[12]

Union-management cooperation may lead to temporary action or to a permanent arrangement. In some cases, for example, unions and employers have jointly hired outside experts to analyze the company's problems and recommend a course of action. In other cases, notably in the garment industry, the union provides expert help by sending its business agents and technicians into a company to help improve its efficiency. These approaches fit the definition of union-management cooperation, since they involve joint action, but they do not lead to permanent arrangements. In other cases, however, the union and the employer set up one or more joint committees to encourage worker suggestions for the improvement of operations or for

---

11. Joseph Shister, "Union-Management Cooperation: An Analysis," in *Insights Into Labor Issues,* Richard A. Lester and Joseph Shister (eds.) (New York: The Macmillan Company, 1948), p. 87.

12. *Ibid.,* pp. 87–91.

the continuing study of production problems. Such programs are intended to be of a continuing nature, and often are incorporated into the labor-management agreement.[13]

Does union-management cooperation mean the end of collective bargaining? Do the identities of the union and the company become submerged in a common enterprise? Is union-management cooperation a form of collusion in which the two parties look after their own interests without regard to the effects on consumers? The answer to all three questions is an emphatic *no*. Enough cases of union-management cooperation are on record to support the conclusion that the companies and unions involved maintain their identities and continue to perform their respective functions as in the days before the cooperative schemes were established. It is possible that the emphasis in collective bargaining has shifted somewhat from the negotiation of agreements to the day-to-day administration of these agreements. But the establishment of joint committees does not preclude the possibility of disagreement, or even of strikes, although it must be admitted that the latter are fairly rare where cooperative relationships have been established.

It is particularly important to distinguish between union-management cooperation, which is associated with efforts to reduce unit costs of production, and union-management collusion. There have been, and undoubtedly still are instances of the latter.[14] In the case of craft unions, the union can agree to deal only with certain employers and the employers in turn to hire only union members. The objective might be to restrict production and raise prices with obvious benefits to management and workers, but at the expense of consumers. Such collusion can be effective only in local market areas, however, and both parties run the risk of prosecution under the antitrust laws if they practice such collusion. The objectives are quite different in the two cases. Collusion is illegal, and it is detrimental to consumers. Union-management cooperation is quite legal and, if it results in improved efficiency, leads to benefits for management, workers, and consumers.

It is worth repeating that relatively few labor-management relationships reach the cooperative stage; the terminal stage for most relationships will be that of acceptance. There are very few instances in which formal schemes of union-management cooperation have evolved in the absence of economic adversity. It is only when a company—and the jobs of its workers—are threatened that the two parties appear to be willing to work jointly towards a solution of their common problems. Labor-management cooperation is still more an exception than the rule even when a company is in serious jeopardy. In most cases the company, if it cannot solve its problems unilaterally, goes out of

---

13. See Sumner H. Slichter, James J. Healy, and E. Robert Livernash, *The Impact of Collective Bargaining on Management* (Washington, D.C.: The Brookings Institution, 1960), p. 845.

14. Melville Dalton, "Some Pros and Cons of Union-Management Cooperation," *Personnel Administration*, November-December, 1965, pp. 39–42.

business, and its workers are faced with the problem of finding new jobs. But in the relatively limited number of cases where union-management coopera-tion has been tried, it seems to have worked well.

Profit Sharing and Union-Management Cooperation

Profit Sharing as an Anti-Union Device

It should not be supposed that profit sharing and union-management co-operation are synonymous. Indeed, profit sharing may be used as a device to keep unions out of a company, or if part of a company has been organized to keep unionism from spreading to the rest of the work force. It is difficult to estimate the exact number of profit-sharing plans in the United States, but there is evidence that they have grown substantially in the past fifteen years.

There are three general types of profit-sharing programs: (a) cash, (b) deferred, and (c) a combination of cash and deferred plans. Under cash plans profits are distributed at the end of the fiscal year. Where a company has a deferred profit-sharing plan, a specified share of company profits is placed in a trust fund each year, and these funds are used as part of employee retire-ment programs. Some companies put only part of the employees' share in the trust fund and the rest is distributed in annual cash payments.

Deferred plans with trust funds require approval by the Internal Revenue Service. Because of this requirement, accurate estimates of the number of such plans in existence can be made. The Council of Profit-Sharing In-dustries estimated that there were about 100,000 deferred profit-sharing plans in the United States in 1972. The number of deferred profit-sharing plans has doubled every four years since 1946. The Council also estimated that between 100,000 and 150,000 cash profit-sharing plans existed at that time. In 1957, 159 companies with profit-sharing plans belonged to the Council of Profit-Sharing Industries.[15] By 1972, there were 1,400 member companies, of which one third had fewer than fifty employees and one half had fewer than 100 employees.[16] In 1957, only 38 per cent of the companies belonging to the Council had recognized trade unions. Spokesmen for the Council were unwilling to release the number of member companies with labor-management agreements in 1972, because in the words of a staff member, "the figure is no longer mean-ingful." Evidently, many member companies have labor-management agree-ments, but the profit-sharing plan does not include the bargaining unit. Unions prefer to negotiate retirement and other fringe benefit programs.

---

15. Joseph B. Meyer (ed.), *Profit-Sharing Manual* (Chicago: Council of Profit-Sharing Industries, 1957), pp. 408–414.

16. Data for 1972 were provided by the Director of Communications of the Council of Profit-Sharing Industries. For further details see *Profit Sharing*, Council of Profit Sharing Industries, Vol. *19* (October 1971), pp. 20–27.

Members of the bargaining unit then know what they can expect in retirement income. One disadvantage of unilaterally determined deferred profit-sharing plans is that employees do not know in advance how much they will receive after retirement.

Where profit-sharing and union-management agreements are found in conjunction, however, it is likely that the labor-management relationship is a mature one, and that the two parties have worked out a successful formula for working together. American unions, in general, have not tried to negotiate profit-sharing plans. Thus, where a company has recognized a union and also operates a profit-sharing plan, it is likely that management has taken the initiative in working out the arrangement.

Profit Sharing and Union-Management Cooperation: the Scanlon Plan

As noted earlier, cooperation exists only where there is *joint* action by the union and management to improve efficiency. There can be cooperation with or without profit sharing. In a number of cases, however, unions and managements have developed profit-sharing schemes based upon formal programs of union-management cooperation. One of the more famous of these is the "Scanlon Plan," named after Joseph N. Scanlon, who developed this form of labor-management cooperation.

What is the essence of the Scanlon Plan? Those who worked most closely with Scanlon in the development of this scheme of labor-management cooperation stress one thing: worker participation. In the words of one of Scanlon's collaborators: "This plan doesn't mean giving people a 'sense of participation'; workers don't want that. This plan means giving them real participation."[17] The Scanlon Plan also is *not* a profit-sharing scheme.

One way to look at the Scanlon Plan is to consider it as a *group incentive* scheme; that is, individual workers are not rewarded for the suggestions they make—a very common procedure in many companies which have no form of labor-management cooperation. Instead, under the Scanlon Plan, every worker in the company benefits from gains in productivity. There is no distinction between "production" and "nonproduction" workers. Office workers, maintenance workers, production workers—everyone in the company—shares in the bonuses, which are an integral part of the group incentive program under the Scanlon Plan.

In a typical Scanlon situation, bonuses are determined by a ratio of total payroll to the sales value of what was produced by that payroll. The ratio is computed for some agreed-upon historical period, and then becomes the basis for computing extra dividends to workers in the form of bonus payments.

---

17. Frederick G. Lesieur, "What the Plan Isn't and Is," in Frederick G. Lesieur (ed.), *The Scanlon Plan* (New York: John Wiley & Sons, Inc., The Technology Press of M.I.T., 1958), p. 39.

The ratio is used to determine a "normal" labor cost. In any month when actual labor costs are below this norm, the difference between the two constitutes the bonus pool. Before payment is made, however, some part of the pool is set aside against possible deficit months in which the labor cost exceeds the norm. In many cases the bonus is split, with 25 per cent going to management and 75 per cent going to the workers in the company.[18]

Thus far two aspects of the plan have been discussed—worker participation and the bonus scheme. But how are productivity gains actually achieved? The answer in its broadest sense has already been implied: gains in productivity result from worker suggestions. But there must be some system for processing these suggestions, and this is achieved through the establishment of joint union-management committees. There may be several kinds of committees, such as screening committees, which examine all worker suggestions, and production committees, which discuss actual operations.[19] Such joint committees epitomize union-management cooperation.

Union-management cooperation under the Scanlon Plan does not mean that management has ceased to operate the company or that the union has stopped representing its workers. What it does mean is that the two parties work together on problems to increase the company's productivity, from which both parties then benefit. The plan will not succeed if either party approaches it in a halfhearted way. Some of the unions and companies that have adopted the Scanlon Plan have become enthusiasts.

The Scanlon Plan has been adopted by several dozen companies in a variety of industries. But the curious might raise the question: "If the Scanlon Plan has worked so well in the companies that have adopted it, why hasn't it spread throughout manufacturing industry?" The answer seems to be that the Plan is not generally applicable. It appears to work best in small and medium-sized manufacturing companies.[20] Not all of these companies are single-plant units; some are multiple-plant firms. But the plan has not been adopted by any of the nation's industrial giants. This suggests that the sort of environment in which the plan has worked is one where workers and management have a fairly close relationship. There is much less specialization in the small or medium-sized concern than is found in the large corporation, with its numerous departments and management hierarchy. The plan seems to work best in those situations where it is physically possible for

18. Elbridge S. Puckett, "Measuring Performance Under the Scanlon Plan," in Lesieur, *The Scanlon Plan*, p. 66. For a specific example of how the ratio is computed, see pp. 67–73 of this article. See also Russell W. Davenport, "Enterprise for Everyman," reprinted from the January 1950 issue of *Fortune* as pp. 17–33 of *The Scanlon Plan*.

19. George P. Shultz, "Worker Participation on Production Problems," *Personnel*, November 1950, p. 5, reprinted in Lesieur, *op. cit.*

20. George P. Shultz, "Variations in Environment and the Scanlon Plan," in Lesieur, *op. cit.*, p. 101.

workers and management to sit down together to discuss problems of mutual concern.

Thousands of firms in the small and medium-sized categories have adopted neither the Scanlon Plan nor some variation of it. Why? One possible answer is that it calls for a considerable amount of "give" on both sides. Management has to be the first to unbend. Workers could easily be sold on the merits of union-management cooperation if they could anticipate additional monetary gains through bonus payments. But union-management cooperation involves the yielding of prerogatives by management. The managers of many concerns feel that they know more about operating the company than the workers, so why sit down with the latter to discuss production problems? Others might feel that they can tap worker ingenuity through a simple scheme of worker suggestions with bonuses paid directly to those whose suggestions are adopted. Such managers might feel that they are tapping the reservoir of worker experience, and yet the workers are kept at arm's length. Management makes all the decisions and the workers do not actually participate in running the firm.

There are no doubt other reasons why the Scanlon Plan has not spread. One characteristic of the American economic and social system is its diversity. It is not likely that any single scheme will be embraced by all businessmen or unions, yet the record of the Scanlon Plan is impressive. Many of the companies that have adopted it were in serious financial difficulty before they elected to try union-management cooperation. Others were not in difficulty, but they realized substantial gains in productivity once the plan was put into effect. There have been cases in which the Plan failed, but these failures can be explained. In some cases the Scanlon Plan was conceived as a substitute for collective bargaining. Where this attitude has been found, the plan has not worked.[21] In other cases, either management or the workers decided to try the plan without being fully convinced of its merits. It appears that a complete commitment is required if the plan is to succeed.

The Scanlon Plan is not foolproof. If the major product of a company is rendered obsolete by technological change—or some other outside disturbance—and the company is not in a position to adapt to some other type of production, the Scanlon Plan alone will not guarantee success. The plan is not a substitute for sound management or for good union leadership. But where the combination of sound management and good union leadership is found, and where the two parties are willing to engage in union-management cooperation without reservation, the evidence suggests that the Scanlon Plan may be more than a scheme for achieving mutual survival. It may be a stimulus to growth and prosperity shared by management and workers alike.[22]

---

21. Schultz, "Variations in Environment," p. 107.

22. For a more skeptical view see Herbert R. Northrup and Harvey A. Young, "The Causes of Industrial Peace Revisited," *Industrial and Labor Relations Review*, October 1968, pp. 40-42.

The Causes of Industrial Peace

Labor-management conflict is as old as the institution of trade unionism, as a voluminous literature dealing with clashes between organized workers and the owners or managers of capital, shows. In the late 1940s, however, Clinton S. Golden, a former union official who had served as a United States labor representative abroad, remarked at a meeting of the National Planning Association: "In my opinion, the time has come when, instead of looking into the causes of conflict that we know and hear so much about, we ought to try to discover *how much peace there is* and *what makes peace.*[23] Mr. Golden's suggestion was adopted by the NPA, and in 1947, the Committee on the Causes of Industrial Peace Under Collective Bargaining was established with Mr. Golden as chairman. For the next six years, the NPA sponsored a series of case studies in a wide variety of manufacturing enterprises extending across the nation. Each case was unique in some respects, but there were also a number of points of similarity. The case studies revealed the diversity of conditions under which industrial peace could be achieved. But they also revealed basic causes of industrial peace common to all of the cases. These causes, listed in the final report on this investigation, are as follows:

1. There is full acceptance by management of the collective bargaining process and of unionism as an institution. The company considers a strong union an asset to management.
2. The union fully accepts private ownership and operation of the industry; it recognizes that the welfare of its members depends upon the successful operation of the business.
3. The union is strong, responsible, and democratic.
4. The company stays out of the union's internal affairs; it does not seek to alienate the workers' allegiance to their union.
5. Mutual trust and confidence exist between the parties. There have been no serious ideological incompatabilities.
6. Neither party in bargaining has adopted a legalistic approach to the solution of problems in the relationship.
7. Negotiations are "problem-centered"—more time is spent on solving day-to-day problems than on defining abstract principles.
8. There is widespread union-management consultation and highly developed information-sharing.
9. Grievances are settled promptly, in the local plant whenever possible. There is flexibility and informality within the procedure.[24]

---

23. From the "Background Statement" by Clinton S. Golden, included in each monograph of the *Causes of Industrial Peace Series* published by the National Planning Association.

24. Charles A. Myers, "Conclusions and Implications," *Fundamentals of Labor Peace—A Final Report* (Washington, D.C.: National Planning Association, December 1953), pp. 93–94.

The National Planning Association attempted to study a representative sample of peaceful relationships. The conditions discussed in the case studies were present in other situations. But the case studies left some questions unanswered. Can peaceful labor-management relations weather severe economic crises? What happens when labor-management peace continues for a long time? How do the employees view these peaceful relationships? Is industrial peace possible only when the environment is favorable? And what is likely to happen when the favorable environment changes?[25] Some of these questions have been answered by Northrup and Young.[26]

Northrup and Young pointed out that the causes of industrial peace listed by the NPA Committee are either "psychological" or they "involve techniques or attitudes." None of the causes is economic.[27] Indeed, they conclude: "The fact is that most of these nine causes are vague and more platitudinal than meaningful. Some are contradictory and others are questionable."[28]

Northrup and Young revisited each plant involved in the twelve original cases some time between 1965 and 1968. Between fifteen and twenty years had thus elapsed between publication of the original case studies and the later review. The findings of the second round of visits are too detailed to be given here.[29]

About half of the companies involved in the NPA studies had experienced severe labor crises since the original reports were published. One of the steel companies involved had experienced two strikes each lasting more than 100 days. In other cases Northrup and Young found a change in formerly cooperative relationships, usually as the result of management turnover. In one case involving a paper company, however, there had been a schism in the union, and the new union, which won bargaining rights, followed more conventional negotiation patterns than the old.

Three of the companies are paper mills, and labor-management relations have been peaceful in these companies. But Northrup and Young attribute this to "the huge investment required in buildings, equipment, and timber reserves; the low capital turnover rate; and the consequently high ratio of fixed costs to total costs. As a result, there is a tremendous pressure on producers to achieve maximum utilization of capital."[30]

In summing up their findings, Northrup and Young concluded that where there was continued industrial peace, it could be explained in economic

25. *Ibid.*, pp. 103–105.

26. Northrup and Young, *op. cit.*, pp. 31–47.

27. *Ibid.*, p. 31.

28. *Ibid.*, p. 43. As noted earlier, however, in his final report on the NPA study, Myers had raised the question: Can peaceful labor-management relations weather severe economic crises?

29. Cf. *ibid.*, pp. 33–43.

30. *Ibid.*, p. 45.

terms. In other cases the old, peaceful relationships broke down, and at times erupted into labor-management warfare.

At the time the original case studies were conducted, the economy was growing rapidly, and labor shortages in industrial areas were not uncommon. The generally favorable economic climate contributed to the peaceful labor-management relations during the period studied. But as economic circumstances changed, as there were turnovers in management and ownership, some of the peaceful relationships were unable to survive. It is fairly clear that the "causes of industrial peace" cannot be accepted as principles to be emulated by companies seeking to avoid labor-management strife. As Northrup and Young[31] stated in concluding:

> The NPA case studies thus stand as interesting histories of particular management-union relationships. Their great value was their attempt to call attention to the constructive aspects of industrial relations and collective bargaining. That they promised much more than they delivered is perhaps symptomatic of the age of prosperity which was their backdrop. The authors—like most of us in that period—failed to comprehend the fleeting nature of the current economic environment and its significance. Because of this failure, the principles enunciated lacked proper sophistication, significance, or generality.

Conclusions

The stages of collective bargaining discussed in this chapter are useful in helping analyze labor-management relations in a wide variety of situations. Not all relationships go through these stages. Some never get beyond the stage of grudging recognition and, in numerous cases, managements have succeeded in keeping unions out of the company by one means or another. In most situations, however, when a union is recognized, there is gradual progress at least to the stage of accommodation. Complete labor-management cooperation and aggressive resistance to unionism are still extremes in the spectrum of labor-management relations. Also, progress is not always in one direction. There have been cases where management has accommodated itself to the union, and the relationship has appeared to be on a sound footing. But, then, for one of a number of reasons—a change in management or union leadership, for example—the relationship deteriorates and goes back to the status of an armed truce. There are also some cases where workers vote to give up their union affiliation. By and large, however, labor-management relations in the United States have been evolutionary. The general pattern has been one of movement from resistance to the union, to recognition, and gradually to acceptance.

---

31. *Ibid.*, p. 47.

Questions and Exercises

1. Describe the stages of collective bargaining.

2. In the "Lennox Case," what assumptions were made by management about the outcome of the union election? What kind of attitude did this lead to in terms of labor-management relations?

3. What did Bakke mean by his concept of "mutual survival"?

4. Does acceptance of a union by management mean the end of "hard" bargaining? Is acceptance of the union synonymous with the "sharing" of management?

5. Union-management cooperation may be said to exist wherever the two parties work *jointly* on one or more phases of the labor-management relationship. According to Shister, what is the objective of this cooperation?

6. Distinguish between union-management cooperation and union-management collusion. Is it true that a large percentage of labor-management agreements in the United States include formal provisions for union-management cooperation?

7. Do profit sharing and union-management cooperation mean the same thing? What are the three general types of profit-sharing programs?

8. About how many deferred profit-sharing plans were in existence in 1972? Has there been much of an increase in profit-sharing over the last quarter century?

9. Do unions typically take the initiative in negotiating profit-sharing schemes? What is the typical attitude of union leaders toward profit-sharing retirement programs?

10. What is the Scanlon Plan? Does the available evidence suggest that the Scanlon Plan can be applied to a wide range of labor-management relations?

11. Where the Scanlon Plan has been adopted, both management and unions often become enthusiastic supporters of this form of labor-management cooperation. What have been some of the obstacles to the more extensive use of this type of program?

12. What led the National Planning Association to establish a Committee on the Causes of Industrial Peace in 1947?

13. In spite of the diversity of the cases studied, there are some causes of industrial peace common to all cases. What were these "causes of industrial peace"?

14. In his final report to the Committee on the Causes of Industrial Peace, Charles Myers raised a number of questions. What are these questions?

15. What were the findings and conclusions of Northrup and Young when they revisited the companies and unions involved in the original *Causes of Industrial Peace* studies?

Suggested Readings

Books

Causes of Industrial Peace Under Collective Bargaining. Washington, D.C.: National Planning Association, Case Studies 1–13, 1948–1953.

Lesieur, Frederick G. (ed.). *The Scanlon Plan . . . A Frontier in Labor-Management Cooperation.* New York: The Technology Press of M.I.T. and John Wiley & Sons, Inc., 1958.

Articles

Dalton, Melville. "Some Pros and Cons of Union-Management Cooperation," *Personnel Administration,* November-December 1965, pp. 3–5, 38–43.

Myers, Charles A. "Conclusions and Implications," *Fundamentals of Labor Peace—A Final Report,* Case Study No. 14, Causes of Industrial Peace Under Collective Bargaining Series. Washington, D.C.: The National Planning Association, 1953.

Northrup, Herbert R., and Harvey A. Young. "The Causes of Industrial Peace Revisited," *Industrial and Labor Relations Review, 22* (October 1968), pp. 31–47.

Porter, Lyman W. "Personnel Management: A Review of the Recent Psychological Literature," *Annual Review of Psychology, 17* (1966), pp. 395–422.

Strauss, George. "Human Relations—1968 Style," *Industrial Relations,* Vol. 7 (May 1968), pp. 262–276.

Sturmthal, Adolf. "Worker's Participation in Management: A Review of the United States Experience," *Bulletin No. 6, Country Study Series.* Geneva: International Institute for Labour Studies, 1969.

19

Nonwage Issues in Collective Bargaining

The list of contract provisions given in Chapter 17 shows that collective bargaining deals with much more than the determination of wages. Increasingly, collective bargaining has been concerned with the "total package" of wages, employee benefits, work rules, supplemental pay practices, and provisions relating to hiring, layoffs, and the recall of workers. Much of this chapter will be concerned with supplemental employee benefits. Not all of these are the result of negotiations; some have been granted unilaterally by employers. Our central concern, however, will be with the nonwage issues involved in collective bargaining.

Supplemental employee payments are referred to by most writers as fringe benefits, although the authors of one of the more comprehensive studies of these payments feel that this term is not descriptive. "Payments that aggregate 20 per cent of total payrolls," they assert, "are decidedly more than incidental"[1] We will see that nonwage benefits now account for a larger proportion of payrolls than they did at the time that Slichter and his colleagues wrote. Also, the use of this term in the present text is due to its familiarity and does not suggest in any way that supplemental benefits are incidental or marginal.

Certain kinds of employee benefits are not of recent origin; some insurance schemes, for example, were negotiated before World War I. But the greatest impetus to the negotiation of employee benefits came during World War II. During that conflict, the Wage Stabilization Board and the Office of Price Administration cooperated to keep wages and prices from rising at a time of acute shortages of manpower and materials. As the war progressed and labor shortages became critical in some areas, however, many employers

---

1. Sumner H. Slichter, James J. Healy, and E. Robert Livernash, *The Impact of Collective Bargaining on Management* (Washington, D.C.: The Brookings Institution, 1960), p. 142.

were more than willing to go along with union demands for benefits with *deferred* payments. This made jobs in their establishments more attractive without creating upward pressure on the wage level at that time. Moreover, the War Labor Board did not object to such agreements. As a result, unions were able to negotiate a number of comprehensive health, welfare, and pension programs. Subsequently, various other kinds of payments for time not worked—such as holiday and vacation pay—were negotiated.

Worker Preferences for Deferred Payments

It has generally been assumed that workers prefer wage increases to deferred payments of various kinds. "Studies, however, indicate that workers often strongly desire to take at least part of any gains in compensation in the form of certain insurance-type benefits"[2] To some extent workers' preferences depend upon the average age of the work force. During the mid-1950s, for example, there was a substantial increase in negotiated fringe benefits. At that time the newly born electronics industry was beginning to expand rapidly in various parts of the country. Both management and the work force in the new electronics companies were young, and employees exhibited little interest in deferred payments. As some of the larger firms in the industry were organized, however, unions followed the standard pattern of negotiating both wage increases and fringe-benefit improvements.

Lester analyzed a number of studies designed to elicit information from workers about their preferences for present wage increases vs. expanded deferred payments. His study showed that, in general, workers prefer a combination of wage increases and deferred payments. Lester also found that "union influence appears to be a factor tending to strengthen worker preference for benefits, resulting in a higher benefit-to-wages mix under collective bargaining."[3] Lester feels that workers value benefit payments more highly than their employers believe they do. This finding, if verified by other studies, could have important implications for wage and bargaining theory.[4]

The Cost of the Fringe-Benefit Package

The U.S. Chamber of Commerce has conducted a biennial survey of fringe benefits since 1949. The 1969 survey showed that for a constant sample of companies, combined benefit costs had increased 77 per cent from 1949 to 1969. According to the survey, fringe payments in 1969 amounted to 31.7 per

---

2. Richard A. Lester, "Benefits as a Preferred Form of Compensation," *The Southern Economic Journal, XXXIII* (April 1967), p. 48.

3. *Ibid.*, p. 494.

4. *Ibid.*

cent of payroll costs, compared with 25.6 per cent of total payrolls in 1959. Of the 31.7 per cent in 1969, 5.4 per cent consisted of legally required payments. The remainder consisted of pensions (10.9 per cent), sick leave and vacations (10.6 per cent), paid holidays and rest periods (3.1 per cent), and profit sharing and bonuses (1.7 per cent).

The average cost of deferred payments in the Chamber of Commerce sample was $2,052 in 1969. These figures support the view advanced by Lester about the revealed preferences of workers for deferred payments. One union, the International Association of Machinists, has made effective use of the Chamber of Commerce study. According to a business publication, it sent copies of the results of the survey to all locals with the question: "Did you get your $2,052 last year in fringe benefits?"[5]

Private Pension Plan

Most workers in the United States today are eligible for Social Security retirement payments starting at age 65—or 62 if they prefer. These benefits were summarized in Chapter 16. In addition, however, about 21 million workers were covered by some form of private pension plan at the end of 1969. This represented an increase of 40 per cent over the 15 million workers who had been covered in 1960. The number of workers covered by private pension plans grew more slowly during the 1960s than during the previous decade, when coverage more than doubled. Moreover, "growth during the 1960s was primarily attributable to increased employment in firms that already had private pension plans; during the 1950s growth resulted largely from the introduction of new plans."[6] As a consequence of the different growth rates in these two decades, worker coverage under private pension plans was relatively stable during the 1960s and amounted to about one third of employment in the private nonfarm sector of the economy.

About 66 per cent of plant workers and 76 per cent of office workers in metropolitan areas were covered by private pension plans in 1960. By 1970, 77 per cent of plant workers and 84 per cent of office workers were covered by such plans. Some plans require worker contributions, but most are noncontributory, that is, financed entirely by employers. In 1960, 54 per cent of metropolitan area workers were covered by noncontributory plans. By 1970, about 65 per cent were covered by pension plans paid for entirely by employers.[7]

Although coverage under private pension plans was relatively stable during the 1960s, there were a number of changes in the character of the

---

5. *Business Week,* December 12, 1970, p. 90.

6. A. E. Davis and Arnold Strasser, "Private Pension Plans, 1960–1969—An Overview," *Monthly Labor Review,* July 1970, p. 45.

7. Lester L. Petermann, "Fringe Benefits of Urban Workers," *Monthly Labor Review,* November 1971, p. 43.

plans, particularly toward the end of the decade. Benefit formulas were liberalized, and early retirement provisions were added to a number of plans. By the end of 1969, "more than three-fourths of the workers were in plans that had a vesting provision and more than nine out of ten with vesting, early retirement or both."[8] To be eligible for these provisions, particularly for vesting, workers had to meet certain age and service requirements. In plans covering 45 per cent of the workers, vesting applied only to those who had been employed by the firm for five to ten years; and 80 per cent of all workers were covered by plans that provided for vesting after periods of employment ranging from five to fifteen years. In addition, in many plans vesting is conditional; it depends upon the type of termination of service. In some cases workers have nonforfeitable rights to their pensions only if their service is terminated by a layoff or other factor beyond the worker's control.[9] Other plans, however, provide for full vesting after specified minimum service requirements have been met. Under these plans, workers are entitled to the retirement benefits that have accrued to them, even if they should voluntarily leave the employ of the company before retirement. Some economists favor the full vesting of all private pension plans on the grounds that forfeiture of accrued pension rights is a barrier to voluntary labor mobility. There is also an equity argument in favor of full vesting. Union spokesmen point out that workers with private pension rights have earned those rights. In general, union leaders believe that workers have a property right in accrued pension benefits.

Vacation and Holiday Pay

Before World War II, only about one fourth of the organized labor force received paid vacations, and in most cases the maximum was one week.[10] By 1953, however, a study by the National Industrial Conference Board showed that 99 per cent of the manufacturing companies and 97 per cent of the nonmanufacturing companies they contacted granted paid vacations.[11] The length of paid vacations also has been increasing.

A 1970 study by the Bureau of Labor Statistics shows a substantial increase in "time off with pay" practices during the 1960s. Although this study was limited to workers in metropolitan areas, many of the results no doubt apply to workers in smaller communities. The sample covered by this study was relatively large—about 14 million plant workers and more than 4 million

---

8. Davis and Strasser, *op. cit.*, p. 45.

9. *Ibid.*, p. 64.

10. Slichter *et al.*, *op. cit.*, p. 426.

11. National Industrial Conference Board, *Fringe Benefit Packages,* Studies in Personnel Policy, No. 143 (1954), pp. 8–9.

office workers. And the sample was stratified by industry and region to ensure representative coverage.[12]

The average number of paid holidays increased from 6.9 in 1960 to 7.8 in 1970 for plant workers, and from 7.8 to 8.4 for office workers. Most of the increases were negotiated during the second half of the decade. Another trend discerned by this study was that toward longer weekends and "floating holidays." If a major holiday falls on Tuesday, for example, the preceding Monday also may be considered a holiday. Similarly, if a holiday falls on Thursday, workers may be given Friday off with pay as well. There is considerable variation in the number of paid holidays by industry. The largest number of paid holidays are found in manufacturing and public utilities, and the smallest in retail trade establishments. There is also considerable regional variation, with the largest number of paid holidays in the Northeast and the smallest in the South.[13]

By 1960, paid vacations were almost universal, and there was a discernible trend toward longer paid vacations during the 1960s. In both 1960 and 1970, for example, more than 95 per cent of plant workers and 99 per cent of office workers received two weeks or more of paid vacation after five years of service. But in 1960, only 74 per cent of plant workers and 82 per cent of office workers were entitled to three or more weeks after fifteen years. By 1970, these percentages had increased to 83 and 92 respectively. Similarly, in 1960, 22 per cent of plant workers and 33 per cent of office workers were entitled to four weeks or more of paid vacation after 25 years of service. By 1970, there had been an increase to 59 per cent for plant workers and 73 per cent for office workers.[14] At the end of the 1960s, paid vacations for long-service workers in some industries, notably steel and autos, were so long they were at times referred to as "furloughs."

Premium Pay Practices

Before the Fair Labor Standards Act was passed in 1938, it was not typical for workers to be paid at premium rates for overtime. The law now specifies that workers are to be paid at the rate of time and one half for all hours in excess of forty in *each* work week. But in some industries unions have negotiated standard work weeks of less than forty hours, and premium pay in these industries begins as soon as the standard number of hours agreed upon has been reached. The law does not specify how the hours are to be spread throughout the week; it only indicates that each work week must stand alone —that there may be no averaging of hours worked over two or more weeks.

---

12. Petermann, *op. cit.*

13. *Ibid.*, p. 42.

14. *Ibid.*, pp. 42–43.

Many agreements call for premium pay for work on Saturdays or Sundays, even if this falls within the forty-hour limit, and some call for premium pay on the sixth or seventh day worked as such. It is also typical for workers to be paid at premium rates if they are required to work on holidays.

Approximately three fourths of the manufacturing firms included in the National Industrial Conference Board's survey provide for shift differentials. Fewer than one third of the nonmanufacturing firms in the sample follow this practice, however. Generally speaking, shift differentials are not large. There is a tendency for third-shift differentials to be slightly above those called for on second shifts. Studies by the Bureau of Labor Statistics indicate a growing trend toward payment of shift differentials in manufacturing but, according to the BLS, this trend has been proceeding much more slowly in nonmanufacturing.

Shift practices vary widely from industry to industry, so any summary statement would be quite unrepresentative. Industries such as steel, which operate round the clock, tend to have standard shifts with premium payments in terms of cents per hour. Other industries generally operate on a single-shift basis, although a second shift might be added if there is a sudden upsurge in production. Some industries work only one shift, but vary hours as necessary in order to meet production schedules. It is only in those industries where second and third shifts are fairly common that premium pay for such work is important.

A majority of agreements covering manufacturing firms and many of those pertaining to nonmanufacturing establishments provide for call-in pay or reporting pay, which means either that workers are paid extra if they have to be called to the job rather than reporting at a scheduled time, or that workers who report and find no work available that day are paid something for reporting.

Insurance Plans

There is more variation in negotiated insurance plans than in any other type of fringe benefit. By 1970, most workers in metropolitan areas—both in plants and in offices—were covered by life, accident, and hospitalization insurance. Many were covered by contributory plans, although an increasing proportion are now covered by noncontributory insurance schemes. In 1960, for example, about half of all workers in metropolitan areas were covered by noncontributory life insurance plans, and this proportion had increased to two thirds by 1970.

A smaller number of workers are covered by accident insurance. Only two thirds of the plant workers in metropolitan areas had accident insurance coverage in 1970, and 47 per cent were covered by noncontributory plans. About the same proportion of office workers had accident insurance, but only 39 per cent were under noncontributory plans.

More than 90 per cent of all metropolitan workers—plant and office—
were covered by hospitalization insurance in 1970, but only two thirds of the
plant workers and slightly more than half of the office workers were covered
by noncontributory programs These percentages do not change substantially
with respect to surgical insurance. A smaller number of workers are covered
by medical insurance schemes, particularly noncontributory plans. In 1970,
about one third of plant workers and 45 per cent of office workers were covered by noncontributory, major medical insurance.

Only a minority of plant workers are entitled to sick leave. In 1960, for
example, 13 per cent of all plant workers in metropolitan areas were entitled
to full pay during a spell of illness. An additional 10 per cent received partial
pay or received pay only following a waiting period. By 1970, 21 per cent of
plant workers were entitled to full pay with no waiting period, and an additional 12 per cent received partial pay or were paid only after a waiting period.
Office workers have had more extensive sick leave coverage. In 1960, 59
per cent received full pay without a waiting period and an additional 8 per
cent were entitled to partial pay or were paid after a waiting period. By 1970,
64 per cent of all office workers received full pay with no waiting period, while
10 per cent were entitled to partial pay or to some pay after a waiting period.

The trends in time off with pay, and the liberalized insurance plans
discussed above, indicate why the fringe-benefit package has become an
increasingly important part of worker compensation and of employers' labor
cost. The Institute for the Future has estimated that by 1985, the fringe-
benefit package will amount to about 50 per cent of total payroll cost.[15] In
view of the trends of the past two decades, this is not an unrealistic projection. And as Livernash has pointed out, this will lead to "future interplay
between private and public provision of benefits." The proportion of the
population not covered by private benefits is becoming smaller but it "is also
becoming far more conspicuous and deprived. Pressure for public benefits
can be expected to mount steadily to alleviate this differential condition."[16]

Guaranteed Annual Wages and Supplementary Unemployment Payments

For a brief time—in 1955 and 1956—there was a flurry of activity in contract
negotiations involving supplementary unemployment compensation. Most
stories in the press discussed the unions' demands for a "guaranteed annual
wage," although that is neither what unions were seeking at the time nor is
it what some unions eventually negotiated. It should be noted that long before,
some companies had adopted guaranteed annual wage plans on their

---

15. E. Robert Livernash, "Wages and Benefits," *A Review of Industrial Relations Research,
Vol. I*, (Madison, Wisconsin: Industrial Relations Research Association, 1970), pp. 120–121.
16. *Ibid.*, p. 121.

own initiative; notable among these are the Procter and Gamble plan adopted in 1923, and the Hormel and Nunn-Bush plans started in the early 1930s.

Guaranteed Annual Wages

The notion of annual wage guarantees is not a new one, although only a small minority of unions have negotiated such agreements. The first guaranteed annual wage was negotiated by the Wallpaper Craftsmen and the National Wallpaper Company in 1894. Between then and 1921, about 15 similar plans were negotiated in the wallpaper industry and between the Brewery Workers Union and various brewers in the Philadelphia area. The total number of workers covered was relatively small, however, and this new union demand made little headway or little impression outside the few firms involved. The issue was revived during the Great Depression, however, and a provision of the Fair Labor Standards Act (Section 7) exempted from overtime pay requirements employers who had a union agreement to provide employment on an annual or semiannual basis. Few firms, except some in highly seasonal industries, have taken advantage of this provision, however.

During World War II, the United Steel Workers tried to negotiate a guaranteed annual wage. The War Labor Board denied their request but recommended that the issue be studied. Such a study, referred to as the Latimer Report after its author, Murray W. Latimer, was subsequently made and published in 1947.[17] The Latimer Report viewed guaranteed wage plans favorably and recommended that they be tied to the federal-state program of unemployment insurance. There was little response to this, however. A survey made by the Bureau of Labor Statistics in 1952 showed that fewer than 1 per cent of all collective bargaining agreements contained a wage guarantee provision.

Supplemental Unemployment Benefits

Actually, not many unions were seeking the kind of guaranteed annual wages that have been established by some firms in seasonal industries such as shoe manufacturing and meat packing. In an industry with fairly predictable annual demand, but with wide seasonal swings, it can be to the advantage of both workers and management to agree on a fixed number of weeks of employment per year. In the unlikely event that the company cannot provide this much employment, it still agrees to pay the workers for a stated number of weeks. By carefully planning its production, the company can estimate its labor requirements closely. It is not faced with the inconvenience and

---

17. Office of War Mobilization and Reconversion, *Guaranteed Wages* (Washington, D.C.: U.S. Government Printing Office, 1947).

added cost of laying off workers during slack seasons, and recalling (or trying to recall) them when business picks up seasonally. Given such circumstances, a guaranteed annual wage works well. In nonseasonal industries, however, unions have pressed for employer-financed supplementary unemployment compensation.

Under the federal-state system of unemployment compensation, unemployment insurance benefits are determined by state legislators. During the early years of the unemployment insurance program, average benefits amounted to almost 45 per cent of the wages earned during the base periods used to compute benefit amounts. But average wages have gone up steadily, and while there have been increases in unemployment benefits, they have lagged far behind the increase in wages. By 1955, for example, average unemployment benefits amounted to about one third of the average base period wage level.

Union leaders insisted that because benefits had lagged behind the rising wage level they were inadequate. Most favored liberalization of payments under the federal-state unemployment insurance program, but some went beyond this and began to press for supplemental unemployment payments by industry. This became one of the most widely publicized bargaining issues of the mid-1950s.

Union spokesmen argued that employer-financed supplements to unemployment compensation would help stabilize the economy by maintaining purchasing power during periods of recession. Employers countered with the argument that by raising labor costs, supplementary unemployment compensation would be self-defeating—it would simply contribute to more unemployment. Commenting on this issue early in 1955, Slichter pointed out that supplementary unemployment compensation in the automobile industry—which would increase the total benefits of unemployed workers to about two thirds of their straight-time weekly earnings—would be roughly equivalent to a 5 per cent wage increase. And, as he noted, there would have been relatively little alarm about a demand for a wage increase of this magnitude.[18]

Slichter did not favor the guaranteed annual wage, largely because he felt it would have injurious effects upon weak firms during recession periods. In his opinion a far more desirable objective, which he thought both unions and management should support, would be to increase unemployment insurance benefits. He suggested that unemployment benefits should amount to about 50 per cent of average wages. Slichter felt this objective would have a number of advantages over negotiated supplementary unemployment payment plans; among other things, it would pool risks without imposing any hardship upon weak firms. However, demands for supplementary unemployment agreements persisted and, in 1955, a number of plans were negotiated.

---

18. Sumner H. Slichter, "Guaranteed Annual Wage—A Dubious Approach to a Desirable Objective," *Barron's*, April 11, 1955.

Supplemental unemployment benefit (SUB) programs were negotiated in the automobile, the farm equipment, the can manufacturing, and the flat-glass industries in 1955.[19] A similar plan covering workers in the merchant marine also went into effect that year, and there were scattered agreements with other firms in durable-goods manufacturing industries. The following year, supplemental unemployment compensation plans spread to the basic steel industry and to the "Big Four" rubber manufacturing firms. By the end of 1956, about 2 million workers were covered by such plans. The debate over supplemental unemployment compensation did not spread widely after the initial plans had been accepted by some companies. A decade after the first SUB plan was negotiated, only 14 per cent of all major agreements contained such a plan. And by 1967, only 2.6 million workers—or 14 per cent of union members in the United States—were covered by supplemental unemployment benefits.[20]

Two kinds of supplemental unemployment plans were negotiated: the *savings* plan and the *insurance* plan.[21] *Savings* plans were instituted in the glass industry. Under this type of plan, each worker has a personal account to which the employer contributes. Payments by the employer to the individual accounts are considered as part of wages. If a worker is temporarily laid off because of slack business or illness he may draw on his account Typically, a ceiling is imposed on the account and, once the company's contribution has reached this amount, the payments are stopped—or perhaps diverted to other fringe benefits such as vacation pay. Slichter has pointed out that "the savings plans are fundamentally a conventional economic device; it is simply a way by which all employees automatically save a part of a wage increase. And there is no new fundamental economic issue."[22]

The *insurance* plan of supplemental unemployment benefits was the one adopted by most unions and companies negotiating such programs—outside of the flat-glass industry. Under the savings plan, the employer contributions are considered as part of wages, and employers are required to pay the unemployment insurance tax on these contributions. Under insurance plans, however, the employers' contributions are considered as part of welfare costs and are nontaxable. The first insurance plan adopted was negotiated by the United Auto Workers and the Ford Motor Company, and it set the pattern for the others that followed. Under this plan, coverage was limited to workers with a certain amount of seniority in the company. Supplemental compensation payments did not begin until a one-week waiting period had

---

19. For a chronology of the early plans, see Joseph M. Becker, *Guaranteed Income for the Unemployed* (Baltimore: The Johns Hopkins Press, 1968), pp. 23–47; 138–141.

20. E. Robert Livernash, "Wages and Benefits," in *A Review of Industrial Relations Research, Vol. I* (Madison, Wisconsin: Industrial Relations Research Association, 1970), p. 124.

21. Sumner H. Slichter, "SUB Plans—Their Economic Impact," *Management Record,* National Industrial Conference Board, February 1956.

22. *Ibid.*

elapsed. Payments were limited to a maximum of twenty-six weeks. More important, payments were also limited by the position of the trust fund and the number of "credits" held by each worker. The company contribution, which was set at five cents per hour worked by each employee subject to the plan, continued until the trust fund reached a stated maximum. Benefit payments were not made from this fund during the first year following the agreement.

During the following decade, SUB plans were modified and liberalized. In some cases, benefits were extended to one year or longer. In 1967 and 1968, benefits granted under some plans were increased substantially. In the rubber industry, for example, benefits were increased to 80 per cent of *gross* pay. And in the auto industry, benefits were raised to 95 per cent of after-tax wages less $7.50 per week.[23]

There were several legal obstacles to be overcome before supplemental unemployment compensation plans became operative. First, it was necessary to obtain state rulings on the integration of supplemental payments and unemployment insurance. Union leaders regard supplemental unemployment payments as deferred wages—something that the worker has earned and to which he has a right. But if they are "wages," as this word is used in most state unemployment laws, can unemployed workers legally draw unemployment benefits? Since most state laws relate benefits to the employment status of a worker, however, the majority of states that took action on this question permitted supplemental payments while an unemployed worker was drawing unemployment compensation. By the time the initial one-year waiting period had been reached, it was clear that this legal obstacle had been successfully hurdled.

It was also necessary for the Internal Revenue Service to decide whether supplemental unemployment benefits were "wages" for tax purposes. The Service ruled that the worker who received such benefits had to include them in his total income for tax purposes, and also that such payments were business costs deductible from company income taxes. Finally, the Wage and Hour and Public Contracts Divisions of the U.S. Department of Labor ruled that companies need not contribute to supplemental unemployment compensation trust funds on the basis of overtime earnings. Since such payments are made to an irrevocable trust fund, they are exempt under Section 7(d)(4) of the Fair Labor Standards Act.

There was some concern when SUB plans first went into operation about their potential impact on the economy. Some writers argued that workers would prefer compensated idleness to unemployment. Others, including Slichter, pointed out that the plans negotiated in 1955 provided payments that amounted to about two thirds of average earnings. Slichter doubted that workers would be willing to forego one third of their income for

---

23. *Ibid.,* pp. 125–126.

an extended "paid vacation."[24] Since benefits were liberalized in the late 1960s, however, some of the early concern has been expressed again. "This degree of liberalization appeared to break an original principle stated by the Ford Motor Company not to weaken the incentive to work."[25]

A new question of "inverse seniority" also has been raised by SUB. Some union spokesmen have suggested that senior employees with full SUB protection be the first to be laid off during periods of recession. This would allow short-service workers, many of whom would not be covered by SUB, to remain on the job.[26] This proposal should appeal to workers, both those who would remain on the job and those who would in effect be getting an extended "paid vacation." But if inverse seniority were widely practiced, it could lead to a variant of the "staggered employment" practice by some New England textile mills during the period of protracted decline in textile employment of the early 1950s.[27] One consequence of staggered employment was that an excessive number of workers became "attached" to the declining textile industry. The widespread practice of inverse seniority could lead to similar conditions in other industries where SUB plans are prevalent.

Work Rules

During the early days of collective bargaining, union demands were largely limited to wages, hours, and working conditions. The latter dealt principally with such matters as workers' safety and sanitation. Subsequently, the emphasis shifted to employee benefits, which became one of the important aspects of collective bargaining during the 1960s. Another important matter in collective bargaining, since about 1955, has been the broad issue of work rules, and there have been numerous labor-management disputes over work rules and working conditions since then.

Work rules are one of the inevitable results of the system of "industrial jurisprudence" which has emerged under collective bargaining in the United States. Work rules cover a wide variety of matters such as work schedules, work speeds, and production methods. Rules have been evolved covering machine assignments; assembly-line speeds; time standards and work quotas under incentive systems; crew sizes; and various work methods. Other rules govern the introduction of new machinery or other technological changes,

---

24. *Ibid.*

25. Livernash, *op. cit.,* p. 126.

26. *Ibid.*

27. Under this arrangement two workers held one job. While one was employed, his alternate would draw unemployment compensation. When the unemployed worker had exhausted his benefit rights he would return to the mill, and the company would lay off his alternate, who would draw unemployment compensation. For further details see William H. Miernyk, *Inter-Industry Labor Mobility* (Boston: Northeastern University, Bureau of Business and Economic Research, 1954), p. 72.

the transfer of workers following technological change, and the impact of such changes on worker earnings.

Few issues in collective bargaining are as complex as those dealing with work rules, and few have led to as much public misunderstanding. Such issues as wage increases, holiday and vacation pay, and the hours to be worked before overtime pay is started are fairly straightforward. They can be understood by anyone, although there can be disagreement over them. But many observers are puzzled by the union position in which union leaders insist on having something to say about work assignments, job transfers, retraining, and similar matters which have been generally considered as employer prerogatives. Does this mean that unions are trying "to take over the front office"? Is it an attempt on the part of union leaders to take an active part in the management of businesses? Union leaders insist that this would be a misinterpretation. They readily acknowledge that work rules limit management's freedom to take unilateral action, but work rules are not negotiated, they assert, to interfere with the management of the firm.[29] The entire program of work rules, as Slichter put it, represents the unions' attempt to introduce civil rights into the work place.

Adding to the complexity of the work rules issue are the frequent charges that such rules lead to "make-work" or "featherbedding" practices. These have become emotionally charged words. Their injection into debates over attempts by either party to make—or to change—work rules have usually led only to further confusion about this aspect of collective bargaining.[30]

How did the practice of negotiating provisions dealing with work rules come into collective bargaining? And what has been the general attitude of unions and managements toward these rules? Perhaps better than anything else, work rules illustrate the evolutionary nature of the collective bargaining process. It is not at all likely that the early unions looked forward to a time when they would have an important voice in such matters as machine assignments, job transfers, the pace of assembly lines, and similar matters now frequently the subject of negotiations. Yet as the position of unions became more secure, their members became increasingly interested in job security.

The principle of seniority was introduced into collective bargaining fairly early and is now incorporated into most agreements.[31] Some work rules are closely tied to the seniority system and are designed to protect the secur-

---

29. For a general discussion of management rights, see Charles C. Killingsworth, "Management Rights Revisited," in Gerald G. Somers (ed.), *Arbitration and Social Change* (Washington, D.C.: Bureau of National Affairs, 1969), pp. 1–19.

30. Restrictions on output are not limited to organized workers. For a graphic account of the limitation of output among unorganized workers, see Stanley B. Mathewson, "Restriction of Output Among Unorganized Workers," in Paul A. Weinstein (ed.), *Featherbedding and Technological Change* (Lexington, Mass.: D. C. Heath and Company, 1965), pp. 2–11.

31. See Frederic Meyers, "The Analytic Meaning of Seniority," in *Proceedings*, Eighteenth Annual Meeting, Industrial Relations Research Association, 1965, pp. 194–202.

ity of workers when they become older and find it more difficult to obtain new employment if laid off. Other work rules were developed as protection against employer "speedups" and deal with such matters as machine assignments and the general pace of the job. Among the most important work rules are those designed to protect the worker against sudden and unexpected technological change. It is these—more than any others—which have led to the charges of featherbedding and make-work.[32]

Many rules governing working conditions, such as those concerned with safety, sanitation, and such matters as heating and lighting, appear to make sense to all concerned. The worker gains added peace of mind if safety hazards are removed, and the employer's liability is also diminished. A worker who can concentrate on his job in reasonable physical comfort is likely to be more productive than one who is too hot, too cold, cramped, or otherwise uncomfortable. Good working conditions generally stimulate productivity, and both labor and management benefit from this. The big disagreement— the one the public appears to have the greatest difficulty in understanding— comes over rules which appear to have an effect upon output.

In popular discussion, no distinction is made between "make-work rules" and "featherbedding," but students of industrial relations often make such a distinction. One classification, developed by Morris Horowitz, is discussed here.[33] Under the general heading of "make-work" rules, Horowitz includes the following:

1. Regulating the number of men per machine or per crew. This would include work rules and practices limiting the number of workers on a single task or a specific machine.
2. Stand-by crews. This includes all rules that require the employment of workers regardless of need.
3. Requiring time-consuming methods of work or requiring that unnecessary work be done.
4. Limiting daily or weekly output, or the speed of work.
5. Requiring that work be performed by a specific craft or occupation. This category includes rules that specify in detail the work of each craft or occupation on the job and penalize employers for any error in assignment.

---

32. Featherbedding is discussed within the framework of conventional economic analysis by Paul A. Weinstein in "Featherbedding: A Theoretical Analysis," in Weinstein, *op. cit.*, pp. 44–54; and by Norman J. Simler, "The Economics of Featherbedding," *idem.*, pp. 55–65. Some of the legal and institutional issues involved are discussed by William Gomberg, "The Work Rules and Work Practices Problem," *idem*, pp. 109–121.

33. Morris A. Horowitz, *Manpower Utilization in the Railroad Industry—An Analysis of Working Rules and Practices* (Boston: Northeastern University, Bureau of Business and Economic Research, 1960), pp. 6–7.

Under the general heading of "featherbedding" rules, Horowitz includes the following:

1. Requiring the payment of extra compensation for no extra work.
2. Requiring the payment of compensation for time spent not working, or for work not performed.
3. Wage guarantees. This includes rules that guarantee a specific minimum amount of compensation per unit of time, regardless of the amount of work performed in that time.

There can be some overlapping—that is, some rules could fall in either category or partly in both. On the whole, however, work rules that impinge in some way upon output or productivity can be classified under one or the other of these main headings. It is important to emphasize that not all work rules are of the "make-work" or "featherbedding" varieties. There are rules that call for work-sharing during slack times, for example, and these must be clearly distinguished from make-work or featherbedding rules, since they do not directly increase the employer's cost. There are many other work rules which protect the security of workers without impinging on output and productivity, and there are some rules dealing with the installation of machinery—or more generally with worker adjustment to technological change—which may or may not have make-work effects. The latter are of particular interest, since it is such work rules that have been at issue in a number of major labor-management disputes in recent years.

Work Rules and Technological Change

More than two decades ago, Sumner H. Slichter made a careful study of union policies toward technological change. His findings are still relevant today.[34] Slichter classified union policies toward technological change into three broad categories: (1) the policy of obstruction, (2) the policy of competition, and (3) the policy of control.

The policy of obstruction, Slichter points out, can be nothing more than a temporary expedient. By preventing the adoption of new processes in organized plants, unions can slow down the rate of technological change. However, if the industry is only partly organized, nonunion plants can adopt the innovations and increase their competitive advantage over unionized plants. Even in highly organized industries, obstruction can only delay— not halt—the installation of new machines or processes. Union leaders have

---

34. Sumner H. Slichter, *Union Policies and Industrial Management* (Washington, D.C.: The Brookings Institution, 1941), pp. 201–281. For a more recent discussion, which includes union acceptance and encouragement of technological change, see Slichter, Healy, and Livernash, *Impact of Collective Bargaining, op. cit.,* pp. 342–371.

long recognized that obstructionist tactics cannot succeed in the long run. Thus most unions, instead of obstructing technological change, have either tried to compete with it or to control it.

At times unions have tried to compete with technological change by liberalizing work rules. When the development of automatic machinery has threatened jobs, some unions have made concessions to employers such as permitting them to operate second or third shifts and accepting cuts in piece rates. This policy might be adopted if there have been substantial job displacements in an industry or if there is a surplus of workers in a particular craft or occupation. Rarely do union leaders believe that the policy of competition can halt technological change. On the other hand, it can slow down the rate at which machines are introduced, and if concessions are made to employers, it can increase the amount of employment on a temporary basis. The hope is that older workers can be kept on the job until they reach retirement age. Then, through gradual attrition, the number of workers in the craft or occupation can be reduced, and younger workers can adapt to the changes without fear of mass unemployment.

The policy of competition, like that of obstruction, is a short-run expedient. Most union leaders recognize this and, in dealing with technological change, they lean toward the policy of control. "In general terms the policy of control simply means that the union seeks to make working conditions and wages on the jobs created by the new technique a matter of agreement between employers and the union."[35] Provisions dealing with the control of technological change vary widely from industry to industry and even among the companies within an industry. In general, unions try to see that workers displaced from jobs through technological change are reassigned to other jobs without loss of earnings. Because there is always a great deal of turnover, with new workers being hired even in declining industries, it is hoped that displaced workers can be absorbed without interfering with the efficiency of the company and without loss to themselves. Slichter believed that the policy of control tended to "promote a more effective utilization of the nation's labor force by requiring employers to transfer and train older employees who otherwise would be laid off."[36] The policy of control has an advantage over other union tactics, since it does not slow down the rate of technological change and thus does not interfere with output or improvements in productivity. But it does impose limits on the employer's freedom to lay off workers displaced by machines. The employer, who will gain from the increased productivity of the new method, is asked to help bear the cost of technological change. Moreover, the union insists on its right to protect the job security of its members—particularly where this does not lead to interference with technological progress.

---

35. Slichter, *Union Policies,* p. 241.
36. *Ibid.,* p. 279.

It is worth repeating that all work rules do not impinge upon output or productivity. As Jack Stieber has pointed out, even "so-called make-work rules, featherbedding and other restrictive practices may, on investigation, turn out to have a sound basis. Like so many other issues which seem to be quite clear on the surface, there are usually two sides to the argument over specific make-work practices."[37] Stieber quotes, with approval, Slichter's[38] attitude toward the complex issue of work rules:

> It is not always easy to determine when a union is "making work." There are some clear cases, such as those in which the union requires the work to be done twice, but the mere fact that the union limits the output of men, or controls the quantity of the work (with effects upon output), regulates the size of crew or the number of machines per man, or prohibits the use of labor-saving devices, does not in itself mean that the union is "making work." In such cases it is necessary to apply a rule of reason and to determine whether the limits are unreasonable. Opinions as to what is reasonable are bound to differ, but failure to apply a rule of reason would be to accept the employers' requirements, no matter how harsh and extreme, as the proper standard.

Specific practices of flagrant featherbedding are often spotlighted in popular discussion of the work-rules issue. No objective student would deny that there are instances where work practices have led to increases in labor costs or to restrictions of output. The extent of actual "make-work" or "featherbedding" practices has undoubtedly been exaggerated, however. As Slichter showed more than two decades ago, unions do not as a general rule try to obstruct technological change or to impose uneconomic work rules on employers. There are exceptions to this, but they should be recognized as exceptions rather than the general rule. Finally, it should be noted that unions have often encouraged employers to make technological changes when the competitive position of a plant or even of an entire industry has been threatened.[39]

Questions and Exercises

1. Why was there a substantial increase in the number of fringe benefits negotiated during World War II?

2. When given a choice between increased wages and an increase in de-

---

37. Jack Stieber, "Non-wage aspects of Collective Bargaining," *Business Topics*, Michigan State University, Graduate School of Business Administration, Spring 1960, p. 31. One of the more widely publicized work-rules disputes has gone on for years between the railroads and the operating crafts. For a discussion of some of the issues involved and efforts to deal with them, see William H. Miernyk, *Trade Unions in the Age of Affluence* (New York: Random House, 1962), pp. 119–121.

38. Slichter, *Union Policies,* pp. 165–166.

39. Slichter, Healy, and Livernash, *op. cit.,* pp. 355–361.

ferred payments, have workers indicated a strong preference for present over future income? According to Lester, what effect have unions had on the benefit-to-wages mix under collective bargaining?

3. During the 1960s, the number of workers covered by private pension plans increased from about 15 million to about 21 million. Does this mean that there was a substantial increase in the number of new pension plans negotiated during that decade?

4. Is it true, in general, that private pension plans do not provide for either early retirement or vesting?

5. Briefly, describe trends in vacation and holiday pay during the 1960s.

6. Is it customary for workers in metropolitan areas to be covered by insurance plans? What types of insurance plans have unions negotiated? Is there a trend toward more or fewer noncontributory insurance schemes in metropolitan areas?

7. What is the difference between (1) a guaranteed annual wage and (2) a supplemental unemployment benefit? Why did some unions press for supplemental unemployment benefit (SUB) plans in the mid-1950s when a federal-state unemployment compensation system already existed?

8. What are the two types of supplemental unemployment plans? Which type has become most prevalent? Were there any legal obstacles to be overcome before supplemental unemployment plans could be implemented?

9. What has happened to benefit payments under SUB plans in recent years? Was this the intent of the companies that agreed to supplemental unemployment benefit plans in the mid-1950s?

10. What is meant by "inverse seniority"? Why has inverse seniority been suggested by some unions? What effect could widespread adoption of inverse seniority have on the number of workers attached to an industry?

11. Some writers have argued that work rules are an inevitable result of a system of "industrial jurisprudence," such as has emerged under collective bargaining in the United States. What is the basis of this argument?

12. Why do union contracts include a seniority clause?

13. Does the negotiation of work rules imply that unions are trying to take over some of management's functions?

14. Is it possible to distinguish between make-work rules and featherbedding? If so, what is the distinction between them?

15. What attitudes have unions adopted toward technological change?

16. Is it true that all work rules impinge in some way upon output or productivity?

17. According to Slichter, is it always easy to determine when a union is "making work"?

Suggested Readings

Becker, Joseph M. *Guaranteed Income for the Unemployed.* Baltimore: Johns Hopkins Press, 1968.

National Commission on Technology, Automation, and Economic Progress. *Technology and the American Economy.* Washington, D.C.: U.S. Government Printing Office, 1966.

Weinstein, Paul A., (ed.). *Featherbedding and Technological Change.* Lexington, Mass.: D. C. Heath and Company, 1965.

Articles

Beier, Emerson. "Incidence of Private Retirement Plans," *Monthly Labor Review,* July 1971, pp. 37–40.

Burck, Gilbert. "That Ever Expanding Pension Balloon," *Fortune,* October 1971, pp. 100 ff.

Davis, Harry E. "Growth of Benefits in a Cohort of Pension Plans," *Monthly Labor Review,* May 1971, pp. 46–50.

Killingsworth, Charles C. "Management Rights Revisited," in Gerald Somers (ed.), *Arbitration and Social Change.* Washington, D.C.: Bureau of National Affairs, 1969, pp. 1–19.

Lester, Richard A. "Benefits as a Preferred Form of Compensation," *The Southern Economic Journal, XXXIII* (April 1967), pp. 488–495.

Livernash, E. Robert. "Wages and Benefits," *A Review of Industrial Relations Research, Vol. 1.* Madison, Wisconsin: Industrial Relations Research Association, 1970, pp. 79–144.

20

The Structure of Collective Bargaining

Earlier chapters have discussed the process of collective bargaining, the content of labor-management agreements, stages of collective bargaining, and the issues involved in typical labor-management negotiations. This chapter is concerned with the diversity of bargaining relationships.

Much of what the public hears about collective bargaining involves the giants of industry and organized labor. When the United Auto Workers negotiate with General Motors, or when the United Steelworkers negotiate with the United States Steel Corporation, the progress of their negotiations is widely reported by the press and other news media. Thousands of negotiations involving smaller companies and smaller unions go virtually unnoticed, however.

The size distribution of American unions was discussed in Chapter 12. There we saw that the American labor movement is made up of a relatively small number of large unions, and a larger number of small unions. The size distribution of unions roughly parallels that of business establishments in the United States. In several major industries, such as steel, autos, and aluminum, a few large firms account for the vast majority of industry sales. Is there a similar concentration of collective bargaining relationships? To what extent do unions deal with individual companies? To what extent do they negotiate with more than one employer at a time? We hear much about "industrywide" collective bargaining, and some business publications express concern about the power of "labor monopolies." To what extent do unions deal with entire industries at one time? What substance is there to the charge that while business monopolies are prohibited by law, labor monopolies enjoy legal immunity and are permitted to flourish? Finally, how do unions behave in industries where a few firms are large and powerful, but the majority are relatively small and lacking in market power?

Some of these issues can be discussed statistically, and there is relatively little room for argument about the conclusions. But the winds of controversy blow strong about others. When considering the latter, an effort is made to present both sides of the debate in this text.

Types of Bargaining Relationships

As collective bargaining developed in the United States various types of bargaining structures evolved. Most of the changes were gradual, as employers and unions adapted to changes in economic circumstances and to shifts in relative bargaining power. The bargaining structures we find today are the result of efforts by the two parties to find the best arrangements both for contract negotiation and the day-to-day administration of agreements.

On the employer's side, "bargaining units" range from a single employer with one or more plants to associations which, in some cases, cover virtually an entire industry. On the union's side, the employee unit may consist of an industrial or craft union, but bargaining can take place at the local, regional, or national levels. At times, several unions work together through a trades department or other special bargaining combination.

Employer bargaining units fall into two broad categories. These are (1) the single-employer unit and (2) the multi-employer bargaining unit. Single-employer units vary from purely local agreements between a union and a small employer with one plant to agreements between a union and a giant corporation with many plants located in a number of regions.

Multi-employer bargaining units are even more varied. In some cases, one union will deal with a large number of small employers. Frequently under such circumstances *form* agreements are used. These are identical agreements signed by different employers, often with very little bargaining involved. Such agreements are likely to be found where there are a large number of small competing firms in a relatively restricted geographic area, in the trucking industry, for example.

Another type of multi-employer bargaining takes place between a union and an association of employers. Most industries have an association or institute that serves as a clearing house for information and performs many functions that have no bearing upon collective bargaining. But in some cases, trade associations also serve as bargaining units for member employers. In other cases, employers band together in bargaining associations which deal with unions but do not perform the information gathering and disseminating functions of the trade association. Finally, there are some pure bargaining associations, made up of employers engaged in various kinds of business activity. The sole purpose of the latter associations is to deal with unions, either as advisers to the employers belonging to the group, or directly, in negotiations. There are also some cases—although these are rather rare— in which a number of employers negotiate jointly with a union without setting up a formal association.

Unions have recently formed coalitions to bargain with large corporations, including conglomerates.[1] Such "coordinated bargaining" typically involved the Industrial Union Department (IUD) of the AFL–CIO, and various local and international unions not part of IUD. Some union spokesmen have claimed that coordinated bargaining has been highly successful.[2] Not all efforts at coordinated bargaining have succeeded, however. A spokesman for the management of Union Carbide has described how his company successfully resisted the efforts of a coalition lead by IUD. He concluded that the cost of the strike the company accepted to resist coordinated bargaining was justified because the strike preserved bargaining at the local plant level.[3]

There are some legal aspects of coordinated bargaining that have not been resolved as yet. In 1968, for example, the National Labor Relations Board ruled that the General Electric Company violated the National Labor Relations Act when it refused to bargain with the Electrical Workers (IUE) because "the unions' bargaining team [contained], as non-voting members, representatives of other unions having contracts with the firm."[4] The issue that has not been decided is whether or not General Electric would have been guilty of refusal to bargain if the cooperating unions had made a prior agreement that no union would sign with the company until the company had agreed to offer to all unions a set of common demands. "If each union is party to an agreement that it will not accept less than the demands agreed upon by all unions, bargaining between the employer and the individual unions is bereft of a substantial part of its utility. The crucial decision will be made not at the bargaining table, but at inter-union conferences."[5] From a purely legal point of view unions may be free to reach such a prior agreement Some may think that this is inconsistent with the "good faith bargaining" provision of the National Labor Relations Act. Goldberg disagrees. He feels that whatever the impact of such coordinated agreements may be on the *bargaining process,* unions have a legal right to reach prior agreements before beginning to negotiate with an employer.[6]

---

1. The rapid expansion of a few conglomerate corporations during the 1960s caused a flurry of concern about the increased concentration of economic power in a few hands. A conglomerate is a purely financial organizational superstructure which may control companies in a wide variety of industries. Two of the larger conglomerates were Ling–Temco–Vought and Litton Industries. Since the conglomerate corporation cuts across industry lines, it may deal with a variety of unions. The stock market decline starting late in 1968 brought to an end the upward spiral of price-earnings (*P/E*) ratios that had gone on throughout much of the 1960s for the conglomerates, and resulted in at least a temporary halt to their growth.

2. See, for example, David Lasser, "Coordinated Bargaining: A Union Point of View," *Spring Proceedings,* Industrial Relations Research Association, 1968; reprinted from *Labor Law Journal,* August 1968, pp. 512–517.

3. Earl N. Engle, "Coordinated Bargaining: A Snare and A Delusion," in *ibid.,* pp. 518–523.

4. Steven B. Goldberg, "Coordinated Bargaining: Some Unresolved Questions," *Monthly Labor Review,* April 1969, p. 56. A complete discussion of the issues is given in Steven B. Goldberg, "Current Decisions of the NLRB and of the Courts," *Proceedings,* Twenty-First Annual Meeting, Industrial Relations Research Association, December 1968, pp. 195–200.

5. Goldberg, "Coordinated Bargaining," *op. cit.,* p. 57.

The Distribution of Bargaining Units in Major Agreements

The most recent study of employer bargaining units is more than a decade old. The details are presented here, however, because the structure of bargaining changes slowly over time.[7] This study, conducted in 1961, was based on 1,733 agreements covering one thousand or more workers. In the aggregate, the agreements covered more than 8 million employees. About 65 per cent of all agreements, covering 53 per cent of the workers in the sample, were of the single-employer type. Thus about one third of all agreements, covering 47 per cent of the workers involved, were of the multi-employer variety. There was considerable variation around these averages from industry to industry, however. It is interesting to note that multi-employer agreements are more prevalent among nonmanufacturing firms than in manufacturing (see Table 20-1).

In some industries—ordnance, chemicals, petroleum, coal, and transportation equipment—there are no multi-employer agreements. In the garment and apparel trades, however, multi-employer agreements outnumber

TABLE 20-1
Distribution of Bargaining Units in Major Agreements, 1961

	Agreements		Workers	
	Number	Per cent of total	Number	Per cent of total
Manufacturing	1,045	60.3	4,351.3	52.4
Single-employer, single-plant	441	25.4	917.3	11.0
Single-employer, multiplant	392	22.6	2,469.4	29.7
Multi-employer	212	12.2	964.7	11.6
Nonmanufacturing	688	39.7	3,956.7	47.6
Single-employer, single-plant	49	2.9	104.7	1.4
Single-employer, multiplant	232	13.4	946.3	11.4
Multi-employer	407	23.5	2,905.8	34.0
Total[a]	1,733	100.0	8,308.0	100.0
Single-employer, single-plant	490	28.3	1,121.9	13.5
Single-employer, multiplant	624	36.0	3,415.6	41.1
Multi-employer	619	35.7	3,870.5	46.6

Source: "Major Union Contracts in the United States, 1961," Division of Wages and Industrial Relations, Bureau of Labor Statistics, *Monthly Labor Review,* October 1962, p. 1137.

[a] Individual items may not add to totals because of rounding.

6. *Ibid.,* p. 57.

7. The interested reader may wish to compare the distribution of bargaining units given in the text with those in Neil Chamberlain, "The Structure of Bargaining Units in the United States," *Industrial and Labor Relations Review,* X, October 1956, pp. 10–11.

those with single employers, and most of the single-employer agreements are with large multiplant firms. A similar distribution of agreements is found in the printing, publishing, and allied industries. The only other manufacturing industry in which the number of multi-employer agreements exceeded single-employer agreements was food and kindred products, and here the difference was small.

In one nonmanufacturing sector—wholesale trade—there was no single-employer agreement in 1961, but there were thirteen multi-employer agreements covering more than 25,000 workers. There were no single-employer agreements limited to one plant on the railroads or airlines or in hotels and restaurants. Multiplant agreements with single employers predominate on the railroads and airlines, while most hotel and restaurant agreements are of the multi-employer variety. In construction, there were only two single-employer, multiplant agreements, while there were 168 multi-employer agreements covering more than 800,000 workers. In most other nonmanufacturing sectors, the majority of single-employer agreements covered more than one plant. This was also true of such nonmanufacturing sectors as mining, transportation (excluding railroads and airlines), utilities, and retail trade. And in most of these sectors multi-employer agreements covered a substantially larger number of workers than those covered by single-employer agreements. The communications sector presents an interesting contrast, however. In communications, there was only one multi-employer agreement (covering about 1,000 workers), while there were 75 single-employer, multiplant agreements covering more than 495,000 workers. This brief discussion shows that there is no single pattern of collective bargaining that applies in all cases. The major characteristic of collective bargaining, when it is analyzed by industry or type of employer, is its diversity.

The structure of bargaining tends to follow the structure of industry. Some industries consist of a relatively small number of large companies which operate more than one plant; in some cases these plants almost blanket the country. It is understandable that a union organizing that industry would attempt to negotiate a single agreement with each of the major employers. Other economic activities, such as trucking, warehousing, retail trade, and construction, are made up of a large number of relatively small firms. In these cases, unions attempt to negotiate a master agreement for all of the employers who have recognized them. This does not mean that each employer signs an identical agreement—there are circumstances under which unions will make adjustments on a regional basis. But even in the latter cases, there is a single *basic* agreement that applies to all employers.

Distribution of Bargaining Units by Size

Most major agreements cover a relatively small number of workers, whereas a few agreements cover a large number of workers. The distribution of bargaining units by sizes is given in Table 20–2. About 59 per cent of the major agreements studied in 1961 covered between 1,000 and 2,500 workers. At the other extreme, nine agreements covered 100,000 workers or more, and seven agreements covered between 15,000 and 100,000 workers.

TABLE 20-2
Distribution of Bargaining Units by Size

Size groups	Agreements		Workers	
	Number	Per Cent	Number	Per Cent
1,000–2,499	1,057	61.0	1,513.4	18.2
2,500–4,999	347	20.0	1,136.3	16.4
5,000–9,999	191	11.0	1,280.1	15.4
10,000–24,999	103	5.9	1,458.2	17.6
25,000–49,999	19	1.1	613.8	7.4
50,000–99,999	7	.4	413.8	5.0
100,000 or more	9	.6	1,892.5	22.8
Total[a]	1,733	100.0	8,308	100.0

Source: "Major Union Contracts in the United States, 1961," Division of Wages and Industrial Relations, Bureau of Labor Statistics, *Monthly Labor Review,* October 1962, p. 1139.
[a] Individual items may not add to totals because of rounding.

A substantial number of agreements covering between 2,500 and 10,000 workers are in manufacturing. Agreements covering 100,000 or more workers in the manufacturing sector are found only in the apparel and garment trades, primary metal industries (steel and aluminum), and transportation equipment (autos). In the nonmanufacturing sector, agreements covering 100,000 workers or more are found in mining and transportation.

Unions have found it necessary to adapt their bargaining strategy to the structure of the industries with which they deal. Single agreements in some industries cover a large number of workers because the firms signing the agreements are large. This is the case, as already noted, in the steel and automobile industries. There are relatively few large garment and apparel firms, yet in this industry a single agreement may cover a substantial proportion of the total work force. The apparel and garment industries are highly competitive, and one of the goals of the unions in this sector is to "take labor out of competition." This is accomplished when competing manufacturers sign a common labor-management agreement.

What can be said about the large number of agreements that fall in the middle range? In this range, there are thousands of firms producing thousands of products, and there are regional variations in costs of production and delivery. It would clearly be more convenient, from the union point of view, to have one or a few master agreements signed by all employers. But such agreements, if they could be negotiated, would require so many exceptions they would lose their original character. The diversity of labor-management agreements found in the United States is merely a reflection of the complexity and diversity of the economy.

The Duration of Agreements

There was a time when most collective bargaining agreements were negotiated on an annual basis. During the early 1950s, however, there was a swing toward long-term agreements. A number of five-year agreements were signed between large unions and large employers. These typically included escalator or cost-of-living adjustment clauses, and some included an annual improvement factor granting automatic wage increases geared to productivity gains. But neither the one-year nor the five-year agreement proved to be entirely satisfactory. "The institutional environment is now dominated . . . by a three-year cycle of three-year contracts with roughly two-thirds of major labor agreements closed in any one year. We now have an 'auto' year, a 'steel' year, and an 'electrical' year."[8]

The three-year agreement is not so long that it locks the two parties into an arrangement that cannot be changed within a reasonable time. But it is sufficiently long to avoid the need for full-scale annual negotiations, and all that such negotiations entail. Since unions and management have experimented in the past with both shorter and longer agreements, it may be that the three-year cycle of three-year agreements comes close to an optimal arrangement.

Continuous or Noncrisis Bargaining

During the early 1960s, new bargaining techniques appeared in the steel, meat packing, and longshoring industries to deal with issues raised by technological change. These techniques have been referred to as "continuous" or "noncrisis" bargaining. While they have not spread to other industries, and while the arrangements negotiated have broken down in some cases, there may be a revival of this approach to collective bargaining as unions and management confront new problems in the future.

One result of the long and difficult strike in the basic steel industry in 1959 was the Human Relations Committee established in 1960 by the United Steelworkers of America and representatives of the nation's larger steel companies. The committee consisted only of union and management representatives; industry spokesmen rejected the idea of asking "outside" members to serve. The objective of the committee was to avoid another confrontation such as the one that had led to a major strike in 1959. The new arrangement

---

8. E. Robert Livernash, "Wages and Benefits," *A Review of Industrial Relations Research, Vol. I* (Madison, Wisconsin: Industrial Relations Research Association, 1970), p. 91.

"enabled the parties to resolve their contractual differences on a noncrisis basis in 1962 and 1963. Complex problems, such as those involving the revision of seniority provisions, were settled by the use of surveys, hearings, and jointly written and recommended sub-committee reports."[9]

Although the steel committee appeared to work well it became, in Stern's words, "a casualty of intraunion politics." This happened in 1965, when I. W. Abel ousted the incumbent David McDonald as president of the Steelworkers, following a bitter election campaign.

A slightly different approach was followed by the Steelworkers and the Kaiser Steel Company. The arrangement negotiated in this case provided for a tripartite Human Relations Committee. The neutral members of the committee were given a relatively broad mandate and allowed to participate in negotiations. Among other things, this committee was concerned with the orderly displacement of labor by new technological developments, with both management and labor sharing in the savings from technological improvements.

The Kaiser plan worked well for a number of years. During its first year of operation, bonuses averaged $700. By 1971, however, union officials estimated that the average bonus had dropped to about $100. Corporate earnings had been declining for a number of years, but union leaders claimed that this was not the sole or even the primary cause of the reduction in bonuses. In their view the bonus plan was based on a faulty formula that related production costs to a 1961 base. Meanwhile, many steelworkers employed by other firms had been shifted to incentive pay plans, and local union leaders in the Kaiser plant claimed that their pay had fallen behind the industry average.

Like some of the other "causes of industrial peace" discussed in Chapter 18, it appears that the initial success of the Kaiser plan was largely due to the flexibility and permissiveness of the management that contributed to its development. Evidently a later generation of management did not share its predecessors' labor relations philosophy. The Kaiser Human Relations Committee became increasingly disenchanted with the plan. On February 1, 1972 the union went on strike and demanded that the plan either be modified or scrapped entirely. According to union spokesmen the plan worked well during its early years. But since the death of Henry J. Kaiser in 1967, they claimed, "bargaining over details of the sharing plan has been much more difficult. . . ."[10]

A tripartite approach was also developed by the Armour Company and the Packing House and Butchers unions. This committee administered an "automation fund" designed to minimize the readjustment problems of workers displaced by technological change. During the 1960s, a number of meatpacking plants were liquidated. But the labor-management agreement spec-

---

9. James L. Stern, "Collective Bargaining Trends and Patterns," *A Review of Industrial Relations Research, Vol. II,* 1971, pp. 128–129.

10. *Wall Street Journal,* February 24, 1972, p. 36.

ified that workers be notified in advance of the shutdown. Originally, the notification period was ninety days, but in 1967 it was extended to six months. Although this program was started before the Manpower Development and Training Act was passed, it has benefited from the expansion of the manpower programs described in Chapter 8. Much of the success of the Armour program has been attributed, however, to the long-range planning and continuous negotiations preceding plant shutdowns.[11]

Another well-publicized case of noncrisis bargaining resulted from the mechanization and modernization agreement between the Pacific Maritime Association and the International Longshoremen's Union (ILWU). The history of labor-management relations on the Pacific Coast was a stormy one before 1959. But in that year the two parties agreed that employers would have a freer hand to modernize. In return, the permanent work force was guaranteed either work or income. Signing of this agreement was followed by a dozen years of "labor peace, employment security, and increased productivity."[12] Throughout this period the "M and M agreement" was widely hailed as an example of innovative bargaining, and other unions were urged by some writers to follow this approach. Unfortunately, the long period of labor peace was shattered on July 3, 1971, by a West Coast dock strike. The strike was interrupted by an eighty day "cooling-off" period, as specified by the Taft-Hartley Act. But it was then resumed in January and continued until February 1972, when the parties reached an agreement, as they put it, "by voluntary means," at a time when Congress was reported to be considering ad hoc legislation to require the strikers to return to their jobs.[13]

One of the issues involved in the long dock strike was the spread of "containerization," or the prepackaging of cargo in ways that allow it to be loaded directly on board ship from railroad cars or trucks, with little or no intervention by longshoremen. There also has been some concern among union leaders about the employment effects of the winding down of the Vietnam war.[14]

Under the settlement, employers agreed to pay a "royalty" of one dollar a ton on all the containers loaded or unloaded by non-ILWU members. The royalty fund is to be used to help cover the cost of a guaranteed thirty-six hour week (either work or pay). The agreement also provided for increased fringe benefits. The imposition of a royalty was expected to raise the cost of containerized shipping and possibly to reduce its volume. Some spokesmen for Teamsters locals threatened to picket the docks if their work became threatened.

---

11. James L. Stern, "Evolution of Private Manpower Planning in Armour's Plant Closings," Monthly Labor Review, December 1969, pp. 21–28.

12. James L. Stern, "Collective Bargaining Trends and Patterns," p. 131.

13. Business Week, February 12, 1972, p. 24.

14. See the report by Albert A. Belman of the 1971 convention of the International Longshoremen's and Warehousemen's Union, Monthly Labor Review, August 1971, pp. 60–62.

The settlement would have increased the cost of wages and fringe benefits during the first year by 20.6 per cent. The Pay Board was faced with a dilemma—either to risk another walkout or to approve an increase that exceeded established guidelines by a substantial margin. The Board did not attempt to reduce the settlement to the guideline level of 5.5 per cent. But with the labor members dissenting, it did order a reduction to 14.9 per cent.[15] Harry Bridges, president of the Longshoremen, had threatened to renew the strike if the full settlement was not approved by the Pay Board. But the union evidently felt that the amount approved by the Board was an acceptable compromise, and the longshoremen remained at work.

Pattern Bargaining

The most prevalent type of collective bargaining, as Table 20–1 shows, is that which results in an agreement with a single employer. But this does not mean that all single-employer agreements are *independent* of one another. Multi-employer agreements tend toward uniformity—at least within an industry and in a given geographic area. Indeed, one reason employers band together for collective bargaining purposes is to achieve a certain degree of uniformity in their relations with labor unions. Unions do not object to this; indeed, most unions favor it. Competing employers are willing to accept uniform agreements —or agreements that tend toward uniformity—so that a relatively strong union will not play off one employer against another. Unions have long insisted that vigorous competition in the product market should not be at the expense of workers. Thus, if they can achieve a degree of uniformity in the agreements they negotiate with various employers, they have to a certain extent "taken labor out of competition."

But what of single-employer agreements? Will not each employer strive for the most favorable agreement from his point of view? Will he not, that is, try to keep his labor costs to a minimum? And where unions deal with one employer at a time, will they not try to obtain the most beneficial contract from the union's point of view in each case?

There was a time—and this is still true under some circumstances—when a favorite union tactic was to "whipsaw" employers. The union would pick one employer and drive a hard bargain. Once the agreement had been signed, the union would use this in its efforts to bring the wages and fringe benefits of other employers "into line." At the next round of negotiations, another employer might be selected and the process would be repeated. Whipsawing, as well as the desire of small employers to meet large unions on more favorable terms, played an important part in the development of multi-employer bargaining.

In many industries, unions have long since abandoned such tactics. They

---

15. *The Wall Street Journal,* March 17, 1972.

still negotiate with one employer at a time but, in some of the largest industries, where employers deal with large and powerful unions, an approach was developed known as *pattern bargaining.* What this means, in brief, is that the union negotiates an agreement with one company in an industry expecting that identical or closely similar agreements will be signed with other employers in the same industry. In recent years pattern bargaining has tended to move beyond the confines of a single industry.

There is a certain amount of rivalry among unions, especially large industrial unions. And if one large union reaches an agreement with a major employer in an industry, it is likely to set a pattern for other unions to follow in other industries. Thus in certain industries—even though the typical bargaining unit is the single employer—there is a greater tendency toward uniformity of agreements than would result if each set of negotiations were entirely independent of all other negotiations.

A single craft union will often deal with a large number of employers. Thus, it is no accident that there is no bargaining between the building trades unions and single-plant construction firms. The union prefers to negotiate with a bloc of employers at a time, since the conditions resulting from the negotiations must be met by all employers. Multi-employer bargaining is a fairly old practice in some craft unions.

With the rise of industrial unionism after 1935, however, pattern bargaining spread. It is to be found in most oligopolistic industries, that is, those industries such as steel, autos, meat packing, and rubber, in which a few large firms account for most of the industry's output. But pattern bargaining is not limited to oligopolistic industries. It is practiced in some highly competitive industries, such as those manufacturing garments, apparel, and textile products. In 1961, for example, single-employer agreements in textiles outnumbered multi-employer agreements by more than four to one, but many of the single-employer agreements were of the pattern variety.

Oligopoly and Pattern Bargaining

The terms "oligopoly" and "monopoly" are sometimes used interchangeably in popular discussion, although it is not correct to do so. Strictly defined, a monopoly is a single seller of a product or service for which there is no close substitute. If the demand for the product is relatively inelastic, that is, if an increase in price is accompanied by a less than proportionate decline in purchases, the firm can increase its total revenue by raising prices and curtailing output. This is precisely what a profit-maximizing monopolist will do. By definition, he has no competitors; thus he is free to set his price and output at levels that will maximize his profits.

In an oligopolistic market, however, there will be not one but a few large sellers. There is a tendency for firms in oligopolistic markets to avoid price competition, but they engage in many other kinds of competition, such as aggressive advertising and merchandising, quality improvements, and production innovations, which will lower their costs without disturbing the price level. Each firm in the oligopolistic market is aware of the fact that if it tries to cut prices its rivals will follow suit and no one will gain. Its management also knows that if it raises prices, independently of cost changes that affect all firms in the market, its rivals are likely *not* to follow this lead, and this firm would then lose customers and revenue. This situation is referred to by economic theorists as *mutual dependence recognized.* But while there is an absence of price competition in oligopolistic markets, there are many other kinds of competition. Unlike the monopolist, who curtails output in order to dispose of his production at the price he has set, each oligopolist is anxious to sell as many units as possible at the ruling market price.

There is a world of difference between these two situations, as most economists have recognized for many years. The behavior of oligopolistic firms in product markets has had a significant influence on their relationships with trade unions. It is not surprising that pattern bargaining has become fairly common in industries predominantly oligopolistic in character. At the same time, there has been a tendency for some writers to exaggerate the extent to which unions have been able to negotiate uniform agreements with all firms in predominantly oligopolistic industries.

Does the practice of pattern bargaining lead to uniform wage and fringe benefit settlements in oligopolistic industries? This is not a simple question to answer. First of all, the concept of a "pattern" in collective bargaining has not been clearly defined.[16] There would be no problem of definition if all companies involved in pattern bargaining started with the same absolute level of wages and fringe benefits. This is not the case, however. Pattern bargaining is largely a post-World War II phenomenon, and the wage and fringe-benefit "package" varied considerably from company to company at the time pattern bargaining became more or less the standard practice in some of our larger industries. Another way to view the pattern, therefore, is to consider the *change* in wages and fringe benefits negotiated. One could say that there is a pattern if the wages and fringe benefits in the "key" bargain were followed quite closely in all other bargains throughout the industry. The ideal would be to measure both. But as Levinson[17] has pointed out,

> any attempt to compare absolute levels among varied firms raises extremely difficult problems of differences in employee-mix, differences in incentive versus hourly earnings, differences in the job content of similar job classifications, and a host of others.

Thus in practice, the term "pattern" typically denotes the major *changes* in wages and fringe benefits negotiated during the "key" bargain. In his analysis

---

16. See Harold M. Levinson, "Pattern Bargaining: A Case Study of the Automobile Workers," *The Quarterly Journal of Economics, LXXIV* (May 1960), p. 297.

17. *Ibid.*

of pattern bargaining in the automobile industry—one that is frequently used to illustrate the concept of pattern bargaining—Levinson found that there is much less uniformity than is popularly believed.

Levinson studied the results of collective bargaining in eighty-five automobile firms in the Detroit metropolitan area—not including the "Big Three" firms of Ford, General Motors, and Chrysler. If pattern bargaining led to uniformity of wage and fringe-benefit changes, one would expect the bargains in these eighty-five firms to follow the settlements in the "Big Three." In fact, however, Levinson found that "only 26 per cent of the companies, employing 40 per cent of the employees in the sample, followed the pattern. . . ."[18] A minority of firms had reached settlements above the pattern, while firms employing about 98 per cent of the workers covered by the sample had reached settlements below the pattern. In general, there was a greater tendency for the larger firms in the sample to follow the pattern than for their smaller counterparts.

Levinson's study was, of course, limited to one industry and one area. But it strongly suggests that pattern bargaining does not lead to uniform wage and fringe-benefit changes, contrary to a fairly widespread belief. Some discussions of pattern bargaining imply that as soon as the "key" bargain has been settled, all other companies in an industry will follow suit. It is true in some oligopolistic industries, the leading firms will settle on similar if not identical terms. But even in such oligopolistic industries as steel and autos, unions deal with hundreds of smaller firms. Levinson's study suggests that in such cases, there can be significant departures from the pattern established by the major firms.

Pattern Bargaining in Highly Competitive Industries

At the other end of the spectrum—in terms of market structure—are the aggressively competitive industries in our economy. Some industries such as textiles, shoes, and apparel, are made up of a large number of firms, no one of which accounts for a substantial share of the industry's total output. Some firms in these industries produce "specialty" products, and thus enjoy a considerable degree of control over the prices they charge, but most of them sell relatively homogeneous products in an open market where prices are determined by the forces of supply and demand. Although there are often a few large firms even in highly competitive industries, they are not in the same position as the dominant firms in such industries as steel, autos, and meat packing. In a highly competitive market, all firms must sell at open market prices.

Characteristically, within an industry whether it is oligopolistic or aggressively price competitive, there will be variations in cost from firm to firm.

---

18. *Ibid.*, p. 299.

One might expect that in price competitive industries, therefore, unions would try to negotiate agreements on the basis of "what the traffic will bear." But even in price competitive industries one can find evidence of something that approximates pattern bargaining. Some textile negotiations, for example, are conducted with associations of employers. The results of these negotiations tend to set a pattern for other firms in the industry. In the apparel industry, the "form" contract is not uncommon. The same contract is presented to a large number of employers, either through an organization of employers or on an individual basis. Such agreements also tend to set a pattern throughout the industry. But as in oligopolistic industries, there are departures from these patterns. The practice of pattern bargaining has not led to uniformity of changes in wages and fringe benefits either in oligopolistic or price competitive industries—although there undeniably has been a *tendency* in this direction. The picture of pattern bargaining sketched by some writers has been misleading. The union is often portrayed as a monolithic giant which, having decided what it is going to get, forces all companies to fall into line. There is obviously some basis for this line of argument—unions have *tried* to obtain uniform agreements wherever possible. But union leaders are realists; they recognize that not every firm in an industry will be able to settle on the same terms, and there is evidence that they have been willing to accommodate themselves to differences among firms in reaching workable agreements.

Multi-Employer Bargaining in the Basic Steel Industry

For many years the agreement between the United Steelworkers of America and the United States Steel Corporation set the pattern of bargaining in this oligopolistic industry. But negotiations were held with each company one at a time. Evidently U.S. Steel, which is generally considered the "price leader" in the industry, did not particularly relish the position it occupied in collective bargaining. "There was an indication as early as 1947 that U.S. Steel considered itself a reluctant dragon so far as its leadership role was concerned."[19] Before 1947, the steel union was not strong enough to bargain on a multi-employer basis. After that year it began to press hard toward this goal, but it was almost a decade before multi-employer bargaining became firmly established in the industry.

As we saw in an earlier section, one result of the long steel strike of 1959 was a new approach to collective bargaining. Since 1959, the union has negotiated with a committee representing eleven major companies, with a separate arrangement for Kaiser Steel. Although the Human Relations Committee did not survive the change in union leadership in 1965, multi-employer bargaining in the steel industry has continued.

---

19. *Collective Bargaining in the Basic Steel Industry* (Washington: U.S. Department of Labor, January 1961), p. 87.

In addition to the dozen giants that account for most of the nation's steel output, about 200 smaller firms are considered to be part of the industry. It appears that whenever possible, the union tries to apply the terms negotiated with the major firms to the smaller companies, and to see that local agreements do not conflict with the provisions of the basic settlement. But there are still extensive variations in wage and fringe-benefit packages among the smaller firms in the industry.

Although the union might lose certain tactical advantages by giving up the ability to "whipsaw" one company at a time, union leaders evidently feel that there is more to be gained from a uniform settlement on basic issues when facing the dominant firms in the industry. Moreover, management, which at one time was reluctant to engage in such bargaining, evidently feels that the position of the industry is strengthened if it faces the union *en bloc* rather than having each company try to negotiate the most favorable terms it can get.

"Industrywide" Bargaining and the "Labor Monopoly" Issue

A theme that recurs frequently in discussions of collective bargaining is that of so-called industrywide bargaining and "labor monopolies." It has been alleged by some conservative groups that while we have outlawed business monopoly, labor monopolies are permitted to flourish. Labor monopolies, it is further argued, pursue their objectives through some form of "industrywide" collective bargaining.

The Opponents of "Labor Monopoly"

The attack on "labor monopoly" has been spearheaded by two business organizations—the National Association of Manufacturers and the U.S. Chamber of Commerce. The NAM[20] has said:

> Monopoly power may be described as a position of power by an individual or group to control the supply and fix the price of needed goods and services. On this basis, there can be no doubt that certain international unions possess monopoly powers in some of the basic industries in the United States. They virtually control the labor supply of these industries and have proved on many occasions their ability to dictate the terms on which the services of labor are available to produce the goods and services the nation needs.

The NAM goes on to say that there are numerous cases in which "employers and their employees must accept the terms fixed by the international unions; the members of the local union and the local bargaining agents have nothing to say about these terms."[21] The cause of all this, in the NAM's view, is the

---

20. *Monopoly Power as Exercised by Labor Unions* (New York: National Association of Manufacturers, no date), p. 5.
21. *Ibid.*

legal immunity of trade unions from the antitrust laws. What cure is advocated by those who accept this extreme view of union power? It is the decentralization of collective bargaining—more specifically, the limitation of collective bargaining to local unions and individual companies.

As noted in an earlier chapter, the center of power in the American trade union movement is the national or international union. This is particularly so in the large industrial unions, and it is not an accident. The complexity of collective bargaining in modern industrial society requires that unions retain staffs of experts to assist their officers in preparing for negotiations. Large companies, too, have their staffs of experts. Collective bargaining has become much more than a matter of table pounding, threats, and counterthreats.[22] The organizations which claim that unions are "labor monopolies" and which "want to bring them under the anti-trust laws" are well aware of this. If the national union could be prevented from participating in collective bargaining, the advantage in negotiations would shift to the side of employers. Indeed, there would be no point in having a national union headquarters if all collective bargaining had to be conducted at the local level.

There have been numerous efforts to pass federal laws that would bar multiple-employer or so-called industrywide collective bargaining. When the Taft-Hartley Bill was being debated, for example, a House Bill (H.R. 3020) that would have prohibited multiple-employer bargaining was passed with a substantial majority, and a similar bill, sponsored by Senator Ball, came within a single vote of being passed in the Senate.

That was a very close call for the kind of collective bargaining that has become widespread in the United States. Despite rejection by the Congress that enacted the Taft-Hartley Act, over President Truman's veto, similar bills have been introduced into succeeding sessions of Congress. The National Association of Manufacturers called for "real bargaining at the local level and an end to the domination of bargaining by international unions."[23] Those espousing this point of view have had, at times, the support of well-known scholars. Roscoe Pound, an eminent legal scholar, wrote that "the employers have no immunities and the statutes as to collective bargaining put the employers in the hands of the unions."[24]

Not everyone who has expressed concern about the labor monopoly problem would go as far as the NAM in limiting collective bargaining. The late

---

22. One indication of the increasing complexity—and growing sophistication—of collective bargaining is the use of computers in the process. Some writers believe that computers will be used increasingly to provide new information rapidly and to explore various alternatives while negotiations are under way. See Stern, "Collective Bargaining Trends and Patterns," p. 169. See also Abraham J. Siegel (ed.), The Impact of Computers on Collective Bargaining (Cambridge, Mass., M.I.T. Press, 1969).

23. Monopoly Power as Exercised by Labor Unions, p. 30.

24. Roscoe Pound, "Legal Immunities of Labor Unions," Labor Unions and Public Policy (Washington, D.C.: American Enterprise Association, 1958), p. 168.

Edward H. Chamberlin,[25] a distinguished economic theorist, argued that labor unions have monopoly power. Yet he said:[26]

> There has been a great deal of discussion as to whether the antitrust laws should be applied to labor. . . . Some partial application is surely possible, but the particular body of law associated with antitrust has actually been developed with reference to product markets, and it would seem on the face of it that the structure and functioning of product markets on the one hand and of labor markets on the other, differ in so many ways that a fresh start may be called for to meet the problems of the latter.

Fritz Machlup argued that outlawing "industrywide" collective bargaining *without at the same time outlawing "industrywide" unions* would be ineffective.[27] Nonetheless, he was emphatic in his belief that there is a considerable amount of business monopoly in our economy, and that if "labor monopolies" are to be abolished, their counterparts on the business side should be abolished also.

Reservations About the Application of Antitrust Laws to Trade Unions

Most of the economists who have expressed concern about the monopoly power of trade unions would be accurately classified as "conservatives." Commenting on this, Archibald Cox, a noted legal educator who served as President Kennedy's Solicitor General, has said: "Much of the support for legislation subjecting unions to the antitrust laws doubtless stems from organized anti-unionism, but too many friends of labor are concerned by some aspects of the problem to condemn these questions through guilt by association."[28] But after a careful analysis of cases involving unions and the antitrust laws, Cox concludes that "a case can be made out for applying the Sherman Act only to those union imposed restraints which fall in the category [of] tampering with the product market for the sake of sheltering employers from competition otherwise than by organizing the employees of competitors and regulating their labor standards."[29] This view also has been advanced by Douglass V. Brown, a distinguished labor economist, who feels that unions

---

25. See, for example, Edward H. Chamberlin, "Labor Union Power and the Public Interest" in Philip D. Bradley (ed.), *The Public Stake in Union Power* (Charlottesville, Virginia: University of Virginia Press, 1959), p. 3.

26. Edward H. Chamberlin, "The Economic Analysis of Labor Union Power," *Labor Unions and Public Policy* (Washington: The American Enterprise Association, 1958), pp. 32–33.

27. Fritz Machlup, "Monopolistic Wage Determination as Part of the General Problem of Monopoly," *Wage Determination and the Economics of Liberalism* (Washington, D.C.: Chamber of Commerce of the United States, 1947), pp. 80–81.

28. Archibald Cox, "Labor and the Antitrust Laws—A Preliminary Analysis," *University of Pennsylvania Law Review, 104,* November 1955, p. 252.

29. *Ibid.,* p. 280.

should be subject to the antitrust laws if they are engaged in the restraint of trade in product markets, but that unions should *not* be subject to the antitrust laws when their activities are limited strictly to the labor market.[30]

One would expect union spokesmen to oppose laws limiting the role of national and international unions in collective bargaining. Former Supreme Court Justice Arthur J. Goldberg, while serving as General Counsel for the Industrial Union Department of the AFL-CIO, wrote: "The truth is that those who make the 'labor monopoly' charge are not really concerned with competition or its negative counterpart monopoly. Their real goal is the weakening of unions and especially those unions which they believe are too strong."[31]

Collective Bargaining with "Marginal" Firms

To what extent are unions willing to recognize the wide variations in costs of production and profitability that exist among individual companies? This is not a simple question to answer. As an ideal goal, many unions would like to see complete uniformity of wages and fringe benefits throughout the industries or occupational groups they represent. But union leaders are too realistic to assume that complete uniformity can be achieved.

There is evidence that when it is necessary to do so, some unions will take into account the competitive position of a company—particularly a smaller company—and reach a settlement below the pattern established elsewhere in the industry. Such union behavior is not widely publicized, and for rather obvious reasons. If it became well known that unions are willing to make concessions, the precedent could be a damaging one—especially when the unions are dealing with the dominant firms in an industry. From a public relations point of view, it might be desirable for the union to let it be known that it is willing to reach "reasonable" settlements with smaller companies, which will permit them to stay in business. But this would conflict with the stated goal of some unions; namely, uniform industrywide conditions.

Even in oligopolistic industries, a certain amount of "price nibbling" among smaller firms is tolerated by the industrial giants; that is, smaller companies can at times depart from the prevailing price in an industry without inviting retaliation from the dominant firms. After all, if the dominant firms account for, say, 80 to 90 per cent of the market, how can such price nibbling damage them? Similarly, even if they are aware of it, the larger firms in an industry might tolerate departures from basic labor-management agreements, although such settlements cannot depart too far from the basic agreements.

All too little is known about the extent to which powerful national unions

---

30. Douglass V. Brown, "Labor and Antitrust Laws," *American Bar Association Proceedings,* August 1955, pp. 23–29.

31. Arthur J. Goldberg, "Labor and Antitrust," pamphlet reprinted from *IUD Digest* (Washington: Industrial Union Department, AFL-CIO, no date), p. 6.

will permit departures from basic agreements in dealing with smaller firms. In this regard, a 1957 study by A. Howard Myers is revealing. It shows that when small companies are confronted with a crisis—especially if there is the threat of liquidation, which would mean the loss of jobs—unions have been willing to make substantial concessions to the employers involved, at least on a temporary basis. Where unions have been convinced that a small firm could not survive an agreement based upon the industry pattern, they have been willing to settle for less in terms of wages and fringe benefits. At least this is what Myers[32] found in a limited number of cases. But there are limits to which such departures from national patterns can be tolerated:

> The national unions cannot allow local self-determination to undermine nation-wide gains or to weaken its national bargaining position. If the sole road to marginal plant labor relations depended upon the destruction of the national union's standards, the union could neither make such exceptions nor allow a local to approve them, even if such concessions were indispensable to the local's survival.

And at times, unions have made such concessions knowing that this would not prevent the ultimate liquidation of the firm, but hoping that the day of reckoning could be put off. This is not necessarily shortsightedness. It does not mean that the union hopes that somehow the company can be strengthened; but the gradual loss of jobs has less of an impact than sudden liquidation.

There is also evidence that in some crisis situations the employees of marginal firms will exert considerable pressure on their union leaders to "go easy" on the company during negotiations.[33] Again, this is not so much because the workers think that by moderating their demands the company can be made to survive. It is often motivated by the desire to stretch out the period of time during which a company gradually goes out of business.

It would be helpful if we had more information about negotiations between unions and small companies. Available studies suggest that under multi-employer collective bargaining, there has been a tendency toward uniformity of wages and fringe benefits, but this is only a tendency. There are significant variations from national patterns even in those industries where we have been told "industrywide" collective bargaining is practiced. The major agreements with the dominant firms clearly reveal the tendency toward

---

32. A. Howard Myers, *Crisis Bargaining* Boston: Northeastern University, Bureau of Business and Economic Research, 1957), p. 71.

33. See Irwin L. Herrnstadt, "The Reaction of Three Local Unions to Economic Adversity," *The Journal of Political Economy, LXII* (October 1954), pp. 425–439. Workers have at times voted to accept pay cuts, and to forego wage increases for a stated period, in order to protect their jobs. For an example of such an arrangement between a local of the International Union of Electrical Workers (IUE) and the Frigidaire Division of General Motors, see the *Wall Street Journal,* January 26, 1972, p. 1.

greater uniformity. But the evidence available suggests that outside this widely publicized area of collective bargaining, there is much more diversity than is commonly believed.

Collective Bargaining in Agriculture

The forgotten men and women of the American labor movement have been the hired farm workers. The earliest attempts at the organization of farm workers were made in 1922, when a union of grape pickers was formed; and there were a number of strikes of agricultural workers during the 1930s. But these early efforts did not produce lasting results. Although organized labor in the United States made its greatest strides after the Wagner Act was passed in 1935, farm workers did not benefit from this legislation. In fact, while union organization was proceeding apace in the nonagricultural sector, the effective organization of farm workers was prevented by legislation that permitted the temporary importation of *braceros*—immigrant farm laborers from Mexico. The ready availability of alternative sources of labor permitted farm employers to treat union organizers with complete impunity.[34]

In 1962, Cesar Chavez established the United Farm Workers Organizing Committee (UFWOC), which became the United Farm Workers of California a decade later. Some of the recent successes achieved by Chavez and his union were mentioned in Chapter 11. There has been a definite change in the labor relations environment in American agriculture. The *bracero* program has been ended, and despite the prospect of somewhat higher food prices if farm organization is successful, there appears to be an increasing amount of public support for farm unions.[35] But many problems still face the United Farm Workers. There has been rapid technological change in agriculture, a phenomenon which is expected to continue. The long-term declining trend in the number of hired farm workers will also continue. One consequence of this decline will be that labor cost will become a smaller part of the total cost of farm production, and this may weaken some of the resistance to union organization.[36]

Although collective bargaining in agriculture is still in its infancy, when compared with bargaining in the nonfarm sector, the principle has been accepted. In terms of bargaining strategy, or the bargaining process itself, little that is new is to be found in the agricultural sector. And there is little reason to believe that there will be a sudden breakthrough in the organization

---

34. See Stern, "Collective Bargaining Trends and Patterns," pp. 160–162.

35. See, for example, Varden Fuller, "A New Era for Farm Labor?" *Industrial Relations,* Vol. 6 (May 1967), pp. 285–302.

36. For a discussion of these and other problems, as well as a concise history of the organization of farm workers, see Karen S. Koziara, "Collective Bargaining on the Farm," *Monthly Labor Review,* June 1968, pp. 3–9. See also other articles in this issue dealing with migratory farm workers and the problems of rural to urban transition for displaced farm workers.

of farm workers, with complete acceptance of collective bargaining. Stern has summarized the current situation in agriculture succinctly: "Bargaining has not yet won widespread acceptance in agriculture, but it has gained a substantial foothold."[37]

Collective Bargaining in the Public Sector

The growth of union membership among public employees was discussed briefly in Chapter 11, and the legal basis for collective bargaining by government employees was described in Chapter 15. Collective bargaining in the public sector is discussed briefly in the present chapter because this type of bargaining adds a new dimension to the pattern of labor-management relations in the United States.

In his survey of recent developments in collective bargaining, Stern pointed out that: "The constancy of behavior in private sector bargaining [during the 1960s] did not extend to the public sector where a fundamental shift in views and conduct took place."[38] But because of recent trends it is possible to exaggerate the extent to which unions representing public employees have been able to follow the lead of those that deal strictly with the private sector. The system of "industrial jurisprudence," which Slichter talked about more than two decades ago, has not yet been duplicated in the public sector.

The notion that public employees should have the right to strike is not one that is widely accepted as yet in the United States. In January 1972, the coal miners of Great Britain—public employees because they work in nationalized mines—went on strike. By the end of February, stockpiles of coal were becoming depleted, and a system of rationing of available electric energy was instituted. The British public considered the "temporary blackouts" to be a nuisance but, by and large, the effects of the strike were accepted with equanimity. A similar situation in the United States undoubtedly would have led to the declaration of a national emergency, and special legislation would have been enacted to bring an end to the strike.

There may be one exception to the above generalization. Public school teachers have gone on strike in a number of communities to achieve collective bargaining demands. When teachers go on strike, children do not, of course, go to school. This may be considered an annoyance, but it is not usually thought of as an emergency. Also, while collective bargaining by school teachers has been highly visible, it is still in its early stages; it may be too early to evaluate its impact.[39] If membership in teachers' unions con-

---

37. Stern, "Collective Bargaining Trends and Patterns," p. 162.

38. *Ibid.,* p. 132.

39. One study of the effects of collective bargaining on teachers' salaries has reached the tentative conclusion that to date, it has had relatively little effect. See Herschell Kasper, "The Effect of Collective Bargaining on Public School Teachers' Salaries," *Industrial and Labor Relations Review, 24* (October 1970), pp. 57–71.

tinues to grow, however, and if teachers' strikes become more widespread, public attitudes could easily change. As George Taylor has pointed out, there has been an increasing use of the strike by state and local employees "even though the right to do so has never been explicitly accorded to them."[40] Until recently, most public employees accepted the notion of a "no-strike" policy as an essential condition of public employment. This is a reflection of what may be called a civil-service mentality. There is a strong likelihood that labor-management relations in the public sector will become more turbulent than they have been in the past as a growing proportion of civil servants become union members. The question of how to deal with disputes — actual or impending — in the public sector is thus of central interest. One "forthright" solution to strikes by public employees, as Taylor has put it, is compulsory arbitration. But this solution is rarely advocated by specialists in the field of industrial relations. Arbitration, which will be discussed more fully in the next chapter, is an integral part of a successful labor-management relationship. But it is one thing to accept arbitration of an existing agreement — something unions and management have long been willing to do — and quite another to accept arbitration of matters that are the subject of negotiations.

It might be possible, at the other extreme, to argue that public employees have the same right to strike as those in the private sector. It is easy to become involved in a morass of legal and philosophical details when discussing this issue, and no attempt will be made to do so in this text. But the conventional view in industrial relations in the United States at present is that while public employees should have every right to organize, some viable alternative to the right to strike must be developed.[41]

The development of alternatives to the right to strike may not be a simple matter. Even if procedures are devised to resolve differences between public employees and management, there is no guarantee that these procedures will function flawlessly. And there may be occasional strikes of public employees simply because the "alternatives" are not working. If strikes are to be avoided in the public sector, review boards, or other agencies established to handle disputes, will have to be flexible to allow for changing conditions in the economy, and for changes in the world of work in general.[42] Taylor has pointed out that: "... public employees are understandably demanding a more effective means of participating in the determination of their employment terms. This should be accorded to them as a matter of simple equity.

---

40. George W. Taylor, "Public Employment: Strikes or Procedures?" *Industrial and Labor Relations Review, 20* (July 1967), p. 617.

41. See David L. Cole, "Devising Alternatives to the Right to Strike," *Monthly Labor Review,* July 1969, pp. 60–62. See also other articles in this issue, by a panel of distinguished specialists in the field of industrial relations, covering a variety of topics dealing with collective bargaining in the public sector.

42. For one suggested plan, see Taylor, *op. cit.,* pp. 633–635.

But it should be possible to do so without sweeping infringements on public rights and without enervating the operation of our kind of political democracy. Strikes are not the answer; new procedures are."[43]

Conclusions

Most organized workers are covered by major agreements negotiated between their unions and single employers, but roughly 47 per cent are covered by multi-employer agreements. The latter are often emphasized in discussions of collective bargaining. Multi-employer bargaining is behind the "labor monopoly" issue, and has led to demands that—for practical purposes—big unions be broken up into little ones.

There appears to be an exaggerated notion of the extent of multi-employer and so-called industrywide collective bargaining. This is not surprising. We have a tendency to generalize and, in viewing complex social and economic situations, it is sometimes easy to generalize unwarrantably. Multi-employer bargaining, and the tendency toward uniformity of agreements, must be recognized. They are an important part of the labor-management scene and a significant reflection of the structure of collective bargaining in this country. At the same time, the tendency toward uniformity should not obscure the great diversity of collective bargaining arrangements and the wide variations in collective bargaining practices that exist in this country.

The most significant change in collective bargaining that has occurred in the United States since the early 1960s is the growth of bargaining in the public sector. Federal, state, and municipal employees are now widely represented by trade unions. Their right to organize has been recognized as a matter of equity. But thorny problems remain. Public employees have not been granted the right to strike either explicitly or implictly. It would be a utopian dream to expect all of the issues that will arise between public employees' unions and their employers to be settled amicably. Scholars in the field of industrial relations appear to agree that it is imperative to develop viable alternatives to the right to strike by public employees. These alternatives—whatever they ultimately may be—will require a degree of flexibility to allow for changes in the social, political, and economic systems.

Questions and Exercises

1. Describe, in general terms, the size distribution of American unions. To what extent does the structure of trade unions in the United States parallel that of business establishments in this country?

---

43. *Ibid.,* p. 636.

2. Labor-management relationships may be described as single employer or multi-employer. Which type of agreement predominates in the United States? Is there any variation in single-employer agreements?

3. Describe some of the various types of multi-employer agreements that have been negotiated in the United States.

4. What is meant by "coordinated bargaining"? What new development in industrial organization led to this type of bargaining? How has coordinated bargaining been viewed by union leaders? Is it a generally accepted view of management that coordinated bargaining is a good thing for both unions and industry?

5. Does the practice of "coordinated bargaining" raise any new legal problems?

6. Until the early 1950s, most labor-management agreements were negotiated on an annual basis. During the early 1950s, however, there was a swing toward five-year agreements. Has this trend continued? If not, what has happened to the duration of labor-management agreements in recent years?

7. What is meant by continuous or "noncrisis" bargaining? How has continuous bargaining worked in the steel industry?

8. Describe the arrangements made by the Armour Company and meat-packing unions to minimize the problems of worker dislocation when plants are shut down. What was the "mechanization and modernization" agreement between the Pacific Maritime Association and the International Longshoremen's Union? After a dozen years of labor peace, there was a West Coast dock strike that lasted more than six months. What were the issues involved? How was this strike settled?

9. What is meant by "pattern bargaining"? Has pattern bargaining led to complete uniformity of wages, fringe benefits, and working conditions in oligopolistic industries? Contrast pattern bargaining in oligopolistic and price-competitive industries.

10. Describe briefly the evolution of multi-employer bargaining in the basic steel industry.

11. Conservative business organizations have charged that organized labor constitutes a "labor monopoly." Why has this charge been made, and what do some business organizations advocate as the proper public policy for dealing with "labor monopolies"? Describe briefly some of the arguments, pro and con, that have been made by lawyers, economists, and others who have discussed the "labor monopoly" issue.

12. Are there any circumstances under which unions will deviate from negotiated patterns in an industry when dealing with marginal firms? If unions make concessions to marginal firms, do they do this typically because they believe they can strengthen the competitive positions of these firms?

13. There has been growing acceptance of the right to organize by public employees. Is it a generally accepted view in the United States that the right to organize also means the right to strike? Assume that you have been asked

to develop an alternative to the strike as a means of settling disputes between municipal employees and local government. Assume further that the two parties already have agreed that compulsory arbitration is not an acceptable alternative. What sort of arrangement would you devise for the settlement of these disputes?

Suggested Readings

Books

American Enterprise Association. *Labor Unions and Public Policy.* Washington, D.C.: the Association, 1958.

Bradley, Philip D. (ed.). *The Public Stake in Union Power.* Charlottesville, Virginia: University of Virginia Press, 1959.

Committee for Economic Development. *The Public Interest in National Labor Policy.* New York: the Committee, 1961.

National Association of Manufacturers. *Monopoly Power as Exercised by Labor Unions.* New York: the Association, no date.

Articles

Brown, Douglass V. "Labor and Antitrust Laws," *American Bar Association Proceedings,* August 1955.

Cole, David L., Theodore W. Kheel, George W. Taylor, Jerry Worf, J. Curtis Counts, and Thomas R. Donahue. "Collective Bargaining in the Public Sector," *Monthly Labor Review,* July 1969, pp. 60–69.

Fuller, Varden. "A New Era for Farm Labor," *Industrial Relations, 6* (May 1967), pp. 285–302.

Hellrigel, Don, Wendell French, and Richard B. Peterson. "Collective Negotiations and Teachers: A Behavioral Analysis," *Industrial and Labor Relations Review, 3* (April 1970), pp. 380–396.

Kasper, Hirschel. "The Effect of Collective Bargaining on Public School Teachers' Salaries," *Industrial and Labor Relations Review, 24* (October 1970), pp. 57–72.

Koziara, Karen S. "Collective Bargaining on the Farm," *Monthly Labor Review,* June 1968, pp. 3–9.

Loewenberg, Joseph J. "Compulsory Arbitration for Police and Firefighters in Pennsylvania in 1968," *Industrial and Labor Relations Review, 23* (April 1970), pp. 367–379.

McKelvey, Jean T. "The Role of State Agencies in Public Employee Labor Relations," *Industrial and Labor Relations Review, 20* (January 1967), pp. 179–197.

Taylor, George W. "Public Employment: Strikes or Procedures?" *Industrial and Labor Relations Review, 29* (July 1967), pp. 617–636.

Ullman, Joseph C., and James P. Betin. "The Structure and Scope of Appeals Procedures for Public Employees," *Industrial and Labor Relations Review, 23* (April 1970), pp. 323–334.

21

The Prevention or
Settlement of Disputes

Most labor-management agreements—perhaps 90 per cent or more—are negotiated quietly and peacefully. But labor peace does not make headlines; labor-management warfare does. The labor disputes with which most of us are familiar are those that occur when negotiations break down and a strike results. But thousands of disputes, most of a minor nature, are settled under the terms of existing agreements. The general public does not know when such disputes occur or how they are resolved. But the day-to-day administration of labor-management agreements is one of the most important, if least known, aspects of collective bargaining. It is important to distinguish between the two major types of labor disputes: (1) those that occur during the lifetime of an agreement, and (2) those that take place when the negotiation of a new agreement breaks down.

Two other species of disputes should be mentioned. The first is the unauthorized or "wildcat" strike that takes place during the life of an agreement. Such strikes are usually spontaneous eruptions, and they are generally settled quite promptly. Responsible union leaders do not condone wildcat strikes. And unions in general are anxious to avoid them, since this is scarcely a good form of public relations. The second kind of dispute, the jurisdictional dispute, involves disagreement between two unions, neither of which may have a specific grievance against the employer. Such disputes—to which the employer is an unwilling third party—are frowned upon by many union leaders. The AFL-CIO, for example, has tried to minimize jurisdictional disputes, and a number of unions have taken steps for the peaceful settlement of jurisdictional rivalry. We will return to the issue of jurisdictional disputes later in this chapter. But for the present we will concentrate on the major types of disputes; the methods that have been developed to avert disputes; and the techniques for the settlement of disputes if they cannot be averted. Sometimes, we will see, disputes can be settled only by a show of force.

The Grievance Procedure

One of the more important parts of the labor-management agreement is the grievance procedure. This is the safety valve built into the agreement to prevent every minor difference of opinion from mushrooming into a major dispute. Even the most carefully worked out agreement cannot provide for every conceivable contingency. Some grievances are of a personal nature; they do not relate to the agreement as such, but if labor and management are to work together, and to live together, there must be a method for settling the many day-to-day disputes that are bound to occur. It was not always so. In the early days of collective bargaining, strikes occasionally erupted without warning, and it was because of this that grievance procedures were developed as collective bargaining matured.[1]

The earliest grievance procedures were evidently negotiated by the International Typographical Union and various publishers with which it dealt. Perhaps the best known early grievance machinery was that developed as part of the Star Island Agreement of 1903 in the flint glass industry. The steps for the settlement of grievances in this agreement closely parallel those commonly followed today.[2] Another famous early grievance arrangement resulted from a spontaneous walkout that took place in the Hart, Schaffner and Marx garment shops in 1911. Discussing this strike, Joseph Schaffner, the head of the firm, pointed out that just a few days before the walkout, he had commented to a friend on the satisfactory state of his industrial relations. When the workers walked out, management's original reaction was one of bewilderment. The employers could not find out what was wrong. Finally, they discovered there was no single cause; the walkout had resulted from the accumulation of a great many grievances some of which, taken alone, would have been quite minor. The strike was settled and steps were taken to establish a grievance system to avoid a repetition in the future. Gradually, out of these and other experiences, grievance procedures were negotiated in a growing number of agreements. Today, a labor-management agreement without a grievance procedure is the exception, and a very rare exception at that.

Types of Grievances

A catalogue of the thousands of grievances settled every year would be an imposing document. But most grievances may be classified under three main headings. These are:

---

1. This section draws heavily upon John A. Lapp, *How to Handle Labor Grievances* (New York: National Foreman's Institute, Inc., 1945).

2. Lapp, *ibid.,* pp. 15–16.

1. Grievances arising from the interpretation of the meaning of words and phrases in labor-management agreements.
2. Grievances resulting from the application of the provisions of agreements in individual cases, including discipline and discharge cases.
3. Grievances affecting individuals or groups of workers and arising out of the day-to-day work environment, and not out of causes covered by the labor-management agreement.[3]

The number of grievances processed every year runs into the thousands. But only a small proportion of serious cases become major issues. Many grievances arise out of purely personal relationships. If a foreman comes to work with a chip on his shoulder, he will be lucky to get through the day without offending some of the workers under his direction. The same is true of individual workers. But all grievances—real or imagined—can impair a sound labor-management relationship unless promptly settled.

Other grievances result from job assignments, changes in rates of pay, discipline or discharge, and a wide variety of other matters covered by the agreement. If a worker feels that he has not been treated justly he is free to file a grievance, which typically goes through the steps described in the following paragraphs. Also, disputes occasionally arise over the meaning of the language in an agreement. In this case, the language in question will usually be changed when a new agreement is negotiated, but there must be some method of settling differences in interpretation during the life of an existing agreement.

Types of Grievance Procedures

The following steps show the typical sequence in a wide variety of grievance arrangements:

1. Shop steward and foreman.
2. Chief steward and personnel officer.
3. Grievance committee.
4. Business agent and general manager.
5. Arbitration.

A worker with a grievance first goes to his shop steward. The latter will listen to the grievance and decide whether it is a bona fide complaint or an unwarranted gripe. If he feels that the grievance is valid, he fills out a grievance form, carefully noting the time and the place and all other relevant facts. The shop steward then goes to the foreman in charge of the aggrieved worker —usually asking the worker to accompany him. Possibly the shop steward

---

3. *Ibid.,* p. 28.

and the foreman can settle the grievance on the spot. Perhaps nothing more is called for than an apology or an indication that there has been a simple misunderstanding. It is likely that under such circumstances, the grievance form is destroyed and does not, therefore, become a matter of record.

But if the grievance cannot be settled at this stage, it will be turned over to the grievance committee, which meets at stated intervals. The committee, which ordinarily is made up of an equal number of representatives of union and management, reviews all grievances before it, at each of its meetings. Some the committee will agree to settle, while others may result in a deadlock. The latter grievances are then turned over to the union's business agent and the general manager, with the stipulation that they be settled within a stated time. Some of the grievances that cannot be settled by the committee will be disposed of by the business agent, who represents the national union, and the general manager. Others must go to arbitration.

Large companies, which deal with large local unions, will often have so many grievances that a full-time umpire is retained by the two parties to settle matters that cannot be handled by the first four steps of the grievance machinery. There are cases where the work load is so heavy that two or more umpires must be retained. In practically all cases, the parties will agree in their contract to abide by the decision of the umpire or arbitrator. Most industrial relations specialists feel that an essential part of a successful grievance machinery is some provision for final and binding settlement. This view is supported by a recent survey of major contract provisions, which showed that 94 per cent of all major contracts contain provisions for final and binding arbitration as the terminal step in the grievance procedure.[4]

The machinery described above is typical of that found in many labor-management agreements. There are some variations. In a few cases, for example, grievances go directly from the foreman to a shop or plant grievance committee; in other cases, where a single union deals with an association of employers, a joint committee will be established to investigate all grievances. Any that cannot be settled will be sent to an impartial umpire or a tripartite board with an impartial chairman.

Ground Rules for the Settlement of Grievances

Most large unions provide their shop stewards with manuals. Among other things, these handbooks tell the stewards how to handle grievances. Typical is the *Shop Steward's Manual* issued by the International Association of Machinists.[5] The IAM *Manual* describes the grievance procedure, quoting the

---

4. Bob Repas, "Grievance Procedures Without Arbitration," *Industrial and Labor Relations Review,* 20 (April 1967), p. 381. This study deals with the unusual case of the Allied Industrial Workers Union in Western Michigan. This union had 79 agreements in this region, but more than 80 per cent *did not* provide for arbitration.

5. Research Department, International Association of Machinists, *Shop Steward's Manual* (Washington, D.C.: IAM, September 1948).

relevant passages from some of its agreements. It then suggests ways by which the shop steward should go about enforcing these contract provisions. Among the "tips on relations with management" which the manual contains are the following: (1) abide by contract rules, (2) make sure that it is a just grievance, (3) get all the facts, (4) write it down, and (5) use a positive, friendly approach.

The shop steward is also exhorted to be a good listener and to disagree amiably; to try to settle at the first stage; to avoid empty threats; and to stick to the facts. If the grievance is settled successfully, he is told not to gloat or brag about his victories over management. Finally, he is urged to get to the roots of the problems from which grievances grow.

The Role of the Shop Steward and the Foreman

A workable labor-management agreement will be written in language that will minimize the number of disputes over interpretation, but the best contract in the world will not minimize grievances unless the foremen and shop stewards are understanding. This is the point of immediate contact between union and management. Good foremen and able shop stewards will, of course, protect the rights of management and workers. But they can also work together to settle minor grievances satisfactorily and thus avoid the time-consuming—and sometimes costly—process of carrying every grievance all the way to the final step of the procedure.

An obstreperous foreman, or a self-seeking shop steward, can do much to keep labor-management relations in a state of constant turmoil. Usually this will not last. Someone higher up the ladder—in the company, the union, or both—will usually find out what is behind a steady flow of grievances. But until this is done, and appropriate steps taken to correct the matter, the work atmosphere can be charged with tension, and at times serious disputes can erupt. But the shop steward and foreman must work within the broader framework of union and management policies, and these, too, at times can magnify rather than minimize the problem of grievance settlement.

A company which decides to adopt a tough attitude toward the union might insist that every grievance—however slight—go all the way to arbitration. In such cases labor-management relations will be constantly strained, and union and management representatives will maintain a constant air of hostility. Nothing short of a change at the top—replacement of the union business agent or international representative, or appointment of a new personnel officer—can change such an environment. But there have been cases where such changes have led to a reevaluation of the entire grievance procedure. Companies have found that they were processing grievances, perhaps at the cost of hundreds of dollars, involving a fraction of this amount. A careful screening of grievances has shown that enormous savings result if only those involving some new principle are processed.

If there is to be steady progress toward minimizing grievances, both unions and management must keep careful records of all grievances and their disposition. If each grievance is classified, and if the entire grievance picture is reviewed at periodic intervals, each side can notice any trends that are developing. If impartial umpires make a majority of awards to the union or to management over some specific issue, the parties might want to consider carefully before sending the next grievance all the way through the machinery. If the two parties are interested in working out and maintaining the best day-to-day relations of which they are capable, they will carefully study the pattern of grievances and the pattern of settlements. As with other phases of collective bargaining, the development of a successful grievance machinery—satisfactory to both parties—is generally an evolutionary process.

Arbitration

There are two general types of arbitration. The first—and by far the most important—is *grievance arbitration.* Grievance arbitration is carried on under an existing agreement. In almost all cases, the decision of the arbitrator is final and binding, although in reaching his decision the arbitrator is limited by his interpretation of the language of the agreement.[6] He must decide the grievance within this framework; he is not permitted to bring in principles or facts other than those introduced by the parties. He can, however, refer to earlier decisions in similar cases. As in the common law, precedent plays an important part in grievance arbitration.[7]

The second kind of arbitration, which is used quite infrequently, is called *wage* or *contract arbitration.* There are some cases when the negotiation of a new agreement reaches a deadlock. Perhaps the two parties can agree on most of the provisions of the new agreement, but neither party is willing to budge on one or a few issues. In such cases—although it must be repeated that this is fairly rare—an arbitrator will be called in to render a decision on the disputed issues. We will consider grievance arbitration first and then turn to a brief discussion of contract arbitration.

Types of Arbitration Arrangements

Some labor-management agreements call for a permanent arbitrator or impartial umpire. The two parties must agree on the arbitrator before the agreement is signed, and it is typical for the agreement to specify that all grievances

---

6. The issue of what is and what is not arbitrable can become a fairly complex one, and when the issue arises it generally has to be settled in the courts. Arbitrators should not be asked to rule on the arbitrability of an issue. "There is a patent contradiction in terms for an arbitrator to announce, after a full hearing has been accorded the matter, that a given issue is not arbitrable. How can it be nonarbitrable when a full scale arbitration hearing has just been held?" R. W. Fleming, "Arbitrators and Arbitrability," *Washington University Law Quarterly, 1963,* p. 219.

7. For an illustration of the interplay between legal precedent and arbitration precedent, see Edgar A. Jones, Jr., "An Arbitral Answer to a Judicial Dilemma: The *Carey* Decision and Trilateral Arbitration of Jurisdictional Disputes," *UCLA Law Review, 11* (March 1964), especially pp. 355–357.

decided by the arbitrator will be final and binding. Whatever the decision, each party agrees to abide by it. This is usually accompanied by a no-strike and no-lockout pledge.

Other agreements provide for *ad hoc* arbitrators. The agreement might specify that an arbitrator will be called in to handle each case that arises, or it might call for the selection of an arbitrator after a certain number of cases have accumulated. To obtain arbitrators, the parties might turn to the American Arbitration Association, which keeps a list of approved arbitrators and can notify the disputants of arbitrators available in a specific area. In other cases, the parties will turn to universities or to priests or other clergymen to decide their cases. The major qualification of an arbitrator—however he is selected—is that he be impartial.

A third variation is the three man arbitration board. Such boards are typically made up of a union representative, a management representative, and an impartial member. In some cases only the impartial member, who serves as chairman, has a vote; in other cases all three members vote although the deciding vote is almost invariably cast by the impartial member. As with single arbitrators, tripartite boards may be either permanent, that is, for the life of an agreement, or they may be selected on an *ad hoc* basis.[8]

One advantage of the impartial umpire, or permanent arbitrator, is that he becomes well acquainted with the company and the union whose disputes he must settle. Many grievances involve technical matters, such as machine assignments, job transfers, the determination of piece rates or incentive pay, and similar matters of a technical nature. If the arbitrator is familiar with the conditions in the company, and if he is familiar with earlier cases that might serve as precedents, he might be able to expedite matters and render decisions in a fairly short time. One disadvantage of permanent arrangements is that the arbitrator might attempt to settle many cases by "splitting down the middle." Most agreements that call for permanent umpires specify that either party can terminate the arbitrator's appointment at its discretion. If too many cases go to one party or the other, the "permanent" arbitrator's appointment might be terminated rather quickly.[9]

In some cases, the parties might feel that an *ad hoc* arbitrator will render more impartial decisions. It is likely that if an arbitrator is called in to settle a single case, he will not be particularly concerned about the distribution of prior decisions. But the selection of an *ad hoc* arbitrator can be a time-consuming process. The parties might find it difficult to agree on a candidate

---

8. In recent years, more than 93 per cent of all decisions by arbitrators have been awards by single arbitrators. There is a tendency for tripartite arbitration boards to be limited to large bargaining units. See Harold W. Davey, "The Uses and Misuses of Tripartite Boards in Grievance Arbitration," in *Developments in American and Foreign Arbitration,* Proceedings of the Twenty-First Annual Meeting of the National Academy of Arbitrators (Washington, D.C.: Bureau of National Affairs, Inc., 1968), pp. 155–157.

9. See, for example, Harold W. Davey, *Contemporary Collective Bargaining,* 2nd ed., Englewood Cliffs, N.J.: Prentice-Hall, Inc., 1959), p. 139n.

who is mutually acceptable. Meanwhile, the grievance remains unsettled until the arbitrator is selected, hearing dates are arranged, the case is heard, and the decision is rendered. *Ad hoc* arbitrators—often university professors— have other duties, and the hearings and other details of arbitrations might have to await their pleasure.

There are advantages and disadvantages to both permanent and *ad hoc* arrangements, and the parties can only decide on the basis of experience which arrangement will work best in each case. Generally, permanent ar- bitrators are found in agreements involving fairly large companies and large unions, where the accumulation of grievances would make it impracticable for the two parties to select *ad hoc* arbitrators for each case.

Types of Arbitrators

In addition to his impartiality, a successful arbitrator must be a judicious person. He must have a good working knowledge of labor law; he must know something about economics; and he must have a good background in the field of industrial relations. It is also helpful if the arbitrator is familiar with the industry or industries in which he works. No effort will be made to develop a detailed classification of various kinds of arbitrators, but one useful distinction might be drawn. Some arbitrators are willing to render judgment on every case brought to them. Such arbitrators feel that their expert knowledge permits them to render sounder decisions than could be reached by the two parties through continued negotiations. Other arbitrators, however, adopt a different view. They feel that it might be relatively easy to render an award in many cases. But at the same time they feel that the two parties will be able to live and work together in greater harmony if they can settle disputed issues themselves. Such arbitrators will decide particularly difficult cases. However, if they feel that more will be gained by refusing to make an award, they will remand the case to the two parties. Representatives of union and manage- ment will then try to hammer out an agreement, knowing that if they fail a second time the case can be returned to the arbitrator.[10]

In some situations, arbitration is a continuation of the day-to-day col- lective bargaining process. There are other cases, however, where arbitration is clearly a judicial process. About the only general statement that can be made about arbitration is that it is essentially a flexible process, which tends to adapt to changing labor-management relationships.

Arbitration is not something that is particularly new in collective bar-

---

10. James Gross has pointed out that since the decisions of arbitrators are influenced by their own values, detailed studies should be made to include "surveys of their social and educational backgrounds, professions, attitudes, and opinions . . . [and] in-depth biographies which will aid in understanding their philosophies and techniques." James A. Gross, "Value Judgments in the Decisions of Labor Arbitrators," *Industrial and Labor Relations Review, 21,* October 1967, p. 72.

gaining. It has been going on for decades.[11] But as R. W. Fleming has recently put it: "Arbitration is still in its swaddling clothes."[12] Arbitration procedures have remained much more flexible than courtroom procedures. As Fleming has noted: "An important characteristic of arbitration is its flexibility in resolving practical problems. Hopefully, this characteristic will assure application of traditional standards of fairness without the imposition of excessive legalisms adopted wholesale from courtroom procedures."[13] Jones has stated emphatically that: "Concern for 'legal' issues simply does not belong in arbitration."[14] Most students of the collective bargaining process would agree with these sentiments.

A successful grievance procedure will include a series of deadlines for the handling of individual cases. Usually, a time is specified for each step in the process. The advantages of a quick settlement are evident. Once a decision is reached the person who filed the grievance must accept it. If there are continued delays, the worker with the grievance is likely to feel that he is being by-passed, and might feel resentful toward both the company and the union. Much the same is true of arbitration. The advantages of fairly prompt decisions are widely recognized. As Arthur Ross has pointed out, however, there has been a tendency for the arbitration process to become more time-consuming. He found that over a ten-year period ending in 1956, the average time between the filing of grievances and arbitration awards increased by more than one half, and had reached more than two hundred days. This he attributed to increasingly elaborate and formal arbitration procedure, delays in the selection of *ad hoc* arbitrators, the overloaded dockets of permanent umpires, and what he considered to be a tendency toward too much arbitration.[15] Ross felt that in many cases there had been "a dangerous trend toward reliance on technicality, reminiscent of the old system of strict pleadings under the common law ... "[16] In his view, there was a tendency for arbitration to lose some of its flexibility which, as noted earlier, most students of industrial relations consider to be one of the virtues of the arbitration process.

---

11. During the late nineteenth century and the early years of the present century, however, "the term 'arbitration' was applied to *any* effort by management and union to resolve a labor dispute by methods other than economic force." It was thus virtually a synonym for what we now call "negotiation" and "conciliation." See Davey, "The Uses and Misuses of Tripartite Boards in Grievance Arbitration," p. 158.

12. R. W. Fleming, "Some Problems of Due Process and Fair Procedure in Labor Arbitration," *Stanford Law Review, 13,* No. 2 (March 1961), p. 251.

13. *Ibid.*

14. Jones, *op. cit.,* p. 356.

15. Arthur M. Ross, "The Well-Aged Arbitration Case," *Industrial and Labor Relations Review, 11,* No. 2 (January 1958), pp. 262–268.

16. *Ibid.,* p. 268.

Contract or Wage Arbitration

Contract or wage arbitration is much less widespread than grievance arbitration. It is one thing for the two parties to agree to have an outsider settle differences of interpretation of *existing* labor-management agreements. It is quite another for them to bring in a disinterested party to break a deadlock during negotiations. There are times, however, when the two parties can agree on most of the provisions being negotiated, but perhaps are deadlocked on one or two. Occasionally, under such circumstances, an arbitrator or an arbitration board might be agreed upon, and the parties will agree to abide by an impartial decision. It must be emphasized that arbitration of this kind is fairly rare, and has been declining. Bernstein found that 103 wage arbitration awards had been reported between 1945 and 1950, but Miller found only 44 such awards during the longer period covered by the years 1953 through 1965.[17]

Why do labor and management object to the arbitration of part of a new agreement, when most successful relationships make extensive use of grievance arbitration? In part, the answer is that such arbitration has not been notably successful in the past. Many union leaders believe that arbitration boards are likely to be biased against the union or its position. And employers object to arbitration of wage matters, for example, because in their view the arbitrators are likely to "split the difference" so that the union is bound to gain something, while the employer is bound to lose. Also, some employers oppose such arbitration because they believe it is an improper delegation of managerial responsibility to someone outside the company. Since, in general, neither labor nor management is favorably inclined toward contract arbitration, it is not surprising that few deadlocks are settled in this way. If necessary, the parties believe, the deadlocks can be broken by a show of force—by a strike.

Compulsory Arbitration

Practically every time there is a major labor dispute, the issue of compulsory arbitration is raised. Editorial writers and others will insist that regardless of how the two parties feel about it, the public must be protected against the disruption of economic activity. A few legislators also become exacerbated during major labor disputes and revive the issue of compulsory arbitration. Fortunately, cooler heads have generally prevailed, although one experience with compulsory arbitration illustrates some of the dangers of this approach.

In 1920, the Kansas Legislature enacted the Kansas Industrial Court Act. This law set up a Court of Industrial Relations, which had the authority to

---

17. Irving Bernstein, *Arbitration of Wages* (Berkeley, California: University of California Press, 1954), p. 25; Richard U. Miller, "Arbitration of New Contract Wage Disputes: Some Recent Trends," *Industrial and Labor Relations Review, 20* (January 1967), p. 264.

investigate labor-management disputes in specified industries, "and, after proper hearing *and trial,* to issue orders compelling adherence to its findings."[18] Both strikes and lockouts were prohibited by law in the industries affected by this act.

A case could be initiated by either party under the Kansas Act, or the court could intervene on its own initiative. Thus the Court of Industrial Relations had greater power than our civil courts, which must wait until someone sets a suit in motion. Either party could appeal the findings of the court—as in the case of civil suits—with decisions going up to the Kansas Supreme Court. During its brief life the Court of Industrial Relations handled a number of labor disputes but there was little satisfaction with its decisions. The United States Supreme Court declared the Act to be unconstitutional and in conflict with the Fourteenth Amendment, in *The Charles Wolfe Packing Company v. The Court of Industrial Relations* in 1923. Among other things, the Supreme Court noted that the Kansas Act "curtails the right of the employer, on the one hand, and of the employee, on the other, to contract about his affairs. This is part of the liberty of the individual protected by the guaranty of the due process clause of the Fourteenth Amendment."[19] After this experience, no other state attempted to provide for compulsory arbitration of labor-management disputes.

One objection to compulsory arbitration, which has been voiced by both labor and management, is that there is no assurance that an industrial court will be impartial in judging labor disputes. Few doubt that our civil courts are impartial in handling most decisions coming before them. Such decisions, however, generally involve relatively private matters, whereas a major labor-management dispute becomes a public matter. Many persons tend to react emotionally to labor-management disputes, and this could apply to the judges of an industrial court as well as to laymen. Another objection is that the members of an industrial court will lack the expertise needed to rule fairly on a wide range of labor-management disputes involving many occupations and industries. Grievance arbitration works well because the arbitrators selected jointly by both parties must know something about the industry and the occupations involved. But the members of an industrial court would have to be experts on *all* industries and occupations. It would be difficult to find anyone with these qualifications. Finally, to be successful, an industrial court would have to have greater powers than the civil court. It would have to be able to initiate action and not wait for one or the other parties to submit their dispute. There is general reluctance to grant a court such sweeping power and authority. Labor unions have solidly opposed any repetition of the Kansas experiment, and similar opposition has been ex-

---

18. John A. Lapp, *Labor Arbitration* (New York: National Foremen's Institute, Inc., 1946), p. 10, italics added.
19. Cited by Lapp, *ibid.,* p. 12.

pressed by the National Association of Manufacturers and the United States Chamber of Commerce.[20] Labor and management agree, however, that where a third party can help in breaking a deadlock this is desirable, so long as the two parties remain completely free to seek or not to seek assistance.

Mediation and Conciliation

Strictly speaking, conciliation means an effort by a third party to keep negotiations going between labor and management in the face of an impending breakdown, whereas mediation implies more active participation in the bargaining process. But this distinction has broken down. Conciliation is now defined as an "attempt by a third party to help in the settlement of disputes between employers and employees through interpretation, suggestion, and advice. In practice, conciliation is synonymous with mediation."[21]

There is a certain amount of grievance mediation in the United States, some of a formal and some of an informal character. There are cases where an arbitrator attempts to mediate a dispute under an existing agreement rather than issuing an award. This is most likely to occur in a relationship that uses a permanent umpire. Typically, however, while such mediation may precede arbitration, it does not preclude the latter.[22] Generally, those who support grievance mediation are of the opinion that voluntary agreement is superior to an enforced award. This undoubtedly is the major argument in favor of grievance mediation. As noted in our earlier discussion of grievance arbitration, one type of arbitrator tries to remand as many cases as possible to the two parties, on the assumption that they will be able to live and work together better if they work out their own differences. Such arbitrators would subscribe to the notion that they should attempt to mediate whenever possible.

There is one difficulty involved in grievance mediation, however. If a permanent umpire has attempted to mediate a dispute and fails, he should not then arbitrate the same issue. There is an old maxim in arbitration circles that: "An arbitrator may mediate but a mediator should never arbitrate." Thus if the umpire has at one point served as a mediator he should step aside if the issue must go on to arbitration. The reasoning behind this is that in his efforts to mediate a difference of opinion, the arbitrator has undoubtedly found some middle ground on which he thinks agreement can be reached. This is likely to affect his decision as an arbitrator.

Compared with arbitration, grievance mediation has certain advantages

---

20. *Ibid.,* pp. 13–14.

21. U.S. Department of Labor, Bureau of Labor Statistics, *Glossary of Current Industrial Relations Terms* (Washington, D.C.: U.S. Government Printing Office, May 1960), p. 5.

22. See William H. McPherson, "Grievance Mediation Under Collective Bargaining," *Industrial and Labor Relations Review, 9,* No. 2 (January 1956), p. 201.

in that it can save both time and money as well as lead to fundamental improvement in the long-run relationship between the two parties. On the other hand, it has been pointed out that unsuccessful grievance mediation lengthens the time between the filing of a grievance and its ultimate disposition through arbitration. Evidently labor and management have not been greatly impressed by the advantages of prearbitration grievance mediation, since relatively few agreements contain provisions calling for this procedure.[23]

Mediation and conciliation are the most important means of settling differences of opinion on *new* agreements, short of a show of economic strength. At times, collective bargaining is accompanied by a great deal of bluster and much publicity. Both labor and management may publicly take adamant positions, and indicate that they will *never* give in unless the other side makes certain concessions. Having adopted this posture it is not easy to back down. But an outsider can then enter the picture—much like the *deus ex machina* in an old Greek drama—and resolve the disputed issue short of a strike.

There is no standard pattern of operations in mediation and conciliation. Each mediator must develop his own techniques. In general, however, the process works somewhat as follows. Since the two parties have reached a deadlock in face-to-face meetings, the first step is generally to separate them. The mediator then sits down with one party and listens to all of its arguments; he weighs and evaluates this position, then repeats the process with the other party. Perhaps at this stage he is able to see areas of agreement which the two parties have overlooked in the heat of negotiations. Then begins a process of going back and forth from one party to the other. He can perhaps encourage a modest amount of "horse trading"—elicit some concessions from both sides. If successful, he will slowly broaden areas of agreement and, at the same time, narrow the areas of disagreement. Perhaps at some point he is able to say to each of the parties that they no longer have an issue at dispute. If he can convince them of this, they can be brought together and settlement can be reached—usually with an appropriate amount of fanfare and publicity.

The mediator must remain completely detached throughout the proceedings. He must be a good listener; he must avoid legalism; and above all he must be sincerely interested in the peaceful settlement of the dispute. At the same time, a good mediator will also know when his efforts are hopeless; at this point he will bow out of the argument gracefully and let the two parties slug it out on their own terms.

Among other things, the Taft-Hartley Act provided for a Federal Mediation and Conciliation Service. If a dispute involving interstate commerce should threaten to cause a substantial interruption in business activity, the Service

---

23. *Ibid.*, p. 212.

may enter the dispute by making available its facilities of conciliation, mediation, and voluntary arbitration. The Service has no power to compel settlement. But in certain types of disputes, the parties have a statutory obligation to "participate fully and promptly in such meetings as may be undertaken by the Service under this Act for the purpose of aiding in the settlement of a dispute." Thus the Federal Mediation and Conciliation Service is involved in all major disputes, although it must be emphasized that it has no power to compel settlement. The Service avoids involvement in minor disputes or in grievance disputes. It will supply a panel of qualified arbitrators upon request, from which the parties can make a selection. In general, however, the Federal Mediation and Conciliation Service was set up to prevent the breakdown of collective bargaining over *new* agreements.

It is difficult to measure the effectiveness of mediation and conciliation. There are outstanding cases in which it is known that mediation has averted a strike and led to a settlement acceptable to both parties. It is impossible to say whether or not such agreement would have been reached without the aid of the mediator. Most students of labor-management relations would undoubtedly agree that the mediator plays an important part in collective bargaining, and that many deadlocks would result in a strike without the intervention of an effective mediator. As Arthur S. Meyer,[24] himself an exceptionally successful mediator, put it:

> Labor disputes are exhausting processes and the mediator, like the participants, will think of nothing so much as of a settlement, any settlement, for according to the conventions of the game, each settlement is a victory and there is little to choose between one and the other. Catalysis is the guiding principle and peace the constant objective.

Despite the best efforts of the two parties—and of mediators—agreement cannot always be reached. When this happens, any remaining differences of opinion are settled by economic force—a strike.

There are also cases in which agreement is reached by union negotiators and representatives of management, with the aid of a mediator, only to have the tentative settlement rejected by the union membership. In the majority of cases of this kind, negotiations are resumed without a strike, and eventual settlement is reached. But on the basis of limited data, it appears that in about one third of the cases in which a mediator has helped the parties reach a tentative settlement, the rank and file have failed to ratify the agreement.[25] In these cases the issue was ultimately settled by a strike.

---

24. Arthur S. Meyer, "Function of the Mediator in Collective Bargaining," *Industrial and Labor Relations Review, 13,* No. 2 (January 1960), p. 165.

25. William E. Simkin, "Refusals to Ratify Contracts," *Industrial and Labor Relations Review, 21* (July 1968), pp. 518–540.

Work Stoppages

When all else fails, labor and management settle their disputes by resorting to a strike or a lockout. Strikes and lockouts are forms of economic warfare. The history of labor-management relations in the United States is dotted with many bitter and violent strikes. Some of the early strikes in the coal and steel industries led to violence and bloodshed. Perhaps the blackest mark in the history of industrial relations was the Ludlow Massacre, which occurred during the Colorado coal strike of 1913 to 1914. Several women and children were killed in the encounter between the state militia and the miners, and a number of miners were killed before this strike was finally settled.

There was also a good deal of violence during the organizational strikes that followed the resurgence of trade unionism after 1935. The famous "Battle of the Bridge," when the United Auto Workers were trying to organize the Ford Motor Company, is a case in point. It was perhaps less than a coincidence that the photographers representing a well-known pictorial news magazine were present to record the affair. In recent years, however, there have been fewer large-scale organizational strikes, and as labor-management relations have stabilized, violence has diminished. Strikes involving violence and bloodshed are quite rare today.[26]

The recent history of work stoppages is summarized succinctly in Figure 21-1.[27] The number of work stoppages reached an all-time peak in 1970, a year in which there were 5,716 strikes. But the largest number of workers—4.6 million—were on strike in 1946. There was a downward swing in the strike cycle until 1964. This was followed by an increase in the number of strikes and in the number of workers involved, which continued until 1970. There was a similar cycle in the number of man-days of idleness due to strike activity with an intervening peak in 1959 due to the long steel strike of that year.

The amount of working time lost due to strikes in the United States has never been large. In the peak year of 1946 it amounted to slightly more than 1 per cent, and for the forty years covered by Figure 21-1 idleness due to strike activity has averaged one fourth of 1 per cent per year. By coincidence, this is the amount of working time lost in 1971.

Can we conclude from the figure below that the economy produced about one fourth of 1 per cent less in 1971 than it would have in the absence of strikes? Some economists would answer this question in the negative, pointing to what has been called the "offset factor" in labor disputes. A stripped-down version of the theory of the offset factor is as follows: Few industries operate

---

26. For a detailed account of the longest strike in American labor history—one frequently punctuated by violence—see Walter H. Uphoff, *Kohler on Strike: Thirty Years of Conflict* (Boston: The Beacon Press, 1966).

27. For comparable details covering the period 1916 to 1930, see *Analysis of Work Stoppages 1960,* U.S. Department of Labor, Bureau of Labor Statistics, Bulletin No. 1302 (September 1961), p. 2.

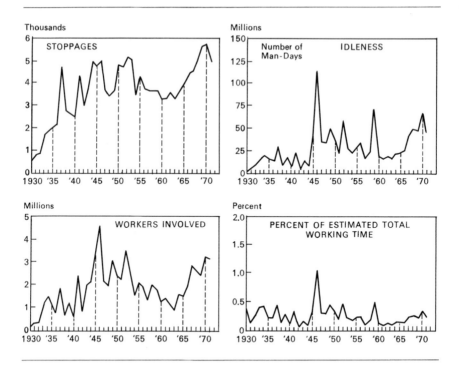

FIGURE 21–1.

Trends in Work Stoppages, 1930–1971. (*Data from U.S. Department of Labor, Bureau of Labor Statistics,* Analysis of Work Stoppages, 1960, *Bulletin No. 1302* [*September 1961*], *p. 4; Monthly Labor Review* [*August 1971*], *p. 119; and "Work Stoppages, 1971," U. S. Department of Labor News Release 72–8.*)

at peak capacity all the time, but in anticipation of a strike, management can begin to step up production months in advance of the strike deadline. The extra production is added to inventory to be used during the course of the strike. Thus, some would argue, strikes might not cost the economy anything in terms of production.[28]

The theory of the offset factor has a great deal of plausibility. If a strike runs longer than either side anticipated, however, the prestrike buildup of inventories might not be sufficient to exactly offset production lost during the strike. During the long steel strike of 1959, for example, certain types of steel were in short supply before the strike ended and some steel users turned to

28. For extended discussion of the theory of the offset factor, with specific application to coal production, see C. L. Christenson, "The Theory of the Offset Factor: The Impact of Labor Disputes Upon Coal Production," *The American Economic Review, XLIII* (September 1953), pp. 513–547, and Christenson, "The Impact of Labor Disputes on Coal Consumption," *The American Economic Review, XLV* (March 1955), pp. 79–112.

foreign producers to satisfy their needs. There is also some evidence that aluminum, and perhaps other metals, were substituted for steel in some construction uses. Thus when steel production was resumed some markets were permanently lost to the steel industry. It is not likely that imports and the substitution of aluminum for steel had significant lasting effects on steel production. These matters are mentioned, however, to indicate the difficulty of measuring with great precision the impact of strikes upon our economy. Yet when we recognize that the time lost due to strikes is a tiny fraction of total working time, and also take into account the offsetting influence of prestrike inventory buildups, it seems safe to conclude that industrial disputes have not seriously retarded economic growth. This is neither an attempt to minimize the seriousness of strikes, nor to suggest that strikes are something which we can simply ignore. Companies involved in strikes can and do suffer losses of revenue. And striking workers are often forced to deplete their savings accounts, and frequently to go deeply into debt, before they are able to return to their jobs. At the same time those who suggest that strikes should be outlawed—usually through compulsory arbitration—fail to recognize that the alternative they suggest could be more damaging to a free society than time lost due to work disputes. Both labor and management insist on the right to settle their differences through a show of economic force, if this becomes necessary. They insist on the "right" to strike so long as this does not jeopardize the health, welfare, or security of society.

What are the major issues that have led to strikes since the end of World War II? Between 1947 and 1959, 73 per cent of all time lost due to work stoppages resulted from strikes over wages, hours, and supplementary benefits. An average for the last two years for which data are available, 1969-1970, shows that idleness due to these causes was down to 62 per cent of the total. From the end of World War II until 1960, about 20 per cent of idleness due to strikes was the result of efforts by unions to obtain union security—generally a union shop agreement—or to strengthen their bargaining position. By 1969-1970, slightly more than 13 per cent of time lost was due to disputes over these issues. There has been an increase in disputes involving work rules or working conditions. During the period 1947 to 1959, less than 5 per cent of time lost due to work stoppages were the result of disputes over working conditions. In 1969-1970, however, more than 22 per cent of mandays idle resulted from disputes over job security, plant administration, working conditions, and "other contractual matters." It is likely that a growing proportion of disputes in the future will involve work rules and working conditions.

The type of strike that leads to the greatest amount of public indignation is the one resulting from interunion and intraunion disputes. This category includes strikes resulting from union rivalry, sympathy strikes, and jurisdictional disputes. Between 1947 and 1960, all strikes involving interunion or intraunion matters accounted for less than 1 per cent of total man-days idle due to work stoppages. In 1969-1970, about 1.8 per cent of idleness due to strikes was the result of interunion or intraunion disputes.

The most highly organized sectors of the economy are manufacturing, mining, construction, transportation, and public utilities. It is not surprising, therefore, that between 50 and 60 per cent of all strike activity is in manufacturing, and that the nonmanufacturing sectors mentioned above account for a disproportionate share of strike activity. Although unions have made some headway in organizing the trades and services, strike activity in these areas has been negligible. This is partly because "white-collar" unions are not strong, and therefore not overly militant; it is also partly a matter of simple arithmetic. Most workers in the trades and services are unorganized, so the strike activity of a small minority expressed as a percentage of the total amount of work time will necessarily be small.

The relatively small amount of time lost due to strikes during the past two decades shows that collective bargaining in the private sector has become a relatively peaceful process. There also has been a tendency for labor disputes to be somewhat shorter than they were in the past. The "average duration of strikes" is a statistic that must be interpreted cautiously. One major dispute lasting for several months can have an appreciable effect on the average. Although there have been a few long strikes in recent years, such as the West Coast dock strike of 1971-1972 most labor disputes have been settled rather quickly. The average duration of strikes in 1969 was 22.5 calendar days; despite the substantial increase in all measures of strike activity in 1970, the average duration increased to only 25 calendar days. Strikes are costly to both labor and management. Although both sides continue to insist on the right to engage in economic warfare when issues cannot be settled at the bargaining table, there seems to be an increasing willingness to settle the strike promptly once it has started.

Strike Insurance and Collective Bargaining

Employers in some industries have banded together to form a single bargaining unit with the object of avoiding union whipsaw tactics. Another approach to the same objective has been the development of "strike insurance." Although not extensively practiced, it has been used by the newspaper publishing, air and rail transportation, and rubber industries. It also has been used by California fruit and vegetable growers and by the Hawaiian sugar cane industry.

The term "strike insurance" has been employed to describe a mutual aid pact that "is a formal private agreement by which competing employers contract that, if one of them is struck, the others will indemnify him by some predetermined amount of money to help him withstand the impact of the strike."[29] Commercial insurance companies have been unwilling to issue

---

29. John F. Hirsch, Jr., "Strike Insurance and Collective Bargaining," *Industrial and Labor Relations Review,* 22 (April 1969), p. 399.

strike insurance because of the possibility of "catastrophe losses" in the event an entire industry is struck. The most widely used method is a "mutual pooling" arrangement designed to spread strike losses throughout a given industry. An insurance company may administer such a plan, but it does so as a trustee and does not assume any of the risk itself.[30]

Needless to say, unions vocally oppose such mutual aid pacts and consider them a violation of the statutory requirement that employers "bargain in good faith." The American Newspaper Guild and other unions have asked for rulings on the legality of strike insurance. They have questioned whether or not strike insurance is a violation of current antitrust laws. Other union leaders have suggested that it may not be wise to press too vigorously for such a ruling, because the courts might find that if employers' strike funds are illegal, union strike funds may also be illegal.[31] Federal agencies, including the National Labor Relations Board, have been unwilling to take the position that strike insurance is illegal.

It is too early to assess the ultimate impact that strike insurance may have on collective bargaining. This will depend on the extent to which it will be used in the future. Mutual aid pacts have no doubt extended the duration of strikes in the few industries in which they have been used. Whether or not this practice will spread to other industries remains a matter of conjecture. Hirsch is of the opinion that if it does, unions will devise a countermeasure, and that in many cases "force and counterforce will leave the parties in the same relative position, but there is not much doubt that the public will be hurt."[32]

Work Stoppages by Public Employees

All measures of strike activity by government employees rose substantially between 1960 and 1970. This was no doubt a consequence of the encouragement of limited collective bargaining provided by President Kennedy's 1962 executive order. The total number of strikes increased from 36 in 1960 to 412 in 1970, and man-days idle increased from 58,000 to more than 2 million. Furthermore, strike activity among public employees has accelerated in recent years. Before 1966, strikes by public employees were increasing gradually. In 1966, however, "public employee strikes and man-days of idleness were more than three times as high as the year before, and the number of workers involved was almost nine times as great."[33]

Most of the increase in strike activity in the public sector was due to work stoppages by local government employees. There was a tenfold in-

---

30. *Ibid.,* pp. 400–401.

31. *Ibid.,* p. 407.

32. *Ibid.,* p. 415.

33. *Government Work Stoppages, 1960–1969 and 1970,* U.S. Department of Labor, Bureau of Labor Statistics, November 1971, p. 1.

crease in local strike activity between 1960 and 1969, and it more than doubled between 1969 and 1970.

In general, work stoppages by government employees do not involve large numbers of workers per stoppage. In 1960, for example, an average of 794 employees were involved in public work stoppages. By 1970, this had increased to 810 workers. Also, strikes by public employees tend to be much shorter than those in the private sector. Between 1960 and 1970, for example, strikes involving local government employees averaged 7.8 days of idleness, and at the state level the average was 5.5 days. As noted earlier in this chapter, strikes in the private sector have averaged more than 20 days in recent years.

Economic issues were responsible for almost two thirds of all public employee strikes in 1970, although the longer stoppages were over the issue of union organization and security. There is also a fairly high degree of concentration in public employee strike activity by occupation. Strikes in public schools and libraries accounted for more than one half of total idleness, and almost two-fifths of all workers involved in government strikes in 1970.

The issue of strikes in public employment was discussed briefly in the last chapter, and George Taylor, a distinguished labor economist, was quoted as saying: "Strikes are not the answer; new procedures are."[34] Essentially, the problem of devising an acceptable alternative to strikes in the public sector is that of avoiding disputes over wage changes or other new contract issues. And these are the issues, as pointed out earlier in this chapter, that do not lend themselves to arbitration. Even if the parties were willing to accept some form of compulsory arbitration—and this does not seem likely in the near future—many problems would remain. These are the problems of devising criteria for wages in public employment.[35]

Ross has discussed some of the measures that might be used as proxies for the criteria used in bargaining over wages in the private sector. He appears to believe that the lack of relevant data is a primary obstacle to third-party settlements of public wage disputes. This may or may not be the case. But the availability of better data on the comparative earnings of public employees, on the "ability to pay" of governmental employers, and other criteria used in private wage negotiations, should lead to improvements in collective bargaining in the public sector. The rapid increase in strike activity by public employees since 1960 should produce increased pressure on union leaders and government agencies to discover workable alternatives to public employee strikes.

---

34. George W. Taylor, "Public Employment: Strikes or Procedures?" *Industrial and Labor Relations Review, 20* (July 1967), p. 636.

35. See David B. Ross, "The Arbitration of Public Employee Wage Disputes," *Industrial and Labor Relations Review, 23* (October 1969), pp. 3–14.

Conclusions

As collective bargaining has matured in the United States, labor and management have developed ways of settling day-to-day differences of opinion without resort to work stoppages. The development of grievance machinery provided an essential "safety valve" for dealing with the problems of individual workers within the terms of existing agreements. Most grievance arrangements today terminate in arbitration, with both parties accepting the arbitrator's decision as final and binding. Less frequently, arbitration is also used for the final settlement of issues upon which the two parties fail to agree during negotiations. In some cases, a strike is ended without all issues settled. In these cases, the parties may agree to arbitration of the unsettled issues after workers have returned to their jobs.

Mediation and conciliation play an important although unmeasurable part in contract negotiations. But there are cases where even with the aid of mediators, agreement cannot be reached and work stoppages result. The few statistics quoted in this chapter indicate that time lost due to strikes involves only a tiny fraction of total working time.

It is not likely that strikes or lockouts in the private sector will become obsolete, at least in the foreseeable future. While there are general expressions of indignation when major strikes occur, and while the hardship suffered by those directly involved should not be minimized, it must be emphasized that the vast majority of all labor-management agreements negotiated each year are settled peacefully. While collective bargaining has become more and more of a peaceful process, both labor and management reserve the right to settle their differences on the economic battleground if there seems to be no other way to reach a solution. Students of industrial conflict seem to agree that so long as the health, welfare, and safety of society are not jeopardized by strike activity, the right to strike, if this becomes necessary, remains one of the essential freedoms of a democracy.

A few industries have used the device of "strike insurance" or mutual aid pacts to spread the cost of strikes against one or a few employers over an entire industry. Union leaders have objected that this represents a lack of good faith bargaining. Neither the courts nor the National Labor Relations Board have been willing to take the position that strike insurance is illegal. Whether or not strike insurance will spread to other industries remains conjectural, but if it does it is not likely to alter the relative power of labor and management in future disputes. One result could be an increase in the duration of disputes, however.

There has been an upsurge in strike activity in the public sector since 1960. Most public employee strikes are at the local level, and they involve relatively small numbers of workers. Strikes by public employees also are considerably shorter than strikes in the private sector. The rapid increase in public employee strikes in recent years has focused attention on the need for an alternative to the strike as a means for settling wage or other new contract disputes. Wage arbitration is not widespread in the private sector, and there is little reason to believe that it will become completely acceptable to public employees and their employers. If the rising trend of disputes in the public sector continues, however, there is likely to be growing public pressure to find alternatives to strikes that will be acceptable to public employees and government agencies.

Questions and Exercises

1. About what proportion of labor-management agreements are negotiated without resort to strikes or lockouts?

2. Distinguish between labor disputes that occur during the lifetime of an agreement and those that take place when the negotiation of a new agreement breaks down.

3. Describe the three major classes of grievances. Indicate the steps of a typical grievance procedure.

4. About what proportion of major labor-management agreements provide for final and binding arbitration as the terminal step in the grievance procedure?

5. What ground rules for the settlement of grievances are included in the IAM's Shop Steward's Manual? Discuss the roles played by the shop steward and the foreman in the settlement of grievances.

6. What are the two general types of arbitration? What are the advantages and disadvantages of *ad hoc* arbitration?

7. About what proportion of arbitration awards in recent years have been made by single arbitrators as opposed to three man arbitration boards? What are the advantages and disadvantages of having an impartial umpire or permanent arbitrator?

8. Discuss briefly the qualifications of a successful arbitrator.

9. What can be said about the trend in contract or wage arbitration? If labor and management are unwilling to allow an arbitrator to decide new contract provisions, how will their differences be settled?

10. What is the general attitude among union leaders and business spokesmen toward compulsory arbitration?

11. Define "mediation" and "conciliation."

12. What role is played in the settlement of labor-management disputes by the Federal Mediation and Conciliation Service?

13. After a mediator has helped negotiators reach a tentative settlement, is this settlement generally accepted by the union rank and file?

14. Describe the trend in work stoppages since 1960. Are labor-management relations becoming increasingly peaceful or increasingly warlike?

15. What is the theory of the "offset factor" in labor disputes? What does

this theory suggest about the economic cost of labor-management disputes?
16. What is meant by "strike insurance"? How extensively has strike insurance been used in the United States? What is the legal status of this method of minimizing the cost of strikes to an individual employer?

17. Figure 25-1 in the text shows relatively little change in man-days lost due to labor disputes over the past ten years. What has been the trend of disputes involving public employees? Do most public employee disputes involve federal, state, or local workers?

Suggested Readings

Books

Lapp, John A. *How to Handle Labor Grievances.* New York: National Foremen's Institute, Inc., 1945.

Lapp, John A. *Labor Arbitration.* New York: National Foremen's Institute, Inc., 1946.

Uphoff, Walter H. *Kohler on Strike: Thirty Years of Conflict.* Boston, Mass.: The Beacon Press, 1966.

Articles

Ashenfelter, Orley, and George E. Johnson. "Bargaining Theory, Trade Unions, and Industrial Strike Activity," *The American Economic Review, LIX* (March 1969), pp. 35–49.

Brown, Douglass V. "Legalism and Industrial Relations in the United States," *Proceedings of the Twenty-Third Meeting,* Industrial Relations Research Association, December 1970, pp. 2–10.

Christenson, C. L. "The Theory of the Offset Factor: The Impact of Labor Disputes Upon Coal Production," *The American Economic Review, XLIII* (September 1953), pp. 513–547.

Davey, Harold W. "The Uses and Misuses of Tripartite Boards in Grievance Arbitration," in *Developments in American and Foreign Arbitration,* Proceedings of the Twenty-First Meeting of the National Academy of Arbitrators. Washington, D.C.: The Bureau of National Affairs, 1968, pp. 152–179.

Hirsch, John S., Jr. "Strike Insurance and Collective Bargaining," *Industrial and Labor Relations Review, 22* (April 1969), pp. 399–415.

Miller, Richard Ulrich. "Arbitration of New Contract Wage Disputes: Some Recent Trends," *Industrial and Labor Relations Review, 20* (January 1967), pp. 250–264.

Ross, Arthur M. "The Well-Aged Arbitration Case," *Industrial and Labor Relations Review, 11,* No. 2 (January 1958), pp. 262–271.

Ross, David B. "The Arbitration of Public Employee Wage Disputes," *Industrial and Labor Relations Review, 23* (October 1969), pp. 3–13.

22

The Economic Consequences
of Trade Unions

Wages in the United States have increased substantially since the end of World War II. Prices have gone up also, but over the past quarter century, price increases have lagged behind wage gains. As a result, there have been impressive increases in "real wages," or money wages adjusted for changes in the cost of living. The details of changes in gross hourly earnings in manufacturing, mining, construction, and retail trade—and changes in the consumer price index—are given in Table 22–1.

The Impacts of Unions on Wages and Prices

If the average layman were asked: "Do you think unions have affected these wage changes?" he would no doubt view the questioner with wonder, then answer "yes." It is widely believed by union leaders, by businessmen, and by the public at large, that unions are supposed to have an impact on wages.[1] Otherwise, one might ask, why would unions exist?

There is less agreement among economists about the effects of unions on wages and prices, however. Some agree with the generally accepted view that unions have an influence on wages. Others believe that the effects of unionism on wages and prices have been exaggerated. Some of these views will be examined in the first part of this chapter. We will consider the impact of unions on wages under two main headings: first, their impact on the wage *level*, then their effect on the wage *structure*.

---

1. Workers in durable manufacturing, mining, and construction are more highly organized than those in nondurable manufacturing and retail trade. Table 22–1 shows a positive association between the degree of organization and hourly earnings.

494

TABLE 22–1

Changes in Selected Gross Hourly Earnings and in the Consumer Price Index, 1947–1971

	Hourly earnings in current dollars			Hourly earnings in constant dollars[a]		
				(1967 = 100)		
	1947	1971	Percent Change	1947	1971	Percent Change
Manufacturing	$1.21	$3.57	195	$1.81	$2.94	62
Durable	1.28	3.80	197	1.91	3.13	64
Nondurable	1.14	3.26	185	1.70	2.69	58
Mining	1.47	4.04	175	2.20	3.33	51
Construction	1.54	5.70	270	2.30	4.70	104
Retail Trade	0.84	2.57	206	1.26	2.12	68
Consumer Price Index	**66.9**	**121.3**	**81**			

Source: *Economic Report of the President* (Washington, D.C.: U.S. Government Printing Office, 1972), pp. 229–247.

[a] Hourly earnings in current dollars divided by the consumer price index.

Unions and the Level of Wages

We will not attempt in this brief section to review the voluminous literature on unions and wages. Instead, some representative views will be examined. A fair sampling of the literature at a time when the effects of unions on wages were being widely debated has been given by Clark Kerr.[2] On the one hand, Kerr notes, such writers as Charles E. Lindblom and the late Edward H. Chamberlin have argued that union pressure on wages definitely leads to inflation. Others, such as the late Sumner Slichter and A. P. Lerner, have taken the more moderate position that unions are only one of *several* causes of inflation. Moving along the spectrum, Lloyd G. Reynolds states that "collective bargaining does not have as much impact on the money wage level as has sometimes been suggested," while Walter A. Morton believes that "unions are a minor factor affecting inflation and may retard it as well as augment it."[3] Milton Friedman has claimed that unions have both a "rigidity effect" and an "upward-pressing effect." But the two largely offset one another, and the "rigidity effect" may be the more important of the two under some circumstances. Finally, Kenneth E. Boulding has argued that "the main effect of

2. Clark Kerr, "The Impacts of Unions on the Level of Wages," *Wages, Prices, Profits and Productivity* (New York: The Fifteenth American Assembly, Columbia University, June 1959), pp. 92–94.

3. *Ibid.*, pp. 93–94.

unionism is to hold down wages and to prevent them from rising faster than they otherwise would. . . . Unions are the opiate of the people under capitalism. That is why you have got to have them."[4]

This bewildering array of opinions advanced by a number of eminent economists shows that we are not dealing with a simple issue. The reaction of noneconomists might be that professional economists rarely seem to agree on anything. But this is far from true. There are wide areas of agreement among economists. The simpler the problem, however, the easier it is to agree.

In one of the early efforts to shed light on this perplexing issue, Rees analyzed the movement of wages in the basic steel industry between 1914 and 1920—a nonunion period—and again between 1939 and 1949, a period during which the United Steelworkers of America was making rapid strides in the industry.[5] He concluded that collective bargaining was not a significant factor in wage increases during the union period. The observed wage increases, in his view, were caused by a tremendous increase in the demand for steel, with an accompanying increase in the demand for steelworkers. In a later study, Rees concluded that "there is considerable evidence that in the United States collective bargaining tends to retard wage increases when strong inflationary pressures are present."[6]

The relationship between unionism and the earnings of steelworkers was examined by Ulman using a different analytical approach. Under conditions of rising prices, he concluded, the steelworkers' union has exerted upward pressure on wages instead of retarding wage increases.[7] Rees remained unconvinced, however, and replied "that collective bargaining is not among the causes of rapid inflation."[8]

Other economists addressed themselves to this question.[9] Ozanne noted that some economists had implied that "our elaborate collective bargaining process is little more than a superstitious ritual, resembling perhaps the fertility dances of primitive peoples," at least so far as its effect on wage levels and income distribution is concerned.[10] After comparing wage movements during the period 1923 to 1929, and again between 1947 and 1945, Ozanne concluded that real hourly earnings of production workers in manu-

---

4. *Ibid.,* p. 94.

5. Albert Rees, "Post-War Wage Determination in the Basic Steel Industry," *The American Economic Review,* June 1951, pp. 389–404.

6. Albert Rees, "Wage Levels Under Conditions of Long-Run Full Employment," *The American Economic Review,* Papers and Proceedings, May 1953, p. 452.

7. Lloyd Ulman, "The Union and Wages in Basic Steel: A Comment," *The American Economic Review,* June 1958, p. 426.

8. "Reply," *idem.,* p. 433.

9. For a partial listing, see Melvin W. Reder, "The General Level of Money Wages," *Proceedings,* Third Annual Meeting, Industrial Relations Research Association (1950), p. 14.

10. Robert Ozanne, "Impact of Unions on Wage Levels and Income Distribution," *Quarterly Journal of Economics,* May 1959, p. 178.

facturing rose more than twice as rapidly during the unionized period than in the earlier nonunion period. He also found that "wage movements in the union period show surprising independence of the market demand for labor."[11] In his view, collective bargaining is more than a ritual. Ozanne believes that unions had a significant impact on wages long before they had organized a substantial part of the labor force. After a careful analysis of wage movements in a single company—the McCormick Harvesting Machinery Company—from 1862 through 1897, Ozanne concluded that "small craft unions had a wage impact grossly underestimated by their numbers as a percentage of the labor force." He also feels that "labor historians may have significantly underestimated union influence in the latter half of the nineteenth century."[12]

More recent studies have turned from the question: *do* unions influence the level of wages, to the question: *how much* do unions affect the wage level? Lewis analyzed the results of ten studies covering eighteen industries over the period 1920 to 1958. He estimated that during the early part of this period unions increased wages by as much as 16 to 25 per cent. Toward the end of the period, he estimated, the impact of unions on wages had declined to the range of 10 to 15 per cent.[13] Hamermesh, using the "relative markup" approach developed by Lewis, estimated the wage effect of unions on clerical workers in manufacturing at about 5 per cent, but the union effect on the wages of blue-collar workers he estimated to be about 20 per cent.[14] Even Rees, who for so long had argued that unions did not have a positive effect on wages, eventually came to the view that the "average effects of all American unions on the wages of their members in recent years would lie somewhere between 10 and 15 per cent."[15] He continued to argue, however, that in "periods of rapid and unexpected inflation . . . even the strongest unions seem to have no effect on relative earnings, or to lose most of the effect they previously had."[16]

In his study of the effects of unions on public sector wages, Ashenfelter found the wages of unionized firemen to be 6 to 16 per cent above those of unorganized firemen. This increase in relative wages was due to a combination of high earnings and reduced hours.[17]

---

11. *Ibid.*, p. 195. See also Robert R. France, "Wages, Unemployment, and Prices in the United States, 1890–1932, 1947–1957," *Industrial and Labor Relations Review,* January 1962, pp. 187, 190.

12. Robert Ozanne, "Union Wage Impact: A Nineteenth Century Case," *Industrial and Labor Relations Review,* April 1962, p. 375.

13. H. G. Lewis, *Unionism and Relative Wages in the United States* (Chicago: The University of Chicago Press, 1963), *passim.*

14. Daniel S. Hamermesh, "White-Collar Unions, Blue-Collar Unions, and Wages in Manufacturing," *Industrial and Labor Relations Review,* 24, January 1971, p. 170.

15. Albert Rees, *The Economics of Trade Unions* (Chicago: The University of Chicago Press, 1962), p. 79.

16. *Ibid.*

17. Orley Ashenfelter, "The Effect of Unionization on Wages in the Public Sector: The Case of Fire Fighters," *Industrial and Labor Relations Review,* 24 (January 1971), p. 201.

Using the econometric techniques that have now become a standard method of wage analysis, Johnson and Youmans examined the relative wage effects of unions by age and education. They found that unions "benefit less educated workers to a greater extent than more educated workers .... The relative wage effects are much greater for very young and for very old workers than for workers in the middle of their working lives . . . [and] unions appear to have greater relative wage effect on the relative wages of Negroes than on those of whites."[18]

One development in collective bargaining received relatively little attention in discussions of the impact of unions on the wage level. This is the automatic wage adjustment or "escalator clause," incorporated into many labor-management agreements during the 1950s. Joseph Garbarino, one of the few economists to consider the effects of escalator clauses, concluded that "automatic wage adjustment systems probably add to the inflationary potential of wage policy (at least so long as they are partial in coverage)."[19]

There is more agreement today that unions have a positive impact on relative wages than there was a decade ago. But a comment made by Kerr[20] at a time when disagreement on this issue was more widespread is still worth quoting:

> . . . I should like to suggest that all of them are right and all of them are wrong. All of them are right to the extent that they suggest that some kinds of unions could have the suggested effects under some kinds of circumstances. All of them are wrong, to the extent they suggest (and some of them do not) that their conclusions are the universal rule. The only universal rule is that there are all kinds of unions operating under all kinds of circumstances and they can have all kinds of effects. But it should also be added that kinds and circumstances and effects can be related—at least to a certain degree. Truth is more likely to emerge from studying the impacts of the unions, than "the impact of the union."

Unions and the Wage Structure

What is the attitude of students of labor economics toward the question: Have unions affected the *structure* of wages? As noted earlier in the text, a major characteristic of wages in the United States is their diversity. There are substantial variations in wages among industries and regions.[21] Even for

---

18. George E. Johnson and Kenwood C. Youmans, "Union Relative Wage Effects by Age and Education," *Industrial and Labor Relations Review, 24* (January 1971), p. 179.

19. J. W. Garbarino, "Economic Significance of Automatic Wage Adjustments," Harold W. Davey et al. (eds.), *New Dimensions in Collective Bargaining* (New York: Harper and Brothers, 1959), p. 172.

20. Clark Kerr, "The Impacts of Unions on the Level of Wages," p. 94.

21. Some of the reasons for these variations are to be found in Martin Segal, "The Relation Between Union Wage Impact and Market Structure," *Quarterly Journal of Economics, LXXVIII* (February 1964), pp. 96–114. The results of this study were discussed in some detail in Chapter 5.

similar or identical occupations, wages are far from uniform *within* a given labor market area. One of the stated goals of some unions is the elimination of wage differentials—at least among workers doing the same job in a given industry. And a few of the stronger unions, such as those in the steel and meat-packing industries, have been quite successful in achieving equal pay for similar work regardless of location. Wage differentials elsewhere have been remarkably persistent, however. Yet one is hard pressed to find agreement among economists about the impact of unions on the *general* wage structure of the United States.

Reynolds and Taft feel that "collective bargaining clearly makes for reduction of wage differentials among firms competing in the same product market."[22] In their view, however, it is the pressure of competition in the product market that is the decisive factor causing a tendency toward wage uniformity. Thus *within a single industry*, Reynolds and Taft conclude: "...the effect of union efforts to reduce wage differentials among rival producers appears to be moderately favorable—not so completely beneficial as unions sometimes allege, but sufficiently so to warrant a positive score for collective bargaining."[23] The impact of unions on the *intra*industry wage structure, at least in highly organized industries, has been to introduce a tendency toward uniformity of pay for similar or identical occupations.

But what of the *inter*industry wage structure? Some industries have become highly organized, whereas others have successfully resisted trade unionism. Have wages increased more rapidly in the highly organized unions? And if so, can we conclude that unions have affected the interindustry structure of wages? Dunlop has attributed interindustry variations in wages to changes in productivity and output, the proportion of labor cost to total cost, competitive conditions in the product market, and changing skill and occupational requirements. In his analysis, Dunlop gives "no distinctive place to the role of labor organization." While he concedes that the influence of unions on the structure of wages cannot be ignored, he concludes that the role of unionization has been neither distinctive nor uniform.[24]

Arthur Ross has argued, however, that "real earnings in the highly organized industries have increased to a greater extent than have those in the less organized industries."[25] Trade unions have had an impact on the wage structure, in his view, and this has been in the direction of widening interindustry differentials. Strong unions have been successful in pushing wages

22. Lloyd G. Reynolds and Cynthia H. Taft, *The Evolution of Wage Structure* (New Haven: Yale University Press, 1956), p. 175.

23. *Ibid.*, p. 179.

24. John T. Dunlop, "Productivity and the Wage Structure," *Income, Employment and Public Policies.* Essays in Honor of Alvin H. Hansen (New York: W. W. Norton, 1948), p. 360.

25. Arthur Ross, *Trade Union Wage Policy* (Berkeley, California: University of California Press, 1948), p. 117.

up in some industries, whereas weaker unions have not been able to achieve the same effect in other industries.

In a later study, Ross and Goldner concluded that "unionization is a source of wage advantage, which operates most effectively under facilitating environmental circumstances."[26] These authors feel that unions have been able to push wages up in expanding industries, particularly in those dominated by a few large and profitable firms. This view has been supported by Garbarino, who has said that "while wage behavior is the result of the operation of a large number of factors . . . the variables of productivity, concentration, and unionization will be capable of explaining the major portion of differential movements."[27] Levinson has argued that the extent of union organization may be more significant than the degree of industrial concentration: ". . . other things equal, wage increases in strongly unionized, highly competitive, nonmanufacturing industries are at least as great as those in the strongly unionized, oligopolistic manufacturing sectors."[28]

Lack of agreement about the effects of unions on the interindustry wage structure stems in part from the statistical difficulties involved. There is general agreement that wages are affected by a number of forces. The difficulty lies in disentangling these forces and in assigning relative weights to each. Few would care to argue that wages in highly organized industries (such as steel and autos) have not increased more rapidly than those in partly organized industries such as textiles. But there are many other differences between the highly organized and the partly organized industries, including differences in market structure, the degree of internal competition, productivity, susceptibility to foreign competition, and various other factors that could impinge upon wages.

What of skill differentials? Have unions widened or narrowed the gap between the wages of skilled and unskilled workers? It should come as no surprise by this time that there are differences of opinion on this score. Some writers have argued that the effect of unions on skill differentials has been neutral;[29] others disagree. Reynolds and Taft are of the opinion that while unions have had only a slight effect on occupational differentials, "to the extent that unionism has had any net effect on occupational differentials, this has almost certainly been in the direction of narrowing them."[30]

---

26. Arthur M. Ross and William Goldner, "Forces Affecting the Inter-Industry Wage Structure," *Quarterly Journal of Economics,* May 1950, p. 281.

27. Joseph Garbarino, "A Theory of Interindustry Wage Structure Variation," *Quarterly Journal of Economics,* May 1950, p. 305.

28. Harold M. Levinson, "Unionism, Concentration, and Wage Changes: Toward a Unified Theory," *Industrial and Labor Relations Review, 20* (January 1967), p. 205.

29. Clark Kerr, "Wage Relationships—The Comparative Impact of Market and Power Forces," in John T. Dunlop (ed.), *The Theory of Wage Determination* (New York: St. Martin's Press, 1957), p. 179; and William Goldner, "Labor Market Factors and Skill Differentials in Wage Rates," *Proceedings,* Tenth Annual Meeting, Industrial Relations Research Association (1957), pp. 8–9.

30. Reynolds and Taft, *op. cit.,* p. 185.

Stieber has pointed out that "occupational earnings differentials . . . have narrowed substantially in steel during the past 50 years much as they have in most other industries."[31] While he insists that the relative earnings differentials between skilled and unskilled workers in basic steel have not been maintained—as some other writers have implied—Stieber is careful to avoid the conclusion that the narrowing in skill differentials in this industry has been the result of union policy. Indeed, he points out the different pressures that exist within the union on this issue. Low-wage workers prefer across-the-board increases, which would continue the trend of narrowing differentials between unskilled and skilled workers. But the higher skilled (and higher paid) workers favor increases that will maintain differentials rather than narrowing them.

On balance, there is less disagreement about the effects of unions on occupational or skill differentials than there is about the impact of unions on the interindustry wage structure. Even those authors who accept the view that there has been a narrowing of skill differentials are of the opinion that this has not been the result of an egalitarian union philosophy. In part at least, the narrowing has been due to the action of various economic forces rather than conscious union policy. [32]

Geographical Wage Differentials

Geographical or interarea wage differentials have been highly persistent in the United States. In general, wage rates tend to be high in the heavily industrialized Middle Atlantic, Great Lakes, and Pacific Coast states. They tend toward the average in New England and in some of the Midwestern states, and wages taper off to their lowest levels in the South. But the geographical wage structure is far more complex than the above summary statement suggests.

The general wage level in New England, for example, is close to the national average. But wages in some industries in New England are higher than in other regions, while the reverse is true for other industries. There is also a considerable amount of wage variation *within* as well as among regions. In general, wages tend to be lower in small communities than in large metropolitan areas. It is not uncommon for wages in a small community in a high-wage *region* to be lower than wages in a large community in a low-wage region. The wage structure may be viewed in a number of ways: industry by industry, occupation by occupation, and area by area. Any way it is viewed, however, the wage structure is complex; but in some ways the geographical wage structure is the most complicated of all.

---

31. Jack Stieber, "Occupational Wage Differentials in the Basic Steel Industry," *Industrial and Labor Relations Review*, January 1959, p. 167.

32. See Richard Perlman, "Forces Widening Occupational Wage Differentials," *The Review of Economics and Statistics*, May 1958, p. 110.

How have unions affected the geographical wage structure? Are variations in geographical wage contours associated with variations in union
strength? This question can be answered with a qualified affirmative. In
general, there is a higher degree of unionism in high-wage than in low-wage
areas. But one cannot simply conclude that unions *cause* wages to be high
in some areas, while the absence of unions causes wages to be low elsewhere.
There are some regions—New England is an example—where unions are
relatively strong, but where wages are not high. The geographical wage
structure is affected by many economic forces. Wages in each region are
influenced by the rate of population growth and by the expansion or con-
traction of industrial and other forms of economic activity. Other factors that
have a bearing on a region's wage level are its "industry-mix," the degree of
competition within its industries, and the degree of unionism. These factors
cannot be isolated to show the precise influence of each. Even when wages
are standardized to eliminate the effects of differences in industry-mix, a
substantial amount of variation remains.[33]

Geographical wage differentials have been persistent. But variation in
wages within regions tends to weaken somewhat the significance of *average*
wage levels on a geographical basis. Reynolds and Taft concluded that
"unionism appears thus far to have had only a slight effect on geographical
differentials; and this effect has not always been in the same direction."[34]
Some unions have adopted the policy of equal pay for equal work, regardless
of location. And the influence of these unions has been in the direction
of narrowing interregional differentials. Other unions, however, have deliberately maintained interregional wage differentials in an effort to obtain what
the traffic will bear in each region. In some industries, unions have succeeded
in organizing the firms in some regions, while they have met with relatively
little success in others. The textile industries provide examples of the latter
situation. Textile mills in the North are predominantly organized, whereas a
minority of textile workers in the South belong to unions. Although North-
South textile wage differentials have narrowed in recent years, this has been
largely a reflection of the weakness of unions in the organized regions, rather
than an indication of growing strength in the predominantly unorganized
South.

The Economic Consequences of Geographical Wage Differentials

Most economists in the United States would probably agree that complete
uniformity of wages is an idle dream of egalitarian reformers. Within reasonable limits, occupational wage differentials can be defended on the grounds

---

33. Paul E. Polzin, "State and Regional Wage Differences," *Southern Economic Journal, XXXVIII*
(January 1972), pp. 371–378.
34. Reynolds and Taft, *op. cit.,* p. 182.

that higher skilled workers must undergo extensive periods of training and they should be rewarded for this. Also, not everyone has the natural aptitudes needed to do skilled work; thus market forces alone would tend to maintain occupational differentials. In a market economy, interindustry differentials are also likely to persist. The ratio of labor cost to total cost varies widely from industry to industry. Some industries require relatively little capital investment, and these tend to be price competitive. Others require huge investments and, in these industries, prices are usually administered. In general, wages are lower in labor-intensive than in capital-intensive industries.

In an economy where market forces determine the allocation of resources, some industries are bound to pay higher wages than others. And even within an "industry," as Dunlop noted in his discussion of wage contours, there will be substantial variation among workers with the same job titles. While some union leaders have talked at times as though they would like to see such differentials eliminated, their actions indicate that they are rarely troubled by occupational and interindustry differentials.

There has been somewhat more controversy about geographical wage differentials, however. Some economists have condemned unions for their efforts to eliminate geographical wage differentials even within a single industry, and they have been equally critical of public policy—notably minimum wage legislation—which in their view interferes with the free market allocation of resources. These economists, in the classical tradition, believe that wage differentials play an important role in economic development. Low wages in some regions, they assert, attract capital to those regions and speed up their industrialization. At the same time, workers in low-wage regions will be encouraged to migrate to relatively high-wage regions. In the long run, this will tend to bring about a more efficient allocation of resources than would be the case if interregional wage differentials were eliminated.

Other economists have tended to question this line of reasoning. They have indicated that labor cost is only one of the determinants of industrial location. And they are doubtful that labor is sufficiently mobile to eliminate geographical differentials through the process of interregional migration, even over fairly long periods of time.[35]

Regardless of how economists feel about them, and despite efforts by some unions to eliminate interregional wage differentials, this goal has not been achieved. As noted earlier, the *average* wage level in a region tells only part of the story. There are wide variations around regional averages. Some

---

35. For an early criticism of union and government interference with geographical wage differentials, see John V. Van Sickle, "The Southeast: A Case Study in Delayed Industrialization," *American Economic Review,* May 1951, pp. 384–393; and "Regional Aspects of the Problem of Full Employment and Fair Wages," *Southern Economic Journal,* July 1946, pp. 35–46. For the contrary view that "low wages appear to be less influential in industrial location and expansion than is popularly believed," see Richard A. Lester, "Southern Wage Differentials: Developments, Analysis, and Implications," *Southern Economic Journal,* April 1947, p. 387.

regions are "high-wage" regions for some industries and "low-wage" regions for others. Some highly unionized industries pay essentially the same wage for similar occupations in all regions. Clearly, there is no simple and direct relationship between average geographical wage levels and the movement of industry.

Some industries are relatively footloose, and plants in these industries are often attracted to low labor-cost areas. Other industries, however, must locate with respect to raw materials or markets and cannot be induced to locate in a particular area simply because wages are low. Locational economics has long been a neglected subject, but there have been rapid advances in recent years. As we have learned more about the forces that determine the location of industry—both those which cause some industries to be migratory, and those which contribute to the relative immobility of others—some of the furor about geographical wage differentials has subsided.[36] The controversy is revived, however, when unions announce that they are going to step up organizational activities in areas where they have made little headway in the past, or when Congress announces that it is contemplating another increase in the statutory minimum wage.

The Overall Impact of Unions on the Wage Structure

Perhaps it will be useful at this point to summarize the discussion of the impact of unions on the wage structure. Such a summary has been given by Reynolds and Taft, who note the following: Unions have had an important impact on *interpersonal* wage differentials. Where they have succeeded in organizing firms, they have insisted on an impersonal wage structure. Wage rates are to be attached to *jobs*, not to individuals.

Unions also have had a significant impact on *interfirm* differentials where the firms are members of a single competitive group. This seems to be the case both in product markets where there is a high degree of price competition and in markets where prices tend to be administered.

The impact of unions on *geographical* or interarea wage differentials has been relatively slight. In some industries, interregional differentials have been largely or entirely eliminated. In others, while interregional differentials have been narrowed they have not been eliminated, and in some industries, unions have pursued a policy of maintaining interregional differentials.

The impact of unions on *occupational* differentials has been relatively slight. Whatever influence unions have had has been in the direction of narrowing differentials. In recent years, however, there has been a tendency for occupational differentials to be maintained, and in some cases there has been a slight widening.

---

36. See Edgar M. Hoover, *An Introduction to Regional Economics* (New York: Alfred A. Knopf, 1971), especially pp. 183–196.

Although this is one of their more debatable conclusions, Reynolds and Taft are of the opinion that the impact of unions on *interindustry* differentials has been relatively minor. If there has been an effect, they believe, it has been in the direction of widening interindustry differentials.[37]

Reynolds and Taft[38] feel that

> the friends of trade unionism as well as its critics have tended to overestimate its actual effects on the wage structure. . . . fears that complete unionization will bring seismic disruption of the wage structure do not seem to be well founded. . . . countries with the strongest union movements appear to have have a wage structure which is more orderly and defensible than the wage structure of countries where unionism has been weak.

Union Wage Policy and Employment

What effect have unions had upon employment? Have unions won wage increases only at the cost of the jobs of some of their members? In establishing their wage *policies,* have unions taken into account the potential "employment effect"? The "law of demand," as we learn it in our first course in economics, tells us that buyers will take more of a good at low than at high prices; that is, demand curves slope downward to the right. If the demand for labor is viewed in terms of such a schedule, one might conclude that there is a simple and direct relationship between employment and wages. And some evidently think this is the case. They point out, for example, that as the coal miners became strongly organized and pushed wages up, employment in this industry fell. Or they point to the New England textile industry and note that as unions became strong in this region and wages rose, much of the industry relocated to the South where unions made much less headway. But the relationship between wages and employment in these cases cannot be explained in terms of a simple demand curve. The latter is a timeless schedule, whereas the events we have described occurred over a fairly long period of time.

Examples can also be cited of highly organized industries, such as shipbuilding, aluminum, aircraft, and electrical machinery, where wages and employment have increased together.[39] Evidently the wage-employment relationship is somewhat more complex than that between the price of a commodity and the quantity of that commodity demanded at any moment of time. The demand for labor is a *derived* demand. Both wages and employment depend upon conditions in the product market; upon changes in labor supply (including hours worked); and upon changes in productivity.[40]

---

37. Reynolds and Taft, *op, cit.,* pp. 193–194.

38. *Ibid.,* pp. 193–195.

39. See Ross and Goldner, "Forces Affecting the Interindustry Wage Structure," pp. 274–275.

40. *Ibid.,* p. 269.

This is not to deny that wages can influence employment, but only to indicate that the connection between them is not a simple and direct one. If wages are pushed up rapidly, management might have an incentive to substitute capital for labor, and this indeed has an employment effect. But it takes time for the employment effect to be realized. It is possible, if not always easy to work out in practice, for a reduction in labor requirements to be geared to normal turnover—to retirement rates and voluntary quits—so that declining employment in an industry *need not* lead to unemployment. Rapid technological progress, as in the bituminous coal industry after 1950, however, has often resulted in substantial unemployment.

In determining their wage policies, do unions take the employment effect into account? What is it that trade unions try to maximize? Assuming that they know the relationship between wages and employment, Dunlop[41] suggests that union leaders might direct wage policy toward a number of goals. For example, the wage policy of a particular union might be designed to achieve:

1. The largest possible wage bill for a particular segment of the economy, regardless of whether all wage earners are employed.
2. The largest possible wage bill from a segment of the economy, including funds from the public support of the unemployed.
3. The largest *private* payroll to employed workers, deducting from their wage income an amount to pay out-of-work benefits to unemployed members.
4. The maximization of employment, even if this means a smaller total wage bill than the union is able to achieve.
5. The highest average wage income for each unit of labor affiliated with the union.

The policy a given union will pursue depends upon conditions in the labor and product markets. A union might pursue one set of goals under certain labor and product market conditions, but it can alter these goals as underlying market conditions change.

Not everyone would agree that unions try to maximize anything. The late Arthur Ross, for example, stated that: "The union is not a business enterprise selling labor. It is a political institution representing the sellers of labor, and there is no necessary reason to assume that it will automatically or mechanically behave in the same fashion as a profit maximizing business enterprise."[42] He concluded that "the volume of employment associated with

---

41. John T. Dunlop, *Wage Determination Under Trade Unions* (New York: Augustus M. Kelly, Inc., 1950), pp. 32–40.
42. Arthur M. Ross, *Trade Union Wage Policy* (Berkeley and Los Angeles: University of California Press, 1948), p. 22.

a given wage rate is unpredictable before the fact, and the effect of a given wage rate upon employment is undecipherable after the fact."[43]

Dunlop views the trade union as an institution responding to economic forces. Ross, however, emphasized the political nature of trade unions, and suggested that union wage policy is determined by the pressures operating on the union's leadership. Union leaders try to reconcile various pressures— to achieve a compromise among them—rather than seeking to maximize wages, employment, or some combination of the two.[44] Other writers have jumped into the fray. After a detailed analysis of the wage behavior of a number of unions in various industries, Shultz and Myers concluded that "some unions, faced with a particular set of labor market and product market conditions, do take into account the probable effect of wage demands on the level of employment for their membership."[45] These situations, the authors contend, are not at all unusual except in periods of full employment and rising prices. Where there is strong competition in the product market, and where an industry is not completely organized, Shultz and Myers maintain that unions must take into account the employment effect in establishing their wage policy.

The Dunlop-Ross debate over the determinants of union wage policy led to a voluminous literature on the subject.[46] Much of the discussion was concerned with the relationship between wages and employment without explicit reference to prices. During the latter half of the 1950s, however, there was a tendency for wages, prices, and unemployment to rise together. This tendency became even more pronounced during the latter half of the 1960s and the early years of the 1970s. The emphasis in economic analysis shifted from a simple wage-employment relationship to the more complex wage-price-*unemployment* relationship.

The Impact of Unions on Prices

The relationship between unemployment and the rate of change in prices, as expressed by the now-famous Phillips curve, was discussed in some detail in Chapter 6, and this discussion will not be repeated here. Instead this section will deal briefly with the impact of unions on the price level.

Between 1951 and 1961, the Consumer Price Index rose 11.8 points, but during the next decade price increases accelerated sharply. The CPI rose by 31.7 points between 1961 and 1971—and more than two thirds of this increase came after 1967. This inflationary outburst led President Nixon to

---

43. *Ibid.,* p. 80.

44. *Ibid.,* pp. 11–12.

45. G. P. Shultz and C. A. Myers, "Union Wage Decisions and Employment," *American Economic Review,* June 1950, p. 379.

46. For a partial list of books and articles dealing with the topic, see M. W. Reder, "The Theory of Union Wage Policy," *Review of Economics and Statistics,* February 1952, p. 34.

institute a 90-day wage-price freeze in August 1971, followed by selective controls on wages and prices administered by wage and price boards.

In general terms, economists attribute rising prices either to "cost-push" or to "demand-pull." The cost-push explanation is usually associated with rising labor costs due to union-negotiated wage increases and with the administration of prices by industrial giants. The demand-pull explanation asserts that "there is too much money chasing too few goods" in the economic system.

It may be instructive to consider changes in some of the components of the Consumer Price Index in an effort to determine the relative importance of cost-push and demand-pull on recent overall price increases. Between 1967—the latest base-year of the CPI—and early 1972, consumer prices rose slightly more than 23 per cent. Food prices rose 20 per cent, and the prices of commodities except food were up about 18 per cent. Durable goods prices increased slightly more than 17 per cent, while nondurables rose a bit more than 18 per cent. Meanwhile, the cost of medical care increased more than 30 per cent, while the cost of all services rose more than 31 per cent. When rent is excluded, service costs were up more than 34 per cent.

Commodity-producing industries tend to be highly organized, whereas the degree of organization in the service sectors is quite low. Yet prices increased more rapidly in the largely unorganized sectors than in those with strong unions. It does not follow that cost-push had nothing to do with recent price increases. There can be little doubt that part of negotiated wage increases are passed on to consumers in the form of higher prices—after an appropriate time lag is taken into account. And unless higher wages are accompanied by increases in productivity, *all* of the increase must eventually be translated into higher prices or reduced profits. But the web of interrelationships between wages, prices, and productivity is a complex one, and it is too much of an oversimplification to argue that price increases can be explained entirely in terms of cost-push.[47] Demand influences, stimulated in large measure by rapidly rising military expenditures, were strong during the latter half of the 1960s. And while cost-push and demand-pull both no doubt played a part in the upward spiral of prices after 1967, the evidence suggests that demand influences were the stronger of the two.

The attitudes of union leaders toward wage stabilization during Phase II of the Nixon price control program were not always easy to determine. We saw in the last chapter that the Longshoremen negotiated a settlement, following a long strike, far in excess of the Pay Board's guidelines of 5.5 per cent a year. And according to I. W. Abel, president of the United Steel-

---

47. As noted in Chapter 6, it is also too much of an oversimplification to think in terms of a simple inflation-unemployment trade-off, since "unemployment and inflation cannot and should not be treated independently of other objectives of economic policy." Frank Brechling, "The Trade-Off Between Inflation and Unemployment," *The Journal of Political Economy, 76* (August 1968), p. 734.

workers of America—and a member of the Pay Board—the Construction Industry Stabilization Committee had approved wage increases far exceeding Pay Board guidelines. Mr. Abel, it should be made clear, was not objecting to wage increases. What he complained to his Pay Board colleagues about was a "double standard," which failed to insure "equality for all sectors in the application of wage controls."[48]

Unions and Distributive Shares

Ever since the days of David Ricardo, economists have been interested in the "laws" of distribution. Out of their speculation came various versions of the theory of marginal productivity. In a free market economy, they asserted, each of the factors of production—in the aggregate—will have its return determined by its marginal product. In the classical and neoclassical periods, it was generally claimed that wages were equal to the value of labor's marginal product. In more recent times, as a result of the development of more sophisticated theories of pricing and distribution, it is asserted that employers will attempt to equate wages with marginal *revenue* product. Most economists would probably now accept the view that the theory of marginal productivity does little to explain what *determines* wages. But there is still strong support for marginal productivity as the basis for a general theory of distribution. This raises the interesting question: Can trade unions affect distributive shares?

A number of analysts have answered this question in the negative. Whatever else unions have been able to do, it is argued, they have not been able to alter the share of total income going to labor as a whole. In the early 1930s, Paul H. Douglas published the results of empirical studies, conducted over a number of years, which showed that labor's share of the national income had been fairly constant.[49] These studies were conducted at a time when unions were relatively weak in the United States, however, and one could not conclude from them that unions have been unable to affect distributive shares.

In *The Theory of Wages*, J. R. Hicks argued that the relative share of national income going to labor could be altered, but this would result from the introduction of labor-saving inventions rather than the direct action of trade unions.[50] More recently, other scholars have concluded that unions cannot affect labor's share through collective bargaining. Cartter has said, for example: "There is scanty evidence that unions ... possess the power to raise general *money* wages above what they would have been in the absence

---

48. *The Wall Street Journal*, February 28, 1972.

49. Paul H. Douglas, *Real Wages in the United States, 1890–1925* (Boston: Houghton Mifflin Company, 1930); and *The Theory of Wages* (New York: The Macmillan Company, 1934).

50. J. R. Hicks, *The Theory of Wages* (London: Macmillan & Co. Ltd., 1932), pp. 121–134.

of unionism, much less real wages or labor's share of total income."[51] And Weintraub has concluded that "over time, *the share of wages in the total of business income remains almost constant.*"[52] Johnson and Mieszkowski feel that unions can affect the distribution of income but "that most, if not all, of the gains of union labor are made at the expense of nonunionized workers, and not at the expense of earnings on capital."[53]

There has been some opposition to this view, however. Robert Ozanne has argued that while labor's share remained relatively constant before unions had achieved significant power in the United States, this share has increased since the end of World War II. At the same time, he said, the share of profits before taxes was increasing during the nonunion period, but has remained relatively stable during the union period.[54] Ozanne does not explicitly state that unions have affected distributive shares but his analysis suggests this conclusion. Clark Kerr, who has a knack for dissecting broad generalizations, has suggested "that a certain kind of trade-unionism under certain conditions will have no effect; that a certain kind of trade-unionism under certain conditions will raise labor's share; and ... a certain kind of trade-unionism under certain conditions will reduce labor's share."[55] Kerr's ultimate conclusion, however, is that trade unionism in the United States has had relatively little effect on labor's share of national income. By supporting a full employment policy, trade unions have tended to *reduce* labor's share. But at the same time, unions have effectively raised the wages paid by some employers who have been temporarily unable to recapture profits. When these forces are balanced off against one another, Kerr suggests, trade unionism has done relatively little to alter the total share of income going to labor as a whole.[56] Kerr has also stated that "labor's share of income, industry by industry, has fared no more favorably in unionized industries than in non-union."[57] Estimates by Close and Shulenburger may raise doubts about the latter conclusion, however. These authors analyzed labor's share in nine

---

51. Allan M. Cartter, *Theory of Wages and Employment* (Homewood, Illinois: Richard D. Irwin Inc., 1959), p. 167.

52. Sidney Weintraub, "A Law That Cannot Be Repealed," *Challenge*, April 1962, p. 17.

53. This conclusion was derived from a sophisticated theoretical analysis, but rather skimpy empirical data. The authors acknowledge that their "empirical estimates are subject to a number of qualifications and limitations." Harry G. Johnson and Peter Mieszkowski, "The Effects of Unionization on the Distribution of Income: A General Equilibrium Approach," *Quarterly Journal of Economics, LXXXIV* (November 1970), p. 560.

54. Robert Ozanne, "Impact of Unions on Wage Levels and Income Distribution," *Quarterly Journal of Economics,* May 1959, p. 195.

55. Clark Kerr, "Trade Unionism and Distributive Shares," *American Economic Review,* May 1954, p. 281.

56. Kerr notes that in Great Britain, wage earners have gained at the expense of salaried workers, and that full employment in Great Britain has led to a smaller reduction in the share of wages than in the share of income going to all employees, that is, wage and salary workers combined. *Ibid.,* p. 291.

57. *Ibid.,* p. 288.

broad sectors and fifty "industries" over the period 1948 to 1965. Labor's share increased more in highly organized sectors than in those where unions are weak. In most of the detailed industries, they found labor's share either to be increasing or nearly constant. Because of statistical difficulties, however, they suggest that the industry results be treated cautiously.[58]

One final note will conclude our discussion of the impact of unions on distributive shares. Given the present state of knowledge, perhaps we cannot answer the question: "Can unions affect distributive shares?" Even those who have argued that labor's share of national income is *relatively* constant have indicated that there has been a *slight* increase in the share going to all employees. But there are statistical difficulties involved in the precise measurement of income distribution. We do not, for example, have a satisfactory breakdown between wages and salaries. There are even greater conceptual difficulties. As Robert Solow has pointed out, "an unknown fraction of society's capital takes the form of the improvement of human abilities and skills.[59] That is, workers today spend a greater part of their lives in education and training than was the case a half century ago. How much of their earnings should then be considered as a return on this investment in human capital and how much as a reward for physical or mental effort? These questions have not been answered by means of statistical analysis, but this does not mean they can be ignored.

Most economists would agree that the effect of unions upon the distribution of income in the United States has not been great. As Solow has noted, however, perhaps the question of distributive shares is far more complicated than has been assumed by those who simply measure the percentages going to "labor" and other factors of production, without taking into account changes in skill distributions, educational attainment, and other changes which make the work force today vastly different from what it was a half century ago.

The Social Impact of Unions

There is often a tendency to view unions as economic institutions without regard to other functions they perform in society. More than three decades ago, Sumner Slichter pointed out that a major function of unions was that of introducing democracy into the work place. This is frequently overlooked by those who are inclined to criticize the institution of trade unionism. Like other man-made institutions, unions have their weaknesses. As one sympathetic critic has noted: "Unions bring rights to the group, not to the person. As a

---

58. Frank A. Close and David E. Shulenburger, "Labor's Share by Sector and Industry, 1948–1965," *Industrial and Labor Relations Review*, 24 (July 1971), pp. 588–602.

59. Robert M. Solow, "A Skeptical Note on the Constancy of Relative Shares," *American Economic Review*, September 1958, p. 630.

result, union government, from the shop level on up, is forced to reconcile the varying demands and needs of union members vis-à-vis each other as well as group needs vis-à-vis the employer."[60] But the fact remains that where unions exist, individual workers are protected from arbitrary treatment by employers, and this cannot be guaranteed in the typical nonunion shop.

The trade union movement was the forerunner of a broader civil rights movement in the United States. When trade unions were struggling to achieve legal recognition they were widely regarded as a threat to the social order. But unions have been to some extent the victims of their own success, and success tends to breed complacency and conservatism. Trade union leaders as a whole have not been notably active in efforts to achieve equality for racial minorities; many have adopted a conservative position with respect to the Vietnam War, and union leaders have been conspicuous by their absence from the ecology movement.[61] They also have turned a deaf ear to the importunings of the leaders of the New Left. Trade unions cannot be regarded as potentially revolutionary institutions today; indeed, they may be more accurately regarded as bulwarks against revolution.

It is always possible to find something to criticize in any institution at any time. But to evaluate institutions fairly, one must view them in historical perspective. In this respect the views of Philip Taft,[62] one of the nation's more eminent labor historians, are worth quoting:

> American labor has always been part of the American community. It has never considered itself a special class. It has supported and shared in the sacrifices and responsibilities during the great crises which have faced Americans in the last 50 years. It has, through its policies, enlarged the rights of freedom of the individual by insisting upon codes of practice embodied in a contract. It has, to be sure, suffered from a variety of defects. Nevertheless, as its achievements are enumerated and compared to those of labor movements elsewhere, one can rightfully conclude that in terms of service for its members, it is the best in the world.

Questions and Exercises

1. Briefly describe general trends in wages and prices since the end of World War II. Compare the trends in money and real wages.

---

60. Paul Jacobs, *Old Before Its Time: Collective Bargaining at 28* (Santa Barbara, California: Center for the Study of Democratic Institutions, 1963), p. 22.

61. Whether or not failure to participate in the ecology movement can be labeled as evidence of conservatism is at least debatable. As Harry Bridges, leader of the Longshoremen's Union put it: "The ecology movement is obviously antiworker, first of all because it is a product of the ruling class. It recognizes no obligation to the worker." Stewart Udall and Jeff Stansbury, "Selling Ecology to the Hardhats," *Washington Post, April 25, 1971.*

62. Philip Taft, "Labor History and the Labor Movement Today," *Labor History, 7* (Winter 1966), p. 77.

2. During the 1950s, there was lively debate among economists about the impact of unions on wages. How did Clark Kerr summarize this debate?

3. More recently, economists have been concerned with measuring the "relative union markup," or relative impact of unions on wages. What were the results of the study conducted by H. G. Lewis on this matter?

4. Hammermesh compared the impact of unions on the wages of clerical and blue-collar workers in manufacturing. What were his findings?

5. Ashenfelter analyzed the impact of unions on the earnings of fire fighters. How much did he estimate union firemen had gained by organizing? How were these gains achieved?

6. According to Johnson and Youmans, what effects have unions had on their members in terms of age and education?

7. What effect have unions had on the *inter*industry wage structure? Contrast these with the effects unions have had on the *intra*industry wage structure.

8. What has happened to occupational differentials over the past half century? To what extent have unions affected changes in occupational differentials?

9. In general terms, describe the geographical wage structure of the United States. What are some of the difficulties involved in characterizing some regions as "high" and others as "low" wage regions?

10. Some economists have defended wage differentials on the grounds that they are a necessary condition of economic development. Is this view widely accepted today?

11. Briefly describe the views of Dunlop and Ross on the institutional nature of trade unions.

12. When formulating wage policy, do unions take into account the potential employment effects of wage changes?

13. Distinguish between the "cost-push" and "demand-pull" explanations of inflation. Which of these forces appeared to exert the greatest influence on prices between 1967 and 1972?

14. What conclusions were reached by Weintraub and by Cartter about the ability of unions to affect the distribution of income? What did Johnson and Mieszkowski have to say about this issue?

15. What findings emerged when Close and Shulenburger examined labor's share by broad sector? What view was expressed by Solow about the constancy of relative shares?

16. Write a brief essay on the social impact of unions.

Suggested Readings

Books

Dunlop, John T. *Wage Determination Under Trade Unions.* New York: Augustus M. Kelly, Inc., 1950.

Hicks, J. R. *The Theory of Wages.* London: Macmillan and Co. Ltd., 1932.

Jacobs, Paul. *Old Before Its Time: Collective Bargaining at 28.* Santa Barbara, California: Center for the Study of Democratic Institutions, 1963.

Lewis, Harold Gregg. *Unionism and Relative Wages in the United States.* Chicago: The University of Chicago Press, 1963.

Reynolds, Lloyd G., and Cynthia H. Taft. *The Evolution of Wage Structure.* New Haven: Yale University Press, 1956.

Ross, Arthur M. *Trade Union Wage Policy.* Berkeley and Los Angeles: University of California Press, 1948.

Articles

Ashenfelter, Orley. "The Effect of Unionization on Wages in the Public Sector: The Case of Fire Fighters," *Industrial and Labor Relations Review, 24* (January 1971), pp. 191–202.

Close, Frank A., and David E. Shulenburger. "Labor's Share by Sector and Industry, 1948–1965," *Industrial and Labor Relations Review, 24,* (July 1971), pp. 588–602.

France, Robert R. "Wages, Unemployment, and Prices in the United States, 1890–1932, 1947–1957," *Industrial and Labor Relations Review,* January 1962, pp. 171–190.

Garbino, Joseph W. "A Theory of Interindustry Wage Structure Variation," *Quarterly Journal of Economics,* May 1950, pp. 282-305.

Hamermesh, Daniel S. "White-Collar Unions, Blue-Collar Unions, and Wages in Manufacturing," *Industrial and Labor Relations Review, 24* (January 1971), pp. 159–170.

Johnson, George E., and Kenwood C. Youmans. "Union Relative Wage Effects by Age and Education," *Industrial and Labor Relations Review, 24* (January 1971), pp. 171–179.

Johnson, Harry G., and Peter Mieszkowski. "The Effects of Unionization on the Distribution of Income: A General Equilibrium Approach," *Quarterly Journal of Economics, LXXXIV* (November 1970), pp. 539–561.

Levinson, Harold M. "Unionism, Concentration, and Wage Changes: Toward a Unified Theory," *Industrial and Labor Relations Review, 20* (January 1967), pp. 198–205.

Ozanne, Robert. "Impact of Unions on Wage Levels and Income Distribution," *Quarterly Journal of Economics,* May 1959, pp. 177–196.

Perlman, Richard. "Forces Widening Occupational Wage Differentials," *The Review of Economics and Statistics,* May 1958, pp. 107–115.

Polzin, Paul E. "State and Regional Wage Differentials," *The Southern Economic Journal, XXXVIII* (January 1972), pp. 371–378.

Reder, Melvin W. "The Theory of Union Wage Policy," *The Review of Economics and Statistics,* February 1952, pp. 34–45.

Ross, Arthur M., and William Goldner. "Forces Affecting the Interindustry Wage Structure," *Quarterly Journal of Economics,* May 1950, pp. 254–281.

Segal, Martin. "The Relation Between Union Wage Impact and Market Structure," *Quarterly Journal of Economics, LXXVIII* (February 1964), pp. 96–114.

Taft, Philip. "Labor History and the Labor Movement Today," *Labor History, 7* (Winter 1966), pp. 70–77.

Index to Names

Index to Subject